# THE SOUTHERN CH

The Civilization of the American Indian Series

THE

# SOUTHERN CHEYENNES

*By Donald J. Berthrong*

UNIVERSITY OF OKLAHOMA PRESS : NORMAN AND LONDON

By Donald J. Berthrong

(editor, with Odessa Davenport) Daniel Ellis Conner, *Joseph Reddeford Walker and the Arizona Adventure* (Norman, 1956)

(editor) W. T. Hamilton, *My Sixty Years on the Plains: Trapping, Trading, and Indian Fighting* (Norman, 1960)

*The Southern Cheyennes* (Norman, 1963)

(editor, with Odessa Davenport) Daniel Ellis Conner, *A Confederate in the Colorado Gold Fields* (Norman, 1970)

*The Cheyenne and Arapaho Ordeal: Reservation and Agency Life in the Indian Territory, 1875–1907* (Norman, 1976)

Library of Congress Catalog Card Number: 63–8990

ISBN: 0–8061–1199–2

*The Southern Cheyennes* is Volume 66 in *The Civilization of the American Indian Series*.

6  7  8  9  10  11  12  13  14  15  16  17  18  19  20  21

*To My Mother and Father*

# FOREWORD

ALMOST FIFTY YEARS AGO George Bird Grinnell published his important work, *The Fighting Cheyennes*. It has stood unrevised and virtually unchallenged as our source of knowledge about the struggles of the Cheyennes to protect their freedom and way of life. The Cheyennes, for nearly two centuries, fought Indians and whites to protect their villages and ranges. Superior numbers of their foes forced them to shift their habitat from the Minnesota River Valley to the Central and Southern Plains. Finally, after the Civil War, in two army campaigns, the Southern Cheyennes were reduced to reservation life, incapable of further armed resistance to the greater military strength of federal and state troops. Essentially, the present volume records the efforts of the Cheyennes to maintain their freedom and tribal integrity.

Some readers, acquainted with Grinnell's writings, will find similarities between this work and *The Fighting Cheyennes*. Grinnell, unlike contemporary scholars, had access to Cheyennes who participated in and remembered events well before the mid-nineteenth century. These Indians are now dead, and we must reluctantly defer to both Grinnell's and the Indians' interpretations of certain events of Cheyenne history. However, historical records unused by Grinnell and unknown to the Cheyennes, whose memories were not infallible, are available to verify or correct much of what Grinnell wrote. Grinnell, impressed by the composite knowledge of his Cheyenne informants and friends, used these records sparingly and preferred Indian tradition to white sources. This led him to present warped and biased versions of some incidents and clashes between the Cheyennes and frontiersmen and troops. Obviously, judicious use of both Cheyenne tradition and historical records will produce greater objectivity.

This volume is not a complete history of the Cheyennes. It is limited both chronologically and topically to the period before 1875 and to those Cheyennes who occupied the Central and Southern Plains. To this division of those people, scholars have affixed the name "Southern Cheyennes." Little attention is paid to those members of the tribe who ultimately took up their abode north of the Platte River and its tributaries and who came into close association with the Sioux. Although trading posts and the overland routes tended to separate the Cheyennes into two divisions, in times of stress and war, visits and flights occasionally obliterated the divisional distinctions until the last quarter of the nineteenth century. Another volume depicting the reservation life of the Southern Cheyennes is needed and will be written at a future date. To combine both the pre-reservation and reservation life of the Cheyennes into one study would do injustice to the vast resources available for their tribal history.

The author is indebted to many individuals and institutions for aid and support. The American Philosophical Society granted funds for research in and collection of materials from the National Archives and the Library of Congress. These funds were supplemented by the Faculty Research Committee of the University of Oklahoma, which made possible further research at those depositories and at various state historical societies. In addition, the Committee provided funds for secretarial assistance, duplication of manuscript records, and the acquisition of many microfilms of manuscript records. The assistance of Mrs. Rella Looney of the Oklahoma State Historical Society, Carmelita Ryan and Mrs. Sarah Jackson of the National Archives, Mrs. Agnes Wright Spring of the Colorado State Historical Society, and Mr. Nyle H. Miller of the Kansas State Historical Society is gratefully acknowledged. My colleagues, Professors Arrell M. Gibson, Edwin C. McReynolds, Gilbert C. Fite, Max L. Moorhead, Charles C. Bush, Edward Everett Dale, and the late Roy Gittinger contributed their advice and knowledge most generously. Miss Opal Carr, Mrs. Sandra D. Stewart, Mrs. Alice M. Timmons, and Mr. Jack D. Haley of the University of Oklahoma Library aided my research by seeking out many necessary materials, as did Mr. Don Rickey, Jr., then of that institution. Mrs. Josephine A. Soukup typed and retyped the manuscript with skill and an unerring eye for details and errors.

The patient understanding and critical judgment of my wife, Edna Marr Berthrong, were indispensable in the long process of achieving the completion of this volume.

DONALD J. BERTHRONG

*Norman, Oklahoma*

# CONTENTS

|  | Foreword | ix |
|---|---|---|
| 1 | Early Migrations of the Cheyennes | 3 |
| 2 | A Way of Life on the Great Plains | 27 |
| 3 | Religion and Government among the Cheyennes | 50 |
| 4 | Cheyennes on the Arkansas River | 76 |
| 5 | An Agent and Treaty Come to the Cheyennes | 100 |
| 6 | The Last Years of Freedom | 127 |
| 7 | Anticipation of War | 152 |
| 8 | Skirmishes and Retaliations | 174 |
| 9 | Massacre at Sand Creek | 195 |
| 10 | Reprisal and Peace | 224 |
| 11 | The Hostiles Come South | 245 |
| 12 | War Returns | 266 |
| 13 | The Treaty of Medicine Lodge: Another Peace Fails | 289 |
| 14 | The End of Freedom | 318 |
| 15 | Reservation Life Begins | 345 |
| 16 | The Last War | 372 |
|  | Bibliography | 406 |
|  | List of Abbreviations Used in Footnotes | 426 |
|  | Index | 428 |

# ILLUSTRATIONS

"Dance of the Soldier Societies"                    *following page* 80
Wolf on the Hill
She Who Bathes Her Knees
Cheyenne Sun Dance
William W. Bent
Charles Bent
George Bent and his wife, Magpie
Governor John Evans
Colonel John M. Chivington
"Herd of Buffalo"

Indian encampment                                   *following page* 208
Camp Weld Conference, 1864
Prisoners captured by Custer
Yellow Wolf
The Bear Above and his wife
Medicine Creek Lodge Council
Black Kettle
Camp Supply

Stone Calf and his wife                             *following page* 368
Cheyennes at the agency, with Chief Friday
Cheyenne and Arapaho chiefs
Tipis of the Cheyennes
Cheyenne drawings
Custer's Washita prisoners
Spotted Tail, Roman Nose, and Old Man Afraid of His Horses
The Battle of the Washita

xiii

# MAPS

Map of Cheyenne Migrations and Lands       *page* 11
Bent's Old Fort                                              95
Map of Emigrant Routes and Army Posts              251

xiv

# THE SOUTHERN CHEYENNES

# 1

## EARLY MIGRATIONS
## OF THE CHEYENNES

IN QUIET REVERENCE before the lodge fire the old people of the Cheyennes recounted for the young their sacred stories, the deeds of the tribal culture-heroes, and their tales of origin. Without a written literature, the Cheyennes orally passed their customs, religious ceremonies, and traditions from generation to generation. A few of these tales concern the origin of the Cheyennes and contain clues to regions previously inhabited by the tribe. Although vague and sometimes contradictory, the traditional accounts can be corroborated in part by historical and archaeological evidence.

The Cheyennes, in common with other Plains Indians, believed the world's surface was once submerged by a flood or deluge. A person floating on the water called the waterfowl together and persuaded them to dive beneath the water's surface and search for earth. Swans and geese failed, but a small duck finally surfaced with mud in its bill. After the mud dried, the earth was created. From the soft earth, the being fashioned figures and created man and woman. Representing summer and winter, this man and woman in their struggles caused climatic and seasonal changes. Later, because the first people created did not reproduce, other persons were created and multiplied and populated the earth.[1]

Nothing in the Cheyenne myths recalls migrations to the North American continent. Rather, it was believed that the first Cheyennes lived underground and were led to the surface by one of their more adventuresome people, who, following a small source of light, discovered the world above them. Lost also from their mythology is the first contact with French fur traders in the Mississippi Valley before

[1] George Bird Grinnell, "Some Early Cheyenne Tales," *Jour. Amer. Folk-Lore,* Vol. XX, No. 78 (July–September, 1907), 170–72.

their removal to the Great Plains. One tale merely places the Cheyennes "way up on the other side of the Missouri River. It is very level and sandy up there." It was a country of little lakes where the Cheyennes depended upon waterfowl and fish for their food.[2]

Other traditional accounts place the Cheyennes far north of the Missouri River on a large lake, where they subsisted largely upon fish caught in willow seines. To supplement their food supply, they collected birds' eggs and young fledglings, and in the fall of the year ate fat skunks. During the winter, the Cheyennes depended upon rabbit meat and used the skins for robes. From the first lake home, the Cheyennes moved to another body of water to the southwest and camped on beautiful prairies near its shores. At this undetermined site, the Cheyennes constructed their lodges of poles, covered with bundles of grass, and sealed their abodes with a plaster of mud, leaving only the entrance and a hole in the roof through which the fire's smoke escaped.[3]

These traditions lend truth to assertions that the Cheyennes early in their history occupied a region populated by Algonquian-speaking peoples. We cannot be more precise than to say that the Cheyennes began their tribal migrations from the shores of the Great Lakes or from the drainage of the upper Mississippi River and its tributaries.[4]

Cheyennes appear originally in historical records on a map attributed to Joliet and drawn, perhaps, before 1673. The map places the "Chaiena," or Cheyenne, fifth in the list of tribes living above the mouth of the Wisconsin River and north of the Sioux, thus occupying a portion of the Wisconsin bank of the Mississippi River. More definite, however, is a visit of a group of Indians named "Chaa," or Cheyennes, to La Salle while he was building Fort Crèvecoeur on the Illinois River. Appearing at the fort on February 24, 1680, the "Chaa" urged the French fur traders to visit their village located high on the

[2] Benjamin Clark, "Extracts from manuscript on ethnography and philology of the Cheyennes," Bureau of American Ethnology, MS No. 3449, p. 9; George Bent to George E. Hyde, August 12, 1911, George Bent Letters, Coe Collection, Yale University Library; Grinnell, "Some Early Cheyenne Tales," *loc. cit.*, 170, 173.

[3] George F. Will, "The Cheyenne Indians in North Dakota," *Proceedings,* MVHA, 1913–14, VII, 68.

[4] George Bird Grinnell, *The Cheyennes Indians: Their History and Ways of Life,* I, 4; Joseph Jablow, *The Cheyenne in Plains Indian Trade Relations, 1795–1840,* 2.

Mississippi River, where beaver and other fur-bearing animals abounded. Adding to the complexity of the early history of the Cheyennes is a letter written on May 9, 1695, by Governor Don Diego de Vargas of New Mexico. Governor de Vargas wrote that while he was absent from Santa Fe, "a band of Apaches from the east, who are called Chiyenes" visited his city and promised to return again in a few months. Some scholars use the Governor's letter to maintain that the "Chiyenes" were Cheyennes who drifted far to the southwest in search of buffalo.[5]

Within a decade after their first visit to French fur traders, Cheyennes began occupation of the Minnesota River Valley. A map drawn by a French cartographer, Jean Baptiste Louis Franquelin, in 1684 and improved in 1688 places the Cheyennes on that stream. From traditions of the Sioux, the Cheyennes lived in the western reaches of the Minnesota River Valley between the Iowas to the east and the Otos to the west and south. In the 1850's the earthworks of the Cheyenne site on the Yellow Medicine River, a southern tributary of the Minnesota, were still visible. Eroded walls surrounded three sides while the fourth was protected by a hill, containing about half an acre of land. Many slight elevations within the enclosure marked the former earthen Cheyenne dwellings.[6]

Franquelin's map and other contemporary evidence tend to destroy the assertion that the Cheyennes occupied the Yellow Medicine River and more westerly sites during the same period. The Cheyennes, Franquelin's map shows, lived at the end of the seventeenth century only on the Sheyenne River in eastern North Dakota. Pierre Charles le Sueur founded Fort L'Hillier in 1700 at the mouth of the Blue Earth River. Shortly after the arrival of Le Sueur's party on the Blue Earth, they were visited by nine Sioux, who told the Frenchmen that the

5 J. V. Brower, *The Mississippi River and Its Source*, MinnHS *Collections*, IX, 72–73; Pierre Margry, *Découvertes et établissements des français dans l'ouest et dans sud de l'Amérique Septentrionale, 1614–1754*, II, 54; Ralph Emerson Twitchell, *The Spanish Archives of New Mexico*, I, 265.

6 Francis Parkman, *La Salle and the Discovery of the Great West*, II, 219–29; T. S. Williamson, "Who Were the First Men," MinnHS *Collections*, I, 245; Stephen Return Riggs, *Dakota Grammar, Texts, and Ethnography, Contributions to North American Ethnology*, IX, 194; George E. Hyde, *Red Cloud's Folk: A History of the Oglala Sioux Indians*, 9; S. R. Riggs, "Mounds of Minnesota Valley," MinnHS *Collections*, I, 119–20.

Minnesota River "was the country of the Sioux of the West, and of the Ayavois [Iowas] and the Otoctatas [Otos] a little further [west]."[7]

When or why the Cheyennes moved farther up the Minnesota River between Big Stone Lake and Lake Traverse and ultimately to the Sheyenne River is unknown. Their removal undoubtedly was caused by pressures from the Sioux or from the Crees and Assiniboins. Intertribal wars in the upper Mississippi River Valley were the result of rivalries between French and English fur traders, who urged their Indian confederates to destroy the tribes trading with their rivals.[8]

Scattered some distance west and northwest of Lake Traverse are a series of sites once utilized by Cheyennes. The first location consists of mounds among the Kettle Lakes region, west of present Sisseton, South Dakota. The Cheyennes also used Bone Hill, a prominence in La Moure County, North Dakota, as an observation point.[9]

The Cheyennes lived for more than a half-century on the Sheyenne River of North Dakota. Their principal village, containing about seventy lodges, was located on the south bank of an old channel of the Sheyenne River, twelve miles southeast of Lisbon, Ransom County, North Dakota. During this period, the Cheyennes fortified their villages, lived in earth lodges more than forty feet in diameter, and possessed a culture not unlike that of the semisedentary Caddoan and Siouan tribes of the eastern Great Plains. While on the Sheyenne River, the Cheyennes acquired the horse and traded for glass beads and metal knives, but apparently still did not possess the gun. At first afoot, later on horses, and armed with bow, arrow, and lance, the Cheyennes soon came to depend for food upon the vast buffalo herds about them, supplementing their diet with beans, corn, and squash.[10]

[7] Grinnell, *Cheyenne Indians,* I, 20–21; SHSWis *Collections,* XVI, 186, 189–90.

[8] Will, "Cheyenne Indians in North Dakota," *loc. cit.* 68; Riggs, *Dakota Grammar,* 194; James Mooney, *The Cheyenne Indians, Memoirs of the American Anthropological Association,* I, 364–65; Jablow, *Cheyenne in Plains Indian Trade Relations,* 6.

[9] George Bent to Hyde, November 30, 1913, Bent Letters, Coe Collection; A. J. Comfort, "Indian Mounds near Fort Wadsworth, Dakota Territory," Smithsonian *Report,* 1871, 389–402.

[10] William Duncan Strong, "From History to Prehistory in the Northern Great Plains," Smithsonian *MC,* Vol. C, 370–76; George Bird Grinnell, "Early Cheyenne Villages," *Amer. Anthr.,* N.S., Vol. XX, No. 4 (October–December, 1918), 361–63; Will, "Cheyenne Indians in North Dakota," *loc. cit.,* 69–70.

The Sheyenne River village was not visited by fur traders or travelers during its occupation by the Cheyennes. It is evident that the La Vérendrye brothers passed some distance north and west of the Sheyenne River during their 1742–43 journey to the Rocky Mountains. Francis Parkman's assertion that the La Vérendryes visited the Cheyennes, known as the "Gens des Chevaux" or "Horse Indians," on October 19, 1742, is untenable.[11]

No conclusive evidence can be cited to date exactly the Cheyenne removal from the Sheyenne River. Previous authorities have speculated, however, that the Cheyennes lived contemporaneously on the Sheyenne and Missouri rivers. Alexander Henry, the younger, a fur trader of the North West Company, writing on November 9, 1800, claimed that about 1740 the Cheyennes were nearly exterminated by the Chippewas. The Cheyennes, Henry explained:

> . . . were a neutral tribe between the Sioux and the Saulteurs [Chippewas] for many years; but the latter, who are of a jealous disposition, suspected they favored the Sioux. A very large party having been once unsuccessful in discovering their enemies, on their return wreaked their vengeance on those people, destroying their village and murdering most of them. . . . The Shians [Cheyennes] having been nearly exterminated abandoned their old territories and fled southward across the Missouri, where they are now a wandering tribe.[12]

Another equally valid source points to the Chippewa destruction of the Sheyenne River village at a later date. In the spring of 1799, "Sheshepaskut" or Sugar, a principal Chippewa chief, related to David Thompson, an explorer and geographer of the North West Company, the details of his tribe's attack upon the Cheyennes. The sixty-year-old chief told Thompson that for years the Chippewas traded with the

11 Francis Parkman, *A Half-Century of Conflict*, II, 22–23n.; Pierre Gaultier de Varrenes de la Vérendrye, *Journals and Letters*, 407; Will, "Cheyenne Indians in North Dakota," *loc. cit.*, 75–76; Grinnell, *Cheyenne Indians*, I, 37.

12 Will, "Cheyenne Indians in North Dakota," *loc. cit.*, 76; Grinnell, *Cheyenne Indians*, I, 16; Grinnell, "Early Cheyenne Villages, *loc. cit.*, 368–73; Meriwether Lewis and William Clark, *Original Journals*, I, 195; Alexander Henry and David Thompson, *New Light on the Early History of the Greater Northwest: Manuscript Journals, 1799–1814*, I, 144; John R. Swanton, "Some Neglected Data Bearing on Cheyenne, Chippewa, and Dakota History," *Amer. Anthr.*, N.S., Vol. XXXII, No. 1 (January–March, 1930), 156–60.

Cheyennes for the latter's surplus corn and vegetables. Once the Chippewas discovered a Cheyenne hunter with the fresh scalp of one of their warriors. At a council, the Chippewas accused the Cheyennes of killing many others of their tribe who had been missing over a period of years and decided to destroy the Cheyenne village.

When spring came, the Chippewas organized a large party of 150 warriors and set out on foot, marching through the forest to avoid detection. Observing carefully the Cheyenne village until their enemies' warriors were absent on a hunt, the Chippewas "entered the Village and put everyone to death, except three Women; after taking every thing we wanted, we quickly set fire to the Village and with all haste retreated for those that fled our attack would soon bring back the whole party, and we did not wish to encounter Cavalry in the Plains." The destruction of the Cheyenne village is dated by various authorities between 1770 and 1790.[13]

Fleeing northwestward into Canada, the Chippewas carried their prisoners to a camp on Rainy River. There one of the Cheyenne women killed herself, and her child was taken to the Rainy River House. If the Rainy River House was definitely the post of the Hudson's Bay Company, we could establish within a few years the final exodus of the Cheyennes from the Sheyenne River. Unfortunately, the Rainy River House was a post maintained either after 1783 by precursors of the North West Company or after 1793 by the Hudson's Bay Company. Since Sugar was sixty years of age when he conversed with Thompson and because the details of the story are so vivid and clear, the attack probably took place in the late 1770's or early 1780's, when Sugar possessed the necessary experience and maturity to lead all the warriors of his band into war.[14]

Nor does the fact that the Cheyennes possessed horses when attacked

[13] David Thompson, *Narrative of Explorations in Western America, 1784–1812*, 261–63; Swanton, "Cheyenne, Chippewa, and Dakota History, *loc. cit.*, 159; Strong, "History to Prehistory in the Northern Great Plains," *loc. cit.*, 371; Jablow, *Cheyenne in Plains Indian Trade Relations*, 7–9.

[14] Arthur S. Morton, *A History of the Canadian West to 1870–71*, 163ff., 174ff., 238–39, 429–30; Grace Lee Nute, *Rainy River Country*, 14–15; Gordon Charles Davidson, *The North West Company*, 10–11, 45; Peter Pond, "Journal," SHSWis *Collections*, XVIII, 314–15n.; Grace Lee Nute, "Hudson's Bay Company in Minnesota Country," *Minn. History*, Vol. XXII, No. 3 (September, 1941), 270–71.

by the Chippewas date the removal. Jonathan Carver, traveling through central Minnesota in 1766, found the Sioux making extensive use of canoes, and when Peter Pond, six years later, visited the same Indians, he found that horses were common among them. Several decades later David Thompson observed that the Sioux had abandoned canoes for horses. The Cheyennes, occupying lands to the west of the Sioux, undoubtedly possessed the horse earlier than their eastern neighbors. Since the Cheyennes had horses before the Sioux, it can only be contended that the former Indians were in possession of horses before the Chippewa attack, and the fact cannot be used to indicate the removal date of the Cheyennes from the Sheyenne River.[15]

Important inferences can be drawn from Cheyenne life on the Sheyenne River. Sometime after 1750 the Cheyennes obtained horses, enabling the tribe to pursue buffalo more successfully. Even so, they still engaged in agriculture sufficiently to trade surplus corn and vegetables with neighboring tribes. When the Cheyennes moved to the Missouri River their economy was mixed. With the horse, they soon adapted to the buffalo culture of the Great Plains environment, in which agricultural possibilities were limited by the lack of water.

Migrating westward, the Cheyennes took up their residence on the Missouri River, near the boundary of North and South Dakota. One of their villages was located on Porcupine Creek, in Sioux County, North Dakota, where they lived in seventy large earth lodges, about sixty feet in diameter, and many smaller ones. This village was substantially larger than that on the Sheyenne River. Either the previous site was only one of several Cheyenne locations, or the tribe was now being joined by other related peoples such as the Sutaios. Continued Cheyenne agriculture is demonstrated by corn fields extending west of the village on both sides of Porcupine Creek.[16]

Archaeological evidence in addition to Cheyenne and Sioux tra-

15 Jonathan Carver, *Three Years' Travel throughout the Interior Part of North America*, 57; Peter Pond, "Journal," *loc. cit.*, 347; Thompson, *Narrative*, 178; Francis Haines, "The Northward Spread of Horses among the Plains Indians," *Amer. Anthr.*, N.S., Vol. XL, No. 3 (July–September, 1938), 433–34; Frederick W. Hodge, *Handbook of American Indians North of Mexico*, BAE Bulletin No. 30, I, 570; Frank Gilbert Roe, *The Indian and the Horse*, 100.

16 Grinnell, "Early Cheyenne Villages," *loc. cit.*, 365, 368–71, 377; Grinnell *Cheyenne Indians*, I, 21–25; Lewis and Clark, *Journals*, I, 212–13.

ditions indicates that the Cheyennes occupied sites on the Missouri River between 1750 and 1780. Living near the Arikaras and Mandans, marrying women of those tribes, the Cheyennes still constructed earth lodges and grew substantial crops of corn, beans, and squash. Old Teton Sioux insist that the Cheyenne village on Porcupine Creek was first established in 1733 and was occupied for fifty years. Then the Cheyennes moved to the Grand River, Corson County, South Dakota, where it is claimed they remained as late as 1840.[17]

This traditional chronology is dubious because about 1781 the Cheyennes escaped a great smallpox epidemic which swept through the Missouri River Indians. Perhaps a small portion of the Cheyennes, however, chose to remain on the Missouri River when the majority of the tribe migrated to better hunting grounds. This assumption can be justified by the ethnological observations of Meriwether Lewis and William Clark. These explorers found living among the Mandans as a chief, a Cheyenne who apparently had severed his relationship with his own tribe.[18]

The Porcupine Creek, Grand River, and other possible Cheyenne villages along both banks of the Missouri River indicate a substantial increase in Cheyenne population. While the Cheyennes lived on the Missouri River, they were undoubtedly joined by the Sutaios, a kindred people with whom the Cheyennes earlier had warred. Southern Cheyennes maintain that only a portion of the Sutaios incorporated into the Cheyenne tribe. Other Sutaios went north from the Missouri and never again were seen by their kinsmen.[19]

Jean Baptiste Trudeau implied that the Cheyennes, in 1794–95, traded beaver skins to French fur traders through the Arikaras. The Cheyennes, Trudeau made clear, ranging along the course of the Cheyenne River, did not trap beaver extensively because they had little contact with white men. Lacking familiarity with white men, the

[17] Grinnell, "Early Cheyenne Villages," *loc. cit.,* 371–72; Grinnell, *Cheyenne Indians,* I, 25–27; George F. Will, "Archaeology of the Missouri Valley," AMNH *Anthropological Papers,* XXII, 311–12; Will, "Cheyenne Indians in North Dakota, *loc. cit.,* 76–77; Clark, "Ethnography and philology of the Cheyennes," *loc. cit.,* 15.

[18] Will, "Cheyenne Indians in North Dakota," *loc. cit.,* 77; Lewis and Clark, *Journals,* I, 212–13.

[19] George Bent to Hyde, February 9, 1914, Bent Letters, Coe Collection; Grinnell, "Early Cheyenne Villages," *loc. cit.,* 377; Hodge, *Handbook of American Indians,* II, 660.

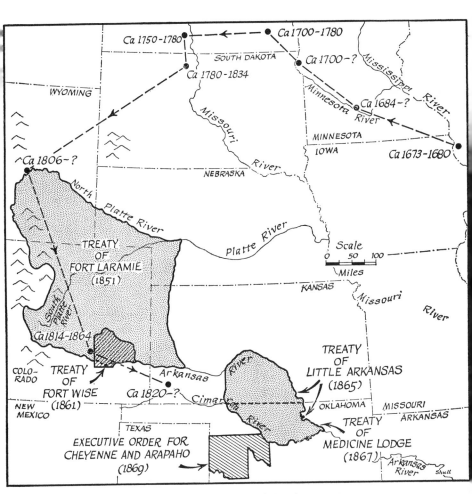

Cheyenne Migrations and Lands

Cheyennes and other nations remote from the Missouri River threw dyed and dressed skins into the river as a sacrifice to the "White Man," a deity among them. To carry on their trade, Trudeau stated, the Cheyennes moved by horse from their villages below the Black Hills on the Cheyenne River. On one occasion, the Cheyennes selected a young man, "The Lance," to receive a Spanish medal from Trudeau, signifying their willingness to live in peace. Trudeau hoped to use the friendly Cheyennes as intermediaries in establishing trade with the Kiowas, Arapahoes, and a Pawnee band who roamed the head-waters of the Cheyenne River above the ranges of the Cheyennes.[20]

By the early 1800's the Cheyennes ranged widely to the southwest of the Missouri River. François Marie Perrin du Lac in the summer of 1802 apparently visited Cheyennes on the Missouri River. At the mouth of the White River, Perrin du Lac came upon "a part of the Chaguyenne [Cheyenne] nation, composed of about one hundred and twenty men. The greatest part of them having never seen a white man, looked at us and our clothing with the greatest astonishment." Perrin du Lac added substance to the contention that the Cheyennes were trapping beaver. "Not content," he wrote, "with hunting on the banks of this river [Cheyenne River], they pass on to the immense savannahs near the Plate [Platte]," where they trapped for beaver. In his discussion of the Cheyennes, Perrin du Lac also noted that "although [the Cheyennes] wandered the greatest part of the year, [they] sow near their cottages maize [corn] and tobacco, which they come to reap at the beginning of autumn. They are in general good hunts-men, and kill great numbers of castors [beaver], which they sell to the Sioux."[21]

Pierre-Antoine Tabeau, more knowledgeable of the fur trade than Perrin du Lac, however, stated that the Cheyennes did not hunt beaver extensively. François Quenneville, Tabeau asserted, spent the winter of 1804–1805 among the Cheyennes, following them "in all their ramblings in the neighborhood of the Black Hills and else-where." While Quenneville traveled with the Cheyennes he saw beaver only three times and collected only eighty-four pounds of pelts from the tribe. This was the first Cheyenne contact, Tabeau main-tained, with a trader, and to please, the tribe "surpassed themselves in the hunt."[22]

Many of Tabeau's details are substantiated by Charles LeRaye, an-other Upper Missouri trader. LeRaye commented that the headwaters

[20] "Trudeau's Journal," *SD Historical Collections*, VII, 453, 455, 461, 470, 472–73. For myths of other tribes, see Alfred L. Kroeber, *Traditions of the Arapaho*, Field Mus. *Anthropological Series*, V, 3; Clark Wissler, *North American Indians of the Plains*, 106–108.

[21] *Travels through the Two Louisianas, and among the Savage Nations of the Mis-souri*, 53, 62–63.

[22] *Tabeau's Narrative of Loisel's Expedition to the Upper Missouri*, 87.

of the Cheyenne River were the home of the Arapahoes, Crows, Kiowas, Omahas, Poncas, and Kiowa-Apaches. But of the Indians occupying the headwaters of the Cheyenne River, "the most powerful of these
tribes are the Chien [Cheyenne], or Dog Indians." On his trading
venture, LeRaye found no Cheyennes lower on the Missouri River
than the first Arikara village. There, in May, 1802, LeRaye found
Cheyennes, Sioux, and three other tribes from the headwaters of the
Cheyenne River trading with the Arikaras.[23]

It is important to note that neither LeRaye nor Tabeau mentioned
the existence of Cheyenne villages on the Missouri River. Tabeau
treated the Cheyennes as a nomadic Plains tribe and claimed that
the Sioux expelled the Cheyennes from the Missouri River villages.
When the Cheyennes and Sioux first met on the Missouri River, the
fur trader wrote, the latter tribe wished to cross the river and camp
near the Cheyennes. Because of Sioux pressure, the Cheyennes gave
up their village on the Missouri, and "abandoned agriculture and
their hearths and became a nomadic people." The Cheyennes and
Sioux waged war, later making peace. Since the peace was only the
"fruit of necessity, the truce is not very sincere and these two nations
live in mutual fear of treachery and always, potentially, in a state
of war."

Dispossessed of their residence on the Missouri River, the Cheyennes
began to frequent the plains east of the Black Hills. From their new
homes, the Cheyennes regularly visited their old and faithful allies, the
Arikaras, for trading purposes. Tabeau lamented that the Cheyennes
possessed so little knowledge of the value of trade goods that trade
with the tribe was very difficult. Still, the Cheyennes controlled the barter of the Arapahoes, and the latter Indians deferred to the judgment of
the Cheyennes. Of the nine Indian tribes inhabiting the upper Cheyenne River, only the Cheyennes visited the Missouri River to exchange robes and furs for trade goods.[24]

Lewis and Clark, while ascending the Missouri River, acquired
from Jean Valle some knowledge of the Cheyennes. Valle, having
traded with the Cheyennes during the winter of 1803–1804, told the
official American explorers that the Cheyennes numbered three hun-

23 "The Journal of Charles LeRaye," *SD Historical Collections,* IV, 159, 165.
24 Tabeau, *Narrative,* 151–58.

dred lodges and lived on the Cheyenne River, engaging in extensive horse-stealing expeditions upon the Spanish settlements. While Lewis and Clark were among the Arikaras in October, 1804, they saw two villages of Cheyennes, designated as the "Shar-ha" and "Weheeskeu," trading with the Arikaras.[25]

Cheyennes also appeared at Fort Mandan, the winter quarters of the Lewis and Clark expedition. The nearby Mandans feared a Cheyenne attack, which did not occur because Lewis and Clark told the Cheyennes to maintain the peace. Lewis and Clark presented these Cheyennes with an American flag and some trinkets, much to the pleasure of the tribe.[26]

On their return voyage down the Missouri River, Lewis and Clark found great numbers of Cheyennes trading among the Arikaras. During August, 1806, not only did Jefferson's representatives hold peace councils with the Cheyennes but Lewis visited a Cheyenne camp. The chief's lodge was made of "20 dressed Buffalow Skins in the same form of the Seeioux and lodges of other nations in this quarter." Lewis' hosts informed him that their band consisted of 120 lodges, and in all probability a majority of the tribe were not at that time trading on the Missouri River.[27]

Information contained within the journals of Lewis and Clark reveals that the Cheyennes had had little previous contact with white men. When Captain Clark presented a Cheyenne spokesman with an American medal, the chief rejected it, saying that "he knew that the white people were all medecine [sic] and that he was afraid of the medal or any thing that white people gave them." Additional persuasion was necessary before the chief finally accepted the medal. In the course of the long council, Clark urged the Cheyennes, Arikaras, and Mandans to "Shake off all intimecy with the Seioux and unite themselves in a strong allience . . . which they all promised to do."[28]

Since Clark did not come into contact with the whole Cheyenne tribe, he seriously underestimated its population. He represented the tribe as containing 350 to 400 fighting men, which would have meant that the Cheyennes numbered between 1,400 and 1,600 persons. Clark

[25] Lewis and Clark, *Journals*, I, 176, 190.    [27] *Ibid.*, V, 350–52.
[26] *Ibid.*, I, 232–33.    [28] *Ibid.*, V, 352–53.

described the Cheyennes as "rich in horses and dogs, the dogs carry a great proportion of their light baggage. They confess to be at war with no nation except the Sieoux," against whom they had been fighting defensive wars for as long as they could remember. Before leaving the council, the Cheyennes requested that traders be sent among them because "their country was full of beaver and they would then be encouraged to kill beaver, but now they had no use for them as they could get nothing for their skins and did not know well, how to catch beaver."[29]

The timidity of the Cheyennes, their lack of beaver-trapping skill, and their request for traders can only mean that this band of Cheyennes previously had little contact with even the far-ranging fur trader. Since the Cheyenne River was devoid of beaver, the Cheyennes, by 1806, must have been hunting south and west of the Cheyenne River, in regions where beaver was plentiful. Lewis and Clark suggest that the Cheyennes were ranging widely by 1806, since they recommended that Cheyenne trade could be developed at the mouths of the Cheyenne and Yellowstone rivers.[30]

A map drawn by Lewis and Clark shows that the Cheyennes were the most populous tribe living about the Black Hills. To the south of the Cheyennes, clustered about the tributaries of the Platte River, were the Kites, a 40-lodge band of Kiowas, and 150 lodges of Arapahoes. There can be no doubt that pressure from the Sioux was a factor in the continuing withdrawal of the Cheyennes to the south and west. Contemporary evidence makes it quite impossible to contend that only the Assiniboins, a Siouan-speaking people, were the sole Siouan tribe to fight the Cheyennes along the Missouri River.[31]

It was the Teton Sioux rather than the Assiniboins who pushed the Cheyennes not only from the Missouri River but also from the Black Hills. One careful scholar maintains that when the Teton Sioux entered the Black Hills, "a favorite winter home of the buffalo about 1765 . . . [they] proceeded to dispossess the Cheyenne and Kiowa whom they found there."[32] Little historical documentation exists, how-

29 *Ibid.,* V, 356–57.

30 *Ibid.,* VII, 100.

31 *Science Magazine,* November 4, 1887; Grinnell, *Cheyenne Indians,* I, 22–23; Clark, "Ethnography and philology of the Cheyennes," *loc. cit.,* 11–12.

32 John C. Ewers, *Teton Dakota: History and Ethnology,* 4.

ever, to validate this early removal of the Cheyennes from the Black Hills.

The younger Alexander Henry in the winter of 1806 met the same Cheyennes whom Lewis and Clark had visited only a few months before. There are some differences in the accounts of Henry when compared with those of Lewis and Clark. Henry, already in the fur trade, noted that the Cheyennes possessed clothing of Spanish origin and that they wintered 200 to 250 miles south of the Black Hills. Near the sources of the Platte and Missouri rivers, Henry stated, the Cheyennes "make their annual hunts of bear and beaver, in company with the Buffalo Indians, or as some call them, the Caveninavish [Arapaho] tribe, a very numerous nation inhabiting that part of the country." After the Cheyennes completed their winter hunt, the tribe disposed of their skins to the Pawnees or Sioux, or to French traders from the Illinois River.[33]

Since both Henry and the Lewis and Clark expedition talked to the same group of Cheyennes, it is difficult to make their accounts correspond. The different geographic locations are not too troublesome when it is realized that little was known by either party of the vast region southwest of the Missouri River. Whether the Cheyennes trapped beaver and traded extensively with fur traders is another matter. To Lewis and Clark, the Cheyennes had deplored their inaptitude in trapping beaver, and they had requested a trader so that he might teach them this skill. Henry, however, stated that two Spanish traders had spent the previous winter among the Cheyennes and had acquired two canoeloads of pelts. Perhaps the Cheyennes spoke to Lewis and Clark as they did to attract American traders among them and gain the benefit from additional competition.

Increased fur-trading activity after the Lewis and Clark expedition led to intermittent conflicts between the Cheyennes and Teton Sioux. These conflicts, however, did not result in the open warfare which typified Assiniboin-Cheyenne relations. In 1812, John Luttig, an employee of Manuel Lisa's Missouri Fur Company, reported that some Sioux ran off Cheyenne horses while the Cheyennes were trading at Fort Manuel, located near the North and South Dakota boundary on the Missouri River. In less than two decades, the Cheyennes had be-

[33] Henry and Thompson, *Journals*, I, 383–84.

come more sophisticated in their trade relations. The Cheyennes, according to Luttig, in February, 1813, possessed a vast quantity of robes and pelts and demanded forty loads of gunpowder instead of the customary twenty in exchange for a prime beaver skin.[34] The Cheyennes were undoubtedly trying to capitalize on the rivalry between the St. Louis and Montreal fur traders. In retaliation, the traders tried to stir up the Indians to steal horses and skins from those tribes trading with their rivals.

Removed from the fur traders, the Cheyennes and the Oglala Sioux, a band of Teton Sioux, collaborated in wars against the Crows. In the first quarter of the nineteenth century the Oglalas lived just east of the Black Hills, while the Cheyennes occupied the lands farther to the west and south. As the two tribes struggled to enlarge their hunting range west of the Black Hills, they came into direct conflict with the Crows for the rich buffalo country along the Powder, Wind, Bighorn, and Yellowstone rivers. A war party of Cheyenne Bow String warriors was wiped out by the Crows in 1819. The following year, the whole Cheyenne nation, supported by Oglalas, moved against the Crows. Led by their medicine-arrows priest, the Cheyennes punished the Crows severely and captured over one hundred young women and boys as captives. The women were taken by Cheyenne men as wives, and the boys were adopted into the tribe. The descendants of the Crow captives were known among the Southern Cheyennes as late as 1905. Hostilities between the Crows and the Cheyennes persisted until 1862, when the former tribe abandoned the hunting grounds east of the Bighorn and south of the Yellowstone.[35]

Another significant factor influencing the Cheyennes' migration was the movement of the Arapahoes, an Algonquian people, once neighbors of the Cheyennes on the Minnesota and Sheyenne rivers.

34 Robert H. Lowie, *The Assiniboine,* AMNH *Anthropological Papers,* Vol. IV, P. 1, 7; Henry and Thompson, *Journals,* I, 385–86; John C. Luttig, *Journal of a Fur-Trading Expedition on the Upper Missouri, 1812–1813,* 123f., 127.

35 George Bent to Hyde, April 10, 1905, Western History Department, Denver Public Library; George Bent to Hyde, February 6, 17, 1912, February 7, 10, 1914; Bent Letters, Coe Collection; Hyde, *Red Cloud's Folk,* 33–34, 66–67, 88–92; Robert H. Lowie, *The Crow Indians,* xiv; F. V. Hayden, *Contributions to the Ethnography and Philology of the Indian Tribes of the Missouri Valley,* 392; Hodge, *Handbook of American Indians,* II, 367–68.

The Arapahoes, affected by the same forces as the Cheyennes, shifted westward just ahead of the Cheyennes to the Missouri River and the Black Hills. By 1796 the Arapahoes were beyond the forks of the Cheyenne River, southwest of the Black Hills, and two decades later they hunted with the Cheyennes between the sources of the North and South Platte rivers. In this movement the Cheyennes helped the Arapahoes to force the Kiowas and Kiowa-Apaches from the Black Hills. Later the Arapahoes aided the Cheyennes in their wars with the Crows. During the movement of the Arapahoes farther from the Missouri River, the Cheyennes served as middle men between the fur traders and their allies.[36]

An English botanist, John Bradbury, in June, 1811, witnessed the arrival of Cheyennes at the Arikara villages. These Cheyennes brought with them a robe from the Arapahoes for trading purposes. As described by Bradbury, the buffalo robe was "curiously ornamented with figures worked with split quills, stained with red and yellow, intermixed with much taste, and the border of the robe entirely hung round with hoofs of young fawns, which at every movement made a noise much resembling that of a rattlesnake when that animal is irritated." The robe brought ten dollars in trade goods for the Cheyenne owner.[37]

From the fur traders at the Arikara villages, Bradbury learned that the Cheyennes had "no fixed place of residence, but resort chiefly about the Black Hills, near the head of the Cheyenne River. . . . Their number is now inconsiderable, as they scarcely muster one hundred warriors." Bradbury gave no explanation of the tremendous decline in the Cheyennes' population. The Cheyennes, Bradbury noted, not only acted as middle men for other tribes but were among the Indians "who make predatory excursions into Mexico, and steal horses from the Spaniards." In turn, these horses were traded to the Arikaras.[38]

[36] William P. Clark, *The Indian Sign Language*, 39–40; James Mooney, *The Ghost-Dance Religion and the Sioux Outbreak of 1890*, BAE *Fourteenth Annual Report* P. 2, 954; Henry and Thompson, *Journals*, I, 530; *Science Magazine*, November 4, 1887; George E. Hyde, *Indians of the High Plains*, 185–86, 188–89; Garrick Mallery, "Pictographs of the North American Indians. A Preliminary Paper," BAE *Fourth Annual Report*, 101–102; Mooney, *Cheyenne Indians*, 367.

[37] Reuben Gold Thwaites (ed.), *Early Western Travels, 1748–1846*, V, 139.

[38] *Ibid.*, V, 139–40, 176.

Friction between the Cheyennes and the Teton Sioux probably also drove the Cheyennes into a close alliance with the Arapahoes. For decades after 1776 the Cheyennes and groups of Teton Sioux clashed periodically. Despite both Cheyenne and Sioux denials of intertribal conflicts, hostilities between the two groups are recorded as late as 1836, when traders of the Pratte-Chouteau Company arranged a truce between them. The peace was short-lived because soon afterward the Cheyennes killed a Sioux warrior and troubles began all over again.[39]

Moving constantly ahead of the Cheyennes, the Arapahoes were as far west as the Bighorn River in 1781. After a Sioux attack in 1792, they shifted southward into the regions held by the Utes, and by 1812 the Arapahoes were firmly established high on the North Platte, where they lived in peace with the Shoshonis to the west and the Kiowas to the south. At the later date, the Arapahoes were beginning their penetration to the Arkansas River. Robert Stuart, a member of the Astoria venture, stated that the Arapahoes, in the summer of 1812, killed Jean Baptiste Champlain and his three hunting companions on that stream.[40]

Shortly after 1812 the Arapahoes were moving southward to the upper Arkansas River in considerable numbers. It is possible that Joseph Philibert contacted the Arapahoes on or near the Arkansas in 1814, when he entered the Indian trade. Thus, the first Cheyenne movement to the Arkansas River was merely a continuation of the Cheyennes' role of middle men to their allies and friends. After a successful venture, Philibert returned to St. Louis, where he was joined by Auguste Pierre Chouteau and Jules DeMun in an effort to exploit the Indian trade of the Arkansas Valley. It was the purpose of Chouteau and DeMun to "go to the headwaters of the Arkansaw river, to trade with the Arapahoes, and other Indians there abouts." The Chouteau–DeMun venture ended in disaster when the party was seized by Spanish authorities and imprisoned at Santa Fe.[41]

39 L. Crawford to P. Chouteau, June 29, 1836, Chouteau-Papin Collection, Missouri Historical Society.

40 Clark, *Indian Sign Language,* 39; Robert Stuart, *On the Oregon Trail,* 82, 119n.; Hyde, *Indians of the High Plains,* 190.

41 Julius [Jules] DeMun to William Clark, November 25, 1817, in 15 Cong., 1 sess., *House Exec. Doc. No. 197;* Clarence E. Carter (ed.), *The Territorial Papers of the United States,* XV, 190.

Traders such as Chouteau and DeMun hoped to assume the Cheyennes' role as providers of trade goods to the Indian groups moving south to the Arkansas River. This is made clear by Dr. Edwin James, the chronicler of the Stephen H. Long expedition. Chouteau and De-Mun with forty-five French hunters, James wrote, met a large encampment of Kiowas, Arapahoes, and "Bad-hearts" on Cherry Creek, near present Denver, Colorado. The Indians were gathered

> . . . for the purpose of holding a trading council with a band of Shiennes [Cheyennes]. These last had been recently supplied with goods by British traders on the Missouri, and had come to exchange them with the former for horses. The Kiawas, Arrapahoes, &c., who wander in the extensive plains of the Arkansa and Red river, have always great numbers of horses, which they rear with much less difficulty than the Shiennes, whose country is cold and barren.

The Cheyennes, James pointed out, did not receive their trade goods directly from the British traders but through Missouri River Indians. Then the Cheyennes in turn traded with the Indians living in the more remote regions of the Plains.[42]

The Stephen Long expedition encountered on July 26, 1820, a large intertribal encampment of Plains Indians on the Arkansas River. Arapahoes, Kiowas, Comanches, Kiowa-Apaches, Cheyennes, and a few Shoshonis were within this village, and chiefs from four of the tribes met with Long. The Indians, James learned, depended almost entirely upon buffalo and wandered widely between the Platte and Red rivers. Bear Tooth, called the "grand chief of the Arapahoes," was the most influential leader of the Arkansas River Indians and largely controlled the five hundred warriors of the intertribal encampment.[43]

The Cheyennes, roaming the Central and Southern Plains with Bear Tooth, were in 1820 far less numerous than the Arapahoes. Captain John R. Bell of the Long expedition stated that the "Chayennes

[42] Edwin James, *Account of an Expedition from Pittsburgh to the Rocky Mountains, Performed in the Years 1819 and '20*, I, 502–503. Hyde (*Indians of the High Plains*, 204) identifies the "Kaskaskias" or "Bad-hearts" as the Gatakas or Kiowa-Apaches.

[43] James, *Expedition to the Rocky Mountains*, II, 60–61, 174–76, 184–85; Captain John R. Bell, *Journal*, 203; Captain John R. Bell to Long, September 14, 1820, Office of the Adjutant General, Letters Received, Records of the War Department, National Archives.

are a small band of the Chayenne nation residing about the head of the Chayenne River." Traditionally, the Cheyennes explain their early appearance on the Arkansas River because of the tribe's desire for wild horses. The Hairy Rope band, the Cheyennes relate, led by Yellow Wolf, Medicine Snake, and Afraid-of-Beavers, were renowned among the tribe for their ability to catch wild horses. This band was the first of the Cheyennes to move south, and roamed as far as the Cimarron River Valley, where wild horse herds were abundant. Captain Bell, however, in 1820, learned that the Cheyennes with Bear Tooth were a "band of seceders from their own nation . . . since on the occurrence of a serious dispute with their kindred on the Shienne river of the Missouri, [they] flew their country, and placed themselves under the protection of Bear Tooth." Whoever these Cheyennes were, their chief exercised exacting discipline over them. Dr. James described the leader as "a man born to command, and to be endowed with a spirit of unconquerable ferocity, and capable of inflicting exemplary punishment upon anyone who should dare to disobey his orders."[44]

Cheyennes were more numerous on the Arkansas River in 1821, when Jacob Fowler led his party from Fort Smith to the Rocky Mountains. Fowler found nine hundred lodges of Kiowas, Comanches, Kiowa-Apaches, Arapahoes, and Cheyennes camping just east of present Nepesta, Pueblo County, Colorado. Two hundred lodges of Cheyennes were present in this vast conclave. The Arapahoes, Fowler stated, possessed far fewer horses than either the Comanches or Kiowas because the former tribe had just sent most of their horses for trading purposes to the Cheyennes of the Cheyenne River. Although Bear Tooth was not mentioned specifically by Fowler, the Arapaho leader possessed considerable influence among the other tribes. When Fowler's camp was threatened by Kiowas and Comanches, two to three hundred lodges of Arapahoes were pitched around the traders to protect them from harm.[45]

During the mid–1820's the Cheyennes were widely scattered from the Missouri River to the Arkansas. Santa Fe traders such as Augustus Storrs, in answer to queries of Senator Thomas Hart Benton, placed

44 Bell, *Journal*, 202–203; James, *Expedition to the Rocky Mountains*, II, 177–78, 186; George Bent to Hyde, October 18, 1908, Bent Letters, Coe Collection.

45 Jacob Fowler, *Journal*, 58–59, 65.

the Cheyennes in 1824 among those tribes of nomadic Indians who bordered on the Arkansas River and who depended upon buffalo for their "support and commerce." In the same year, James Ohio Pattie, traveling with Bernard Pratte's trading group, noted Cheyenne utilization of the Republican and Smoky Hill valleys, a region later to become the prized hunting ground of the Southern Cheyennes.[46]

General Henry Atkinson, in the summer of 1825, ascended the Missouri River to make peace treaties with the Missouri River Indians and those tribes inhabiting the Northern Plains. Atkinson did not meet the Cheyennes as expected at the Arikara villages and encountered them first at the mouth of the Teton River. Fifteen Cheyenne chiefs and leaders arrived at Atkinson's camp on July 4, 1825, and were described by Major Stephen Watts Kearny as "decidedly the finest looking Indians we have seen." On July 6, 1825, the Cheyennes signed their first treaty with the United States, acknowledging the sovereignty of the United States and its right to regulate all trade. The document was signed by four Cheyenne chiefs—Wolf-with-the-High-Back, Little Moon, Buffalo Head, and One-Who-Talks against-the-Others—and nine warriors.[47]

Months later, General Atkinson wrote his formal report, which justifies the assumption that a majority of the Cheyennes were still living west of the Black Hills. The Cheyennes, we learn, appeared at the mouth of the Teton River with the Saones, a division of the Teton Sioux. Since the Cheyennes preferred to hold their council there, it is possible that the Saones, Oglalas, and Cheyennes were hunting in the summer of 1825 west of the Black Hills, in the region of the upper Powder and Bighorn rivers. Atkinson's report estimated the Cheyenne population at 3,000 persons, of whom 550 to 600 were warriors. The Cheyennes, wrote Atkinson, possessed "an abundance of horses and mules," were armed with bows and arrows and guns, and

. . . inhabit the country on the Cheyenne river, from near its mouth, back to the Black Hills . . . and rove at pleasure, according to the

[46] 18 Cong., 2 sess., *Sen. Exec. Doc. No. 7; Niles' Register,* Vol. XXVII (January, 15, 1825), 312–16; Thwaites (ed.), *Early Western Travels,* XVIII, 49.

[47] Henry Atkinson to Colonel Roger Jones, Adjutant General, June 23, 1825, Office of the Adjutant General, Letters Received; Journal of S. W. Kearny, entry dated July 4, [1825], Missouri Historical Society; 7 U.S. Stat. 255–57.

direction which buffaloe are to be found. . . . Their principal rendez-vous is towards the Black Hills, and their trading ground at the mouth of Cherry river, a branch of the Chayenne, 40 miles above its mouth.

Despite direct contact with the Cheyennes, Atkinson added little to the knowledge of the tribe already obtained by Lewis and Clark. The information brought back by the Atkinson expedition led Superintendent William Clark at St. Louis to recommend the mouth of the Cherry River as a logical site for trade with the "Cheyenne nation."[48]

Santa Fe traders during the late 1820's pleaded for protection from predatory Indians along their route of travel. Men such as Alphonso Wetmore, a trader from Franklin, Missouri, pointed out that the Pawnees, Cheyennes, Arapahoes, Kiowas, and Comanches harassed their wagon trains. Wetmore's party, en route to Santa Fe during the summer of 1828, encountered a small party of Kiowas four days beyond the Cimarron River. From the Kiowas, the traders learned that they "had been on a gentleman-like horse stealing expedition against the Chians [Cheyennes], in which they were first successful, but when they believed that [they] had escaped with their booty, the Chians were down upon them, and retook the cavalry [horses] and a few scalps." This incident substantiates traditional Cheyenne and Arapaho accounts which say that about 1826 the two tribes began raiding the Kiowas and Comanches for horses.[49]

Since more Arapahoes than Cheyennes were living on the Arkansas River, they rather than the Cheyennes are prominently mentioned in raids upon the Santa Fe caravans. Troops commanded by Major Bennet Riley were sent from Fort Leavenworth in June, 1829, to protect the Santa Fe traders. Three to four hundred warriors, whom Major Riley thought were Kiowas, Comanches, Arapahoes, and perhaps Pawnees, attacked Riley's command on the American side of the Arkansas River. The journal of Major Riley does not mention the existence of Cheyennes along the Santa Fe route in 1829, but if the Arapahoes were present, so were the Cheyennes. Two years later

48 19 Cong., 1 sess., *House Exec. Doc. No. 117*, 6, 10; Journal of Kearny, July 4, [1825], *loc. cit.;* Clark to James Barbour, secretary of war, December 8, 1835, St. Louis Superintendency, Records of the Office of Indian Affairs, National Archives.

49 Major Alphonso Wetmore, "Diary of a Journey to Santa Fe, 1828," *MHR*, Vol. VIII, No. 4 (July, 1914), 180, 192; Grinnell, *Cheyenne Indians*, I, 31.

William M. Gordon, writing to William Clark, noted that the Arapahoes and Gros Ventres "are the same people, speak the same language, and have 1,200 warriors. They inhabit the country from the Santa Fe trail to the head of the Platte. . . . They harrass the Santa Fe traders, and those engaged in the fur trade."[50]

Thomas Fitzpatrick, the first Indian agent for the upper Platte and Arkansas rivers, also knew that the Arapahoes preceded the Cheyennes to the Arkansas River. Writing in 1847, Fitzpatrick reported that the Cheyennes claimed land above Bent's Fort for a distance of fifty miles. He believed, however, that the Arapahoes had a superior claim because

> . . . the Aripahoes were in possession of their country, and north to the South Fork of Platte and beyond, without any tribe to dispute their claim. The Chyennes at that time were living on the south side of Missouri River, between the Chyenne and White rivers, and along the Black Hills. But the Sioux coming in such numbers from the North, drove the Chyennes further south, on to the river Platte, both branches of which they still occasionally resort.[51]

Since trading opportunities were available on the Arkansas River, Bent, St. Vrain and Company began the establishment of Bent's Fort. Clearly, this post was not established primarily to trade with the Cheyennes, since they were far less numerous than the Arapahoes, Comanches, and Kiowas. And the Cheyennes did not follow William Bent to the Arkansas, because members of the tribe were on that stream for about a decade and a half before Bent's Fort was completed. Much historical confusion has arisen because of information provided by George Bent, son of William Bent.

It was Charles rather than William Bent who first came in contact with the Cheyennes. In 1824, Charles Bent was trading with the Sioux on the Missouri River, and in the following year Charles Bent and

[50] Fred S. Perrine, "Military Escorts on the Santa Fe Trail," *NMHR*, Vol. III, No. 3 (July, 1928), 286, 293; Otis E. Young, *The First Military Escort on the Santa Fe Trail, 1829;* William Gordon to Clark, October 3, 1831, and Riley to Clark, September 28, 1831, William Clark Papers, Kansas State Historical Society, Vol. VI, 301, 330–35.

[51] LeRoy R. Hafen, "A Report from the First Indian Agent of the Upper Platte and Arkansas," *New Spain and the Anglo-American West*, II, 134. The original of this document is Fitzpatrick to William H. Harvey, superintendent of Indian affairs, October 19, 1847, Upper Platte Agency, Records of the Office of Indian Affairs, National Archives.

Andrew Dripps were issued a license to trade at the mouth of the Yellowstone and other sites. There also is evidence that Charles Bent remained in the Missouri River fur trade as late as 1828. Competition of the American Fur Company and the Rocky Mountain Fur Company undoubtedly was too strong for Charles Bent and his partners to overcome, and a decision was made to shift to the Arkansas River.[52]

In the early 1830's the Bents, in partnership with Céran St. Vrain, began to trade along the upper Arkansas River. Meeting Cheyennes led by Yellow Wolf, Little Wolf, and Wolf Chief, the Bents were told that they should establish their permanent post near the buffalo range. Yellow Wolf promised that if this were done, his Hairy Rope band would trade with the Bents.[53] Bent's Fort was begun about 1833 and completed the following year to take advantage not only of the Cheyenne trade but also of the larger numbers of Arapahoes, Kiowas, and Comanches hunting and living in the region drained by the Arkansas River.

Erroneous dating of Bent's Fort stems from the letters of George Bent and from conversations of Porcupine Bull with George Bird Grinnell. In 1912, Grinnell visited the Cheyenne and Arapaho reservation in Oklahoma and talked to Porcupine Bull, whose father, White Faced Bull, had been a friend of Yellow Wolf. In this conversation Porcupine Bull told Grinnell that the Cheyennes first met the Bents at their temporary stockade at the mouth of the Purgatoire River in 1828 and that the Bents and St. Vrain immediately began the construction of Bent's Fort. (Porcupine Bull and his wife stayed with Grinnell for several weeks, and for their information, Grinnell paid the two old Cheyennes fifty cents each. Grinnell, needless to say, received no additional information from the Southern Cheyennes.)[54]

By January, 1834, traders on the Missouri River had heard that Charles Bent was constructing his post on the Arkansas River. Wil-

---

52 James Kennerly, "Diary," MoHS *Collections,* Vol. VI, 69; Abstract of Licenses [1825], St. Louis Superintendency, Records of the Office of Indian Affairs, National Archives; J. P. Cabanné to P. Chouteau, Jr., September 22, 1828, Chouteau-Papin Collection, Missouri Historical Society.

53 LeRoy R. Hafen, "When Was Bent's Fort Built," *Colo. Magazine,* Vol. XXXI, No. 2 (April, 1954), 105, 114–17; David Lavender, *Bent's Fort,* 385–86n.

54 George Bent to Hyde, April 14, 1908, November 29, 1912, Bent Letters, Coe Collection.

liam Laidlaw, writing from Fort Pierre, was worried that Bent, if successful, would draw Indians away from the trading posts on the upper Missouri. "The Chayennes," Laidlaw declared, "have remained in that part of the Country [Arkansas River] depending I have no doubt on that very establishment and if kept up I have very little doubt but that a great many Sioux will follow their example." So few Cheyennes appeared at Fort Pierre in the winter of 1833–34 that Laidlaw could not acquire the necessary horses for Chouteau outfits trading in the Rocky Mountains. On December 13, 1834, William Clark, as superintendent of Indian affairs at St. Louis, issued a license to Charles Bent to trade with Indians at Bent's Fort.[55]

To take advantage of Cheyenne and Sioux trade on the North and South Platte rivers, Bent, St. Vrain and Company, between 1835 and 1839, built Fort St. Vrain on the south bank of the South Platte River a short distance below St. Vrain's Fork. This completed the withdrawal of the Cheyennes from the Missouri River trade, a fact recognized by the traders who now were forced to use the Sioux as middle men in obtaining horses from the Cheyennes.[56]

The early migrations of the Cheyennes were not the result of a single factor. Hostile pressure and migration of neighboring tribes, desire for trading opportunities, necessity of an adequate food supply, and freer access to horses resulted in the movement of the Cheyennes. Warfare with the Chippewas and Assiniboins pushed the Cheyennes onto the prairies and plains. Pressure and intermittent warfare with the Teton Sioux drove the Cheyennes beyond the Black Hills. Following the Arapahoes, who preceded the Cheyennes south and west, the latter Indians raided for horses in the Spanish settlements and continued to serve as middle men between the Arapahoes and the Missouri River traders. When Bent's Fort and Fort St. Vrain were constructed in the 1830's, the Cheyennes no longer needed the goods provided by the posts of the Missouri River and shifted their residences and trade to the Platte and Arkansas rivers.

[55] Laidlaw to Pierre Chouteau, January 10, 1834, Fort Pierre MSS Letter Book, 1832–35, Chouteau Collections, Missouri Historical Society; Hafen, "When Was Bent's Fort Built," *loc. cit.*, 117.

[56] George Bird Grinnell, "Bent's Old Fort and Its Builders," KSHS *Collections*, 1919–1922, XV, 41–42; Honoré Picotte to Jacob Halsey, January 17, 1839, Chouteau-Papin Collection.

# 2

## A WAY OF LIFE
## ON THE GREAT PLAINS

CHEYENNES OF THE MINNESOTA RIVER WERE, perhaps, the descendants of the Sand Hill Men, or Ní-ŏm-a-hé-tăn-iu, and lived in palisaded villages. Later, these Algonquian-speaking people knew themselves as Tsĭs-tsĭn-tsĭs'-tas, or Tsĭs-tsĭs-tăs, meaning "we belong here," or simply the "people." A second division of the tribe, the Sutaio or Sŭh'-tai, once lived near the Cheyennes and after wars, made peace, and were eventually assimilated into the Cheyenne nation. No Cheyennes in the twentieth century knew when the Cheyennes and Sutaios joined, but as late as the 1830's the Sutaios maintained separate camps, continued their own tribal organization, spoke their own dialect, and brought different traditions and culture-heroes into the tribe's lore.[1]

The search for subsistence, according to Cheyenne tales, led the tribe to the buffalo ranges. Far to the north and east of the Missouri River, the Cheyennes existed in one large camp where everyone was hungry. They depended upon fish and waterfowl in the little lakes. Then two chief's sons made a journey in search of game. While crossing a large river, a serpent held the youths in the water, but a man killed the serpent and conducted them to his lodge. After the younger Cheyenne accepted a beautiful young woman as his wife, the man told them to look to the north. In that direction they saw a field of corn; to the east, a country covered with buffalo; to the south and southwest, deer, elk, and horses; and finally to the west they observed an abundance of birds. Together, the younger Cheyenne, his newly acquired wife, and the older youth returned to their village, mindful of instructions never to allow their people to express sympathy for

---

[1] Clark, "Ethnography and philology of the Cheyennes," *loc. cit.,* 19; George Bent to Hyde, August 5, 1911, Bent Letters, Coe Collection; Grinnell, "Some Early Cheyenne Tales," *loc. cit.,* 169.

birds or animals. After the three companions arrived at the Cheyenne village, buffalo and game appeared. Eventually a woman sympathized with a tormented buffalo calf and the animals disappeared, as did the three young people who had brought days of abundance to the Cheyennes.[2]

Cheyenne legends often contain the theme of hunger and the search for a plentiful food supply. Culture-heroes encountered beings who pointed out animals, and who provided seeds and instructions for their use. Corn, supposedly, was not grown by the Cheyennes until they moved to the Missouri River. Unable to prevent the Arikaras from stealing their corn, the Cheyennes abandoned its cultivation. One tale accounts for the decline of corn's importance to the Cheyennes by having Standing-on-the-Ground, who brought the sacred Medicine Hat to the Sutaios, reprimand the Cheyennes. "I told you to watch this corn," spoke Standing-on-the-Ground, "but I can see that some one has been stealing it. That takes the power of raising corn from you."[3]

The Cheyennes, however, raised crops of corn and vegetables while living on the Minnesota and Sheyenne rivers. Garden crops were indispensable until the horse extended the range of their hunts and enabled the Indians to depend upon buffalo for food. Buffalo-bone hoes, grinding stones, and mullers found at the Sheyenne River village indicate a primary dependence upon agriculture, supplemented by hunting. Cheyennes ate buffalo, deer, bear meat, fish, turtles, and dogs. Grown dogs were eaten only when all other food supplies were exhausted, but fat puppies were considered a delicacy among the Cheyennes.[4]

Located between the woodland Indians on the east and the semi-sedentary Indians of the eastern Plains, the Cheyennes in eastern North Dakota partook of both groups' cultures. Pottery on the Shey-

[2] Grinnell, "Some Early Cheyenne Tales," *loc. cit.*, 173–78.

[3] Clark, "Ethnography and philology of the Cheyennes," *loc. cit.*, 24; Grinnell, "Some Early Cheyenne Tales," *loc. cit.*, 189–92.

[4] David I. Bushnell, Jr., *Villages of the Algonquian, Siouan, and Caddoan Tribes West of the Mississippi*, BAE *Bulletin No. 77*, 21–22; Elman R. Service, *A Profile of Primitive Culture*, 112; Strong, "History to Prehistory in the Northern Great Plains," *loc. cit.*, 375; William Mulloy, "The Northern Plains," in *Archaeology of Eastern United States* (ed. by James B. Griffin), 135.

enne River was produced by the methods of the Arikaras, Mandans, and Hidatsas. Yet it is suspected that the decorations link Cheyenne pottery with that of the Indians occupying the eastern woodlands. But the basic culture of the Cheyennes by 1770 links them more closely with their western neighbors on the Missouri River, where, probably, other Cheyenne camps already existed. Although the Cheyennes used birch bark, shell knives, and stemmed arrow points, which set them apart from the Missouri River Indians, their utilization of earth lodges demonstrates close contacts with the adjacent western Indian tribes.[5]

Once the Cheyennes were on the Plains, rapid cultural change took place. After only about two generations, Cheyennes living in 1804–1806, near present day Scottsbluff, Nebraska, on the North Platte River, had completely adapted to the new environment. No longer did these Cheyennes live in fortified villages or earth lodges. They utilized no pottery and practiced no agriculture, lived in buffalo-hide tipis, and traded extensively for many of their necessities. Movement by the Cheyennes onto the Plains, however, was gradual.[6]

Living on the Great Plains, the Cheyennes' way of life assumed characteristics commonly shared by other Indian groups dwelling in that environment. Differences between tribes existed in languages, in social, political, and religious ceremonies. Yet similarities were important among the tribes, ranging from the Sarsis and Plains Crees on the north to the Comanches on the south, and from the Nez Percés and Utes on the west to the Osages and Iowas on the east. The parallel characteristics of the Plains Indians have been delineated by Clark Wissler. Flesh of the buffalo was the indispensable source of food, and was eaten raw, cooked, or as pemmican. Tipis, serving as shelters, were made of dressed buffalo hides stretched over a conical framework of poles. During formal tribal gatherings and ceremonies, the tipis were arranged according to bands in specified places within the camp circle. Transportation of property was provided first by dog

[5] Strong, "History to Prehistory in the Northern Great Plains," *loc. cit.,* 374–75; Mulloy, "The Northern Plains," *loc. cit.,* 135.

[6] Strong, "History to Prehistory in the Northern Great Plains," *loc. cit.,* 376; William Duncan Strong, *An Introduction to Nebraska Archaeology,* Smithsonian *MC,* Vol. XCIII, No. 10, 272–73; Waldo R. Wedel, "Culture Sequence in the Central Great Plains," Smithsonian *MC,* Vol. C, 327; Grinnell, *Cheyenne Indians,* I, 27; Hyde, *Indians of the High Plains,* 47.

travois and later by horses. Movement by water was limited to ferrying, either by bullboats or by rafts. There was no weaving either of cloth or baskets, and only incidental use was made of pottery. The dressing of the skins of buffalo and large game animals was the women's chief industry. Circular shields made of toughened buffalo hides, elaborate eagle-feather headdresses, and decorated shirts fringed with animal hair were utilized by warriors during their military activities. The Sun Dance, worship of buffalo, belief in the efficacy of the medicine bundle, and military societies characterized religious practices and ceremonial organizations. Artistic expression was confined to painting upon rawhide, embroidering with quills or beads, and the use of a few rectangular and triangular designs in complex patterns.[7]

Dependence upon the buffalo for food increased rapidly as the Cheyennes migrated onto the Great Plains. Two vast buffalo herds roamed the Plains—one south and one north of the Platte River. There were "almost inconceivable numbers in the heyday of the living herds" which supplied the Indians with an abundance of food. Travelers on the Plains, striving to remain credible, made possible the inaccurate estimates of 15,000,000 buffalo. Lewis and Clark, passing the mouth of the White River in August, 1806, saw the Plains "darkened with buffalo," yet offered the opinion that only 20,000 animals were within their view.[8]

The veteran traveler on the Santa Fe Trail, Josiah Gregg, commented that during his experience between 1831 and 1840, "I have never seen them [buffalo] anywhere upon the Prairies so abundant as some travellers have represented—in dense masses, darkening the whole country. I have only found them in scattered herds, of a few scores, hundreds, or sometimes thousands in each, and where in the greatest numbers, dispersed far and wide; but with large intervals between." The explorer John C. Frémont, while moving up the Platte River on July 4, 1842, was surrounded by buffalo "on every side; ex-

7 Wissler, *Indians of the Plains*, 13, 18f.; Wissler, "Diffusion of Culture in the Plains of North America," *Congrès International des Américanistes, XVᵉ Session*, II, 39–40; Robert H. Lowie, *Indians of the Plains*, 5–6.

8 Frank Gilbert Roe, *The North American Buffalo: A Critical Study of the Species in Its Wild State*, 520; LeRoy R. Hafen and Carl Coke Rister, *Western America*, 543; Lewis and Clark, *Journals*, III, 267.

tending several miles in the rear, and forward as far as the eye could reach."[9]

Tremendous buffalo herds continued to exist into the 1870's. Colonel Richard Irving Dodge in May, 1871, driving a wagon between Fort Zarah and Fort Larned in Kansas, became engulfed by a herd migrating to the north. Describing this herd later, Dodge wrote: "From the top of Pawnee Rock, I could see from six to ten miles in almost every direction. The whole mass was covered with buffalo, looking at a distance like one compact mass. . . . I have seen such sights a number of times, but never on so large a scale."[10]

Following the migrations of the buffalo, the Cheyennes became less dependent upon their gardens for food. Except for the hoofs and bones, the whole buffalo was consumed. The tongue and nose were delicacies, liver seasoned with gall was enjoyed, and intestines filled with chopped meat were roasted or boiled. The lungs were dried and roasted, marrow of the bones was consumed, blood was cooked in the bluffalo rennet until it attained jellylike consistency, and even the hide of the bull buffalo was roasted and eaten. Buffalo meat was roasted or boiled after the kill, but a portion was sliced and dried on racks. Pemmican was made by the Cheyennes after an additional roasting of the dried meat. After pulverizing the hardened flesh, the Cheyenne women added melted fat, bone marrow, and powdered, dried, wild cherries. Among the Cheyennes pemmican was limited to rather immediate use and was not stored as emergency food for times of privation. Elk, deer, wild sheep, and antelope supplemented buffalo meat, as did young dogs.[11]

Hunting was the chief labor of Cheyenne men. A successful hunt meant food for the band; failure meant privation and hardship. Because of its crucial importance, careful preparation and strict discipline were necessary during a communal hunt. When buffalo were plenti-

9 Gregg, *Commerce of the Prairies*, 71; Frémont, *Report of the Exploring Expedition to the Rocky Mountains in the Year 1842, and to Oregon and North California in the Years 1843–'44*, 23.

10 *The Plains of the Great West*, 120–21; Richard I. Dodge to William T. Hornaday, September 21, 1887, in Hornaday, "The Extermination of the American Bison, with a Sketch of Its Discovery and Life History," *Smithsonian AR*, 1887, II, 390.

11 Grinnell, *Cheyenne Indians*, I, 254–56; Wissler, *Indians of the Plains*, 27–29.

ful, individuals and small parties were not permitted to kill the game. Chiefs decided when the buffalo surround would occur, and the soldier societies enforced the chiefs' commands. Violators were severely whipped, and if they persisted, their tipi was destroyed and their horses killed. Before acquiring efficient firearms, the Cheyennes used lances and bows and arrows. Riding along the right side of the buffalo, the Indians thrust the lance for the kidneys rather than the heart. A single arrow, if well placed, killed a buffalo because some Cheyenne bows were powerful enough to pass entirely through an adult animal.[12]

When the buffalo grew fat, planning began for the great hunt. First a favorable site for a hunting camp was selected near water, with timber for drying scaffolds, level enough for stretching and drying of hides, and in the proximity of the buffalo feeding grounds. In the hunting camp, the soldier bands controlled the village. Sometimes the grass was burned to concentrate the buffalo, diminishing the laborious buffalo drive. If possible, the Indians maneuvered the herd into a narrow valley, where all the males of the tribe strong enough to kill animals silently moved into assigned positions. At the proper moment the hunt leader gave the signal, and the mounted men rushed in, closing off the buffalo from escape. The slaughter began, each Indian grimly determined upon his work, and soon the warriors' task was accomplished.[13]

The men returned to the camp proclaiming their hunting prowess, and the women began their work. The hide was stripped from the carcass, the meat separated from the bones and packed on animals, and all was carried back to the camp. Choice portions were feasted upon and women began the drying process. More laborious still was the dressing of the hides for tipi covers or for robes. Generally buffalo hides taken in the summer were made into lodge-skins, and those in the winter into robes. Depending upon the wealth of a man, a lodge could require from eleven to twenty-one buffalo hides. Cowhides were preferable for lodge-skins and robes, while older bull hides were used for moccasin soles, parfleches, and shields. After the hide was firmly

[12] George Bent to Hyde, May 7, 1906, Bent Letters, Coe Collection; Grinnell, Cheyenne Indians, I, 262–64.

[13] Richard I. Dodge, Our Wild Indians, 287–90.

pegged in place, all flesh and gristle were removed, the hair was worked from the hide, and the hide was thinned down on the hair side with a fleshing instrument until of uniform thickness. The hide was then roughened and dried before the tanning mixture was applied, consisting of brains, liver, soapweed, and grease. Allowed to dry overnight, the hide was softened the following day by working the skin over a taut sinew or through the hole of a buffalo shoulder blade. After the skins were sewn together with sinew and raised on the lodgepoles, the new tipi covering was thoroughly smoked by a smudge fire built inside the lodge for added resistance to moisture and rain.[14]

From the buffalo and other animals, Cheyenne women fashioned many of their household utensils. Spoons and ladles were made from horns of the buffalo or mountain sheep. Water was carried in the paunch of the buffalo, or in the bladder and pericardium. Well-tanned buffalo robes served as bedding for the Cheyennes and as coverings for back rests, the frames of which were made of willow shoots laced together with buffalo sinew. Parfleches, made of heavy buffalo rawhide, not only carried pemmican but served as trunks for transportation of Cheyenne household goods. Rawhide was made simply by removing the fat, muscle, and connective tissue from the hide, and then bleaching the skin in the sun for several days. Afterward, if desired, the hair was removed with an adz. Rawhide was indispensable for the manufacture of various receptacles and for binding together the wood and stone parts of implements.[15]

Bones of animals or edged stones, before acquisition of metal, provided the cutting surfaces for Cheyenne implements. Shoulder blades of buffalo made adequate hoes for the cultivation of corn and garden crops. Scrapers early consisted of flat, oval stones, chipped down to an even edge, sometimes large enough to be used with both hands. Other scrapers were made from the cannon bone of a buffalo, cut diagonally with the edge notched for greater effectiveness. After contact with white traders, old gun barrels were split, opened, and pounded flat,

[14] George Bent to George B. Grinnell, January 16, 1906, Western History Department, Denver Public Library; Clark, "Ethnography and philology of the Cheyennes," *loc. cit.,* 2; Grinnell, *Cheyenne Indians,* I, 213-17, 226-30; Reginald and Gladys Laubin, *The Indian Tipi: Its History, Construction, and Use,* 119-20.

[15] Grinnell, *Cheyenne Indians,* I, 211-13; Lowie, *Indians of the Plains,* 62-63.

then notched or toothed. An adz consisted of a flint cutting edge bound to elk horn, and in later times the flint was replaced with metal. Large stone mauls were used as axes to break trees into suitable size for fuel, to drive tent pins, and to break large bones of animals. Hammers were used to break bones before they were boiled for grease, and to pulverize chokecherries, dried roots, and dried meat. Usually a maul or a hammer consisted of an oval, grooved stone bound with rawhide to a wooden handle.[16]

While still semisedentary and living in the woodlands or on the fringes of the Great Plains, the Cheyenne women made crude pottery, rendered serviceable either by mixing the clay with a form of glue or by firing. On the Missouri River, the Cheyennes also used earthenware dishes, but as the tribe became nomadic and as trade contact increased on the Missouri, metal camp-kettles gradually replaced less durable clay pottery.[17]

Skins and hides of animals in large numbers were sewn by women into clothing for their families. When trade cloth and blankets became more abundant in the nineteenth century, the use of leather for clothing declined. Moccasins, while the Cheyennes still lived in the woodlands, were made from a single piece of deerskin and without a sole. After movement onto the Plains, the one-piece moccasin was retained, and a parfleche sole was sewed on its outside. In historic times the upper part of a moccasin was commonly cut from one piece of deerskin, and a parfleche sole of buffalo hide was sewed to it. Beading, porcupine quillwork, or other ornamentation was placed on the upper before it was attached to the sole. Winter moccasins in addition had attached above the foot opening a loose piece of leather, which was drawn up and around the ankle for protection against snow. During extremely cold weather, Cheyennes sometimes made one-piece moccasins from old buffalo robes with the hair on the inside.

Fringed men's leggings reached from the ankle to the crotch and somewhat higher on the outside and were tied to a belt by strips of deerskin. Cheyenne men wore the breechcloth as a sign of sex, and they said they would lose their manhood if they took it off. Little boys,

[16] Grinnell, *Cheyenne Indians*, I, 210–11, 214–15.

[17] Strong, "History to Prehistory in the Northern Great Plains," *loc. cit.*, 373–74; Grinnell, *Cheyenne Indians*, I, 235–41.

as soon as they walked, wore only the string on which the breech-cloth hung. Even when some Cheyenne men adopted trousers, it was still customary to wear the breechcloth. Deerskin shirts, worn as cere-monial war clothing, were sleeved, fringed, and reached halfway to the knees. Commonly they consisted of well-tanned leather made from the skins of deer, antelope, or mountain sheep. Cheyenne war shirts were trimmed along the seams with enemy hair or scalps, and elabo-rately beaded or ornamented with porcupine quills.

Men wore hair ornaments made from beaten silver coins attached to the scalp lock. A man's hair braids were wrapped with bands of otter fur or with brass wire when it was available through traders. Eagle feathers were worn in the hair by older men, and eagle tail feathers were greatly prized for war bonnets, often long enough to trail to the ground. Before glass beads were obtained from traders, necklaces of elk and deer teeth and fish vertebrae were worn.

Women's dresses were shirts or smocks, sometimes ornamented with porcupine quills or elk teeth, made of leather from the skins of deer, sheep, antelope or elk, and reached down midway between the knee and ankle. The sleeves, cut cape-like, hung down to the elbows. Wom-en also wore moccasins and leggings, the latter made secure by a leather string used as a garter. After puberty, Cheyenne women wore a type of breechcloth tied about the thighs and waist. Young girls after maturity and young women also wore a protective rope tied around the waist, passed between the thighs, and wound around the thighs almost to the knees during the night and when traveling. Vio-lation of the woman's rope meant punishment even by death by the males of her family. Of course, in winter, buffalo robes were indis-pensable for all members of the Cheyenne family.[18]

It was the duty of women to perform all the tasks necessary when the village moved. Before acquisition of horses, dogs were used as beasts of burden, either carrying the loads on their backs or dragging the laden travois. As described by an old Cheyenne, these dogs "though big, were not like wolves. They were of different colors— black, white, yellow, and spotted. They had long bodies, and feet that turned out," and were strong enough to pull two children on a travois. As horses became plentiful, larger travois were adapted for

18 Grinnell, *Cheyenne Indians*, I, 131, 219–24; Lowie, *Indians of the Plains*, 46–53.

them. The horse increased the mobility of the Cheyennes and enabled them to live in larger and more comfortable tipis, but increased mobility also necessitated household artifacts that could be readily dismantled for quick movement. When the camp moved, women took down the lodge, packed the travois, and while on the march carried small children on their backs. Other children too young to care for themselves were transported in cradleboards hung from saddles or travois poles. En route to the new camp, the women tended, perhaps, a half-dozen ponies.[19]

At the new campsite, women continued their strenuous duties. White men often sympathized with the women. Viewing women at work setting up camps, Lewis H. Garrard in 1846 wrote:

> After a ride of two hours, we stopped, and the chiefs fastening their horses, collected in circles, to smoke the pipe and talk, letting their squaws unpack the animals, pitch the lodges, build fires, arrange the robes, and when all was ready, these "lords of creation" dispersed to their several homes, to wait until their patient and enduring spouses prepared some food. I was provoked, nay, angry to see the lazy, overgrown men, do nothing to help their wives; and, when the young women pulled off their bracelets and finery, to *chop wood,* the cup of my wrath was full to overflowing, and in a fit of honest indignation, I pronounced them ungallant, and savage in the true sense of the word. A wife, here, is indeed, a helpmeet.[20]

Garrard did not understand the Cheyennes' rigid sexual division of labor. The duty of Cheyenne men was the hunt and war, and the women's share of the community's labor was care of the household and the welfare of the family.

Cheyenne women ruled the camps, spurred men on to necessary duties, and checked them when unwise actions were contemplated. Although the women did not take part in tribal councils, their influence was immediate upon their husbands. Arguing, cajoling, and persuading, the Cheyenne women carried their points about tribal concerns. Traditions exist of women accompanying the Cheyenne war parties and of heroic women striking the tribe's enemies. The women

[19] George Bent to Hyde, September 14, 1910, Bent Letters, Coe Collection; Grinnell, *Cheyenne Indians,* I, 56, 105; Lowie, *Indians of the Plains,* 40–41.
[20] Lewis H. Garrard, *Wah-to-yah and the Taos Trail,* 106–107.

who had participated in war were set apart from other females of the tribe and may have constituted a society, or class.[21]

Women who decorated thirty robes or who made a lodge without assistance were highly respected by the Cheyennes. Customarily a Cheyenne women was initiated into a quilling society, where she learned the ceremonies and the proper ways of decorating robes, lodges, and war shirts. The work of women devoted to ceremonial decorations upon robes, lodges, or other articles was considered highly important and corresponded to men's bravery and success in war.[22]

When the female child reached puberty, her family announced the fact to the camp and, if wealthy, gave away a horse. If the father's lodge contained a sacred medicine bundle, a shield, or anything else of a sacred character, it was removed or the young woman occupied a menstrual lodge. Ceremonial rites, initiating the girl into women-hood, were usually performed by her grandmother, and thenceforth the young woman wore the protective rope. At this stage of the girl's life her informal and formal relationships changed. After puberty a sister no longer talked to older brothers and began to receive instruc-tions from her mother on proper conduct. Chastity was emphasized by the Cheyenne mother, and sexual relations out of marriage were reprehensible to the Cheyennes. "It is silly," instructed one Cheyenne mother, "to exchange too many glances and smiles with this young man, especially in the presence of people. He will think you are too easy and immoral."[23]

Soon after maturity, courtship began for the Cheyenne maiden. The suitor awaited the young woman and attracted her attention by tug-ging at her robe or by standing at a distance and whistling to her. After a time the young lovers exchanged rings or other tokens of af-fection. Young men played flutes to influence their girls or wore a tail of the white-tailed deer as a powerful love charm. Courtship often lasted from one to five years. The offer of marriage, however, was made by some elderly relative of the suitor to the girl's father. In some cases the family allowed a brother or cousin to approve finally a mar-

21 Grinnell, *Cheyenne Indians*, I, 128–29, 156–57, 159.

22 *Ibid.*, I, 159–60.

23 Clark, "Ethnography and philology of the Cheyennes," *loc. cit.*, 3, 23; Truman Michelson, "The Narrative of a Southern Cheyenne Woman," Smithsonian *MC*, Vol. LXXXVIII, No. 5, 4n.; Grinnell, *Cheyenne Indians*, I, 129–31.

riage arrangement. Although the young woman was permitted to reject a suitor, or even elope, the Cheyenne girl more often respected the wishes of her family. Acompanying the proposal of marriage from the suitor were presents, consisting of horses, a war bonnet, or in some cases all of the young warrior's hunting and war paraphernalia. Custom required an early decision, usually within a day. If the family's decision was favorable, the presents were distributed among the family's members. In turn the young woman's family sent presents to the bridegroom-to-be, and if wealthy in horses, the father gave his daughter horses which remained her property.

A simple marriage ceremony took place a day or two after the accepted proposal. The bride was brought to her father-in-law's lodge wearing new, fine clothing. It was customary for the girl's mother to lead the horse on which the bride rode, and following behind were other women of the family leading other horses. After being carried into the father-in-law's lodge on a blanket, the bride was redressed in wedding clothes provided by the mother-in-law. Shawls, dresses, rings, bracelets, leggings, and moccasins were presented to the bride, who then returned to her own people. The bride's family prepared a feast, and toward the evening hour a new lodge was erected near those of her people. For a time, the bride could wear the protective string or rope and it was respected by her husband. If the bride and groom were strangers, this custom in effect substituted for the normal premarriage courtship and permitted the couple to adjust to each other. At first the bride's mother watched her daughter closely and kept her near her husband day and night "to prevent any gossip from [the] . . . husband's people."[24]

Cheyenne men practiced polygamy, but tribal customs often controlled the selection of additional wives. When a second wife was taken, she was usually related to the first and was often her younger sister. Sororate marriages, although not compulsory, added strength to the enlarged circle of relations. Marriages of two brothers and two sisters were also encouraged because this brought the two families even more closely together. Old Cheyennes explained that if the second wife was not related to the first, trouble would develop and the

[24] Michelson, "Narrative of a Cheyenne Woman," *loc. cit.*, 6–7; Grinnell, *Cheyenne Indians*, I, 131–45.

older woman was likely to leave her husband's lodge. Few men, if any, took more than five wives because of limitations of wealth and food.[25]

Incompatible marriages led to divorces. The separation was formally announced during a dance or a meeting of the husband's soldier society. Usually the husband danced to a traditional song, approached the drum with a stick, struck the drum, and threw the stick into the air, exclaiming: "There goes my wife; I throw her away! Whoever gets that stick may have her!" Frequently a wife eloped with another man, and the husband expected and received payment for his loss. If compensation was not paid, the aggrieved husband could kill the new husband's horses or seek other vengeance. More often, an intermediary would determine an acceptable gift and no difficulties ensued. Only a chief, whose dignity might be compromised, could not seek revenge against his erring woman and her new spouse. The marriage records of old Cheyenne women indicate that a brisk interchange of husbands was not uncommon during the second half of the nineteenth century.[26]

Death of the husband marked the end of the family's tipi or lodge. Early Cheyenne women expressed their sorrow by cutting their hair short and slashing their heads and calves with knives. Wives, mothers, and sometimes sisters practiced mutilation to the extent of cutting off a finger. A man's best horse was killed near the grave, or under the tree containing the scaffold, and the man's spirit departed to "the camp in the stars, where he met his friends and relatives and lived in the camp of the dead." Even after self-mutilation ceased, the wives' braids of hair were cut by an old woman. People came to the tipi, carried away its contents, and the remaining furnishings and tipi were destroyed by fire. The widow and her children returned to the lodges of her father or brothers. In time the relatives provided a lodge, and a brother furnished the food until a son learned to hunt and support his mother and sisters. A widow controlled her remarriage, usually stipulating the support and care of her children.[27]

25 Service, *Profile of Primitive Culture*, 124–25; Grinnell, *Cheyenne Indians*, I, 153.

26 Grinnell, *Cheyenne Indians*, I, 153–55; see also Heirship Files, Cheyenne and Arapahoe Agency, Records of the Office of Indian Affairs, National Archives.

27 Michelson, "Narrative of a Cheyenne Woman," *loc. cit.*, 9; Grinnell, *Cheyenne Indians*, II, 160–63.

Indians possessed great love and affection for their children. Warriors fought to the death protecting their camps and families from enemies. While occupied with war, Cheyennes commonly preferred male children, "since they would be more useful" to the family and the tribe. Attrition of the male population was greater than that of the females, accounting for the acceptance of polygamy. Miscarriages were considered murder when caused by the deliberate actions of the expectant mother. Before the reservation period a soldier society whipped women after the fetus was lost.[28]

Cheyenne children were rarely subjected to physical punishment and were regulated by tribal restraints or sanctions. They were not directly instructed in right or wrong but were controlled by the desire of the respect or approbation of their fellow tribesmen. Ridicule for violation of marriage rules, taboos, or improper conduct while at war was sufficient to cause a Cheyenne to follow the customs of his tribe.[29]

Cheyenne children were nursed by their mothers until they reached the age of four or five. Customarily, a paternal relative named the child on its day of birth, or within a few days. Boys were named after animals, birds, or physical phenomena; girls' names were derived from the same sources but always ended in the word "woman." If a child possessed an unusual physical or mental characteristic, he or she was given a descriptive nickname such as Crooked Foot or White Woman. Often Cheyennes retained their childhood name for life, but many also changed their names at adulthood. Men may have changed their names to agree with visions or upon encountering an unusual animal, person, or experience.[30]

Dependent upon the mother for food, children accompanied the mother while she performed her camp duties. When sufficiently strong, the child was laced to a baby-board or cradle-board and carried upon the mother's back. When the baby reached an age of three to six months, its ears were pierced at the Sun Dance or some other tribal

[28] Sister M. Inez Hilger, "Notes on Cheyenne Child Life," *Amer. Anthr.*, N.S., Vol. XLVIII, No. 1 (January–March, 1946), 60–61.

[29] John H. Provinse, "The Underlying Sanctions of Plains Indian Culture," in *Social Anthropology of North American Tribes* (ed. by Fred Eggan), 355–56.

[30] Hilger, "Notes on Cheyenne Child Life," *loc. cit.*, 65–66, 67–69; Grinnell, *Cheyenne Indians*, I, 107–108.

function. A brave warrior was asked to perform the ceremony, and upon its completion, an appropriate gift was presented to him by the child's father. The ear-piercing symbolized lightning striking the child, thus making it invulnerable to arrows and enemies in time of war.[31]

A child's life among the Cheyennes was both pleasurable and purposeful. Young children played. at the camp's edge, grubbing in the dirt, making mud images, and sliding down the snowy hills in the winter. Boys engaged in athletic contests, practicing with bow and arrow, throwing sticks, wrestling, or participating in the wheel game. Young girls were given dolls to be dressed and sung to in imitation of the mother's activities. Childlike, the girl carried her back-load of twigs, and as she matured was taught the skills of dressing robes, quilling, and beadwork. Grandmothers and aunts, constantly advised the girl to remain near the lodge.

Boys began their warrior training early by dividing into rival camps, mounting attacks upon the other's village, using buffalo hair for scalps, and dancing over their victories. With riding sticks, boys repelled the attacks upon their simulated villages, or if the buffalo hunt took place near the village, they rode to the killing ground and returned to camp with their small load of meat. Mimic camps were supplied with fish by the use of crude fish traps or with birds by hunting with bow and arrow. Enjoyable as the play was to the youth, it was the training of a future hunter. Stalking birds and small game with infinite patience, older boys used blunt arrows to learn the skills necessary for hunting larger game animals. The first large bird or rabbit bagged by the young Cheyenne was exhibited to his family with pride, and he received the plaudits of his elders.

When the Cheyenne youth reached the age of twelve, his training became more formal. His grandfather began the instruction in the duties of a man. For Cheyenne men, the most desired attributes were bravery in war and success on the hunt. Elders treated boys with more consideration than females because they might be killed on their first

31 Grinnell, *Cheyenne Indians*, I, 104–106; George A. Dorsey, *The Arapaho Sun Dance: The Ceremony of the Offerings Lodge*, Field Mus. *Publication 75*, *Anthropological Series*, IV, 180; Sister M. Inez Hilger, *Arapaho Child Life and Its Cultural Background*, BAE *Bulletin No. 148*, 24–28.

war party and they desired to make them comfortable and happy. Physical discipline was rarely used because the youth would soon be a warrior and entitled to the respect of his kinsmen. The youth was also taught to respect his elders, obey their wishes and commands, and carry out their instructions without question. It was important to care for the camp's horses, to maintain his arms, and not to quarrel or brag about his prowess. Fathers, uncles, grandfathers, and wise old men talked to the boys as they played about the camp. If the elders' advice was heeded, the youth would grow up to be a good man, a brave warrior, and a respected member of the tribe.

During early adolescence, the preparation for man's duties culminated in the youth's first buffalo hunt. Previously instructed, the youth knew the habits of the buffalo, how to ride, how to shoot the buffalo, and was prepared to accept the orders of the hunt's leader. Often the youth killed a buffalo calf and returned with his first load of meat for his people. His efforts were praised by his father and a feast was given. Sometimes the father presented a horse to a poor man and proudly announced, "My little boy has killed a calf. He is going to be a good man and a good hunter. We have had good luck."

The next important phase of a boy's life began when he accompanied his first war party. A year or two after the first buffalo hunt the youth was prepared to engage his people's enemies. If the father's wealth permitted, a horse was given away at the beginning and conclusion of the venture. The youth was urged to be unafraid, fight with valor, and try to kill the enemy. The first coup, the youth was told, "will make a man of you, and the people will look upon you as a man." When the party returned, the boy became a man among the Cheyennes.[32]

To kill an enemy was important only because it reduced the number of opposing hostiles. Scalping a fallen foe was likewise of little merit. It was more important to touch the enemy with the bare hand or the coup stick; this was the bravest feat a warrior could perform. White observers seeing warriors rush toward a prostrated enemy concluded that they raced to obtain a scalp. Three coups could be counted upon an enemy by the Cheyennes, and the first to reach the foe received

[32] Grinnell, *Cheyenne Indians,* I, 106–26, 312–35; Service, *Profile of Primitive Culture,* 126–27.

the greatest distinction. Entering combat without a weapon used to kill an opponent at a distance was the ultimate proof of bravery. It was braver to carry only a hatchet or war club rather than a lance or bows and arrows. It was likewise creditable to ride over an enemy on foot or to capture a gun, shield, or other weapon of the hostile warriors. The scalp itself was a mere trophy, and any other part of the enemy's body could serve in its place during ceremonies rejoicing a victory.[33]

Success in war brought not only status to the warrior but also wealth. War parties were formed to take vengeance upon hostile tribes—a vengeance expressed by killing an enemy warrior and by capturing horses. Horses constituted wealth and war yielded this wealth to the Cheyenne warrior. Possession of horses enabled the warrior to hunt and engage extensively in warfare on the Plains; therefore, the horse herds of the Pawnees, Utes, Crows, or even the Kiowas and Comanches before 1841, were the raiders' prime targets. Sons needed horses to follow in the pattern of the father-warrior, and without transportation the family was relegated to the more menial camp duties of the tribe. Fast, nimble ponies assured success on the hunt, feasts to publicize the prestige of the family, and the means to start the offspring properly upon military careers. Horses became a basis for property distinctions among the Cheyennes, and this basis was best maintained by military activity. The relationship of war and its fruits was obvious to the young Cheyenne brave, and outstanding military careers led to wealth and preferment within the councils of the tribe.[34]

Once he had become a man, the young Cheyenne was expected to seek a vision of a "guardian spirit" to safeguard him on the warpath and bring success to his hunt. The pursuit of visions was undertaken by the Cheyennes of recognized maturity and was not a manifestation of the transition from adolescence into manhood. To attain the vision, or in some cases to gain the powers of a shaman, the man engaged in self-torture. Among the Cheyennes, who practiced self-torture to a greater extent than other Plains tribes, it was a common sight in the camp circle to see men tormenting their bodies in quest of a vision.

[33] George Bird Grinnell, "Coup and Scalp among the Plains Indians," *Amer. Anthr.*, N.S., Vol. XII, No. 2 (April–June, 1910), 296–310.

[34] Bernard Mishkin, *Rank and Warfare among the Plains Indians, Monographs of the American Ethnological Society*, Vol. III, 57–63.

Commonly, one or more buffalo skulls were attached to skewers inserted beneath the skin of the back before the dancer made the circle about the lodges of the assembled tribe.[35]

Several years after his first war party, the young warrior sought out his "medicine." An older man, wise in the ways of the spirits who ruled the earth, instructed his pupil in the proper ways of self-sacrifice which would ensure the spirits' pleasure. In preparation, the novice cut a pole and obtained a rope, a bundle of sinews, and small wooden pins, hiding them near an appointed hill. Early in the morning, the older man and his young friend set out and carried the paraphernalia to the hilltop. The pole was firmly planted in the ground, the rope was secured to the pole's top, and pins were attached to the rope by sinew. Offering his knife and the pins to the sun and sky, then placing them on the earth, the older man prayed to the spirits to aid the initiate. The flesh on each breast was punctured with the knife and the pins passed through the flesh. Before leaving his charge, the instructor told the youth to throw his weight against the rope, look at the sun, pray constantly, and try to tear the pins from his flesh. The ordeal of one young Cheyenne is recorded:

> All through the long summer day I walked about the pole, praying to all the spirits, and crying aloud to the sun and the earth, and all the animals and birds to help me. Each time when I came to the end of the rope I threw myself back against it, and pulled hard. The skin of my breast stretched out as wide as your hand, but it would not tear, and at last all my chest grew numb, so that it had no feeling in it; and yet, little by little, as I threw my whole weight against the rope, the strips of skin stretched longer and longer. All day long I walked in this way. The sun blazed down like fire. I had no food, and did not drink; for so I had been instructed. Toward night my mouth grew dry, and my neck sore, so that to swallow, or even to open my mouth in prayer hurt me.

When the sun was setting, the older man reappeared and stated that the pins could not be torn free. The skin was cut from the breasts, freeing the pins, and once again the spirits were supplicated to hear the youth's prayers. As instructed, the youth slept on the hilltop and

[35] George A. Dorsey, *The Cheyenne: The Sun Dance*, Field Mus. *Publication 103, Anthropological Series*, Vol. IX, No. 2 (May, 1905), 175–77.

dreamed of a conversation with a wolf. The wolf boasted of the superior intelligence and skill of wolves and predicted the brave would have these skills. The wolf finished by telling the young Cheyenne to carry a little wolf hair in his medicine bundle and to make his quiver and bow case from wolf hair.[36]

Visions, however, were not related to torture in many early tales but most frequently occurred after fasting or during adversities. The practice of self-torture while seeking a vision of a guardian may have intruded into the Cheyennes' religious practices during the contact with the Sioux on the Missouri River and its tributaries. The plasticity of Cheyenne culture has been previously demonstrated as the tribe migrated from the woodlands to the prairies to the plains. The possibility is present, therefore, that the association of self-torture and vision is not deeply rooted in Cheyenne history.[37]

After having proven himself as a warrior and hunter, the young Cheyenne thought of acquiring a wife. Perhaps at a dance, the warrior gazed across the fire at some maiden and later met her as she performed her household duties. Their mothers discussed their children's merits and the required gift was agreed upon. The proposed union was referred to old men and women to determine the degree of the blood relationship if any. If they were found to be as much as sixteenth cousins, the plans were canceled; if not, the marriage was consummated.[38]

The husband, wife, and their children formed the primary or elementary family, normally living and eating together in a single tipi. Even when enlarged through sororal polygamy or when maintained in case of death by sororate or levirate, the elementary family possessed the strongest kinship ties and was responsible for the transmission of tribal heritage. The extended family or household consisted of the wife's parents, grandparents, her married sisters and their

---

[36] George Bird Grinnell, *When Buffalo Ran*, 78–83.

[37] Ruth Fulton Benedict, "The Vision in Plains Culture," *Amer. Anthr.*, N.S., Vol. XXIV, No. 1 (January–March, 1922), 5–6; A. L. Kroeber, "Cheyenne Tales," *Jour. Amer. Folk-Lore*, N.S., Vol. XIII, No. 50 (July–September, 1900), 163, 188, 190; Grinnell, "Some Early Cheyenne Tales," *loc. cit.*, N.S., Vol. XX, No. 78, 199, and N.S., Vol. XXI, No. 82, 282.

[38] John H. Seger, "Cheyenne Marriage Customs," *Jour. Amer. Folk-Lore*, N.S., Vol. XI, No. 43 (October–December, 1898), 298–99.

children, and unmarried brothers. Occupying several tipis and camping together, the extended family was the primary economic unit within the Cheyennes and was well adapted to the hunting, nomadic life on the Plains. The extended family contained several hunters and enough women to dress the hides and preserve the meat during the more bountiful hunting season.

Relationships of all persons allied by blood or marriage were well understood by the Cheyennes. These relationships also controlled the mode of behavior between all relatives to prevent conflict. Based upon generations within the circle of kindred individuals, fathers-in-law were classified with the grandfather, the mothers-in-law with the grandmother, and children-in-law with the grandchildren. Children of brothers became "sons" and "daughters"; the children of sisters became "nephews" and "nieces"; while the offspring of sons, daughters, nephews, and nieces became "grandchildren." A married man classified his wife's brothers and sisters in the same category as his brother's and sister's spouses, but the husband of his wife's sister became his "brother" and the wife of his wife's brother became his "sister."

The kinship system established proper behavioral patterns for the Cheyennes. Parents, of course, were responsible for the training and welfare of their children, the father caring for the education of the sons and the mother caring for the daughters. Parents of the opposite sex were given more affection, but the relationship was never one of familiarity. In general, the same relationship existed between "parents" and "sons" and "daughters" but on a more limited basis because of separate family residences.

Between brothers in the immediate family, bonds of affection and responsibility were great. An older brother looked after his young brother, and the latter was expected to accept the former's advice. There was no formality between brothers, and they often engaged in gentle teasing. Sisters grew up closely, sharing their duties and helping each other at all times. This early harmony was often important because frequently they remained together during their entire lives, holding their possessions in common and sharing the same husband. An older sister cared for a younger brother, but conversely an older brother paid little attention to his sister's life. Yet the older brother was required to respect his sister, was interested in her welfare, and often determined her marriage. Since cousins were "brothers" and "sisters" in the Cheyenne kinship system, mutual attitudes and behavior varied according to closeness of blood or marriage ties. Men marrying sisters called each other "brother" and had common responsibilities within the household and toward each other's children. Avoidance of conflict was necessary within these relationships, but distant "brothers" and "sisters-in-law" could quarrel and disagree because immediate family affections were not jeopardized.

It was expected among the Cheyennes that a man's sister should be vitally interested in his children. In the case of a female child, the aunt often named the child and aided in the rearing, teaching the girl how to conduct herself with young men. The attitudes of the mother's brother were very similar, and he felt great affection for his nephews and nieces, looking after them out of his respect for his sister. The relationship between the nephew and the uncle, however, was closer. The uncle had ceremonial duties toward his nephew, such as supervising the youth's search of his vision or discussing the youth's violations of tribal customs. In common with most societies, grandparents were permitted to demonstrate great affection and even spoil their children's offspring. Grandchildren looked up to their grandparents and treated them with deference because of the age differential. From the grandfather, the grandson learned the tribal myths and ritual observances, and the grandmother aided in the domestic training of her granddaughter.

Relationships between spouses of brothers and sisters reflect both conflict and mutual co-operation. Among primitive people, joking relationships or licensed familiarity existed between potential wives and husbands. Certain liberties were permitted between a man and his brother's wife and between a man and his wife's sister, both of whom might become his wife through levirate or sororate.[39] Brothers-in-law living in the same camp basically had identical duties within the family. They were expected to aid each other and help each other's wives when necessary. When not in each other's presence, the brothers-in-law respected each other's character and reputation. When together, they were expected to to joke "roughly," play tricks, call each other uncomplimentary names in good spirit and without anger, and

[39] Robert H. Lowie, *Primitive Society,* 102.

47

exchange presents. If one of the brothers-in-law failed to fulfill his duties and obligations, he could be the target of the other's jests. Social behavior among sisters-in-law corresponded to that of the brothers-in-law.

In sharp contrast to the relationship between brother and sister was the social behavior of a brother and sister-in-law. They were permitted to joke crudely with each other, make obscene remarks, and indulge in sexual play. Information varies but it is probable that sexual intercourse between brothers and sisters-in-law was practiced among the Cheyennes, especially during the Sun Dance. This deportment was acceptable among the tribe because levirate and sororate made brothers-in-law and sisters-in-law possible husbands and wives. The Cheyennes recognized this fact by stating: "The sister-in-law is like a wife."

The Cheyenne system of social behavior was based upon respect and joking relationships which represent opposite modes of conduct. Basically they represent "alternate ways of adjusting social conflicts" arising within immediate or extended family relationships. Of the two, respect relationships were the more fundamental because they involved the elementary family and parents by marriage. Since parents were responsible for transmission of tribal heritage, authority was vested in the parents, who enjoyed the obedience and respect of their children. The respect relationship was illustrated when brothers and sisters protected each other's interests. When conflicts were probable, as between the mother-in-law and son-in-law, avoidance and respect combined to assure harmony within the camp. Since sexual differentiation was not a factor between the father-in-law and son-in-law and because economic and martial co-operation was often necessary, there was respect but avoidance was not feasible. Since close social contact was usually absent between the daughter-in-law and her parents by marriage, respect dominated their relationship. Of an older generation, the wife's father-in-law was respected but not avoided, and the mother-in-law's interest in grandchildren required free and respectful exchanges.

Joking relationships were the means of preventing hostilities within the Cheyenne camps. Thrown into continuous contact, brothers-in-law and sisters-in-law inevitably clashed. Still, close collaboration was essential among these relatives by marriage despite rivalry and conflicts. Thus obligatory pranks, jests, satiric exchanges, and sexual play served to "organize hostility in socially desirable ways" since respect could not totally eradicate conflicts.

Remembering the pattern of matrilocal residence and bilateral classification of relationships, these modes of behavior can be summarized in the following categories: Respect relationships dominated where there was a possibility of conflict and a social necessity to prevent it. Mild joking relationships obtained where conflict was probable but no strong reason was present to prevent it. Avoidance relationships controlled the Cheyennes' behavior where it was absolutely necessary to minimize hostility and where there was a difference in generations. Obligatory joking relationships were required where conflicts were inevitable and where harmony was essential but no differences in generation were involved.[40]

[40] Fred Eggan, "The Cheyenne and Arapaho Kinship System," in *Social Anthropology of North American Tribes,* 35–96.

49

# 3

## RELIGION AND GOVERNMENT
## AMONG THE CHEYENNES

CHEYENNE RELIGION NOT ONLY WAS IMPORTANT to the individual but also integrated the tribe. The whole system of beliefs, practices, and actions by which the Cheyennes sought to understand powers beyond those of humans may be called supernaturalism. Striving to learn the causes of nature's workings, the Cheyennes personified the elements and attributed to birds, animals, and other natural objects supernatural powers which were transferred through visions to man. Prayers offered to these natural objects were not offered to the bird or animal itself but to the powers it possessed.[1]

Feeling helpless in the face of nature's powers, the Cheyenne believed that his existence depended upon a dispensation from nature in the form of the arrival of some creature to the praying and fasting Indian; this creature became his guardian spirit and gave him some powers of the omnipotent universe. A dog, saved by the compassion of a Cheyenne youth, guided him to success on the warpath; a bear led a Cheyenne woman back to her village; a great raven rescued a boy from freezing to death; and for reuniting a family of mice, a young Cheyenne warrior attained great stature at war.[2] The Indians' perpetual contact with the phenomena and power of nature explains their preoccupation with the spirits and the rituals which pervaded Cheyenne life.

The Cheyennes venerated two principal gods: Heammawihio, or the Wise One Above, and Ahktunowihio, a god who lived under the ground. Powerful spirits lived at the four cardinal points of the com-

---

[1] Lowie, *Indians of the Plains*, 154; Grinnell, *Cheyenne Indians*, II, 87.

[2] Clark Wissler, *The Relation of Nature to Man in Aboriginal America*, 90–91; Benedict, "The Vision in Plains Culture," *loc. cit.*, 1–23; Ruth Fulton Benedict, "The Concept of the Guardian Spirit in North America," American Anthropological Association *Memoirs*, No. 29 , 15ff.; George Bird Grinnell, *By Cheyenne Campfires*, 83–141.

pass. As the Cheyennes addressed their deities, their pipes were pointed first to the sky, then to the earth, to the east, to the south, to the west, and to the north, asking of the great spirits to smoke and hear their prayers and requests. Although the god in the sky and the one in the earth possessed like, beneficial powers, the former's primacy was well recognized. Praying to Ahktunowihio, the god of the earth who dwelt beneath the ground, they sought from him food, water, plants, herbs, and other necessities of life. Nivstanivoo, or the sacrifice to the four directions, was offered for a long life and to acquire the favor of these spirits, who exercised a great influence over the Indian's fortunes.[3]

Unlike Christianity and some Eastern religions, the beliefs of the Plains Indians were not greatly concerned about the hereafter. No reward or punishment awaited the spirit, or tăsŏŏm, after death. Sharing the aboriginal belief of the soul's immortality, they thought that the dead continued to live much as they did on earth. The place of the dead was reached by following the Hanging Road, the Milky Way, where the Cheyennes chased buffalo, hunted game, played games, went to war, and lived in white lodges as they did before death. These beliefs rested upon the reports of persons who, when unconscious or deliriously ill, had related their adventures while supposedly dead.[4]

Natural phenomena were personified by the Cheyennes and bestowed with powers. Hoimaha lived far to the north and appeared as a man, entirely white, who brought snow and cold to the earth. The Thunderbird caused thunder and lightning, retreating to the south in the winter, returning in the spring with the sun to bring heat and rain. Powerful spirits dwelt in springs, rivers, hills, and high bluffs. Although these spirits were not harmful to man, they were pacified by offerings lest they become offended and injure members of the tribe. Monsters of various kinds lived underwater, and occasionally a ghost appeared to frighten people.[5]

Central to the Cheyennes' religious beliefs and rituals were the powers of animals or birds. In particular, the buffalo was greatly ven-

3 Grinnell, *Cheyenne Indians*, II, 88–91.
4 *Ibid.*, II, 91–93; Lowie, *Indians of the Plains*, 164–65.
5 Grinnell, *Cheyenne Indians*, II, 94–103.

erated by the Cheyennes. The Wise One Above was offered the pipe and was asked to send buffalo so that the people could eat. Then the pipe was presented to a buffalo skull, which was asked to come back to life to furnish meat for food, skins for lodges, and to run over smooth ground so that the hunt would not injure the horses and hunters.[6]

Early in their tribal history the Cheyennes practiced a ceremony assuring a successful buffalo hunt. Preliminary to the hunt, a tipi was erected in the vicinity of the buffalo herd, and a virgin, covered with a buffalo robe, was placed within the tipi. A shaman, wearing a robe and carrying a straight pipe, walked toward the herd, singing as he approached it. The buffalo were drawn toward the shaman, and at a signal the hunters drove the herd into a circling run. When the first buffalo fell, an old man cut a piece of fat from the animal and the fat was carried by a young man to the tipi and given to the virgin, who covered it with her buffalo robe. This rite, introduced to the Cheyennes by the Sutaios, became the Ceremony of the Buffalo or Ceremony of the Buffalomen.

The central rites of the ceremony were performed by a priest of the Buffalomen. Utilizing a medicine bundle kept in the Sacred Hat Tipi, the priest was aided by his wife and several assistants. It was customary for any person to make a vow to sponsor the Ceremony of the Buffalo on behalf of his children, relatives, or himself if they were sick and desired health. Both the pledger and his wife were conducted through the ritual by the priest, his wife, and assistants.

The Ceremony of the Buffalo lasted an evening and the following day. The first evening was used to perform the ceremonial smoking, feasting, and offering of food and prayers. On the next day, the pledger and his wife were painted, a sweat lodge constructed, sand prepared within the lodge for tracing symbolic designs, a buffalo skull placed upon an earthen mound, and a pyramid of stones and logs assembled to heat stones for the sweat lodge. Within the sweat lodge the sacred pipe was ceremonially smoked, food was offered to the spirits of the four cardinal directions and was consumed by the principals of the ceremony, a series of songs was sung, and a sweat bath was taken. The pledgers broke their fast by partaking of food in the tipi where

[6] *Ibid.,* II, 103–104.

the preparations for the rite had taken place, and the ceremony was concluded when the priest gave the vow-makers a portion of his medicine root.

Afterward, the pledgers gave gifts to the individuals who conducted the ceremony. Portions of the ceremony were similar to the Sun Dance, Arrow Renewal, and Massaum, as well as to personal rituals practiced for healing, war, and hunting success. The tribal adoption of the Ceremony of the Buffalo resulted from its assumed effectiveness, and led from specific personal practices to general application for purposes other than fortune on a buffalo hunt.[7]

Many other animals and birds possessed great powers. The mule-deer aided the medicine man in curing the sick, the white-tailed deer was a potent aid in love affairs, the lowly skunk's skin was used by the Cheyenne doctors as a wrapping for their medicine bundles, and the bear was a great medicine animal. Eagles, ravens, hawks, owls, and magpies all were powerful in war because they possessed ability to capture and gain sustenance from the flesh of their prey. Of all the birds, the eagle, especially the gray eagle, had the greatest powers. A man wearing a war bonnet of gray eagle feathers was protected from either arrows or bullets.[8]

Many observers simply classified all Indians who possessed exceptional healing powers and those who conducted ceremonies as "medicine men." Two distinct categories, however, emerge upon closer examination: Those concerned with curing diseases, discovering the presence of the enemy, and recovering stolen and lost property are properly classified as shamans or medicine men, while those who conducted tribal ceremonies are more accurately classified as priests. In some Plains tribes the functions of shamans and priests overlapped, but among the Cheyennes their duties and privileges can be distinguished.[9]

Since disease resulted from both natural and supernatural causes, the shaman understood and used medicines and prayers. The shaman's knowledge was obtained from Heammawihio, who instructed

[7] Robert Anderson, "The Buffalo Men, A Cheyenne Ceremony of Petition Deriving from the Sutaio," *Southwestern Journal of Anthropology*, Vol. XII, No. 1 (Spring, 1956), 92–104.

[8] Grinnell, *Cheyenne Indians*, II, 103–108.

[9] Lowie, *Indians of the Plains*, 161–64.

the healer in the use of roots and herbs. When the shaman received his powers, his wife became an assistant and was also taught the secrets of curing the ill. Sometimes a younger man seeking shamanistic powers prevailed upon a practitioner to share his knowledge. The novice was instructed in the use of roots and herbs. For the information, the student paid his teacher property, usually in the form of horses, saddles, clothing, and arms.

Different shamans possessed various powers for the curing of the ill. The sick person's family and relatives collected the gifts and approached the proper doctor, offering him a pipe. If accepting, the shaman began his long ceremony with the purification of himself and his patient by the burning of sweet pine leaves or sweet grass mixed with ground juniper, dried and pulverized mushrooms, and powdered bitterroot. A song of invocation was sung, a rattle was shaken, and the shaman prayed to drive the bad spirit from the lodge. Because it was believed that the disease was limited to a specific location in the body, a rattle would be shaken over the afflicted place to drive the evil spirit out, and the shaman also used his mouth to suck the cause of the disease from the patient's body. Practicing his magic, the shaman by sleight of hand appeared to produce buffalo hair, stones, and lizards, thought to be the causes of the disease, from the sufferer's body. After additional purifying, songs were sung, and medicine was given to the patient. Often a sweat lodge was used in the medical treatments. The medicine man directed the construction of the lodge and the ceremonies during the sweat bath. When the sweating was finished, the participants plunged into the river.

Cheyenne doctors practiced limited surgery. They were particularly skillful in healing wounds, in extracting arrowheads, and in the setting of broken or fractured bones. Even though the bones of a limb were hopelessly shattered, the Cheyennes did not permit amputation. A few of the shamans cured humans bitten by a snake, perhaps understanding the use of pressure points in the human anatomy, thus preventing the venom from circulating in the victim's blood.

Many shamans also applied their curative powers to horses. The crucial importance of horses to the Cheyennes made their cure an event of significance among the tribe. Medicine men were sought out not only to cure ailing animals but also to imbue additional speed and endurance in the mounts. When warriors left for war, the shaman was requested to protect the animal from injury, and when a race was to be run, the medicine man was asked to bring misfortune to the opponent's animal.[10]

Not all of the Cheyennes' ceremonialism or ritualism was conducted in common with other tribal members. Cheyennes prayed individually and offered personal sacrifices to the supernatural powers. In times of danger, difficulty, or illness the Cheyennes made vows to perform some sacrifice or ceremony. Warriors about to join battle with their enemies sacrificed bits of their skin or flesh while praying for the success of their ventures.

Taboos imposed by medicine men were burdensome to the Cheyennes. Leaders of war parties and possessors of medicine war-pipes could not ask for food and water. Some warriors were proscribed from eating the ham or neck meat of buffalo; others could not eat food removed from the fire by metal implements. The failure of Roman Nose to observe the latter taboo led to his death. Roman Nose was among the large party of Cheyennes, Sioux, and Northern Cheyennes who had surrounded Major George A. Forsyth and his scouts on the Arikaree Fork of the Republican River. Before the fighting began, a woman cooking food had removed some bread from a fry-pan with a metal fork. Roman Nose, unaware of this, ate some of the bread, and then his attention was called to the fact by a Dog Soldier. Tall Bull, a Dog Soldier chief, advised Roman Nose to perform his purification rites, but Forsyth's scouts had been already discovered; so the latter had only time enough to make his normal preparations for battle.

Previously, Roman Nose's war bonnet had protected him in battle because of its strong medicine. The bonnet had been made for the noted Cheyenne warrior by White Buffalo Bull, a great medicine man, and it consisted of a single buffalo horn in front and forty black and red eagle feathers in back. As instructed by White Buffalo Bull, Roman Nose held the bonnet four times to the sun and then to the root and offered the bonnet four times to the sun and then to the cardinal points. Roman Nose completed his preparations by painting himself according to White Buffalo Bull's instructions—yellow across his forehead, red across his nose, and black across his mouth

[10] Grinnell, *Cheyenne Indians*, II, 126ff.

and chin. However, the warrior knew his war bonnet's medicine had been broken and announced: "I have done something that I was told not to do. My food was lifted with an iron tool. I know that I shall be killed today." Mounting his horse, Roman Nose rode to where the scouts were besieged. In the charge that followed, Roman Nose was shot through his body just above the hips. He dragged himself to the river's bank, where he was later found and carried off by some young warriors. True to his premonition, Roman Nose died at sundown.[11]

Distinct from shamans were priests, whose duties and competence concerned the conducting of rituals. Priests among the Cheyennes led the tribe in the observance of the Arrow Renewal, the Buffalo Hat, the Sun Dance, and the Massaum, also called the Crazy or Animal Dance. Priests were treated with respect by the Cheyennes. It was expected that the ceremonial leaders would in turn conduct themselves with dignity and accept the responsibilities of their positions. To these men were entrusted the myths of the sacred fetishes and the knowledge required to perform the elaborate rituals. One priest among the Cheyennes, the keeper of the medicine arrows, had duties which involved the "most solemn religious ceremony the Cheyennes knew." The arrows, in the belief of the Cheyennes, were received from Mŭt-sĭ-l-ū-ĭv, meaning Sweet-Root-Standing, also known as Sweet Medicine, Sweet Root, or Medicine Root. Although Cheyenne myths conflict in some details, Sweet Medicine received the medicine arrows from a supernatural being, and they became inextricably linked with the tribe's welfare.[12]

The arrows represented subsistence and safety to the Cheyennes. Two of the arrows' shafts, called "buffalo arrows," were painted red and symbolized the procurement of food. The other two arrows, called "man arrows," had black shafts and represented war or the means of obtaining victories over the tribe's enemies. As long as these fetishes were properly worshiped, the Cheyennes were assured of a good life

---

[11] George Bent to Hyde, May 10, 1906, Bent Letters, Coe Collection; George Bird Grinnell, *The Fighting Cheyennes*, 277–86.

[12] George Bird Grinnell, "Great Mysteries of the Cheyenne," *Amer. Anthr.*, N.S., Vol. XII, No. 4 (October–December, 1910), 545; Clark, "Ethnography and philology of the Cheyennes," *loc. cit.*, 17; Grinnell, "Some Early Cheyenne Tales," *loc. cit.*, N.S., Vol. XXI, No. 82, 269–71, 280.

and victory over their foes. The office of the arrow-keeper remained within one family, passing from the priest to his son or younger brother, as designated before the priest's death. If no successor was available within the priest's family and none was appointed before his death, another man was free to assume the care of the medicine arrows. When taking charge of the arrows, the priest sacrificed strips of skin from his body, but this custom terminated in 1883 when the custody shifted from Black Hairy Dog to Little Man.[13]

The Arrow Renewal ceremony was performed to prevent evils from befalling the tribe, to end tribal hardships, and sometimes as an atonement or sacrifice for a crime or death. When the Cheyennes were at war and many of their men were killed, or if a man were murdered, the arrows were renewed. An individual warrior in great danger often pledged to sponsor an Arrow Renewal ceremony if he escaped or recovered from a serious wound.

Unlike other major ceremonials among the Cheyennes, the Arrow Renewal was not performed regularly. Necessity determined its performance, but the consent of the arrow-keeper or priest was always required. When the ceremony was set, the whole tribe was summoned to congregate. If some did not respond to the invitation, it was the duty of the soldier societies to force their attendance. It was permissible for the soldiers to destroy lodges and kill horses, but if the people still refused, they became outside of the beneficial influence of the medicine arrows. Great care was taken in arranging the lodges on the inside of the camp circle. In the center of the camp circle a shelter or shade was raised to serve as a headquarters for the soldier societies. The Arrow Renewal was not only a religious event; it was also a time for feasting, visiting, and renewing acquaintances, and a propitious time for curing the sick. Shamans constructed their sweat lodges and restocked their supplies of roots and herbs. Warriors renewed their shields or made new ones if the ceremony took place in the spring when the bull hide of the buffalo was in its best condition.

At the time appointed for the arrows' renewal, the soldiers ordered the people to remain quietly in their lodges. A large tipi was raised

13 Clark ("Ethnography and philology of the Cheyennes," *loc. cit.,* 17) says that Black Hairy Dog, or Black Haired Dog, was the son of Medicine Arrows, who was prominent during the 1860's and 1870's.

and the shelter removed. The man who had pledged to sponsor the renewal of the arrows brought a bundle of arrow shafts to the keeper of the arrows. Then the pledger went into the village and offered a pipe to four old men skilled in arrow-making to come and renew the arrows. Many feared to participate in the renewal of the arrows because the responsibility was great, and if an error was made during the renewal ceremony, great misfortune would visit the malefactor. The exacting procedures of the refurbishing took four days and were witnessed by the pledger, members of his soldier society, old chiefs, and men who had previously taken part in the ceremonies. On the morning of the fifth day the arrows were displayed in the front of the renewal lodge, the buffalo arrows pointing upward and the man arrows downward. Men were permitted to approach the arrows and look at them, but women were denied this privilege.[14]

Tragedy struck the Cheyennes in 1830 when the Pawnees captured the medicine arrows. Pawnees, while camping and hunting along the Platte River, were attacked by the whole Cheyenne nation. As the Pawnees prepared their defenses, a Pawnee warrior, grievously ill, asked to be placed on the battlefield so that he could be killed while fighting his enemies. It was customary for the Cheyennes to follow the medicine arrows into battle when the entire tribe moved against the enemy, since it was the most powerful medicine of the Cheyennes. Bull, a Cheyenne medicine man, led the Cheyenne charge against the Pawnees with the medicine-arrows bundle attached to his lance. Friends of the Pawnee warrior brought him to the battlefield, where he was charged by Bull. Avoiding Bull's lance thrust, the Pawnee wrested the lance and the sacred bundle from the Cheyenne medicine man and gave them to Big Eagle, a Pawnee chief. The Cheyennes fought desperately to recover the medicine arrows, and failing, they left the Platte in despair for their own country.

In time the Cheyennes made substitute medicine arrows for those lost to the Pawnees. For more than three decades the Cheyennes tried through negotiation to recover the medicine arrows and finally did regain several of their fetishes. As late as 1866, Black Kettle and Big Head tried through Edward W. Wynkoop to obtain the return of

---

[14] George Bent to Hyde, February 15, 1905, Western History Department, Denver Public Library; Grinnell, "Great Mysteries of the Cheyennes," *loc. cit.,* 545–50.

two of the arrows from the Pawnees, promising in return to make peace and give the Pawnees one hundred fine ponies and other presents. Cheyenne and Pawnee traditions vary widely concerning when and how the medicine arrows were returned to the Cheyennes. When several of the arrows were recoverd, the substitutes were placed on a high butte in the Black Hills. The many misfortunes of the Cheyennes during the nineteenth century were directly attributed to the loss of the sacred medicine arrows to the Pawnees.[15]

The other Cheyenne fetish was the sacred buffalo hat, or Is'sïwŭn. Brought into the tribe by the Sutaios, the buffalo hat had great powers over the welfare of the camp. If properly respected, the buffalo hat brought abundant food, good health, and adequate clothing and shelter to the Cheyennes. Standing-on-the-Ground brought the buffalo cap to the Cheyennes after he had taken the power of growing corn away from the tribe. From Standing-on-the-Ground the Cheyennes learned that the sacred hat protected them from sickness, and that if the "cap is abused, or hurt, the buffalo will disappear, because the cap is the head chief of the buffalo." A guardian of the buffalo hat was selected by Standing-on-the-Ground, and he was instructed in its proper care.[16]

As in the case of the medicine arrows, the priesthood of the buffalo hat was hereditary. The man selected was quiet, brave, and responsible because the care of the fetish was extremely important to the Cheyennes' welfare. The lodge occupied by the priest entrusted with the buffalo cap was sacred, out of deference for the powers symbolized by the sacred hat. No one could stand in the presence of the hat as it hung in its keeper's lodge; people spoke in low voices in the tipi, and

[15] Two dates are offered for the loss: 1830 and 1833. See George Bent to Hyde, February 6, 1905, Western History Department, Denver Public Library; George Bent, "Forty Years with the Cheyennes," (ed. by George E. Hyde), *The Frontier* (November, 1905), 3–4; George A. Dorsey, "How the Pawnees Captured the Cheyenne Medicine Arrows," *Amer. Anthr.*, N.S., Vol. V, No. 4 (October–December, 1903), 644–58; Grinnell, "Great Mysteries of the Cheyenne," *loc. cit.*, 550–62; Grinnell, *Fighting Cheyennes*, 70–73; Commanding Officer, Fort Harker, to Commanding Officer, Fort Kearny, August 15, 1866, Fort Harker, Letters Sent, United States Army Commands, Records of the War Department, National Archives.

[16] Standing-on-the-Ground is also named Red Tassel, Straight Horns, or Erect Horns in some Cheyenne tales. Grinnell, "Some Early Cheyenne Tales," *loc. cit.*, N.S., Vol. XX, No. 78, 192–94.

children were instructed not to play near the lodge. The lodge in which the buffalo hat was kept was also a sanctuary: no enemy or person who entered it could be harmed.

The buffalo hat was made from the skin of a buffalo cow's head and covered with blue beads, to which two carved and painted buffalo horns were attached. It could be shown only on three occasions: in times of general sickness; when the medicine arrows were renewed; and when worn during war. The beads on the hat were used to predict success at war. If beads appeared above the general surface, the number indicated those who would be killed, and if some of the beads were missing, a corresponding number of the war party would not return.

In 1869, when the buffalo hat's keeper Half Bear was on the verge of death, its care was entrusted temporarily to Broken Dish, a close friend of the priest. Half Bear's son Coal Bear, absent at the time of his father's death, returned four years later to assume his duties. When Broken Dish refused to give the hat to Coal Bear the Fox Soldiers intervened and returned the hat to its rightful custodian Coal Bear. A wife of Broken Dish had removed one of the hat's horns, but the loss was not discovered until it had been in the care of Coal Bear for sometime. Kept among a family related to Broken Dish by marriage, the horn remained among the Southern Cheyennes until 1908, when Three Fingers, a Southern Cheyenne chief, returned it to the buffalo hat's keeper, who traditionally lived among the Northern Cheyennes.[17]

Predictions of disaster followed the desecration of the buffalo hat. The family of Broken Dish died out; the Northern Cheyennes, allies of the Sioux, were forced to surrender to General Nelson A. Miles in the spring of 1877 and were removed to the Cheyenne and Arapaho Reservation in Indian Territory. Disease struck the Northern Cheyennes, and under Dull Knife they attempted to flee to their Northern homes. Pursued, captured, and incarcerated at Fort Robinson, Dull Knife's people broke out again in January, 1879, only to be further decimated. The broken remnants of the Northern Cheyennes were gathered at Fort Keogh, Montana Territory, but none doubted that

[17] George Bent to Hyde, October 30, 1913, Bent Letters, Coe Collection.

the destruction of tribal power was the consequence of the loss of the medicine arrows and the desecration of the buffalo hat.[18]

Two of the more important Cheyenne ceremonials were the Massaum ceremony or dance and the Sun Dance. The Massaum ceremony was brought to the Cheyennes by Sweet Medicine and in older times was celebrated to bring food to the camps in times of starvation. Although the ceremony propitiated the earth, the source of human sustenance, it also was intended to cure the sick and assure victory in war. Undertaken for the benefit of a man who pledged to sponsor the Massaum ceremony, general benefits also redounded upon the tribe. Priests conducted the rituals and passed the instructions down from generation to generation. By the early twentieth century, when its significance was told to white men, portions of the ritual had been lost and some of the old meanings forgotten. The whole ceremony lasted over four nights, beginning with the selection of a green cottonwood trunk for the center pole of the Massaum lodge. For the second day's rituals a great double lodge was raised and prepared under the direction of the chief priest.

At daybreak on the second day sacred objects were brought into the lodge. Opposite the eastward-facing entrance a buffalo skull was placed, and a wolf-skin and the Box Elders' bundle flanked the skull. A cross with arms pointing in the cardinal directions was marked with gypsum, and two mounds of dirt were sprinkled with black paint and two with red paint. These mounds represented the four hills upon which the earth rested and in which dwelled the spirits who watched and held up the earth. A central part of the second day's ritual concerned the buffalo skull and the digging of a shallow trench, into which the skull was finally placed, originally symbolizing the buffalo's appearance on earth. During the third and fourth day various rites were performed to assure abundance of food, but also during the fourth day the buffalo skull was painted and the yellow-wolf effigy created. On the fifth and concluding day an Indian wearing a yellow wolfskin and another in a gray wolfskin circled the camp, beginning

18 Grinnell, "Great Mysteries of the Cheyenne," *loc. cit.*, 562–70; Grinnell, *Fighting Cheyennes*, 70, 359ff; see also Mari Sandoz, *Cheyenne Autumn*, for a popular account of the trials of the Northern Cheyennes.

the dance. Two persons representing foxes danced in the camp circle, followed by men taking the role of elk and white-tailed deer. The Contrary society members joined the dance, bringing to the rites their clownish antics, which were enjoyed by the viewers. A group of Indians dressed as buffalo joined the dancing and were circled by the wolves and the Contraries portraying hunters. Meat was hung from the lodgepole, and the fox-dancer on the fourth leap seized the food, symbolizing tribal success on the buffalo hunt. A procession of dancers to a stream concluded the Massaum ceremony.[19]

At midsummer the Cheyennes observed the ceremony known among them as the Medicine Lodge, or the Sun Dance. The rituals of the Sun Dance were of such central importance that the entire tribe was involved and attendance was compulsory for every adult male. The dance diffused into the Plains region from the Arapahoes, Cheyennes, and Oglala Sioux, with the former tribes sharing its innovation. The Cheyennes probably received the Sun Dance from the Arapahoes, but the Cheyennes claim that they adopted the ceremony subsequent to the Sutaio incorporation into their tribe.[20]

Held once a year, the Sun Dance usually occurred when the tribe left winter camps and congregated for the summer buffalo hunt. During the Sun Dance period, other ceremonies took place for both the tribe and the individual. Social dances were held, the young men and women courted, and warriors renewed their medicine. The aims of the ceremony varied from tribe to tribe, or participant to participant. The Sun Dance was an expression of religion and a "free show" performed for the pleasure and entertainment of the whole tribe.[21]

Vows made when a man or woman was in distress initiated the Sun Dance. During this critical time supplications for supernatural aid were made, and the Sun Dance also presented an additional opportunity to seek favors from powerful spirits. After the camp circle was established, a lodge was raised near its center. Secret preliminary rites were first conducted by the priest, followed by instructions to the

---

[19] Grinnell, *Cheyenne Indians*, II, 204–10, 285ff.

[20] Leslie Spier, "The Sun Dance of the Plains Indians: Its Development and Diffusion," AMNH *Anthropological Papers*, Vol. XVI, Pt. 7, 459, 495; Hodge, *Handbook of American Indians*, I, 252, 254; Dorsey, *The Cheyenne: The Sun Dance*, 186.

[21] Robert H. Lowie, "Ceremonialism in North America," *Amer. Anthr.* N.S., Vol. XVI, No. 4 (October–December, 1914), 628–29; Lowie, *Indians of the Plains*, 180.

pledger, preparation of the ceremonial costumes, and rehearsal of painting and songs. As these preparations were in progress, others of the tribe hunted for buffalo, whose tongues and hides were required later in the ceremonies. Still others of the tribe gathered the timbers and brush for the Sun Dance structure, which was erected at the center of the camp circle.

The first great spectacle of the Sun Dance began with the search for the Sun Dance pole, the counting of coup upon the tree, and its felling. The pledger and priests left the secret lodge at this point and joined in the tying of the medicine bundle and offerings to the forks of the dance pole. The pole was raised and the Sun Dance lodge was completed. Warriors danced in the Sun Dance lodge and an altar was built. The pledger and those associated with him, having denied themselves both food and drink, began the dance and seriously besought the supernatural powers for aid, constantly looking toward the sun or the offerings attached to the central pole. These dances continued for several days and culminated in the torture dance when wooden skewers were thrust through the flesh of the breast or back. The skewers were fastened by sinews to ropes which were in turn tied to the Sun Dance pole. Rising to their toes, blowing whistles, the dancers strained against their ropes until the flesh was torn away from the skewers. Whether the torture dance was a central part of the Cheyenne Sun Dance is debatable. "The suffering of the Medicine Lodge," Grinnell wrote, "was not for the purpose of making warriors or to show endurance, nor was it any part of the ceremony. Instead, it was . . . a sacrifice of self to bring good fortune or to avert misfortune in the future, or else was the carrying out of some instruction received in a dream." Others maintain that torture was so common during the Sun Dance that it was a fundamental element within the whole ceremony.[22]

The Cheyennes called the Sun Dance ceremony the "new-life-lodge" or "renewing the earth." The rites signified the "rebirth of life on the earth, the return of the season of growth." Since it was also a time

---

[22] Spier, "Sun Dance of the Plains Indians," 461–62, 491; Dorsey, *The Cheyenne: The Sun Dance*, 175–77, 181; George Bird Grinnell, "The Cheyenne Medicine Lodge," *Amer. Anthr.*, N.S., Vol. XVI, No. 2 (April–June, 1914), 245–47; Grinnell, *Cheyenne Indians*, II, 211.

when the whole tribe was blessed by the spirits, all of the Cheyennes desired and were expected to attend the ceremonies. The reason was simple enough: Misfortune could befall those who did not participate in the Sun Dance, and an individual's ill-luck could extend to other members of the tribe.[23]

In the days of their freedom on the Great Plains, warriors pledged to sponsor a Sun Dance if they survived imminent danger. Later, on reservations, Cheyennes vowed to sponsor a Sun Dance if a life within a Cheyenne family was preserved. The dance could be vowed by a man or woman, who would be the principal of the ceremony. Pledges to carry out a Sun Dance were made more than once, and during the ceremony the pledger became known as the lodge-maker and "reanimator," through whom the tribe was reborn and nature reproduced her kind. Those who had previously sponsored a Sun Dance formed a fraternity and possessed common ownership of the Sun Dance medicine bundle.

Before the Sun Dance, the lodge-maker's military society chose from previous sponsors a director of the rites, who became the ceremonial grandfather of the lodge-maker. By sponsoring the Sun Dance, the pledger purchased the privilege of participating in the medicine-bundle ceremonies at later Sun Dances. These privileges came at considerable costs to the pledger and his soldier society, and the former became the keeper of the medicine bundle until the next Sun Dance, when he received gifts from the next initiate. An additional consideration in the purchase of the privileges was the required surrendering of the pledger's wife to the ceremonial grandfather during preliminary rites. If it was impossible for the lodge-maker's wife to fulfill the ceremony, another woman was selected as the co-participant.[24]

Since the Sun Dance depended upon an individual vow, it was not necessarily an annual event. Among the Southern Cheyennes the dance was usually held during July, but whatever month it was celebrated, the grass was in full growth and the cottonwoods were in full

[23] Grinnell, "Cheyenne Medicine Lodge," loc. cit., 247–48; Dorsey, The Cheyenne: The Sun Dance, 57.

[24] Spier, "Sun Dance of the Plains Indians," 481; Dorsey, The Cheyenne: The Sun Dance, 57–58, 69, 131, 150, 165; Grinnell, "Cheyenne Medicine Lodge," loc. cit., 255; Grinnell, Cheyenne Indians, II, 215–17.

leaf. The duration of the dance varied, depending upon the length of time the chief priest of the Sun Dance had fasted when he had been the lodge-maker. Usually the ceremonies lasted from five to eight days. On the appointed day Cheyenne bands began moving to the site selected for the camp circle. Always the camp was located on the south bank of a stream, its opening pointed east, and since the whole tribe was present, the circle was a mile in diameter. Fellow members of the lodge-maker's soldier society arranged the tipis in an orderly fashion along the inner circumference of the camp circle.[25]

The participants in the Cheyenne Sun Dance were fairly numerous. The lodge-maker and his female associate were the focus of most of the rituals. The lodge-maker was present throughout all the rites, and the woman during most of them. In the pageantry of the dance, the pledger's role was emblematic of the Sutaio culture-hero Erect Horn or Red Tassel, and the chief priest represented the spirit who had originally taught the ceremonies to Erect Horn. In the ceremonies and dances, it was obligatory for all members of the pledger's warrior society to take part and optional for other warrior society members.

With the camp circle in order, the ceremonies preliminary to the sacred rites began. Members of the warrior societies marched about the camp while those of the pledger's warrior society hunted. A lodge belonging to a fellow warrior society member was designated as the "warrior's tipi." To this tipi the priests of the Sun Dance repaired and planned the ceremony so that it would be carried out properly. After the meeting of the priests, the lodge became the "priests' tipi," and it was moved fifty steps within the camp circle where it became the "lone-tipi," or the "only" lodge. Within the "lone-tipi" the pledger and his woman listened and learned the duties and ceremonies of the Sun Dance. On the second day the pledger formally invited a former lodge-maker to act as the chief priest for the rituals, and in the "lone-tipi" instructions in the secrets of the ceremony began.

During the second and third days the rites largely venerated the earth. Five times the powers of the earth were acknowledged, for they sustained the buffalo, and thus the Cheyennes. With elaborate cere-

25 Dorsey, *The Cheyenne: The Sun Dance*, 59–62.

mony the Sun Dance lodge's center pole was selected, and although treated as an enemy and counted coup upon, the tribal chiefs through one of their members addressed the designated tree: "The whole world has picked you out this day to represent the world. We have come in a body to cut you down, so that you will have pity on all men, women, and children who may take part in this ceremony. You are to be their body. You will represent the sunshine of all the world." By the time the center pole was brought to the selected site of the lodge, the timbers to support the roof were in place. During the fourth day bundles of vegetation were placed in the forks of the pole, a piece of dried buffalo meat was secured to one of the bundles by a broken arrow, and a rawhide image of a human was attached. Spectators crowded forward, especially women, and tied small offerings to the center pole. The painted, decorated pole was raised into place, the remainder of the lodge's construction was quickly completed, and the materials for the Sun Dance altar were assembled. That evening the lodge was formally dedicated, and some dancing took place, marking the beginning of the dance proper.

The Sun Dance altar was assembled on the fifth day of the dance. A buffalo skull served as the altar's center, around which were placed rectangular strips of sod, symbolizing the four medicine spirits at the cardinal points and the sun, all of which was surrounded by foliage from cottonwoods and plum bushes, representing useful vegetation. To the Cheyennes the altar was the whole of the earth, "the supreme medicine being," and the lodge represented the heavens. Five times the dancers were painted during the fifth and sixth days, each painting and dance dedicated to some phenomenon of nature exercising influence over the lives of the Cheyennes. Upon the dancers' bodies yellow, pink, white, and black base paints were applied, and designs of the sun, moon, flowers, and plants were superimposed in recognition of nature's blessings. During these rituals men undertook their torture to complete their vows. A final pipe was smoked; the dance and rites to the spirits of the four directions were performed; and the chief priest, his wife, and the sponsors of the Sun Dance entered a sweat bath for purification. With the removal of the dance paint and the breaking of the fast, the Sun Dance was concluded. The Cheyennes were now reborn, the spirits looked with favor upon their people, and days of plenty were contemplated.[26]

Military societies of the Cheyennes not only had ceremonial functions such as their participation in the Sun Dance but also were largely responsible for protecting the tribe and maintaining tribal discipline. These societies of the Plains Indians were organized on either an age-grade basis or continuous membership in a specific society. A Cheyenne warrior remained within his society until he no longer took to the warpath. Three common characteristics were shared by all military socities: they functioned as police and soldiers, possessed age qualifications, and if the tribal camp was in danger the societies' membership could not leave the battlefield. Membership in the ungraded or continuous societies was voluntary, not dependent on age, and intersociety rivalry was common.[27]

Sweet Medicine in Cheyenne mythology established their military societies. As recounted in a Cheyenne tale: "When Sweet-Root [Sweet Medicine] changed himself into a wolf, he foretold the Wolf-Soldiers; when he became the fox, he foretold the Fox-Soldiers; the dog, the Dog-Soldiers; and the bull, the Red-Shields or Bull-Soldiers." At a later time the prophet of the Cheyennes organized still another warrior society, the Thunder-Bows, also known as the Bowstrings. A sixth society was founded by Owl-Man, a Cheyenne warrior, after the tribe's contact with white men. This society danced with guns, indicating its origin subsequent to white contact and the acquisition of firearms and gunpowder.[28]

26 *Ibid.,* 64ff., 111; Grinnell, *Cheyenne Indians,* II, 218ff. Spier, "Sun Dance of the Plains Indians," *loc. cit.,* can be used to compare the Cheyennes' Sun Dance with that of other Plains tribes.

27 For a general introduction and map showing the distribution of the age-grade and continuous membership societies, see Clark Wissler (ed.), *Societies of the Plains Indians,* AMNH Anthropological Paper, Vol. XI, iv–viii, and the editor's chapter, "Societies and Ceremonial Associations in the Oglala Division of the Teton-Dakota," 69, 74; Lowie, *Indians of the Plains,* 96–104; Grinnell, *Cheyenne Indians,* II, 49.

28 The names and numbers of Cheyenne warrior societies vary widely in both secondary sources and manuscripts. For the variations, see Grinnell, "Some Early Cheyenne Tales," *loc. cit.,* N.S., Vol. XXI, No. 82, 308, 311–12; George A. Dorsey, *The Cheyenne: Ceremonial Organization,* Field Mus. *Publication No. 99, Anthropological Series,* Vol. IX, No. 1, 3–29; Robert H. Lowie, "Plains Indians Age-Societies: Historical and Comparative Summary," in Wissler (ed.), *Societies of the Plains Indians,* 894; Clark,

The Dog Soldiers, also called the "Dog Men," were unquestionably "the most important, distinct, and aggressive of all the warrior societies." Comprising half of the Cheyenne warriors, the Dog Soldiers controlled the whole tribe. But the constant recurrence of the Dog Soldiers' exploits in the white man's records, especially during the wars on the Plains, can only be explained by the observers' unfamiliarity with the total organization of the Cheyenne warrior societies. The Dog Soldiers became numerically the most important of the societies in the early part of the nineteenth century. Sometime before 1850 all adult male members of the Flexed Leg band joined the Dog Soldiers, and they became a band within the tribe, camping together in the tribal camp circle, while the other soldier societies' members were scattered among the camps of other bands. Many Dog Soldiers were half-blood Sioux, which accounts for the band named the "Cheyenne Sioux" in the tribal camp circle. The Dog Soldiers were not governed by the usual band chiefs but by their own military chiefs. For these reasons the Dog Soldiers had greater cohesion and strength than other bands and soldier societies.[29]

Between the ages of thirteen and sixteen boys were initiated into a warrior society. The youth, invited by the society, was free to join almost any of the soldier organizations, but frequently he chose his father's society. It was an important event in the young man's life, and in recognition his family presented gifts to the society's chief or some other member of the society or tribe.[30]

Primarily, the soldier societies were military associations, and the members were collectively known as warriors. Although the soldier societies contained most of the adult males, there were some Cheyenne men who did not belong to any of the organizations. Comradeship was present between the society's members. They addressed each

"Ethnography and philology of the Cheyennes," *loc. cit.*, 5; Mooney, *Cheyenne Indians,* 413; Grinnell, *Cheyenne Indians,* II, 57–62; Karl N. Llewellyn and E. Adamson Hoebel, *The Cheyenne Way: Conflict and Case Law in Primitive Judisprudence,* 99; George Bent to Hyde, May 7, 1906, Bent Letters, Coe Collection.

[29] Mooney, *Cheyenne Indians,* 412; Dorsey, *Cheyenne: Ceremonial Organization,* 20; Grinnell, *Cheyenne Indians,* II, 63ff.; Llewellyn and Hoebel, *The Cheyenne Way,* 100; Dorsey, *The Cheyenne: The Sun Dance,* plate VI, opposite p. 62; George Bent to Hyde, January 23, 1905, Western History Department, Denver Public Library.

[30] Edward S. Curtis, *The North American Indian,* VI, 105; Grinnell, *Cheyenne Indians,* II, 49.

other as "friend" or "brother" and mutually protected each other in battle. Each of the associations had its own distinctive sacred symbol, decorations, paint, dances, and songs. The societies were led by a chief and seven assistants, all of whom were elected by the society's members for their bravery and success in war. Deeds of valor were recognized by extending to the warrior the privilege of wearing a buckskin coat fringed with the hair of the enemy. Esteemed were those warriors who led their fellows in successful battles with enemies, who scalped four live foes, and who rescued comrades left behind on the battleground; but reserved for the highest distinction were those who led their brothers to victory after an initial defeat. Being a chief of a soldier society carried with it great responsibilities. Only the bravest of the warriors accepted these offices because they not only planned the battle actions but were expected to lead their followers in conflict and by example rally the spirits of the warriors when disaster was impending. Succinctly stated, "death was always expected— a soldier chief was chosen to be killed."[31]

Three of the warrior societies admitted four maidens as associates into their organizations. From prominent families, preferably those of chiefs, the young women had duties confined to the society's ceremonial functions. They participated in the soldiers' dances, were present at the feasts, and sat in front of the war chiefs in all the councils. Sweet Medicine gave the soldier societies the privilege of allowing four maidens in their association but required that they be "chaste and clean." Two of the societies, the Dog Soldiers and the Bowstrings, were unwilling to assume the risk and permitted no women in their organizations.[32]

A small number of Cheyenne warriors were set apart and known as Contraries. They were not a military society but only several men selected for their strength, bravery, and leadership. Painted red and wearing clothing of the same color, the Contrary carried into battle the contrary bow, really a lance shaped like a bow with two strings. As the Contrary warrior moved into battle, he carried his lance, sometimes called the "thunder-bow," in the hollow of his left arm. As long

[31] Lowie, "Plains Indian Age-Societies," *loc. cit.,* 895; Dorsey, *Cheyenne: Ceremonial Organization,* 15–16; Grinnell, *Cheyenne Indians,* II, 51.

[32] Dorsey, *Cheyenne: Ceremonial Organization,* 16; Grinnell, *Cheyenne Indians,* II, 50.

as he maintained the lance in that position, he was allowed to maneuver freely and retreat. Once he shifted the thunder-bow to his right hand and blew his whistle, he could no longer retreat but had to charge the enemy and fight until he was killed or until the foes left the field.[33]

The life of the Contrary was not pleasant. He lived by opposites, acting and talking exactly in reverse when addressed by another member of the tribe. At one time Contraries did not marry, but later in Cheyenne history they did take wives. The warrior, whose lodge was painted red, was not expected to mingle with crowds of people. He could not joke or have a good time and was treated with deference by the rest of the tribe. No one other than the Contrary could touch the thunder-bow or eat from his dishes. At tribal councils his food was specially prepared and served to him separately. If two Contraries lived in the same camp, they might associate with each other; otherwise, a Contrary was alone. A man became a Contrary only when a vision made it clear that he could not escape from the responsibilities of the office. Duties of the office called for a warrior in the prime of life, and when unable to perform his heroic deeds in battle, the Contrary made a buffalo sack and put the thunder-bow away. The transference of the office required the payment of a large amount of property because of the office's great power, importance, and esteem.[34]

Cheyenne tribal authority also found expression among the council of forty-four chiefs. Three divergent tales, quite contradictory, give the origin of the Cheyenne tribal chiefs. About 1750 the Cheyennes encountered a hostile tribe, defeated them, and took as captive the wife of their enemy's chief. From this woman they learned of the council of forty-four and then elected members of the Cheyennes to fill the offices. Another tale has a Cheyenne woman, captured by the Assiniboins, bring the tribal council of chiefs to the Cheyennes upon her return. The woman observed that forty-four chiefs existed among the Assiniboins, and when she returned to the Cheyennes she appointed forty-four Cheyenne headmen to the office of chiefs. The Cheyennes followed the custom of replacing those who died, thus constantly

[33] George Bent to Hyde, December 31, 1906, Colorado State Historical Society, Denver, Colorado.

[34] Grinnell, *Cheyenne Indians*, II, 79–86; Dorsey, *Cheyenne: Ceremonial Organization*, 24–26.

maintaining the tribal chiefs' council. Still another tale, ascribed to Elk River, a Northern Cheyenne born about 1810, uses a common theme of deserted children solving the necessity for tribal authority. The children's father, after killing his wife, deserted a son and daughter, leaving them alone and apart from the tribe. After making their way back to the main camp, the children were accused by the father of their mother's death and as punishment they were staked to the plains and left to die. Saved by a spirit in the form of a dog, they were directed by another spirit, this one in human form, to call the Cheyennes to them. With powers to kill buffalo by simply looking at the animals, the children sent the message to the Cheyennes by a crow. When the tribe returned, the children directed a lion and a bear to kill their father. The daughter then instructed the tribe in its proper form of government, first selecting five men as head chiefs, and ultimately appointed forty-four chiefs in all, who, in council, governed the Cheyennes.[35]

Within the Cheyenne chiefs' council there were four head chiefs, two doorkeepers of the chiefs' tipi who were also called "servants," and thirty-eight undifferentiated members of the chiefs' council. All of the chiefs possessed a ten-year term of office. During the winter of the tenth year, messengers were sent among the Cheyenne camps to inform the people that a new chiefs' council was to be chosen in the spring. The council was not a democratically chosen body but rather a self-perpetuating institution. Warriors of the military societies elected their leaders, but no such election took place in the case of the tribal chiefs. Since the four head chiefs, or principal chiefs, had dual religious and secular functions, the maintenance of the office necessitated the selection of some person trained in the dual roles. A son or younger brother was often a logical successor, and the office seemed almost hereditary. In case of death and no son of sufficient age, another man filled the office until the son proved himself worthy of the position. When a principal chief died or resigned without selecting his successor, the chiefs' council was empowered to fill the office, and the new chief was likely to be picked from among the warriors who were not members of the council. It is not entirely clear from descriptions

[35] Mooney, *Cheyenne Indians*, 371–72; Grinnell, *Cheyenne Indians*, I, 345–46; Llewellyn and Hoebel, *The Cheyenne Way*, 68–73.

of the composition of the chiefs' council that the priest-chiefs were also the principal chiefs of the Cheyennes. It well may have been that the principal chiefs were four members of the previous chiefs' council who were elected to another ten years in office.[36]

Selection of chiefs was an important matter and evoked much discussion. Full details of the chiefs' council powers in religion are not fully known, nor do we know exactly how it functioned internally as the tribe's "supreme official authority." Two functions clearly within the province of the chiefs were moving the camp and determining the time and place of the communal buffalo hunt. Through a military society, the chiefs controlled the movement of the camp and the tribal hunt. When the tribe scattered and lived as bands, chiefs were still available to make these decisions. Since each band normally was represented by four chiefs in the council, the chiefs exercised the same powers for their band which the council of forty-four did for the whole of the Cheyennes.

Men of good judgment and even temperament were appointed to chieftainship. Such qualities were desirable because the chiefs, although vested with ultimate authority, managed affairs by gaining tribal acquiescence to their decisions. When the chiefs' decisions were approved by the military societies, defectors felt the weight of tribal opinion, and punishments carried tribal sanction. A sense of mutual respect existed between the tribal chiefs and the chiefs of the military societies. Tribal chiefs, whose wisdom, social recognition, and status placed them at the pinnacle of authority, realized their dependence upon the warriors of the military societies for carrying out the council's decisions. As a Cheyenne warrior remarked, the fighting men "are the ones who will have to do the work."

A decision made in 1840 to make peace with the Kiowas and Comanches reflects the interdependence of the tribal chiefs and military societies. A small Cheyenne raiding party intent upon stealing horses from the Kiowas, Comanches, or Kiowa-Apaches stopped at a large encampment of Arapahoes. In the camp were some Kiowa-Apaches

[36] Llewellyn and Hoebel, *The Cheyenne Way*, 74–75; Clark, *Indian Sign Language*, 101–102; Mooney, *Cheyenne Indians*, 402–403; Dorsey, *Cheyenne: Ceremonial Organization*, 12–15; Grinnell, *Cheyenne Indians*, I, 337, 340–41; Maurice Greer Smith, *Political Organization of the Plains Indians, with Special Reference to the Council, University Studies* of the University of Nebraska, Vol. XXIV, Nos. 1 and 2, 26–27.

visiting Bull, an Arapaho chief, and the Kiowa-Apaches stated that the Kiowas and Comanches desired to make peace with the Cheyennes. The Cheyennes declined an offer of Bull to smoke a pipe of peace with the Kiowa-Apaches, but Seven Bulls, the Cheyenne raiding party's leader, called off the raid and conveyed the peace message to the Cheyenne camp. A Cheyenne council was called, and when the chiefs were unable to decide the issue, the decision was referred to the Dog Soldiers. Finally the Dog Soldiers allowed White Antelope and Little Old Man, two of the bravest chiefs within the society, to make the decision. The two chiefs declared for peace and carried their verdict to the chiefs' council. Accepted by the chiefs, the Dog Soldiers' decision was implemented by peace with the Kiowas, Comanches, and Kiowa-Apaches, a peace which subsequently was never broken.[37]

Obviously the making of peace with powerful enemies was of crucial importance to the Cheyennes. We do not know completely what motivated the Dog Soldiers' decision in this case. Perhaps peace would lead to a greater opportunity to trade horses, to share more easily common sources of trade goods, to make an alliance which could resist more effectively white encroachment on the Southern Plains, or to form a union which could bring greater pressure against mutual enemies to the west. Young warriors with reluctance curtailed one activity, horse raiding, which brought wealth and status. War likewise brought acclaim to the fighter, yet the machinery of Cheyenne government functioned smoothly and prevented a clash between civil and military authorities and between warriors' interests and those of the whole tribe. At no time did the chiefs relinquish their authority, because the Dog Soldiers were delegated the right to decide for peace or war, and their decision was reported back to the tribal council, which reported the decision to the whole tribe through High-Backed-Wolf, the principal chief of the council.[38]

The band, rather than a clan or gens, determined individual place of residence. It was composed of unrelated, extended family households and was not exogamous; that is, it permitted marriage within

[37] Grinnell, *Fighting Cheyennes*, 63–69.

[38] Jablow, *Cheyenne in Plains Indian Trade Relations*, 75–76; Llewellyn and Hoebel, *The Cheyenne Way*, 73, 89–91, 93–94; Grinnell, *Fighting Cheyennes*, 65; Grinnell, *Cheyenne Indians*, I, 340–43.

the band, except for close relatives. There is some evidence that Cheyenne bands descended from common ancestors and that at one time exogamy was practiced. Within the period of white contact, however, the Cheyennes used the band organization and did not maintain either clans or gentes.[39]

The band, as a living unit, was an adaptation to the Plains environment. Ecologically, the Plains could not provide subsistence for a large tribal group, except during a few summer months, and small groups could more easily fatten their ponies. At other times of the year the tribe was forced to separate and yet maintain a concentration of people sufficient to repel hostile war parties. Cheyennes, and other Plains Indians, thus adopted the band as a means of meeting both necessities.[40]

Four Cheyenne bands originally occupied segments of the camp circle, separated by lines drawn from the cardinal points. The camp circle opening always faced east, and the bands occupied their same assigned places. The earliest disposition of the bands clockwise around the camp circle began with the Aorta band occupying the southeastern quadrant, the Hairy band the southwestern quadrant, the Dog Men the northwestern quadrant, and the Eater band the northeastern quadrant. Later ten bands constituted the full camp circle. The bands increased in numbers when two branched off from the Dog Men, three separated from the Hairy band, and the Sutaios were incorporated into the Cheyennes. One scholar using composite information maintains that before the reservation period, the Cheyennes were organized into thirteen bands, the additional number resulting from the division of older bands.[41]

Bands were not completely stable either in size or in membership. If a man married outside of his band, his tipi was normally located

[39] A clan is an exogamous family grouping which traces its descent through the female line, while the gens functions similarly through male descent. See George Bird Grinnell, "Social Organization of the Cheyennes," *International Congress of Americanists, Thirteenth Session . . . 1902,* 135; Lewis Henry Morgan, *The Indian Journals, 1859–1862,* 95; Mooney, *Cheyenne Indians,* 408–409; Grinnell, *Cheyenne Indians,* I, 90–92.

[40] George Bent to Hyde, April 30, 1906, Bent Letters, Coe Collection; Eggan, "Cheyenne and Arapaho Kinship System," *loc. cit.,* 85.

[41] Mooney, *Cheyenne Indians,* 402–403, 411; Grinnell, *Cheyenne Indians,* I, 88–89; Dorsey, *Cheyenne Sun Dance,* 61–62, and plate XIX.

with his wife's band. Among the Dog Soldiers, after they became a distinct band, there was considerable intermarriage, and it was much the same among the Sutaios. A man often maintained an affiliation with the band into which he had been born, and he also had the option of joining another band if he thought it presented better opportunities. Rivalries developed between bands as their numbers rose and fell. Antagonism between band members and chiefs, for example, led to families' breaking away and joining another band. When the tribe divided into its Northern and Southern divisions, the Eaters for the most part remained in the North, but other bands seemed to divide according to individual choice.[42]

Cheyenne life on the Plains early in the nineteenth century was well adapted to tribal existence. Their institutions were both meaningful and integrated. They had worked out a practical governmental system and a religion or supernaturalism related directly to the environment in which they lived, established a satisfying economy, maintained an orderly family and kinship system, and made alliances with powerful and friendly tribes which assured that they would not be exterminated by their native foes.

[42] Grinnell, *Cheyenne Indians*, I, 96–97; Eggan, "Cheyenne and Arapaho Kinship System," *loc. cit.*, 84–85.

# 4

## CHEYENNES
## ON THE ARKANSAS RIVER

THE CHEYENNE REMOVAL to the Arkansas River did not bring peace
to the tribe. The early and mid–1830's were a time of widespread
intertribal wars on the Southern and Central Plains in which the
Cheyennes frequently participated. To quell the turmoil, Secretary
of War Lewis Cass sent two expeditions to the Plains. The first, led
by General Henry Leavenworth and Colonel Henry Dodge, traveled
too far to the south and did not come into contact with the Arkansas
River Cheyennes. Its success, however, led Cass in 1835 to send Colonel
Dodge to the Central Plains to council with the Cheyennes, Arapahoes,
and their warring neighbors. In addition to terminating the Indians'
wars, Cass hoped to protect the frontier settlements and facilitate the
Santa Fe trade.[1]

After departing from Fort Leavenworth on May 29, 1835, Dodge's
expedition reached the Platte River and held a council with the Pawnees. From them Dodge learned that they were at war with the Cheyennes, Arapahoes, and Sioux and were willing to negotiate a peace
with the two former tribes. Guided by Captain John Gantt, a fur
trader, the expedition passed through the buffalo range of the Platte
River. The command's official chronicler, Lieutenant Gaines P. Kingsbury, noted that the region from the forks of the Platte to the foot of
the mountains was "neutral ground . . . and is only frequented by the
war parties of different nations. The Arepahas [*sic*] and Cheyennes
sometimes move into this country for a short time during the summer
to hunt buffalo." Information derived from Gantt and John Dougherty, the expedition's interpreter, reveals that the Cheyennes as yet

---

[1] *American State Papers*, Military Affairs, V, 358, 373–82; Louis Pelzer, *Marches of
the Dragoons in the Mississippi Valley*, 34–38; Edwin C. McReynolds, *Oklahoma: A
History of the Sooner State*, 142–48.

did not dominate the buffalo range south of the Platte and east of its southern branch.[2]

Traversing a wide arc by way of the main valley of the Fontaine qui Bouille, or Fountain Creek, the expedition encountered no Indians until the Arkansas River was reached. After camp was established on the Arkansas River about thirty miles from the mountains, three Arapahoes and a Blackfoot appeared and informed the dragoons that the Arapahoes, Gros Ventres, and Blackfeet had already assembled in anticipation of the forthcoming councils.[3]

Colonel Dodge and his soldiers arrived at Bent's Fort on August 6, 1835, and found two villages of Cheyennes occupying both banks of the Arkansas River. Because many of the Cheyennes were drunk on whisky obtained from Mexican traders, Lieutenant Kingsbury's description of the tribe was most critical. "They are," he wrote, "very fond of whiskey, and will sell their horses, blankets, and everything else they possess for a drink of it. In arranging the good things of this world in order of rank, they say that whiskey should stand first, then tobacco, third, guns, fourth, horses, and fifth, women." Bent, St. Vrain and Company enjoyed a brisk buffalo robe trade at their post with the Cheyennes, Arapahoes, Comanches, and Gros Ventres of the Prairie. The partners, Captain Lemuel Ford explained, purchased the robes "for about 25 cents worth of goods and sell them at St. Louis for five & six dollars."[4]

The Cheyennes explained to members of the Dodge expedition that their recent departure from the Missouri River was the result of Sioux hostility. Shortly after General Atkinson's 1825 treaty councils, the Cheyennes had shifted in considerable numbers to the South Platte and had taken up their residences with the Arapahoes. The Cheyennes, Captain Ford predicted, would incorporate themselves into the Arapa-

2 "Journal of a march of a detachment of dragoons, under the command of Colonel Dodge, during the summer of 1835," *American State Papers, Military Affairs,* VI, 138. Comparison of the published journal with a manuscript copy in the Office of the Adjutant General, Letters Received, reveals only minor variations in punctuation and spelling. See also Dodge to General E. P. Gaines, October 15, 1835, Office of the Adjutant General, Letters Received.

3 Lemuel Ford, "Captain Ford's Journal of an Expedition to the Rocky Mountains," *MVHR,* Vol. XII, No. 4 (March, 1926), 564–65; "Journal of Colonel Dodge," *loc. cit.,* VI, 140.

4 "Journal of Colonel Dodge," *loc. cit.,* VI, 140; Ford, "Journal," *loc. cit.,* 566–67.

ho nation for protection and success in wars. Ford's assumption was based upon his estimate of Arapaho and Cheyenne population. The Captain maintained that in 1835 the Arapahoes outnumbered the Cheyennes on the Arkansas River by almost one thousand persons. This information was incorrect because three years later Charles Bent told Superintendent William Clark that the Cheyennes, led by Yellow Wolf, Whirlwind, and White Crow, numbered 2,800 persons, while the Arapaho population did not exceed 1,600.[5]

The Cheyennes at the time of Dodge's arrival at Bent's Fort were in a state of confusion. "The Cheyennes," wrote Lieutenant Kingsbury, "are a bold and warlike band of Indians ... [and] had just killed their principal chief, and had separated into three villages, and were wandering about the prairie without any leader." High-Backed-Wolf, the principal chief in question, who had signed the 1825 treaty with General Atkinson as "the wolf with the high back," had recently been killed by relatives in a dispute over a stolen wife. Within a few days, however, enough Cheyennes were at Bent's Fort for Colonel Dodge to initiate the councils.[6]

Cheyennes, Arapahoes, Gros Ventres, and a few Blackfeet listened to Colonel Dodge as he opened the talks. The Colonel of the dragoons voiced the Pawnees' desire for peace and urged the Arapahoes to act as mediators between the Cheyennes and the Comanches. Little Moon, the second signer of Atkinson's treaty, replied for the Cheyennes. He was willing to consider continuing amicable relations with the whites but not with other Indians. Two large war parties were out—one against the Comanches, the other against the Pawnees and Arikaras—and until they returned, Little Moon refused to commit himself upon Dodge's request for an intertribal truce. The Cheyenne spokesman welcomed the Pawnee emissary accompanying Dodge's expedition and hoped that the Pawnee leader would "give each band a medicine

[5] "Journal of Colonel Dodge," *loc. cit.*, VI, 140–41; William Clark to C. A. Harris, April 30, 1838, William Clark Papers, Missouri Historical Society.

[6] "Journal of Colonel Dodge," *loc. cit.*, VI, 140–41; Grinnell, *Cheyenne Indians*, I, 30; George Bent to Hyde, October 18, 1908, Bent Letters, Coe Collection. Llewellyn and Hoebel (*Cheyenne Way*, 146–473), although familiar with the "Journal of Colonel Dodge," chose to ignore the discussion of High-Backed-Wolf's murder since it is contrary to later Cheyenne assertions of the veneration of the tribe for their chief. See also 7 U.S. Stat. 256.

arrow." Obviously, Little Moon was trying to regain the medicine arrows captured from the Cheyennes by the Pawnees in 1830.

The Pawnee representative, backed by one hundred warriors, succinctly stated the Pawnee grievances against the Cheyennes. Three or four peace treaties had already failed, and the Pawnee told the conclave that the Cheyennes "have stolen our horses and killed our people." No firm peace commitment was made by the Cheyennes although they presented twelve horses to the Pawnees as a gift.

Colonel Dodge urged the Cheyennes to select chiefs. When no Cheyennes stepped forward, the Colonel asked Little Moon to select three chiefs, who, with himself, would be recognized by the United States as the leaders of their tribe. Little Moon selected White Crow, Flying Arrow, and Walking Whirlwind, all of whom were presented with medals and informed by Dodge that they "were chiefs, and would be regarded as such by the whites." These men, the expedition's journal comments, "were not only the choice of the Cheyenne nation, but the very men that the traders who were acquainted with them would have selected." This marked the beginning of intervention by the United States into the leadership of the Cheyennes. The fact that these four chiefs were selected by whites did not bring them into disrepute, however, among their fellow tribesmen, because two years later Walking Whirlwind and White Cow, or White Crow to Dodge, were recognized as leading chiefs by Charles Bent.

Two day's march from Bent's Fort a village of fifty to sixty Cheyenne lodges was encountered. The expedition stopped for a day since the people had not been present at Bent's Fort. Large quantities of buffalo meat were drying on racks, and a large herd of horses, many of which had been recently captured from the Comanches, surrounded the village. Of these Cheyennes, Captain Ford was much more complimentary than Lieutenant Kingsbury had been of those living near Bent's Fort. Ford observed that "the Shians are very neat in the dressing & also clean about their Lodges [and] excell any Indians for cleanliness Dress & Beauty .... Their femailes are handsome & modest [and] their dress show[s] considerable taste." Again Colonel Dodge asked the Cheyennes to select a chief upon whom a medal would be bestowed; the appointee became known as the White Man's Chief.

While the dragoons were at the Cheyenne village, a mixed party of

130 Pawnee Loups and Arikaras charged the camp, firing their guns into the air as a sign of peace. Lieutenant Kingsbury, viewing the feasting and exchanging of presents, thought the dragoons had brought peace. Captain Ford was more skeptical and believed that the Pawnees and Arikaras "came here for the purpose of Stealing the Shian horses but on finding the dragoons in the vicinity thought it best to make it a campaign of peace."

Once more Dodge urged the Indians to make peace. In his discourse, Dodge assured the Cheyennes that they were a poor people and possessed no lands desired by the United States government. The Cheyennes must have wondered if Colonel Dodge were blind. Buffalo were abundant, a vast herd of ponies surrounded their village, and they had forty guns in their lodges even after giving a like number as presents to their temporary guests, the Pawnees and Arikaras. Formerly the Arikaras and Cheyennes had been friends, but when the Cheyennes allied themselves with the Arapahoes, the Arikaras began to steal Cheyenne horses. Finally, the Cheyennes trapped a twenty- or thirty-man raiding party and wiped it out, except for one warrior who returned to his people. To please Colonel Dodge, the Cheyennes agreed to try to arrange a peace with the Arikaras and Pawnees. Perhaps Dodge was successful in arranging a temporary truce, but neither the Cheyennes nor the Pawnees have any tradition of a permanent peace in this period of their history.[7]

The Cheyennes respected the Pawnees and likened their struggle to "two buffalo bulls, both pushing hard; first one would push the other, until he got tired, and then the other would push harder and drive back his opponent." Certainly there was no cessation of hostilities between the two tribes during the 1850's. Either in 1851 or 1852 the Pawnees killed Alights-on-the-Cloud, a prominent Cheyenne chief. The Cheyennes then gathered their allies the Arapahoes and Brulé Sioux, and smaller numbers of Kiowas, Kiowa-Apaches, and Crows, and followed their sacred medicine arrows and buffalo hat into battle against the Pawnees. The 1853 war against the Pawnees ended in dis-

[7] "Journal of Colonel Dodge," *loc. cit.*, VI, 142, 144; Ford, "Journal," *loc. cit.*, 568–69; Dodge to General Roger Jones, October, 1835, Office of the Adjutant General, Letters Received, and reprinted in *American State Papers*, Military Affairs, VI, 144–46; George E. Hyde, *Pawnee Indians*, 139. The "Journal of Colonel Dodge" is also found in 24 Cong., 1 sess., *Sen. Exec. Doc. No. 209* and *House Exec. Doc. No. 181*.

"Dance of the Soldier Societies," a Cheyenne ritual. From a painting by Dick West. *Courtesy Philbrook Art Center.*

Wolf on the Hill, Cheyenne chief. From a painting by George Catlin.
*Courtesy The Smithsonian Institution.*

She Who Bathes Her Knees, wife of Wolf on the Hill. From a painting by George Catlin. *Courtesy The Smithsonian Institution.*

"Sun Dance, Third Day." From a painting by Dick West. *Courtesy Philbrook Art Center.*

*Left above,* William W. Bent, proprietor of Bent's Fort and, later, Indian agent. *Courtesy State Historical Society of Colorado.*
*Right above,* Charles Bent. From a sketch by Theodore R. Davis, *Harper's New Monthly Magazine,* February, 1868.
*Below,* George Bent and his wife, Magpie, niece of Black Kettle, 1868. *Courtesy George E. Hyde.*

John Evans, governor of Colorado territory. *Courtesy State Historical Society of Colorado.*

Colonel John M. Chivington, leader of the United States Army force at Sand Creek. *Courtesy State Historical Society of Colorado.*

"Herd of Buffalo," the Cheyenne commissary. From a painting by Captain Seth Eastman. *Courtesy Ayer Collection, Newberry Library.*

aster for the Cheyennes. The warriors of the combined tribes could not drive their enemies from a strong defensive position, and the battle raged indecisively for hours. Then a body of horsemen appeared— Potawatomis armed with new rifles, who alternately advanced by platoons, firing and retreating. The Plains Indians were no match for the well-organized Potawatomi warriors, so the former fled from the battleground. In 1854, however, the Cheyennes revenged their defeat when they and the Kiowas cut off 113 Pawnees and killed them almost to the man.[8]

At first the Cheyennes were at peace with the Kiowas and Comanches on the Arkansas River, but by 1827 or 1829 the Cheyennes were at war with their southern neighbors. The source of the war was horse raiding, which was initiated by the Cheyennes, aided by Arapahoes, Gros Ventres, and Blackfeet. Bull Hump, a Comanche war chief, retaliated in 1829, seeking and running off Cheyenne horse herds north of the Arkansas River. When Bull Hump thought he was safely camped on the Arkansas River, Yellow Wolf, leading a Cheyenne raiding party, discovered the Comanches and ran off the ponies stolen from the Cheyennes and some of the Comanches' herd. Those Comanches who had horses tethered in their camp gave chase. When the Comanches drew near, the Cheyennes with guns whirled and charged their pursuers, killing several in the melee. Yellow Wolf and Little Wolf rode proudly into the main Cheyenne camp on the South Platte with the Comanche scalps, and general hostilities ensued.[9]

The antagonism of the Cheyennes also extended to the Kiowas, who were closely allied to the Comanches. About 1833 the Cheyennes attacked a Kiowa village near present Denver, Colorado, when the Kiowas were en route to trade horses for elk teeth and ermine with the Crows. The Kiowas escaped without serious casualties, losing only a woman with a white captive child. Four years later the Bowstring soldiers became anxious to raid the Kiowas' pony herds and take a few scalps. Before they could leave, an Arrow Renewal ceremony was necessary because of a tribal murder. Gray Thunder, the medicine-

---

[8] Grinnell, *Fighting Cheyennes*, 72, 78–81, 93–96; Hyde, *Pawnee Indians*, 104n., 106n., 177–79; St. Louis *Missouri Republican*, September 26, 1851.

[9] George Bent to Hyde, March 6, 1905, Western History Department, Denver Public Library; George Bent to Hyde, October 22, 1908, Bent Letters, Coe Collection; Grinnell, *Fighting Cheyennes*, 38–43.

arrow priest, at first refused to renew the arrows, but the Bowstrings beat him with their quirts until he fulfilled their request. He warned the society, however, that their first war venture would be ill-fated.

Despite the warning of Gray Thunder, small parties of Bowstrings left the Cheyenne camps and later joined into one large group. Making their way south on foot, the Cheyennes found the Kiowa village in the Washita River Valley. A Kiowa hunter discovered the Bowstring scouts and sounded the alarm in his village. Kiowas and Comanches under Satank surrounded the Cheyenne raiders and killed the entire party. The Kiowas, however, record the fight as taking place on Sweetwater Creek in the Texas Panhandle. They lost six warriors while forty odd Bowstrings were scalped, stripped, and laid out in a row by the victors.[10]

An Arapaho trading party soon afterward visited the Kiowa and Comanche camps while they were dancing in celebration of their success. The Arapahoes recognized the scalps of two of the Bowstrings and brought the news back to the Cheyennes. Infuriated by their losses, the Cheyennes sent runners to all of their tribesmen and asked their aid in wiping out the Kiowas. Porcupine Bear, a Dog Soldier chief, tried to organize the Cheyennes for vengeance, but when he and his relatives killed a Cheyenne warrior in a drunken brawl, they were forced to move away from the main Cheyenne village.

Little Wolf, a Bowstring chief, continued to incite the other soldier societies to seek revenge. At a great encampment of the Cheyennes near the Forks of the Platte River, the final decision was left to the Red Shield society, which declared for a tribal move against the Kiowas. Guns and ammunition were obtained at Bent's Fort, and the Arapahoes, camping near the post, agreed to join the Cheyennes.

The whole Cheyenne tribe, reinforced by many Arapahoes, moved toward the North Canadian River, protected by the powers of their medicine arrows. The medicine arrows' protection, however, was negated when Porcupine Bear's outlaw camp accidentally came across and wiped out a small Kiowa hunting party. Scouts from the main camp finally located the main Kiowa and Comanche camp about

[10] George Bent to Hyde, January 23, February 17, 1905, Western History Department, Denver Public Library; Grinnell, *Fighting Cheyennes*, 43–44; James Mooney, *Calender History of the Kiowa Indians*, BAE *Seventeenth An. Report*, 271–72.

twenty miles from the mouth of Wolf Creek. A group of Kiowa women, digging roots opposite the camp, was immediately attacked, and twelve of them were killed. Unable to surprise their foes, and their medicine broken, the Cheyennes still went into battle. Breaking into small groups, the Cheyennes and Arapahoes charged to the edge of the village, where the Kiowa warriors occupied rifle pits in the creek-bed sand. Behind the perimeter defense Kiowa women constructed a breastworks, in case the attackers broke through the outer defenses. The fighting surged back and forth all day; all of the tribes lost important chiefs and warriors. As the sun set, the Arapahoes and then the Cheyennes rejoined their women and children, retreating toward the North Canadian River. According to the memory of old Cheyennes, the tribe lost twelve warriors and their foes fifty to sixty men.[11] This was the last serious conflict between the Cheyennes and their southern foes.

The Southern Plains Indians all had good reasons to seek peace. Smallpox struck the Kiowas, Comanches, and Kiowa-Apaches during the summer of 1839. A year later, at the "Council House tragedy," Texans killed twelve important chiefs and twenty other leaders of the Comanches, an event illustrating the Texans' determination to free their frontier of Indian resistance. Since the Cheyennes realized that they could not wipe out their enemies, and since the Comanches and Kiowas needed allies to resist the expansion of the Texas frontier, there were advantages in amity for all of the tribes.

The Arapahoes and Kiowa-Apaches acted as intermediaries before the peace council. Little Raven, a principal chief among the Arapahoes, who married a Kiowa-Apache woman in 1840, played a leading role in bringing the five tribes together at the "Treaty Ground," a site a few miles below Bent's Fort. Little Mountain and Satank of the Kiowas, Bull Hump and Shavehead of the Comanches, and Leading Bear of the Kiowa-Apaches smoked the peace pipe with their recent foes. Three days after the chiefs met, the five tribes camped together and exchanged presents; Satank alone gave away 250 horses to his new allies. In anticipation of trade during 1841, Charles Bent

11 Grinnell, *Fighting Cheyennes*, 48–62; Mooney, *Calender History of the Kiowa, loc. cit.*, 273; George Bent to Hyde, January 23, February 17, 1905, Western History Department, Denver Public Library.

mentioned that the Comanches made peace with both the Cheyennes and Arapahoes and were expected to trade at his post.[12] These remarks of Charles Bent confirm the traditional Indian accounts of an intertribal peace on the Southern Plains that originated in 1840.

Overland travelers along the Oregon Trail came into increasing contact with Cheyennes. A few members of the 1839 Peoria Party, who had turned back at Brown's Hole, were seized by Sioux on the South Platte. Four hundred Cheyennes appeared at the Sioux village and held off the young Sioux warriors while the whites made good their escape.[13]

A year later Father Pierre-Jean de Smet, the famed Belgian Jesuit missionary, also found the Cheyennes hospitable. Traveling with an American Fur Company party under Andrew Dripps, Father De Smet stayed for a time with forty lodges of Cheyennes on the Laramie River. The Cheyennes, De Smet wrote, were civil to whites and were distinguished by their cleanliness and decency. Cheyenne men, according to the priest, were "of good stature, and of great strength; their nose is aquiline, and their chin strongly developed. The neighboring nations consider them the most courageous warriors of the prairies." The decline in Cheyenne power was accounted for by the missionary as a consequence of a "dreadful war" with the Sioux which reduced the Cheyennes to a wandering people, "lest the Scioux should come again to dispute with them the lands which they might have chosen for their country."

While De Smet visited the Cheyennes, he was embraced by a Cheyenne chief who informed him that three of the chief's best, fat dogs had been killed for a feast. The good father did not shrink from dog meat and on the contrary found it "very delicate and extremely good; it much resembles that of a young pig." The Cheyennes gave Father De Smet a large serving, which consisted of two thighs and paws, with five or six ribs. According to the laws of the feast, the guest was

---

[12] Mooney, *Calender History of the Kiowa, loc. cit.*, 274–76; Ernest Wallace and E. Adamson Hoebel, *The Comanches: Lords of the South Plains*, 277, 293–94; Jablow, *Cheyenne in Plains Indian Trade Relations*, 72ff.; Grinnell, *Fighting Cheyennes;* 63–69; Charles Bent to M. Alvaras, March 15, 1814, in "The Charles Bent Papers," *NMHR*, Vol. XXX, No. 2 (April, 1955), 155.

[13] LeRoy R. Hafen and Ann W. Hafen (eds.), *To the Rockies and Oregon, 1839–1842*, 63–64.

required to eat all of his food, but the priest was saved from embarrassment when he found he could pass the unconsumed portion to another guest along with a present of tobacco.[14]

Father De Smet returned to the Rockies in the spring of 1841 with the Bidwell-Bartleson party and Thomas Fitzpatrick's fur traders. On the Platte, the caravan had an Indian scare after Nicholas Dawson, one of Bidwell's men, wandered away from the wagons to hunt. When he returned to the wagon train, Dawson was minus his mule, rifle, and pistol, and reported excitedly that he had been surrounded by thousands of Indians. The frightened emigrants stampeded, and only with difficulty did Fitzpatrick persuade them to form a hollow square and picket their animals within the enclosure. When the thousand Indians appeared, they were forty Cheyenne warriors. De Smet said that there were eighty Cheyennes in the party, who were camped peacefully a short distance away on the Platte. Fitzpatrick, parleying with the Cheyennes, learned that the Indians did not desire to harm Dawson and disarmed him to keep him from shooting them. Dawson's version was quite different. He had been surrounded, forced to dismount at lance-point, beaten, and stripped of his possessions and clothing. Coming back to camp, Dawson borrowed a horse and gun and threatened to shoot the first Indians he encountered. Fortunately, Fitzpatrick had already talked with the Indians, and the fur trader "by some forcible language" ordered Dawson to desist. Later Dawson's property was returned to him by the Cheyennes, who also presented the emigrant with a present for each article returned, and Fitzpatrick told Dawson that he "ought to be satisfied to have got off with [his] life." Dawson agreed that the Cheyennes were not hostile, only "thievish." From such misunderstandings demands quickly arose for troops to protect the overlanders from the depredations of the Plains Indians.[15]

14 De Smet to Rev. Father Roothan, February 7, 1841, in Thwaites, *Early Western Travels*, XXVII, 160–61; Hiram Martin Chittenden and Alfred Talbot Richardson, *Life, Letters and Travels of Father Pierre-Jean De Smet, S. J., 1801–1873*, I, 211–12.

15 Jay [James] Monaghan, *The Overland Trail*, 200–205; John Bidwell, "The First Emigrant Train to California," *Century Magazine*, Vol. XLI, No. 1 (November, 1890), 116; Chittenden and Richardson (eds.), *De Smet's Life and Travels*, I, 311–12; Nicholas Dawson, *Narrative of Nicholas "Cheyenne" Dawson to California in '41, & '49, and Texas in '51*, 11–12.

In this era of Manifest Destiny it was easy for expansionists in Congress, led by Thomas Hart Benton and Lewis F. Linn, to secure appropriations for the exploration and protection of the frontier. Lieutenant John Charles Frémont, Benton's newly acquired son-in-law, was given command of the first official exploration of the Oregon Trail. Guided by Kit Carson and Lucien Maxwell, on June 10, 1842, Frémont's expedition left Cyprian Chouteau's trading post on the Kansas River. Two days out on the Platte, Cheyennes were seen for the first time by Frémont. Two Cheyenne warriors and a thirteen-year-old boy came into camp on their return from an unsuccessful horse-stealing raid against the Pawnees. Frémont was unimpressed by the Cheyennes, noting that they were "miserably mounted on wild horses from the Arkansas plains, and had no other weapons than bows and long spears." The warriors were chagrined by their lack of success and rationalized their failure by accusing the Pawnees of being cowards, "who shut up their horses at night."

The Cheyennes rode with Frémont to the forks of the Platte, where the expedition divided. Frémont and Charles Preuss, the expedition's cartographer, Maxwell, and the Cheyennes swung southwest, while the main body of men proceeded up the North Platte. For four days Frémont continued up the South Platte without incident, noticing many buffalo carcasses which indicated the presence of Indians. On July 8 the three Cheyennes who were riding a mile in the rear began whipping up their horses. Fifteen or twenty Indians were bearing down rapidly. Unable to reach a clump of timber, the explorers and their Indian friends prepared to make a stand. Just as Maxwell was about to fire, he shouted at the leading warrior in Indian language: "You're a fool, God dam you, don't you know me?" Wheeling, the Indian approached Frémont, struck his breast, and exclaimed, "Arapaho." The Arapahoes appeared disappointed that the Indians with Frémont turned out to be Cheyennes because they had hoped for a few Pawnee scalps.

In the confusion of the charge, the Cheyennes lost their pack horse used to carry their shields, spears, and gifts received from Frémont. The Cheyennes were mortified by their unsuccessful raid upon the Pawnees, and one of them said: "Our people will laugh at us returning to the village on foot, instead of driving back a drove of Pawnee horses." Not far away there was a village of Arapahoes, in which there were twenty Cheyenne lodges, containing the families of Frémont's Cheyenne friends.[16]

Leaving the Arapaho village, Frémont continued up the South Platte toward Fort St. Vrain. En route, Jim Beckwourth was encountered hunting horses. Baptiste Charbonneau, Sacagawea's son and an employee of Bent, St. Vrain and Company, entertained the party at his island post forty or fifty miles below Fort St. Vrain with mint juleps, boiled buffalo tongue, coffee, and "the luxury of sugar." Fort St. Vrain was reached on July 10, 1842, and there the small party was hospitably received by Marcellus St. Vrain, the younger brother of the Bents' partner. This post, supplied out of Bent's Fort, was maintained to take advantage of the trade with the Arapahoes, Cheyennes, and Sioux who frequented the abundant buffalo herds ranging east of the South Platte. At Fort St. Vrain, Frémont obtained a few horses and mules before he left to rejoin the main body of his expedition at Fort Laramie.[17]

While Frémont was absent, other members of the expedition learned disquieting information. The Sioux, Cheyennes, and Arapahoes in the region were in an ugly mood. Early in 1841, Henry Fraeb and his band of hunters had built a trading post on the Green River in Wyoming. Needing meat, the hunters led by Fraeb wandered toward the Overland Trail and met the Bidwell-Bartleson party, from whom the mountain men obtained a supply of trading whisky. While Fraeb was out hunting, a party of 500 Cheyennes, Arapahoes, and Sioux attacked a Snake village with whom the remainder of Fraeb's party were living. In this battle 3 trappers were killed, and the victors ran off 160 ponies. Jim Bridger immediately sent word to Fraeb to return and join him at the post which he was constructing on the Green River.

While Fraeb and his hunting party were on their way to join

16 For the role of Thomas Hart Benton in Western expansion, see Elbert B. Smith, *Magnificent Missourian, The Life of Thomas Hart Benton,* and William Nisbet Chambers, *Old Bullion Benton: Senator from the New West;* see also Allan Nevins, *Frémont, the West's Greatest Adventurer,* I, 92–93; Frémont, *Report,* 9–10, 18, 23–29; Charles Preuss, *Exploring with Frémont: The Private Diaries of Charles Preuss,* 15, 18.

17 George Bent to Hyde, March 19, 1906, Bent Letters, Coe Collection; Rufus B. Sage, *His Letters and Papers, 1836–1847,* II, 57; Frémont, *Report,* 29–35.

Bridger, they were intercepted by the big war party of Cheyennes, Arapahoes, and Sioux. Hopelessly outnumbered, the mountain men dug in behind their horses and tree stumps on a small tributary of the Little Snake River, near the present Wyoming–Colorado state line. Jim Baker, one of Fraeb's men, gave an account of the fight, in which the Cheyennes and Sioux did most of the fighting while the Arapahoes encouraged their allies. Baker recalled:

> Old Frappe [Fraeb] was in command. The Indians made about forty charges on us, coming up to within ten or fifteen paces of us every time . . . . Old Frappe kept shouting, "Don't shoot until you're sure. One at a time." Old Frappe was killed, and he was the ugliest looking dead man I ever saw, and I have seen a good many . . . . Well, when the fight was over there were about a hundred dead Injuns. There were three of our party killed.

Other accounts vary in the casualties suffered, but the Indians lost from five to ten times the number of mountain men killed. The tribes in 1842 were still furious at their losses and were scouring the country west of the Red Buttes looking for whites. Experienced mountain men such as Jim Bridger and Thomas Fitzpatrick made wide detours to the south when coming east in 1842, to avoid the enraged Cheyennes, Arapahoes, and Sioux. Kit Carson was brave but not foolish enough to ignore the danger; he made out his will at Fort Laramie in case Lieutenant Frémont decided to press on. Preuss thought it unwise to risk the lives of twenty-five people, "just to determine a few longitudes and latitudes and to find out the elevation of a mountain range."[18]

Frémont knew that Fitzpatrick had succeeded in guiding Dr. Elijah White and his party through the dangerous country, so Frémont saw no reason to turn back. It took all of Broken Hand's (Fitzpatrick's)

---

[18] Bidwell, "The First Emigrant Train to California," loc. cit., 119; Howard Stansbury, Exploration and Survey of the Valley of the Great Salt Lake of Utah, 239–40; Grinnell, Fighting Cheyennes, 72; LeRoy R. Hafen, "Fraeb's Last Fight and How Battle Creek Got Its Name," Colo. Magazine, Vol. VII, No. 3 (May, 1930), 100–101; Charles Edmund DeLand, "Basil Clement (Claymore)," SD Historical Collections, XI, 291; Lavender, Bent's Fort, 400n.; Frémont, Report, 41–42; Preuss, Exploring with Frémont, 21–22.

skill, however, to obtain an unmolested passage from 350 Oglala Sioux, Cheyenne, and Arapaho warriors who surrounded the white party near Independence Rock. At the parley, the Indians assured Fitzpatrick that "this path was no longer open, and that any party of whites which should thereafter be found upon it would meet certain destruction." When Sioux chiefs warned Frémont at Fort Platte that their young men were on the warpath, the Pathfinder (Frémont) predicted that if he and his men were killed, the Great White Father "before the snow melts will sweep away your villages as the fire does the prairie in the autumn." Preuss grumbled and confided in his diary that if he had foreseen these events, "I should not have come along. I see no honor in being murdered by this rabble."

Frémont's luck did not desert him west of Fort Laramie. Before he reached the upper reaches of the North Platte, the big village of Oglalas, Cheyennes, and Arapahoes had dispersed, some going off to fight Crows, others retreating into higher ranges looking for game and grass. Almost without incident, Frémont terminated his westward penetration at Frémont Peak, an eminence in the Wind River Mountains, in mid-August and returned to the mouth of the Kansas River by October 1, 1842, completing his first exploration of the Far West.[19]

During the summer and fall of 1842, the Cheyennes were scattered from the North Platte to the Arkansas River. One small band of Cheyennes, numbering only seventy to eighty people, remained on the Arkansas River just below Bent's Fort. Rufus Sage found still another small village near Fort St. Vrain on the South Platte. Among the Cheyennes, evidences of tribal degradation was apparent to observers. Sage commented in 1842 that formerly the Cheyennes were "a much better people, but the contaminating effects of intercourse with the whites have made a disposition, naturally bad, immeasurably worse . . . they are treacherous and unworthy of trust, at all times and in all places." At Fort Lupton, Tall Soldier's Cheyennes were in possession of three white men's scalps. They requested and were denied a "scalp-feast" by Lancaster P. Lupton, owner of the post. During the

19 LeRoy R. Hafen and Francis Marion Young, *Fort Laramie and the Pageant of the West, 1834–1890*, 98–99; Frémont, *Report*, 40–41, 47, 50–79, 145–46; Preuss, *Exploring with Frémont*, 29.

winter of 1842–43, Sage also learned that three Cheyennes were killed by their fellow tribesmen during a drunken brawl.[20]

Fierce competition among the fur and hide traders who used whisky freely caused much of the trouble for the Indian tribes. The going rate on the Plains was four and one-half pints of diluted whisky for one Indian buffalo robe. Uncut whisky sold in St. Louis at ten to fifteen cents per gallon, and the robes brought the traders about five dollars in St. Louis. Major trading outfits as well as irresponsible traders poured whisky down the throats of their customers. Whisky, wrote Frémont, "will purchase from an Indian everything he possesses—his furs, his lodge, his horses, and even his wife and children."[21]

On the other great trading thoroughfare, the Santa Fe Trail, similar conditions existed. The Bents and St. Vrain carved out a permanent trading area and maintained it in the face of vigorous competition. John Gantt and his partner, Jefferson Blackwell, in 1832, opened a trading post five miles east of the mouth of Fountain Creek on the Arkansas River. Gantt, known as "Baldhead" among the Cheyennes, introduced the tribe to whisky on the Arkansas River. By 1835 the Gantt and Blackwell post was in ruins, but in 1842, George Simpson, J. B. Doyle, and Alexander Barclay built a new post, named "Pueblo," which became the center for a notorious nest of illegal whisky-traders. Within a decade the Cheyennes, previously opposed to the use of liquor, were known to be a tribe of drunkards.[22]

Even Jim Beckwourth, "Yellow Crow" to the Cheyennes, was somewhat abashed over the consequences of the whisky traffic; it did not, however, deter him from plying his Indian customers with whisky. Beckwourth reckoned the profits this way:

[20] Joseph Williams, *Narrative of a Tour from the State of Indiana to the Oregon Territory in the Years 1841–42*, in Hafen and Hafen (eds.), *To the Rockies and Oregon*, 279–80; Rufus Sage, *His Letters and Papers*, I, 256–58, II, 54–55, 60; LeRoy R. Hafen, "Old Fort Lupton and Its Founder," *Colo. Magazine*, Vol. VI, No. 6 (November, 1929), 220–44.

[21] Frémont, *Report*, 39–40; Hafen and Young, *Fort Laramie*, 50, 63; Bernard De Voto, *Across the Wide Missouri*, 31; Rufus Sage, *His Letters and Papers*, I, 257–58.

[22] Arthur J. Fynn, "Fur and Forts of the Rocky Mountain West," *Colo. Magazine*, Vol. IX, No. 2 (March, 1932), 50–51; Grinnell, "Bent's Old Fort," *loc. cit.*, 44–45; Rev. Moses Merrill, "Diary," NSHS *Transactions and Reports*, IV, 181; George Bent to Hyde, July 25, 1911, Bent Letters, Coe Collection.

Let the reader sit down and figure up the profits on a forty-gallon cask of alcohol, and he will be thunderstruck, or rather whisky struck. When disposed of, four gallons of water are added to each gallon of alcohol. In two hundred gallons there are sixteen hundred pints, for each one of which the trader gets a buffalo robe worth five dollars![23]

For a season Beckwourth traded for Bent, St. Vrain and Company, and then about 1842 he decided to strike out on his own. With a partner, Beckwourth got together one hundred gallons of alcohol and some fancy trade articles and sought out the Cheyennes. When he found the Outlaw band on the South Platte, he placed his alcohol and trade goods in the lodge of the chief, Old Bark, so that the younger warriors would not appropriate his goods without payment. After a few disagreements, orderly trading began, and women brought their robes, while warriors pledged a horse or mule for whisky. Beckwourth bought four hundred robes, thirty-eight horses and mules, and much fancy handwork of the Cheyenne women. After packing up the robes on the horses and mules, Beckwourth brought out five more gallons of whisky for the crowd. In appreciation, the Cheyennes produced forty very fine robes—the kind "the young squaws finish with immense labor to present to their lovers."[24]

Charles Bent, the senior member of Bent, St. Vrain and Company, defended with vigor his company's interest against such interlopers as Beckwourth and the Mexican traders. In particular, Bent complained to Superintendent D. D. Mitchell, who was formerly an employee of the American Fur Company, that unlicensed traders operating out of Pueblo were disrupting legitimate trade. Also large parties of Mexican traders frequently passed over onto American soil and stirred up the Indians against the licensed traders. Beckwourth's trade alone amounted to robes worth three thousand dollars on the St. Louis market. Thoroughly irritated by his loss of profits and trade, Charles Bent informed the Superintendent at St. Louis that there are "several renegade Americans, who have built houses on the Arkansas River .... This [Pueblo] is also a harbor for all Mexican traders .... The

[23] James P. Beckwourth, *The Life and Adventures of James P. Beckwourth,* 305.
[24] George Bent to Hyde, January 7, 1905, Bent Letters, Coe Collection; Beckwourth, *Life and Adventures,* 312, 314–20.

only mode to put a stop to the liquor trade from Mexico is to establish a military post" on the Arkansas.[25]

Bent's suggestion for a military post met with no response from
the Indian officials or the army. Mexican traders appeared wherever
the Cheyennes camped. One outfit from Taos and Santa Fe appeared
at Fort Laramie, where they competed for robes with licensed American traders. Later another caravan from New Mexico found a Cheyenne encampment on the South Platte. In the orgy that followed, eight
Cheyennes were killed by their own people. Generally, responsible
traders agreed that the chiefs opposed the use of liquor but were
unable to check its acquisition by their young men. Although Charles
Bent heartily disapproved of the whisky trade, this did not stop his
brother William from making liquor an important staple in his
trading stock at Bent's Fort.[26]

In response to Bent's complaints, four companies of dragoons
marched along the American portion of the Santa Fe Trail in the
spring of 1843. Captain Philip St. George Cooke, commanding the
dragoon expedition, noted that the Cheyennes ranged between the
upper waters of the Platte and Arkansas rivers, following the buffalo,
and were "generally armed with guns which they procure at the trading houses—sundried brick 'forts'—of American trading companies
on both rivers, exchanging buffalo robes and some beaver." The warlike Cheyennes, numbering about five thousand persons, lived in
friendship with the Arapahoes, with whom they often intermarried.[27]

Also in 1843, John C. Frémont undertook his second expedition into
the Far West. Frémont gathered some of the same companions from
his first reconnaissance, included a twelve-pound brass howitzer in
his equipment, and departed from Kaw Landing on May 29, 1843.
He saw no reason to retrace his previous route and charted his course
up the Kansas and Republican rivers and then across to the South

[25] Bent and St. Vrain to Mitchell, January 1, 1842, Charles Bent to Mitchell, May 4,
1843, William Clark Papers, Kansas State Historical Society. Copies of these letters are
also in St. Louis Superintendency, Records of the Office of Indian Affairs, National
Archives. Beckwourth, *Life and Adventures*, 320; Lavender, *Bent's Fort*, 214–25.

[26] Dripps to Harvey [October, 1844], Clark Papers, Kansas State Historical Society;
George Bent to Hyde, July 25, 1911, Bent Letters, Coe Collection.

[27] William E. Connelley (ed.), "A Journal on the Santa Fe Trail," *MVHR*, Vol. XII,
Nos. 1 and 2 (June, September, 1925), 72–98, 227–55.

Platte. Traversing the heart of the central buffalo range, Frémont saw no Indians until an Arapaho village of 160 lodges was encountered between Forts Lupton and St. Vrain. Even a side trip from Fort St. Vrain to Pueblo failed to reveal any concentration of Indians.[28]

Frémont explained the absence of Indians along the Republican River by declaring it a "war ground" for the mutually hostile eastern and western Indians. Indians, however, were using the range in the summer of 1843 and were found by traders, including Rufus Sage. The latter agreed with Frémont's generalization and wrote: "The region lying upon the head branches of the Kansas River is considered very dangerous,—it being the war-ground of the Pawnees, Caws, Cheyennes, Sioux, and Arapahos." Sage and his companions, unlike Frémont, were searching for Indians and were led to a six- or seven-hundred-lodge encampment of Arapahoes, Cheyennes, and Sioux. This village, containing about five thousand Indians, was en route to the South Platte to trade the robes acquired from an early summer's hunt.[29]

Not until Frémont approached Fort Bridger did the party come into contact with Cheyennes. Previous to Frémont's arrival in the region, Cheyennes had tried unsuccessfully to raid the horse herds of the Shoshonis near Fort Bridger. An observer reported that the Cheyennes made a "beautiful sight" as they "formed in the shape of a crescent driving stolen horses at full speed before them. A party of skirmishers following close behind, sig-zagging or as it is called 'making snake' along the line, which they endeavored to prevent the pursuers from breaking." After losing their stolen ponies back to the Shoshonis, the large Cheyenne war party turned upon Frémont's party but did not attack because of "his bold stand and the howitzer's death dealing bombs." Seventy Cheyennes and Arapahoes charged Frémont's camp but pulled up short when they saw the men were not Indian foes. Their mistake was excused by Frémont, who explained that the Cheyennes and Arapahoes "had been on a war party, and had been defeated, and were consequently in the state of mind which aggravates their innate thirst for plunder and blood."[30]

28 Frémont, *Report*, 105–107, 111–19; Nevins, *Frémont*, I, 138–39, 142–46.

29 Frémont, *Report*, 114–15; Sage, *His Letters and Papers*, II, 262, 265–70.

30 Theodore Talbot, *Journals*, 41–42; Frémont, *Report*, 126–27; John Charles Frémont, *Memoirs of My Life*, I, 196.

After a year-long journey which carried Frémont as far west as central Oregon, the expedition reached Bent's Fort on July 1, 1844. Frémont's party rested four days at Bent's Fort and then went into camp twenty miles below the post on the Arkansas River. There the travelers were met by a large party of Cheyennes and Sioux who were returning from a visit to the Kiowa and Comanche country south of the Arkansas. Prior to meeting Frémont, these Cheyennes and Sioux had encountered on the Smoky Hill River a party of Delawares who were returning from a successful hunt in the Rocky Mountains.

These tribes were not at war with each other in 1844. But the vastly superior force of Cheyennes and Sioux followed a Delaware family to their camp and immediately opened fire. The Delawares retreated into a ravine, tied up their horses, and rejected Cheyenne peace overtures. Why the Cheyennes and Sioux persisted in their attack is not clear; perhaps the temptation of the Delawares' skins and pelts was too strong to be resisted. Because Cheyennes had no taste to face the guns of the Delawares, Medicine Water, as a ruse, gave his nephew Alights-on-the-Cloud a shirt of mail and told him to ride close to the Delawares to draw their fire. The strategem worked. The Cheyennes then rushed the Delawares and killed the whole hunting party. Fearing retaliation, the Cheyennes asked Frémont to carry a peace message to the Delawares. Amicable relations were restored in 1845, when some Delawares, accompanying Frémont on his third expedition, met the Cheyennes at Bent's Fort. Yellow Wolf and Old Bark apologized to the Delawares, and the latter chief accepted from the Delawares "a curious pipe," which he said he would "always reverence as great medicine . . . [to] be handed down to our children as a memorial of this day, when we reestablished our firm friendship with our brothers towards the rising sun."[31]

Frémont's reconnaissance parties were not strong enough to impress the Plains Indians that the United States was capable of defending the overland routes. Colonel Stephen Watts Kearny and 250 dragoons, with Thomas Fitzpatrick as their guide, departed from Fort Leavenworth on May 1, 1845, to quiet the Indians along the Oregon

[31] Frémont, *Report*, 287–88; Preuss, *Exploring with Frémont*, 138; Grinnell, *Fighting Cheyennes*, 75–78; George Bent to Hyde, November 22, 1908, Bent Letters, Coe Collection; 29 Cong., 1 sess., *Sen. Doc. No. 438*, 4; Frémont, *Memoirs*, I, 424–25; 30 Cong., 1 sess., *Sen. Exec. Doc. No. 23*, 16.

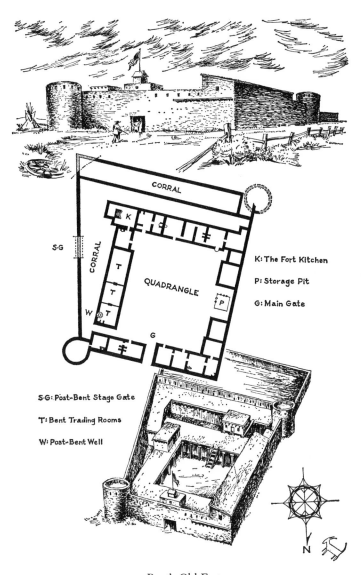

CORRAL

CORRAL

S·G

QUADRANGLE

T
T
T

K
G
P
W
G

K: The Fort Kitchen

P: Storage Pit

G: Main Gate

S·G: Post-Bent Stage Gate

T: Bent Trading Rooms

W: Post-Bent Well

N

Bent's Old Fort

95

Trail. On the main route Kearny's dragoons met with Pawnee, Sioux, Cheyenne, and Arapaho Indians. These tribes were firmly told that "the road opened by the dragoons must not be closed by the Indians, and that the white people travelling upon it must not be disturbed, either in their persons or property."

On Chugwater Creek, a tributary of the Laramie River, the dragoons visited an interesting band of Cheyennes. As described by Captain Cooke, these Cheyennes were led by a "patriarch, with the garrulity of age, and the shadow of an authority which had descended to the active warriors, and even sages of the first and second generations, addressed his two hundred descendants and connexions, and enforced the excellent advice given them by the colonel; and, with still greater emphasis, acknowledged a liberal largess."

Later Captain Cooke wrote vivid descriptions of this mid-July visit to the Cheyenne village. Cooke, like Frémont in 1844, noted that the Cheyennes still possessed "numerous wolf-dogs" used for transporting smaller camping articles from place to place. The hunters brought in horseloads of meat, while

> . . . a bevy of red ladies sitting [i.e., sat] around a white, well-dressed buffalo-robe, extended on a frame; they had shells containing different dyes, with which they were ornamenting it, in many quaint and regular figures: either from native modesty, or possessing the boasted easy self-possession of civilized refinement, they did not interrupt their embroidery at our approach, or exhibit any of that curiosity or excitement which we might flatter ourselves our sudden and warlike visit had inspired.

Captain Cooke envied this

> . . . happy, secluded community . . . a patriarchal family numbering two hundred; all descended—save those who joined to them by marriage—from this old chief . . . . Children were very numerous; like Arabs, they indulge in a plurality of wives. They wear their hair long, and are partial to our caps of fur: happy for them, if they remain far distant from whites, and follow no less innocent fashions than that of a headdress.[32]

[32] S. W. Kearny, *Report of a summer campaign to the Rocky mountains, &c., in 1845,* 29 Cong., 1 sess., *House Exec. Doc. No. 2,* 211, 216; St. Louis *Missouri Republican,* September 1, 1845; *Niles'-Register,* Ser. 5, Vol. XIX, No. 8 (October 25, 1845); 123; Philip St. G. Cooke, *Scenes and Adventures in the Army: Or, Romance of Military Life,* 395–97.

The well-intentioned wishes of Captain Cooke did not come true. Less than a year after Kearny's expedition, a flood of travelers and troops passed through the Cheyennes' country. President James K. Polk began fulfilling the "manifest destiny" of the United States. Following the President's suggestion, Congress declared that "a state of war exists" between the United States and the Republic of Mexico. During June, 1846, Fort Leavenworth served as a staging post for the "undisciplined mob that called itself the Army of the West." When assembled at this post on the Missouri frontier under the command of Colonel Kearny, the Army of the West consisted of the First Dragoons, eight companies of mounted volunteers, two artillery companies, and a company of rangers from St. Louis. Kearny's column of 1,658 men had as its objective Santa Fe, the capital of the Province of New Mexico and the terminus of the Santa Fe Trail.[33]

News of the war disturbed the Santa Fe traders. Many, such as Albert Speyer, hastened on ahead of the troops to Santa Fe, seeking to arrive before the war closed down the commercial exchanges. Speyer was carrying, in addition to merchandise, two wagonloads of guns and ammunition to Mexico. On the regular Santa Fe route, where the trail parallels the Cimarron River, five Cheyennes visited Speyer's train. The Indians reported that just ahead, five hundred lodges of their people were trading with the Comanches. At the lower Cimarron Springs, described by Adolphus Wislizenus, a German physician accompanying Speyer's caravan, "a whole crowd of Shayenes—warriors, squaws, and papooses—made their appearance. The warriors sat down to a smoke and a talk, were fed, and received some presents; the squaws, some of whom were quite handsome, sold ropes, moccasins, &c., to our men, and we all parted in friendship." The Cheyennes were at peace with the Santa Fe traders in 1846, and this was a status they did not desire to break when they observed the miles of tents gathering in July at Bent's Fort.[34]

[33] Otis E. Young, *The West of Philip St. George Cooke, 1809–1895,* 176; Pelzer, *Marches of the Dragoons,* 142.

[34] Max L. Moorhead, *New Mexico's Royal Road: Trade and Travel on the Chihuahua Trail,* 152–54; A. Wislizenus, *Memoir of a Tour to Northern Mexico, Connected with Col. Doniphan's Expedition, in 1846 and 1847,* 5, 13; John Taylor Hughes, *Doniphan's Expedition and the Conquest of New Mexico and California,* 139n.; Lavender, *Bent's Fort,* 257.

Cheyennes and Arapahoes hung around the fort for handouts because they alleged that the seasonal hunt had been poor. This does not correspond with what the Americans saw as they passed over the Santa Fe Trail east of Bent's Fort. A detachment guarding a forward supply and provision train encountered a tremendous buffalo herd at Pawnee Rock. Thomas Forsyth, an old trapper and hunter, from the top of the rock stated that "buffalo were so thick that the ground were covered as far as the eye could see, in every direction," and estimated that at least five hundred thousand animals were upon the surrounding plains.[35]

Thirty-five miles below Bent's Fort, Kearny's troops passed through the "Big Timber." This was a scattered and thin grove of large cottonwood trees which extended about a mile in width and three to four miles along the north bank of the Arkansas River. A junior officer of the Army of the West commented that among these cottonwoods "the Cheyennes, Arapahoes, and Kioways sometimes winter, to avail themselves of the scanty supply of wood for fuel, and to let their animals browse on the twigs and bark of the cotton-wood. The buffaloes are sometimes driven by the severity of the winter, which is here intense for the latitude, to the same place to feed upon the cotton-wood." So favorable was the site that William Bent thought of transferring his establishment to the Big Timbers.[36]

To impress the Indians at Bent's Fort, small delegations were brought to the troops' encampment. Although Cheyennes are not mentioned as being present, their allies, the Arapahoes, were at the fort in considerable strength. One Arapaho chief came to visit Kearny and looked at the "big guns." Expressing his admiration for the Americans, the Arapaho signified that "the New Mexicans would not stand a moment before such terrible instruments of death, but would exscape [sic] to the mountains, with the utmost dispatch." When the troops departed from Bent's Fort on August 1 and 2, 1846, they left behind Lieutenant James W. Abert, sick with fever, who lamented

[35] Susan S. Magoffin, *Down the Santa Fé Trail into Mexico: The Diary of Susan Shelby Magoffin, 1846–1847*, 49; Hughes, *Doniphan's Expedition*, 139–40n.; Jacob S. Robinson, *A Journal of the Santa Fe Expedition under Colonel Doniphan*, 12–13.

[36] W. H. Emory, *Notes of a Military Reconnaissance, from Fort Leavenworth, in Missouri, to San Diego, in California*, 30 Cong., 1 sess., *House Exec. Doc. No. 41*, 13.

being denied temporarily from entering "upon a field full of interest to the soldier, the archeologist, the historian, and the naturalist." During his convalescence, Lieutenant Abert observed the Cheyennes closely and left behind a valuable record of Cheyenne life during the era of the Mexican War.[37]

37 Magoffin, *Down the Santa Fé Trail*, 67; Hughes, *Doniphan's Expedition*, 181; George Rutledge Gibson, *Journal of a Soldier under Kearny and Doniphan, 1846–1847*, 173; Abraham R. Johnston, *Marching with the Army of the West, 1846–1848*, 26, 92–93, 142–43; J. W. Abert, *Report of Lieut. J. W. Abert of His Examination of New Mexico in the Years 1846–'47*, 30 Cong., 1 sess., *Sen. Exec. Doc. No. 23*, 3. Abert's report is also found in Emory's *Military Reconnaissance*, 419–548.

# 5

## AN AGENT AND TREATY
## COME TO THE CHEYENNES

THE MEXICAN WAR MARKS THE BEGINNING of a transitional era for the Cheyennes. Earlier the Cheyennes' contact with whites had been limited to traders and occasional army expeditions of exploration and protection of the overland routes. Within a few years American population began to shift west of the lands of the Cheyennes, and the great thoroughfares to the Far West passed directly through the Cheyennes' hunting grounds and areas of occupation. More soldiers, more travelers, more roads, and more contact with whites were the inevitable results of American penetration into the regions beyond the Great Plains, with increasing control over the Cheyennes through agents and treaties by the federal government for the protection of its citizens and their interests.

From the Cheyennes, Lieutenant Abert learned that the tribal leaders sensed the dangers to their old way of life posed by the ever-increasing contact with American frontiersmen. Through interpreters Abert conversed with Old Bark and Yellow Wolf, entertaining his Cheyenne friends with hardtack soaked in molasses and water. Yellow Wolf, whose Cheyenne name was Yellow Coyote, in particular impressed the young Lieutenant as a man of considerable influence and depth of insight. The Cheyenne chief was greatly concerned with the declining population of the tribe and the decreasing number of buffalo. Unless the Cheyennes adopted the white man's way of life, Yellow Wolf believed that his people would ultimately perish.

To prevent tribal extinction, Yellow Wolf proposed that the United States aid the Cheyennes in changing their means of subsistence. He suggested that the government build a protecting fort, give all adult males a mule, teach them to cultivate the land and raise cattle. He realized that the Cheyennes would not adapt to the new way of life quickly because many "would not be content to relinquish the delights of the chase ... [but] the old men and squaws might remain at home cultivating the grounds, and be safely secured in their fort from the depredations of the hostile tribes."[1]

The Cheyennes claimed that although they committed fewer depredations than other tribes, they were ignored by the government. They were jealous of the Pawnees, who were not deterred from killing and robbing American citizens by government presents. Yellow Wolf and other chiefs with whom Abert conversed claimed they needed aid because their tribe was rapidly declining in numbers and in less than two decades they had lost half of their people. In 1845 the Cheyennes of the Central Plains suffered from the ravages of measles and whooping cough. And the tribe was hungry in 1846. Their spring and summer hunts in the Arkansas River Valley were unsuccessful because they succeeded in killing only a few old, tough bulls. There was, of course, no scarcity of buffalo this early on the Plains, but the herds were shifting from the ranges through which white travel was increasing. No longer able to hunt adequately in the immediate vicinity of the Arkansas River, the Cheyennes came to depend upon the ranges in the valleys of the Smoky Hill and Republican rivers.[2]

Two Cheyennes fascinated Abert. The largest Cheyenne seen by Abert was Big Left Hand, who stood six feet, two and one-half inches, and who, because of his enormous weight, could find no pony able to carry him during the buffalo chase. Big Left Hand became the best arrow-maker in his village. Young warriors going on a hunt or war party obtained their arrows from him, and upon their return, gave him a portion of the meat or spoils from their foray. Big Left Hand was also a shaman among the Cheyennes, claiming the power to cure snake bites by chewing coreopsis and spitting upon the wound. At Bent's Fort, however, the whites placed their reliance on alcohol, and maintained that "if they can make a person drunk soon after the bite, he is safe."

Equally interesting was Slim Face, or Mi-ah-tose, a famed warrior, whose piercing eyes scrutinized everything about him. When, in 1844, Mexican liquor was flooding into Cheyenne and Arapaho camps, Slim Face was selected by his people to go east and seek means of checking

---

[1] Abert, *Report*, 5–6.　　　　[2] *Ibid.*, 6.

the illegal whisky trade. Accompanied by William Bent, Slim Face carried his protest to the Superintendent of Indians Affairs at St. Louis. The appeal was futile, but Slim Face was filled with wonder at the multitude of white men in the fur emporium of the West. Procuring a long stick, Slim Face sat down on a busy corner, cutting a notch in the stick for each passing person. The crowds soon exceeded the stick's capacity for notches, and in awe Slim Face threw away his counter.[3]

Another and even more excellent view of Cheyenne life in 1846 is obtained from the writings of Lewis H. Garrard. For three months Garrard, a seventeen-year-old youth, lived and traveled with the Cheyennes of the Arkansas River. His native perspicacity was undoubtedly sharpened by the knowledge of his host, William Bent, and the latter's employee, John S. Smith. Garrard's first glimpse of Cheyennes came while still on the Santa Fe Trail, riding with Céran St. Vrain's wagon train bound for Bent's Fort. Two Cheyenne scouts from a war party against the Pawnees appeared, "innocent of clothing, with the exception of a cloth around the loins, and a pair of moccasins, and a robe which was drawn around while walking; but, on sitting down, it was permitted to fall off, leaving the body nude from the waist upwards." The youthful adventurer envied the Cheyennes for their free and happy life "on the untamed plains, with fat buffalo for food, fine horses to ride, living and dying in a state of blissful ignorance." With less perception, as one might expect from the young, Garrard stated: "Religion they (the Cheyennes) have none, if, indeed, we except the respect paid the pipe; nor do we see any signs or vestiges of spiritual worship."[4]

Near Bent's Fort, Garrard began observing Cheyenne camp life. He met intermarried whites such as William Bent and John Simpson ("Blackfoot") Smith.[5] With Smith, Garrard visited his first Chey-

[3] *Ibid.*, 7–14. Grinnell ("Bent's Old Fort," *loc. cit.*, 59–60) claims Slim Face carried his protest to Washington, but this is unlikely because William Bent proceeded no farther than St. Louis.

[4] Garrard, *Wah-to-yah*, 19–25, 82–83, 120.

[5] William Bent, a younger brother of Charles, in 1835 married Owl Woman, daughter of White Thunder, keeper of the medicine arrows. By this marriage Bent had four children. When Owl Woman died, Yellow Woman, a younger sister, became Bent's

enne tipi, carefully observing the Indian custom of not passing between the fire and his host, who was seated in the back of the lodge. Infringement of the custom, the Cheyennes held, dissolved the friendship. Garrard found some Cheyenne foods "hard to stomach—others quite palatable." Smith wagered that his young companion would find dog meat "the best you ever hid in your 'meatbag.'" Contrary to his prejudice, Garrard "broke the shackles of deep-rooted antipathy to the canine breed . . . [and] ever after remained a staunch defender and admirer of dogmeat." Garrard especially enjoyed a Cheyenne delicacy made of wild cherries, buffalo bone marrow, and meat patted into balls. Other foods served to Garrard consisted of buffalo hide and meat chips saved while the robe was being dressed. These chips were placed in a wooden bowl with boiling water poured over them, and Garrard found the flavor comparable to Irish potatoes. The Cheyennes also served their guest meat boiled several hours with fungus from decaying logs, which imparted an oysterlike taste to the flesh of the buffalo.[6]

For several weeks Garrard traveled with the Cheyennes while Smith traded with Lean Chief's people. Periodically, the village moved to a new camping site. Since the band was small, consisting of only eighteen lodges, the Cheyennes moved quickly. Young men drove in the horses, while the women took down the lodges and packed the travois. Soon Garrard saw nothing at the old site except "eighteen thin pillars of smoke . . . marking where had been the lodges; pieces of old, cast-off robes, and the usual *debris* of a deserted Indian camp; which with a few snarling coyotes, and large gray wolves, were all the signs of life remaining of the noisy, bustling town." At this date, dogs were still used for transportation but were not equipped with travois. They were packed with small quantities of meat or some other articles not easily injured. Smith and Garrard traded with the Chey-

wife and bore him a fifth child. John Smith arrived on the Arkansas River in 1830, after living for a number of years among the Blackfeet. Smith married a Cheyenne woman and was especially adept in trading with the Cheyennes. See Grinnell, "Bent's Old Fort," *loc. cit.,* 46–47; Lavender, *Bent's Fort, passim;* H. L. Lubers, "William Bent's Family and the Indians of the Plains," *Colo. Magazine,* Vol. XIII, No. 1 (January, 1936), 19; Garrard, *Wah-to-yah,* 95n.

[6] Garrard, *Wah-to-yah,* 95–107, 118–19, 134–35.

ennes for mules and then returned to Bent's Fort. When they re-
visited Lean Chief's camp, William Bent came with them, bringing a
full line of goods to trade for robes.[7]

Even with Smith as his companion, Garrard was not completely
safe from danger. On one of the trading trips to a Cheyenne village
on Horse Creek, Smith and Garrard passed through an unfriendly
Arapaho camp led by Coho and Beardy. Although the warriors had
in their possession "several scalps, two prisoners, and thirty, or more,
horses and mules," the Arapahoes were for some reason unhappy.
One leader of the camp declared that the "whiteman was bad, that
he ran the buffalo out of the country, and starved the Arapaho." Smith
regaled the Arapahoes with his friendship for them, pointed to his
Cheyenne wife, and claimed that it was his intention "to live and die
with the Cheyenne, for he had thrown away his brothers in the
States. The Cheyenne lodge was his home—they smoked the same
pipe—the broad prairie supported them both." Unmoved by Smith's
eloquence, the Arapahoes' leader retorted: "The whiteman has a
forked tongue." As the Arapaho warriors left Smith and Garrard,
only the trader's insight into Indian character prevented the Indians
from including Smith's animals among the horses and mules stolen
in New Mexico.[8]

Approvingly, Garrard often cast his eyes upon the Cheyenne maidens. He appreciated the care they took of their appearance and their
daring on horseback. Their brass bracelets, shell earrings, and fine
complexions, "eclipsed by a coat of flaming vermillion," also increased
their attractiveness to Garrard. In Old Bark's camp, Garrard danced
with the young people and did not evict Tobacco's teen-aged daughter when she sought to share his robe. Garrard's sojourn with the
Cheyennes ended abruptly when news arrived at Bent's Fort that
Charles Bent had been murdered on January 19, 1847, in an uprising
at San Fernando de Taos. The Cheyennes knew and respected William Bent's eldest brother and offered to send a large party to "scalp
every Mexican within reach." William Bent rejected their offer and
gathered a twenty-three-man party of employees and free trappers to
avenge his brother's murder. With the vengeance-seekers rode Gar-

[7] *Ibid.,* 95–96, 98, 103–105, 106f.
[8] *Ibid.,* 136–37, 164–65.

rard, but before they reached Taos, Colonel Sterling Price stormed the Taos pueblo and killed two hundred Mexicans and Indians.[9]

When Garrard returned to Bent's Fort in April, 1847, he had little opportunity to visit with the Cheyennes. During late April and early May, 1847, most of the Cheyennes were on the Platte, and only fifty lodges of the tribe remained on the Arkansas. The Cheyennes caused no trouble, but the Comanches and Arapahoes were attacking the trains along the Santa Fe Trail and were causing considerable concern to the traders and military officers. The Arapahoes were troublesome at Bent's Fort, but no open hostilities occurred there. Satisfied with his adventures, Garrard left Bent's Fort about mid-June, 1847, and traveled with a government train to Fort Leavenworth.[10]

With less appreciation and much less understanding, another young man visited the country of the Cheyennes in the summer of 1846. Francis Parkman, a twenty-two-year-old Bostonian, swung through the Plains via Fort Laramie, and passed Fort St. Vrain, which was "fast tumbling into ruins," to Pueblo. The latter post was far from pleasing to the fastidious Easterner, who described Pueblo as "a wretched species of fort, of most primitive construction, being nothing more than a large square inclosure, surrounded by a wall of mud, miserably cracked and dilapidated." With some exaggeration, Parkman observed that several thousand Arapahoes and their horses camping near the post were rapidly disposing of the corn which grew in the fields about Pueblo. With foresight, the Indians always left enough of the crop "to serve as an inducement for planting the fields again for their benefit the next spring."

Parkman saw few Cheyennes during his tour of the Plains. The main body of the tribe was absent from the Arkansas, hunting buffalo on the northern tributaries of the Arkansas. If he had observed them, he probably would not have described them much differently from the Arapahoes whom he encountered five days below Bent's Fort. All the time he was with the Arapahoes, Parkman was uneasy and complained that the village was filled with the stench of meat and women busy dressing robes. His comments on these Indians were unflatter-

[9] *Ibid.*, 105, 143, 176–85, 207; Grinnell, "Bent's Old Fort," *loc. cit.*, 77–81; Lavender, *Bent's Fort*, 281–83.
[10] George Frederick Ruxton, *Ruxton of the Rockies*, 272–73; Garrard, *Wah-to-yah*, 34, 36, 339, 346–48.

ing. They had "bad faces—savage and sinister. In complexion, form, and size, and feature inferior to the Sioux . . . [the women were] very ugly and dirty, like the men."[11]

With a portion of the Oregon country already acquired and Colonel Kearny gathering the Southwest to the United States, more systematic control over the Indians of the Central Plains was necessary. Again the hand of Senator Benton became visible when he suggested the appointment of Thomas Fitzpatrick, the Indians' "Broken Hand," as Indian agent for the Upper Platte and Arkansas rivers. Approval of Fitzpatrick's appointment was made on August 3, 1846, while he was still serving as a guide for Kearny's troops. The appointment, however, was not officially conferred upon Fitzpatrick until he visited the nation's capital carrying Kit Carson's dispatches from the Army of the West. Soon after accepting his commission on November 30, 1846, Fitzpatrick set out for St. Louis, where he discussed Indian affairs with Thomas A. Harvey, superintendent of Indian affairs.[12]

In St. Louis, Fitzpatrick suggested to Harvey the desirability of holding treaties with the Plains Indians. Two councils were advocated by Fitzpatrick: one on the Republican River with the Pawnee, Osage, and Kansas tribes who preyed upon travelers and citizens; and the second for the Sioux, Cheyennes, Arapahoes, Pawnees, Poncas, and Omahas at Fort Laramie. As a side benefit, Fitzpatrick thought that at the latter treaty, he might bring peace between the Sioux, Cheyennes, and Arapahoes, who were constantly warring upon the Pawnee, Ponca, and Omaha Indians. Fitzpatrick also sought money with which to buy presents for the Indians, because without gifts, he knew that nothing substantial could be achieved with the Plains Indians. Depredations committed near Bent's Fort and on the Santa Fe road, in the face of large bodies of troops, led Fitzpatrick to maintain that the tribes would not be easily intimiated by a demonstration of force.

11 *The Journals of Francis Parkman*, II, 450, 465, 468ff.; Francis Parkman, *The Oregon Trail, Sketches of Prairie and Rocky Mountain Life*, II, 30, 319–22.

12 Benton to William Medill, April 9, August 27, 1846; Fitzpatrick to Robert Campbell, August 24, 1846, enclosed with Campbell to Medill, September 24, 1846, Upper Platte Agency, Records of the Office of Indian Affairs, National Archives; Fitzpatrick to Harvey, February 4, 1847, St. Louis Superintendency, Records of the Office of Indian Affairs, National Archives; Hafen (ed.), "A Report from the First Indian Agent of the Upper Platte and Arkansas," *loc. cit.*, 122.

Among the Indians of his jurisdiction, Fitzpatrick estimated that there were 300 lodges of Cheyennes and 350 lodges of Arapahoes. Thus, the Cheyennes, according to Fitzpatrick, numbered in the winter of 1846–47 approximately 2,400 persons, or about 800 more than mentioned by Lieutenant Abert.[13]

Indian trouble along the Santa Fe route caused Fitzpatrick to proceed to Santa Fe instead of going directly to Bent's Fort as originally planned. At Santa Fe, Fitzpatrick engaged John Smith as his interpreter at the maximum salary allowed by the government, twenty-five dollars a month. Finally, on August 29, 1847, Fitzpatrick arrived at Bent's Fort, where he was greeted by a portion of the Arkansas River Cheyennes and a few Arapahoes.[14]

Fitzpatrick immediately sought to determine which tribes were committing the depredations on the Santa Fe Trail. Yellow Wolf spoke for the Cheyennes and identified the Comanches as the principal culprits. Gratified that the "great father" had finally noticed his people, Yellow Wolf promised the agent that ". . . the Cheyenne warriors shall be ready at a moment's warning to assist in punishing those bad people, the Camanches." The Indian agent assured Yellow Wolf that their "great father," the President of the United States, had enough soldiers to do his own fighting and ardently urged the Cheyennes not to embroil themselves in intertribal wars.

Yellow Wolf repeated his request made to Abert the year before, that the Cheyennes be aided in adopting agriculture and cattle raising. Not even the death of one of the Cheyennes' best and wisest men at the hands of the whites had caused the tribe to take revenge upon the whites. Old Tobacco, who had been John Smith's and Garrard's host, had sought in the spring of 1847 to warn a government train of the Comanches' hostility. As the friendly Cheyenne chief entered the train's camp, he was fired upon and mortally wounded. The dying chief urged his family and relatives not to avenge his death,

13 Fitzpatrick to Harvey, January 3, April 30, 1847, St. Louis Superintendency, Records of the Office of Indian Affairs, National Archives.

14 "Appendix to the Report of the Commissioner of Indian Affairs," 30 Cong., 1 sess., *Sen. Exec. Doc. 1*, 238–41. This report is in the form of a letter from Fitzpatrick to Harvey, September 18, 1847 (hereafter cited as Fitzpatrick, "Report for 1847"; see also, Lavender, *Bent's Fort*, 302; Hafen (ed.), "A Report from the First Indian Agent of the Upper Platte and Arkansas," *loc. cit.*, 128.

because ". . . his friends had killed him without knowing who he was."[15]

Fitzpatrick closed his first council with the Cheyennes and Arapahoes by reprimanding the latter tribe because many of their warriors had already joined the Comanches. An Arapaho chief to whom the Indian agent addressed his remarks admitted that many of his braves were absent on the warpath. For twenty-four years Fitzpatrick had worked and traded among the Plains Indians, and these experiences had taught the Indian agent not to place too much confidence in their professions of friendship. "Circumstances and necessities," Fitzpatrick wrote, "may seem to change their disposition; but ingratitude, low mean cunning, cowardice, selfishness and treachery, are the characteristics of the whole race." Fitzpatrick believed the Cheyennes were sincere in their friendship at the time, but he doubted that agriculture would be a success among them since it was "too laborious" for the Indians' habits.[16]

In a series of reports written in 1847, Fitzpatrick reviewed the status of the Plains Indians and suggested plans for their control. The Cheyennes claimed the Arkansas River and the surrounding country without exact limits. Together with their allies, the Sioux and Arapahoes, they claimed the whole region along the eastern base of the Rocky Mountains and between the Missouri River and northern boundary of New Mexico to the western fringe of white settlements. The Cheyennes warred over a great region—into New Mexico, into the mountains against the Utes and Shoshonis, and toward the lands occupied by the Pawnees and other more easterly tribes. In 1847 the Cheyennes were less numerous than their confederates, the Arapahoes, and about one-third as powerful as the Sioux bands with whom they were also allied.[17] Of these Indians, Fitzpatrick thought the Arapahoes were the most dangerous, not that they were braver or more courageous than

[15] Garrard, *Wah-to-yah*, 138ff.; Fitzpatrick, "Report for 1847," 241–42.

[16] Fitzpatrick, "Report for 1847," 243. In Hafen (ed.), "A Report from the First Indian Agent of the Upper Platte and Arkansas," 133, the leader of the hostile Arapahoes is identified as "Coho, or the lame." During the winter of 1847–48, Coho, on several occasions, vigorously denied that he and his band were raiding with the Comanches (see Fitzpatrick to Harvey, February 13, 1848, Upper Platte Agency, Letters Received).

[17] Using the approximation of eight people to a lodge, the Cheyennes' population was 2,000; the Arapahoes, 2,800; and the Sioux, 6,400.

the Cheyennes and Sioux, but because of the confidence acquired in their succcessful conflicts with the whites moving over the Santa Fe route. The friendship of the Cheyennes could easily change to hostility since they were under heavy pressure from the Kiowas and Comanches, who told their northern neighbors that the emigrants from the United States were "as easily killed as elk or buffalo, and [were] not at all to be compared with the Texans."[18]

To insure peace on the Central Plains, Fitzpatrick presented a positive program. First, the illegal liquor trade had to be stamped out. The new Indian agent felt that major traders such as Bent, St. Vrain and Company, and Pierre Chouteau, Jr., and Company, would cooperate, since they had already learned that "traffic in spirituous liquors was becoming very unprofitable." Fitzpatrick singled out John Ruchare, Parkman's John Richard, as one of the more notorious liquor peddlers among the Indians from the Platte to the Arkansas. On the latter river the posts at Pueblo and Hardscrabble were the centers from which whisky poured into the Indian camps.

For the task of protecting the caravan routes, Fitzpatrick urged the formation of a highly mobile body of troops under the command of an experienced officer. These troops would consist of 250 mounted riflemen, 100 well-disciplined dragoons, 100 Mexican lancers and would be supported by two or three mountain howitzers with trained gun crews. The core of the command would be recruited from old trappers skilled in Indian fighting, who would train the neophytes in the arts of punishing their Indian foes. The Indian agent's suggestions were reasonable and based upon personal knowledge of the Indians, their habits, and the terrain in which they lived. Little notice, however, was paid to Fitzpatrick's recommendations.[19]

During his residence at Bent's Fort, Fitzpatrick succeeded in preventing a Cheyenne war party from attacking the frontier of New Mexico. The Indian agent also witnessed an incident of conflict between the Cheyennes and Arapahoes. While observing a dance, Fitzpatrick saw an old woman enter the dance circle, "bleeding from every pore, her face, legs, and arms bleeding profusely," and ask for

18 Fitzpatrick, "Report for 1847," 244.
19 Fitzpatrick, "Report for 1847," 246–48; Jackson Taylor, Jr., "Early Days at Wetmore and on the Hardscrabble," *Colo. Magazine*, Vol. VIII, No. 3 (May, 1931), 116.

vengeance upon an Arapaho who had killed her only son. Cheyenne warriors broke up the dance, mounted their best horses, and later that night they returned with "two Arapahoe scalps, and a squaw as prisoner." In a few months the Cheyennes and Arapahoes settled their differences, drawing from Fitzpatrick the comment that even the relations between Indian allies were always precariously balanced. Although pleased with the Cheyennes' and Arapahoes' willingness to abide by his instructions, the Indian agent stated that the "best and surest method to keep them in this pleasing mood would be to show them the symptoms of our ability to chastise offenders."[20]

Nothing Fitzpatrick could do deterred the Cheyennes and Arapahoes from carrying war to the Pawnees, for whom the Indian agent had little sympathy. After the Cheyennes and Arapahoes had patched up their temporary grievances, the two tribes sent a large combined war party against the Pawnees. The basic source of the conflict was struggle for former Pawnee buffalo ranges. "The Platte river," wrote Fitzpatrick, "the headwaters of the Kansas, and even southwest to the Arkansas were formerly the hunting grounds of the Pawnees, but now these districts are generally occupied by numerous bands of Sioux, Cheyennes, and Aripahoes, who are gradually nearing the Pawnees, with a full determination of 'wiping them out.' This the Pawnees have all brought on themselves, as they are too rascally to live in peace with any other nation." Persistently the Pawnees maintained the struggle and raided the Cheyennes' horse herds. When Fitzpatrick entreated with the Cheyennes to abandon "their abominable and cruel war" with the Pawnees, their spokesman replied: "What, do you wish us to remain here inactive whilst our brethren are being murdered and plundered by our enemies? No: we will [go] forward and seek revenge."[21]

While Fitzpatrick was assuming his duties as Indian agent, the War Department made its first efforts to protect the Santa Fe trade. In the spring of 1847, Fort Mann was constructed just west of present

[20] Hafen (ed.), "A Report from the First Indian Agent of the Upper Platte and Arkansas, *loc cit.*, 128, 132; Fitzpatrick to Harvey, December 18, 1847, February 15, 1848, Upper Platte Agency, Letters Received.

[21] Fitzpatrick to Harvey, December 18, 1847, June 24, 1848, Upper Platte Agency, Letters Received.

Dodge City, Kansas, and in that fall it was occupied by a battalion of Missouri volunteers under Lieutenant Colonel William Gilpin. During the season's travel, forty-seven Americans were killed, 330 wagons were lost, and 6,500 draft animals were captured on the road to New Mexico. Early in the winter of 1847–48, Gilpin stationed his three companies of infantry at the little stockade called Fort Mann and took his cavalry to winter quarters at Big Timbers. Impressed by this show of strength, the Cheyennes and Arapahoes broke off their relations with the Kiowas and Comanches and tried to persuade the Kiowas to abandon their alliance with the Comanches.

With little to do during the winter months, Gilpin spun some fantastic schemes. He urged Fitzpatrick to select the most stable of the Cheyennes who had previously requested aid in adopting agriculture and to settle them at the Cimarron cutoff of the Santa Fe Trail on the Arkansas River. Gilpin naively reasoned that those Cheyennes would not only provide food for troops and travelers but would also protect the route from raiders. The suggestion brought a vigorous dissent from the Indian agent. "No policy," Fitzpatrick criticized, "could be more uncertain or dangerous than to employ Indians in any shape or form in this country for the purpose of attempting to tranquilise it. Their well known faithlessness and treachery and between whom no difference exists in regard to villany ought to be forever a bar against such proceedings." The "fickleness and uncertain disposition" of Indians rendered the success of any agricultural efforts most problematical. In reply, Gilpin spitefully criticized the agent's lack of co-operation and refused to provide Fitzpatrick with an escort of troops for a trip to the Platte River.[22]

Before leaving Bent's Fort late in February, 1848, the Indian agent held a council with his charges. When Fitzpatrick expressed his sorrow to some Kiowa chiefs for their hostilities against the United States, they promised to break their alliance with the Comanches and join the friendly Cheyennes on the Arkansas River. With Fitzpatrick out of the way, Colonel Gilpin and his volunteers "thoroughly ransacked" the country between the Arkansas and Canadian rivers along the Santa

---

22 Gilpin to Fitzpatrick, February 8, 14, 1848; Fitzpatrick to Gilpin, February 10, 1848, Upper Platte Agency, Letters Received; Gilpin to General R. Jones, AG., U. S. A., August 1, 1848, in 30 Cong., 2 sess., *House Exec. Doc. 1,* 136–40.

Fe Trail, rendering it unfit for Indian occupation. When Gilpin returned to Fort Mann on May 30, 1848, he found the Kiowas, Cheyennes, and Arapahoes waiting to talk peace. The Comanches, however, were not overawed by Gilpin's efforts and continued to harass government trains east of the Arkansas River. Nor was Fitzpatrick impressed with Gilpin's success, for he maintained that five hundred men properly led could put the Santa Fe Trail "in such a state of safety that one man, with his wife and child, could pass to New Mexico, or the Rocky Mountains, unmolested."[23]

After completing his first tour through his agency, Fitzpatrick laid down a series of suggestions to assure peace and safety on the overland routes. Military posts should be established on the Platte and Arkansas River, each with a battalion of troops led by experienced men who knew both the country and the Indians. After his brush with Gilpin and the Missouri volunteers, the Indian agent was more certain than ever that the troops in the field should be composed in part of old trappers.[24]

Fitzpatrick returned to Bent's Fort again in November, 1848, to resume contact with the Indians of the Southern and Central Plains. At the post and in its vicinity, numerous groups of Cheyennes, Arapahoes, Kiowas, and Kiowa-Apaches awaited the arrival of their agent for a "Big Talk." Without presents or the means to obtain them, Fitzpatrick did not want to hold talks with the Indians, but he could not avoid them. As before, the Indians complained to Fitzpatrick about the destruction and dispersal of game and the cutting of timber from the river bottoms by the ever-growing flood of emigrants on the overland routes. With his Indians dispersed in their winter camps and making no signs of hostility, Fitzpatrick prepared to visit the Platte River. Starting in mid-February for Fort Laramie and less than a hundred miles out, Fitzpatrick was overtaken by a party of Kiowas who informed him that trouble was possible. The Comanches had heard that a body of troops was marching toward Bent's Fort, intent upon liberating all prisoners held by the tribes. Fitzpatrick tem-

[23] Gilpin to Jones, August 1, 1848, 30 Cong., 2 sess., *House Exec. Doc. No. 1*, 136–40; Fitzpatrick to Harvey, October 6, 1848, in *Report of the Commissioner of Indian Affairs, 1848*, 30 Cong., 2 sess., *House Exec. Doc. No. 1*, 470–73.

[24] Fitzpatrick to Medill, August 11, 1848 (Copy), Upper Platte Agency, Letters Received.

porarily returned to the Arkansas, held a council, and secured the co-operation of the Indians, but later assured his superintendent that the prisoners could not be freed without payment of ransom. The Indian agent set out again for the northern portion of his agency, leaving a message warning Major Benjamin L. Beall of the First Dragoons not to use force lest a serious Indian war break out along the Santa Fe route.[25]

Gold in California brought the forty-niners swarming through the Plains Indians' country, and the emigrants spread cholera through the Indian tribes. For the most part, the passage of the emigrants through the Indian country was peaceful, and only occasionally were the whites annoyed by Indians begging for food or tobacco. During the late spring and early summer of 1849, the Cheyennes were as usual scattered from the Platte to the Arkansas River. Near the Pawnee villages, five hundred Cheyennes took provisions from a government wagon train, leaving as payment some "bead-work, moccasins, sashes, &c." Later in June, other Cheyennes were hunting along the North Platte and were in contact with California-bound travelers. Cholera spread from the emigrants to the Plains Indians. How many Indians died during the epidemic cannot be ascertained. The traditional enemies of the Cheyennes, the Pawnees, were swept off like "chaff before the wind," and more than eleven hundred of them died during the summer of the California gold rush. Several Sioux bands also suffered severely from the ravages of cholera. Thus the Cheyennes who camped and hunted along the Platte rivers during the summer, may either have acquired the disease from other Indians or directly from the emigrants on the trail.[26]

While the Cheyennes moved south from the Platte rivers, men and women were stricken by "big cramps," or cholera, fell from their horses in agony, and died. They fled in terror all the way to the Arkansas River, and slowly the epidemic abated. At Bent's Fort the Cheyennes joined a peace conclave and celebrated the cessation of hostilities between the Kiowas and Osages. During the dances, a Kiowa warrior

25 Fitzpatrick to Mitchell, May 22, 1849, Upper Platte Agency, Letters Received.

26 Ralph P. Bieber (ed.), *Southern Trails to California in 1849*, 371–74; J. Goldsborough Bruff, *Gold Rush: The Journals, Drawings, and Other Papers of J. Goldsborough Bruff*, 18, 26; *Annual Report of the Commissioners of Indian Affairs for 1849*, 107.

and an Osage dropped to the ground clutching their stomachs. Soon the tribes were in flight. William Bent sent his wife, Yellow Woman, and three of his children away from the Santa Fe road with the Cheyennes. Before the epidemic ran its complete course, the Cheyennes lost half of their people. All was confusion among the Indians of the Southern and Central Plains, and Céran St. Vrain informed the Indian agent at Santa Fe that never had he seen a "worse state" of affairs during all of his time in the Southwest.[27]

The value of the trade on the Arkansas had been declining for several years. Fort St. Vrain and Fort Lupton had been abandoned a few seasons earlier. Such events, however, reflected only a general trend. The trading season of 1848, for example, had been profitable on the Arkansas River. Two firms, one of which was Bent, St. Vrain and Company, had invested $15,000 for goods at St. Louis prices and when they had completed their trade, the two outfits had gathered thirteen thousand buffalo robes which brought $39,000 on the St. Louis market in March, 1849. In all probability, the cholera epidemic totally ruined trade during the 1849 season at Bent's Fort. The Comanches and some Arapahoes were openly hostile to Bent and his traders, and the Cheyennes of the Arkansas River had been decimated by cholera. Despondently, William Bent ordered his people to strip the fort of its valuable goods while he rolled powder kegs into the fort's main rooms and applied the torch to the wooden ceilings. The adobe fortress, gutted by explosion and fire, smoldered for days. Although the date—even the year—of the destruction of the fort is in dispute, evidence seems to point to the year 1849. On or about August 22, 1849, a party of Santa Fe traders heard an explosion and when they arrived at Bent's Fort, they found the building still burning. No longer was Bent's Fort to be the mecca of the robe trade for the Cheyennes and other Indians on the Arkansas River.[28]

[27] Thaddeus A. Culbertson, *Journal of an Expedition to the Mauvaises Terres and the Upper Missouri in 1850*, BAE Bulletin No. *147* (ed. by John F. McDermott), 133, 137; James S. Calhoun, *The Official Correspondence of James S. Calhoun*, 42; George Bent to Hyde, January 23, 1905, Western History Department, Denver Public Library.

[28] Lavender, *Bent's Fort*, 313–16; St. Louis *Missouri Republican*, October 2, 1849; Fitzpatrick to Mitchell, December 18, 1847, May 22, 1849, Upper Platte Agency, Letters

The wave of emigrants and disease gave the Indians additional grievances. Despite troops at Fort Kearny and Fort Laramie, Thomas Fitzpatrick felt that a treaty was urgently needed. These views were supported by Superintendent D. D. Mitchell at St. Louis, who dispatched Fitzpatrick to Washington to urge the pressing necessity of the treaty upon Commissioner Orlando Brown. Because the news of the destruction of Bent's Fort had not yet reached St. Louis, they thought the tribes could be cheaply assembled at either Bent's Fort or Fort Laramie. Mitchell's arguments for a treaty were reasonable. Most of the tribes were not bound firmly to the United States by peace treaties, and the government was unable to "whip them into friendship" by force. Infantry was useless for action against the Plains Indians, and cavalry rapidly became infantry when mounts broke down. Further, Mitchell stated, a treaty would cost less than a six months' war on the Plains. It was August 27, 1849, before Mitchell received official approval to hold a treaty, and at that late date the Plains Indians were scattered on their fall hunts. Mitchell therefore hoped to hold a treaty during the next summer and in the meantime instructed Fitzpatrick to distribute a portion of the available presents to hold the Indians in check.[29]

During the delay the plans for the treaty became more elaborate. By March, 1850, Mitchell proposed that the tribes be assigned, with their consent, to specific geographic areas with boundaries marked by rivers and mountains. Confined to their own regions and held responsible for all depredations committed within their assigned lands, individual tribes could be more easily controlled and punished for violations of the treaty. The superintendent estimated the cost of the

Received. Grinnell ("Bent's Old Fort," *loc. cit.,* 82) maintained the post was not destroyed until 1852. This assertion is based upon George Bent to Hyde, February 26, 1906, Western History Department, Denver Public Library, George Bent to Hyde, June 29, 1914, Bent Letters, Coe Collection, and an erroneous deduction from *Report, Commissioner of Indian Affairs, 1850,* 51–52.

29 Mitchell to Brown, August 27, 1848, Clark Papers, Vol. IX, 223–24, Kansas State Historical Society; Mitchell to Fitzpatrick, August 1, 31, 1849, Mitchell to Brown, August 1, 1849, Upper Platte Agency, Letters Received; Mitchell to Brown, October 13, 1849, in 31 Cong., 1 sess., *House Exec. Doc. No. 5,* Vol. III, Pt. 2, p. 1070; Hafen and Young, *Fort Laramie,* 178.

treaty at two hundred thousand dollars. Senator David R. Atchison of Missouri, chairman of the Senate Committee on Indian Affairs, on March 18, 1850, called for favorable action on a bill to approve and appropriate funds for the Indian treaty. Congress, however, was in the midst of the great debate leading to the Compromise of 1850, and final approval with an appropriation of one hundred thousand dollars was not obtained until February 27, 1851.[30]

While Congress delayed, Fitzpatrick worked hard keeping the Indians quiet and preparing them for a big peace council. From March 15 to April 15, 1850, Fitzpatrick held frequent meetings with the Sioux, Cheyennes, Arapahoes, Kiowas, and Kiowa-Apaches at Big Timbers. Excepting only the Comanches, Fitzpatrick thought the tribes would "enter into amicable arrangements with the government." The Indian agent began his final preparations for the treaty in the summer of 1851, after Commissioner Luke Lea had designated Mitchell and Fitzpatrick as commissioners to treat with the Indians at Fort Laramie.[31]

Arriving at Fort Atkinson, a small military post on the Santa Fe Trail, on June 1, 1851, Fitzpatrick found only a few Indians waiting for his arrival. Runners sent out to the various tribes returned within two weeks bringing with them major portions of all the tribes, so that the country around Fort Atkinson on either side of the Arkansas was "literally covered with lodges." Talking to each tribe separately, Fitzpatrick was assured by the Cheyennes and Arapahoes that they would go to Fort Laramie, but the Kiowas, Comanches, and Kiowa-Apaches refused to risk their horses and mules on such a long journey through a country inhabited by "such notorious horse thieves as the Sioux and Crows." The three dissenting tribes, however, indicated that they were willing to sign a treaty if it were held in their own country.

An unfortuante incident occurred at Fort Atkinson which threatened to negate the Indian agent's successful diplomacy. An army de-

[30] Mitchell to Brown, October 26, 1849, March 9, 1850, in 31 Cong., 1 sess., *Sen. Misc. Docs. No. 70*, Vol. I, pp. 1–5; *Report, Commissioner of Indian Affairs, 1851, Sen. Exec. Doc. No. 1*, Vol. I, 47–48; see also, 9 U. S. Stat. 572.

[31] *Report, Commissioner of Indian Affairs, 1850*, 51–52; Lea to Mitchell, May 26, 1851, Office of Indian Affairs, Letters Sent, Vol. XLIV, 103, Records of the Office of Indian Affairs, National Archives.

tachment commanded by Colonel Edwin Vos Sumner arrived soon after Fitzpatrick concluded his talks. The officers of the command relaxed their discipline over the troops, and for two days the Indians mingled freely with soldiers in the military camp. Rarely, Fitzpatrick commented, had he seen such "free and unrestrained intercourse" permitted even by traders and trappers among the Indians. The Indian agent feared that such familiarity would lead to unpleasantness and he was right. A Cheyenne warrior, accused of "some unseemly conduct" towards an officer's wife, was given a "good sound flogging with a large carriage-whip" by the offended husband. This exasperated the whole Cheyenne camp, and its leaders asked for a suitable gift to assuage the warrior's injured pride. Some Kiowas and Comanches informed Fitzpatrick and Sumner that the Cheyennes had invited them to help wipe out the whites. When Sumner heard the news, he "planted his whole command within striking distance of the Cheyenne encampment." Many of the Cheyennes pulled down their lodges and fled; others went to Fitzpatrick inquiring the cause of Sumner's action. The Cheyenne delegation denied any hostile intent and accompanied the Indian agent to Sumner's tent, where the incident was closed when the Cheyenne warrior "received a blanket for his wounds."[32]

Some of the Cheyenne warriors were less ready to settle down. Shortly after the whipping took place, Kit Carson was leading a wagon train for Lucien Maxwell with goods for Santa Fe. Carson's train passed through the Cheyenne camps near Fort Atkinson, and its warriors ignored Carson's signs of friendship. Small groups of Cheyenne braves gathered about the wagons, and Carson inquired why the Cheyennes wanted his scalp. The few whites with Carson were nervous, but Carson saved the day by bluffing the Indians, telling them to clear out. One member of the wagon crew remembered: "There were red fellows enough there to eat us up, and at one time I could almost feel my hair leaving my head." Under the cover of darkness, Carson sent one of the young Mexican teamsters on foot to Sumner's camp. The next morning when the Cheyennes reappeared, the boy's footprints told the Indians that the troops had been alerted,

---

[32] *Report, Commissioner of Indian Affairs, 1851*, 32 Cong., 1 sess., *House Exec. Doc. No. 2*, 332–35; St. Louis *Missouri Republican*, September 13, 1851.

and the braves allowed Carson's train to pass on untroubled.[33] There is no evidence that the Cheyennes allowed the incident to prevent their attendance at the councils of the Treaty of Fort Laramie.

By the end of July, 1851, Cheyennes, Arapahoes, Oglala and Brulé Sioux began gathering at Fort Laramie, although the councils were not to begin until September 1. On August 30, Superintendent Mitchell's party arrived, escorted by a detachment of dragoons. Along with Mitchell came Colonel Samuel Cooper, from the Office of the Adjutant General, A. B. Chambers, editor, and B. Gratz Brown, reporter, of the St. Louis *Missouri Republican*. The Cheyennes impressed the officers of the dragoons and the newsmen. Editor Chambers described the Cheyennes as "a stout, bold, athletic set of people—more cleanly and better supplied with horses and implements of war, than the other tribes." They bore themselves proudly and were treated with respect by all of the whites and the army officers. These actions, Chambers wrote, caused the Cheyennes to have "great contempt for the white man and the power of the government and [they] do not hesitate to express it freely."[34]

Tensions mounted as the Indian foes of the Cheyennes and their allies began to appear. Even as the Shoshonis were en route under Jim Bridger's care, a party of undisciplined Cheyenne warriors killed two Shoshoni scouts. At Fort Laramie an Indian battle was narrowly avoided. As the Shoshonis came into view, a Sioux warrior whose father had been killed by a Shoshoni chief a few years before, grabbed his bow and arrows, jumped on his horse, and rushed toward the Shoshoni chief. Before the Sioux reached his enemy, a French interpreter threw the Sioux from his horse, disarmed him, and stood over the prostrate warrior. The Shoshonis, led by their redoubtable chief, Washakie, stood their ground, guns in hand, while the Sioux fingered the arrows in their quivers. Although the Sioux and their allies outnumbered the Shoshonis more than five to one, each Shoshoni, or Snake, warrior had a gun furnished by Jim Bridger, while not one out of a hundred Sioux possessed firearms. If the Sioux warrior had been

---

[33] Edwin L. Sabin, *Kit Carson Days*, II, 627–29; St. Louis *Missouri Republican*, September 13, 1851.

[34] Hafen and Young, *Fort Laramie*, 179; Percival G. Lowe, *Five Years a Dragoon, '49 to '54 and Other Adventures on the Great Plains*, 76–77.

allowed to attack the Shoshoni chief, the warrior would have been killed and a general fight would have quickly taken place. The two hundred and seventy dragoons escorting the Indian commissioners and their entourage would have been powerless to stop the Indians, and no peace would have been possible. Bridger told one of the dragoons that it was fortunate for the Plains Indians that the Sioux warrior had not accomplished his purpose, because "there wouldn't have been room to camp 'round here for dead Sioux."[35]

Ten thousand Indians congregated at Fort Laramie. So vast were the horse herds that they roamed for miles about the fort, and when more room was needed, the treaty grounds were shifted thirty-five miles below the post to the mouth of Horse Creek. The Americans were treated to Indian pageantry never before seen by whites. On September 6, nearly a thousand Sioux warriors riding in a column, four abreast, rode to the commissioners' tents, bearing an old American flag given to them, they claimed, by William Clark. Later in the day, several hundred Cheyennes repeated the Sioux performance and received gifts of tobacco and vermilion from Mitchell. During the Sunday respite from councils, the Oglalas hosted the Cheyennes, Arapahoes, and Shoshonis to a great dog feast and dance which lasted until dawn on Monday morning. These manifestations of friendship among former enemies led Mitchell to have high hopes for a successful treaty.[36]

On September 8, a cannon boomed out the signal that the formal talks would begin. Indian chiefs assembled in the tent of the commissioners and peace pipes were smoked. Superintendent Mitchell spoke for the government and made known to the Indians the purposes of the treaty. The "great father" wanted safety for his white children as they passed over the roads, the right to build protecting military posts, and sought to define a territory for each tribe in which it could live and hunt. Each tribe was also requested to select a chief who would exercise control over his nation and who would be responsible for the tribe's actions. The Cheyennes designated Wan-ne-sah-ta,

35 Lowe, *Five Years a Dragoon*, 79–83; Lavender, *Bent's Fort*, 321–22; St. Louis *Missouri Republican*, September 26, 1851.

36 St. Louis *Missouri Republican*, September 26, October 5, 1851; Hafen and Young, *Fort Laramie*, 183; Mitchell to Lea, September 7, 1851, Clark Papers, Vol. IX, 347, Kansas State Historical Society.

or Who-Walks-with-His-Toes-Turned-Out, the keeper of the medicine arrows, as their tribal representative. In return, and as compensation for the whites' destruction of the buffalo ranges and grass, Mitchell promised the tribes a total of fifty thousand dollars per year for fifty years, to be expended for goods and provisions.[37]

Fitzpatrick advised the Indians to discuss the treaty among themselves and asked each tribe to make its own decision. For nine days the Indians counciled, feasted, and entertained each other and their white hosts. One hundred young Cheyenne warriors, on September 9, gave a wonderful exhibition of horsemanship and war maneuvers. Painted, stripped as if for battle, and armed with guns, lances, or bows and arrows, the warriors, without more than hand signals from their leaders, carried out precise turns, charges, and individual charges upon mock enemies. Songs, dances, and coup-counting concluded the Cheyenne demonstration, some of the Cheyenne men claiming as many as twenty-five to thirty heroic deeds against their enemies.[38]

During the interlude of formal negotiations, more Indian tribes arrived. Alex Culbertson and Father De Smet brought the Crows, and delegations from the Assiniboin, Minnitaree, and Arikara tribes moved, on September 10, to Fort Horse Creek. Father De Smet immediately began to work for the conversion of pagan souls. Among the Oglala, Father De Smet's words were greeted with a "general whispering and embarrassed laugh." When the priest asked the cause of the levity, an Oglala chief arose and responded: "We are great liars and thieves; we have killed; we have done all the evil that the Great Spirit forbids us to do; but we did not know those beautiful words; in the future we will try to live better, if thou wilt but stay with us and teach us."[39] Although spoken by an Oglala, the speech could have come from any of the tribes assembled at Horse Creek.

The Indians found the missionary's appeals persuasive and presented him with hundreds of children for baptism. Happily, the Jesuit baptized 253 Cheyenne infants. The Cheyennes did not abandon their own christening ceremonies, however. De Smet saw a Cheyenne

[37] St. Louis *Missouri Republican*, October 1, 24, November 2, 1851; Hafen and Young, *Fort Laramie*, 184–88.

[38] St. Louis *Missouri Republican*, November 2, 1851; Hafen and Young, *Fort Laramie*, 188–89.

[39] Chittenden and Richardson (eds.), *Travels of Father De Smet*, II, 674–78.

mother give a warrior a knife, extend her child on carefully prepared animal skins, and hold her child while the man made "two to five incisions in the rim of each ear" of the child from which ornaments were later hung. When the ear-piercing was finished, the warrior and those assisting in the ceremony were given horses by the child's family.

Father De Smet, Brown, and Chambers also witnessed the Cheyennes' reparations for the death of the two Shoshoni scouts. The Cheyennes erected a large shelter from the skins of six lodges. There the chiefs of the Cheyennes and forty Shoshonis gathered for a feast consisting simply of corn, "crushed and thoroughly boiled." "The dogs were spared this time," the Jesuit wrote, because the guest tribe, an exception among the Indians, never ate flesh of dogs. When the feast was over, the Cheyennes brought out presents of tobacco, blankets, knives, and cloth, and presented them to their guests. The two scalps were also placed near the presents and returned to the brothers of the dead Shoshoni scouts. The brothers were assured that the scalp dance had not taken place, and they were deeply affected by sorrow for their relatives' deaths. The aggrieved Shoshonis nevertheless "embraced the murderers, received the donations and distributed a larger portion of them to their companions." Somewhat later, each of the two tribes adopted children from the other tribe, while Indian eloquence strengthened the hand of new-found friendship.[40]

On September 17, 1851, the Treaty of Fort Laramie was ready for the signatures of the Indians and the American commissioners. The general provisions of the treaty provided for peaceful relations, roads, forts, and Indian responsibility for depredations committed in their territories. The Cheyennes and Arapahoes were jointly assigned the lands whose boundaries began at the Red Buttes, up the North Platte to the "main range of the Rocky Mountains," south to the headwaters of the Arkansas, down that stream to the crossing of the Santa Fe Trail, northwest to the forks of the Platte, then back to the point of origin at the Red Buttes. The treaty neither stipulated that the Indians abandon their claims to other lands, nor that they surrender the privileges of hunting, fishing, or traveling through lands to which they had prior claims. Four Cheyenne chiefs, including Yellow Wolf,

[40] Chittenden and Richardson (eds.), *Travels of Father De Smet*, II, 679–80; St. Louis *Missouri Republican*, October 29, 1851.

signed the Treaty of Fort Laramie, and their signatures were attested to by John S. Smith for the Cheyennes and John Poisal for the Arapahoes.[41]

Much to the consternation of the Indians and the commissioners, the wagon train bringing the treaty goods did not arrive for three days after the treaty had been concluded. The chiefs of the tribes were the first to receive their presents and paraded, "for the first time in their lives, pantalooned; each arrayed in a general's uniform, a gilt sword hanging at his side. Their long, coarse hair floated above the military costume, the whole was crowned by the burlesque solemnity of their painted faces." Once the remaining presents were distributed, the Indians drifted off, some down the Platte where buffalo were plentiful. The Cheyennes kept well together and moved up Horse Creek, followed soon afterward by the Arapahoes. Fitzpatrick selected eleven Indian chiefs, including Little Chief, White Antelope, and Alights-on-the-Cloud of the Cheyennes, and took them to St. Louis and Washington to impress them with the might of the United States.[42]

Superintendent Mitchell was delighted with the ease in which the treaty had been accomplished. "The different tribes," wrote Mitchell to Commissioner Lea, "although hereditary enemies, interchanged daily visits, . . . smoked and feasted together; exchanged presents, adopted each others children according to their own customs . . . to prove the sincerity of their peaceful and friendly intentions." One problem remained unsolved when intermarried whites and mixed bloods began their demands for land. Many of these men came among the Indians as employees of traders, acquired Indian wives, and as the number of their children increased, were forced to seek a more reliable and rewarding occupation than the hazards of the declining fur trade. At the Treaty of Fort Laramie the whites and mixed bloods asked the commissioners for land in the Cheyenne and Arapaho country, but the two tribes denied the request since many of the intermarried whites were related to other tribes. In Washington the eleven

---

[41] Charles J. Kappler (comp. and ed.), *Indian Affairs: Laws and Treaties*, II, 594–96; Mitchell to Lea, November 11, 1851, Clark Papers, Vol. IX, 359–61, Kansas State Historical Society; St. Louis *Missouri Republican*, November 9, 1851.

[42] Chittenden and Richardson (eds.), *Travels of Father De Smet*, II, 683, 688; Lowe, *Five Years a Dragoon*, 89; Hafen and Young, *Fort Laramie*, 195–96; St. Louis, *Missouri Republican*, October 22, 1851; Grinnell, *Fighting Cheyennes*, 74.

chiefs thought the agricultural settlements made by the mixed bloods might be valuable examples for their peoples.[43]

Congress found the treaty too generous to the Indians. When the Senate ratified the document on May 24, 1852, it reduced the annuities from fifty to ten years, an action requiring the tribes' approval. A portion of the Cheyennes ratified the amended treaty in August, 1853, when Fitzpatrick read the new documents to the chiefs at the ruins of old Fort St. Vrain. Fitzpatrick acquired the marks of the chiefs present and returned the document to his superiors. In 1858 Congress held that the treaty was incomplete; the subsequent appropriations have been interpreted to mean that "the government considered itself bound by its provision and appropriated money regularly to carry them out."[44]

The Cheyennes completed their first land treaty with the United States without significant cost. Their buffalo range was still intact, annuities added to their wealth, and traders on the Platte and Arkansas rivers served them adequately. Fitzpatrick's report for 1853, however, carried information portentous for the Cheyennes' future. In his description of the South Platte, the Indian agent pointed out that "mineral wealth likewise abounds in the sands of the water courses, and in the gorges and cañons from which they issue; and should public attention ever be strongly directed to this section of our territory, and free access be obtained, the inducements which it holds will soon people it with thousands of citizens, and cause it to rise speedily into a flourishing mountain State."[45]

A stable peace for the Plains Indians was completed in July, 1853, when the Kiowas, Comanches, and Kiowa-Apaches signed a treaty similar to that of Fort Laramie. No specific region was assigned to the three tribes, their territory being vaguely described as south of the Arkansas River. Hoping, perhaps, to revive his fortunes in the Indian trade, William Bent laid plans to build another post on the

[43] Mitchell to Lea, November 11, 1851, Clark Papers, Vol. IX, 359–61, Kansas State Historical Society; St. Louis *Missouri Republican*, November 30, 1851; 32 Cong., 1 sess., *House Exec. Doc. No. 2*, 336.

[44] 11 U. S. Stat. 749; James C. Malin, *Indian Policy and Westward Expansion*, University of Kansas *Humanistic Studies*, Vol. II, No. 3, p. 93; *Report, Commissioner of Indian Affairs, 1853*, 33 Cong., 1 sess., *Sen. Exec. Doc. No. 1*, Part I, 366.

[45] *Report, Commissioner of Indian Affairs, 1853*, 366.

Arkansas. During the winter of 1852–53, Bent set stone-cutters to work preparing stone for the wall of his new fort. His presence on the Arkansas protected the Cheyennes from an attack from troops stationed at Fort Atkinson. Lieutenant Henry Heth, commanding officer at the fort, believed that the Cheyennes had murdered a man on the Santa Fe road, and he prepared to attack their village. When Bent learned that the man had been killed for his money by his traveling companions, Lieutenant Heth called off the attack. In June, 1853, Bent wagoned in the hardware for his new post at Big Timbers, and his establishment was ready to renew trade relations with the Indians bordering the Arkansas River.[46]

New Bent's Fort did not prosper because the Indian trade never rose to the levels of the 1830's and 1840's. The reasons were graphically stated by Fitzpatrick in his 1853 report. The Cheyennes, Arapahoes, and Sioux, the Indian agent wrote, "are actually in a *starving state.* They are in abject want of food half the year. . . . Their women are pinched with want and their children constantly crying out with hunger." More and more, these Indians clustered around the traders, seeking food, accepting employment, and living on the proceeds of their wives' prostitution.[47]

Emigrant and trading roads already encircled the Cheyennes' country, but a constantly increasing American population on the Pacific coast led to demands for better roads and a cry for a transcontinental railroad. Secretary of War Jefferson Davis, exercising his discretion as permitted in the 1853 railroad survey appropriation act, surveyed only three of the five suggested railroad routes. In the maneuvering that followed, Thomas Hart Benton succeeded in pushing three railroad surveying parties through the lands of the Cheyennes. Secretary Davis passed over Frémont and appointed Captain John Gunnison to head the survey of the thirty-eighth parallel route.[48]

[46] Kappler, *Laws and Treaties*, II, 600–602; Heth to Captain Irwin J. McDowell, April 14, 1853, Upper Platte Agency, Letters Receiver.; Lavender, *Bent's Fort*, 323–24.

[47] Lavender, *Bent's Fort*, 329; *Report, Commissioner of Indian Affairs, 1853*, 368.

[48] For the background of the railroad surveys, see, Lewis H. Haney, *A Congressional History of Railways in the United States, 1850–1887*, 54; Robert R. Russel, *Improvement of Communication with the Pacific Coast as an Issue in American Politics, 1783–1864*; George L. Albright, *Official Explorations for Pacific Railroads, 1853–1855*, 119–32; Nevins, *Frémont*, II, 461–62.

On the edge of the Great Plains, Captain Gunnison divided his party, sending one portion up the Kansas and Smoky Hill rivers and the other over the Santa Fe road. Before the two units rejoined at the mouth of Walnut Creek, Captain Gunnison's party saw Fort Riley being constructed at the juncture of the Republican and Kansas rivers and still another post near the site later to be occupied by Fort Zarah at the mouth of Walnut Creek. Few Cheyennes were encountered along the Arkansas when Captain Gunnison traveled along its course in mid-July, 1853, because the Cheyennes, Arapahoes, Kiowas, and Kiowa-Apaches had gone "to wipe out the Pawnees."[49]

When Secretary of War Davis refused to appoint Frémont to head the thirty-eighth parallel survey, Benton prevailed upon Lieutenant Edward F. Beale to travel over the proposed route on his way to assume his duties as superintendent of Indian affairs for California. Beale and his party preceded Captain Gunnison to the Rocky Mountains and arrived on May 25, 1853, at Fort Atkinson, where Cheyennes and Arapahoes were waiting for Indian Agent Fitzpatrick. At the post Beale and his companions found the commanding officer embroiled in settling disputes between the Cheyennes and emigrants. No observations were made concerning activity at new Bent's Fort, but the walls of the old fort were covered with messages "from parties who had already passed here to their friends in the rear."[50]

Undaunted by Jefferson Davis' snub, Frémont organized his own surveying party and arrived at new Bent's Fort in November, 1853. Beyond Fort Riley Frémont maintained a vigilant watch over his stock, but still Cheyennes ran off five of his animals. When the Cheyenne village at Big Timbers was reached, "the animals and some of the thieves were found." Candidly, the Cheyennes told Frémont that they had watched his camp carefully, and while the herd's guard warmed himself at a fire, they stole five animals and if they had had another hour, "they would have stolen a great many more." S. N. Carvalho, an artist with Frémont's expedition, saw 250 Cheyenne lodges

[49] *Reports of Explorations and Surveys to Ascertain the Most Practicable and Economical Route to the Pacific Ocean*, 33 Cong., 1 sess, *Sen. Exec. Doc. No. 78*, II, 16, 19, 25, 28; Marvin H. Garfield, "The Military Post as a Factor in the Frontier Defense of Kansas, 1865–1869," *KHQ*, Vol. I, No. 1 (November, 1931), 53, 54.

[50] Nevins, *Frémont*, II, 461–62; LeRoy R. and Ann W. Hafen (eds.), *Central Route to the Pacific*, 17–20, 95–96, 98–100.

at Big Timbers, estimating the camp's occupants at one thousand people, which was actually one-half of the true size of such a large encampment. The artist found a chief's daughter particularly beautiful, attired in "costly robes, ornamented with elk teeth, beads, and colored porcupine quills." After sketching the maiden, Carvalho persuaded her to give him one of her brass bracelets, which he coated with mercury much to the girl's delight. Other women of the tribe also requested Carvalho to turn their brass jewelry into silver, but they had to be content with demonstrations of "lucifer matches" and burning alcohol. The Cheyennes wanted this white shaman to live with them, and Carvalho was convinced that "they would have worshipped me as possessing most extraordinary powers of necromancy."[51]

Army posts, railroad surveying parties, and increased emigrant travel through the Cheyenne country following the Treaty of Fort Laramie were indications that the white frontier was drawing ever nearer to the lands of the Cheyennes. The tribesmen were still free to war and hunt, but their freedom was becoming more constricted, and within a decade whites would begin to claim Cheyenne lands.

[51] Nevins, *Frémont*, II, 462; S. N. Carvalho, *Incidents of Travel and Adventure in the Far West; with Colonel Frémont's Last Expedition*, 71.

# 6

## THE LAST YEARS OF FREEDOM

INTERTRIBAL WARS, punitive army expeditions, and problems with emigrants and settlers marked the last decade of freedom for the Cheyennes. Frémont's party, while resting at new Bent's Fort, witnessed the Cheyennes celebrating a small victory over their enemies, the Pawnees. Twelve or fifteen Pawnee scalps were brought into the Cheyenne village, each waving on the end of a long scalp pole. Men and women took part in the scalp dance, "grotesquely attired in wolf, bear, and buffalo skins; some of them with horns of the buffalo, and antlers of the deer, for head ornaments." The tribe, however, was still smarting from its 1853 defeat at the hands of the Pawnees.[1]

In the summer of 1854, a large intertribal war party was raised by friends and relatives of the warriors lost in the Pawnee battle. A large encampment, twelve to fifteen hundred lodges, gathered at the Pawnee Fork on the Santa Fe Trail. A Kiowa warrior whose brother had been killed sent out the formal summons for war. Old Bark, also called Ugly Face, Old Whirlwind of the Cheyennes, Little Raven, Bull, and Storm of the Arapahoes accepted the Kiowa and Comanche war pipe. The Cheyennes, Arapahoes, Kiowas, and Comanches furnished the greater number of warriors and they were re-inforced by small numbers of Sioux, Osages, and Crows.[2]

The allies were supremely confident of victory as they moved north from the Arkansas River. When John W. Whitfield, Thomas Fitzpatrick's successor as Indian agent, asked them to return to their camp, they replied that they were going to " 'wipe out' all frontier Indians

---

[1] Carvalho, *Travel and Adventure in the Far West*, 69.

[2] George Bent to Hyde, January 19, 1905, Bent Letters, Coe Collection; Mooney, *Calender History of the Kiowa*, 297; Grinnell, *Fighting Cheyennes*, 102–103; *Report, Commissioner of Indian Affairs, 1854*, 90.

they find on the Plains." But the war party never reached the Pawnees and was routed by a hunting party of Sac and Fox Indians accompanied by a few Potawatomis. Probably on a tributary of the Kansas River, the Plains Indians met eighty warriors from the eastern reservations, who, from a well-protected position and "all well armed with rifles with which 'they hit every time,' " repulsed the superior force of Plains Indians. The bows, arrows, and lances of the Cheyennes and their friends proved impotent weapons against the Sac and Fox rifles, and when the three-hour battle ended, the Plains Indians suffered at least sixteen killed and one hundred wounded. The Kiowas, the instigators of the avenging effort, suffered the worst casualties, having twelve of their warriors killed, including Black Horse, a prominent war chief. The six Sac and Fox Indians killed were accounted for undoubtedly by the Osages, who, like the reservation Indians, possessed efficient rifles.[3]

Only a few Cheyennes actually took an active part in the fight, and the Arapahoes "stood off and looked on." Old Whirlwind of the Cheyennes, however, added greater renown to his war prowess, going into battle wearing a large feathered war bonnet to the front of which was attached a little stuffed hawk. In his later years Old Whirlwind recalled that this was his hardest fight, because his war pony kept trying to charge up close to the beleaguered foes, and Old Whirlwind found rifle "balls were flying thick around me. The feathers were cut from my war bonnet, yet the hawk that was on it in the front was not hit, and I was not hit. . . . Hé-ămmă-vī'-hĭo and the hawk protected me."[4]

During these years of the 1850's, the Cheyennes were not yet divided into two divisions, north and south. They utilized the North Platte, the South Platte, and the Arkansas rivers for their residences. There is continuous evidence that the various Cheyenne bands shifted from the north to the south with complete freedom, hunted extensively along the South Platte and the tributaries of the Kansas River, and held their medicine lodge ceremony and other religious rites as a united tribe. This view is sustained by Agent Whitfield's 1854 report, but he added the whole tribe had not camped together since the Treaty

[3] George Bent to Hyde, n.d., Western History Department, Denver Public Library; *Report, Commissioner of Indian Affairs, 1854*, 90.

[4] Grinnell, *Fighting Cheyennes*, 104; Clark, *Indian Sign Language*, 397–98.

of Fort Laramie. From the Arkansas River Cheyennes, Whitfield recovered Mexican prisoners taken during a spring raid earlier in 1854, and in council the Cheyennes promised to cease raiding if the "Mexicans would let them and their buffalo alone."[5]

Whitfield distributed annuity goods on the Arkansas and the South Platte before traveling on toward Fort Laramie. About fifty miles below that post, he met twenty-five lodges of Sioux in full flight. They reported that Sioux Indians had wiped out a detachment of soldiers in a fight. This conflict was a Sioux affair, but the consequences later involved the Cheyennes. Despite the Treaty of Fort Laramie, travel along the Platte route continued to irritate the Indians. During the 1853 season, fifteen thousand Americans moved past Fort Laramie, destroying game and bringing diseases to the Indians. After Miniconjou Sioux seized the ferryboat near Fort Laramie, Lieutenant Hugh B. Fleming sent a detachment of soldiers from the fort to recover the boat. In anger, a Sioux warrior shot at the sergeant leading the detachment. When Lieutenant Fleming led a larger group of soldiers to demand the offender, a skirmish took place in which three Miniconjou warriors were killed and three wounded, while the soldiers took two prisoners.[6]

Shortly before Whitfield arrived at Fort Laramie, a Miniconjou warrior, embittered by the skirmish with Lieutenant Fleming, shot an arrow at a Mormon emigrant. Missing, the warrior notched another arrow, shot again, and brought down the Mormon's cow. Both the Mormon and a Brulé chief named Bear reported the incident to Lieutenant Fleming, the commanding officer at Fort Laramie. Lieutenant Fleming selected Lieutenant John L. Grattan, a young West Pointer, to lead twenty-nine men and an interpreter to bring the Miniconjous to Fort Laramie until Indian Agent Whitfield arrived.

Lieutenant Grattan was on record at Fort Laramie as having little respect for the Plains Indians' ability to fight. When some citizens had failed to recover horses belonging to the post interpreter earlier in the summer, Grattan had boasted that with thirty men he could defeat the whole Cheyenne nation. Backed by two mountain how-

[5] *Report, Commissioner of Indian Affairs, 1854,* 92.

[6] Hafen and Young, *Fort Laramie,* 201, 209–10; Eugene Bandel, *Frontier Life in the Army, 1854–1861,* 23–24.

itzers, Grattan and his detachment, on August 19, 1854, rode to a Brulé camp where the Miniconjou warrior was living. A council with the Indians not having produced the desired results, the two howitzers were fired into the village but with little effect. Whether the Indians or the soldiers fired the first shot is not known, but once the soldiers had discharged their weapons they were overwhelmed by the Indians. Bear, the Brulé chief, was killed early in the fight, and his infuriated warriors killed and mutilated twenty-eight men of the command within a mile or so of the village. Lieutenant Grattan's body, found later with twenty-four arrows protruding from it, was identified only by his watch.[7]

Agent Whitfield, after learning of the "Grattan Massacre," recommended a "genteel drubbing" for every Indian tribe from Texas to Oregon, and the army needed little urging to field an expedition to punish the Sioux. A year after Lieutenant Grattan's death, Colonel William S. Harney led six hundred men from Fort Kearny toward the Sioux country. Thomas S. Twiss, the new Indian agent for the Upper Platte, meanwhile tried to separate the hostiles from the friendly Indians, gathering about four hundred lodges of Sioux thirty-five miles above Fort Laramie.[8]

At Ash Hollow, Colonel Harney learned that Little Thunder and his Brulés were camped on Blue Water Creek. Little Thunder tried to parley his way out of a tight spot, but Harney would have none of it. The troops and dragoons killed at least eighty-six men, women, and children, wounded five, and seized seventy women and children as prisoners. Harney moved farther into the heart of the Sioux country and found the Indians more conciliatory. At his winter quarters on the Missouri River at Fort Pierre, Colonel Harney held peace councils from March 1 to 5, 1856, with the Sioux. Harney also made certain demands upon the Cheyennes and Arapahoes peremptorily, ordering the two tribes to make peace with the Pawnees and Sioux, to hunt only in their own country, and to withdraw completely from the

[7] 34 Cong., 1 and 2 sess., *Sen. Exec. Doc. No. 91*, 11–12; Bandel, *Frontier Life in the Army*, 24–28; Hafen and Young, *Fort Laramie*, 222–29; *Report, Commissioner of Indian Affairs, 1854*, 92–98; *Engagement between United States Troops and Sioux Indians*, 33 Cong., 2 sess., *House Exec. Doc. No. 63*, 1–27.

[8] *Report, Commissioner of Indian Affairs, 1854*, 96; *Report, Commissioner of Indian Affairs, 1855*, 400–401.

Platte route. Failure to comply with these commands, Harney warned, would force him to make war upon them and "sweep them from the face of the earth."[9]

Chiefs of the Cheyennes and Arapahoes living near Fort Laramie acquiesced to Harney's demands. Major William Hoffman, commanding officer at the fort, who conveyed Harney's demands, remained skeptical even after the Cheyennes and Arapahoes had sent runners to the South Platte and Arkansas bands informing them of the council's outcome. "The Cheyennes," Major Hoffman warned, "are an unruly race and I have little confidence in their promises of good conduct unless they are kept in dread of immediate punishment for their misdemeanors."[10]

While Colonel Harney was "pacifying" the Sioux, Indian Agent Whitfield found the five tribes of his reduced agency scattered, confused, and uncertain in their relations to the United States. When Whitfield arrived at new Bent's Fort late in June, 1855, he was convinced that the Cheyennes were raiding and robbing trains along the North Platte. Only with difficulty were the Cheyennes of the Arkansas and South Platte found, and then they were more than four hundred miles from Bent's Fort on the Little Blue River. Whitfield waited for the Cheyennes, and after the council he was more concerned than ever. Fifteen chiefs talked with their agent and when they found that he brought them no guns or ammunition, they asked him why he had bothered to come at all. It took all of the influence of William Bent to keep the Cheyennes quiet and to persuade them to accept their annuities. Bent's long friendship with the Cheyennes did not spare him from the anger of the Cheyennes; they had threatened to scalp him if Whitfield did not produce guns and ammunition among their annuities. An agreement was reached only after the In-

[9] Bandel, *Frontier Life in the Army*, 28, 84; Major W. Hoffman to Colonel S. Cooper, November 29, 1854, 33 Cong., 2 sess., *House Exec. Noc. No. 36*, 3–5; St. Louis *Missouri Republican*, September 27, 1855; Philip St. George Cooke to Major O. F. Winship, September 5, 1855, 34 Cong., 3 sess., *Sen. Exec. Doc. No. 59*, 4; *Report of General Harney, Commander of the Sioux Expedition*, 34 Cong., 1 sess., *Sen. Doc. No. 1*, Pt. 1, pp. 49–51; *Council with the Sioux Indians at Fort Pierre*, 34 Cong., 1 sess., *House Exec. Doc. No. 130*, 1–39; Pleasonton to Hoffman, March 5, 1856, Office of the Adjutant General, Letters Received.

[10] Hoffman to Pleasonton, March 31, 1856, Fort Laramie, Letters Sent, United States Army Commands, Records of the War Department, National Archives.

dian agent promised to include guns and ammunition in the next year's goods. At best, Whitfield believed he had only delayed a "destructive war on the plains," which would eventually take place.[11]

From knowledge derived at Bent's Fort, Indian Agent Whitfield wrote a summary of the condition and economic activity of the Indians in the Upper Arkansas Agency. The total population of the agency numbered 11,470, in which number were included 3,150 Cheyennes and 2,400 Arapahoes. From their camps on the South Platte and Arkansas rivers, the Cheyennes could field a force of 900 warriors and their allies, the Arapahoes, 500. The Cheyennes lived in 350 lodges and possessed seventeen thousand horses. The Cheyennes enjoyed an income of $15,000 from the 40,000 buffalo, 3,000 elk, 25,000 deer, and 2,000 bear killed annually whose skins and hides were the staples in their exchanges with the traders.[12]

Whitfield used every means at his disposal to placate the Cheyennes. He believed the test would come the next season on the Santa Fe Trail when the travelers and emigrants would pay the customary toll of sugar, coffee, and whatever else struck the Indians' fancy. Only a "sound chastisement," in Whitfield's opinion, would bring the Plains Indians to their senses, because "every present made them they regard as an acknowledgment of their superior power and given to deprecate their wrath. At this time they have no respect for the government."[13]

Until this time routes of travel had occupied merely the fringes of the Cheyenne country, but in the mid–1850's plans were developed for wagon roads to push through the heart of the Cheyenne buffalo range. Under the supervision of Lieutenant Francis T. Bryan, one survey was begun in the summer of 1855 and completed through the region of the Kansas, Solomon, and Smoky Hill rivers to Bent's Fort on the Arkansas. William Bent tried to arrange for Cheyenne and Arapaho guides for Lieutenant Bryan, but the tribes, having already

[11] John W. Whitfield to Alfred Cumming, August 1, 1855, Upper Arkansas Agency, Letters Received.

[12] Whitfield to [Cumming?], August 15, 1855, Upper Arkansas Agency, Letters Received. Twiss, in responding to a circular, informed the superintendent that there were 1,400 Cheyennes and 1,600 Arapahoes in his agency (see Twiss to Cumming, November 14, 1855, Upper Platte Agency, Letters Received).

[13] Report, Commissioner of Indian Affairs, 1855, 435–36.

witnessed the effect of other roads on the buffalo herds, refused to aid the Lieutenant. The next year saw the construction of bridges on the Fort Riley-Bent's Fort road, and the penetration of white settlers into the Smoky Hill Valley began. Later in the 1856 season, Lieutenant Bryan also surveyed a road through the northern portion of the Cheyenne country via the Platte River, the South Platte, and Lodgepole Creek and returned by way of the Cache la Poudre, the South Platte, and the Republican rivers.[14] The surveying added to Cheyenne suspicions that the whites were about to spoil their prime buffalo ranges.

Specific incidents, however, involved the Cheyennes in difficulties with the army. In April, 1856, a small party of Cheyennes came to the Upper Platte bridge, near present Casper, Wyoming, to trade. A misunderstanding arose over some stolen horses allegedly in the possession of the Cheyennes. An officer tried to take three Cheyennes as prisoners. One of the Cheyennes, trying to escape, was shot down, and the other fled with his band to the Black Hills where they killed an old trapper. Dull Knife, a Cheyenne chief, visited Fort Laramie on May 24, 1856, and promised to surrender the two men who had killed the trapper, and expressed the Cheyennes' desire for peace.[15]

Dull Knife, however, did not speak for all of the Cheyennes. Some Cheyennes who normally lived on the North Platte joined the Arkansas River bands who were camping on the headwaters of the Republican and Smoky Hill rivers. William Guerrier was trading among these Cheyennes in May, 1856, when the warrior wounded at the Platte bridge arrived in the camps. The chiefs warned Guerrier to be cautious and ordered their young men to guard the trader. Guerrier heard the chiefs haranguing their people, urging them to avoid more difficulties with the whites.[16]

Warriors from these camps ignored their chief's pleas. In June, 1856, Cheyennes and Arapahoes attacked an emigrant train on the Little

14 34 Cong., 3 sess., *House Exec. Doc. No. 1*, Vol. II, 370; W. Turrentine Jackson, "The Army Engineers as Road Surveyors and Builders in Kansas and Nebraska, 1854–1858," *KHQ*, Vol. XVII, No. 1 (February, 1949), 40–44; W. Turrentine Jackson, *Wagon Roads West*, 125.

15 Hoffman to Captain H. Heth, May 24, 1856, Fort Laramie, Letters Sent; *Report, Commissioner of Indian Affairs, 1856*, 87.

16 Grinnell, *Fighting Cheyennes*, 111–12; Hoffman to Pleasonton, June 18, 1856, Fort Laramie, Letters Sent.

Blue River, mortally wounding one man. After the attack the same party came to Fort Kearny, where Captain H. W. Wharton accused them of the attack. The warriors maintained that the Kiowas had committed the depredations and were highly incensed when the captain seized three hostages, two Cheyennes and one Sioux. As the prisoners were being conducted to the guard house, they made a dash for freedom; two escaped without harm, but one of the men, a Cheyenne, had to be carried away by his mounted friends. Indian Agent Twiss and Captain Wharton were firmly convinced that the Cheyennes and Arapahoes from the Arkansas River were guilty. The commanding officer of Fort Kearny explained: "The Cheyennes have been pursuing this same outrageous course for some years past, but this time in open and daring violation of the treaty just made by them it calls most loudly for punishment."[17]

For three more months the Cheyennes and Arapahoes remained quiet. On August 24, 1856, the real troubles started. The Cheyennes and Arapahoes were concentrated on the Platte road in sufficient numbers to cause the Pawnees to take protection at Fort Kearny and abandon their usual summer buffalo hunt. Some young warriors from the Cheyenne camps stopped a mail wagon just below Fort Kearny. They sent a young halfblood to ask the driver for tobacco while they gathered around. The driver, sensing trouble, whipped up his horses, drew his pistol, and made a dash for the fort, but he was wounded in the arm by an arrow. Older members of the village, hearing the shooting, rode out, severely quirted the young warriors, and drove them back into camp.[18]

Captain Wharton quickly sent Captain George H. Stewart and forty-one men of the First Cavalry, with several guides, to track down the Cheyennes. The Cheyenne camp, under Little Grey Head and

[17] Twiss to Commissioner of Indian Affairs, July 15, 1856, Upper Arkansas Agency, Letters Received; Wharton to Pleasonton, June 7, 1856, quoted in Alban W. Hoopes, "Thomas S. Twiss, Indian Agent on the Upper Platte, 1855–1861," *MVHR*, Vol. XX, No. 3 (December, 1933), 361; Wharton to E. V. Sumner, June 11, 1856, Office of the Adjutant General, Letters Received; Hoffman to Pleasonton, July 20, 21, 28, 1856, Fort Laramie, Letters Sent.

[18] Grinnell, *Fighting Cheyennes*, 112; *Report, Commissioner of Indian Affairs, 1856*, 99; Captain John H. Dickerson to Colonel J. J. Abert, December 15, 1856, 35 Cong., 1 sess., *House Exec. Doc. No. 2*, Vol. II, 530–31.

Little Spotted Crow, was found about fifteen miles from Grand Island on the Platte. Dividing his detachment, Captain Stewart hit the Cheyennes, who immediately scattered. The troopers killed ten Cheyennes and wounded eight or ten more before they made good their escape.[19]

In retaliation for Stewart's attack, the Cheyennes ripped up the Platte River route. It appears that the infuriated Cheyennes committed at least three different strikes. On August 25, they destroyed a small, four-wagon train about thirty miles below Fort Kearny, killing Almon W. Babbitt, secretary of Utah territory, two men, one child, and carrying off Mrs. Wilson, the child's mother. When Mrs. Wilson was unable to ride with the fast moving warriors, she was killed by the Cheyennes. The second attack took place five days later, eighty miles above Fort Kearny when the Cheyennes killed Mrs. William Schvekendeck, wounded one man, and carried off Schvekendeck's four-year-old son as a captive. Then, on September 6, Cheyennes attacked some Mormons returning East, killed two men, a woman, and a child, and seized another woman as a prisoner. There were other unconfirmed Cheyenne attacks reported to Captain Wharton, and the newspapers claimed the Cheyennes killed eighteen whites in a series of depredations.[20]

After these attacks the Cheyennes moved away from the Platte to the sources of the Republican River. There they were encountered by Lieutenant Bryan and his surveying party, and the Cheyennes manifested a spirit of hostility until they saw the strength of Bryan's escort. In the camp were warriors who had survived Captain Stewart's fight. Passing through the heart of the buffalo range on the Republican and its tributaries, Lieutenant Bryan noted that the abundant grass in the streams' bottom lands afforded subsistence for "immense herds of buffaloes and elks," making it a favorite hunting ground for the Cheyennes, Comanches, and Kiowas. These tribes, however, expressed

[19] Stewart to Wharton, August 27, 1856, in Kansas *HC*, IV, 491–92; Hoffman to Sumner, July 10, 1857, Fort Laramie, Letters Sent.

[20] Wharton to Cooper, September 8, 1856, in Kansas *HC*, IV, 492–94; Hafen and Young, *Fort Laramie*, 278–79; Twiss to Cumming, in *Report, Commissioner of Indian Affairs, 1856*, 99–101; Grinnell, *Fighting Cheyennes*, 113; Hoopes, "Thomas S. Twiss, Indian Agent," *loc. cit.*, 361; Hoffman to Sumner, July 10, 1857, Fort Laramie, Letters Sent.

their intention of preventing any road along the Republican, necessitating in the Lieutenant's opinion the establishment of posts to "overawe them."[21]

As the Cheyenne raiders satiated their vengeance, they returned to their main camps on the upper Republican, where the chiefs and principal men tried to calm the tribe. After the villages moved to Beaver Creek near the South Platte, delegations were sent to Indian Agent Twiss at Fort Laramie to give their side of the story. They denied that their young men had intended to do harm to the mail driver, because the Cheyennes could have killed him with ease if they had desired. When struck by Captain Stewart's troops, the Cheyennes only "ran away, leaving their horses, bows, and arrows," rather than fight. The chiefs claimed, however, that they could not control their young men, "hot for the war path," who had seen "their friends killed by the soldiers after they had thrown down their bows and arrows and begged for life."

Twiss exacted four conditions from the chiefs. The Cheyennes would abandon their attacks upon the Platte route, treat the emigrants passing through the Cheyenne country as friends, cease wars with the Indian enemies, and prevent any other act likely to disturb peace and harmony between the Cheyennes and the United States. The talks continued for two days and came to a successful conclusion when the Cheyennes and Major Hoffman agreed to exchange a few prisoners. Twiss was convinced that the Cheyennes were once more peaceful and that the older chiefs had "organized a party of their own relatives and friends who will kill any war parties that may attempt to leave the Cheyenne village." To add further strength to his assertions, Twiss also persuaded the Cheyennes to deliver other white captives to him whom they had taken during their August and September raids on the Platte route.[22]

The army officers paid little attention to the peace councils of Twiss. Because the Indian agent and the officers on the frontier had been

---

[21] *Report, Commissioner of Indian Affairs, 1856*, 100; 35 Cong., 1 sess., *House Exec. Doc. No. 2*, Vol. II, 470–71, 475.

[22] *Report, Commissioner of Indian Affairs, 1856*, 99–103; Hoffman to Twiss, September 25, 1856, Fort Laramie, Letters Sent.

feuding about jurisdiction over the hostile Plains Indians, the army was not likely in 1856 to pay much attention to Twiss's accomplishments. General Persifer F. Smith, commanding the Department of the West, stated that the Cheyennes must be "severely punished . . . no trifling or partial punishment will suffice." Because winter was fast approaching, General Smith recommended that the punitive expedition be delayed until 1857, at the "springing of the first grass." Secretary of War Jefferson Davis endorsed the General's views and instructed the department command to make "needful arrangements" for a campaign against the Cheyennes.[23]

The new Secretary of War, John B. Floyd, by April 10, 1857, implemented his predecessor's decision and notified Secretary of the Interior Jacob Thompson that Colonel Edwin V. Sumner and Lieutenant Colonel Albert Sidney Johnston were preparing to conduct expeditions "to keep the peace of the plains and to punish past offences against the United States, especially those committed by the Cheyenne and Kioway Indians." Whether the Cheyennes were determined to keep the peace or to wage war depends upon the documents read. Twiss continued to insist that there was no danger of the Cheyennes continuing their depredations on the Plains.[24]

Other evidence points to a lingering desire for more revenge among the tribe. Relatives of the warriors killed by Stewart continued to harangue the camps, reminding the warriors of the injuries suffered at the hands of the whites. Two medicine men, White Bull and Dark, assured the Cheyennes that they had the power to give their people a victory over the Americans. Tim Goodale, a mountain man turned Indian trader, was told in the spring of 1857 by Long Chin, a Brulé chief, that the Cheyennes had offered his band horses and mules if the Sioux would keep the Cheyennes' old men, women, and children and allow their warriors to join in raiding against the emigrant trains.

---

23 Hoopes, "Thomas S. Twiss, Indian Agent," *loc. cit.*, 359–61; Hoffman to Major George Deas, Fort Laramie, Letters Sent; Twiss to George W. Manypenny, November 7. 1856, Upper Platte Agency, Letters Received; Smith to Cooper, September 10, 1856, and Indorsement by Secretary of War Jefferson Davis, October 24, 1856, in Kansas *HC*, IV, 489–90, 494.

24 Alban W. Hoopes, *Indian Affairs in the West, 1849–1860*, 215; Hoopes, "Thomas S. Twiss, Indian Agent," *loc. cit.*, 362.

From a Cheyenne woman married to a white man, Goodale learned that the Cheyennes were ready for peace or war depending upon the actions of the army.[25]

William Bent warned the Cheyennes that the army was preparing an expedition against them. The Cheyennes replied that they had no intention of meeting the troops in a decisive fight. They would instead place their women and children in safety, scatter into small bands from the Arkansas to the Platte rivers, and "kill all they want, and get plenty of white women for prisoners."[26]

Colonel Sumner divided his command and sent one column west under Major John Sedgwick via Bent's Fort, Fountain Creek, and the South Platte. On Cherry Creek, Major Sedgwick's command observed six or eight Missourians prospecting for gold, and here, too, Fall Leaf, the Delaware chief and scout, acquired his gold to be displayed later on the Kansas frontier. Colonel Sumner took the remainder of the command west by way of the Platte rivers to Fort Laramie and then dropped back down to the South Platte, where the two columns were joined for movement on to the High Plains. When organized on the South Platte, Sumner commanded about four hundred cavalry and infantry supported by four mountain howitzers.[27]

En route to their rendezvous neither column had sighted the Cheyennes. Sumner knew that he would have to move fast to find his quarry, and he left his baggage train on the South Platte. Ahead of Sumner's three columns, the Delaware and Pawnee scouts scoured the country for signs of Cheyennes. Eleven days out from the South Platte, Fall Leaf and his Delawares found fresh signs of Indian camps on the Solomon River. On July 29, 1857, the Delaware chief sent one of his warriors back to Sumner with information that a small party of Indians was just ahead. Sumner, "Bull o' the Woods" to his men, was

[25] Grinnell, *Fighting Cheyennes*, 117; LeRoy R. and Ann W. Hafen (eds.), *Relations with the Indians of the Plains, 1857–1861*, 18, 18–19n.

[26] George Bent to Hyde, November 14, 1912, Bent Letters, Coe Collection; Hafen and Hafen (eds.), *Relations with the Indians of the Plains*, 18–19.

[27] Robert M. Peck, "Recollections of Early Times in Kansas Territory," Kansas *HC*, VIII, 486–94; Hafen and Hafen (eds.), *Relations with the Plains Indians*, 49–67, 98–112n.; Sumner to AAG., September 20, 1857, Office of the Adjutant General, Letters Received; Lowe, *Five Years a Dragoon*, 246–62.

afraid that the Cheyennes would escape, so he pushed his cavalry ahead rapidly, leaving the infantry and artillery to struggle along as rapidly as they could.

White Bull and Dark, the Cheyenne medicine men, had convinced their tribesmen that the soldiers' guns would not fire. The Cheyennes, therefore, made no effort to abandon their village, and the warriors rode directly toward the troops. Sumner, too, was confident. The Colonel rode to the head of his cavalry and exhorted them: "My men! the enemy is at last in sight. I don't know how many warriors the Cheyennes can bring against us, but I do know that if officers and men obey orders promptly, and all pull together, we can whip the whole tribe. . . . Bugler, sound the advance." Halting long enough to observe the Cheyennes' movements, several officers sighted a "swarm" of warriors gathering in a cottonwood grove. A glint of a rifle barrel or lance point was seen by the cavalry, and Cheyenne warriors, stripped of clothing except for a "gee-string" rode toward the cavalry in a "well-formed line of battle." The outnumbered troopers, seeing the Cheyennes advancing, wished the supporting infantry and howitzers were closer at hand.

As the Cheyennes and the cavalry closed, Fall Leaf whipped up his horse and sped midway between the combatants. Pulling up, Fall Leaf fired at the Cheyennes who returned several answering shots. Sumner then shouted to a subordinate, "Bear witness, . . . that an Indian fired the first shot." Deploying his troops to meet a Cheyenne flanking movement, Sumner felt free to begin the battle.

Sumner's booming voice ordered his men to "sling-carbine" and "draw saber." Seeing cold steel, the Cheyennes checked their advance. Sensing his warriors' hesitation, a fine-looking Cheyenne leader "dashed up and down in front of their line, with the tail of his war-bonnet flowing behind, brandishing his lance," trying to stem the mounting panic among the Cheyenne braves. Not even their medicine men, though, could restore courage to the Cheyenne warriors as they fled the field. Sumner reported that Indians ". . . stood, with remarkable boldness, until we charged and were nearly upon them, when they broke in all directions, and it was impossible to overtake many of them." The medicine men's power applied only to guns, not to flashing sabers; the medicine was broken and the "Fighting Cheyennes" lived to fight another day.[28]

In terms of casualties, the Cheyennes were not badly whipped. One trooper thought thirty Cheyennes were killed, but Sumner counted nine dead warriors, and later the Cheyennes claimed only four warriors were killed in the brief skirmish and chase. Sumner's losses were smaller than the Cheyennes', since his casualties were limited to two troopers killed, one lieutenant, later to be the famed Confederate cavalryman Jeb Stuart, and eight enlisted men wounded. Leaving his artillery, one company of infantry, and the wounded behind, Sumner pressed on. Two days' march brought the command to the Cheyenne village, where 171 lodges were still standing. So fast was the Cheyenne flight that they left behind fifteen to twenty thousand pounds of buffalo meat, their winter food supply. Destroying the lodges and other equipment, Sumner followed the trail for forty miles until the Cheyennes scattered in every direction. Sumner believed that the Cheyennes would flee south, and he marched his men to the Arkansas River, arriving at Fort Atkinson on August 9, 1857, where he hoped he could intercept the tribe.[29]

After the fight with Sumner, part of the Cheyennes fled north and others south. Sumner's wagon train, after re-provisioning at Fort Laramie, waited for the command near Lodgepole Creek. There, four Cheyenne warriors, thinking the train to be emigrants, came in hoping to get food. In a scuffle the wagon master and his men seized two of the Cheyennes and shackled them to the wagons. Scouting toward the creek, they observed in the distance a band of Indians moving much too fast to be encumbered with lodges. Another portion of the Cheyennes passed south of the Arkansas River ahead of Sumner's troops and joined the Kiowas.[30]

[28] Peck, "Recollections," Kansas *HC*, VIII, 494–98; Lowe, *Five Years a Dragoon*, 267; Sumner to AAG., August 9, 1857, 35 Cong., 1 sess., *House Exec. Doc. No. 2*, Vol. II, 96, 99; *Report, Commissioner of Indian Affairs, 1857*, 147.

[29] Peck, "Recollections," *loc. cit.*, 498; 35 Cong., 1 sess., *House Exec. Doc. No. 2*, Vol. II, 96–97; *Report, Commissioner of Indian Affairs, 1857*, 147; Grinnell, *Fighting Cheyennes*, 121; George Bent to Hyde [1905?], Western History Department, Denver Public Library; Sumner to AAG., August 9, 1857, Office of the Adjutant General, Letters Received.

[30] Lowe, *Five Years a Dragoon*, 269, 273–83, 286–89; Jackson, *Wagon Roads West*, 196–97; *Report, Commissioner of Indian Affairs, 1857*, 145–46.

While Sumner was hunting the Cheyennes, a new Indian agent for the Upper Arkansas Agency, Robert C. Miller, was making his way west to distribute annuity goods. The Kiowas were also disaffected in the summer of 1857 and demanded their goods as soon as the agent reached Fort Atkinson. Miller nearly had to call upon the Comanches for protection when the Kiowas appeared with "bows strung and their hands full of arrows, impatient for the least excuse to make an attack." After the distribution of goods to the Kiowas and Comanches, Miller moved on to Bent's Fort. Miller had already distributed to the Arapahoes their share of the goods and had moved on to meet the Cheyennes.[31]

Knowing that the Cheyennes and Sumner might meet and fight, William Bent wanted no part of the goods. Messengers from Miller and Bent could not find the Cheyennes, so Bent moved away from his post and established a temporary stockade on the Purgatoire River. Finally two Kiowa-Apaches came to Bent's Fort and announced that the Cheyennes were camping on the Smoky Hill. But by the time Miller's emissaries reached the Cheyennes, Sumner had already fought the tribe. The Cheyennes, according to Miller's informants, were badly beaten and in an ugly mood. The Cheyennes joined the Kiowas, whom Miller knew were already restless, and the two tribes threatened to come back to Bent's Fort "to help themselves to the goods, and take the scalp of the agent and everyone with him." Trying to be conciliatory, Miller sent messengers to the Cheyennes, who replied that "they would not come to the Fort, except to fight, they did not want to make peace nor did they desire presents."[32]

Certain that the agent and public property were in jeopardy, Sumner decided to move to Bent's Fort, "with the elite of my cavalry, in the hope that I may find the Cheyennes collected in the vicinity, and, by another blow, force them to sue for peace." He arrived at Bent's Fort on August 18, 1857, and took over the Cheyenne annuity goods. The Colonel reasoned that the government would not sanction an expedition to punish the Cheyennes and at the same time send the tribe arms, ammunition, and supplies. The guns, flints, and powder

31 *Report, Commissioner of Indian Affairs, 1857*, 142–44.

32 Miller to Cumming, July 20, 25, 1857, Upper Arkansas Agency, Letters Received; *Report, Commissioner of Indian Affairs, 1857*, 145–46; Lavender, *Bent's Fort*, 333.

were either destroyed or taken back to Fort Leavenworth, while the perishable goods and clothing were distributed among the friendly Indians as an advance on the next year's annuity payments. At Walnut Creek, on the way back to Fort Leavenworth, Sumner received a message ordering him to send his serviceable units to join the Utah expedition. Thus ended the first punitive expedition against the Cheyennes.[33]

The view that Sumner's campaign, "chastised a few Indians, embittered the feelings of many, and failed to overawe any," is true only in part. Four Cheyenne chiefs, White Antelope, High-Back-Wolf, Tall Bear, and Starved Bear, gathered at Bent's Fort late in October, 1857, and pleaded their cause to their friend, William Bent. Claiming they represented the South Platte and Arkansas River Cheyennes, the chiefs reviewed their life since the Treaty of Fort Laramie. The Cheyennes, they claimed, had ceased to war upon all other Indians except the Pawnees and Utes, who were not represented at Fort Laramie. They also asserted that they did not deserve to be attacked by the army. At Fort Kearny, two of their warriors had been seized and one wounded "in six different places; this we all let pass in peace." Later, another of their men was starved to death in the guardhouse at Fort Laramie. The Kiowas, the Cheyennes alleged, caused all of the troubles on the Little Blue early in June, 1856, and the Cheyennes did not deserve the punishment meted out by Captain Stewart. This officer, the Cheyennes claimed, "charged on us and all of us but a few young men fled without making the least resistance leaving behind all of our Lodges and other property which they destroyed and killed five of our people and took a great many horses." In spite of these grievances, the Cheyennes did not retaliate, although they had many opportunities.

Explaining the subsequent depredations, the four Cheyenne chiefs insisted: "We Arkansas and South Platte Band of Cheyannes Indians have never committed but very few depredations, it is true some of our Young Men have joined the North Platt Band of Cheyannes but we have nothing to do with them we are separate and distinct

33 Sumner to AAG., August 11, 1857, 35 Cong., 1 sess., *House Exec. Doc. No. 2*, Vol. II, 97–98; Sumner to Miller, August 19, September 3, 1857, Office of the Adjutant General, Letters Received; *Report, Commissioner of Indian Affairs, 1857*, 146–48.

142

Bands they have their own rules and regulations." William Bent supported the contentions of the Cheyennes and advocated that steps be taken to end the misunderstandings. The old Indian trader later told Superintendent John Haverty that the Arkansas River Cheyennes were behaving themselves and that the North Platte band were the ones who "commenced the fracus and ortof shared a part of the thrashing." Indian Agent Miller came to share Bent's view in the spring of 1858, believing that the Arkansas River band were penitent for their wrongs and sufficiently punished by the whipping administered by Sumner. Since the government could not adequately protect the Santa Fe road, the Cheyennes, Miller held, should be paid their annuity goods, lest they revenge themselves on the emigrants along the route.[34]

Before anything could be done to restore amity with the Cheyennes, the vanguard of the Pike's Peak gold rush reached Cherry Creek. Evidence of loose gold had been observed in the streams rising in the mountains of Colorado since 1850, and Americans soon flooded in to avail themselves of the precious metal. By June 24, 1858, over a hundred men, comprising the Green Russell and Missouri parties, were at the mouth of Cherry Creek, and by mid-July they were joined by fortune hunters from Lawrence, Kansas. The invasion of the Cheyenne and Arapaho lands continued through the fall of 1858, and before the end of the year four town sites were established along Cherry Creek alone. In slightly more than a year after the arrival of the first prospecting parties, over a hundred thousand "fifty-niners" swept toward the region later to become the state of Colorado. Perhaps less than one-half of the gold-seekers ever reached the mines of western Kansas territory, but enough remained to inundate the lands of the Cheyennes and Arapahoes.[35]

Surprisingly, Indians along the Arkansas and Platte rivers committed few depredations upon the gold-seekers in 1858 and 1859. Rather than fight, the Cheyennes and Arapahoes sought another treaty with the government by which they could find "permanent homes where

[34] Hoopes, *Indian Affairs in the West*, 216; White Antelope, *et al.*, to Col. Hafferdy [John Haverty], October 28, 1857; William Bent to Hafferday [Haverty], December 11, 1857; Miller to Charles E. Mix, April 30, 1858, Upper Arkansas Agency, Letters Received.

[35] LeRoy R. Hafen (ed.), *The Southwest Historical Series*, IX, Introduction.

they would not be intruded upon by the whites." William Bent had never seen the Indians so quiet, as Indian Agent Miller distributed Indian annuity goods at the mouth of Pawnee Fork. "Colonel Sumner has worked a wondrous change" in the disposition of the Cheyennes, Miller reported, proving the "salutary effect of a good whipping." To Miller, the Cheyenne chiefs said that, "They had eyes and were not blind. They no longer listened to their young men who continually clamored for war." The chiefs desired peace, a home protected from white encroachments, until "they had been taught to cultivate the soil and other arts of civilized life." In the event of another treaty, the Cheyennes expressed a desire to be "assigned the country about the headwaters of the south Platte."[36]

Colonel Sumner, too, found no hostility among the Cheyennes in the summer of 1858. In the vicinity of Fort Atkinson about mid-August, Sumner met "a party of Cheyennes, who were perfectly humble." The presence of troops undoubtedly reminded the Cheyennes of their unhappy experience of the previous summer. Few Indians, of course, had been killed in 1857, but they had lost heavily in lodges, equipment, and food and had forfeited a year's annuity goods. Two months later, Bent, in writing to an Indian Bureau official, commented upon the pleasant relations with the Cheyennes and Arapahoes but mentioned that they were "molesting me very mutch . . . [and] they wish you to do something for them concerning theair contry The whites are abought taking posesion of it. The whites I am told are abought laying off town lots or towns, I am yousing all of my influence to keep the Indians quiet and I have suxceeded in doing so."[37]

During the winter of 1858–59, prospectors and town-site speculators turned their attention to acquiring title to the Cheyenne and Arapaho lands. Correspondents of Representative Samuel R. Curtis of Iowa thought extinguishment of Indian title to the whole region "would be the surest if not the only course to insure friendly relations between the miners & settlers and the Indian tribes." Representative Curtis, whose son was at Cherry Creek, wrote to Governor James W. Denver

[36] Miller to A. M. Robinson, July 20, 1858; William Bent to Robinson, August 4, 1858; *Report, Commissioner of Indian Affairs, 1858,* 96–100.

[37] Sumner to AAG., October 5, 1858, Office of the Adjutant General, Letters Received; William Bent to [Mix?], October 20, 1858, Upper Arkansas Agency, Letters Received; *Report, Commissioner of Indian Affairs, 1858,* 99.

of Kansas territory requesting the Governor to use his influence for
the purchase of the region of the "new Gold mines of Kansas & Nebraska," so that "the settlement of titles and the security of homes
may be pressed forward to the aid of organization of Society."[38]

Miners settling down in their winter quarters mixed easily with
the Indians. Hearing of the whites' holiday of Christmas, Indians
drove into the settlements on Cherry Creek one hundred ponies for
wagers on horse races between their animals and those of the miners.
The Indians offered to bet 150 animals on a trotting mule in their
possession against any American trotting horse. Having no trotter,
the miners thought of importing a trotting mule from Missouri. In
January, 1859, five hundred Arapaho warriors and their women and
children were feasted by the miners at Auraria with roast oxen,
dried apples, coffee and bread. Rufus C. Cable, witnessing the feast,
was amazed at the Indians' prodigious eating capacity. "I have never
seen men," wrote Cable, "eat till now. I have heard that one man
could eat an antelope at one meal, and I verily believe one Indian,
called 'Heap of Whips,' could eat a whole ox." John S. Smith, Bent's
old trader, was, however, turned out of Denver, early in 1859, for
breaking his Indian wife's back when she requested permission to
dance with miners.[39]

Little Raven, an important Arapaho chief who was respected by
many of the early settlers, pledged that he would keep peace and
order among his people. Loss of stock was, of course, blamed upon
the Indians. Thousands of Indians supposedly camped along Cherry
Creek near Denver, early in May, 1859, and when they moved "no
more Indian outrages" took place.[40]

Some travelers came into contact with Cheyennes during the spring
of 1859. One village of Cheyennes, located at the mouth of the Cache
la Poudre, availed themselves of the opportunity to trade with the
1859 variety of American tourists. Two well-known journalists, Albert D. Richardson of the Boston *Journal* and Horace Greeley of the
New York *Tribune,* eyed the Cheyennes with suspicion when some

38 David Dickinson and John D. Sarver to Col. [Samuel R.] Curtis, January 27,
1859; Curtis to James W. Denver, February 6, 1859, Upper Arkansas Agency, Letters
Received.
39 LeRoy R. Hafen (ed.), *Colorado Gold Rush,* 147–48, 208, 219, 349.
40 Hafen (ed.), *Colorado Gold Rush,* 357.

of the tribe visited them on Sappa Creek. The stagecoach carrying the two newspapermen overturned, scattering their baggage. Cheyennes gathered about, and were described by the Easterners as, "instinctive thieves, and we watched them with drawn revolvers," until the baggage was safely stored in the nearby station.[41]

With the influx of settlers into the gold fields, the officials of the Indian Bureau realized the importance of an Indian agent who could control the tribes living between the Platte and Arkansas rivers. Superintendent A. M. Robinson selected William Bent, who assumed his duties during the summer of 1859 and whose appointment Congress confirmed on April 27, 1860. As Indian agent for the Upper Arkansas Agency, Bent began by assembling and transporting the annual annuity payments to the South Platte. On July 19, 1859, William Bent and his son Robert, who was serving as the transportation contractor, found only forty-five lodges of Cheyennes at Beaver Creek waiting for their goods. The great majority of the tribe, reduced to starvation, had left for the Republican and Smoky Hill rivers in search of buffalo. Bent moved up the South Platte slowly, waiting for his runners to find the tribes, and finally, after a long delay, he reasoned that the Cheyennes and Arapahoes were watching for him on the Arkansas River. The Indian agent had no desire to see the Kiowas and Comanches because he believed those tribes would be, "purtay Saucy but as I have bin appointid agent I feel it my dutay to see all of the Indians under my Agency if they sculp me."

While Bent was traveling about in search of the Cheyennes and Arapahoes, he presented in a series of letters his views on the problem of those tribes. He was certain that they would have to adopt agricultural activities in the very near future, because "the game are now to scarce for them to depend upon it for subsistence." This conclusion was reached also by the Cheyennes and Arapahoes who had already "passed theair laws amongst themselves that they will do anything that I may advize." The Indian agent closed one letter by saying that the "Indians bother me so that I shall have to close You must excuse my bad spelling as I have bin so long in the wild world I have almost forgotten how to spell." After waiting for a month on the

---

[41] LeRoy R. Hafen (ed.), *Overland Routes to the Gold Fields, 1859*, 161, 255–57.

South Platte, the Cheyennes and Arapahoes appeared, and Bent distributed their annuity goods to them.[42]

Bent knew the Cheyennes and Arapahoes better than any other white man. Despite the many irritations stemming from white occupation of the gold regions and decline of game, the two tribes faithfully and carefully maintained the peace. Beneath the surface, however, Bent warned: "A smouldering passion agitates these Indians, perpetually fomented by the failure of food, the encircling encroachments of the white population, and the exasperating sense of decay and impending extinction." In 1859 the two divisions of the Cheyennes and Arapahoes began to emerge. One group lived between the North and South Platte rivers, the other between the latter stream and the Arkansas. The settlers and routes to the gold fields along the South Platte placed barriers between the two divisions and began limiting the freedom of movement between the two groups. The recommendations made by William Bent in 1859 for the most part applied to the Southern Cheyennes and Arapahoes.

The only solution for preventing "difficulties and massacres" was to withdraw the Cheyennes and Arapahoes from contact with the whites and transform them into an "agricultural and pastoral people." For the Southern Cheyennes and Arapahoes, Bent believed that the tribes would be satisfied with the lands bordering on the Arkansas River, extending from Fontain Creek towards the Raton Mountains. Bent also mentioned that the tribesmen desired to make provisions for the "half-breeds, the children of white men intermarried with the Cheyennes and Arapahoes," which, of course, included Bent's five children by Owl Woman and Yellow Woman. The Indians of his agency, Bent stressed, were already "pressed upon all around by the Texans, by the settlers of the gold region, by the advancing people of Kansas, and from the Platte, are already compressed into a small circle of territory. . . . A desperate war of starvation and extinction is therefore imminent and inevitable, unless prompt measures shall prevent it."[43]

42 Lavender, *Bent's Fort*, 340, 417n.; William Bent to Robinson, July 23, August 1, 1859, Upper Arkansas Agency, Letters Received; *Report, Commissioner of Indian Affairs, 1859*, 137.
43 *Report, Commissioner of Indian Affairs, 1859*, 137–39.

William Bent pressed hard for a treaty during the winter of 1859–60 as he wintered at his post on the Arkansas River. The Kiowas were ready to go to war, and this angered the other tribes. The Cheyennes and Arapahoes, in particular, offered to punish the Kiowas, and although Bent thought "it would be the cheapest plan to get rid of the Kiowas," he would not approve of the intertribal war. The Cheyennes and Arapahoes, though peaceful, became more restless about white encroachments. "The whites," wrote Bent, "by their large, extensive settlements and towns on the Arkansas, Cherry Creek, and South Platte, appropriated the best part of the Cheyenne and Arapaho country and their principal hunting grounds." The two tribes authorized Bent to approach the government for a treaty and offered to meet commissioners on the South Platte during the 1860 annuity payment.[44]

The Kiowas needed a whipping, at least in the opinion of Bent. During the summer of 1860, two columns of troops went after the Kiowas, one column under Major John Sedgwick swinging through a five-hundred-mile arc south of the Arkansas and having no success. The other, under Captain S. D. Sturgis, had only one brush with the Indians. Either on the Republican or Solomon River, Sturgis had a running fight with a large band of six to eight hundred Kiowas, Comanches, and some Cheyennes. Little Chief and White Antelope, forty-five years later, remembered Sturgis' expedition and told George Bent that at one time the Cheyennes had very nearly lured the Indian scouts with Sturgis into an ambush, but the warriors showed themselves prematurely, and Sturgis was able to rescue his scouts.[45]

Bent's insistence upon a treaty finally brought a response from the Bureau of Indian Affairs. Superintendent Robinson persuaded Bent to remain in his position until the treaty was completed. After some delays Commissioner A. B. Greenwood arrived at Bent's Fort to conduct the negotiations. The Arapahoes were waiting patiently for the treaty, but when the councils were to begin, the Cheyennes were re-

[44] William Bent to Robinson, November 25, 28, December 17, Upper Arkansas Agency, Letters Received.

[45] Lavender, *Bent's Fort,* 344; Hafen and Hafen (eds.), *Relations with the Plains Indians,* 196–254; George Bent to Hyde, March 6, 1905, Western History Department, Denver Public Library; William Bent to Robinson, November 28, 1859, Upper Arkansas Agency, Letters Received.

ported as being 250 miles away hunting buffalo on the Plains. White Antelope, Black Kettle, and four or five lesser chiefs appeared without their bands about September 18, and the talks began.

Essentially amenable to the proposals made by Commissioner Greenwood, the Cheyennes and Arapahoes consented to a greatly reduced reservation. The Cheyenne chiefs explained that even if their absent tribesmen dissented, they, the principal chiefs, would later sign the treaty and allow the others to locate themselves elsewhere. Once the tentative agreement was reached, William Bent tendered his resignation to the Commissioner and it was accepted. Bent's resignation was not a protest, but he must have had some doubts. How would the warriors, absent from the treaty councils, react? The old trader knew that many of the young men were spoiling for war and might well repudiate the actions agreed to by White Antelope, Black Kettle, and the other chiefs.

Commissioner Greenwood departed from Bent's Fort on September 20, 1860, with the understanding that the chiefs would sign the treaty as soon as they could make its provisions known to the rest of the Southern Cheyennes. Albert G. Boone, grandson of Daniel Boone, was, upon the suggestion of William Bent, appointed the new Indian agent for the Upper Arkansas Agency. Boone has been criticized for his role in the final signing of the treaty. The new Indian agent, however, only followed the agreements already attained by Greenwood and Bent. A majority of the Arapahoes were compliant, and the peace chiefs of the Cheyennes, headed by Black Kettle, were willing to sign the document with or without the consent of the warriors.[46]

The Treaty of Fort Wise, signed on February 18, 1861, by the chiefs of the Southern Cheyennes and Arapahoes, is an interesting document. By its provisions the tribes ceded all the Fort Laramie treaty lands except for a reservation bounded by a line beginning at the mouth of Sand Creek, continuing up the north bank of the Arkansas River, across the Arkansas at the mouth of Purgatoire River, then up

[46] 12 U. S. Stat. 59; Greenwood to J. Thompson, October 25, 1860, in *Report, Commissioner of Indian Affairs, 1860,* 228–30; Hafen and Hafen (eds.), *Relations with the Plains Indians,* 284–89; Lavender, *Bent's Fort,* 346.

the west bank of that river to the northern boundary of New Mexico territory. The reservation line then went west until it reached a north-south line which intersected the Arkansas River five miles east of the mouth of the Huerfano River. This north-south line was then projected north to upper Sand Creek and then followed Sand Creek down to its mouth on the Arkansas River.

The secretary of the interior was given the power to assign lands of the reservation in severalty to members of the two tribes. Within every tract assigned, each family would be given a reasonable amount of water and timber. Those lands assigned to tribal members could not be "alienated in fee, leased, or otherwise disposed of," except to other tribal members or to the United States, and then only with the approval of the secretary of the interior. Anticipating local and state government in Colorado territory, the lands held in severalty were exempted from "taxation, levy, sale, or forfeiture," until Congress permitted such actions.

For the huge cession, the United States agreed to pay $450,000 over a period of fifteen years. In addition, the United States agreed to expend $5,000 for five years for the establishment and maintenance of saw mills, grinding mills for grain, a mechanic shop, and their necessary employees. The cost of agricultural implements, the breaking and fencing of land, the building of houses, and other improvements, of course, would be borne by the Indians from the cession purchase money. For the protection of the Cheyennes and Arapahoes, the reservation was closed to all white persons except government employees and legal traders. The government guaranteed the Cheyennes and Arapahoes "quiet and peaceful possession" of the reservation, their persons, and property during the tribesmen's good behavior.

Two provisions of the treaty reflect private interests. Robert Bent and Jack Smith, the son of John S. Smith, were given 640 acres of land along the Arkansas River. This concession was approved by the United States Senate. Another provision, allowing town-site speculators of Denver and other adjacent towns to purchase land for their speculative ventures at $1.25 per acre, was disallowed.[47]

President Abraham Lincoln proclaimed the treaty effective on De-

[47] Kappler (ed.)., *Laws and Treaties*, II, 807–11.

cember 15, 1861.[48] With this act the mining frontier had closed in on the Southern Cheyennes. They could either abide by the treaty's provisions or lose its benefits and fall outside of the protection offered by the United States. Now the days of freedom were at an end.

[48] 12 U. S. Stat. 1168–69.

# 7

## ANTICIPATION OF WAR

CALM JUDGMENT AND EFFICIENT MANAGEMENT of Colorado Indian affairs might have avoided the tragic massacre at Sand Creek. After the Treaty of Fort Wise, however, circumstances prevented adequate supervision of Indian affairs on the Plains. The Civil War was upon the nation, and Confederate agents, such as Albert Pike, hoped to use the Plains Indians to disrupt the Santa Fe commerce, isolate New Mexico, and cut off the North from California. A recommendation to Confederate President Jefferson Davis in May, 1861, suggested the seizure of Cheyenne Pass, Fort Laramie, Fort Wise, and the mail route to California.[1] Suspicions arose, roving Indians were eyed with distrust, troops were stripped from western army posts, inefficient and sometimes corrupt men administered Indian affairs, and the Cheyennes, especially the young warriors, balked at remaining within the limits of their reservation. The Dog Soldiers refused to sign the Treaty of Fort Wise, insisting that they would never agree to live on a reservation.

In the spring of 1861, Indians committed depredations in Colorado territory. From Denver, on April 25, 1861, Indian Agent Boone informed Superintendent Robinson that: "Daily and hourly I am receiving complaints of burning ranches, killing stock as well as many cases of outrages of the gravest character perpetrated on white women." Boone alerted Major John Sedgwick to have two companies of cavalry available at a moment's notice to quiet the settlers' fears. Since there were Kiowas, Comanches, Cheyennes, and Arapahoes in the vicinity of Denver, the Indian agent could not be certain which tribe

[1] Grinnell, *Fighting Cheyennes*, 126; U. S. War Department, *The War of Rebellion. A Compilation of the Official Records of the Union and Confederate Armies,* Series I: Vol. 3, 579 (hereafter cited as *O. R., I*).

was guilty of the depredations. Boone also noted that the Cheyennes and Arapahoes were preparing war parties to attack the Shoshonis and Pawnees.[2] Fears subsided, however, and no troop action was necessary in the spring and summer of 1861.

Governor William Gilpin, of Colorado territory, feared the Indians and Confederates, thousands of the latter being present in the territory's mines. On June 19, 1861, Gilpin offered Commissioner of Indian Affairs William P. Dole a plan in which the territorial capital would be the administrative center for the Indians living on the Central and Southern Great Plains and in the mountains of Colorado and New Mexico territories. The Governor stressed the necessity of immediate approval of the Treaty of Fort Wise, so that the Cheyennes and Arapahoes could be restricted to their reservation. For better control, territorial Governor Gilpin recommended that the "half breed band of Cheyennes and Arapahoes" who lived between the North and South Platte rivers, and who frequently occupied central Colorado territory, be placed under his jurisdiction. This Cheyenne-Arapaho band and the Oglala Sioux claimed a right to live permanently on the South Platte and Cache la Poudre, where they killed stock and threatened the settlers. Gilpin believed the only effective way to control the twenty-five thousand Indians in the region surrounding Denver was a system of five Indian agents under his personal supervision.[3]

Concern over Indian affairs mounted during the fall of 1861. Arapahoes under Big Mouth pillaged a Mexican train at Coon Creek, thirteen miles west of Fort Larned. Little Wolf's band of Cheyennes, "unable to resist the temptation" of several barrels of whisky, shared in the spoils, which included flour, sugar, tobacco, and blankets. Captain J. Hayden, commanding Fort Larned with only thirty-seven infantrymen, admitted his inability to protect the Santa Fe route against mounted Indians and suggested that Indian Agent Boone seize Big Mouth and twenty-five or thirty of his warriors as hostages against further depredations.[4] Such an incident, however, was of no great import. The Cheyennes and Arapahoes, without respect for Mexicans,

2 Boone to Robinson, April 25, 1861, Upper Arkansas Agency, Letters Received.

3 William Gilpin to Dole, June 19, 1861, in *Report, Commissioner of Indian Affairs, 1861*, 99–101.

4 Hayden to Boone, September 1, 1861, Upper Arkansas Agency, Letters Received.

did not consider them within the groups protected by the United States.

To preserve the peace, Boone advised Commissioner Charles E. Mix that basic revisions were necessary in Indian policies. First, to keep the Indians on their reservation, agricultural implements and animals should be supplied to them in addition to "a few honest farmers" who could instruct the Indians in adapting to an agricultural way of life. Indian agents residing among their charges should be well qualified to aid the Indians in industrial and agricultural occupations. The non-intercourse provisions of the statutes between Indians and illegal traders should be vigorously enforced. Care, however, was necessary in accepting the testimony of an Indian against the whites, limiting it to "extreme or criminal cases" because the Indians' "natural want of intellect and hatred & jealousy to the white race." Boone, with years of experience among the Indians, stated that much of the trouble on the frontier stemmed from an illegal whisky trade and "low depraved beings" who intermarried with the Indians. These intermarried whites, in Boone's opinion, were the chief means by which illegal whisky venders made their inroads into the tribes. An important theme in Boone's recommendations was his theory that if authorities controlled the whites who came in contact with the Indians, the Indians would be more easily supervised. No traders except those licensed by the government officials should be allowed in the Indian country. More rigid inspection of annuity goods was necessary to eliminate articles of no use to the Indians and provisions "not worth transportation." Another problem, which intensified with passage of time, was the "swarm of petifogging traders" who appeared at the annuity payments pretending to trade, but who "have whisky smuggled at a distance for the purpose of buying the goods supplied by the govt after the distribution." These and other whites detrimental to peace and Indian welfare, Boone insisted, should be removed from the Indian country by the Indian agent.[5]

Two tasks faced Agent Boone in the fall of 1861. He had to acquire Cheyenne and Arapaho approval of the Senate amendment and check Confederate inroads upon the Indians of his agency. The Arapahoes signed the amending document late in October and appeared "well

[5] Boone to Mix, September 6, 1861, Upper Arkansas Agency, Letters Received.

satisfied." The Cheyennes, remaining on their hunt, were not as easily assembled and were less amenable than the Arapahoes. After two days of hard counciling, the Cheyennes revealed that they had vowed never to sign another treaty. But, after promising thirty-six sets of uniforms, six of them to be complete with epaulets, and permission for the chiefs to visit Washington, Boone persuaded the Cheyennes to sign the amendment.[6]

Through the Yamparika Comanches, Albert Pike sought to bring other Plains Indians under Confederate influence. Boone worried not only about the Confederate sympathy among the Comanches, but was also deeply concerned that the feeling might spread to other Indians of his agency. William Bent, installed at his strong Purgatoire River stockade, threw his weight against a Confederate alliance with the Cheyennes and Arapahoes. He told the tribe to stay out of the "white man's fight," and there is no evidence that the Confederates succeeded in acquiring the support of the Plains Indians. Nevertheless, the threat was strong enough to cause Governor Gilpin to suggest the establishment of a garrison at Fort Wise.[7]

As one of his last acts as Indian agent, Albert G. Boone took a careful census of the Upper Arkansas Agency Indians. The Cheyennes numbered 1,380 individuals, of whom there were 425 men, 480 women, and 475 children, occupying 250 lodges. Commenting to Commissioner Dole, Indian Agent Boone maintained that most people "from a birds eye view or seeing them assembled" overestimated their actual numbers. These Cheyennes were led by five chiefs: Lean Bear, White Antelope, Little Wolf, Left Hand, and Tall Bear. Boone evinced little sympathy for or understanding of his agency's Indians. The men of the tribes, wrote Boone:

"abhor labor, the women do all the drudgery; they are an indolent community, lay around, pilfer & beg, great lovers of whiskey, sugar and think it very strange that I have not allowed it to be brought and

6 Boone to Dole, October 26, November 2, 1861, Upper Arkansas Agency, Letters Received.
7 Boone to Mix, October 19, 1861, Boone to Dole, October 26, 1861, Gilpin to Dole, June 19, 1861, in *Report, Commissioner of Indian Affairs, 1861*, 99–101, 104–106; Gilpin to Colonel E. R. S. Canby, October 26, 1861, *O. R.*, I: Vol. 4, 73; Lavender, *Bent's Fort*, 348. Albert Pike, in 1861, was serving as commissioner of the Confederate States to the Indian nations and tribes west of Arkansas.

traded for such commodities as they have to sell, often offering a good Pony or mule for one Bottle. They are very licentious, they worship the Sun, Earth and Smoke and swear by the Pipe."

Some jealousy and conflict, stemming from the Treaty of Fort Wise, existed between the Arkansas River group and the other division of the Cheyennes and Arapahoes. The Platte bands insisted that the Arkansas River division had no authority to cede lands to the United States, and they were also jealous of the additional goods and annuities due the Arkansas River division from the treaty's provisions. Of all the Cheyennes, Boone found only Black Kettle capable of fully understanding matters crucial to the welfare of the whole tribe.[8]

Even after leaving office, Albert Boone continued to advise Commissioner Dole on means of allaying Indian discontent. Early in 1862, the Cheyennes and Arapahoes complained that Kiowas and Comanches hunted extensively on their reservation and destroyed their grass and timber. To avoid the problem, Boone suggested that the tribal annuities be subsequently paid at Fort Larned, where the buffalo were more numerous and where the Indians would be farther removed from white settlements along the upper Arkansas River Valley. This course would also remove the Cheyennes and Arapahoes farther from the Utes, with whom they were constantly at war. Their war parties en route to the mountains moved through the white settlements, where they stole and killed the whites' stock. These incidents naturally irritated the whites, and only with considerable effort could Boone, while Indian agent, prevent hostilities from breaking out between the settlers and Indians of the Upper Arkansas Agency.[9]

Without visiting his charges, the new Indian agent, S. G. Colley, began immediately to recommend a new policy for controlling the Cheyennes and Arapahoes. Colley, a cousin of Governor Gilpin, described the Cheyenne and Arapaho reservation as "a very large tract of valuable land . . . not surpassed in fertility in the United States,"

[8] S. G. Colley was appointed Indian agent for the Upper Arkansas Agency on August 26, 1861, but the notice of the change did not reach Colorado territory until mid-November, 1861. Gilpin to Dole, October 8, 1861, in *Report, Commissioner of Indian Affairs, 1861,* 104; Colley to Gilpin, December 19, 1861. "Census Returns of the Different Tribes of Indians in the Upper Arkansas Agency up to the First of November, 1861," Boone to Dole, November 16, 1861, Upper Arkansas Agency, Letters Received.

[9] Boone to Dole, January 18, 1862, Upper Arkansas Agency, Letters Received.

abounding in rich pastures but deficient in game. The Indians, however, viewed this land in quite a different way, as did later Colorado
settlers. Without buffalo near at hand and uninterested in agriculture, the young disdained the reservation. Yet, according to Colley,
the tribal chiefs and leading men, meaning the treaty signers, were
anxious to live upon the reservation and begin agricultural activities.
Eager to placate United States officials, the chief's desired an uninter-
rupted flow of presents and annuity goods, but their control over the
warrior societies was minimal. On the whole, Colley's approach to a
solution of Indian problems was unrealistic, yet one of his suggestions
was feasible. A few mixed-blood Cheyennes could farm, but full bloods
could not or would not engage in a way of life whose duties, by tradition, devolved upon women. Hoe corn, cultivate gardens—no self-
respecting warrior could stand the derision of his comrades even for
presents or the agent's approbation. Quite sensibly Colley advocated
a shift from agriculture to stock raising. Cheyennes cared for their
pony herds with great attention. Their reservation, with abundant
pasturage, could sustain cattle herds not only in the summer but
during the winter without supplementing the forage from the grasses
of the Great Plains. Unless some food supply was soon found to replace
the depleted game on their reservation, Colley predicted that the Cheyennes and Arapahoes would war against their white neighbors. The
buffalo range was east and north of the assigned reservation, and if
the Indians left the reservation to hunt, contacts, depredations, and
conflicts were inevitable.[10]

Historians, without proof, have maintained that the Cheyennes and
Arapahoes planned, in 1862, to initiate a war against the whites. No
evidence exists, however, that the entire Cheyenne and Arapaho tribes
contemplated a concerted war against Colorado territory. Dissatisfactions were present, but more so among the Cheyennes and Arapahoes
living between the North and South Platte rivers than those living
on the Arkansas. The latter groups wintered near the Great Bend
of the Arkansas River hunting buffalo available in the region. Cheyennes and Brulé Sioux of the Upper Platte Agency raided along the
South Platte early in the summer of 1862, but a company of the Second Colorado Volunteers, under Colonel Jesse H. Leavenworth and

[10] Colley to Gilpin, December 19, 1861, Upper Arkansas Agency, Letters Received.

accompanied by John Evans, governor of Colorado Territory, chased the frightened Indians to their hunting grounds of the upper Republican River.[11]

Cheyennes and Arapahoes along the Arkansas in the summer of 1862 were well disposed toward the United States. Colonel Jesse H. Leavenworth, at Fort Larned, in August, 1862, saw no reason to fear the Cheyennes and Arapahoes but thought the Kiowas and Comanches "more than half disposed to take up the hatchet." The Indians expected Agent Colley to distribute their annuity goods and agreed to return to the Cimarron Crossing on October 1, and in the meantime to hunt peacefully on the buffalo range north of the Arkansas River. The little trouble that arose while the Indians were assembled at Fort Larned was caused by the activities of "interested parties residing in the neighborhood and on Indian lands, hoping if the Indians received their goods they would be able to purchase for little or nothing whatever the Indians received from the Government."[12]

Recognizing the limitations of the Treaty of Fort Wise, Governor Evans advocated an extension of its terms to all the Cheyenne and Arapaho bands. Evans realized that the consent of all Cheyennes and Arapahoes to the cession would be necessary because the tribes recognized no boundaries marking off ranges for particular bands. The Governor also felt that the reservation was sufficiently large to accommodate the whole of the confederated tribes. The Cheyennes and Arapahoes disliked Evans' efforts to terminate their war parties against the Utes. Some chiefs regarded the Governor's actions as "unwarranted intervention," and only with reluctance did they agree to abandon Ute warfare.[13]

Allotment of land and stock raising were the means Evans and Colley hoped to use in settling the Cheyennes and Arapahoes upon

[11] Jerome C. Smiley, *Semi-Centennial History of the State of Colorado,* I, 413; Hubert Howe Bancroft, *History of Nevada, Colorado, and Wyoming,* II, 459; Ray C. Colton, *The Civil War in the Western Territories: Arizona, Colorado, New Mexico, and Utah,* 149; Colley to Dole, January 22, 1862, Upper Arkansas Agency, Letters Received; *Report, Commissioner of Indian Affairs, 1862,* 132. LeRoy R. Hafen, *The Overland Mail, 1849–1862,* 248; Denver *Rocky Mountain News,* June 24, 28, 30, July 5, 11, 19, September 25, October 30, 1862.

[12] Leavenworth to Captain Thomas Moonlight, August 8, 13, 1862, *O. R.,* I: Vol. 13, 547–49, 567–77.

[13] *Report, Commissioner of Indian Affairs, 1862,* 230–31.

their reservation. The land reserved under the Treaty of Fort Wise "is a choice grazing country . . . [the Cheyennes and Arapahoes can] readily learn to take care of cattle and sheep. They keep large droves of ponies in good condition. By this means the Indians of the plains may all readily be taught to procure a livelihood for themselves." Education of Cheyenne and Arapaho children was also advanced by Evans as a means of "civilizing" these Indians. At the school the children would be removed from parental influence. "If we civilize" the Cheyennes and Arapahoes, Evans concluded, "it must be by suspending the wild influences of their aboriginal state and condition, in their children."[14]

Policy was being formed to reduce the independence of the Cheyennes. As time passed, elaborations were added to Evans' suggestions, but three main elements of his program were maintained. First, because principal chiefs were made responsible to the government for the actions of their tribe, there was a recognition of the superior force of the white man's laws and treaties. Second, an allotment of land to destroy communal land rights restricted the Indians' claims to vast hunting ranges. Third, education, which removed parental and tribal influence, increased the children's affinity for white culture.

During the winter of 1862–63, Colorado territorial officials decided to drive the Cheyennes and Arapahoes from the South Platte. The Sioux outbreak in August, 1862, along the Minnesota River produced a flurry of fear along the western frontier and was viewed in Colorado as "positive evidence of the brutal and treacherous character of the Indian tribes." No effects, however, were felt in Colorado territory. Indian Agent Colley reported to Governor Evans on December 31, 1862, after distributing the annuity payment at Fort Lyon, that the Arkansas River Cheyennes and Arapahoes were peaceful and had departed for their hunting grounds on the Pawnee and Republican rivers. But Friday and his band of Arapahoes were "very much dissatisfied with the reservation on the Arkansas" and had returned to "their old haunts" on the Cache la Poudre, where they wanted the government to establish for them a small reservation. Colley maintained that the Treaty of Fort Wise had already made adequate pro-

14 Evans to Dole, August 6, 1862, Upper Arkansas Agency, Letters Received; *Report, Commissioner of Indian Affairs, 1862*, 231.

vision for them on the Arkansas River. A few Cheyenne depredations on the Santa Fe mail route were dismissed by Colley as caused by whites providing the Cheyennes with whisky.[15]

Seeking a reason to force Friday's band to accept the Arkansas reservation, Governor Evans sought information from former Indian agent Albert G. Boone. Commissioner Greenwood, Boone recalled, ordered him to extend a cordial invitation to all the Cheyennes and Arapahoes to sign the Treaty of Fort Wise, and, if some refused, to "make the Treaty over their heads." When Boone arrived at Fort Wise to conclude the agreement, he waited for the Platte bands to appear, but the Cheyennes and Arapahoes in attendance were unwilling to delay longer, describing those absent as "only a small band who lived and hung around Ft. Laramie scarcely ever going on the hunt and begging for a living, refusing to live on their own land." Boone admitted to Governor Evans that he knew that there was no partition of land between the various Cheyenne and Arapaho bands. Although the Platte bands did not make the cession and agree to the reservation, by implication they could move onto the Arkansas River reservation.[16]

With this information at hand, Governor Evans began his program to consolidate all Cheyennes and Arapahoes in Colorado territory upon the Arkansas River reservation. Paramount of importance in Evans' mind was the necessity of validating the Treaty of Fort Wise with the nonsigning bands. As the Governor explained to Commissioner Dole: "If this is not done the mining country of the Territory and in fact all the settled portion of Colorado are subject to Indian title and by our Organic Act not under the Territorial Government at all. Our laws are null and we are in anarchy."[17] Thus the crucial issues did not involve the Arkansas River Cheyennes and Arapahoes,

[15] Hafen, *Overland Mail,* 248; Denver, *Rocky Mountain News,* February 26, 1863; Colley to Evans, December 31, 1862, Upper Arkansas Agency, Letters Received.

[16] Boone to Evans, January 16, 1863 (Copy), Upper Arkansas Agency, Letters Received.

[17] Governor Evans was referring to the statute, passed on February 28, 1861, which states in part: "That nothing in this act contained shall be construed to impair the rights of person or property now pertaining to the Indians in said Territory, so long as such rights shall remain unextinguished by treaty between the United States and such Indians, or to include any territory which, by treaty with any Indian tribe, is not, without the consent of said tribe, to be included within the territorial limits or jurisdiction of any State or Territory; but all such territory shall be excepted out of the boundaries

but rather those living on the Platte rivers. Governor Evans continued his argument to the commissioner by stressing the fact that Friday had previously agreed to accept the treaty provisions but then had refused. Resistance came not from the Indians but "a few interested advisers who think they are gaining something by their disaffection." With the Indian bureau's approval, Evans sought authority for Indian Agent Colley to call the small Platte bands to the Arkansas reservation, "saying that their country has been ceded &c." If only the Washington officials co-operated, Evans had no doubt that the non-signing Cheyennes and Arapahoes, "poor wanderers over a country too large for them to traverse in a year," would quietly accept the provisions of the Treaty of Fort Wise. In order to impress the Cheyennes, Arapahoes, and Utes with the power of the United States, a delegation of chiefs from those tribes was sent to Washington in February, 1863.[18]

Settlement was advancing along the South Platte in the spring of 1863, and individuals were filing pre-emption notices at the Denver land office. Until the title to Indian lands was extinguished, John Pierce, surveyor general of Colorado and Utah territories, terminated further receipt of claims to land under the Pre-emption Act of 1841. The worried official asked his superior in Washington if surveys should proceed regardless of the confused status of Indian title to lands along the South Platte.[19]

In May and June, 1863, one Colorado territory settler wrote two utterly confused letters to Washington officials which revealed white attitudes toward Cheyenne and Arapaho title to lands held under the Treaty of Fort Laramie. The settler, Benjamin F. Hall, argued that the Cheyenne country was on the Cheyenne River in Dakota

and constitute no party of the Territory of Colorado until said tribe shall signify their assent to the President of the United States to be included within said Territory, or to affect the authority of the Government of the United States to make any regulations respecting such Indians, their lands, property, or other rights, by treaty, law or otherwise, which it would have been competent for the Government to make if this act had never passed." An editorial in the Denver *Rocky Mountain News,* May 7, 1863, called attention to the fact that the mining districts were still in unceded Indian country.

18 Evans to Dole, March 19, 1863, Upper Arkansas Agency, Letters Received; Denver *Rocky Mountain News,* February 26, 1863.

19 Pierce to J. M. Edmunds, Commissioner, General Land Office, April 13, 1863 (Copy), Upper Arkansas Agency, Letters Received.

territory, and that the Cheyennes and Arapahoes, the latter merely a Blackfoot band, had wandered down to the Arkansas River some thirty years previously in search of buffalo, then were prevented by the Sioux from returning to their true lands. "Now these stray Indians," Hall stated, "as all Indians do, make claim of the country & magnify their numbers; but they are very weak." Hall wanted any future negotiations with the Cheyennes and Arapahoes limited to inducing the tribes to return to their original habitat. "It is high time," the citizen concluded, "that this Indian business was conducted with more care for the interests of civilization. If every stray band of Indians is to be treated with as a nation and given reservations and annuities, it will retard the settlement of the great west and be too heavy upon the Treasury."[20]

Governor Evans was determined to protect the Colorado territory settlements when the Cheyennes and Arapahoes began their raids. Cheyennes seized food and burned the hay, about December 5, 1862, at a mail station fifty-five miles east of Fort Lyon. Colonel John M. Chivington was requested to furnish protection for the mail route. The matter was dropped when Indian Agent Colley learned that the guilty Cheyennes "left for a remote part of the country." Manifestations of Indian restlessness appeared in March, 1863, when Cheyennes raided ranches near the mouth of the Cache la Poudre, making off with food and other goods but committing no other violence upon the settlers. A detachment of the First Colorado Cavalry was immediately dispatched to apprehend the raiders. On Bijou Creek, three days' march from the Cache la Poudre, the cavalry found twenty-one lodges of Cheyennes, who protested their innocence, claiming Cheyennes under Buffalo, or Long Chief, had committed the robbery. Lieutenant George W. Hawkins, in charge of the detachment, could not continue the pursuit because of the lack of forage. En route, Lieutenant Hawkins reported that: "The Indians talk very bitterly of the whites—say they have stolen their ponies and abused their women, taken their hunting grounds, and that they expected they would have to fight for their rights." Governor Evans learned also in the spring of 1863, that the Indians were warning the settlers from the South Platte

[20] Benjamin F. Hall to Dole, May 24, 1863, Hall to Secretary of the Interior [J. P. Usher], June 1, 1863, Upper Arkansas Agency, Letters Received.

that the country still belonged to them and that they were determined to occupy the region even if they had to fight the whites.[21]

Colonel Leavenworth, at Fort Lyon, thought the demand for additional volunteer troops in Colorado was unnecessary. Two companies of cavalry at Fort Lyon, one at Fort Garland, and one at Camp Collins, later Fort Collins in Larimer County, Colorado, on the Overland Mail route, would protect the territory. "All the rest retained," wrote Colonel Leavenworth, "are to protect new town lots, and eat corn, at $5.60 per bushel."[22]

Before more depredations were committed, Governor Evans, in May, 1863, again stressed the Indian threat. He sent a special messenger to Washington and also warned General John M. Schofield, commanding general for the Department of the Missouri, that troops in Colorado territory might shortly need re-enforcement. Using Hawkins' earlier information, Evans stated that the Indians had delivered the ultimatum to the whites: Fight or leave. A careful watch was kept on a secret Cheyenne, Arapaho, and Sioux council held one hundred miles north of Denver; but even Colonel Chivington touring southern Colorado found no immediate cause for alarm, commenting that although the Indians were more restive than usual, no outbreak was imminent if the Colorado officials followed a "firm and prudent course" As a precaution, however, Chivington distributed his cavalry and light artillery among the various military posts in Colorado.[23]

Greater danger was seen along the Santa Fe route by Colonel Leavenworth. On June 11, 1863, near Fort Larned, there was a large concentration of Indians representing the Comanches, Kiowas, Kiowa-Apaches, Cheyennes, Arapahoes, and Caddoes. Disaster would result, Colonel Leavenworth believed, if anything aroused the Indians. The source of trouble was whisky being carried in great quantities by Mexican wagon trains along the route to Santa Fe. "Let a few Indians threaten one of these Mexican trains," the old officer wrote, "but with a show, and compel them to give them one canteen of whisky,

---

21 *Report, Commissioner of Indian Affairs, 1863,* 122, 128–29; Colton, *Civil War in the Western Territories,* 150.

22 Leavenworth to Major General E. V. Sumner, March 22, 1863, *O. R.,* I: Vol. 22, pt. 2, p. 172.

23 Evans to [Schofield], May 30, 1863, Chivington to [Schofield], June 1, 1863, *O. R.,* I: Vol. 22, pt. 2, pp. 294, 302–303.

and fearful, indeed, may be the consequences. There is whisky enough in one train that I met to-day to intoxicate every Indian on the plains." Leavenworth seized the train, placed a guard about it, and notified his superiors that he would take similar action against all other trains loaded with whisky until he received instructions on their disposition. Indian Agent Colley, supporting Leavenworth's estimate of the situation, stated that if the New Mexican trains were "allowed to carry whisky to the extent seen to-day, that he very much fears of the consequences, as they will sell, more or less, to the Indians."[24]

To control the Indians, Leavenworth asked for larger garrisons at Fort Larned and Fort Lyon. A wagon master, a veteran of eighteen years on the trail, reported to Leavenworth that he had never seen the Indians so "impudent and insulting." Kiowas and Comanches had stripped the saddle from the wagon master's mule, taken all of his men's blankets, cut open the sacks of provisions, and committed "many other outrages." Leavenworth sent for the chiefs of all the tribes about Fort Larned to tell them bluntly that "if they cannot stop their young men from committing these robberies, I shall." The Indians were also irritated by "a great number of white men [who] are now engaged in killing Buffalo merely for their hides." Whisky and buffalo hunters could cause a serious outbreak, and, if possible, Leavenworth wanted to prevent a disaster.[25]

A crisis developed at Fort Larned on the morning of July 9, 1863, when a sentinel shot and killed an Indian. Immediately, Leavenworth sent out runners to bring in the chiefs of all tribes in the vicinity and also asked all officers commanding troops along the Santa Fe Trail to concentrate their commands at Fort Larned to meet the anticipated emergency. When the dead Indian was examined by chiefs of the Kiowa-Apache, Arapaho, and Kiowa Indians, the corpse was identified as Little Heart, a Cheyenne. Since few Cheyennes were in the vicinity of Fort Larned, Leavenworth reported, "we escaped a collision for the moment. What may happen it is impossible for me to say." No immediate results occurred from the shooting of the Cheyenne

---

[24] Leavenworth to Curtis, June 11, 1863, *O. R.,* I: Vol. 22, pt. 2, pp. 316–17.

[25] Leavenworth to H. Z. Curtis, June 24, 1863, Leavenworth to Lieutenant John Williams, June 27, 1863, *O. R.,* I: vol. 22, pt. 2, pp. 335–36, 339–40; Leavenworth to Dole, June 27, 1863, Upper Arkansas Agency, Letters Received.

warrior, but the incident created dissatisfaction among tribal leaders, who later counciled with Colorado territorial officials.[26]

While Leavenworth was desperately trying to keep the Indians calm, Governor Evans was keeping a wary eye on them along the South Platte. The big Indian council previously mentioned by Governor Evans broke up by mid-June, 1863. Arapahoes under Friday and Many Whips, camping on the Cache la Poudre, had been invited at the council by the Sioux to fight the whites, but the invitation was declined. Evans still felt it was better to keep the Indians quiet by "a distribution of the comforts of life." Information gleaned earlier led Governor Evans to suggest a treaty with the Cheyennes, Arapahoes, and Sioux who occupied Colorado territory. The treaty, it was undoubtedly hoped by Governor Evans, would serve the dual purpose of keeping the Indians at peace and concentrating the Cheyennes and Arapahoes on the Arkansas River reservation, where the Governor noted only one Indian family had settled.[27]

Colorado officials were successful in the summer and fall of 1863 in obtaining peace with the Utes. But efforts to treat with the Cheyennes, Arapahoes, and Sioux proved far less successful. In June, 1863, Governor Evans invited Indian agents Colley and Loree to Denver to prepare for the treaty with the Cheyennes and Arapahoes. On June 24, 1863, Governor Evans met a delegation of Arapahoes representing all of the tribe from the upper Platte rivers. Although these chiefs absolutely refused to accept lands on the Arkansas, they still agreed to council with the governor. The Cheyennes were another matter. Reportedly, they were in an ugly mood, meditating war, and likely to refuse any kind of a talk. Still, Evans believed that if they had not yet commenced hostilities, he could convince the Cheyennes to attend the meeting.[28]

---

[26] Leavenworth to the Commanding Officers of any Troops on the Santa Fe Road, July 9, 1863. Leavenworth to AAG., District of the Border, July 15, 1863, *O. R.,* I: Vol. 22, pt. 2, pp. 361, 400–401; Denver *Rocky Mountain News,* July 30, 1863; Colley to Dole, July 27, 1863, Upper Arkansas Agency, Letters Received.

[27] Evans to Dole, June 15, July 22, 1863, Upper Arkansas Agency, Letters Received; *Report, Commissioner of Indian Affairs, 1863,* 122–23.

[28] Hafen, *Overland Mail,* 251–52, 255; Evans to Dole, June 24, 1863, Colorado Superintendency, Letters Received by the Office of Indian Affairs, Records of the Office of Indian Affairs, National Archives, Washington, D. C. (hereafter cited as Colorado Superintendency).

Runners were sent out to collect the Cheyennes and Arapahoes for a treaty council to begin September 1, 1863, on the headwaters of the Republican River. It took Governor Evans only a few days to work out his plans for the anticipated treaty—Loree and Colley to serve with him as commissioners. The entire Cheyenne and Arapaho tribes were to be gathered on the Arikaree Fork of the Republican River, represented by their chiefs, headmen, and delegates. To attract the tribes to the treaty, the year's annuity goods would be distributed there. Elbridge Gerry and Antoine Janisse were sent to the Upper Platte bands, and another runner, to be selected by Agent Colley, carried the invitation to the Arkansas River group. The emissaries were instructed to invite the Indians to the treaty and to determine what modifications were necessary to the Treaty of Fort Wise, but they were to avoid carefully any commitments which the commissioners could not fulfill.[29]

Before Governor Evans left Denver to confer with the Cheyennes and Arapahoes, he was well aware that Agent Colley had failed in his attempt to get the Arkansas River Cheyennes to attend the treaty. Fearing total failure, Governor Evans still was determined to proceed and to obtain notification later from those who refused to attend the councils. From Fort Lyon, Agent Colley, after sending John Smith unsuccessfully to gather up the Arkansas River Cheyennes and Arapahoes, declared that the Cheyennes "utterly refuse to go to the Res [Arikaree] Forks; the reasons they give are, that they are making their lodges, that their horses are poor, and that from where they are it is impossible for them to go for the want of water." Further, Northern Arapahoes were at Fort Lyon, "poor and hungry," obtaining an inadequate food supply from the officers at the post.

Why the Cheyennes and Arapahoes refused to meet Governor Evans is problematical. Grinnell claims the Cheyennes harbored no resentment over the killing of Little Heart, who was drunk and who tried to ride over the sentry. The Cheyennes, in Grinnell's account, regarded the shooting of Little Heart as justifiable, accepted Colley's presents, and considered the affair closed. John S. Smith's version of the incident is vastly different. Going to Fort Larned, Smith found 160 lodges of Cheyennes and 200 of Arapahoes gathered in the vicinity

---

[29] Evans to Dole, July 13, 14, 17, 1863, Colorado Superintendency.

of the post on Pawnee River. The Cheyennes were enraged by the death of Little Heart, and only the persuasions of the Arapahoes kept them quiet. Agent Colley's presents satisfied a portion of the Cheyennes for a time, but five months later many still were embittered because of the shooting.[30] However, Smith's report may have been colored by the fact that Governor Evans was, late in 1863, trying hard to prove the hostile intentions of the Plains Indians.

Antoine Janisse became sick and failed to bring in the band of Cheyennes living on the upper reaches of the Yellowstone River. Agent Colley received no satisfaction in August from the Cheyennes and Arapahoes remaining on the Arkansas River. Elbridge Gerry, a trader from the South Platte and a grandson of the signer of the Declaration of Independence, found a great portion of the Cheyennes in August, 1863. Gerry, called White Eyes by the Cheyennes, traversed the Plains for six hundred miles before he encountered 150 lodges of Cheyennes near the sources of the Smoky Hill River. These constituted the bands reported to be resentful of the Treaty of Fort Wise who saw no necessity of abandoning the chase for a reservation. Yet, by "kindness and persuasion," Gerry obtained a positive assurance from the chiefs and headmen that they would attend Evans' treaty.

The Cheyennes denied ever promising Gerry that they would attend Governor Evans' treaty council. Long Chin, a Dog Soldier chief well acquainted with Gerry, merely told Evans' messenger that following the Sun Dances held earlier on Beaver Creek, the Cheyennes were too scattered on their summer hunts to attend a treaty. Long Chin, an uncle of George Bent, never mentioned a second conference with Gerry, as was reported in the Report of the Commissioner of Indian Affairs.[31]

Gerry then turned north to Julesburg, Colorado territory, joined the commissioners, and conducted them to the treaty grounds on the Arikaree. Only four lodges of Cheyennes came to the meeting place, but

30 Evans to Dole, August 25, 26, 1863, John Evans Collection, Indian Affairs, Colorado Division of State Archives and Public Records, Denver, Colorado (hereafter cited as Evans Collection). Evans to Dole, September 22, 1863, Smith to Colley, November 9, 1863, Colorado Superintendency; Colley to Evans, August 22, 1863, *Report, Commissioner of Indian Affairs, 1863*, 131; Grinnell, *Fighting Cheyennes*, 132.

31 *Report, Commissioner of Indian Affairs, 1863*, 124; George Bent to Hyde, April 30, 1906, Bent Letters, Coe Collection.

they assured the commissioners that the Cheyenne delegation was on its way. When no delegation appeared, Gerry went out in search of the Cheyennes and found them on Beaver Creek in western Colorado territory. The village now contained 240 lodges, and many noted Cheyenne chiefs attended Gerry's council. Dog Soldier Chiefs White Antelope and Bull Bear, Little Robe, Two Wolves, and Tall Bear were in the Beaver Creek village representing both the Arkansas and Platte divisions.[32]

The chiefs now adamantly refused to sign another treaty. White Antelope said he never signed the Fort Wise treaty; Black Kettle made the same statement. The general consensus of the Cheyennes now was that the Treaty of Fort Wise was a "swindle." The killing of Little Heart was also urged as a reason for refusing to treat. "They said," wrote Gerry, "that the white man's hands were dripping with their blood, and now he calls them to make a treaty." Confident that the buffalo would last many years, the Cheyennes wanted no other country than the region of the Republican and Smoky Hill rivers and its buffalo range, which they denied selling. They refused to occupy the Arkansas River reservation, because of the scarcity of game; the North Platte was not suitable, and the South Platte was lost to the whites. Gerry finally persuaded Bull Bear, the Dog Soldier chief, to accompany him to the treaty ground if the tribal council was agreeable. When the Cheyennes counciled and refused Bull Bear permission to go with Gerry to meet the commissioners, Evans' hopes for another treaty ended.[33] The Governor of Colorado territory would have to find another way to clear Cheyenne and Arapaho title to the lands between the Arkansas and Platte rivers.

Actually, unless Governor Evans was trying to pacify the restless elements with the Cheyennes and Arapahoes, a new treaty was hardly necessary. Even before joining Evans for the treaty effort, Agent Loree had acquired the signatures of three Arapaho and two Cheyenne chiefs from the Upper Platte Agency on an agreement by which those chiefs promised to recognize the Treaty of Fort Wise and any other treaty subsequently made by their people. For their signatures, no

---

[32] If the village was as large as reported, it would constitute two-thirds of the Cheyennes in the Upper Platte and Upper Arkansas agencies.

[33] *Report, Commissioner of Indian Affairs, 1863*, 129–30.

presents or other considerations were made, and annuities were merely distributed. As Agent Loree was returning to his post after the abortive treaty, he found a large encampment of Cheyennes on the Cache la Poudre. The agent found the Indians bitter, and Spotted Horse's life was endangered because other chiefs accused him of selling their land. Not all the resistance to the treaty originated with the Indians, for old traders at Fort Laramie, including Joseph Bissonnette, had advised the Cheyennes to delay signing any document until 1864, when the Indians said they would get "heap horses—and a big treaty." Further, the Cheyennes said the whites were at war killing each other off, and the Indians would retake the country of the Plains in the spring of 1864.[34]

His treaty plans frustrated, Governor Evans moved systematically to prove that the Plains Indians were hostile. His motivation was simply to force a situation which would enable him to clear Indians from all settled regions of Colorado territory. The Cheyennes and Arapahoes had, by the Treaty of Fort Wise and the August, 1863, agreement at the Upper Platte Agency, given Evans a legitimate claim to the lands east of the Rocky Mountains and between the Arkansas and Platte rivers.[35] But Evans knew he could not have both the Cheyenne-Arapaho land and peace. If the Indians' hostility could be proved, military actions against them could be justified; the Cheyenne and Arapahoes could be forced to the Arkansas reservation; and the remaining hostile tribes could be ejected from Colorado territory, since their lands, under the Treaty of Fort Laramie and other agreements, lay north of the Platte and south of the Arkansas. Thus mere antagonism to the Indians and bad judgment do not explain completely the actions of Governor Evans late in 1863 and in 1864.

Reports from Fort Lyon in the fall of 1863 contained nothing that seemed to indicate an open threat of war. Kiowas and Comanches were accused in September of hostilities near the Cimarron Crossing

---

34 Evans to Dole, September 22, 1863, Evans Collection, *Report, Commissioner of Indian Affairs, 1863,* 125, 131–32. Spotted Horse and Shield signed Loree's document, and they were probably only minor chiefs among the Platte River Cheyennes; see, Hafen and Hafen (eds.), *Relations with the Plains Indians,* 176ff. Loree to Evans, October 24, 1863, Colorado Superintendency.

35 See Dole to S. E. Browne, United States District Attorney, Colorado territory, February 27, 1863, in Denver *Rocky Mountain News,* April 2, 1863.

on the Arkansas River. Major Scott J. Anthony, commanding at Fort Lyon, thought that, if necessary, he could chastise the Indians and would try "by all fair means to avoid an Indian war." John M. Chivington justified his distribution of troops in Colorado territory by pointing out the Indian depredations, the need for protecting the mail and transportation routes, and the gold-bearing resources of the territory. Chivington welcomed an official investigation and denied that he had retained troops needed in Kansas and Missouri because of a "sinister design." Several days later Major Anthony stated that the raids had ceased. From Yellow Buffalo, a Kiowa chief, and Little Raven, a leading Arapaho chief, Major Anthony heard that runners from the Sioux and the Cheyennes of the Platte had invited the Arkansas River Indians to join an all out attack on both the Arkansas and Platte routes, timed for the spring of 1864. All the tribes, except the Cheyennes, refused the war pipe. Because the Cheyennes agreed to join the Sioux, Major Anthony expected trouble on the Platte, but not on the Arkansas.[36]

As the Indians prepared for winter quarters, Major Anthony found the tribes on the Arkansas River quiet. A prolonged drought had dried up the Arkansas River for four hundred miles; buffalo and game were scarce, and the Indians fully realized their dependence upon the government for food and subsistence. En route up the Arkansas River to his headquarters at Fort Lyon, Major Anthony, using John S. Smith as an interpreter, visited the chiefs of the Kiowa, Comanche, Kiowa-Apache, Caddo, and Arapaho Indians. The Arkansas River Cheyennes were not mentioned by Major Anthony; obviously they were still hunting on the Republican and Smoky Hill rivers. Again the chiefs expressed their desire for peace, explained the hostile acts of their young men to the Major's satisfaction, and maintained their refusal to smoke the war pipe. Only the Northern Cheyennes, the chiefs claimed, had accepted the Sioux invitation to hostilities. Two thousand Arapahoes, including some Northern bands, under Little Raven, Left Hand, and Neva were moving toward Fort Lyon to re-

36 Anthony to Lieutenant George H. Stilwell, September 2, 14, 1863, Chivington to Schofield, September 12, 1863, O. R., I; Vol. 22, pt. 2, pp. 507–508, 527–29, 532–33. George Bent insisted that the Cheyennes also refused the Sioux war pipe (see, George Bent to Hyde, September 26, 1905, Western History Department, Denver Public Library).

ceive their annual annuities. Northern Arapahoes had recently made forays near Boone's and Maxwell's ranches, but Major Anthony refused to punish the Indians after learning the facts of the situation from John Smith. Major Anthony summed up the condition of the Indians as destitute. The government, wrote Anthony, "will be compelled to subsist them to a great extent, or allow them to starve to death, which would probably be much the easiest way of disposing of them."[37]

After returning from the Arikaree Fork, Governor Evans restricted contact between the troops and the Indians camping around the military posts. The Governor requested that the posts' commanding officers deny Indians rations or the right to trade except with the written permission of the Indian agent. Colonel Chivington readily agreed to Evans' request and stressed his willingness to "act in concert with all officers of the Indian Bureau in carrying out the policy of the Government with the Indians." By November 7, 1863, Governor Evans had begun to take added precautions against an Indian outbreak. Writing to Indian Agent Colley, Evans ordered him to withhold all arms and ammunition from the tribes of his jurisdiction.[38]

Information gathered in November of 1863 sustained Evans in his belief that the Indians would commence hostilities the following spring. Evans did not panic as suggested by Grinnell. Rather, the Governor began exploiting the supposed war threats as a means of pushing the Cheyennes onto the Arkansas reservation. Agent Colley blamed the Sioux for the anticipated trouble and was not certain to what degree the Sioux were able to create intense disaffection among his agency's tribes. The Cheyennes and a portion of the Kiowas, Colley feared, would join in an attack against the settlements on the South Platte and Arkansas rivers, but the whites could depend upon the Comanches, Kiowa-Apaches, and most of the Arapahoes for aid.[39]

Evans had three sources of information, in addition to Colley, with which to justify his conclusion of an Indian war. Based upon his long

37 Anthony to [Stilwell], September 24, 1863, *O. R.,* I; Vol. 22, pt. 2, pp. 571–72.

38 Evans to Stilwell, September 21, 1863, Chivington to Dole, November 6, 1863, Evans to Colley, November 7, 1863, Colorado Superintendency; Evans to Chivington, September 21, 1863, Evans Collection.

39 Grinnell, *Fighting Cheyennes,* 135; Colley to Evans, November 9, 1863, Colorado Superintendency.

experience with the Indians, John Smith believed that the threat of Indian hostilities was real. Large bands of Sioux, never known to come so far south before, were on the Arkansas and Smoky Hill rivers. Little Raven, the Arapahoes' influential and pro-white chief, professed fear of going in the vicinity of the Cheyenne and Sioux, doubting their friendship and afraid of being named a party to attacks certain to occur. The same day, November 9, that Smith submitted his information to Agent Colley, Governor Evans, with Smith as his interpreter, talked to Roman Nose, a signer of the August, 1863, agreement, and two or three minor chiefs of the Platte Arapahoes. Roman Nose professed friendship for the whites, which Smith doubted, and admitted that the Sioux, Cheyennes, and Kiowas wanted war. Both on this occasion and two days later, Roman Nose insisted that he would never accept the Arkansas River reservation and would only agree to another treaty if a new reservation were established on the Cache la Poudre.[40]

Robert North, a white who had lived among the Arapahoes since boyhood and married into the tribe, also confirmed the possibility of war. North, shortly before, had returned an Arapaho woman who had been a captive of the Utes to the Arkansas River Arapahoes. This feat gained North the confidence of the Indians, and they allowed him to participate in a "big medicine dance," held fifty-five miles below Fort Lyon. There North, talking to the chiefs of several Plains tribes, learned that the Comanches, Kiowa-Apaches, Kiowas, Northern Arapahoes, all of the Cheyennes, and the Sioux had pledged each other to commence a war as soon as they acquired ammunition in the spring of 1864. Those who opposed the decision were silenced and threatened with death. The Indians agreed to pretend friendship for the whites until they were ready, then strike. Governor Evans, convinced of the truthfulness of North's report, promised Commissioner Dole that he would ferret out each step of progress in "this foul conspiracy among those poor degraded wretches."[41]

[40] Smith to Colley, November 9, 1863, Colorado Superintendency; Evans to Dole, November 9, 11, 1863, Evans to Loree, November 24, 1863, Evans Collection.

[41] For additional information on Robert North, see Grinnell, *Fighting Cheyennes*, 134n. Evans to Dole, November 11, 1863, Colorado Superintendency. North's statement is printed in *Report, Commissioner of Indian Affairs, 1864*, 224–25, but Evans' comments are deleted.

Governor Evans took his case personally to Washington. His November communications were undoubtedly before Commissioner Dole when Evans arrived at the nation's capital in December, 1863. Governor Evans sought to strengthen Colorado territory's Indian defenses and wanted permission to hold another treaty with the Cheyennes and Arapahoes to avert war. It was the hope of the Governor to cede those tribes a reservation other than that on the Arkansas River, "which they utterly refuse to occupy."[42] It does not appear that Evans was successful in obtaining his request, for authority to carry out these plans is not mentioned in later correspondence or documents.

By the winter of 1863-64, Evans was convinced Indian hostilities would begin in the spring. If all went well, the Indians could be defeated and Colorado territory cleared of hostiles. Evans and the Colorado settlers now could only wait for the Indians to make their move.

[42] Evans to Edwin M. Stanton, December 14, 1863, in Denver *Rocky Mountain News,* August 31, 1864, and Evans Collection; Evans to Dole, December 20, 1863, Colorado Superintendency.

# 8

## SKIRMISHES AND RETALIATIONS

DURING THE SEVERE WINTER OF 1863–64, the Cheyennes and Arapahoes caused no difficulties. Although the tribes lost many of their ponies, their winter hunts were still successful. As usual, traders on the Arkansas River were preying upon the Indians, paying seventy-five cents worth of trinkets or two dollars in food per robe, which was one-fourth of actual value. Worse yet, the Indians found whisky plentiful at Fort Lyon, where the men of the tribes traded the robes off their backs for a bottle of whisky on the coldest winter's day. Sutlers at the post extended credit to Indian chiefs for liquor and contributed to a shocking amount of "dissipation, licentiousness, and venereal diseases" among the Indians of the Arkansas River.[1]

Special Indian Agent H. T. Ketcham was appalled by what he saw in the spring of 1864 when he visited Forts Larned and Lyon. Ketcham castigated both the whites who lived among the Indians and the soldiers at the posts. At Fort Larned, the special agent watched a white man, after draining a whisky bottle, hit an Indian in the face with the empty bottle because the Indian had looked on "wistfully and longingly" as the white enjoyed the intoxicant. Other whites incited the Indians to steal ranchers' stock and then bought the animals from the Indians. Concluding his letter to Governor Evans, Ketcham maintained:

> While citizens and soldiers are permitted to enter their villages with whisky in day time & at night; to make the men drunk & cohabit with the squaws, disseminating venerial [sic] diseases among them; while the Commanding Officer at the Post [Fort Larned] continues to get drunk every day & insult and abuse the leading men of the Tribes, &

[1] H. T. Ketcham to Evans, April 4, 1864, Colorado Superintendency.

make prostitutes of their women; you cannot expect to have any permanent peace with these Indians. . . .[2]

As the Indian agents began their duties early in 1864, there was no mention of impending Indian hostilities. Indian Agent Colley hoped to initiate agriculture on the Arkansas River reservation by renting land on shares or hiring Mexicans who understood the principles of irrigation to farm the Indians' lands. Corn was selling for $3.50 a bushel on the Arkansas, and the yield was twenty bushels to the acre even when planted on newly-broken sod. It was clear, however, to the Indian agent that even the Arapahoes, less turbulent than the Cheyennes, were still unprepared to adopt an agricultural economy. At Fort Laramie late in February, 1864, Indian Agent Loree reported that the Sioux, Cheyennes, and Arapahoes were quiet and "well disposed toward the whites." Army officers objected to the sale of ammunition to the Indians, but Loree knew no other way of feeding the Indians than allowing them to buy sufficient ammunition with which to hunt.[3]

On March 26, 1864, Major General Samuel R. Curtis, commanding officer of the Department of Kansas, withdrew every man who could be spared from the Indian frontier to meet a Confederate force ominously poised south of the Arkansas River. Almost immediately Governor Evans began to worry about the defenseless condition of the settlements in Colorado territory. Dutifully, Indian Agent Colley, at Fort Larned during March, 1864, learned from Cheyennes and Arapahoes that the Sioux intended to raid the Platte and Arkansas settlements during the spring and early summer. Hoping to add some concrete proof to his assertion that the Indians were aroused, Governor Evans suggested that the Indian agent place spies among the Indians of the Arkansas River to learn their intentions.[4]

More worrisome to Colley was the possibility of renewed intertribal hostilities. Earlier, a small party of Cheyennes and Arapahoes

---

[2] Ketcham to Evans, July 1, 1864, Colorado Superintendency.

[3] Colley to Dole, Rebruary 4, 1864, Colorado Superintendency; Loree to Chivington, February 29, 1864, *O. R.*, I: Vol. 34, pt. 2, p. 469.

[4] Evans to Colley, March 15, 1864, Evans Collection; Curtis to Evans, March 26, 1864, *O. R.*, I: Vol. 34, pt. 2, pp. 742–43; William Frank Zornow, *Kansas: A History of the Jayhawk State*, 115–17.

had raided a Ute village and had run off fifty or sixty head of stock. The Utes, pursuing the horse thieves, overtook them five or six miles west of Fort Lyon, recaptured their stock and killed three Cheyennes and an Arapaho. The Arapahoes also became suspicious of the Kiowas when a number of Arapaho warriors failed to return following a joint raid for animals into Texas. When some Arapaho ponies turned up in the Kiowa herd, the Arapahoes were convinced that their warriors had been killed by the Kiowas. Unless the Arapaho warriors returned soon to their camps, Colley believed that the two tribes would go to war, and the Indian agent wrote: "If the Indians go to war among themselves, I fear that it will extend much farther." Nothing, however, in any of Colley's information linked the Arkansas River Cheyennes to any plan to attack the settlements or overland routes. In the Upper Platte Agency the only dissatisfaction voiced by the Indians was their general antagonism to Indian Agent Loree.[5] Yet, two weeks later, the incidents began which led to the Sand Creek Massacre.

By April 7, 1864, Major General Curtis at Fort Leavenworth was informed of the theft by Indians of 175 head of stock belonging to Irwin, Jackman and Company, government contractors, from their herd wintering on the Smoky Hill River. The information was relayed to Brigadier General Mitchell at Omaha, who in turn instructed Lieutenant Colonel William O. Collins at Fort Laramie to "recapture the stock," and punish "the scoundrels." Colonel John M. Chivington was also notified of the theft and was ordered not to let "district lines prevent pursuing and punishing" the Indians.[6]

Colonel Chivington, commanding the District of Colorado, acted quickly. According to his intelligence, a party of Cheyennes had, on April 5, stolen 175 head of cattle from the Irwin-Jackman herd near the headwaters of Sand Creek. Herders trailed the stock about fifteen miles until the trail left Sand Creek and turned due east toward the headwaters of the Smoky Hill River. Lieutenant George S. Eayre was dispatched on April 8 from Camp Weld, two miles from Denver,

---

[5] Robert M. Wright, "Reminiscences" (Typescript), Kansas State Historical Society, Topeka, Kansas; Evans to Chivington, March 16, 1864, enclosing an extract of a letter, Colley to Evans, March 12, 1864, Mitchell to Captain John Williams, AAG., Department of Kansas, March 24, 1864, O. R., I: Vol. 34, pt. 2, pp. 633–34, 720.

[6] Mitchell to Commanding Officer, Fort Laramie, April 7, 1864, Curtis to Chivington, April 8, 1864, O. R., I: Vol. 34, pt. 3, pp. 85, 98.

with fifty-four men and two twelve-pound howitzers to recover the stock and chastise the Indians if necessary. At Beaver Creek one of the herders joined Eayre's detachment and guided the troops to the upper reaches of Sand Creek, where they were snowed in for several days. Resuming their march, the troops came, on April 14, upon a large, distinct trail which led northwest toward the Republican River's headwaters. In Eayre's opinion the trail was made by at least one hundred cattle, and it led to a small Cheyenne camp of five lodges. By the time an officer and two men arrived at the camp to demand the stolen stock, the Cheyennes had fled. A lone warrior was observed on the column's flank, and two men were sent out to cut off the brave's flight, but the warrior evaded capture and seriously wounded one of the volunteers. Pressing on, Eayre's troops continued on the trail for three more days and discovered a larger, but also deserted, Cheyenne village. In their flight the Cheyennes left behind a four-mile trail of robes, dried meat, lodges, and camp equipment, all of which Eayre burned. In this village nineteen head of Irwin–Jackman cattle were recovered. On April 18, Lieutenant Eayre began his march back to Camp Weld.[7]

It is possible that the Cheyennes did not steal the Irwin-Jackman stock. Kit Carson, for example, testified before the Special Joint Committee of Congress investigating the Sand Creek Massacre, that irresponsible herders often covered their negligence in watching their herds by accusing Indians of theft. George Bent, one of the sons of William Bent, claimed that the cattle must have strayed away from the main herd and been picked up later by the Cheyennes. The Cheyennes, Bent further insisted, had no reason to steal the stock for food, because buffalo were still plentiful on the plains. Both Crow Chief's band, the first village struck by Eayre, and Beaver's village, the larger encampment of Cheyennes, were totally innocent of the theft and were unaware of any difficulty with the whites. The camps, warned of

[7] Chivington to AAG., Department of Kansas, April 9, 1864, Eayre to Chivington, April 18, 23, 1864, Chivington to Curtis, April 25, 1864, *O. R.*, I: Vol. 34, pt. 3, pp. 113, 218–19, 291; pt. 1, pp. 880–82; Report of the Joint Special Committee appointed under Joint Resolution March 3, 1865, "Condition of Indian Tribes," 39 Cong., 2 sess., *Sen. Report No. 156*, 72 (hereafter cited as *Sand Creek Investigation*); Denver *Rocky Mountain News*, April 27, 1864; Grinnell (*Fighting Cheyennes*, 139) contains several errors in his account of the first Eayre expedition.

the approaching troops, did not wish to fight and in their flight lost their lodges and much of their food and camp utensils.[8]

While Lieutenant Eayre was operating on the Republican River, trouble also broke out along the South Platte. Alerted to the alleged pillaging of the Irwin-Jackman herd, Major Jacob Downing, stationed at Junction Ranch, pursued a band of Indians, apparently Cheyennes, on April 11, destroying their lodges and camp equipment. Neither Eayre's nor Downing's actions resulted in loss of life to the Cheyennes, and if the difficulties had proceeded no farther, no general war would have resulted.[9]

A more decisive turn of events occurred on April 12 when Lieutenant Clark Dunn, First Colorado Cavalry, had a running fight with a small party of young Cheyenne Dog Soldiers. These warriors were moving north from Beaver Creek to join the Platte River Cheyennes in response to the latter's invitation. In the summer of 1863, Brave Wolf, a Northern Cheyenne, had been killed by the Crows, and his friends notified the Southern Cheyennes of an avenging war party which the latter could join if they desired. As the Dog Soldier party moved toward the South Platte, they picked up four stray mules and included the animals in their own herd. After crossing the South Platte near the mouth of Kiowa Creek, they were met by Lieutenant Dunn and forty men of the First Colorado Cavalry near Frémont's Orchard.[10]

W. D. Ripley, a rancher from Bijou Creek, came to Camp Sanborn, a temporary post on the South Platte, on the evening of April 11 to complain that Indians were running off all the stock along the creek and that he had barely escaped with his life. Early the next morning, Captain George L. Sanborn dispatched Lieutenant Dunn with forty men, and, accompanied by Ripley, they set out to recover the stock. Proceeding up the South Platte, searching the low hills along the stream's south bank as they went, they observed Indians with a horse herd on the north bank late in the afternoon. What happened

[8] *Sand Creek Investigation*, 96; George Bent to Hyde, January 18, 1906, Western History Department, Denver Public Library; George Bent to Hyde, April 12, 1906, Bent Letters, Coe Collection; Grinnell, *Fighting Cheyennes*, 139–40.

[9] Downing to [Chivington], April 12, 1864, *O. R.*, I: Vol. 34, pt. 3, p. 146.

[10] George Bent to Hyde, March 26, 1906, Western History Department, Denver Public Library. Another copy of this letter is in the Bent Letters, Coe Collection.

during the encounter varies widely in the accounts of the Indians and the whites.[11]

The Cheyennes maintained that Dunn's men attacked without warning. In the fight three warriors were wounded, but the whole party escaped capture and fled back to the main camp on the head of Beaver Creek, a tributary of the Republican River. Little Chief, who was present at the fight, insisted that the soldiers left the field of action first, and that the Cheyennes decapitated an officer, stripped off his jacket, and took other trophies. Captain Eugene F. Ware, on May 21, 1864, while stationed at Cottonwood Springs, saw a Cheyenne chief in some Brulé Sioux camps displaying a sergeant's jacket and other effects and asking those Sioux to join the Cheyennes in the war against the United States Army and the white settlers. William Bent also blamed Dunn's command for the initial hostilities. Before a congressional committee, Bent testified that while Dunn was under orders to disarm any Indians met, the Lieutenant intercepted seven Cheyennes driving some animals along the South Platte, including some strays belonging to whites. Lieutenant Dunn approached the Indians, Bent claimed, in what appeared to be a friendly manner, but then he and his men attempted to seize the Indians' weapons. As the Indians broke away, the soldiers opened fire, wounding two, one of whom fell from his horse. Others in the Cheyenne party picked up their fallen comrade, and together they successfully escaped.[12]

Testimony of army officers conflicts sharply with that of the Cheyennes and their friends. Lieutenant Dunn claimed that the fight took place on the South Platte's north bank about three miles below Frémont's Orchard. After Ripley had identified some of the animals in the Indians' herd as his, Dunn ordered four of his men and Ripley to prevent the Indians from driving the herd into the sand hills north of the Platte. Alone, the Lieutenant dismounted and approached the

11 George L. Sanborn to Chivington, April 12, 1864, Report of Lieutenant Clark Dunn, First Colorado Cavalry, April 18, 1864, Chivington to Evans, April 15, 1864, *O. R.*, I: Vol. 34, pt. 1, pp. 883–84, pt. 3, 166; *Sand Creek Investigation*, 68.

12 George Bent to Hyde, September [?], 1906, MSS of Colorado State Historical Society, Denver, Colorado. In this letter Bent claims that Little Chief, who was present at the Dunn fight at Frémont's Orchard, told him that the Cheyennes killed three soldiers and could have killed more if they had so desired. Eugene F. Ware, *The Indian War of 1864*, 194; *Sand Creek Investigation*, 93; Grinnell, *Fighting Cheyennes*, 142.

Indians, who were in battle array with their weapons ready for use. Dunn's demand for Ripley's stock brought a "scornful laugh" from the chief. Although Dunn was without an interpreter, he still tried to tell the chief that he was under orders to disarm all Indians he met and attempted to seize a warrior's arms. The Cheyennes opened fire upon the troops and it was returned immediately by Dunn's men. Superiority in numbers and weapons were with the Indians, but despite this advantage, Dunn's troopers chased the Indians fifteen miles before the chase was abandoned. In the fight, Dunn claimed to have killed eight or ten warriors while his losses were two men dead and two others severely wounded.[13]

After the fight near Frémont's Orchard, an aide of Chivington warned other posts in Colorado territory of the alleged stock stealing and stated, "there is but one course for us to pursue, . . . to make them behave or kill them." To an officer commanding a post along the Indians' anticipated line of flight, Lieutenant George H. Stilwell wrote: "Be sure you have the right ones, and then kill them." Colonel Chivington's short note to Lieutenant Colonel Collins at Fort Laramie briefed the latter on Dunn's skirmish and told Collins that the Cheyennes had fled "with stolen stock in your direction. Look out for them and kill them." In his communication to General Curtis, Chivington was less vindictive, stating that he would chastise the Cheyennes severely, unless instructed otherwise by the general.[14]

Lieutenant Dunn was barely back at Camp Sanborn before rumors of more raids and killings were heard at the post. Captain Sanborn immediately sent thirty men under Lieutenants Dunn and Chase to track down the raiders. The detachment proceeded to Elbridge Gerry's ranch on the north bank of the South Platte at the mouth of Crow Creek where the trader told the troops that it would be impossible to follow the Indians because a heavy snow had obliterated the trail. Perhaps Gerry was trying to protect the Dog Soldiers with whom he had traded during the winter of 1863–64 when he informed Captain Sanborn that the Indians, both Cheyennes and Sioux, in the vicinity

[13] Report of Lieutenant Clark Dunn, April 18, 1864, *O. R.,* I: Vol. 34, pt. 1, pp. 884–85; *Sand Creek Investigation,* 68–69.

[14] George Stilwell to Captain S. H. Cook and Captain W. H. Backus, April 13, 1864, Stilwell to Lieutenant G. W. Hawkins, April 13, 1864, Chivington to Collins, Chivington to Curtis, April 13, 1864, *O. R.,* I: Vol. 34, pt. 3, pp. 149, 150, 151.

of his ranch knew nothing of a war party supposedly lurking along the South Platte. Lieutenant Dunn, however, pressed on to the area where the men were supposedly murdered and found no murdered men and no sign of a fight. A trail made by forty cattle was picked up leading up Beaver Creek, a tributary of the South Platte, and past a point where the Indians would have swung east toward the headwaters of the Republican River. This tenuous evidence led Lieutenant Dunn to assume that the Indians committing the depredations were from the Arkansas River. Seemingly, it did not occur to Dunn that the Indians were merely taking an indirect route back to the Republican River village. But, more important, the Southern Cheyennes, at least in the mind of Dunn and his superiors, were linked to the raids on the South Platte.[15]

Fear of an Indian attack also spread to the Arkansas Valley. Albert G. Boone, the former Indian agent, hearing of the raids on the South Platte, asked Chivington not to leave the Arkansas River settlements defenseless by withdrawing all troops to defend the Platte route. To protect the settlers near Boone's ranch, Chivington sent a small detachment of troops to re-enforce those garrisoning Camp Fillmore.[16]

Cheyennes living near Fort Lyon were anxious to remain at peace while the attacks were occurring on the South Platte. Some stray horses from Fort Lyon were picked up by the Cheyennes, and they made no effort to return the animals. Captain David L. Hardy was sent out with a troop of cavalry with orders to recover the animals and fight the Cheyennes if necessary. Indian Agent Colley independently sent John Prowers, an intermarried white and clerk of William Bent, to the Cheyennes and instructed him to determine their attitudes. Prowers reported back before Captain Hardy and told Colley that although the Sioux had offered the war pipe to the Cheyennes, the latter declined to join their allies in a war against the whites or the army. Two Cheyennes who came back to Fort Lyon with Prowers told Colley that they were "very much frightened" that the consequences of the depredations on the South Platte would extend to

[15] George Bent to Hyde, March 26, 1906, Bent Letters, Coe Collection; Sanborn to Chivington, April 15, 1864, Gerry to Sanborn, April 14, 1864, Report of Lieutenant Clark Dunn, April 18, 1864, *O. R.,* I: Vol. 34, pt. 3, pp. 167–68, pt. 1, pp. 887–88.

[16] Boone to Chivington, April 16, 1864, Stilwell to G. L. Shoup, April 16, 1864, *O. R.,* I: Vol. 34, pt. 3, pp. 188–90.

their band. Captain Hardy returned to Fort Lyon with all of the
strayed stock except three mules which were with a band hunting on
the Smoky Hill. The Captain reported that the Cheyennes not only
returned the stock but that they were thoroughly alarmed and "appeared to be very anxious to keep on good terms with the whites."[17]

It was quite different on the Platte, where news of raids kept Major
Downing and his command in the saddle much of the time. On April
19, Indians drove inhabitants from a ranch and took what they wanted.
All agreed that the Indians were Cheyennes. Downing was unsuccessful in an attempt to intercept the raiders and commented to his superiors that unless more troops were dispersed along the Platte road
near the scenes of the depredations, he could never mount effective pursuits because of the distance from Camp Sanborn to the trouble spot.
The Cheyennes, Major Downing wrote, were at the bottom of the
raids, and he requested enough troops to "wipe out" those troublesome Indians. Ranchers and settlers along the Platte were terrified by
the raids and threat of war, and the Major also feared that unless the
route were protected, immigration to Colorado would soon stop.[18]

After his return to Camp Sanborn, Major Downing wrote a de-
tailed report to Colonel Chivington of his futile effort to track down
the latest group of looters. At Morrison's ranch Downing had learned
that ten lodges of Cheyennes had camped in the vicinity just before
the last raid. Although several lodges of Sioux were also close by,
Downing did not disturb them because the Major had been informed
that the Sioux did not approve of the Cheyennes' actions. Downing,
by marching in a loop north of the Platte, hoped to pick up fresh
signs of the Cheyennes, but he was unsuccessful. During his march
all the evidence gathered by Downing seemed to agree that the party
consisted of forty or fifty Cheyennes and possibly a few Kiowas. Failing to find a fresh trail, Downing returned to Camp Sanborn and
distributed his troops to the posts and stations above and below the
post, retaining a portion of the post's garrison with which to scour
the sand hills along the South Platte if necessary. Although the Cheyennes as a tribe discountenanced the attacks already committed, this

[17] Colley to Evans, April 19, 1864, Upper Arkansas Agency, Letters Received; Captain Samuel H. Cook to Stilwell, April 22, 1864, O. R., I: Vol. 34, pt. 3, p. 262.

[18] Downing to Chivington, Sanborn to Chivington, April 20, 1864, O. R., I: Vol.
34, pt. 3, pp. 242–43.

did not alter Downing's determination to punish any Cheyenne found on the South Platte—whether a member of a raiding party or not. Through Captain Sanborn, Downing ordered a few lodges of Cheyennes trading at Gerry's ranch to move away from the South Platte. Downing informed Chivington that, at the proper time, he was prepared to go to the main Cheyenne village and "compel them to surrender the depredators, or clean them out."[19]

Reports from Lieutenant Eayre and Major Downing made it reasonably certain that the Cheyennes were operating out of their villages on the Republican River. But as more troops were dispersed along the Platte route, fewer Indians were observed for a few weeks. Then, late in April, raiding commenced again. Cheyennes ran off eight hundred dollars' worth of horses from the Moore and Kelley Overland Stage station, west of Julesburg. Troops sent in pursuit destroyed eleven Cheyenne lodges and many fresh buffalo robes, but no Indians or horses were taken. As usual, because the cavalry could not maintain the chase, the Indians made good their escape to the Republican River. Downing expressed the opinion to Chivington that his command could whip the raiders if they were caught, but the cavalry's horses simply did not have enough stamina to maintain a protracted chase. The Major was also fearful that unless the raiding was soon checked, the Sioux would join the Cheyennes, a contingency that Downing wished to avoid "till we get through with the Cheyennes."[20]

Hoping to discover a Cheyenne camp close enough to strike, Downing sent out a party of scouts across the Platte to the north. Following his scouts, Major Downing with forty men captured an Indian prisoner, half-Cheyenne–half-Sioux. Downing's first impulse was to shoot the prisoner but the Indian's life was spared when he promised to lead the troops to a camp containing some of the raiders. After a march to Cedar Bluffs, about sixty miles north of the South Platte, the command reached the Indian camp early on the morning of May 3 while the Indians were still asleep. The Major deployed ten men to seize the horse herd, five men to hold the command's horses, and with twenty-five dismounted troopers, Downing attacked the village.

[19] Downing to Chivington, April 21, 1864, *O. R.*, I: Vol. 34, pt. 3, pp. 250–52.
[20] Downing to Chivington, April 26, 27, 1864, *O. R.*, I: Vol. 34, pt. 3, pp. 304, 314.

The surprised Cheyennes fled their village to a canyon where, because of the Indians' superior numbers, the troops could not dislodge the warriors. In his report, Major Downing claimed that he had killed twenty-five Cheyennes, wounded thirty or forty more, and suffered only one killed and one wounded among his command. If he had mountain howitzers, the Major thought that he could have "annihilated the entire band." Major Downing complimented his entire command, and especially Lieutenant Dunn, for their "great gallantry," against the Cheyennes, and the Major believed that the Cheyennes were "pretty severely punished in this affair, yet I believe now it is but the commencement of war with this tribe, which must result in exterminating them."

Slightly more than a year later, Downing recapitulated the account of his attack upon the Cheyenne camp at Cedar Bluffs to a congressional committee. The Cheyenne village contained fifteen large lodges and several smaller ones, which would mean a village population slightly in excess of one hundred people. Normally such a camp would contain only twenty-five warriors, and Downing explained the greater number of Cheyennes in the engagement by stating that many of the warriors living in the village did not possess lodges of their own. To Downing's knowledge, no women or children were killed, no prisoners were taken, but the command did capture one hundred Indian ponies.[21]

Runners soon brought the news of the fight at Cedar Bluffs to the Cheyennes living on the Arkansas River. The Southern Cheyennes still professed that they wanted "no trouble but if the troops come after them they will have to fight." Indian Agent Colley feared trouble with the Southern Cheyennes, but the other tribes along the Arkansas River pledged neutrality in the event of hostilities.[22]

During early May, 1864, Major Edward W. Wynkoop, commanding at Fort Lyon, heard of no depredations committed by any Indians attached to the Upper Arkansas Agency. So peaceful was the situation at Fort Lyon that Major Wynkoop saw no reason to keep a surplus of ordnance stores at his post. As yet, Chivington's office did

---

[21] Downing to Chivington, May 2, 3, 1864, O. R., I: Vol. 34, pt. 3, p. 407, pt. 1, pp. 907–908; Sand Creek Investigation, 69.

[22] Colley to Evans, May 1, 1864, Upper Arkansas Agency, Letters Received.

not possess information linking the Upper Arkansas Agency Cheyennes to the South Platte raids. One of Chivington's aides instructed Wynkoop to question the Cheyennes and determine "whether they participated in any of the thefts committed by that tribe, either on the waters of the Platte, Republican, or Smoky Hill. If they did, they should be punished; if not, and if they commit no offense, of course they will not be molested, but must be watched." It was known, however, in Denver that a "young Bent," either George or Charles, who had previously served in the Confederate Army under General Sterling Price, had joined the Cheyennes, and Major Wynkoop was told to put him in irons in the Fort Lyon guardhouse.[23]

Lieutenant George S. Eayre, after reprovisioning and adding more men to his detachment, left Camp Weld in late April, 1864, to look for the Cheyennes. This time, Eayre's column contained one hundred men supported by two mountain howitzers. On a tributary of the Smoky Hill River on May 1, Eayre found a fresh trail made by an Indian band of one hundred lodges coming from the direction of the Republican River. The Lieutenant was convinced that the Cheyennes had not yet joined the large encampment, and since his mounts were still fresh, he determined to follow the trail, trusting that his next report to Colonel Chivington would be of a "more interesting character." It was obvious that Lieutenant Eayre was spoiling for a fight, and this assumption was supported by Lieutenant Augustus W. Burton, a member of Eayre's command, who stated that Eayre's orders from Denver instructed him to "kill Cheyennes whenever and wherever found."[24]

For two weeks Eayre sought out the Cheyennes, narrowly missing large Dog Soldier and Sioux camps on the Solomon and Smoky Hill rivers. Then on May 16, 1864, when the column was within three miles of the Smoky River, four hundred Cheyenne warriors attacked the detachment. The Cheyennes and the troops, according to Eayre's re-

---

[23] Wynkoop to Chivington, May 9, 1864, Maynard to Wynkoop, May 16, 1864, *O. R.,* I: Vol. 34, pt. 3, pp. 531–32, 630; George Bent, "Forty Years With the Cheyennes" (ed. by George Hyde), *The Frontier,* October, 1905, February, 1906, 22; George Bent to Hyde, March 9, 1905, February 26, 1906, Western History Department, Denver Public Library.

[24] Eayre to Chivington, May 1, 1864, Major T. I. McKenny to Charlot, June 15, 1864, *O. R.,* I: Vol. 34, pt. 4, pp. 101, 403.

port, fought for more than seven hours before the Indians were driven off. At first Eayre thought that he and his men had killed three chiefs and twenty-five warriors, but several weeks later the Lieutenant stated that "many of the Indians were killed, including one of the chiefs." Whether the fight took place at an old site known as Big Timbers, on Goose Creek in present Wallace County, Kansas, or on Ash Creek, as claimed by Wolf Chief, is not of crucial importance.[25] The consequences of the conflict, however, were decisive, because the killing of Lean Bear, a renowned Cheyenne chief, was bitterly resented by the tribe.

Lieutenant Eayre's reports were so phrased that his superior immediately assumed that the Cheyennes had initiated the fight. According to Cheyenne history, the 250 lodges under Lean Bear, Wolf Chief, and Black Kettle had not yet heard of the raids on the Platte or of Eayre's first expedition. Three white men, testifying a year later, stated that Lieutenant Eayre struck first and made no effort to council in peace with the Cheyennes or their chiefs. Trooper Asbury Bird of the First Colorado Cavalry, for example, does not state that Lean Bear was shot down in cold blood, but it becomes apparent that Eayre wasted little time before the shooting began. William Bent, for the most part, supports the contentions of Wolf Chief. Unaware of any serious difficulties, Lean Bear went in advance of his warriors, greeted the soldier, and showed his medal received at Washington in 1862. After one of the soldiers with Lieutenant Eayre shot the chief off his horse, a running fight took place, with the soldiers making their way to Fort Larned. When Bent and Eayre met near Fort Lyon, the young officer told the old Indian trader that he and his men had killed seventeen Cheyenne and Sioux warriors in a fight.

Much of the testimony offered by Major Wynkoop corroborates Bent's information. Obtaining his information from troops with Eayre and from the Cheyennes, Wynkoop stated that Lean Bear was brought to Eayre's column by a sergeant and was then killed. It was common knowledge, Major Wynkoop told the congressmen, that Lieutenant

[25] Eayre to Chivington, May 19, 1864, Wynkoop to Maynard, May 27, 1864, Shoup to [Evans], May 30, 1864, Thomas J. McKean to Charlot, May 25, 1864, O. R., I: Vol. 34, pt. 1, pp. 934–35, pt. 4, pp. 38–39, 207–208; George Bent to Hyde, March 26, 1906, Bent Letters, Coe Collection.

Eayre was operating under orders from Colonel Chivington "to kill all Indians he came across." John S. Smith, Bent's former employee and, in 1864, an interpreter for the Upper Arkansas Agency, volunteered the information that Lean Bear approached the troops alone and was shot down.[26]

More than forty years later, Wolf Chief, who participated in the fight with Eayre, remembered the incident well. When the column of soldiers was sighted, a camp crier alerted the village and Lean Bear with some other leaders rode out to meet them. As the soldiers drew up in a battle line, Lean Bear and Star rode to the front of the soldiers; the former only intended to show some papers obtained in Washington two years previously and to tell the soldiers that his camp was friendly. When the two Cheyenne leaders were twenty or thirty feet away from the troops, Eayre issued a command and the soldiers shot Lean Bear and Star from their horses. The troops then rode forward and poured another volley into the chiefs' bodies. Eayre's howitzers quickly opened up on the Cheyennes, and the running fight was terminated when Black Kettle, always in favor of peace with the whites, ordered the warriors away from Eayre's command.[27]

Now practically all the Cheyenne between the South Platte and Arkansas rivers had real grievances. Major Downing, despite his insistence to the contrary, had killed two women and two children at Cedar Bluffs; Lieutenant Dunn had fought young Dog Soldiers at Frémont's Orchard; and Lieutenant Eayre had killed Lean Bear, five other Cheyennes, and six Sioux. Black Kettle and the other Cheyenne peace chiefs could no longer hold their young men in check. As soon as Eayre's column was out of sight, the Cheyennes formerly under Lean Bear began their war councils, and many of the band decided to regroup toward the north and carry the war to the whites.[28]

On the day after the Eayre fight, a settler rode forty miles to Salina, Kansas, bringing information that Indians had just attacked ranches along the Fort Riley–Fort Larned road. At the Cow Creek station

26 George Bent to Hyde, April 12, 1906, Bent Letters, Coe Collection; *Sand Creek Investigation*, 59, 72, 75–76, 83–94.

27 George Bent to Hyde, March 6, 1905, Western History Department, Denver Public Library; Grinnell, *Fighting Cheyennes*, 145–46.

28 Parmeter to AAG., Department of Kansas, May 17, 1864, *O. R.*, I: Vol. 34, pt. 3, p. 643.

an Indian attack was repulsed, and at the Walnut Creek ranch Indians appeared and demanded that the attendant leave immediately or be killed. The ranch keeper, whose wife was a Cheyenne woman, was informed by the Cheyennes that they intended "to kill all the whites they could find," and spared the man only because of his Cheyenne wife, whom they took back to her people. H. L. Jones, deputy United States marshal at Salina, upon hearing of the attacks, organized a posse of citizens and, accompanied by fifteen mounted troops, began an investigation of the reports. The posse and troops found the station keeper at Cow Creek dead with "the arrow still sticking in his body." Proceeding farther along the road, the Jones party found the ranches and stations "deserted and sacked."[29]

One week later rumors began drifting into Cottonwood Springs that a company of troops had been nearly wiped out 180 miles to the south. Since Chivington had been without communication from Eayre for nearly a month, it was assumed that Eayre's command was in trouble. Other massacres came quickly. A telegraph operator at Plum Creek, the third station west of Fort Kearny, reported Indians concentrating on Boxelder Creek, where ten soldiers had been "butchered." Some 1,640 Cheyenne warriors, it was warned, were swarming north to the Platte route to "kill all white men and soldiers" on the Overland road. Not all of the Cheyennes, however, were ready for war, because during the interval between Eayre's fight and the reports from the Platte, a large camp of Cheyennes was establishing itself in a village sixty miles east of Fort Lyon.[30]

Governor John Evans immediately demanded troops to defend Colorado territory from a "powerful combination of Indian tribes, who are pledged to sustain each other and drive the white people from this country." From old Indian traders and Indians themselves, Evans learned that the Cheyennes, Kiowas, and Comanches had allied to carry out "their hellish purposes." No such alliance was known to the army officers at Fort Larned, and Evans, of course, made no mention that Colorado troops had goaded the Cheyennes into the attacks—

[29] Jones to T. O. Osborn, United States marshal for the state of Kansas, May 31, 1864, O. R., I: Vol. 34, pt. 4, pp. 149–50.
[30] Maynard to Wynkoop, May 23, 1864, Chivington to Major George M. O'Brien, John Pratt to Charlot, May 21, 1864, Wynkoop to Maynard, May 21, 1864; O. R., I: Vol. 34, pt. 4, p. 14, pt. 3, pp. 711–12; Ware, *Indian War of 1864*, 193.

attacks which would well serve Evans' scheme to clear Indian title from Colorado territory. Evans begged Major General Curtis in the "name of humanity" not to withdraw the troops concentrating at Fort Lyon to the east, but to allow them to chastise the Indians on the Smoky Hill and Republican rivers until they abandoned hostilities.[31]

With the reports filtering into his headquarters, Colonel Chivington feared that the Indians were to "give our out settlements a bad time this season," and ordered all but two companies of the First Colorado Cavalry to gather on the Arkansas River. To Major Wynkoop at Fort Lyon, Chivington sent a dispatch, warning that the greatest vigilance was necessary. "The Cheyennes," wrote Chivington, "will have to be soundly whipped before they will be quiet. If any of them are caught in your vicinity kill them, as that is the only way."[32]

The Cheyennes, after avenging the death of Lean Bear, ceased raiding for almost a month. During the lull the Cheyennes moved their villages to Medicine Lodge Creek, so that their women and children could live in safety while the warriors made war. To meet the threat of war, Major General Curtis ordered Brigadier General Robert B. Mitchell, commanding the District of Nebraska, to keep the Platte route open, while Colonel Chivington was directed to deal with the Indians and Confederates along the Arkansas River in Colorado territory and western Kansas. Chivington arrived at Fort Lyon on June 11, 1864, and immediately evaluated the situation for his superior officer. The Cheyennes and Kiowas, in Chivington's opinion, were "determined on war, and will have to be soundly thrashed before they will be quiet," but the Comanches and Kiowa-Apaches were resisting their neighbors' entreaties to join in a war against the whites. If so ordered by Major General Curtis, Chivington stated that he, with his troops could, "keep the route between Larned and Lyon Clear of Indians and rebels, and . . . can make campaign into Texas, or after Indians on Smoky Hill and Republican."[33]

[31] Evans to Curtis, May 28, 1864, Evans Collection.

[32] Chivington to Charlot, May 28, 1864, Chivington to Wynkoop, May 31, 1864, *O. R.*, I, Vol. 34, pt. 4, pp. 100–101, 151.

[33] George Bent to Hyde, March 26, 1906, March 20, 1913, Bent Letters, Coe Collection; Statement of Robert North, June 15, 1864, in *Report, Commissioner of Indian Affairs, 1864*, 228; Chivington to Charlot, June 11, 1864, *O. R.*, I, Vol. 34, pt. 4, pp. 318–19; Grinnell, *Fighting Cheyennes*, 152.

An alleged Cheyenne raid near Denver, on June 11, 1864, caused an outburst of frenzied hatred of Indians in Colorado territory. In the afternoon of that day, Nathan Ward Hungate, his wife, and two young daughters were murdered by Indians. Hungate, an employee of Isaac P. Van Wormer at the latter's ranch, and a hired hand, named Miller, were working that afternoon several miles from the ranch house. Observing smoke and flames from his home, Hungate rode to his family; Miller, fearing the Indians, carried the alarm to Denver, some thirty miles to the northwest. When appraised of the attack, Van Wormer set out alone and, coming to his property, found the buildings burned, the stock run off, the body of Hungate some distance from the house, and the bodies of Mrs. Hungate and the two young girls bound and thrown in a well. Loading the bodies on his wagon, Van Wormer brought them to Denver, where they were exposed to public view.[34]

Such evidence as existed pointed to the Cheyennes as the murderers of the Hungate family. Just previous to the attack on Van Wormer's ranch, Indians on Coal Creek had raided a train belonging to J. S. Brown and Thomas J. Darrah, and four days later, six warriors ran off stock from an emigrant train sixty-five miles from Denver on Bijou Creek. The freighters trailed the Indians, whom they identified as Cheyennes, and met a man who had just visited the Van Wormer ranch. From this individual, named Johnson, Brown and Darrah learned that "About 100 yards from the desolated ranch they [Johnson and others] discovered the body of the murdered woman and her two dead children, one of which was a little girl of four years and the other an infant. The woman had been stabbed in several places and scalped, and the body bore evidences of having been violated. The two children had their throats cut, their heads being nearly severed from their bodies. Up to this time the body of the man had not been found, but upon our return down the creek [Boxelder], on the opposite side, we found the body. It was horribly mutilated and the scalp was torn off. . . ."[35]

[34] Elmer R. Burkey, "The Site of the Murder of the Hungate Family by Indians in 1864," *Colo. Magazine*, Vol. XII, No. 4 (July, 1935), 139–42; Susan R. Ashley, "Reminiscences of Early Colorado," *Colo. Magazine*, Vol. XIV, No. 2 (March, 1937), 74–75.

[35] Evans to Chivington, June 11, 12, 1864, Brown and Darrah to Evans, June 11, 1864, Brown, D. C. Corbin, and Darrah to Maynard, June 13, 1864, Maynard to Charlot,

A pursuit of the Indians was ordered, but the Indians escaped. When Colonel Chivington learned of the murders, he added some instructions for the detachment's commander, Captain Joseph C. Davidson. Davidson was ordered to co-operate with Lieutenant Dunn, who was reported within eight miles of the tragic scene, and Chivington concluded his order with the admonition not to "encumber your command with prisoner Indians."[36]

Were the Hungate murders committed by the Cheyennes, and were they a prelude to the long anticipated Indian war? In all probability the Cheyennes had nothing to do with the Hungate killings. Robert North, Governor Evans' informant, believed that the murders were instigated by John Notee, an Arapaho who had been angered when he had been forced to return some stock previously stolen from the Van Wormer ranch. Knowing undoubtedly that Evans wanted to pin the murders on the Cheyennes, Notee told the governor that, although he was uncertain, he believed most of the raiders were Cheyennes and Kiowas. Later, in the summer of 1864, when a delegation of Arkansas River Cheyennes and Arapahoes were asked who committed the Hungate murders, Neva, an Arapaho chief, without hesitation, identified the leader as Roman Nose, also known as Medicine Man, and three other Northern or Platte River Arapahoes.[37]

Governor Evans, in the fact of near panic in Denver, began organizing the Colorado militia and sought permission from the War Department to raise a regiment of one hundred days' volunteers. Both Robert North and William McGaa, alias Jack Jones, a mountain man and Indian trader, told Governor Evans what he wanted to hear. North reported that he had heard several plains tribes discussing war, confident that they would drive the whites out of the country and

June 13, 1864, E. Reynolds to Commanding Officer, District of Colorado, June 15, 1864, *O. R.*, I: Vol. 34, pt. 4, pp. 319–20, 353–55, 405.

[36] Maynard to Davidson, June 11, 1864, Davidson to Maynard, June 19, 1864, Chivington to Davidson, June 12, 1864, *O. R.*, I: Vol. 34, pt. 4, pp. 320–21, 330, 462.

[37] AAAG., District of Colorado to Lieutenant Colonel W. O. Collins, to Lieutenant G. H. Hardin, to Lieutenant G. H. Chase, November 8, 18, 1864, Department of the Missouri, District of Colorado, Letters Sent, United States Army Commands, Records of the War Department, National Archives, Washington, D. C. (hereafter cited as District of Colorado, Letters Sent); Statement of Robert North, June 15, 1864, in *Report, Commissioner of Indian Affairs, 1864,* 228; *Sand Creek Investigation,* 89; Evans to E. M. Stanton, Secretary of War, June 14, 1864; *O. R.*, I: Vol. 34, pt. 4., p. 381.

regain their lost lands. The Indians were also disgruntled because they had been cheated by a few traders, and the hostiles believed the time for counciling had passed; those Indians who refused to join the alliance would be treated as enemies. McGaa's charges were more serious. Claiming to know all of the Cheyenne leaders, McGaa accused the Cheyennes of committing depredations upon emigrant trains for eight years—murdering men, ravishing women, and killing children in six or eight instances to his personal knowledge. The Cheyennes, the mountain man claimed, were the ringleaders of the war which had been brewing for two or three years, and for that purpose, the Cheyennes secretly had begun gathering ammunition in the fall of 1863. In league with the Arapahoes and Sioux, the Cheyennes intended to war upon the whites, impoverish the frontiersmen in Colorado territory, and force them to leave the Indians' country.[38]

In mid-June, 1864, Governor Evans was still unwilling to declare all Cheyennes and Arapahoes hostile despite the earlier depredations and skirmishes. He advocated the establishment of camps in which the friendly Indians could be segregated from the hostiles, so that the latter could be pursued and punished until the war was terminated. "I have ordered," Governor Evans wrote in explanation to Commissioner of Indian Affairs Dole, "camps for friendly Indians at Fort Lyon, Fort Larned, and on the Cache la Poudre, and hope all the friendly Sioux may come to Fort Laramie; then, as we whip and destroy," the hostiles will join the friendly Indians at the established camps, bringing the war to a rapid end. Dole's successor as commissioner of Indian affairs, Charles E. Mix, however, rejected Evans' plan because he feared that Congress would not appropriate the necessary funds to defray the costs of feeding the Indians at the camps. The new commissioner, rather, instructed Evans to "use every endeavor to keep peace with the Indians, gather the Indians only on the buffalo range, and contract no debt for feeding Indians on reservations."[39]

Before his plan was rejected, Governor Evans began to separate the

[38] Statement of Robert North, in *Report, Commissioner of Indian Affairs, 1864*, 228; Statement of William McGaa, June 13, 1864, *O. R.*, I; Vol. 34, pt. 4, p. 423.

[39] Evans to Dole, June 15, 1864, Evans to Curtis, June 16, 1864, Evans Collection; Mix to Evans, June 23, 1864, in *Report, Commissioner of Indian Affairs, 1864*, 230.

hostile and friendly Indians. Through Indian agents, interpreters, and traders, Evans informed the peaceful Indians to gather at their appointed havens of safety; the Arkansas River Cheyennes and Arapahoes were told to proceed to Fort Lyon; the Upper Platte members of the same tribes to Camp Collins on the Cache la Poudre; the Kiowas and Comanches to Fort Larned; and the Sioux to Fort Laramie.[40]

Officers under Major General Curtis also thought peace with the Indians could be maintained. Major T. I. McKenny, inspector general of the Department of Kansas, suggested that war could be averted through a policy of conciliation with the Indians, adequate guards of troops for the mail and wagon trains, and a termination of "these scouting parties that are roaming over the country who do not know one tribe from another, and who will kill anything in the shape of an Indian." In McKenny's opinion it would require "but few murders on the part of our troops" to unite all the Plains tribes in a general war against the whites. To further insure the peace, McKenny suggested that incompetent officers such as the commanding officer at Fort Larned, a "confirmed drunkard," should be immediately replaced. Major Henry D. Wallen, commanding officer of Fort Sumner, confirmed McKenny's contention that although an "expensive Indian war" between the whites and the Cheyennes, Kiowas, and a band of Arapahoes was imminent, "It can be prevented by prompt management."[41]

Since Governor Evans and Major General Curtis received their information from different sources during June, 1864, they did not agree upon the immediate danger of an Indian war. Evans asked the General to approve a simultaneous attack upon the hostile Indians from the south by Chivington, from the east by Curtis, and from the north by Mitchell. Obviously distressed, Evans asked Curtis for information to show "that my evidence of Indian hostilities are not well founded." The territorial Governor of Colorado firmly argued that "multiplied and numerous assurances from friendly Indians, Indian traders, and people who suffer, and our troops, who have had several engage-

---

40 *Sand Creek Investigation*, 55–56; Evans to Colley, June 29, 1864, in *Sand Creek Investigation*, 55.

41 McKenny to Parmeter, June 15, 1864, Wallen to AG., Kansas City, Missouri June 20, 1864, *O. R.*, I: Vol. 34, pt. 4, pp. 402–404, 476.

ments with them" proved the danger of a war and he could not understand how Curtis could believe otherwise.[42]

Late in June a few scattered Indian forays took place. A stage coach, on June 27, was attacked between Fort Larned and Fort Lyon, but the escort drove the Indians off, killing several warriors. A day later, a wagon train somewhere between Julesburg and Fort Laramie suffered the loss of all its mules. Curtis, caught between these annoying hostilities and Governor Evans' agitation for vigorous retaliation, was apparently trying to prevent the antagonists from committing the act which would lead to a full-scale Indian war. Generally, Curtis reported that the Indians were quiet, "but the Cheyennes were preparing for mischief." Unimpressed by the rumors of a general war or by the Indians' fighting ability, Curtis ordered Chivington to attend to the Indians if they were actually hostile and commented that a "good company or two, with two howitzers well attended," were sufficient to destroy any band of Plains Indians.[43]

Nothing occurred before July, 1864, to make an all out Indian war on the Plains inevitable. The land hunger of the Colorado territorial officials, irritating clashes with troops, and travel through the heart of the buffalo range made the Indians restive, but there is little convincing evidence that the factions inclined to war among even the Cheyennes carried with them the sympathy of the majority. But one thing was clear: if either the Indians or the whites made a few more mistakes of aggression, bloodshed on the Plains would certainly come.

---

[42] Evans to Curtis, June 22, 1864, *O. R.*, I; Vol. 34, pt. 4, pp. 512–13.

[43] Curtis to Brigadier General Thomas J. McKean, June 27, 1864, Curtis to Major General H. W. Halleck, June 28, 1864, Lieutenant John Pratt to AAG., District of Nebraska, June 28, 1864, Curtis to Chivington, June 29, 1864, *O. R.*, I: Vol. 34, pt. 4, pp. 575, 585, 595–96.

# 9

## MASSACRE AT SAND CREEK

THE LULL IN INDIAN HOSTILITIES was broken on July 17, 1864, when large war parties struck the overland roads at widely separated points. At last, Governor Evans' Indian war seemed at hand. On July 17, an unidentified band of Indians swooped down upon the Overland route, attacking the Bijou, Beaver Creek, and Kelly's stations on the South Platte River. Sources vary considerably in the effect of the attacks; the press claimed five men lost their lives; Governor Evans claimed three men were killed; and Captain Sanborn, the investigating officer, established that only one man was actually killed. Much of the stock stolen from the stations was quickly recovered by Lieutenant George H. Chase, but neither he nor Captain Sanborn intercepted the war parties estimated by Granville Ashcraft, the latter's guide, as consisting of at least 150 warriors. When Captain Sanborn completed his scout toward the Republican River, he admitted that the Indians in their raids killed five and wounded one emigrant.[1]

Brigadier General Mitchell, who was at Cottonwood Springs when the troubles began, quickly moved up the South Platte to Julesburg. From the freighting post Mitchell asked for authority to raise two hundred volunteers from the ranchers along the Platte who understood "the Indian character and the country, and [who] are accustomed to fighting Indians." The request was denied by Major General Curtis, who merely urged Mitchell to use his cavalry and the Colorado militia to protect the route and to stop the trains from proceeding into the danger spots. Four days after the initial attacks, on July 21, Major General Curtis decided to take personal command

[1] Denver *Rocky Mountain News*, July 18, 23, 27, 29, 1864; Evans to Curtis, July 18, 1864, Sanborn to Maynard, July 21, 1864, Sanborn to Chivington, July 28, 1864, *O. R.*, I: Vol. 41, pt. 2, pp. 256, 323, pt. 1, pp. 73–74.

of the troops operating against the hostile Indians in his department.[2]

Major General Curtis hurried to Fort Riley to ascertain the gravity of the Indian peril. Since stage service was already disrupted over Butterfield's Overland Despatch route, which ran up the Smoky Hill Valley, Curtis was not able immediately to gauge the extent of the raids; the General did not know, for example, that the Indians had already run off stock from Fort Larned and the Walnut Creek station. At Fort Larned, previous to Curtis' movement, Indians and troops had engaged in a skirmish, and the warriors went on to attack Walnut Creek station, fifteen miles below the post. There it was reported that Indians killed ten men and scalped a man and a boy who escaped with their lives by feigning death. Shortly afterwards Indians also besieged four large trains, consisting of nearly four hundred wagons, at Cow Creek, where two more men were killed and three hundred head of stock were seized by the Indians. After some fighting the troops with Curtis relieved the train, which then proceeded on to Fort Larned. The unidentified Indians raided widely, small parties of warriors appearing within thirty miles west of Fort Riley.[3]

The new evidence did not change the opinion of Curtis, who was still convinced that the Indians did not intend a general war but were only out on stock raids. If the press and official reports were accurate, the Indian raids on the Kansas frontier were more serious and successful than those along the Platte route. In a period of a few days following July 17, Indians on the Kansas frontier killed twelve men, wounded three, and ran off about six hundred head of animals. There is no doubt that the Cheyennes were implicated in both the raids on the South Platte and those on the Santa Fe road. George Bent saw the warriors bringing the plunder to the large Indian villages along the Solomon River, and scalp dances were held regularly as the war parties returned fresh from new successes. Warriors and their women decked themselves in dresses and shirts made from silk cloth taken from captured wagon trains. And, a little later, William Bent in-

2 Denver *Rocky Mountain News*, July 27, 1864; Mitchell to Curtis, July 19, 1864, Curtis to Mitchell, Curtis to Evans, July 20, 1864, Curtis to Major S. S. Curtis, July 21, 1864, *O. R.*, I: Vol. 41, pt. 2, pp. 276, 302, 322.

3 Lawrence, Kansas *Daily Tribune*, August 7, 1864; *Rocky Mountain News*, August 1, 3, 1864; Curtis to Major General Henry W. Halleck, July 23, 26, 28, 1864, *O. R.*, I: Vol. 41, pt. 2, pp. 368, 413, 445.

formed Indian Agent Colley that the raiders on the South Platte consisted of 150 braves who no longer would take the advice of their "peace chiefs."[4]

Gathering a force of four hundred men, Major General Curtis marched from Fort Riley to Fort Larned and established two new posts en route. As usual, because the Indians quickly scattered as the troops appeared, the department commander could only hope that he would be able to catch and administer a "severe chastisement" to the Indians for their recent outbreak. After arriving at Fort Larned on July 29, Curtis dispersed his troops to protect the Santa Fe route; the new troops, however, did not prevent the Indians from successfully attacking another train at the Cimarron Crossing, where the warriors killed and scalped two men.[5]

The opinion of Indian Agent Colley was typical of the attitudes of the Colorado territorial officials. Colley, who had never had much sympathy for his charges, was thoroughly disgusted and wrote that no Indian could be trusted. Now, the Indian agent stated, "a little powder and lead is the best food for them."[6]

At Fort Larned, Curtis charged that Colonel Chivington was more interested in Colorado politics than in performing his duties as commanding officer of the District of Colorado. Chivington denied political aspirations and excused his absence from the trouble spots along the Arkansas River by claiming that he needed to return to Denver and quiet the terror and alarm among the people at the territorial capital. Chivington's denial and plea had the hollow ring of falsehood. Pro-statehood politicians in Colorado territory were confidently planning not only to submit their constitution for ratification, but also to hold a general election offering a full slate of candidates for office; Chivington was the pro-state faction's candidate for congressman. Headed by Governor Evans and Henry M. Teller, the pro-statehood faction engaged the anti-statehood group in a bitter,

[4] George Bent to Hyde, February 28, 1906, Bent Letters, Coe Collection; Curtis to Halleck, July 23, 26, 1864, *O. R.*, I: Vol. 41, pt. 2, pp. 368, 413.

[5] The new posts were Fort Ellsworth, later called Fort Harker, on the Smoky Hill River and Fort Zarah, at the confluence of Walnut Creek and the Arkansas River. Curtis to Governor Thomas Carney, Curtis to Halleck, July 28, 1864, Chivington to Curtis, August 8, 1864, *O. R.*, I: Vol. 41, pt. 2, pp. 445–46, 613–14.

[6] Colley to Evans, July 26, 1864, in *Report, Commissioner of Indian Affairs, 1864*, 230, 253.

unscrupulous campaign. Deep, festering political feuds and hatreds resulted, and the constitution was rejected by a decisive three-to-one vote; Chivington was now a marked man.[7]

With the Indians scattered and out of range of his troops, Curtis could do very little. The General estimated the toll of the Indian raids at twelve killed, six wounded, and about 150 head of government stock stolen. The two travelers scalped at Walnut Creek on July 18 were expected to live, "although one of them had the skin taken off to his ears and had eighteen wounds besides." From inadequate information Curtis accused the Kiowas, Comanches, and Big Mouth's Arapahoes, as well as members of other Plains tribes, of instigating the attacks on the Santa Fe route. When even the friendly Indians fled, fearing indiscriminate attacks by the militia among Curtis' force, there was no reason for Curtis to remain at Fort Larned. As one of his last actions before returning to his headquarters at Fort Leavenworth, Curtis created the District of the Upper Arkansas and placed Major General James G. Blunt in command. Even if Curtis had desired to stay on at Fort Larned, the threat of William Quantrill and Major General Sterling Price of the Confederate Army demanded his personal attention.[8]

The Indian situation was not taken lightly by Curtis. He re-enforced the garrisons of posts along the Santa Fe road with as many troops as he could spare and still meet the Confederate threat. Curtis admitted that during his tour of western Kansas, he found the Indians of the Upper Arkansas Agency in "defiant array" and feared that the tribes would unite to "destroy trains and murder our white people." In his letter to Major General Blunt, the commanding officer frankly stated that all of the agency's tribes had been "implicated in the stealing of stock, and most of them with the murders." Curtis also advised Blunt to separate those Indians opposed to the war from the hostiles and to

[7] Elmer Ellis, "Colorado's First Fight for Statehood, 1865–1868," *Colo. Magazine*, Vol. VIII, No. 1 (January, 1931), 23–26; Chivington to Curtis, August 8, 1864, *O. R.*, I: Vol. 41, pt. 2, pp. 613–14.

[8] Curtis to Chivington, Curtis to Evans, July 30, 1864, Special Field Orders No. 3, Headquarters, Department of Kansas, July 31, 1864, General Orders No. 1, Headquarters, District of the Upper Arkansas, Colonel James H. Ford to Curtis, July 31, 1864, *O. R.*, I: Vol. 41, pt. 2, pp. 483–85, 491, 529; Albert Castel, *A Frontier State at War: Kansas, 1861–1865*, 184ff.

keep a force in the field "to annoy, catch, and kill, so as to make war a burden to the savages and prevent them from procuring their usual supplies of buffalo meat."[9]

Detachments of the Eleventh Kansas Cavalry had no success in either finding or harassing the hostile Indians. Captain Henry Booth reported that on a scout along upper Walnut Creek and the Smoky Hill River, only a few deserted Indian camps were found, and he was of the opinion that the Indians were living somewhere upon the Saline, Solomon, or Republican rivers where buffalo were plentiful. Within two days after Captain Booth returned to Salina, Kansas, for a short rest, Indians, on August 7, 1864, raided an outpost of his command and made off with all of his detachment's horses. Captain Booth returned immediately to the field, but four days scouting between the Smoky Hill and Saline rivers netted no Indians. When the Captain and his men returned to Salina on August 11, a report awaited him that four men had just been killed near Beaver Creek, forty miles west of Salina. These buffalo hunters, surprised by Indians, were surrounded, killed and scalped.[10]

Near Fort Lyon, Major Wynkoop was also in trouble. Kiowas and Comanches attacked a wagon train within seven miles of the post and also caused some settlers to withdraw from their exposed residences. William Bent reported to Major Wynkoop that both Satanta and Little Mountain, Dohasan's son, were in the vicinity, and although the latter, when seen by Bent, appeared "very anxious for peace," the old trader thought "it may all be a suck-in." From his residence on the Purgatoire River, Bent also complained that "his old squaw," referring to his Cheyenne wife, Yellow Woman, "ran off a few days ago, or rather went off with Jo. Barraldo, as she liked him better than she did me. If I ever get sight of the young man," the aging Bent fumed, "it will go hard with him." Faced by an estimated force of one thousand Kiowa and Comanche warriors, Major Wynkoop was powerless to do more than protect his post.[11]

Indian Agent Colley, at Fort Lyon with Major Wynkoop, could

[9] Curtis to Blunt, August 9, 1864, *O. R.*, I: Vol. 41, pt. 2, pp. 629–31.

[10] Booth to Curtis, August 5, 7, 11, 1864, Blunt to Curtis, August 8, 1864, *O. R.*, I: Vol. 41, pt. 1, pp. 189–90, 233–35, pt. 2, pp. 611–12, 659.

[11] Colley to Evans, August 7, 1864, Wynkoop to Maynard, August 9, 1864, Bent to Colley, August 7, 1864, *O. R.,* I: Vol. 41, pt. 1, pp. 233–34, pt. 2, p. 735.

not identify the Indians lurking around the post. Within the space of little more than a week following August 11, Indians chased in a single soldier to the post, fought a fifteen-man detachment, losing two warriors, stampeded the horse herd of the Upper Arkansas Agency, and killed two men who were traveling between the agency buildings and Fort Lyon. While these incidents were occurring, the Indian agent noted that not even the friendly Arapahoes whom he had been feeding came to his post, and it looked to Colley that all of the tribes of the Upper Arkansas Agency required punishment.[12]

Smashing into emigrant and freighting trains, stage coaches, and ranches along the Platte route, following August 8, 1864, the Indians made the depredations on the Santa Fe Trail appear harmless. These savage attacks stretched from old Julesburg to Kiowa station, a distance of 250 miles. There can be no doubt that these raids were carefully planned and executed by Cheyennes, Arapahoes, and Sioux, because George Bent observed warriors returning to their villages loaded with plunder from the wagon trains and ranches.[13]

Cheyennes and a few Sioux carried out the first raid near the Plum Creek station. On the night of August 7, 1864, E. F. Morton, of Sidney, Iowa, with ten wagon loads of merchandise and household goods, and Michael Kelly, of St. Joseph, Missouri, with six wagons loaded with corn and machinery, stopped one-half mile east of the station. On the following morning, about one hundred Cheyennes rode down upon the unsuspecting travelers, surrounding the trains, killed or captured the people, and carried away any goods that struck the warriors' fancy. No one knows how many lives were taken by the Cheyennes in this tragedy; the minimum estimate runs to eleven dead and two captives, while the maximum indicates that at least eighteen men were killed and five women and children taken prisoner. Four hours later a small party of Cheyennes attacked the Fred Smith ranch, killed the hired man, burned the store, and ran off the loose stock.[14]

Those settlers and ranchers who were warned fled to army posts,

<hr />

[12] Colley to Evans, August 12, 26, 1864, in *Report, Commissioner of Indian Affairs, 1864,* 230, 231–32.

[13] George Bent to Hyde, February 28, 1906, Bent Letters, Coe Collection; Grinnell, *Fighting Cheyennes,* 155.

[14] Denver *Rocky Mountain News,* August 19, 1864; Omaha, *The Omaha Nebraskian,* August 17, 1864; Captain Henry Kuhl to Chivington, August 8, 1864; Lieutenant

but not all escaped the arrows and bullets of the Cheyennes. Between Fort Cottonwood and Fort Kearny six men were killed either on the opening day of the raids or shortly thereafter. The isolated settlements on the Little Blue River in Nebraska territory were severely punished by large war parties of Cheyenne, Sioux, and Arapaho warriors. Engaged in farming, stock raising, and station tending for overland travelers, these frontiersmen and their families felt secure from Indian raids. But before sunset on August 10, 1864, braves from the three tribes killed a family of eight, and seven other people met a similar fate. Farther to the west, on the same day, two men were killed and a train burned thirty-five miles west of Fort Kearny. Then on August 12, eighty wagons gathered together for safety at the Little Blue station were attacked, and nine men were killed. Less successfully, the Indians raided the Pawnee Ranch on two occasions, shot one man, and scalped him before he died.[15]

As the Indians struck, Governor Evans described Colorado territory in a "desperate condition." The raids along the Arkansas and Platte rivers set the stage for Governor Evans to issue his controversial proclamation. In the *Rocky Mountain News* of August 10, 1864, the Governor prepared the way for his official proclamation. He appealed to the patriotic citizens of Colorado territory to defend their homes against the "merciless savages," defining any man who killed a hostile Indian a patriot but at the same time warning citizens not to disturb friendly tribesmen. Approvingly, the editor of the newspaper commented: "A few months of active extermination against the red devils will bring quiet and nothing else will."[16]

Thomas Flanagan to Captain D. J. Craigie, November (?), 1864, *O. R.,* I: Vol. 41, pt. 3, p. 615, pt. 1, p. 244; Leroy W. Hagerty, "Indian Raids Along the Platte and Little Blue Rivers, 1864–1865," *Neb. History,* Vol. XXVIII, No. 4 (October-December, 1947), 240–41n.; James Green, "Incidents of the Indian Outbreak of 1864," NSHS *Publications,* XIX, 5–6.

[15] George Bent to Hyde, February 28, 1906, Bent Letters, Coe Collection; Curtis to Carney, August 10, 1864, N. A. Gillespie to Curtis, August 10, 1864, *O. R.,* I: Vol. 41, pt. 2, pp. 641, 642; George K. Otis to Dole, August 31, 1864, in *Report, Commissioner of Indian Affairs, 1864,* 254–55; Hagerty, "Indian Raids," *loc. cit.,* 241–45; Green, "Indian Outbreak of 1864," *loc. cit.,* 14–15n.; Root and Connelley, *Overland Stage,* 353–54; Hafen, *Overland Mail,* 258; *Sand Creek Investigation,* 90; Denver *Rocky Mountain News,* August 10, 1864; Omaha, Nebraska *Advertizer,* August 11, 1864.

[16] Evans to Curtis, August 8, 1864, *O. R.,* I. Vol. 41, pt. 2, p. 613; Denver *Rocky Mountain News,* August 10, 1864.

On August 11, 1864, Governor Evans published his official statement. In it Evans informed the public that friendly Indians had been instructed to gather at Forts Lyon, Larned, and Laramie and Camp Collins. Since his messengers to the Indians had returned and since most of the tribes remained away from the designated posts, Evans declared those Indians remaining on the Plains hostiles and at war with the government. All citizens of Colorado territory were authorized by Evans, either individually or in organized parties, to avoid those Indians at peace, but "to kill and destroy, as enemies of the Country, wherever they may be found, all hostile Indians." As compensation, the Governor empowered the citizens of Colorado territory to seize as their own all property of the hostiles, recapture stolen property for redemption by original owners, and pay for themselves and their horses under existing militia legislation. "The conflict is upon us," concluded the Governor, "and all good citizens are called to do their duty for the defence of their homes and families." Fearing that Colorado territory would have to depend exclusively upon its unorganized citizenry, Evans wrote to Secretary of War Stanton: "Pray authorize me to raise and mount a regiment of 100 day men to fight the Indians. Otherwise we are helpless."[17]

With mail and travel into Denver temporarily terminated, Governor Evans was confident that Major General Curtis could no longer deny that a general alliance for war existed among the Plains Indians. The available troops both in Nebraska territory and Colorado territory were too few to cope with the threat of Indian raids. Evans sought to have the two Colorado volunteer regiments returned from their tour with Curtis' eastern forces to defend their own people. Only fifty cavalry were available for immediate duty at Fort Kearny, and Brigadier General Mitchell, marooned at Fort Cottonwood, was powerless to do more than concentrate settlers and wagon trains at strong points for self-defense.[18]

[17] Denver *Rocky Mountains News*, August 17, 1864; "Massacre of Cheyenne Indians," Report of the Joint Committee on the Conduct of the War, 38 Cong., 2 sess., *Report No. 142*, p. 47 (hereafter cited as *Massacre of Cheyenne Indians*); *Report, Commissioner of Indian Affairs, 1864*, 230–31; Evans to Stanton, August 10, 1864, Telegram, Evans Collection.

[18] Evans to Stanton, Evans to Dole, August 10, 1864, Evans to Curtis, postscript by Otis, August 11, 1864, Evans Collection; Denver *Rocky Mountain News*, August 13,

After a three-day delay Governor Evans was authorized to raise a regiment of mounted "100 days' men" to protect the Colorado settlements. These recruits would be the nucleus of Chivington's troops at Sand Creek. Chivington was willing to use any means to kill off the raiders. When he learned in Denver that about four hundred Ute warriors were on their way to attack the Cheyennes, Arapahoes, and Sioux, Chivington told another district commander that he would place no obstacles in the way of the Utes in their passage through his jurisdiction. "Now," wrote Chivington, "if these red rebels can be killed off by one another, it will be a great saving to the Government, for I am fully satisfied that to kill them is the only way to have peace and quiet."[19]

As some of the raiders moved with their plunder to the Republican River, it was assumed that they would soon move south of the Arkansas River and break off their raids. But the eight-hundred-mile expanse of the Overland route from Fort Kearny to South Pass remained under Indian attack by Cheyennes, Arapahoes, Kiowas, and the Yankton and Brulé Sioux. On the eastern portion of the emigrant road, Captain Edward B. Murphy and his company of the Seventh Iowa Cavalry were joined at Little Blue station on August 14, 1864, by a company of Nebraska volunteers. The two units tried to begin a scout towards the Republican River but at Elk Creek were met by a large party of warriors estimated at 250 to 500 strong. A sharp skirmish began, and when the troops' howitzer became disabled, the whites retreated to Fort Kearny. The Cheyennes' version of the fight with Captain Murphy varies widely from those of the white participants. Captain Murphy's men encountered, according to George Bent's information, some Sioux hunters upon whom the whites began to fire. The shooting attracted many other warriors, and the whites quickly fled from the field of action.[20]

The Indians pressed their attacks to within thirty miles of Denver,

---

1864; Chivington to Curtis, John Pratt to Charlot, Mitchell to Curtis, August 12, 1864, *O. R.,* I: Vol. 41, pt. 2, pp. 671–73.

[19] Evans to Stanton, Charlot to Evans, Chivington to Commanding Officer, Camp Collins, Colorado territory, August 13, 1864, *O. R.,* I: Vol. 41, pt. 2, pp. 694–95.

[20] Curtis to Halleck, Mitchell to Curtis, August 18, 1864, *O. R.,* I: Vol. 41, pt. 2, pp. 762, 765; W. H. Stoner, *et al.,* to J. B. Weston, n. d., in NSHS *Publications,* XIX, 16–17; Grinnell, *Fighting Cheyennes,* 155–56.

and wagon trains in the Arkansas Valley were also struck. Frantically Governor Evans called for aid from Major General Curtis, claiming that ranches were being burned and settlers killed by the Indians. Farmers, frightened by the sporadic raids, did not gather their crops, and with the Overland route closed, Colorado territory was in danger of starvation. For a six-week period, from August 15 to September 29, 1864, no mail arrived in Denver from the East.[21]

While the Indians' activities were near their peak, sufficient troops to protect the settlements and the roads simply were not available. Major General William S. Rosecrans refused to free the Second Colorado Cavalry from duty to the east, and the "100 days' regiment," or the Third Colorado Cavalry, was still organizing. Flushed with success, the young warriors of the Cheyennes planned still more raids. Two Cheyenne chiefs, Long Chin and Man-Shot-by-a-Ree, old friends of Elbridge Gerry, appeared at the latter's ranch on August 20 and warned the trader to remove his stock quickly because eight hundred to one thousand Cheyenne, Arapaho, Kiowa, Comanche, and Kiowa-Apache warriors intended to sweep the South Platte Valley clean. Gerry's friends stated that first the warriors would raid for stock, then divide into smaller parties and strike the settlements at Fort Lupton, Latham, Junction, the Cherry Creek area, and Pueblo. The old men and chiefs of the tribes, the Cheyennes informed Gerry "were opposed to the war, but the young men could not be controlled; they were determined to sweep the Platte and the country as far as they could; they know that if the white men follow up the war for two or three years they would get rubbed out, but meanwhile they would kill plenty of whites." Again Governor Evans feared the worst. He dashed off a telegram to Secretary of War Stanton: "Unlimited information of contemplated attack by a large body of Indians in a few days along the entire line of our settlements."[22]

[21] Evans to Stanton, Evans to Curtis, August 18, 1864, *O. R.,* I: Vol. 41, pt. 2, pp. 765–66; Root and Connelley, *Overland Stage,* 330; Hafen, *Overland Mail,* 260–61.

[22] Curtis to Charlot, Curtis to Captain G. L. Gove, August 20, 1864, Halleck to Rosecrans, August 19, 1864, Curtis to Rosecrans, August 21, 1864, Rosecrans to Curtis, August 22, 1864, John C. Anderson to Major W. F. Wilder, August 21, 1864, Curtis to Major S. S. Curtis, August 22, 1864, Evans to Stanton, August 22, 1864, *O. R.,* I: Vol. 41, pt. 2, pp. 779, 788–89, 793, 797, 808, 809; Augusta Hauck Block, "Lower

It is improbable that Gerry made the long ride through to Denver warning the settlers of their peril. However the news came, though, the farmers and ranchers vacated their exposed homes, gathered at the larger settlements, and sent out strong patrols of citizens and militia to watch for the hostiles. Ironically, Elbridge Gerry and his neighbor, Antoine Reynal, or Raynal, suffered the loss of their herds while other stock losses were minimal. Five days after the first alarm, confidence of safety returned to the settlers and they drifted back to their farms and ranches as the small parties of warriors disappeared from the South Platte.[23]

Indians living south of the Arkansas River did more damage than those camping on the Solomon or Republican rivers after August 20, 1864. Three trains were intercepted by strong parties of warriors above Fort Larned on the Santa Fe Trail, and at least eleven men were killed during these three incidents. In addition two more men were killed in a separate attack between Fort Lyon and Fort Larned. Near the Cimarron River still another wagon train was surrounded by a strong party of Indians. Mexican trainmen, allowed by the warriors to proceed to Fort Union, told army officers that the white men with the train "were killed and their bodies most horribly mutilated, heads cut off, hearts cut out, and evidently placed in the center of their 'dance circle' while . . . [the Indians] held their fiendish war dance around them, and kicked the mutilated bodies about the praries." Colonel J. C. McFerran, chief of staff for the Department of New Mexico, depicted life unsafe upon the Santa Fe Trail even within sight of large bodies of troops. Brutal outrages, the Colonel charged, were committed by members of the Comanche, Cheyenne, Kiowa, Arapaho, and Kiowa-Apache tribes, and conditions were likely to worsen unless the savages were chastised.[24]

Opinion was unanimous that the Plains Indians needed punish-

Boulder and St. Vrain Valley Home Guards and Fort Junction," *Colo. Magazine*, Vol. XVI, No. 5 (September, 1939), 188; *Report, Commissioner of Indian Affairs, 1864*, 232.

[23] S. E. Browne to Evans, Gerry to Evans, August 22, 1864, Browne to Evans, Browne to Chivington, Browne to Evans, August 24, 1864, *O. R.*, I: Vol. 41, pt. 2, pp. 843, 844–45, 864–65.

[24] Anthony to Captain H. G. Loring, Captain N. S. Davis to Commanding Officer, Fort Union, New Mexico territory, August 23, 1864; Anthony to Lieutenant J. E. Tappan, August 29, 1864, McFerran to Carleton, Carleton to Brigadier General Lorenzo Thomas, August 28, 29, 1864, *O. R.*, I: Vol. 41, pt. 2, pp. 827, 828–29, 926–28.

ment. From the beginning of the outbreak on August 7 through August 28, 1864, at least fifty people had lost their lives on the Platte route alone. By the latter date, Major General Curtis felt that mail coaches with escorts could resume their normal operations. The road east of the ninety-ninth meridian was now safe, and although bands of Indians continued to harass the route west of Fort Kearny, the attacking Indians were using greater caution because of the greater frequency of patrolling troops.[25]

Leaving militia units to protect the road, Major General Curtis, on September 3, 1864, began a two-week scout south of the Platte River. Not only did Curtis intend to reconnoiter in force, but he felt that his 628 troopers, supported by five mountain howitzers and Pawnee scouts, were strong enough to punish any Indian concentration found on the Plains. The command began its search for Indians at Plum Creek, marched to the Republican River, and arrived on the Solomon River, where the column was divided into two smaller forces, on September 7. Brigadier General Mitchell took a majority of the troops west and then turned north to Fort Cottonwood, while Curtis led the smaller unit down the Smoky Hill to Fort Riley. Neither of the two columns found any significant Indian villages, although Mitchell passed just east of a large Indian encampment at "Big Timbers" where Black Kettle and other Cheyenne and Arapaho chiefs were sending out peace messages. Mitchell's patrols scouted the Republican and Platte rivers intensely, but except for two small skirmishes no contact was established with Indians. Curtis, after returning to Fort Riley, found it impossible to devote any more time to the Indians since Confederate Major General Sterling Price, with fifteen thousand men, was moving north into Missouri. Blunt and Mitchell were left in the field to protect the communication routes and, if possible, punish the warring Indians.[26]

[25] Curtis to Halleck, August 28, 1864, Chivington to Curtis, August 30, 1864, Curtis to Saunders, August 31, 1864, *O. R.,* I: Vol. 41, pt. 2, pp. 914–15, 946, 964.

[26] Curtis' Field Order for Troop Movement, September 2, 1864, Curtis to Major S. S. Curtis, September 13, 1864, Colley to Evans, September 4, 1864, Mitchell to Charlot, October 14, 1864, Flanagan to Craigie, November [?], 1864, Curtis to Halleck, September 13, 1864, Mitchell to Curtis, September 16, 1864, Curtis to Halleck, September 17, 1864, *O. R.,* I: Vol. 41, pt. 3, pp. 36, 180, 195–96, pt. 1, pp. 243, 244–47, pt. 3, pp. 179–80, 218, 234. Grinnell (*Two Great Scouts,* 72) implies that the total effective force taken by Curtis into the field consisted only of 180 men.

Again, Major General Curtis thought the Indian danger less serious than did Governor Evans. Repeatedly, in the field, Curtis wrote that the Indians were not concentrated, and that "bands of hunters, steal and scalp," or that the Indians were scattered into "small, shy bands." The hostiles, thought to be in western Kansas, seemed to be moving south. To Kansas citizens Curtis stated that the number of Indians involved was small and that settlers on the frontier could defend themselves by adequate enclosures against the Indians' "dashing charge and immediate retreat." Soon after Curtis left western Kansas, Ben Holladay, the stage line operator, was ready to resume operations over the Platte route, and even Colonel Chivington, by mid-September, admitted that the Indian threat to the Overland route and the road to Denver was clear, and coaches could travel with "perfect safety . . . with proper precaution." As travel resumed, Chivington began shifting troops and his attention south toward the Arkansas River, where he thought a "large force" of Indians still threatened the frontier.[27]

Black Kettle, fulfilling his earlier promise to William Bent, sought to bring peace between the Cheyennes and the whites. Late in August, 1864, the chiefs' council agreed to negotiate peace and sent One Eye and Minimic as messengers to Major Wynkoop and Indian Agent Colley. The chiefs admitted that their tribe was hostile and that they possessed seven white prisoners. The letter carried by One Eye and Minimic and written by George Bent for the chiefs contained two conditions: first, that the Cheyennes would exchange their prisoners for those Indians held by the whites; and, second, that peace would be restored not only with the Cheyennes but with all of the other Plains Indians. From the Cheyenne emissaries, Colley and Wynkoop learned that three Cheyenne and two Arapaho war parties were still out, but were expected back to the Indian camps on the headwaters of the Smoky Hill River where Cheyennes, Arapahoes, and Brulé and Oglala Sioux were living in large villages.[28]

[27] Curtis to Halleck, Curtis to Major S. S. Curtis, September 13, 1864, Curtis to J. D. Brumbaught, *et al.*, Ben Holliday [*sic*] to Curtis, Curtis to Holliday, September 23, 1864, Chivington to Curtis, September 13, 23, 1864, *O. R.*, I: Vol. 41, pt. 3, pp. 179–80, 181, 260, 294–95, 334–35.

[28] George Bent to Hyde, March 14, 1905, Western History Department, Denver Public Library; Denver *Rocky Mountain News*, September 28, 1864; Black Kettle and

Major Wynkoop immediately placed One Eye and Minimic in the guardhouse at Fort Lyon so that they would be available as guides to the Indian camps. Organizing 130 cavalry, supported by a section of artillery and with the messengers to guide the column, Wynkoop marched to the headwaters of the Smoky Hill River about 140 miles northeast of Fort Lyon. Confronted by a formidable array of six to eight hundred Cheyenne, Arapaho, and Sioux warriors, Wynkoop sent one of the messengers forward and asked for a council with the chiefs. Although Black Kettle and the other peace chiefs prevented the Dog Soldiers from beginning a fight with Wynkoop's column, they could not gain unanimous consent from the assembled tribes to terminate the war with the whites. The Major told the chiefs that he could not make a peace treaty, but that the delivery of their prisoners would lead to a meeting with Governor Evans and "peace with their white brothers." Wynkoop then retired with his men to a strong position twelve miles from the Indian villages and awaited the final decision of the councils. Within the time specified by Wynkoop, the Cheyennes and Arapahoes surrendered four of their seven prisoners: Laura Roper, Isabella Eubanks, and Ambrose Usher, seized on the Little Blue River, and Daniel Marble, captured on the South Platte, all of whom were young children. The other prisoners, the chiefs said, were not in the camps on the Smoky Hill, and they hoped these could be surrendered at a later date.[29]

Major Wynkoop was willing to make peace with the Indians. Taking a moderate position, the Major anticipated that the surrender of the prisoners would lead directly to the settlement of Indian troubles in Colorado territory. While Wynkoop was meeting the Indians and hoping for peace, Colonel Chivington was planning to strike the Smoky Hill villages. The Third Colorado Cavalry was fully recruited and organized, lacking only the necessary ordnance. To complete the preparation of the regiment for field action, Chiving-

other Chiefs to Colley, August 29, 1864, in *Report, Commissioner of Indian Affairs, 1864,* 233; Colley to Evans, September 4, 1864, Wynkoop to Tappan, September 18, 1864, *O. R.,* I: Vol. 41, pt. 3, pp. 195–96, 242–43.

[29] George Bent to Hyde, March 14, 1905, Western History Department, Denver Public Library; Denver *Rocky Mountain News,* September 21, 28, 1864; Wynkoop to Tappan, September 18, 1864; *O. R.,* I: Vol. 41, pt. 3, pp. 242–43; Edward W. Wynkoop, MSS Colorado History, 104–108, Colorado State Historical Society, Denver, Colorado.

"Prairie Indian Encampment." From a painting by John Mix Stanley. *Courtesy Detroit Institute of Arts.*

Camp Weld Conference, September 28, 1864, Denver. Kneeling, left to right: Major Edward W. Wynkoop, Lieutenant Silas Soule; seated, left to right: Neva (Arapaho), Bull Bear (Cheyenne), Black Kettle (Cheyenne), One Eye (Cheyenne), unidentified; standing, left to right: unidentified, unidentified, John Smith (interpreter), White Wolf (Kiowa?), Bosse (Cheyenne), last two men not identified. *Courtesy State Historical Society of Colorado.*

"The Indian Campaign—Prisoners Captured by General Custer." From a sketch by Theodore R. Davis, *Harper's Weekly,* December 26, 1868.

Captain J. W. Abert's sketch of Yellow Wolf, Cheyenne chief. From Abert's *Report* of 1846–47.

Captain J. W. Abert's sketch of The Bear Above and his wife. From
Abert's *Report* of 1846–47.

Council at Medicine Creek Lodge. From a sketch by J. Howland, *Harper's Weekly,* November 16, 1867.

Black Kettle, Cheyenne chief. *Courtesy Division of Manuscripts, University of Oklahoma Library.*

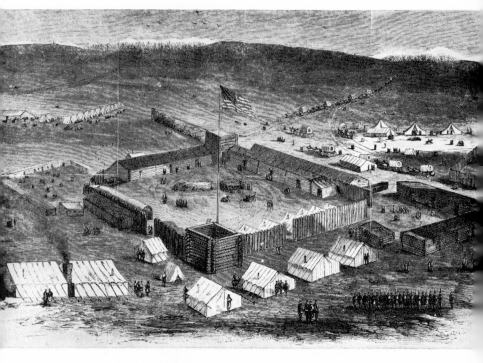

Camp Supply, Indian territory, about 1870. *Courtesy Denver Public Library, Western Collection.*

ton sought to divert guns and ammunition intended for the Department of New Mexico for use against "Indian warriors congregated eighty miles from Fort Lyon 3,000 strong."[30]

Major General Blunt, unaware that Wynkoop was working for peace, was in the field looking for hostiles. Blunt knew that his superior officer, Major General Curtis, believed that: "Before any peace can be granted the villains who have committed the crimes must be given up, and full indemnity in horses, ponies, and property must be granted as the Indians can indemnify. Something really damaging to them must be felt by them." Cheyenne chiefs led by Black Kettle, Bull Bear, and White Antelope, after the council with Wynkoop, traveled to either Fort Lyon or Fort Larned, where they received food for their people and assurances of peace. No longer fearing soldiers, the camps left the Smoky Hill River and moved closer to Fort Larned on the Pawnee Fork.[31]

Hearing of the large Indian concentration close at hand, Blunt led an expedition from Fort Larned. His advance party, early on the morning of September 25, 1864, discovered a warrior camp on Walnut Creek about ten miles below the main villages. Blunt immediately sent Major Scott J. Anthony forward with two companies of the First Colorado Cavalry. Before the detachment could attack the camp, strong parties of warriors surrounded Anthony's detachment. The cavalrymen panicked, and only the suggestion made by Fall Leaf, the Delaware chief and scout, that the troopers dig in saved Anthony's two companies.

Unaware that Anthony was in desperate trouble, Blunt continued to march northward with his main force. Before the troops came within earshot of the fighting, fifty Cheyenne warriors, under Standing-in-Water, rode up to Blunt's column and were permitted to ride with the troops. When Blunt and the Cheyennes came in view of Anthony's detachment holding off several hundred warriors, Standing-in-Water and his party quietly slipped away, and the General quickly relieved the beleaguered troopers. Seeing the large force of

[30] Wynkoop to Carleton, Chivington to Curtis, September 19, 1864, *O. R.,* I: Vol. 41, pt. 3, pp. 260, 261.

[31] George Bent to Hyde, April 13, 1913, Bent Letters, Coe Collection; Curtis to Blunt, September 22, 1864, *O. R.,* I: Vol. 41, pt. 3, pp. 314–15.

soldiers, the Cheyennes attacking Anthony fled, as did the main Indian camp. In the skirmish Anthony lost two men killed and seven wounded, while nine dead Indians remained on the field, and more, according to Blunt's report, were killed but carried away by their fellow warriors. Blunt's command pursued the Cheyenne and Arapaho camp, estimated at four thousand, of whom fifteen hundred were warriors, for several days without success as the Indians headed back to the Smoky Hill River.[32]

At Camp Weld, near Denver, on September 28, 1864, while Blunt was chasing the main villages, an important council took place. Major Wynkoop brought a delegation of seven chiefs, including Black Kettle, White Antelope, and Bull Bear of the Cheyennes, to meet the Colorado territorial officials. Governor Evans headed the delegation for the government, and with him were Colonel Chivington, Colonel George L. Shoup, Indian Agent Simeon Whitely, Major Wynkoop, and John S. Smith as interpreter. The Cheyenne and Arapaho chiefs did not deny that their tribes had engaged in hostilities during the spring and summer of 1864 and also admitted that two women and one infant were still prisoners in Cheyenne camps. Governor Evans also forced the chiefs to admit that they could not control their young warriors, but the chiefs promised to aid the army in bringing those members of their tribes who continued the struggle under control. The latter promise the chiefs interpreted as an agreement for peace with at least the repentent portions of the tribes. The leaders of the Cheyennes and Arapahoes did not understand Governor Evans' fine distinction that since he could not undertake a comprehensive peace pact, all bands of the tribes were to be considered at war with the United States Government.

Specific raids and fights were also discussed at Camp Weld. White Antelope denied that the Cheyennes initiated hostilities by attacking Lieutenant Dunn's troops at Frémont's Orchard. The young Cheyenne warriors, led by a great warrior, Fool Badger's son, were only trying to return two stray animals to their owners. The Hungate family was not killed by the Cheyennes but by a party of Arapahoes,

---

[32] George Bent to Hyde, January 29, 1913, Bent Letters, Coe Collection; Blunt to Charlot, September 29, 1864, *O. R.,* I; Vol. 41, pt. 1, p. 818; Grinnell, *Fighting Cheyennes,* 161–64.

under Friday, who were permitted to remain undisturbed on the Cache la Poudre. White Antelope acknowledged that his people did raid the trains west of Fort Kearny in August but did not directly acknowledge responsibility for the attacks along the Little Blue River. Not all of the Cheyennes were in agreement at Camp Weld, because Bull Bear, a Dog Soldier chief, near the end of the council proclaimed: "I am young and can fight. I have given my word to fight with the whites. My brother (Lean Bear) died in trying to keep peace with the whites. I am willing to die in the same way, and expect to do so."

Colonel Chivington spoke only as the council was concluding. His statement undoubtedly contributed to the Cheyennes' belief that they would not be disturbed if they placed themselves under the protection of Major Wynkoop. Chivington explained that although he was not "a big war chief," he commanded all the troops in the surrounding territory, and that his "rule of fighting white men or Indians is to fight them until they lay down their arms and submit to military authority. They [the Indians] are nearer to Major Wynkoop than any one else, and they can go to him when they get ready to do that." As had Evans', Chivington's contributions to the council clouded the meaning of the agreement. The officer perhaps meant that when all of the Cheyennes and Arapahoes laid down their arms— and not before—they would be considered at peace with the whites.[33]

Why did Governor Evans and Colonel Chivington refuse to accept the Indians' peace proposals at Camp Weld? Governor John Evans wanted a land cession from the Cheyennes and Arapahoes as much as he wanted peace. Clearing Indian title to Colorado territory would give additonal justification for the Republican political faction seeking statehood. John M. Chivington, the former Methodist minister lately turned soldier, and a man of political aspirations, knew the appeal of a successful Indian fighter at the frontier ballot box. Further, Chivington's political fortunes rested upon the success of the Evans' pro-statehood group.

Those who deny that Evans and Chivington acted with duplicity at Camp Weld shift the responsibility for subsequent events upon

---

[33] *Sand Creek Investigation*, 87–90; Denver, *Rocky Mountain News*, October 5, 1864.

Major General Curtis. As Major Wynkoop was bringing the Indian delegation to Camp Weld, Chivington telegraphed Curtis, informing him that the Third Colorado Cavalry was ready, but since winter was approaching, the Cheyennes and Arapahoes wanted peace. Curtis' reply to Chivington's request for orders was better than the Colorado official expected. No peace was the essence of Curtis' answering telegram. From the Indian delegation at Camp Weld, Curtis wanted the ringleaders of the raiders delivered up, full restitution of stock, and hostages. "I want no peace," wired Curtis:

> till the Indians suffer more. Left Hand is said to be a good chief of the Arapahoes, but Big Mouth is a rascal. I fear agent of Interior Department will be ready to make presents too soon. It is better to chastise before giving anything but a little to talk over. No peace must be made without my directions.[34]

Governor Evans treated the Camp Weld council as a discussion to determine the Indians' attitudes. Carefully, he wrote to Indian Agent Colley that the only band of Cheyennes and Arapahoes considered at peace with the United States were those under Friday camped on Cache la Poudre. Until peace was granted to the others by military authority, neither Evans nor the Indian agents could properly intervene in Indian affairs. Much the same point was made by Governor Evans concerning the proceedings at Camp Weld to Commissioner of Indian Affairs Dole. Since the Indians were considered to be in a state of war, Dole agreed that civil authority was temporarily in abeyance. The Washington official, however, reminded Evans that as superintendent of Indian affairs, "it is your duty to hold yourself in readiness to encourage and receive the first intimations of a desire on the part of the Indians for a permanent peace, and to co-operate with the military in securing a treaty of peace and amity." With thinly-veiled criticism, Dole concluded: "I cannot help believing that very much of the difficulty on the plains might have been avoided, if a spirit of conciliation had been exercised by the military and others."[35]

[34] Curtis to Chivington, September 28, 1864, *O. R.*, I: Vol. 41, pt. 3, p. 462.

[35] Chivington to Curtis, September 26, 1864, *O. R.*, I: Vol. 41, pt. 3, p. 399; Evans to Colley, September 29, 1864, Chever to Dole, September 29, 1864, Evans Collection;

The councils at Camp Weld did not terminate the skirmishes between the Cheyennes and the whites. During the second week of October, 1864, an Indian warrior in full paint and war dress was seen lurking about the Wisconsin ranch. A scout with the troops at Valley station volunteered to lead them to a camp of Indians at a spring about twelve miles from the post. Captain David H. Nichols, commanding officer of a detachment of the Third Colorado Cavalry at Valley station, decided to have a "little surprise party" for these Indians and quietly left his post with forty troopers and two guides. At dawn on October 10, the Indian camp, consisting of only two lodges occupied by six men, three women, and one fifteen-year-old boy, was found. The Indians were cut off from their horses and the volunteers "went for them in earnest, and in a very short time they raised the white flag but too late. They went under, one and all." In the lodges Captain Nichols found certification of the good character of the camp's leader, Big Wolf of the Cheyennes, a scalp and the bloodstained clothing of a white man, and freight bills taken on the Overland route. Chivington issued no reprimand to Nichols for killing the Indian women and affirmed his previous orders, instructing Nichols to: "Kill all the Indians you come across."[36]

Soon after the killing of Big Wolf, parties of Cheyennes were seen on the Platte road. On October 14, near Plum Creek station, forty Cheyennes, allegedly under White Antelope, attacked a small scouting detachment led by Captain Henry H. Ribble. Before the eight-man party could reach safety, the Indians killed two, wounded two, and killed most of the cavalry's horses. It is doubtful if White Antelope, a principal chief of the Cheyennes, led these forty warriors, because this chief was reportedly with Black Kettle at the time, leading a portion of the Cheyennes to Sand Creek. Other members of the tribe split away from Black Kettle after the three chiefs returned from Denver and took up their camps on the Solomon River. It is possible, therefore, that employees of the Overland Stage Company were justified in demanding that the army pursue the Indians "to their fastnesses, and slay without sparing all who can fight. A winter

Dole to Evans, October 15, 1864, in *Report, Commissioner of Indian Affairs, 1864*, 256.

[36] Nichols to Chivington, October 11, 1864, Chivington to Nichols, October 14, 1864, *O. R.*, I: Vol. 41, pt. 3, pp. 798–99, 876.

campaign well devised would utterly break their power and learn [*sic*] them to fear if not respect our Government."[37]

Assured by Major Wynkoop of protection, Black Kettle and White Antelope of the Cheyennes, with Left Hand of the Arapahoes, led their bands to Fort Lyon. In hopes of gaining approval of his action, Wynkoop justified his issuance of food and protection on the grounds that he would have the Indians under close surveillance and would be able to detect any evidence of hostility. Because of these unauthorized actions, Major Wynkoop was replaced by Major Scott J. Anthony as the commanding officer at Fort Lyon. In the orders directing him to his new station, Anthony was ordered to investigate "the unofficial rumors that reach headquarters that certain officers have issued stores, goods, or supplies to hostile Indians," in violation of orders from Major General Curtis. Major B. C. Henning, in command of the District of the Upper Arkansas, informed the new commander at Fort Lyon that Major General Curtis "will not permit or allow any agreement or treaty with the Indians without his approval . . . [or] allow any Indians to approach any post on any excuse whatever." Two days after Anthony received his orders transferring him from Fort Larned to Fort Lyon, Colonel Chivington moved the Third Colorado Cavalry to the Bijou Basin, about sixty miles east of Denver, in preparation for a move against the Cheyennes and Arapahoes.[38]

On November 2, Major Anthony assumed command of his new post. Nearby, Anthony found Left Hand, Little Raven, Neva, and other Arapaho chiefs with over 650 of their people. When these people surrendered their arms and captured stock to Anthony, he permitted them, as unarmed prisoners, to remain near the post. The Cheyennes, however, were not given the same privilege, because the major informed the Cheyenne leaders that he could not protect

[37] Captain W. W. Ivory to Lieutenant L. J. Boyer, October 14, 1864, Holladay to Curtis, October 1, 1864, B. M. Hughes to Curtis, October 10, 1864, *O. R.,* I: Vol. 41, pt. 1, pp. 841–42, 843ff., pt. 3, pp. 549–50, 768.

[38] *Massacre of Cheyenne Indians,* 15, 31, 82, 87; Annual Report of John Evans, Colorado Superintendency, *Report, Commissioner of Indian Affairs, 1864,* 222; Special Orders No. 4, Headquarters District of the Upper Arkansas, October 17, 1864; Henning to Anthony, October 17, 1864, Chivington to Wynkoop, October 16, 1864, *O. R.,* I: Vol. 41, pt. 4, pp. 62, 23; Denver *Rocky Mountain News,* October 19, 1864.

them if they continued to camp near Fort Lyon. Four days later
Black Kettle and eight other Cheyenne chiefs visited Major Anthony
and informed him that six hundred Cheyennes were camped thirty-
five miles to the northeast of Fort Lyon on Sand Creek and that a
much larger camp with two thousand of the tribe were seventy-five
miles from the post. In this interview, Major Anthony denied the
tribe asylum at Fort Lyon and suggested that they move to within
twenty-five miles of the fort, where they would be safe "until his
superior officers had indicated their plans." Anthony transmitted his
reports to Major General Curtis, and the latter officer made no change
in his standing orders.[39]

Without exception during mid-November, army officers advocated
a punitive campaign against the hostile elements of the Cheyennes.
Governor Evans left Denver on November 23 for the national capital
to seek more arms and troops to protect the lines of western communications. It is highly probable that Governor Evans was informed
by Colonel Chivington of the latter's determination to march against
the Cheyennes camped near Fort Lyon. Most significant is a letter
written by Major General Curtis to Major General Carleton a day
before the Sand Creek Massacre. From the letter's context, it is apparent that Chivington had not informed his superior military officer
of his intentions, and, just as important, Curtis recognized that some
of the Cheyennes and Arapahoes deserved protection from winter
campaigns. Curtis wrote: "They [the Cheyennes and Arapahoes]
insist on peace or absolute sacrifice, as I choose. Of course, they will
have to be received, but there still remains some of these tribes and
all of the Kiowas to attend to, and I have proposed a winter campaign for their benefit. This, if successful, must be secret and well
arranged beforehand." Three days after Chivington struck the Cheyennes at Sand Creek, Curtis still had no information from his district commander. Curtis continued to approve the withholding of a
treaty from all the Indians except those who were willing to surrender members of the tribe guilty of the depredations, along with

[39] Wynkoop MSS Colorado History, 111–12; George Bent to Hyde, April 17, 1905,
Western History Department, Denver Public Library; George Bent to Hyde, April 30,
1906, Bent Letters, Coe Collection; Anthony to AAAG., District of the Upper Arkansas,
November 6, 16, 1864, Henning to Anthony, November 5, 1864, *O. R.,* I: Vol. 41, pt.
I, pp. 912–15.

their arms and horses. At the proper time, Curtis informed Major Henning, a campaign would be undertaken against the hostiles, and to assure its success, the march of his troops would be masked from the view of the public. Curtis confessed to Governor Evans that he was "entirely undecided and uncertain as to what can be done with such nominal Indian prisoners," referring to the Cheyennes and Arapahoes who were trying to surrender at Fort Lyon. All that Curtis knew of Chivington's movements was that the latter was near Fort Lyon trying to find some Indians who recently had attacked a wagon train and that Chivington had his volunteer regiment with him.⁴⁰

The decision to attack the Cheyennes and Arapahoes near Fort Lyon must have been made early in November. During the first week of that month, Colonel George L. Shoup began collecting the regiment's scattered detachment, and on November 14 the Third Colorado Cavalry received marching orders. A week later the troops were concentrated at Camp Fillmore on the Arkansas River, where, on November 23, Chivington joined the regiment and assumed command—much to the dissatisfaction of many of the men. As Chivington's command marched down the Arkansas River, mail was detained; a guard was posted around Bent's ranch; and once Fort Lyon was reached, no one was permitted to leave the post. Later, when queried on these acts, Chivington replied that Curtis, Mitchell, and Blunt had failed in their campaigns because the Indians had been forewarned. At Fort Lyon, Major Anthony added 125 men from the post's garrison and approvingly stated: "I believe the Indians will be properly punished—what they have for some time deserved."⁴¹

At eight o'clock on the evening of November 28, Chivington moved his column out of Fort Lyon. The strength of the force numbered between 700 and 750 men, supported by four twelve-pound mountain howitzers. As guides Chivington took from Fort Lyon Jim Beck-

⁴⁰ Denver *Rocky Mountain News*, November 23, 1864; Henning to Charlot, November 19, 1864, Curtis to Evans, November 24, 1864, Curtis to Carleton, November 28, 1864, Curtis to Henning, December 2, 1864, Curtis to Evans, December 5, 1864, *O. R.* I: Vol. 41, pt. 4, pp. 621, 671–72, 709, 751, 771–72.

⁴¹ Major Hal Sayr, "Major Hal Sayr's Diary of the Sand Creek Campaign" *Colo. Magazine*, Vol. XV, No. 2 (March, 1938), 52–55; *Massacre of Cheyenne Indians*, 108; Chivington to Curtis, December 16, 1864, Anthony to Lieutenant A. Helliwell, November 28, 1864, *O. R.*, I: Vol. 41, pt. 1, p. 948, pt. 4, p. 708.

wourth and Robert Bent, the eldest son of William Bent and Owl Woman. When the cold proved more than Beckwourth could endure, Chivington forced Robert Bent to lead the troops to the Cheyenne village. By daylight on November 29, the troops were in position to attack.[42]

Chivington carefully deployed his troops before the signal to attack was given. The Third Colorado Cavalry was placed in the center and units of the First Colorado Cavalry on the flanks of the battle line. By surprise and superior valiance the cavalry swept through the village, forcing the Indians to regroup a mile above the encampment. Chivington conceded officially that the Indians "stubbornly contested every inch of ground" as they gathered, and in the fighting they were driven from one position to another for five miles, until they "finally abandoned resistance and dispersed in all direction, and were pursued by my troops until night fall." When the fighting ceased, Chivington estimated that five to six hundred Indians were killed on the battlefield, about the same number of animals captured, and the lodges with all equipment destroyed. These losses to the Indians Chivington contrasted to the ten dead and thirty-eight wounded troops. In justification of the attack, Chivington insisted that the worst of the Cheyennes were concentrated in the camp, since his troops found scalps of white men and women as well as clothing belonging to white people. "On every hand," Chivington confidently concluded, "the evidence was clear that no lick was struck amiss." Throughout his official reports and the subsequent investigation, Chivington continued to insist that the action was taken against a superior force of Indian warriors numbering never less than seven hundred braves. And the field commander of the troops always main-

42 George Bent to Hyde, March 9, 1905, Western History Department, Denver Public Library; *Sand Creek Investigation*, 95–96; J. P. Dunn, *Massacres of the Mountains, A History of the Indian Wars of the Far West*, 396; "Sayr's Diary," *loc. cit.*, 55. The exact number of troops with Chivington cannot be determined. Hubert Howe Bancroft (*History of Nevada, Colorado, and Wyoming*, 466 and 466–67n.) states that there were nine hundmen men in Chivington's command and relies upon a private letter, Colonel George L. Shoup to (?), December 3, 1864, in *Sand Creek Investigation*, 92, and the Denver *Rocky Mountain News*, December 14, 1864. In the three investigations of the Sand Creek Massacre, officers estimatel the strength of the force from seven hundred to one thousand men and officers. For Chivington's official statement, see Chivington to Curtis, December 16, 1864, *O. R.*, I: Vol. 41, pt. 1, p. 949.

tained that "I saw but one woman killed, and one who had hanged
herself; I saw no dead children." In his testimony Chivington asserted that when the attack was made on the Indian camp, the
greater number of women and children made their escape while
the warriors remained behind to fight.[43]

In many places, Chivington's official reports and statements are
erroneous. Both John S. Smith and Edmond G. Guerrier, for example,
from their own personal knowledge, later stated that the village
contained from eighty to one hundred lodges and about five hundred
people, two-thirds of whom were women and children. And Smith,
elaborating upon the fighting, believed that never more than sixty
warriors made any effort to resist the attack.[44]

Cheyennes at a later date also contributed information at variance
with Chivington's observations and testimony. At sunrise on November 29, some Indian women observed what they first thought was a
herd of buffalo moving toward their camp. When the figures became
discernible as men, the women awakened Edmond Guerrier and
told him that "there were a lot of soldiers coming." The Indians observed a detachment of troops swinging between the camp and the
horse herd; this was Captain Luther Wilson with 125 men sent by
Chivington to cut off the camp's ponies from the warriors. Their
mission accomplished, Wilson's men opened fire, and soon the main
body was raking the village with artillery and small-arms fire which
sounded to the Cheyennes like hail on the taut lodgeskins. At the
outset of the attack, Black Kettle raised both an American and a
white flag over his tipi as signs that the Indians were friendly, but
they were ignored completely.[45]

[43] Chivington to Curtis, Chivington to Editors [*Rocky Mountain News*], Chivington
to Curtis, November 29, December 16, 1864, *O. R.*, I: Vol. 41, pt. 1, pp. 948–51; *Massacre of Cheyenne Indians*, 102, 103.

[44] *Sand Creek Investigation*, 60, 65; *Massacre of Cheyenne Indians*, 6, 103; *Report of the Secretary of War*, Communicating, In compliance with a resolution of the
Senate of February 4, 1867, a copy of the evidence taken at Denver and Fort Lyon,
Colorato Territory, by a military commission, ordered to inquire into the Sand Creek
massacre, November, 1864, 39 Cong., 2 sess., *Sen. Exec. Doc. No. 26*, 69, 106 (here-
inafter cited as *Military Commission*).

[45] *Sand Creek Investigation*, 66, 67, 60; Denver *Rocky Mountain News*, December
14, 1864; George Bent to Hyde, April 14, 1906, Bent Letters, Coe Collection; George
Bent to Hyde, March 14, 1905, Western History Department, Denver Public Library.

Confused and not believing that the soldiers would press the attack further, the Indians concentrated near Black Kettle's lodge. When the troops continued their volleys into the milling crowd, the Indians began to scatter and run for cover. Black Kettle, his wife, and White Antelope remained until all hope that the attack would cease had ended; Black Kettle, followed by his wife, ran up the dry creek bed. The woman fell behind her husband, and the chief continued on until he joined a small group of warriors who had already dug rifle pits in the sandy stream's bottom. Surrounding the braves, the cavalry dismounted and closed upon the warriors. The combatants fought hand-to-hand with knives, clubbed rifles, and carbines. "The Indians," wrote Major Anthony two days after the conflict, "fought desperately, apparently resolved to die upon that ground, but to injure us as much as possible before being killed. We fought them for about six hours along the creek for five miles." Many of the warriors who fought in the rifle pits survived the combat, and as darkness came, they gathered with other survivors of the massacre in a ravine ten miles above their former village. Lightly clothed, without shelter, the wounded men and women gathered grass for fires to avoid freezing to death. Black Kettle went back in search of his wife, believing her dead; miraculously she still lived, despite her nine wounds. White Antelope, however, did not survive. As Black Kettle left, old White Antelope, seventy-five years old, began singing his death song:

> Nothing lives long
> Except the earth and the mountains,

until he was shot down, unresisting, by the soldiers. On the morning of November 30, the survivors of the Sand Creek Massacre slowly made their way to the Cheyenne village on the upper Smoky Hill River.[46]

Chivington grossly exaggerated the number of Indians killed by his volunteer troops. The Colonel persisted in stating that he left between four and six hundred Indians dead at Sand Creek. Edmond

[46] Report of Major Scott J. Anthony, December 1, 1864, Report of Colonel George L. Shoup, December 7, 1864, *O. R.*, I: Vol. 41, pt. 1, pp. 951, 956; Lorah to J. C. Anderson, December 1, 1864, in Denver *Rocky Mountain News*, December 14, 1864; George Bent to Hyde, April 14, 1906, Bent Letters, Coe Collection; Grinnell, *Fighting Cheyennes*, 177–80.

Guerrier, who was with the Indians both during the assault and for four weeks after, said that at the first counting there were 148 missing, about 60 men, the balance women and children. There are many other contemporary accounts taken from the battlefield and from the testimony of Indians at a later date. George Bent, twenty-five years after the tragedy, wrote to Samuel F. Tappan that 137 Indians, twenty-eight of whom were men, the rest women and children, were killed at Sand Creek. Ten men who participated in the fighting estimated the Indian deaths from 150 to 200.[47]

Does Colonel Chivington bear the responsibility for the mutilations and atrocities committed by his troops at Sand Creek? Chivington and other field commanders were under a general field order issued by Major General Curtis, which read in part: "Indians at war with us will be the object of our pursuit and destruction, but women and children must be spared." Defenders of Chivington's career deprecate and disavow statements attributed to him by his political opponents as malicious slander. At least four men, nevertheless, testified that Chivington wanted no prisoners and might have saved the women and children. Sam E. Browne, United States district attorney and a political opponent of Chivington, heard the Colonel exclaim during the public speech in Denver "kill and scalp all, little and big; . . . nits made lice." Before the troops left Fort Lyon, Lieutenant Joseph A. Cramer, First Colorado Cavalry, protested that an attack upon Black Kettle's village would be a betrayal of Major Wynkoop's and Major Anthony's pledges. In reply Chivington shouted: "Damn any man who sympathizes with the Indians," and that "he [Chivington] had come to kill all Indians, and believed it to be honorable to kill Indians under any and all circumstances." Old Jim Beckwourth heard Chivington exhort his men: "Men, strip for action. . . . I don't tell you to kill all ages and sex, but look back

[47] Chivington to Curtis, November 29, December 16, 1864, Anthony to Tappan, December 15, 1864, Wynkoop to Tappan, January 15, 1865, O. R., I: Vol. 41, pt. 1, pp. 948, 949, 954, 961; *Massacre of Cheyenne Indians*, 102–103; *Sand Creek Investigation*, 60, 66; George Bent to Samuel F. Tappan, March 15, 1889, MSS of the Colorado State Historical Society, Denver, Colorado; Anthony to [brother], December 30, 1864 (Copy), MSS of the Colorado State Historical Society, Denver, Colorado; Diary of Samuel F. Tappan, MSS, January 1, 1865 (Microfilm copy), Colorado State Historical Society, Denver, Colorado; *Military Commission*, 11.

on the plains of the Platte, where your mothers, fathers, brothers, and sisters have been slain, and their blood saturating the sands of the Platte." After the fight, Lieutenant Clark Dunn asked Chivington what disposition should be made of Jack Smith, mixed-blood son of Interpreter John S. Smith, and Chivington replied: "Don't ask me; you know my orders; I want no prisoners."[48]

There can be no doubt that troopers and officers of the Third Colorado Cavalry scalped and mutilated the corpses of the fallen Indians. One lieutenant was seen scalping successively three women and five children, after they had been captured and held as prisoners. Several officers of the First New Mexico Infantry agreed in essence with a deposition which related that "in going over the battle-ground the next day I did not see a body of a man, woman, or child but was scalped, and in many instances their bodies were mutilated in the most horrible manner." During the course of the subsequent inquiries, Chivington, personally confronting his accusers, could not shake witnesses from their testimony that soldiers had scalped and mutilated Indians. But, if no one testified that Chivington urged his men to commit these acts, neither is there evidence in the official transcripts to show that the commander attempted to check the bloody carnage.[49]

Information reaching the headquarters of Major General Curtis undoubtedly led him to believe that Indian traders and Chivington's

48 Major General S. R. Curtis, General Field Orders, No. 1, Headquarters, Department of Kansas, July 27, 1864, *O. R.*, I: Vol. 48, pt. 1, pp. 503–505; *Sand Creek Investigation*, 71, 74; *Military Commission*, 68–69, 47, 71. It seems incontestable that Jack Smith was captured and later killed (see George Shoup to Web [Shoup], December 1, 1864, in Denver *Rocky Mountain News*, December 14, 1864); George Bent to Hyde, March 9, 1905, Western History Department, Denver Public Library; *Massacre of Cheyenne Indians*, 10; *Military Commission*, 22, 71; Anthony to Tappan, December 15, 1864, *O. R.*, I: Vol. 41, pt. 1, p. 954.

49 Little Bear, a survivor of Sand Creek, told George Bent that most of the atrocities were committed just after the initial attack while the warriors were pinned down in the rifle pits in the stream bed of Sand Creek (see George Bent to Hyde, April 14, 1906, Bent Letters, Coe Collection). *Sand Creek Investigation*, 71; *Military Commission*, 23. It has often been asserted that Captain Silas S. Soule was assassinated for his testimony against Chivington, (see MSS Autobiography of Samuel F. Tappan, Kansas State Historical Society, Topeka, Kansas; Wynkoop MSS Colorado History, 114). For particularly reprehensible acts committed by the Colorado troops, see *Sand Creek Investigation*, 53ff.; Diary of S. F. Tappan, *loc. cit.*

political foes would utilize the Sand Creek Massacre to their advantage. Early in January, 1865, Curtis requested and received Chivington's resignation from the army. Curtis hoped that this action would head off discontent building up in the East and among the anti-statehood faction of Colorado territory. These efforts failed, and Major General Henry W. Halleck ordered Curtis to investigate Chivington's conduct, which had led to a "series of outrages" that contributed to general Indian hostilities. In his reply to Halleck's order, Curtis admitted that Chivington "may have transgressed my field orders . . . and otherwise acted very much against my views of propriety," but denied that Chivington's action increased Indian hostility on the Plains.[50]

Curtis was much more critical of Chivington in correspondence with Governor Evans. "I abominate the extermination of women and children," Curtis emphatically informed Evans. Still, as in the correspondence with Halleck, Curtis insisted that no matter how much Chivington had erred, his severity and lack of judgment had made no new Indian foes but, on the contrary, had reduced the number and badly frightened those who warred against the United States. To Evans, Curtis also admitted that "the popular cry of settlers and soldiers on the frontier favors an indiscriminate slaughter, which is very difficult to restrain. I abhor the style, but so it goes from Minnesota to Texas." Neither the military commission nor later congressional investigation treated Chivington so kindly, and the weight of historical judgment has heaped opprobrium upon the action of Chivington and his Colorado volunteers.[51]

Flushed with success after his punishing attack at Sand Creek, Chivington anticipated further actions against the Cheyennes and Arapahoes immediately. As it was, Chivington had already killed nine Cheyenne chiefs, the most prominent of whom were White Antelope, War Bonnet, and old Yellow Wolf, in addition to Left Hand, an Arapaho chief. Some of Chivington's subordinates, such as Major Anthony, desired to follow up the first attack and strike

[50] J. M. Chivington, General Orders No. 1, Headquarters, District of Colorado, January 4, 1865, Halleck to Curtis, January 11, 1865, Curtis to Halleck, January 12, 1865, O. R., I: Vol. 48, pt. 1, pp. 416, 489, 502–503.

[51] Curtis to Evans, January 12, 1865, O. R., I: Vol. 48, pt. 1, pp. 503–505.

either the larger Cheyenne village on the Smoky Hill or Little Raven's Arapahoes, who were heading for the Pawnee Fork. Anthony rejected as utterly false Chivington's contentions that the heavy snow and the exhausted condition of his command's horses prevented any more active campaigning. "The massacre," wrote a disappointed Anthony, "was a terrible one and such a one as each of the hostile tribes on the plains richly deserve. I think one such visitation to each hostile tribe would fovever put an end to Indian war on the plains, and I regret exceedingly that this punishment could not have fallen upon some other band." Chivington's one-hundred-days' men, however, had served their enlistment and were marched to Denver, where they were received joyously by a grateful citizenry. The war did not cease, and Major Anthony's judgment that the "road and settlements above us are in worse condition than before the arrival of Colonel Chivington's command" was only too correct.[52]

---

[52] Chivington to Curtis, November 29, 1864, Report of Major Anthony, December 1, 1864, Anthony to Tappan, December 15, 1864, *O. R.*, I: Vol. 41, pt. 1, 948, 952, 954; "Sayr's Diary," *loc. cit.*, 56; Grinnell, *Fighting Cheyennes,* 173; Anthony to [brother], December 23, 30, 1864 (Copies), MSS of the Colorado State Historical Society, Denver, Colorado.

# 10

## REPRISAL AND PEACE

THE SURVIVORS OF the Sand Creek Massacre fled to join their kinsmen on the Smoky Hill River. Practically the whole of the Southern Cheyenne tribe was in these camps, re-enforced by the Dog Soldier band. Runners were quickly sent to their allies, Spotted Tail's and Pawnee Killer's people of the Sioux and the Northern Arapahoes. Even those Cheyennes previously friendly to the whites now thirsted for white blood and vengeance. Temporarily Black Kettle was shoved aside by the Cheyennes, and his place as chief was given to Leg-in-the-Water and Little Robe, a son of the Cheyenne chief of the same name killed by Chivington's men. Black Kettle, however, also wanted war, and he was absent from the camps seeking war pledges from the half-blood Cheyennes and Sioux. Soon the Sioux, Northern Arapahoes, and Cheyennes were camping together on the Republican River. Army officers estimated that by late December, 1864, two thousand warriors were concentrated in these villages, and they braced themselves for vigorous attacks along the overland routes.[1]

Old Jim Beckwourth tried to make peace with the Cheyennes. His efforts were rejected by the tribe when Leg-in-the-Water replied for his people:

> But what do we have to live for? The white man has taken our country, killed our game; was not satisfied with that, but killed our wives and children. Now no peace. . . . We have now raised the battle-axe until death.[2]

By the time Beckwourth reached the Cheyennes, they and their allies

[1] George Bent to Hyde, January 12, 1906, Bent Letters, Coe Collection; Anthony to [his brother], December 30, 1864, MSS of the Colorado State Historical Society; Henning to Tappan, December 14, 22, 1864, *O. R.*, I: Vol. 41, pt. 4, pp. 862, 919.
[2] *Military Commission,* 73–74.

had already committed their retaliatory raids on the Platte road.

The Sand Creek Massacre drove the Arkansas River and Dog Soldier bands into a union closer than any obtained for several decades. For about twenty years the Dog Soldiers, led by Tall Bull, White Horse, and Bull Bear, had ranged between the Platte and Republican rivers, rarely visiting the Arkansas River. Consisting of one hundred lodges and representing about five hundred people, the Dog Soldiers traded with such men as Elbridge Gerry and tried to persuade Black Kettle's people to join them in moving back to their old lands north of the Platte. Sometimes the Dog Soldiers threatened to use force to make the Arkansas River bands join them, but the threats were never carried out. Now the other Cheyennes were determined to fight, even though they were aware that extermination could follow.[3]

From George Bent and Edmond Guerrier came some information concerning the Cheyennes' plans. Small parties of warriors from the combined villages scouted the country to determine if the army planned a campaign against them and if troops were in the field. Only Little Raven's Arapahoes remained apart from the hostiles as the councils decided on a war greater in extent than in 1864, and as the tribes prepared a large store of food for their people to use while the warriors carried their forays to the whites.[4]

Once the war councils were concluded, nothing was left to chance. Small raiding parties were prohibited, the camps were controlled by the soldier societies, and the movement of the camps was well disciplined. Unobserved, the great villages moved close to the South Platte, and on January 6, 1865, more than a thousand warriors of the combined tribes were ready to wipe out the garrison at Fort Rankin and the stage station at Julesburg. As a decoy a smaller party of warriors attacked a train near Valley station, the fourth post west of Julesburg, and killed a dozen men.[5]

[3] *Military Commission*, 102ff.

[4] Livingston to Charlot, January 2, 1865, *O. R.*, I: Vol. 48, pt. 1, pp. 398–400; Grinnell, *Fighting Cheyennes*, 181–82.

[5] Fort Rankin became Fort Sedgwick after September, 1865. George Bent to Hyde, May 3, 1905, MSS of the Colorado State Historical Society; Moonlight to Curtis, January 7, 1865, *O. R.*, I: Vol. 48, pt. 1, pp. 23–24; Denver *Rocky Mountain News*, January 11, 1865.

The sand hills flanking the flat bottom land of the South Platte shielded the massed warriors from the view of the troops at Fort Rankin and the inhabitants of Julesburg. The Indians hoped to decoy Fort Rankin's garrison into the sand hills by a ruse, then surround and annihilate them. Big Crow, a chief of the Cheyenne Crooked Lance society, selected ten warriors and slipped quietly down to the fort before daybreak. At dawn Big Crow and the warriors rushed a couple of sentinels outside the fort's walls. The trick worked. Captain Nicholas J. O'Brien dashed out of the fort with his cavalry and a few civilians in pursuit of the mounted Indians.

As a precaution the soldier societies held their massed warriors in a single column waiting for Big Crow and his party to accomplish this mission. Once the younger warriors caught sight of Captain O'Brien and his cavalry chasing Big Crow's party, nothing could restrain the young men, who whipped their ponies and charged into the flats. Seeing the Indians surging from the sand hills, Captain O'Brien wheeled his men around and made for the fort; before the troops could reach it, the warriors on the fastest ponies, led by Big Crow, were upon the cavalry, some of whom dismounted to fight. The troops on foot were quickly overrun and the remainder of the cavalry soon surrounded by the thousand Indian warriors, who killed all but fourteen to eighteen of O'Brien's sixty men. Once inside the stockade, the rest of the garrison and the survivors prepared for defense, but the Indians had no stomach for a frontal assault on the small post. Inside the walls of Fort Rankin were the maintenance men, the freight warehouse employees, and the passengers of the early morning stage from Julesburg. The victorious warriors charged one mile up the South Platte to Julesburg, where they looted with abandon, seizing whatever took their fancy.[6]

The Indians carried away load after load of plunder on their ponies from Julesburg. Howitzer shots from Fort Rankin did not disturb them as they piled the sacked food and provisions on their horses; not knowing what to do with canned goods, they left those articles on the warehouse shelves. One of the passengers of the morning stage

[6] George Bent to Hyde, April 24, 1905, Western History Department, Denver Public Library; Ware, *Indian War of 1864*, 448, 450; Curtis to Halleck, January 9, 10, 1865, *O. R.*, I: Vol. 48, pt. 17, pp. 1, 23, 486.

had been an army paymaster on his way to pay the troops stationed in Colorado territory. The officer abandoned his strongbox in his haste to reach Fort Rankin, and the payroll was found by the Indians. One warrior gleefully chopped up bundles of the "green paper" and scattered the currency into the wind. Not George Bent; he carried away as much money as his pockets could hold. After taking possession of as much loot as possible, the Indians moved off and gathered on Frenchman Creek, where Beckwourth found them sometime between January 9 and 12, 1865.[7]

Little information arrived from Captain O'Brien at Omaha, for he reported only that he had just been in a "desperate fight" with Indians. Hastily Brigadier General Mitchell left his headquarters at Omaha and began to move troops into the danger spot. Because there were not enough troops under Major General Curtis' command to open the Platte route, soon neither freight nor mail was arriving in or departing from Denver. Colonel Moonlight, commanding the District of Colorado, was forced to "submit to the howl and sneer of parties who cannot believe but that I ought to start after the savages with nothing more than my headquarters outfit."[8]

Large war parties of warriors continued to scour the road for unwary travelers and unprotected settlers. In raids after January 14, 1865, Indians burned all the ranches and stations west of Fort Rankin for eighty miles. Riding in parties up to five hundred strong, the warriors seized fifteen hundred cattle and killed eight people, including one woman and two children at Wisconsin Ranch, fifty-six miles west of Fort Rankin. The small detachments of cavalry at Valley station, Junction station, and Fort Rankin risked their lives when they ventured from their stockades, and were powerless to do more than escort refugees from the Indians to safety at their posts.[9]

After several weeks of raiding, the Indians held another council.

---

[7] George Bent to Hyde, May 3, 1906, Bent Letters, Coe Collection; *Military Commission,* 72.

[8] O'Brien's telegram dated January 8, 1865, is transmitted in Mitchell to Curtis, January 8, 1865, Moonlight to Lieutenant W. R. Newkirk, January 9, 1865, Moonlight to Charlot, January 11, 1865, *O. R.,* I: Vol. 48, pt. 1, pp. 463, 470, 490–92.

[9] Lieutenant J. J. Kennedy to Moonlight, January 16, 17, 29, 1865, Lieutenant Albert Walter to Moonlight, February 1, 1865, Livingston to Pratt, February 5, 1865, *O. R.,* I: Vol. 48, pt. 1, pp. 40–44.

The overwhelming majority of the Cheyennes and their allies decided to continue fighting and planned to move their villages north, out of range of troops certain to take to the field against them. Evidently Black Kettle, with about eighty lodges of Cheyennes, had had enough revenge and plunder and decided not to accompany the main body. Black Kettle soon led his people south of the Arkansas River and joined the Kiowas, Comanches, and Little Raven's Arapahoes. The Cheyennes, Sioux, and Arapahoes from the north moved their camps from Frenchman Creek and re-established their village on the South Platte River, opposite and between Fort Rankin and Valley station. On January 28, 1865, the Cheyennes enveloped the road west of Julesburg; the Sioux took the road east of the station; and the Arapahoes concentrated their activities near Julesburg itself. Few stations or settlers were left when the Indians completed this foray. Before the Indians left the South Platte, they decided to make one more swing over the road. One thousand warriors, on February 2, moved down the South Platte to Julesburg where the buildings were burned, 3,500 sacks of corn were destroyed or carried away, and several thousand dollars of provisions and other stores were seized. This attack alone cost Ben Holladay's company over $115,000, and the single cavalry company at Fort Rankin dared not leave the stockade while the Indians were present in such overwhelming numbers.[10]

The victories and plunder eased the stinging memory of Sand Creek. Fresh meat from the whites' cattle herds fed the camps; the people ate flour, corn meal, hams, bacon, dried fruit, and molasses from Julesburg; and the warriors dressed themselves and their families from the clothing and materials taken from the freighting station and the captured trains. George Bent was constantly asked the use of unfamiliar items by the curious tribesmen. The evening after Julesburg was burned, the warriors held their last victory dance on the South Platte, in full view of the soldiers and civilians huddled together in Fort Rankin. Telegraph poles were cut down by the warriors for their fires, and throughout the night Lieutenant Eugene F. Ware observed the Indian braves "circling around the fire, then

---

[10] George Bent to Hyde, May 3, 1905, MSS of the Colorado State Historical Society; Grinnell, *Fighting Cheyennes*, 188–93; Root and Connelley, *Overland Stage*, 360–61; *Sand Creek Investigation*, 94; George Bent to Hyde, January 12, 1906, Bent Letters, Coe Collection.

separately stamping the ground and making gestures . . . , and finally it was a perfect pandemonium lit up with the wildfire of burning telegraph poles. We knew the bottled liquors destined for Denver were beginning to get in their work and a perfect orgy was ensuing."[11]

The chiefs and soldiers decided to move north. On the day of the burning of Julesburg, the camps began shifting to Lodgepole Creek where they were joined by the warriors. No permanent camps were pitched since the tribes intended to keep traveling until the Tongue River country was reached. On the road between the North and South Platte rivers, there was only one station—Mud Springs—which consisted of a stage station, a telegraph office, and a small detachment of troops. When Indian scouts appeared on February 4, the telegraph operator immediately wired for aid from Fort Laramie and Camp Mitchell.[12]

Relief troops were quickly despatched from Fort Laramie. A hard twelve-hour ride brought Lieutenant William Ellsworth and thirty-six men of the Eleventh Ohio Cavalry to Mud Springs. Together with the ten whites already there, the cavalry barricaded themselves inside the building and held off the Indians. They gained a respite when they released their horses from the corral, and, as hoped, the Indians turned to rounding up the scattered stock and rejoined their camps on Rush Creek. Lieutenant Colonel William O. Collins, the commanding officer at Fort Laramie, realized that the small detachment under Lieutenant Ellsworth could do little in checking the Indians' plundering. Collins, therefore, led 120 men from his post toward Mud Springs on the evening of February 4. Dissatisfied with the slow march of the cavalry, Collins picked twenty-five of his best mounted men and rode more rapidly to the relief of the beleaguered station. The main body of troops arrived at Mud Springs on the morning of February 6, and as soon as the cavalry straggled in, Indian warriors tried to cut them off, beginning a six-hour skirmish. Neither the Indians nor the cavalry desired to risk a charge, so the combatants deployed themselves in the ravines and rocks, firing as targets appeared. Shooting blind from behind their cover, the Indians rained

11 Ware, *Indian War of 1864*, 512–13.

12 Mud Springs is now a station on the Chicago, Burlington, and Quincy Railroad near present Simla, Morrill County, Nebraska.

arrows upon the troopers and their horses, wounding a few. Lieutenant Colonel Collins reported that it was necessary for his men to fight by taking cover "under banks and creep to favorable position, watch for an Indian's head, shoot the moment it was shown, and pop down at the flash of his gun. . . . It was common to see a soldier and an Indian playing bo-peep in this manner for a half hour at a time." Although the Indians held a superiority of five to one, they could not maintain their position on the high ground near the station when charged by Collins' command. During the early afternoon of February 6, the Indians began withdrawing into the hills, having wounded seven men while suffering four times as many casualties.

Scouts sent out the next morning found the deserted camps on Rush Creek. These villages, Collins reported, covered several miles, and here the Indians had slaughtered over one hundred cattle and had left behind debris of empty oyster, meat, and fruit cans. Evidently Collins' appearance had caused the camp to move before it was ready, because quantities of meat drying on racks and skins pegged down preliminary to tanning were left behind on the ground. Trailing the Indians was easy as Collins followed with his troops. Opposite the mouth of Rush Creek on the North Platte, the Indians re-established their camps, hoping to rest their people and ponies. But on the following morning, February 8, a mounted warrior sentinel signaled from a bluff south of the camps: "Enemies. Across the river."

From a high hill overlooking the Platte Valley, George Bent saw Collins' white-topped wagons moving slowly across the flat river bottoms. Four cavalry companies were escorting the wagons, "and toward this train the Indians were hurrying, looking like little black ants, crawling across the river on the ice." Collins overestimated the attacking force of warriors, thinking that more than two thousand foes swarmed out of the hills to meet his one hundred and fifty men. The troopers dug in hastily and fought from cover except for one charge to dislodge some braves on a nearby hill. In this foray, two troopers were killed and one of the corpses was later found with ninety-seven arrows protruding from it. Indecisive fighting continued until sundown, but the Indians returned the next morning in far less numbers to delay the troops until their families had time to move their camps. In the two engagements, Collins lost two killed, sixteen wounded, and ten men disabled from frostbite, while he estimated Indian casualties from 100 to 150. George Bent remembered that only two Indians were killed and two others wounded. Vastly outnumbered, Collins wisely decided to return to Fort Laramie and offer no further resistance to the Indians' northward trek.

The Cheyennes, Sioux, and Northern Arapahoes moved leisurely toward the Black Hills, stopping to hunt on the Niobrara and White rivers. When the northern edge of the Black Hills was reached, the Brulés under Spotted Tail and Pawnee Killer moved farther to the east; the Northern Arapahoes went to the Tongue River; and somewhat later the Southern Cheyennes joined the Oglala Sioux and Northern Cheyennes on the Powder River.[13]

Indian scouts confirmed in late February that the Indians had reached their northern hunting grounds. The Cheyennes in particular still thirsted for more white blood, and when warm weather came, they intended "to clean the country" of whites. A woman captive, after her freedom had been purchased from the Indians, told the officers at Fort Kearny that the hostile tribes intended to leave their families on the Powder River, and then the warriors were "determined to make war to the knife."[14]

Reorganization of army commands brought Major General John Pope to the Military Division of the Missouri and Major General Grenville M. Dodge to the Department of the Missouri. To these officers was assigned the task of protecting the western roads along the Platte and Arkansas rivers. As they assumed their commands, a new factor entered into Plains Indian policy. Congress, in 1862 and 1864, had granted charters to the Union Pacific Railroad for the construction of a railroad across the Plains. Secretary of the Interior Jacob P. Usher, looking forward, saw that railroad construction would require "the removal of Indians who inhabit the valleys of the Platte and Republican Rivers." To protect the surveying and construction

[13] George Bent to Hyde, May 3, 1905, MSS of the Colorado State Historical Society; George Bent to Hyde, May 4, 1906, Bent Letters, Coe Collection; Collins to Pratt, February 15, 1865, *O. R.*, I; Vol. 48, pt. 1, pp. 92–98; Grinnell, *Fighting Cheyennes*, 193–203.

[14] Mitchell to Dodge, February 28, March 6, 1865, *O. R.*, I: Vol. 47, pt. 1, pp. 1014–15, 1105.

parties, Usher recommended abolishing the Upper Platte Agency and prohibiting the Indians from inhabiting much of the Central Plains.[15]

Soon words and not bullets were flying as Indian Agent Jesse Leavenworth tried to protect the Indians of the Upper Arkansas Agency from more army attacks. From his headquarters at Fort Larned, Leavenworth insisted that every Cheyenne and Arapaho chief who had held out for peace had been killed by Chivington. He was confident that if the army committed no more "outrages on these Indians, I can give peace to the frontier at once [and] . . . save millions to the government."[16]

The army officers were unimpressed by Leavenworth's pleas and assertions. Late in January, 1865, Brigadier General Mitchell scoured the upper reaches of the Republican Valley for Indians and found none. Although intelligence was available that the Cheyennes and their allies had left for the Black Hills or Powder River country, Major General Dodge thought that some of the hostiles were still living between the Arkansas and Platte rivers and ordered Colonel James H. Ford to move against those Indians. Dodge believed that the Indians should be punished but not in the manner as at Sand Creek. He therefore instructed Ford to capture the women and children and concluded: "I do not consider such fights as Chivington's to be of any benefit in quelling Indian disturbances or of any credit to our service."[17]

An Indian council led Leavenworth to maintain that the southern frontier of Kansas and the Santa Fe route were safe from all Indian tribes except the Cheyennes. Leavenworth's plea for co-operation from the army officers was transmitted to Secretary of War Edwin M. Stanton, who contended that "the military have no authority to treat with the Indians. Their duty is to make them keep the peace by punishing them for hostilities." Free to act, Major General Dodge sent remounts for Ford's cavalry and distributed companies of the Second United States Volunteers, recruited from Confederate pris-

[15] Usher to Stanton, January 12, 1865, *O. R.*, I: Vol. 48, pt. 1, 498–99.

[16] Leavenworth to Dole, January 9, 19, 1865, Upper Arkansas Agency, Letters Received; *Report, Commissioner of Indian Affairs, 1865*, 387–88.

[17] Curtis to Evans, January 30, 1865, Dodge to Pope, February 9, 1865, Dodge to Ford, February 15, 1865, *O. R.*, I: Vol. 48, pt. 1, pp. 687, 793–94, 862–63.

oners at Rock Island, Illinois, who preferred active service to imprisonment, among the frontier posts so that more Federal troops could be made available for field duty.[18]

Colonel Ford kept strong scouting parties out from his posts in the District of the Upper Arkansas and found no concentration of Indians, but only fresh signs of roving warrior parties between the Platte and Arkansas rivers. Rejecting Leavenworth's hope for a cessation of hostilities, Ford suggested: "One good thrashing will gain a peace that will last forever." Unless the Indians were severely chastised, the Colonel insisted, "they will be as proud, defiant, and troublesome as though they were the victors," and he suggested that no more presents be given to the Indians because: "Everything that is done to ameliorate their condition only prolongs the war. Every blanket given them is only aiding and encouraging them to commit further depredations." Ford's attitude matched those of his superiors. Major General Dodge planned to send eight hundred to one thousand cavalry against any Indians found on the frontier along the Santa Fe road.[19]

Failing to obtain satisfactory cooperation from either Pope or Dodge, Leavenworth hastened to Washington. Accompanied by Senator James R. Doolittle of Wisconsin, Leavenworth visited Major General Halleck, army chief of staff, to press his case for peace with the Indians of his agency. No such promise could be extracted from Halleck, who only required of Major General Pope that: "None but officers of good judgment and discretion should be allowed to command any expedition into the Indian country." Throughout the period of March to early May, 1865, the contest between Agent Leavenworth and army officers continued. The military commanders feared to send their troops against the Indians because of the indecision of their superiors in Washington and because Leavenworth's peace efforts seemed capable of success.[20]

18 Ford to Dodge, February 20, 21, 1865, Halleck to Dodge, February 23, 1865, Dodge to Ford, February 23, 1865, *O. R.,* I: Vol. 48, pt. 1, pp. 923, 926, 960, 961.

19 Ford to AAG., Department of the Missouri, February 28, 1865, Ford to Dodge, March 3, 1865, Dodge to Carleton, March 3, 1865, *O. R.,* I: Vol. 48, pt. 1, pp. 1011–12, 1082, 1096–97.

20 Leavenworth to Dole, May 6, 1865, Upper Arkansas Agency, Letters Received; Halleck to Pope, March 13, 1865, Pope to Halleck, April 20, 1865, *O. R.,* I: Vol. 48, pt. 1, p. 1162, pt. 2, p. 141.

Late in April, 1865, Indians identified by Leavenworth as Cheyennes and Sioux raided the Cow Creek station on the Santa Fe road, driving off the stock. Almost immediately Secretary of War Stanton and Secretary of the Interior Usher released Pope and Dodge from their indecision. Stanton informed Pope that Leavenworth had no authority to make any treaty with the Indians and stated that there was no reason why Dodge should not proceed vigorously with his long-delayed campaign. Colonel Ford assembled his troops hastily and informed Leavenworth that his orders contained instructions "to pay no attention to any peace movements or proposition."[21]

Before Ford's command could take the field, another obstacle prevented an Indian campaign. President Andrew Johnson authorized Senator Doolittle's congressional committee to act as a commission to make a treaty of peace with the hostile Indians, subject to presidential approval. In the spring of 1865, few Cheyennes were on the Southern Plains, and they were those bands attached to Black Kettle. Unaware that the President had approved a peace treaty with the Indians of his agency, Leavenworth, nevertheless, continued to seek information on the temper of his wards. Leavenworth sent George Ransom, his Negro servant, from Council Grove to the North Canadian River. Upon Ransom's return the Indian agent learned that the Indians were watching carefully for troop movements and were holding a vast encampment at Fort Cobb on the Washita River. In this meeting, attended by Kiowas, Comanches, Kiowa-Apaches, Arapahoes, and Cheyennes, only the latter desired to continue hostilities.[22]

After a week on the Plains, the congressional committee thoroughly agreed with Leavenworth that peace was not only possible but necessary. The committee also entertained the hope that the five tribes of the Upper Arkansas Agency would accept a reservation south of

[21] Leavenworth to Dodge, April 26, 1865, Pope to Dodge, enclosing telegram Stanton to Pope, April 29, 1865, *O. R.*, I: Vol. 48, pt. 2, pp. 217, 243–44; AAAG., District of the Upper Arkansas to Leavenworth, May 6, 1865, *Report, Commissioner of Indian Affairs, 1865*, 389–90.

[22] Senators James R. Doolittle (Wisconsin), L. S. Foster (Connecticut), and E. G. Ross (Kansas) of the Joint Special Committee of Congress were assigned the duty of investigating Indian affairs on the Plains (see *Sand Creek Investigation*, 1); Doolittle to the President of the United States, May 27, 1865, in *Report, Commissioner of Indian Affairs, 1865*, 391; Stanton to Doolittle, May 29, 1865, Leavenworth to Ford, May 30, 1865, *O. R.*, I: Vol. 48, pt. 2, pp. 669, 687–88.

the Arkansas River and east of Fort Bascom. Major General Alexander McD. McCook, assigned by Pope to accompany the senators and congressmen, also suspended Ford's campaign because of insufficient troops and the likelihood that an attack would result in a general Indian war. When Dodge learned of McCook's order, he asked Pope for additional instructions. Pope evaded the issue by stating that McCook did not have authority to interfere in troop movements and told Dodge that he "must do as you think best about Ford."[23]

Dodge, after consulting with Ford, thought it wise to delay the movement of the troops. For the time being, Dodge conceded that it was better to wait until the congressional committee had failed or succeeded. The senators, however, were embarrassed while waiting at Fort Lyon for confirmation of their treaty powers by an Indian attack on Fort Dodge and murders along the Santa Fe road. For some reason the senators had not yet received the presidential authorization for the treaty and sent a telegram seeking confirmation. Secretary of War Stanton again sent the authorization and explained that the President and the War Department were anxious to avoid Indian hostilities, establish peaceful relations with the Indians, and secure protection for frontier citizens.[24]

After waiting ten days for the congressional committee to achieve some tangible results, Major General Dodge began again to criticize any peace policy not based upon punishment for the tribes' past actions. Dodge wanted to push his cavalry into the heart of the Indian country, force the hostiles to respect the power of the government, and make them sue for peace. "Any treaty," wrote Dodge on June 17, 1865, "made now by civilians, Indian agents, or others will, in my opinion, amount to nothing, as the Indians in all the tribes openly express dissatisfaction with them and contempt for them." Both Pope and Dodge saw to the heart of the problem; a lack of harmonious action between the Departments of War and Interior "establishes conflict of authority, alarms and confuses the people to be protected against

---

23 McCook to Pope, McCook to Ford, May 31, 1865, Dodge to Pope, Pope to Dodge, June 3, 1865, *O. R.,* I: Vol. 48, pt. 2, pp. 707–708, 754.

24 Dodge to Pope, June 8, 1865, *O. R.,* I: Vol. 48, pt. 2, pp. 820–21; Doolittle, Foster, and Ross to Andrew Johnson, June 11, 1865, Stanton to Doolittle, June 15, 1865, in *Report, Commissioner of Indian Affairs, 1865,* 392.

the Indians, and puts in the popular mind two of the great administrative Departments of the government in opposition to each other in matters of common public interest."[25]

While Senator Doolittle and his colleagues were at Old Bent's Fort, Indians began a series of attacks. On June 8, 1865, and also a few days later, Indian horse raiders ran off all but eight of the animals from the post herd of Fort Dodge. At Cow Creek the day after the first raid on Fort Dodge, one hundred warriors besieged four wagon trains on the Santa Fe road, and, on June 11, perhaps the same body of warriors chased Lieutenant R. W. Jenkins and a small escort into Fort Zarah. On the latter date, two military messengers riding between Forts Zarah and Larned were scalped and mutilated by warriors. Army scouts and traders pointed out that these depredations and raids were committed by Indians living south of the Arkansas River, since their trails did not lead toward the Smoky Hill or Republican rivers. In spite of these hostilities, Doolittle and his committee insisted that it was their duty "to pacify this country . . . , and we must succeed; we know it is more just, more honorable, more humane, and vastly more economical to make peace with all the tribes." The almost daily skirmishes between the Indians and Colonel Ford's troops added substance to the belief of Dodge and Pope that nothing less than a thorough punishment of the Indians would bring peace.[26]

Following these raids, Major General Dodge pleaded for permission to use his troops. He pointed out to Secretary of the Interior Harlan that when Leavenworth first attempted to find his charges, "they robbed him, stole his mules, and he hardly escaped with his scalp." Dodge asserted that he had then been ready to punish the Indians, but the congressional committee had checked his preparations. Less than two weeks after Senator Doolittle left Fort Larned, the Indians were back on the attack, raiding "posts and trains all along the line, running off stock, capturing trains, &c., murdering

[25] Dodge to Pope, June 17, 1865, Pope to Harlan, June 19, 1865, O. R., I: Vol. 48, pt. 2, pp. 911–12, 933–35.

[26] Ford to Dodge, June 12, 14, 1865, Major W. F. Armstrong to Tappan, Jenkins to Captain Elisha Hammer, Hammer to Tappan, Captain Theodore Conkey to Tappan, June 12, 1865, Willans to Dodge, June 17, 1865, O. R., I: Vol. 48, pt. 1, pp. 308–309, 312, 313–14, 315–16, pt. 2, p. 914; Doolittle to Leavenworth, June 12, 1865, in Report, Commissioner of Indian Affairs, 1865, 393.

men, and showing conclusively that they were determined on war
at all hazards." Injustices to the Indians were recognized by Dodge,
who felt that another contributing factor to the troubles was the
doubtful character of the Indian agents; most of them the General
believed to be swindlers. Although Dodge did not accuse Leavenworth of being corrupt, he noted that the Indian agent had been
dismissed from the army, and: "He 'blows hot and cold' with singular
grace. To my officers he talks war to the knife, to Senator Doolittle
and others he talks of peace. Indeed he is all things to all men." Dodge
also informed Harlan that he had ordered his field commanders to
obtain an informal cessation of hostilities if possible, but that he was
utterly opposed to any permanent peace treaty until the Indians had
paid for the outrages committed in their raids.[27]

Indian Agent Leavenworth kept in touch with the Indians of his
agency largely through traders. Of the tribes within his jurisdiction,
Leavenworth insisted, only the Cheyennes and Arapahoes desired to
continue the war. In an effort to gain additional information, Leavenworth sent Jesse Chisholm to the Indians, and Chisholm requested
that Colonel Ford not send troops south of the Arkansas as such an
act would endanger Chisholm's life. Major General Dodge disregarded Chisholm's request and ordered the new commanding
officer of the District of the Upper Arkansas River, Major General
John B. Sanborn, to send a column into the Southern Plains. "The
place," Dodge told the Secretary of the Interior, "to make treaty is
down in the heart of their country where we can dictate the terms;
not they in our country."[28]

The struggle by Dodge to punish the Indians met still another
roadblock. The troops could not move immediately because of inadequate supplies and provisions. Before the troops could move, Senator
Doolittle had visited with Kit Carson and William Bent in New
Mexico territory. These two veterans of the Indian trade told Doolittle
that, if authorized, they could make peace with the Indians of
Leavenworth's agency. William Bent stated that he would guarantee

[27] Dodge to Harlan, June 22, 1865, *O. R.*, I: Vol. 48, pt. 2, pp. 971–74.
[28] Leavenworth to Ford, June 27, 1865, H. J. Tibbitts to Ford, June 28, 1865, Sanborn to Dodge, July 12, 1865, Dodge to Sanborn, July 13, 1865, Dodge to Harlan,
Dodge to Sanborn, July 13, 1865, *O. R.*, I: Vol. 48, pt. 2, pp. 1009, 1021, 1074, 1076,
1075–76.

the peace "with his head." Senator Doolittle asked members of the Cabinet to suspend all army operations until Bent and Carson had an opportunity to treat with the Indians.[29]

While Doolittle's letter was in transit, four Kiowa men and four women arrived at Leavenworth's headquarters at the mouth of the Little Arkansas River, purporting to be a delegation from the Indians of the Upper Arkansas Agency. They pledged that the five tribes would discontinue all hostilities, remove from the Santa Fe road, and allow all travelers and wagon trains to move unmolested. Sanborn offered the opinion that his troop movement should not take place while the conversations were in progress; Dodge, however, reacted differently. Immediately, the commanding officer of the Department of the Missouri sent Leavenworth an extract of Secretary of the Interior Harlan's July 11, 1865, letter which "suspended all intercourse" between the Indians and their agents unless sanctioned by appropriate army officers. Sanborn could merely implement his superior's attitude and informed Leavenworth that the interview with the Kiowas would have to be terminated immediately, "unless there is a moral certainty that it will result in a peace with these tribes honorable to the government and advantageous to the tribes themselves."[30]

Major General Dodge did not want to grant the Indians a respite. "Every day is now precious," he told Sanborn, who was now to push his troops into the Indian country as soon as possible. Sanborn was not empowered to make a formal treaty once in the Indian country and was instructed only to negotiate a cessation of hostilities, leaving the permanent treaty to an authorized peace commission. Leavenworth's insistence that a peace was possible without the use of troops did not impress Dodge, who ordered Sanborn to continue his preparations for an expedition. Dodge justified his stand because he had "no faith in their [the Indians] continual application for peace. It has been this way for three months, and they continue to rob and steal." To Sanborn, Dodge outlined his conditions for the cessation of hostilities. The Indians must "deliver up the stolen Government stock

[29] Doolittle to Secretary of State William H. Seward and Stanton, July 18, 1865, O. R., I: Vol. 48, pt. 2, p. 1094.

[30] Sanborn to Dodge, Sanborn to Leavenworth, July 22, 1865, O. R., I: Vol. 48, pt. 2 pp. 1115–16.

and property, . . . control their entire tribes, keep off our lines of communication, and desist entirely from any and every act of hostility."[31]

Major General Pope vacillated as Dodge and Sanborn completed their gathering of supplies and troops. On July 28, 1865, Pope wrote to Dodge, "A permanent settlement of Indian difficulties is what we want," and ordered that Sanborn contact the Indians so that peace commissioners could be on hand. Dodge explained to Pope that it would take ten days to contact Sanborn and said: "I put no faith in any treaty made with these Indians until they are whipped and made to give up stolen stock. It appears to me a treaty is a bid for them to commence again as soon as we take our troops off." Pope's replying telegram approved Dodge's position and concluded that Sanborn was not to be held back. Six days later, on August 4, Pope reversed his position and ordered Sanborn to suspend all movements against the Indians of the Upper Arkansas Agency and arrange for a peace treaty with the Indians.[32]

Through friendly Wichita and Caddo Indians, Agent Leavenworth finally persuaded Indians of his agency to meet him at the mouth of the Little Arkansas River. On August 2, 1865, Dohasan of the Kiowas and Poor Bear of the Kiowa-Apaches, accompanied by seventy-five of their people, arrived at Leavenworth's camps and told the Indian agent that more of the tribes were on the way. From a Cheyenne woman living with the Kiowas, Leavenworth confirmed his feeling that it would be difficult to persuade the Cheyennes to accept peace. Leavenworth assured the Indians that no attack would take place upon them until they had an opportunity to talk with Sanborn. More Indians continued to gather at the mouth of the Little Arkansas as Jesse Chisholm brought in the Comanches. When Major General Sanborn arrived at Leavenworth's quarters on August 15, 1865, no Cheyennes were present. By the terms of the truce, the Kiowas, Comanches, and Kiowa-Apaches pledged themselves to refrain from all "violence or injury to the frontier settlements, and to travellers on the Santa Fe road, or to other lines of travel, and to

31 Dodge to Sanborn, July 24, 27, 1865, *O. R.,* I: Vol. 48, pt. 2, p. 1117, pt. 1, p. 360.

32 Pope to Dodge, July 28, 29, 1865, Dodge to Pope, July 29, 1865, Pope to Sanborn, August 4, 1865, *O. R.,* I: Vol. 48, pt. 1, pp. 360–61.

remain at peace." Big Mouth of the Arapahoes also signed the truce agreement, but was uncertain whether the Cheyenne and Arapaho bands on the Platte would come south even after they heard that a truce had been signed. The signators of the truce agreed to use all of their influence upon those Cheyennes living south of the Arkansas River to persuade them to join in the cessation of hostilities. It was also agreed that the tribes and treaty commissioners would meet on October 4, 1865, on Bluff Creek, a tributary of the Salt Fork of the Arkansas River, to sign a permanent peace treaty.[33]

Black Kettle, Little Robe, Storm, and Little Raven of the Cheyennes and Arapahoes did not participate in the first truce parley. On August 16 those chiefs, with their bands, visited the Cow Creek station and, upon learning of the truce negotiations, joined Leavenworth and Sanborn at the mouth of the Little Arkansas. There, on August 18, Little Robe, Black Kettle, three other Cheyenne leaders, and some Arapaho chiefs agreed to a truce somewhat different than that signed by the other three tribes. As signers of the truce on the part of the United States government, Leavenworth and Sanborn implicitly recognized that the Sand Creek Massacre was the cause of Cheyenne and Arapaho hostilities. The chiefs signing the document stated that they hoped to restore peace between their bands and the government and, if possible, include their whole tribes under the terms of the truce. Finally, Black Kettle, Little Robe, and the other Cheyennes and Arapahoes indicated their willingness to meet at Bluff Creek with the peace commissioners.[34]

Preparations for the treaty councils began immediately after the truce was signed. Major General Pope recommended to Secretary of the Interior Harlan that Kit Carson and William Bent were indispensable for the success of the treaty, and Major General Dodge suggested that his subordinate, Major General Sanborn, represent the military arm of the government among the commissioners. Dodge was pessimistic; he saw no chance for a lasting peace unless the

[33] Leavenworth to Sanborn, August 4, 10, 1865, Sanborn to Dodge, August 17, 1865, *O. R.*, I: Vol. 48, pt. 2, pp. 1164, 1176, pt. 1, pp. 362–63; *Report, Commissioner of Indian Affairs, 1865*, 394–95.

[34] "Treaty with Arrappahoes and Cheyennes," dated August 18, 1865, enclosed with Leavenworth to Doolittle, August 23, 1865, Scott J. Anthony Manuscripts, Colorado State Historical Society; *Report, Commissioner of Indian Affairs, 1865*, 395.

Indians were protected from their agents and traders—and then only if the Indians agreed upon the free, unmolested transit of goods and people over the Arkansas, Platte, and new Smoky Hill routes. The Smoky Hill road was suggested by D. A. Butterfield, and over it Butterfield's Overland Despatch line went into operation between Leavenworth and Denver in September, 1865. Later, when the hostile Cheyenne bands came south, the road would become a bitter bone of contention because it extended through the heart of the Cheyenne buffalo range north of the Arkansas River.[35]

The full treaty commission, gathered at the mouth of the Little Arkansas River, consisted of Major General Sanborn, president of the treaty commissioners, Major General W. S. Harney, Kit Carson, William Bent, Indian Agent Leavenworth, James Steele, representing the Bureau of Indian Affairs, and Superintendent Thomas Murphy of the Central Superintendency. It was deemed inadvisable to meet the Indians at Bluff Creek as originally planned, so runners were sent to bring the Indians to the Arkansas River. The council was delayed nearly a week while the Indians traveled to the treaty grounds near present Wichita, Kansas. By the evening of October 11, 1865, the Cheyennes and Arapahoes who were living on the Southern Plains had arrived to begin their discussions with Sanborn and the other commissioners.[36]

Previously, William Bent had insisted that no war with the Arkansas Indians was necessary. To Senator Doolittle's committee Bent had testified: "If the matter were left to me I would guarantee with my life that in three months I could have all the Indians along the Arkansas at peace, without the expense of war." Bent also recommended a new reservation between the Smoky Hill and Republican rivers for the Cheyennes and Arapahoes; this proposal was rendered impractical by the establishment of the Butterfield Overland Despatch route. Any reservation for the Indians of the Upper Arkansas Agency now would have to be located south of the Arkansas River and away

35 Pope to Harlan, August 21, 1865, in *Report, Commissioner of Indian Affairs, 1865*, 396; Dodge to Sanborn, in Dodge to Major George C. Tichenor, August 24, 1865, Dodge to Pope, August 24, 1865, *O. R.*, I: Vol. 48, pt. 1, pp. 363–64, pt. 2, p. 1208; Hafen, *Overland Mail*, 282–83.

36 Samuel A. Kingman, "Diary of Samuel A. Kingman at Indian Treaty of 1865," KHQ, Vol. I, No. 5 (November, 1932), 445.

from the rich buffalo lands between the Platte and Arkansas rivers.[37]

Major General Sanborn opened the talks with the Cheyennes and Arapahoes in a conciliatory tone. He conceded that the Cheyennes and Arapahoes, by the actions of Chivington, had been "forced to make war." For the suffering of the two tribes, the government was willing to make a restitution of property and to bestow lands upon the chiefs and those survivors of Chivington's massacre who had either parents or husbands killed. Both Black Kettle and Little Raven, Cheyenne and Arapaho spokesmen, commented quickly that they doubted the wisdom of making a treaty either ceding or accepting land when so few of their people were present. In the case of the Cheyennes, Black Kettle stated that only eighty lodges of the tribe were present, while about two hundred lodges normally associated with the Arkansas River and Dog Soldier bands were absent and living north of the Platte River. Sanborn and Leavenworth, however, overcame these objections by telling the tribes that only those bands actually represented were bound by the treaty, and those absent could assent to the treaty at any time within the next five months.

Black Kettle's speech to the commissioners reflected both a desire for peace and a fear of the white man's armies. "Your young soldiers," Black Kettle told the commissioners, "I don't think they listen to you. You bring presents, and when I come to get them I am afraid they will strike me before I get away. When I come in to receive presents I take them up crying." The Cheyenne chief also asked that honest agents be sent among them, that traders be restored to the tribe, and that the Cheyennes and Arapahoes be permitted to hunt buffalo north of the Arkansas River. Undoubtedly, William Bent's presence and request that the Cheyennes and Araphoes sign whatever proposition the commissioners offered led to their accepting the treaty, for on October 14, 1865, Black Kettle and six other leaders from his band placed their marks upon the Treaty of the Little Arkansas.

The treaty established peace between the United States and the two tribes and provided for mutual redress of injuries done either to Indians or United States citizens. Although the southern boundary for the new Cheyenne and Arapaho reservation was ambiguous, the commissioners meant that the reservation began at the mouth of the

[37] *Sand Creek Investigation*, 95.

Cimarron River on the Arkansas River, went up that stream to a point opposite Buffalo Creek, then north to the Arkansas River, and down that river to the confluence of the Cimarron and Arkansas rivers. After title held by other Indian tribes was cleared from this land, the Cheyennes would receive $40.00 per capita when established on the reservation and $20.00 before their occupation for a period of time not to exceed forty years. One half-section of land was granted to each Cheyenne signator on the reservation, and 160 acres of land were granted to those survivors of Sand Creek who had suffered the loss of husbands or parents. These lands were protected for alienation for a period of fifty years. Thirty-one mixed-bloods among the Cheyennes and Arapahoes were each granted a section of land in the old Fort Wise Treaty reservation in Colorado territory. The Cheyennes and Arapahoes, signing the treaty, ceded to the United States all other lands claimed by their tribes and retained only the right to that range between the Arkansas and Platte rivers unoccupied by white settlers.

The treaty's sixth article repudiated "the gross and wanton outrages" of Chivington's massacre and explained the unusually liberal terms of the document for the Cheyennes and Arapahoes. Those bands agreeing to the treaty were also required to use their "utmost endeavor" to persuade the unrepresented bands to accept the provisions of the treaty. Three days after the Cheyennes and Arapahoes signed the papers, an amendment was added which declared the Cheyennes, Arapahoes, and Kiowa-Apaches to be confederated tribes for purposes agreed upon in the original document.[38]

To prevent any violation of the treaty by army units, William Bent, upon the request of the Cheyennes and Arapahoes, was permitted to spend the winter in their camps. General Pope ordered all officers in his divisional jurisdiction to take cognizance of Bent's advice. If they acted to the contrary for any reason, Pope ordered that an immediate and full statement of facts be sent to his headquarters.[39]

Peace was restored by this treaty to only a small fraction of the

[38] The proceedings of the councils are printed in *Report, Commissioner of Indian Affairs, 1865*, 517–27; Kappler (ed.), *Laws and Treaties*, II, 887–89.

[39] Pope to William Bent, October 30, 1865, Department of Missouri, Letters Sent, United States Army Commands, Records of the War Department, National Archives, Washington, D. C. (hereafter cited as Department of the Missouri, Letters Sent).

Cheyennes. To make it effective, the hostiles still north of the Platte River had to be persuaded to sign and recognize its provisions. There was little chance that the Treaty of the Little Arkansas would end the Indian wars on the Southern and Central Plains. Prophetically, Samuel Kingman, a secretary at the treaty councils, wrote after leaving Bent and Carson: "Their fate as com[missione]rs will be that they died of too large views."[40]

[40] Kingman, "Diary," *loc. cit.,* 450.

# 11

## THE HOSTILES COME SOUTH

THE TREATY OF THE LITTLE ARKANSAS was signed, but peace was still only a hope. None of the two hundred lodges of Arkansas River and Dog Soldier bands north of the Platte demonstrated any willingness to forget the Sand Creek Massacre. Isolated from Black Kettle's band and their agents, they did not participate in or even know the terms of the truce and treaty signed by their fellow tribesmen in the fall of 1865.

Hostile Cheyennes undoubtedly were among the small parties of warriors who harassed army posts and animal herds during the months of March and April, 1865. These attacks spanned the distance from the Platte Bridge, on the upper North Platte River, to Fort Rice, on the Missouri River in Dakota territory. Both Major General Alfred Sully and Brigadier General P. Edward Connor were convinced that the Cheyennes were the prime instigators of the widespread depredations. From Little Thunder, a Brulé chief who surrendered with sixty lodges of his people by mid-April, 1865, Brigadier General Connor learned that the Cheyennes were among the Sioux north of the Black Hills, "trying to induce the Sioux in that country to join them in a war against the whites, and that they [the Cheyennes] are determined to continue their hostility."[1]

Major General Pope hoped to send two strong expeditions against the Cheyennes and their allies. He planned for Major General Sully, moving west from Fort Pierre and Brigadier General Connor, marching north from Fort Laramie, to invade the heart of the hostiles' buffalo range and force them to sue for peace. From scouts and

[1] Mitchell to Dodge, March 10, 1865, Colonel C. A. R. Dimon to Major DeWitt C. Cram, Sully to AAG., Division of the Missouri, May 13, 1865, Connor to Dodge, April 14, 1865, *O. R.*, I: Vol. 48, pt. 1, pp. 1143, 208–209, pt. 2, pp. 434–35.

Indians surrendering at army posts, Pope and his field commanders tried to keep informed on the location of the bands carrying on the raids. Their villages, Colonel Thomas Moonlight stated, were on the Wind and Bighorn rivers, from which the Cheyennes were raiding as far west as South Pass. With unwarranted optimism Major General Pope anticipated that only the Cheyennes would remain at war during the summer of 1865 and commented, "With them we can easily deal."[2]

Although the army officers chose the wrong locations for the Cheyennes, Major General Pope and other officers were correct in predicting that the tribe would continue to exact more vengeance for the Sand Creek Massacre. During the early months of 1865, the Cheyennes camped and hunted buffalo on the Powder and Little Powder rivers and later moved to the Tongue River in the foothills of the Big Horn Mountains. There, in May, the chiefs held war councils with their northern kinsmen and Oglala Sioux. The chiefs conveyed their decisions to the soldier societies, permitting them to raid in small parties and setting June as the beginning of a large movement against the Platte road.[3]

On May 3, 1865, Colonel Moonlight began a two-week scout to find the Cheyennes' camps or to intercept the raiding warriors. With five hundred cavalrymen, and guided by Old Jim Bridger, Moonlight's command made a wide arc between Fort Laramie and the Platte Bridge, touching the Powder and Wind rivers. Neither Bridger's Indian lore nor a march of 140 miles in a four-day period brought Moonlight any results; no warriors or Cheyenne camps were found. On May 13, while Moonlight was on his scout, troops near Julesburg fought Indians for six hours, but the warriors escaped into the sand hills. Then within five days after Moonlight returned to Fort Laramie, the whole route west of the post was infested by parties of warriors. Five hundred braves, on May 22, tore down the telegraph line paralleling the Sweetwater River, and, less than a week later, large war parties began a series of raids at the Sweetwater Bridge and St.

[2] Pope to Connor, April 28, 1865, Pope to Grant, May 18, 1865, *O. R.,* I: Vol. 48, pt. 2, pp. 237–38, 492–94.

[3] George Bent to Hyde, October 12, 1905, Western History Department, Denver Public Library; George Bent to Hyde, May 11, 1906, Bent Letters, Coe Collection.

Mary's stations, routing the troop detachment at the latter post on May 27, and destroying four hundred yards of telegraph line.[4]

Continuing the attacks, a party of one hundred warriors descended upon the Platte Bridge station on June 3. When the warriors opened fire on the station from cover across the North Platte, Lieutenant Colonel Preston B. Plumb, later United States senator from Kansas, hearing the rifle shots, selected ten troopers from his command at Camp Dodge and ten from Platte Bridge to drive the Indians away. A running fight ensued during which a party of sixty warriors dashed from concealment to cut off the detachment's stragglers. Re-enforcements from the posts appeared, and the Indians wheeled and scattered. Smaller groups of troopers took up the chase, some of them in turn cut off by Indians still lurking in the ravines. Two soldiers were killed—one of them scalped—before the cavalrymen could fight and ride their way out of the traps. During the engagement one Indian was killed, and six others were wounded.[5]

These encounters were undertaken by warriors without controlling directions from the chiefs' councils. As the warrior parties returned to their villages, the chiefs ordered no more war parties to leave the camps, and hunting was restricted. The Crazy Dogs of the Northern Cheyennes were appointed as tribal police to enforce the decision of the intertribal war council. The Cheyennes dismantled the Medicine Arrow and Buffalo Hat lodges; the medicine men renewed the protective powers of the warriors' medicine bundles; the soldier societies held their war dances; and the tribes moved toward the appointed rendezvous on Crazy Woman's Creek. The Cheyennes in particular boasted that the failure of Major General Sully to fight them was caused by his fear of their bravery.[6]

For a period of six weeks the Cheyennes, Sioux, and Arapahoes committed no new depredations. During the lull the Indians, numbering about three thousand warriors, held their final war councils in the hills north of the North Platte River and decided to attack the

[4] Moonlight to Price, June 6, 1865, Lieutenant Martin B. Cutler to Lieutenant Eugene S. Sheffield, May 18, 1865, Dodge to Pope, May 22, 1865, Lieutenant H. C. Bretney to Moonlight, June [?], 1865, *O. R.* I: Vol. 48, pt. 1, pp. 255–56, 269–70, pt. 2, p. 544, pt. 1, p. 294.

[5] Plumb to Taber, June 4, 1865, *O. R.*, I: Vol. 48, pt. 1, pp. 305–306.

[6] George Bent to Hyde, May 15, 1906, Bent Letters, Coe Collection.

Platte Bridge post in strength. The post, however, was protected by a fourteen-foot pine log stockade, in which were stationed 120 troopers of the Eleventh Kansas Cavalry under Major Martin Anderson. Storming a stockade with so many troops inside was not in the Indians' minds a likely way to take scalps. Major Anderson and his men were fully aware of the large concentration of warriors lurking in the hills and exercised great care not to be taken by surprise. Early on the morning of July 25, 1865, a group of warriors unsuccessfully attempted to stampede the post's horse herd. When an effort to lure the troops from the stockade also failed, the younger warriors became impatient.[7]

On the following morning, news arrived at the Platte Bridge that a small army wagon train was coming in from the Sweetwater Bridge station. Lieutenant Caspar Collins of the Eleventh Ohio Cavalry volunteered to lead twenty-five men to escort the train to safety. Two other officers with forty men stationed themselves near the bridge to hold it open for Collins and the wagons. As Collins and his small detachment rode toward the wagon train, six hundred Cheyennes swarmed from the sand hills on the left and front; three times that number of Sioux charged from the ravines on the right; and two hundred Arapahoes attempted to seize the bridge. Seeing that it was impossible to reach the wagon train, which had reached a point about three miles west of the bridge, Collins ordered his men to retreat, and twenty of the detachment reached the bridge safely.[8]

Lieutenant Collins and the wagoners were not so fortunate. Riding a spirited horse that bolted toward the charging warriors, the young officer was observed being carried by his runaway mount, with an arrow protruding from his forehead, through the ranks of the Indian warriors. Sergeant Amos J. Custard of the Eleventh Kansas Cavalry, in charge of the wagon train, sent five of his men forward to the Platte Bridge, three of whom survived the Indian gauntlet, made a corral of his wagons, and tried to hold off the Indians. Some accounts state that the men in the wagon train fought for five hours;

[7] S. H. Fairfield, "The Eleventh Kansas Regiment at Platte Bridge," Kansas *HC*, VIII, 356–57; Grinnell, *Fighting Cheyennes*, 222–23.

[8] Agnes Wright Spring, *Caspar Collins: The Life and Exploits of an Indian Fighter of the Sixties*, 81–87; Fairfield, "Eleventh Kansas at Platte Bridge," *loc. cit.*, 357–58.

others note that the fighting lasted only an hour. Two more soldiers were killed when a party from the Platte Bridge post tried to repair the telegraph line connecting the outpost to the east. In all, the Indians killed twenty-nine soldiers, including Lieutenant Collins, and captured 250 mules.[9]

When re-enforcements arrived on July 27 from Deer Creek station, thirty-five miles to the east of Platte Bridge, Major Anderson sent out parties to bring in the bodies of those killed by the Indians. The body of Lieutenant Collins was found about one-half mile beyond the bridge with his "arms bound to his body by telegraph wire, his hands and feet cut off, his tongue and heart cut out, and otherwise horribly mutilated." At the wagon train, those who died with Sergeant Custard were "lying upon their faces, their bodies pinioned to the ground with long spears. They had been stripped and cut up in a shocking manner. The wagoner was strapped to his feed-box, and hot irons from the hubs of the wagon-wheels were placed along his back, apparently when he was alive. . . ." The Indians, however, apparently considered the fight no victory, because they threw away the soldiers' scalps as they left the battlefield, indicating that they had lost more warriors than enemies killed. Before withdrawing completely from the Overland road, the Indians killed seventeen travelers and captured a teen-age girl and a two-year-old female child.[10]

Even before these raids occurred, Brigadier General Connor was determined to launch a campaign against the hostiles. He expressed his opinion to Major General Dodge early in July, 1865, that none of the warlike Indians were to be trusted: "They must be hunted like wolves." And, to Colonel Nelson Cole, who would later lead a column of troops into the hostiles' country, Connor wrote that his subordinate would "not . . . receive overtures of peace or submission from Indians, but [you] will attack and kill every male Indian over twelve years of age." Plagued by lack of horses and supplies, Connor

---

9 George Bent to Hyde, May 3, 10, 1905, MSS of the Colorado State Historical Society, Denver, Colorado; George Bent to Hyde, May 22, 1906, Bent letters, Coe Collection; Connor to Major J. W. Barnes, July 27, 1865, *O. R.,* I: Vol. 48, pt. 1, p. 357; Spring, *Collins,* 89, 94–95.

10 Fairfield, "Eleventh Kansas at Platte Bridge," *loc. cit.,* 359–60; Spring, *Collins,* 93–94; Price to Dodge, August 8, 1865, *O. R.,* I: Vol. 48, pt. 1, p. 358; Denver *Rocky Mountain News,* August 10, 16, 1865.

could not complete the preparations until after the Indians had struck. Toward the end of July, about three thousand men were assembled at Fort Laramie and at Omaha, Nebraska territory. With these troops it was planned that Connor would command one column and march north from Fort Laramie to the Tongue River. A second column, under Lieutenant Colonel Samuel Walker, was directed to proceed north from Fort Laramie, skirt the western edge of the Black Hills, and join Connor's column on the Tongue River. The third wing of the expedition, consisting of 1,400 men under Colonel Nelson Cole, was ordered to move from Omaha to the Loup Fork of the Platte, then circle the Black Hills along their eastern and northern fringes, and cross the Little and Big Powder rivers to the Tongue River.[11]

On July 30, 1865, Brigadier Connor's column marched out of Fort Laramie. With his troops went Jim Bridger, Nicholas Janisse, and other traders as guides and a company of Pawnee Scouts commanded by Captain Frank J. North. The Powder River was reached on August 11, and four days later, at the juncture of the Bozeman Trail and Powder River, a post was constructed on that stream and named Camp Connor, later to be the site of Fort Reno. Columns of smoke from an Indian village were seen in the distance, and scouting parties reported Indian signs along the Powder River.[12]

On August 16 a detachment of the Pawnee Scouts accompanied by Captain North and a few other officers discovered the trail of a war party returning from the North Platte. The Pawnees followed the trail for a day and came within striking range of the Cheyennes. The Indian scouts, riding "like mad devils, dropping their blankets behind them, and all useless paraphernalia, rushed into the fight half naked, whooping and yelling, shooting, howling. Some twenty-four scalps were taken. . . . There was a squaw with the party; she was scalped and killed with the rest." Returning to Camp Connor, the Pawnees rode in triumph and waved the bloody scalps of their enemies from the ends of scalp poles. In addition to the Cheyennes' horses, the Pawnees recovered government animals and plunder from the Chey-

11 Connor to Dodge, Connor to Cole, July 3, 4, 1865, Cole to Grant, February 10, 1867, *O. R.*, I: Vol. 48, pt. 1, pp. 1045, 1049, 366–80; H. E. Palmer, "History of the Powder River Indian Expedition of 1865," NSHS *Transactions and Reports*, II, 203.

12 Price to Dodge, August 8, 1865, *O. R.*, I: Vol. 48, pt. 1, p. 358; Palmer, "Powder River Expedition," *loc. cit.*, 205–208.

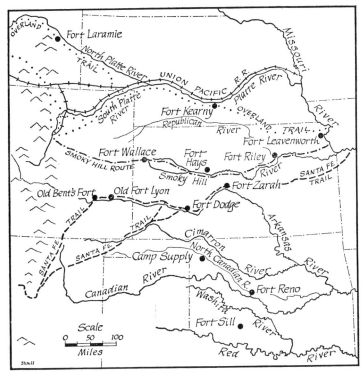

Emigrant Routes and Army Posts

ennes' recent raids along the North Platte. Contrary to the statements that all the Cheyennes were "rubbed out" by the Pawnees, the Cheyennes remembered that they lost only five warriors.[13]

The Pawnee Scouts patrolled the Powder River and found one well-defined trail used by many warrior parties returning from the North Platte. Along this trail the Pawnees and soldiers had several skirmishes with the Cheyennes and warriors from other tribes. Captain North narrowly escaped death one day when he was jumped by a small party of Cheyennes. Another skirmish resulted in the death of a brave old Cheyenne warrior identified as Red Bull by Nick Janisse. Cut off from his comrades by North's Pawnees, Red

[13] Palmer, "Powder River Expedition," *loc. cit.*, 208; Connor to Dodge, August 19, 1865, *O. R.*, I: Vol. 48, pt. 1, p. 358; Grinnell, *Two Great Scouts*, 92; George Bent to Hyde, July [?], 1906, Bent Letters, Coe Collection.

Bull held the Pawnees off with only his bow and arrows until they were exhausted. Although North admired the courage of the old warrior, he ordered his scouts to kill Red Bull.[14]

Operating in advance of the supply base at Camp Connor, Captain North sought additional troops because Cheyennes seemed to be plentiful in the vicinity. Six companies of the Sixth Michigan Cavalry under Colonel James H. Kidd were sent forward by Connor. These troops, however, were in a surly mood and previously had threatened mutiny and injury to their officers, blaming them for their continuation on active service. The Pawnees carefully watched the Cheyenne camps and directed the Michigan troops to warrior concentrations. A small patrol under Lieutenant James Murie was sent ahead of the main detachment and succeeded in keeping the Cheyennes under observation. Dangerously exposed, Lieutenant Murie waited in vain till dusk for the other troops to appear, finally, under the cover of darkness, riding back to Camp Connor, where the column's commanding officer charged Colonel Kidd with cowardice. Brigadier General Connor reasoned that the Indians were fully aware of his troops and were no longer concentrated within striking distance of Camp Connor. Leaving behind the unruly Sixth Michigan and the supply train, Connor decided to push ahead with the major portion of his command and track down the Cheyenne, Sioux, and Arapaho villages thought to be located either lower on the Powder or west on the Tongue.[15]

Brigadier General Connor's column moved out of Camp Connor on August 22, 1865, and traveled north until a large Indian trail was found leading westward. Connor sent Captain North ahead with ten Pawnees and also ordered Jim Bridger to do some independent scouting. When both the Pawnees and Bridger found plenty of Indians, Connor personally led 250 troopers and 80 Pawnee Scouts in an attack on the camp discovered by Jim Bridger. After a successful surprise attack in which the Pawnees gained sixty scalps and Connor captured over a thousand ponies, it was learned that the village did

[14] George Bent to Hyde, September 23, 1913, Bent Letters, Coe Collection; Connor to Dodge, August 21, 1865, *O. R.*, I: Vol. 48, pt. 1, p. 358; Grinnell, *Two Great Scouts*, 97–99; Palmer, "Powder River Expedition," *loc. cit.*, 209.

[15] Connor to Dodge, August 21, 1865, *O. R.*, I: Vol. 48, pt. 1, p. 358; Grinnell, *Two Great Scouts*, 99–102; Palmer, "Powder River Expedition," *loc. cit.*, 209.

not belong to either the Cheyennes or Sioux but to Black Bear's Northern Arapahoes. Because the time was approaching for the rendezvous with the other two columns, Connor moved his contingent down the Tongue River to the appointed place. As yet the greater number of hostiles were unpunished, and Connor hoped that either Walker's or Cole's column had intercepted them or that the combined commands could still bring the Indians to bay.[16]

Connor waited impatiently on the Tongue River for information from the two missing columns. Before any news arrived from Walker or Cole, Connor learned that a surveying expedition led by Colonel James A. Sawyers was in trouble en route between Sioux City, Iowa, and Virginia City, Montana territory. Sawyers' party consisted of about fifty civilians, three companies of escorting troops, and eight emigrant families. When it had reached a point about fifty miles southeast of Camp Connor, parties of Indians began to harass the wagon train. On August 13, a young man, Nathaniel D. Hedges, was surprised while scouting ahead of the wagons, riddled with arrows, and scalped by Cheyennes. On the two days following, some five to six hundred Dog Soldiers and Crooked Lances of the Arkansas River Cheyennes, Northern Cheyennes under Dull Knife, and Red Cloud's Oglala Sioux surrounded the party and attempted to stampede the stock. After forming a wagon corral and digging rifle pits, the road surveyors and their escort repulsed several Indian charges. When the assaults failed, the Indians asked for a parley. George and Charles Bent represented the Indians, who agreed to withdraw when Sawyers offered a wagonload of bacon, sugar, coffee, flour, and tobacco for safe passage. Most of the Cheyennes withdrew, but the Sioux, dissatisfied with their share of plunder, attacked the train again on August 16 and were again beaten off.[17]

Messengers to Camp Connor brought additonal cavalry protection, and the post was reached without difficulty. Determined to push on, Sawyers was given a cavalry escort from Camp Connor through the dangerous area. On the Tongue River, however, on August 31, Sawyers' party was attacked by Black Bear's Arapahoes, who killed

---

16 Palmer, "Powder River Expedition," *loc. cit.*, 209. Stanley Vestal, *Jim Bridger, Mountain Man,* 231–34; Grinnell, *Two Great Scouts,* 105–11.

17 George Bent to Hyde, September 21, 1905, Western History Department, Denver Public Library.

an escorting cavalry officer. For several days the Arapahoes alternately withdrew and attacked, killing several wagon drivers. Finally the Indians signaled their desire for a talk, and in the agreement which followed, three Arapaho warriors were given as hostages to accompany Sawyers' party to Connor's camp farther down on the Tongue River. By this act the Arapahoes hoped to recover the ponies seized by Connor, but the officer only sent more troops to protect the surveyors until his camp was reached.[18]

Through the first week of September, Connor still had no word of the location of the commands of Cole and Walker. One party was sent out to the mouth of the Yellowstone River and returned without discovering the missing troops. Finally, on September 8, Connor sent Captain North with twenty Pawnees to the Powder River and small detachments in other directions to search for the other columns. By this time the commands of Cole and Walker had joined. Rations for Cole's men had been exhausted a week before—consumed during the long march east and north of the Black Hills. Cole saw no Indians or signs of their camps until his command reached the Powder River. On September 1, while the column was in bivouac, four to five hundred warriors swept out of concealment toward the horse herd. A small detachment of soldiers under Captain E. S. Rowland of the Second Missouri Light Artillery reached the horses first, but were immediately cut off by the warriors and killed to the man except for Captain Rowland, who was saved as the main body of Cole's troops arrived. The Indians, mainly Sioux and a few Cheyennes, waited for a better chance for a successful attack as Cole's column rode down the west bank of the Powder River.

Swarms of warriors hovered about the flanks of the column and prevented scouts from operating to the fore. An early sleet storm killed over two hundred of the cavalry's weakened mounts, and the Indians became bolder daily. On September 5 parties of warriors ranging in numbers from ten to one hundred braves engaged portions of the Twelfth Missouri Cavalry and Second Missouri Light Artillery and tried to lure the Missourians from their strong defensive positions.

[18] James A. Sawyer[s], "Wagon Road From Niobrara to Virginia City," 39 Cong., 1 sess., *House Doc. No. 58,* 22–26; Albert M. Holman, *Pioneering in the Northwest,* 16–33; Dodge to Pope, September 15, 1865, *O. R.* I: Vol. 48, pt. 2, p. 1229; Grinnell, *Fighting Cheyennes,* 208–209.

A year later Colonel Cole recalled that the hills, divides, and ravines were literally covered with warriors whose leaders, watching from higher ground, used red flags and signal glasses to deploy their men. When the Missourians refused to fall into their trap, the Indians prepared a massive charge.

One thousand Sioux and Cheyennes tried to ride over the troops. Roman Nose, the Cheyenne war leader, led the charge. Wearing his protective war bonnet, Roman Nose rode along the whole length of the troops' line, emerging unscathed although his white war pony was shot out from under him. Since the Indians possessed few guns, the troops could not be destroyed by the warriors, and they withdrew when Cole brought his artillery into action.[19]

After this fight Walker's command proceeded ahead of Cole's troops up the Powder River. On September 8, Walker's troops were again attacked by Indians in strength, but the warriors did not try to hold the field after Cole came forward to support Walker. That night another sleet storm killed more than four hundred horses and mules of the column, so for all practical purposes the command was left afoot. Captain North reported to Connor on September 11 his discovery of large numbers of dead animals, and immediately fears arose for the missing elements of the Powder River expedition. Two days later, two Pawnees and several troopers found Cole's and Walker's men—so weak from starvation and exposure that the march to Camp Connor took seven days despite the relatively short distance left to traverse. Disgusted and footsore, having suffered without rations for fifteen days, the men were at last safe at Camp Connor, where supplies left behind by Connor restored their spirits and strength.

Connor, in his march to the Tongue River, enjoyed no success against the Indians. He then retreated to Camp Connor where the three wings of the Powder River expedition began their return to Fort Laramie, arriving there on October 4. During his fights with the Indians on the Powder River, Cole reported that he had killed and wounded between two and five hundred Indians—a statement consistently denied by Indian informants. The only effect of the

[19] George Bent to Hyde, May 10, 1905, MSS of the Colorado State Historical Society, Denver, Colorado; George Bent to Hyde, May 16, 1906, Bent Letters, Coe Collection; Grinnell, *Fighting Cheyennes*, 214.

expedition was to force the warriors to protect their women and children, thereby terminating their raids along the North Platte River. Certainly the warriors were not impressed by the ineffective efforts of Connor's expedition, and the hostiles made no effort to join those bands who sought peace.[20]

After their encounters with the Powder River expedition, the disaffected Arkansas River Cheyennes began to drift south. Perhaps the troops disturbed them, or, after a year's absence, perhaps these Cheyennes desired to return to their accustomed hunting grounds. During the first week of November, 1865, large bands of Indians were observed crossing the Platte road, heading south. When they reached the Smoky Hill road, the warriors killed six people, burned five stations, and harassed travelers. Among the braves who destroyed Downer station was one of the sons of William Bent. These raids have been interpreted as evidence of the Dog Soldiers' contempt for the peace concluded at the Treaty of the Little Arkansas. Writers also speculate that Charles Bent did nothing when Dog Soldiers tortured a man at Downer station, but nothing in the contemporary documents can be cited to maintain either assertion. These Cheyennes knew nothing of the treaty and up to this time had signed no document which bound them to its provisions.[21]

The Cheyennes maintained later that the depredations along both the Platte and Smoky Hill rivers were in retaliation for attacks by soldiers along the first stream. Superintendent Murphy was convinced that if the Cheyennes had been allowed to proceed south unmolested, they would not have committed their raids. The superintendent was also aware that the Cheyennes still harbored a "Spirit of retaliation," and he asked William W. Bent to suggest a plan so that future troubles could be prevented. Although the old trader was not in immediate contact with the Cheyennes, he ventured the opinion that:

[20] Cole to Grant, February 10, 1867, *O. R.* I: Vol. 48, pt. 1, pp. 366–80, and supporting letters of subordinate officers, *ibid.*, 380–81; Palmer, "Powder River Expedition," *loc. cit.*, 221–27; Grinnell, *Fighting Cheyennes*, 212–15.

[21] George Bent to Hyde, September 3, 1913, Bent Letters, Coe Collection; Cummings to Cooley, December 4, 1865, Upper Arkansas Agency, Letters Received; Thomas Murphy to Cooley, November 29, 1865, Central Superintendency, Letters Sent, Field Office Files, Records of the Office of Indian Affairs, National Archives, Washington, D. C. (hereafter cited as Central Superintendency II).

... theair are a portion of those Chayns north which are anxious to get to those south and be friendly and peasable but I think that this portion of them are overpowered by a band called the Dog Soldiers who privents them from coming if it ware possible that I cold get to see them I think I wood be able to get most of them to join those south and remain quiet.

Bent also suggested that the Dog Soldiers by some means be kept separated from the bands of Black Kettle and Little Robe, who had not broken the peace; otherwise, he feared the government would have to fight another costly war with the Cheyennes when spring came.[22]

In the nation's capital, officials began taking steps to reunite the bands of the Arkansas River Cheyennes. Major Edward W. Wynkoop was assigned to the Interior Department on special duty, "to bring about a union of the Cheyenne and Arapahoe Indians who have been north of the Platte River during the past season, with that portion of said tribes on the Upper Arkansas river with whom treaties have been recently negociated." Major General Dodge was ordered to co-operate with Wynkoop in every way consistent with the safety of the Overland routes.[23]

During the winter months of 1865–66, the Cheyennes frequently moved their villages and camped all the way from the tributaries of the Republican to the Cimarron River. Some warriors joined Black Kettle's village on the Cimarron and gave no evidence of a desire to continue the war. One camp of Dog Soldiers reportedly was located seventy-five miles south of Fort Larned in mid-January. The commanding officer at Fort Larned, Major Hiram Dryer, learned from traders that these Dog Soldiers desired peace, and if Dr. I. C. Taylor, at that time Indian agent of the Upper Arkansas Agency, had per-

22 George Bent to Hyde, May 16, 1905, MSS of the Colorado State Historical Society, Denver, Colorado; Murphy to Cooley, November 29, December 10, 1865, Central Superintendency II; Leavenworth to AAG., Washington, D. C., Headquarters of the Army, Letters Received, United States Army Commands, Records of the War Department, National Archives, Washington, D. C.; William Bent to Murphy, November 21, 1865, Upper Arkansas Agency, Letters Received.

23 James Harlan to Cooley, December 6, 1865, Upper Arkansas Agency, Letters Received; AAG., Department of the Missouri, to Dodge, December 27, 1865, Department of the Missouri, Letters Sent, United States Army Commands, Records of the War Department, National Archives, Washington, D. C.

formed his duties, a cessation of hostilities could have been arranged with some of the soldier societies.[24]

Major Wynkoop arrived on the Arkansas River in mid-February, 1866, to council with those Cheyennes who had not participated in the Treaty of the Little Arkansas. Wynkoop, with Indian Agent Taylor and escorted by a company of cavalry, immediately went to the camps of the Cheyennes, Kiowas, and Kiowa-Apaches on Bluff Creek. There, on February 25, Wynkoop found Black Kettle, Medicine Arrows, and Big Head, the latter two being important leaders of the bands who had just come south. Of the signers of the treaty, only Little Robe was absent, for he and Ed Guerrier were searching on the Solomon River for some Dog Soldiers who had declined to follow the others to the peace talks.[25]

Major Wynkoop addressed his remarks to Medicine Arrows and Big Head and suggested that they and other leaders accept the Treaty of the Little Arkansas. The two chiefs at first objected and refused to sign the treaty. They stated that they had been unaware of the treaty while in the north, and had been attacked by troops while moving south—an act which they interpreted as nullifying the treaty. Big Head was even more specific. He opposed the treaty because it permitted travel over the Smoky Hill road, which ran through the Cheyennes' best hunting ground. Overland travel and emigrants would drive away the buffalo, and he and his people did not want to live south of the Arkansas in the country of other tribes; they preferred to live in the midst of their traditional buffalo range north of the Arkansas River. Wynkoop finally prevailed, and the leaders of the soldier societies living on Bluff Creek signed a paper accepting the terms of the Treaty of the Little Arkansas. During the talks Wynkoop also, through Indian traders, freed Mary Fletcher, a sixteen-year-old girl captured on the Platte route in August, 1865.

[24] Bent to Dryer, January 19, 1866, Dryer to AAG., District of Kansas, January 26, 1866 (Copy), Upper Arkansas Agency, Letters Received; Dodge to Pope, January 21, 1866 (Copy), Central Superintendency, Letters Received, Records of the Office of Indian Affairs, National Archives, Washington, D. C. (hereafter cited as Central Superintendency III).

[25] Captain R. S. Morris to AAAG., District of Kansas, February 18, 1866, Fort Dodge, Letters Sent, United States Army Commands, Records of the War Department, National Archives, Washington, D. C.

All of the benefits of the Treaty of the Little Arkansas could be destroyed, however, by a few killings committed either by the Indians or the whites. During the talks at Bluff Creek, Wynkoop and Major Dryer learned that a few days earlier, four Cheyennes had killed and scalped a youth six miles east of Fort Dodge. Completing their duties at Bluff Creek, Wynkoop and Dryer investigated the incident. The boy's father, they discovered, had swapped ten one-dollar greenbacks for ten ten-dollar bills by convincing the Indians that it was a fair trade. The Indians, upon learning they had been cheated, returned to the settler's home and killed his son in revenge. The chiefs of the Cheyennes agreed to surrender the four braves committing the murder, but it does not appear that the army officers exerted much pressure in attempting to gain custody of the culprits. One officer, in concluding his report, wrote, "I think this case needs no comment."[26] Under different conditions, had peace not been strongly desired, the incident could have easily produced serious reprisals.

Some Cheyennes were as yet uninformed of the Bluff Creek talks. Early in March, 1866, four hundred Cheyenne, Sioux, and Arapaho warriors appeared on the Butterfield Overland Despatch route and prepared to raid for stock. Before the forays were undertaken, Little Robe and Guerrier arrived at their camps and persuaded the Dog Soldiers to talk with Wynkoop. Wynkoop completed his duties when, on April 4, Little Robe and those of the soldier societies who had not signed the articles of the Treaty of the Little Arkansas marked the necessary document. In letters to Major General Pope and Commissioner Cooley, Wynkoop represented the whole of the Southern Cheyennes at peace and the routes of travel through their country perfectly safe. Wynkoop took this position because the agreements had been made not only with the Cheyenne chiefs but also with the warrior societies. The special agent, with some overemphasis, claimed the Cheyennes "exhibited a fervent desire for peace, endorsing the actions of their chiefs at the mouth of the Little Arkansas and of the council held by myself on Bluff Creek. They it is true, yield the Smoky Hill Country with great reluctance; it is their favorite hunting ground

[26] Captain G. A. Gordon to AAG., District of Kansas, March 5, 1866, Fort Dodge, Letters Sent; Wynkoop to Pope, March 12, 1866, Dodge to Pope, March 14, 15, 1866 (Copies), Upper Arkansas Agency, Letters Received.

and the bones of their fathers repose there." As long as the government fulfilled its promises, Wynkoop predicted, the Cheyennes would observe the peace.[27]

Although the Cheyenne warriors remained quiet during the spring and early summer of 1866, doubts arose over the permanence of the treaty. A trader was told by the Dog Soldiers that they would not accept their share of the annuity goods, and while they would not molest travel along the Platte or Santa Fe roads, they would go to war before surrendering the Smoky Hill country where buffalo and game were plentiful. The same information came from William Bent, John Smith, and Ed Guerrier, who believed that although the Cheyennes wanted to remain at peace, they would never leave the Smoky Hill, where "they would live or die." The Cheyenne determination to retain the Smoky Hill country at any cost, Indian Agent Jesse Leavenworth complained from his agency, was not reflected in Wynkoop's newspaper reports and statements. Concerning the Bent brothers, who had long ridden with the hostile Cheyennes, Leavenworth informed Superintendent Murphy that Charles, supposed in popular accounts to be committed to savagery, was peacefully settled down on his father's Westport farm, and that George had promised to leave the Cheyenne camps.[28]

William Bent in May, 1866, journeyed to Washington to urge exact compliance with the terms of the Treaty of the Little Arkansas. He felt slighted because no mention had been made of his services in gathering the Cheyennes and influencing them to accept the terms of the treaty. The old agent, however, had more important reasons to be in Washington while the treaty was under consideration by the United States Senate. His children stood to gain valuable lands in the Arkansas Valley if the treaty were approved, and Bent also felt the fulfillment of the pact's provisions was required because "my reputation as a man with them [the Cheyennes and Arapahoes] was at

27 Douglas to AAG., District of Kansas, March 8, 1866, Fort Dodge, Letters Sent; Murphy to Cooley, March 19, 1866, Wynkoop to Pope, April 5, 1866, Wynkoop to Cooley, April 8, 1866, Upper Arkansas Agency, Letters Received.

28 Murphy to Cooley, May 2, 1866, Central Superintendency II; Leavenworth to Murphy, May 22, 1866, Central Superintendency, Letters Received, Field Office Files, Records of the Office of Indian Affairs, National Archives, Washington, D. C. (hereafter cited as Central Superintendency I).

stake." Unless the treaty was adhered to by governmental officials, Bent predicted "a more bloody and terrible Indian war, than has ever before taken place upon the plains; the New Mexico trade will be entirely cut off and an amount of expense will ensue to the government and damage to its citizens that it is impossible to estimate."[29]

While ratification of the Treaty of the Little Arkansas was being delayed by the United States Senate, the Cheyennes continued to insist that they would not give up the Smoky Hill country. Under pressure from warriors, Black Kettle was forced to repudiate the cession of that region in the 1865 treaty. Superintendent Murphy maintained, however, that war could be avoided only if that concession remained. To allay Indian dissatisfaction, Major Wynkoop was instructed to purchase $1,000 worth of annuity goods for immediate distribution among the Cheyennes and Arapahoes. He was told by Commissioner Cooley to express regret over the delay in the ratification of the treaty and to warn the Cheyennes and Arapahoes that: "If the government is obliged to open war upon them *all* the people will suffer terribly, and such chastisement will be made that there will be nobody left to make war."[30]

Major Wynkoop hurried to the Smoky Hill road and found that something had to be done—and quickly—to avoid trouble. Indian Agent Taylor was worthless, since he remained at Fort Zarah, "constantly in a state of intoxication." Taylor's complaints that Wynkoop was trying to undermine his influence among the Indians were ignored as were his assertions that Black Kettle, in exchange for permission to hunt in the Smoky Hill Valley, guaranteed unmolested travel over the road. On August 14, 1866, Wynkoop held his first council with the eight Cheyenne chiefs, including some leaders of the soldier societies. The conversations were amicable, and while the chiefs admitted that it was difficult for the tribe to give up its last hunting ground, they declared that if "any of their young men here-

[29] Robert Campbell to Cooley, May 22, 1866, Upper Arkansas Agency, Letters Received. See four letters, William Bent to Cooley, May 29, June 4, 7, and 9, 1866, in Upper Arkansas Agency, Letters Received, the first three of which are neither in Bent's handwriting nor his frontiersman's rendition of English diction and grammar.

[30] Murphy to Cooley, July 6, 1866, Central Superintendency II; Harlan to Cooley, July 25, 1866, Upper Arkansas Agency, Letters Received; Cooley to Wynkoop, July 25, 1866, in *Report, Commissioner of Indian Affairs, 1866*, 278–79.

after . . . committed any act offensive to the whites they would confiscate his property or if necessary for an example, *kill him."* The Cheyennes asked Wynkoop to obtain for them six hundred ponies with the money to be paid as remuneration for Sand Creek losses and to return two Indian children taken by the troops of Chivington. William Bent, back on the Arkansas River in late August, 1866, mentioned that the Cheyennes wanted these children returned to their families, and they knew that one was in Denver and the other was being exhibited in a side show somewhere in the United States. In writing to Major General Pope, Bent seemed unaware of any significant restlessness among the Cheyennes and insisted that all of the government's obligations to the Cheyennes had to be met.[31]

Drunken and incompetent, Indian Agent Taylor, from his headquarters at Fort Zarah, tried to convince his superiors that he possessed the key for ending the Cheyenne problem. First he recommended that the troops exterminate the Dog Soldiers as the only solution for a permanent peace. Then, to impress Superintendent Murphy with his influence among the Cheyenne warriors, Taylor informed the superintendent that after a frank talk with the Dog Soldiers, he had persuaded them to follow the majority of their tribe to hunting grounds south of the Arkansas River.[32]

There is good evidence that Taylor's statements were creations of his imagination. Late in August, 1866, parties of Cheyenne warriors began visiting Fort Wallace and the stations along the Smoky Hill road. These warriors, under Spotted Horse and Roman Nose, bluntly warned the stage company employees to leave the country in fifteen days. Lieutenant A. E. Bates, the commanding officer of Fort Wallace, sent William Comstock, an army scout and guide, to determine the truth of these stories. The warriors told Comstock that as soon as the "medicine lodge" ceremonies were over, the soldier societies were

[31] Wynkoop to Cooley, August 11, 14, 1866, Taylor to Cooley, August 15, 1866, William Bent to Pope, August 28, 1866 (Copy), Upper Arkansas Agency, Letters Received. Among the better-known Cheyennes attending the Fort Ellsworth council were Black Kettle, Little Wolf, Big Head, White Beard, later known as Grey Beard, and Roman Nose.

[32] Taylor to Murphy, September 30, 1866, in *Report, Commissioner of Indian Affairs, 1866,* 280–81; Taylor to Murphy, October 1, 1866, Upper Arkansas Agency, Letters Received.

determined that either the whites would abandon the Smoky Hill road or the Cheyennes would close it. Although there were no incidents resulting in loss of life either to whites or Indians, on September 19 a party of Cheyennes led by Spotted Horse stampeded the horse herd of the cavalry at Fort Wallace.[33]

Additional evidence of the warriors' determination not to give up the Smoky Hill country was revealed during the series of councils held to gain tribal approval of Senate amendments to the Treaty of the Little Arkansas. The Bureau of Indian Affairs sent W. R. Irwin and Charles Bogy as special agents to meet the Cheyennes and Arapahoes at Fort Zarah during mid-October. To assure the success of the talks, William Bent was given the contract to purchase and haul a vast store of annuity goods to the post on the Arkansas River. Bent believed that the amendments, the principal one of which was that the Cheyenne and Arapaho reservation be entirely outside of the boundaries of Kansas, would be easily approved. Superintendent Murphy disagreed and maintained that the Dog Soldiers certainly would not approve the amendment and would immediately begin to raid.[34]

At a crucial point in the talks, which began on October 16, 1866, the soldier societies asserted their power over the peace chiefs. Black Kettle, Little Robe, and other chiefs were forced by the warriors to withdraw their assent to the amendments since the Dog Soldiers were not numerous enough to coerce the whole tribe. From whisky peddlers Cheyenne braves purchased enough liquor to make them ugly, and the officials were powerless to stem its flow. Charles Bent was deeply involved in troubles and constantly urged the warriors not to give up the Smoky Hill country. At one point, while drunk, Charles threatened to kill his father and his brother George, the latter now disassociated from the warrior societies. William Bent, deeply cha-

---

[33] Bates to AAAG., District of the Upper Arkansas, August 28, 30, 1866, Fort Wallace, Letters Sent, United States Army Commands, Records of the War Department, National Archives, Washington, D. C.; Lieutenant R. E. Flood to AAAG., District of the Upper Arkansas, September 20, 1866, Office of the Adjutant General, Letters Received.

[34] Irwin to Cooley, September 26, 1866, Upper Arkansas Agency, Letters Received; Murphy to Cooley, October 6, 1866, Central Superintendency II; Kappler (ed.), *Laws and Treaties*, II, 888.

grined by his son's behavior, wanted Special Agent Irwin to arrest Charles, but the young Bent was allowed to roam freely and without restraint, protected by his popularity among the Cheyenne warriors. Major Wynkoop, replacing Taylor as agent to the Cheyennes, Arapahoes, and Kiowa-Apaches, believed the only chance to gain assent to the amendments was to separate those who declined from the more amenable groups and then to exact submission from the recalcitrant. William Bent gave up all hope of concluding the talks successfully, sold his store of goods to David A. Butterfield, and left Fort Zarah.

While these abortive councils were taking place, news arrived at Fort Zarah that forty Cheyenne warriors led by Bull Bear had recently killed two station keepers and burned the station at Chalk Bluff on the Smoky Hill road. Temporarily, Irwin, Bogy, and Wynkoop abandoned further talks and began working on the chiefs again. Wynkoop softened up Black Kettle and Little Robe by feasting those of the tribe who still remained for several days and finally received assurance from the chiefs that they would return by mid-November to Fort Zarah. In the interim the special agents bought an additional $14,000 worth of presents for the Indians in the hope that the massive pile of goods would overcome the timidity of the chiefs and that they would sign the amendments.[35]

When the councils were renewed at Fort Zarah on November 13–14, the chiefs readily assented to and signed the amendments to the Treaty of the Little Arkansas. The chiefs' willingness to sign the documents probably stemmed from the fact that the warriors had moved north and west from Fort Zarah, and thus the chiefs were freed from coercion. The chiefs would not, however, meet every request of the special agents. They refused to surrender Fox Tail, Medicine Arrows' son who had killed an employee of William Bent at Fort Zarah before the councils resumed. Nor, the chiefs stipulated,

[35] D. Street to Major Chauncey McKeever, October 23, 1866; Wynkoop to Brevet Major General J. W. Davidson, October 25, 1866, W. R. Irwin to Commissioner Lewis V. Bogy, November 3, 1866, Lieutenant James Hale to AAAG., District of the Upper Arkansas, December 19, 1866, Upper Arkansas Agency, Letters Received; Hoffman to AAG., Department of the Missouri, November 1, 1866, Fort Leavenworth, Letters Sent, United States Army Commands, Records of the War Department, National Archives, Washington, D. C.

should the Cheyennes be punished for every lapse in their good behavior, and in justification they pointed to the government's failure to deliver the two missing children and the long delay in the indemnity payment for the Sand Creek Massacre.[36]

After Indian Agent Wynkoop shifted his headquarters to Fort Larned, he reported that the Cheyennes seemed well satisfied by the results of the councils at Fort Zarah. Major General Winfield Scott Hancock, commanding the Department of the Missouri, was unwilling to forget the depredations on the Smoky Hill road. He ordered the surrender of those Indians guilty of killing the station keepers and stealing the stock at Fort Wallace. "If they [the Cheyennes] do not respond properly," Hancock threatened, "we will attack them also." Immediate plans to launch an expedition against the Cheyennes were delayed so that Wynkoop could complete his investigation and verify without doubt which tribe was guilty of the forays.[37]

The ratification of the Treaty of the Little Arkansas and its amendments brought one conflict to a close. At the same time, another series of events was occuring which would result in the resumption of war in the spring of 1867.

[36] Charles Bogy to Commissioner Bogy, November 5, 15, 1866, Charles Bogy and Irwin to Commissioner Bogy, November 15, 23, 1866, Upper Arkansas Agency, Letters Received; Lieutenant John P. Thompson to AAAG., District of the Upper Arkansas, "Statement of John S. Smith," August 15, 1867, Office of the Adjutant General, Letters Received.

[37] Wynkoop to Commissioner Bogy, November 26, 1866, Wynkoop to Murphy, December 2, 1866, Upper Arkansas Agency, Letters Received; Hancock to Davidson, October 21, 29, 1866, Hancock to Carleton, Hancock to Ben Holladay, October 23, 1866, Department of the Missouri, Letters Sent.

# 12

## WAR RETURNS

WHEN INDIAN CONFLICTS seemed inevitable during the summer of 1866, William Tecumseh Sherman, commanding officer of the Military Division of the Missouri, decided upon a personal inspection of the trouble spots. From the information derived on the spot, Sherman believed that he and his subordinate, Major General Winfield Scott Hancock, assigned to the Department of the Missouri, could better cope with the problems of the frontier. Once in the Indian country, Sherman was unimpressed by the alleged presence of hostile Indians. From Fort McPherson, Sherman commented: "As usual, I find the size of Indian stampedes and stories diminishes as I approach their location." In the heart of the region most frequently harassed by Indians, Sherman saw little danger. The telegraph lines were operating, travelers were moving unmolested, and stages were running daily. "I have met," wrote the general, "a few straggling parties of Indians who seem pure beggars, and poor devils, more to be pitied than feared."[1]

By the time Sherman reached Fort Laramie, his views had changed. Some citizens had been killed along the Platte route, and it was the army's duty to protect the roads and travelers. He therefore countermanded General Hancock's orders and re-enforced the garrisons east of Fort Laramie and along the Smoky Hill route. True, people were killed, but in Sherman's accurate and matter-of-fact analysis, their deaths were unnecessary. Travelers started out in strong parties and moved for days without seeing an Indian. Someone thinking the danger "all humbug, rides off a ways and finds himself surrounded

[1] Sherman to General John A. Rawlins, August 21, 24, 1866, in *Protection Across the Continent*, 39 Cong., 2 sess., *House Exec. Doc. No. 23*, 5–6, 6–8 (hereafter cited as *Protection Across the Continent*).

and gone." The difficulties between the Indians and whites arose from many sources: the chiefs could not control their young warriors who committed the acts of murder and horse stealing; mutual distrust existed between the Indians and their white neighbors; the Indian regarded treaties as "waste paper"; and the miners killed Indians "just as they would kill beasts." In the opinion of Sherman, the only solution was army control over the western tribes.[2]

The longer Sherman remained in Colorado territory, however, the more convinced he became that there was no danger of an Indian war. He had traveled from Fort Laramie to Fort Garland to Fort Lyon without an escort. Sherman finally came to believe that the ranchers and farmers of the territory were exploiting the rumors of hostilities in order to sell their grain and cattle to anticipated army expeditions and enlarged garrisons. At Fort Lyon Sherman concluded: "The Utes are hunters and peaceable, and the Cheyennes and Arapahoes are off after buffalo. God only knows when, and I do not see how, we can make a decent excuse for an Indian war. . . . All of the people west of the Missouri river look to the army as their legitimate field of profit and support and the quicker they are undeceived the better for all."[3]

Completing his tour, Sherman submitted his recommendations to General Grant. The Indians, Sherman maintained, should be controlled by the army, restricted to reservations, and established away from the overland routes and railroads. The Cheyennes and the five other tribes of the Central and Southern Plains, Sherman proposed to settle south of the Arkansas River and east of Fort Union. When the Sioux were shifted north of the Platte and west of the Missouri rivers, Sherman explained to Grant, citizens would have exclusive "use of the wide belt, east and west, between the Platte and the Arkansas, in which lie the two great railroads, over which passes the bulk of the travel to the mountain territories." Sherman hoped to place the Cheyennes and their neighboring tribes near more civilized Indians, thereby inducing them to practice agricultural pursuits;

2 Sherman to Grant, Sherman to Rawlins, August 31, 1866, in *Protection Across the Continent,* 8–11.
3 Sherman to Rawlins, September 21, 1866, Headquarters of the Army, Letters Received, Records of the War Department, National Archives, Washington, D. C.; Sherman to Rawlins, September 30, 1866, in *Protection Across the Continent,* 16–19.

otherwise, they would have to be fed. Sherman realized his policy would keep some of the tribes quiet, while the more restless "will be as hard to keep to their reservations as the wild buffaloes."[4]

Sherman's hope for peace on the Plains faded during the winter of 1866–67. First the Sioux trapped and cut down Brevet Lieutenant Colonel William J. Fetterman on December 21, 1866, on the Bozeman Road near Fort Phil Kearny. Then Sherman was informed of Major General Hancock's evidence that the Cheyennes were restive and responsible for the killings on the Smoky Hill road during the previous summer. Late in December, 1866, the general wrote his brother that he supposed clashes with the Sioux and Cheyenne were unavoidable and speculated that "they must be exterminated, for they cannot and will not settle down, and our people will force us to it." Winter, however, was no time to campaign, so Sherman waited for approval of his plan to remove all the Indians from between the Platte and Arkansas rivers.[5]

Early in December, 1866, Major General Hancock singled out the Cheyennes as the target for a spring campaign. Convinced that they had committed the past summer's attacks and murders on the Smoky Hill road, he wished to renew the demands for the surrender of those warriors guilty of the forays. Hancock, believing that the punishment of any one tribe would probably serve to check additional depredations, suggested the Cheyennes as the object of the expedition since they "appear to be as deserving of chastisement as any other."[6]

With additional evidence accumulated during the winter of 1866–67, Hancock justified a campaign against the Cheyennes. From guides, interpreters, and wagon drivers Hancock established, to his own satisfaction, that the Cheyennes were the principals in destroying

---

[4] Sherman to Rawlins, November 5, 1866, in *Annual Report of the Secretary of War, 1866,* 39 Cong., 2 sess., *House Exec. Doc. No. 1,* 18–23.

[5] Hafen and Young, *Fort Laramie,* 353–53; Sherman to Grant, December 28, 1866, in 39 Cong., 2 sess., *Sen. Exec. Doc. No. 15,* 4; Sherman to John Sherman, December 30, 1866, William T. Sherman Papers, Library of Congress, Washington, D. C.; Sherman to Rawlins, January 11, 1867, Headquarters of the Army, Letters Received.

[6] Hancock to AAG., Military Division of the Missouri, December 2, 1866, Department of the Missouri, Letters Sent; Hancock to Wynkoop, December 17, 1866, Wynkoop to Hancock, December 26, 1866, in *Reports of Major General Hancock upon Indian Affairs with Accompanying Exhibits,* 14–15, 15–17 (hereafter cited as *Reports of Hancock*).

the Chalk Bluff station. While Hancock was gathering the necessary information, Indian Agent Leavenworth informed him that sixty-five warriors from Black Kettle's camp, including George and Charles Bent, were on their way to fight Pawnees. These Cheyenne warriors, however, turned aside at Fort Harker on January 1, 1867, wounded a Kaw army scout, and ran off forty horses. Hopefully Hancock told Sherman that he wished the Cheyennes to refuse to turn over those guilty of previous depredations so that he might be able to demonstrate the power of the army to the Plains Indians. Hancock, less forthright to Leavenworth, stated that certain demands would be placed before the Cheyennes which they would be given time to consider.[7]

Since the Cheyennes were obviously hostile, Sherman and Hancock sought ways to suppress sale of guns and ammunition to the tribe David A. Butterfield, former operator of the Overland Despatch line, provided the backing for traders who were selling arms by the case to Indians along the Arkansas River. Butterfield possessed a permit from the Indian Bureau giving him the right to sell guns and ammunition to any tribe living in peace with the United States. Warriors visiting Fort Dodge carried new revolvers and boasted that if war came in the spring they would possess plenty of arms and ammunition. Because these weapons were sold to the Indians for as much as twenty times their cost, the profits explained the traders' insistence upon unrestricted trade with the Indians.[8]

In January, 1867, the Indian bureau and the army officers in the West bitterly debated the sale of arms to Indians after departmental commanders received discretionary power to permit sale of weapons to peaceful Indians for hunting. Sherman, however, viewed Butterfield's permit for unlimited sale of arms and ammunition to the

[7] For these documents, see *Reports of Hancock,* 115–26; Leavenworth to Hancock, January 12, 1867, Hancock to Leavenworth, January 17, 1867, Statement of E. K. Page, agent for the Kansas Indians, February 22, 1867, *Reports of Hancock,* 12–13, 13–14, 126; Hancock to Sherman, January 14, 1867, Department of the Missouri, Letters Sent.

[8] Statements of Bogy, Irwin, Leavenworth, Bent, and Wynkoop to Butterfield, November 15, 1866 (Copy), Headquarters of the Army, Letters Received; Captain Henry Asbury to AAG., Department of the Missouri, January 14, 1867, Major Henry Douglass to AAG., Military Division of the Missouri, January 13, 1867, Office of the Adjutant General, Letters Received.

Arkansas River tribes as "monstrous" and appealed through General Grant to the President for a revocation of such permits. Angered by the sale of arms to the Indians, Major General Hancock, upon orders received from General Sherman, on January 26, 1867, banned all sales of weapons and ammunition to Indians living on the Arkansas River. In turn, Commissioner of Indian Affairs Lewis V. Bogy complained to Secretary of the Interior Orville H. Browning that sale of arms to peaceful Indians was within the power of the Indian agents and approved by statutes. Unless such interference ceased, Bogy was certain the result would be "nothing less than the destruction of our entire western settlements," because the tribes would be deprived of subsistence provided by their hunts.[9]

In Hancock's opinion, Bogy's views were nonsense. It was dangerous to supply arms to Cheyennes and Kiowas who had recently committed "robberies, murders, and other brutal outrages against our citizens." Common sense, Hancock insisted, dictated that guns and ammunition in great quantities should not be sold to Indians who threatened the frontier's safety.[10]

The Cheyennes' agent, Edward W. Wynkoop, vigorously denied that his charges had committed any act of violence since their councils with Special Agents Irwin and Bogy. "I have been among them constantly," Wynkoop wrote to the commissioner, "and never knew them to feel better satisfied or exhibit such a pacific feeling." Nevertheless, an impressive amount of information came to Hancock's headquarters that seemed to prove Wynkoop wrong. It was also known that four hundred lodges of Brulés and Northern Cheyennes camping again on the tributaries of the Republican River were in constant communication with the Dog Soldiers living on Pawnee Fork. Army officers reported from their posts during February and

[9] Colonel E. D. Townsend to Sherman, January 19, 1867, Sherman to Grant, January 12, 1867, Office of the Adjutant General, Letters Received; General Orders No. 2, Headquarters, District of the Upper Arkansas, January 26, 1867, Lewis Bogy to Browning, January 23, February 4, 1867, in *Letter of the Secretary of the Interior communicating in compliance with a resolution of the Senate of the 8th instant, information touching the origin and progress of Indian hostilities on the frontier*, 40 Cong., 1 sess., *Sen. Exec. Doc. No. 13*, 7–11, 18–20, 52–55 (hereafter cited as *Causes of Indian Hostilities, 1867*). For the authorization of Butterfield to sell arms, see *ibid.*, 41–42.

[10] Hancock to AAG., Military Division of the Missouri, March 6, 1867, in *Reports of Hancock*, 1–11.

March, 1867, that the Cheyennes had run off stock from a party of buffalo hunters, had compelled a rancher to cook them a meal, threatening to kill the man when no sugar was available, and had stolen forty head of mules and horses from a wagon train within twenty miles of Fort Dodge. One trader reported at Fort Dodge that when the Cheyennes confiscated his entire stock of trade goods, they held target practice with new rifles and revolvers and informed him that they had plenty of ammunition in their camps.[11]

For greater control over the Indians, the War Department sought to transfer them to its jurisdiction. The plan formulated by Colonel E. S. Parker, an aide-de-camp to General Grant, urged that the army could administer Indian affairs with greater efficiency, more honesty, and with greater justice both to the Indians and frontiersmen. The bill embodying Parker's ideas was later killed by the Senate Committee on Military Affairs. To Sherman the defeat of the bill, which both he and Grant supported, relieved the army of all responsibility for peace on the western frontier. "We surely cannot be held responsible for the Peace of the Frontier," Sherman wrote to his brother, "if it is adjudged we are trespassers everywhere in Indian Territory, and have no right to forsee and prevent collision & trouble. After the Indians do mischief it is too late to apply the remedy."[12]

From the outset of the planning, Sherman approved of Hancock's campaign against the Cheyennes. Sherman wanted the troops in the field before the spring grasses could strengthen the Indians' horses, because, as he wrote to Grant, the time to strike is now; "an Indian with a fat pony is very different from him with a starved one." At a conference in St. Louis on March 8, 1867, Hancock discussed the proposed expedition and gained his superior's complete assent. Hancock then warned Indian Agent Wynkoop that the purpose of his march

---

[11] Wynkoop to Bogy, February 21, 1867, in *Causes of Indian Hostilities, 1867,* 75; Douglass to AAAG., District of the Upper Arkansas, February 24, 1867, March 19, Fort Dodge, Letters Sent; Keough to AAAG., District of the Upper Arkansas, January 1, 1867, Fort Wallace, Letters Sent; Asbury to AAAG., District of the Upper Arkansas, February 27, March 6, 1867, Office of the Adjutant General, Letters Received.

[12] Parker to Grant, January 24, 1867, Grant to Stanton, February 1, 1867, in *Causes of Indian Hostilities, 1867,* 40–41, 42–49; Extract from Washington *Chronicle,* February 4, 1867, in 39 Cong., 2 sess., *Sen. Exec. Doc. No. 16,* 17–18; Sherman to John Sherman, February 24, 1867, Sherman Papers; *Congressional Globe,* 39 Cong., 2 sess., pt. 2, p. 1224.

would be to demonstrate to the Indians that the government possessed the power to punish any tribe that molested travelers. Wynkoop was instructed to inform the Indians of his agency that the general was fully prepared for war, but if those Indians "abandon their habit of infesting the country traversed by our overland routes, threatening, robbing, and intimidating travellers," no punitive action would be taken. Sherman explained the purpose of Hancock's expedition to the general staff in Washington; it would move into the country of the Cheyennes and Kiowas, confer with the Indians, and if they offered to fight, grant them their wish. If the Indians offered to remain at peace, subject to their treaties and agents, Hancock would not disturb them, but would only point out to them the wisdom of keeping their young warriors off the main emigrant roads. Sherman, believing that a clash was most likely, pointed out: "Our troops must get among them, and must kill enough of them to inspire fear, and then must conduct the remainder to places where Indian agents can and will reside among them, and be held responsible for their conduct."[13]

On March 22, 1867, Hancock began moving his troops to Fort Riley, intending to assemble as he moved west an effective unit of 1,400 men. As finally constituted at Fort Larned, the command consisted of eleven troops of the newly-organized Seventh Cavalry, six companies of infantry, a battery of artillery, a pontoon train, fifteen Delaware scouts under Fall Leaf, and three frontiersmen, including James Butler (Wild Bill) Hickok, as couriers. The explorer Henry M. Stanley, later to gain fame in Africa, and Theodore Davis, of *Harper's New Monthly Magazine,* rode with Hancock's column.[14]

Hancock's expedition was not free to chastise the Cheyennes or other Indians unless they inaugurated hostilities. Hancock could not demand the surrender of Fox Tail or those warriors who had raided

[13] Sherman to Grant, February 18, 1867, Sherman to Lieutenant Colonel George K. Leet, Headquarters of the Army, Letters Received; Hancock to Wynkoop, Hancock to Leavenworth, March 11, 1867, Department of the Missouri, Letters Sent. Hancock's letters were written on March 4 but delayed until March 11, after Hancock had conferred with Sherman in St. Louis.

[14] *Reports of Hancock,* 17ff.; James W. Dixon, "Across the Plains with General Hancock," *Journal of the Military Service Institution of the United States,* Vol. VII, No. XXVI (June, 1886), 195; Henry M. Stanley, *My Early Travels and Adventures in America and Asia,* I, 3ff.; Theodore Davis, "A Summer on the Plains," *Harper's New Monthly Magazine,* Vol. XXXVI, No. 213 (February, 1868), 292ff.

six months before and could only give the Indians a chance to fight
if they so desired. In his field orders Hancock established the rules
for his troops while marching through Indian country: no straggling
was allowed; hunting was permitted for meat only; and no officer,
other than Hancock, was allowed to council with the Indians.
Somehow, as one reads Hancock's order to his troops, the impression
is gained that Hancock hoped for a fight as he told his men: "We
shall have war if the Indians are not well disposed towards us," and,
"No insolence will be tolerated from any bands of Indians whom
we may encounter."[15]

Wynkoop's messengers found the Cheyennes and other tribes without difficulty. F. F. Jones, an interpreter and guide at Fort Dodge,
visited Bull Bear's camps, which contained two hundred lodges of
Cheyennes and ten lodges of Sioux. Bull Bear denied that his camp
and the much larger village of Sioux nearby had any intention of
initiating a war and said they were gathered "to make medicine."
The information brought back by Ed Guerrier substantiated the
report of Jones, and to both men Bull Bear indicated his willingness
to council with Hancock whenever he was notified.[16]

When Hancock arrived at Fort Larned with his command on
April 9, 1867, the chiefs were reported on their way to the post for
talks. The Cheyenne chiefs were delayed by a severe storm until
April 12, when Tall Bull, Bull Bear, White Horse, Little Robe, and
ten other tribal leaders appeared at Fort Larned, prepared to meet
Major General Hancock. Although the Cheyennes never counciled in
the evening, they acceded to the wishes of the general and gathered
around a roaring fire near Hancock's tent. Hancock and his junior
officers were in their glittering parade-dress uniforms, while the
Indians, with their agent, Wynkoop, and his interpreter, Ed Guerrier,
sat on the opposite side of the fire, many of the chiefs dressed in army
overcoats, some with blazing red trade blankets, and all with their
faces and bodies painted. The firelight playing upon their ornaments
impressed Stanley, who described them: "To the hideous slits in their

[15] Sherman to Hancock, March 14, 1867, Office of the Adjutant General, Letters Received; General Field Orders No. 1, Headquarters, Department of the Missouri, In
the Field, March 26, 1867, *Reports of Hancock,* 95–96.
[16] Douglass to AAG., Department of the Missouri, March 31, 1867, Fort Dodge,
Letters Sent.

ears were hanging large rings of brass; they wore armlets of silver, wrist rings of copper, necklaces of beads of variegated colours, breast ornaments of silver shields, and Johnson silver medals, and their scalp locks were adorned with a long string of thin silver discs."[17]

The chiefs listened to Hancock's speech, translated slowly by Guerrier, with "grave and taciturn countenances." They had heard these words many times before: peace was desired by their Great Father; the Indians must return their captives; railroads and wagon roads must not be molested; and they should support the chiefs who favored peace. Only once did the Cheyennes break their silence, and then to express their disbelief when Hancock promised to punish whites guilty of crimes against the Indians.

Before the Cheyennes' spokesman rose, they accepted and smoked the peace pipe. Tall Bull, brief and noncommittal, spoke in reply to Hancock's speech. He recognized the peace arranged by Wynkoop, assured the general that he and his troops were free to pass through the Cheyenne range, and failed to discuss either the roads or railroads passing up the Smoky Hill Valley. Hancock interrupted Tall Bull to state that he was going to march his troops to their camps. Again Hancock stressed that the young warriors must be kept off the roads, and in particular, the General warned the Cheyennes, "if you should ever stop one of our railroad trains, and kill the people on it, you would be exterminated."[18]

Tall Bull made no effort at Fort Larned to dissuade Hancock from marching his command to the Indians' camps. Privately, however, the chief urged Wynkoop to reason with Hancock and stress that the women and children, with memories still fresh of the Sand Creek Massacre, would most certainly flee as the troops appeared. Wynkoop's appeals failed, and the command, on April 13, 1867, moved up Pawnee Fork. Small parties of warriors kept the column under surveillance while others burned the grass near their camps so that Hancock would be forced to pitch his tents some distance away. Before the

[17] Hancock to AAAG., Military Division of the Missouri, May 14, 1867, Department of the Missouri, Letters Sent; George Bent to Hyde, June 5, 1906, Bent Letters, Coe Collection; Dixon, "Across the Plains with General Hancock," loc. cit., 196; Davis, "A Summer on the Plains," loc. cit., 294; Stanley, Early Travels, I, 29.

[18] Hancock's and Tall Bull's speeches are found in Reports of Hancock, 45–48, and shorter versions in Stanley, Early Travels, I, 30–35.

troops made camp for the night, Pawnee Killer, a Brulé chief, and White Horse of the Cheyenne Dog Soldiers joined Hancock's column and assured the general that their people would remain in their village and that the chiefs would be available for council on the following morning. Hancock, aware that Pawnee Killer was considered a friendly chief, agreed to meet the Cheyennes and Sioux in council. At nine-thirty o'clock, on the morning of April 14, Bull Bear appeared and told Hancock that the other chiefs were delayed by a buffalo hunt. When the chiefs failed to come by eleven o'clock, Hancock began to doubt the sincerity of the Indians and told Bull Bear that he was going to march his column to the village.[19]

A few miles out of their camp, the troops were met by a battle line of Cheyenne and Sioux warriors. Lieutenant Colonel George A. Custer depicted the array as "one of the finest and most imposing military displays, prepared according to the Indian art of war, which it has ever been my lot to behold." For more than a mile, the chiefs had spaced their warriors across the line of the column's march, with other braves organized into reserves and couriers. Armed with lances bearing crimson pennants, bows strung, quivers full of arrows, breech-loading rifles and revolvers ready, the warriors waited quietly for further commands from their chiefs. Outnumbered more than four to one by Hancock's cavalry and infantry, the Cheyennes and Sioux were prepared to sell their lives to protect their women and children.[20]

As Hancock deployed his command, his officers observed that the chiefs had selected a position in which their warriors could operate effectively. Indian Agent Wynkoop, who had ridden out with Hancock from Fort Larned, broke some of the tension when he rode forward alone and assured the Indians of their safety. After he had urged the Indians to keep their people in camp, Wynkoop escorted Roman Nose and other chiefs back and met Hancock and Custer midway between the lines. Roman Nose acted as sole spokesman

[19] George Bent to Hyde, June 5, 1906, Bent Letters, Coe Collection; *Report on Indian Affairs by the Acting Commissioner for the Year 1867*, 311; *Reports of Hancock*, 20–21; George A. Custer, *My Life on the Plains*, 42–44.

[20] The number of warriors varies from Hancock's "several hundred" to Davis' count of 329. *Reports of Hancock*, 21; Stanley, *Early Travels*, I, 37; Davis, "A Summer on the Plains," *loc. cit.*, 295; *Report, Commissioner of Indian Affairs, 1867*, 311; Custer, *Life on the Plains*, 44–45; see also Custer's letter to his wife, in Elizabeth B. Custer, *Tenting on the Plains*, 559–60.

for the Cheyennes and Sioux. From the manner in which the warrior leader addressed Hancock, observers thought it was a matter of indifference to him whether he fought or parleyed. When Hancock demanded to know if the Indians wanted peace or war, Roman Nose replied: "We don't want war; if we did, we would not come so close to your big guns." Roman Nose, according to both George Bent and Guerrier, threatened to kill Hancock and was only prevented by Bull Bear, who prevailed upon the warrior to consider the consequences upon their women and children. To the discerning eye of artist Theodore Davis, Roman Nose was a fine specimen of Indian manhood, "six feet in height and finely formed," armed with a carbine, which hung at the side of his pony, four revolvers in his belt, while in his left hand he grasped a strung bow and a number of arrows.[21]

Breaking off the conference, Hancock ordered the march resumed to the Indian encampment. Two hundred and fifty Cheyenne and Sioux lodges were still standing in a beautiful grove of trees on the north branch of Pawnee Fork. Only the warriors and their chiefs remained there; the women and children had fled to safety when the warriors and the chiefs delayed Hancock's command. Approaching the Indian village, Hancock sent for the chiefs, and Roman Nose, Bull Bear, Grey Beard, Tall Bull, Medicine Wolf, and White Horse came readily. The general was irritated by the flight of their people and demanded that the chiefs send messengers out immediately to order them to return. Since the chiefs stated that their own horses were worn-out and poor, Hancock furnished fresh mounts for the runners. After nightfall, the Cheyennes returned to their village accompanied by Guerrier, whom Hancock ordered to report the activities of the chiefs and warriors every two hours.[22]

During the night the chiefs and warriors also prepared to flee, and Guerrier delayed his reports to give his friends additional time to depart. When Guerrier's message finally did reach Hancock, he

[21] George Bent to Hyde, June 12, 1906, Bent Letters, Coe Collection; *Report, Commissioner of Indian Affairs, 1867*, 312; Stanley, *Early Travels, I*, 37–38; Davis, "A Summer on the Plains," *loc. cit.*, 295.

[22] George Bent to Hyde, June 5, 1906, Bent Letters, Coe Collection; Davis, "A Summer on the Plains," *loc. cit.*, 295; *Reports of Hancock*, 22; Grinnell, *Fighting Cheyennes*, 252–53.

ordered Custer with his Seventh Cavalry to surround the village, but by that time the Indians had vanished. At about three o'clock on the morning of April 15, Custer dashed off a note to his wife stating that the Indians had fled in great fear, and that at daylight he was under orders to "overtake them and bring them back if possible and hold the council. If they refuse to come, and are disposed to fight, I am to accommodate them. . . . I do not anticipate war, or even difficulty, as the Indians are frightened to death, and only ran away from fear."[23]

Before Custer began his pursuit of the fleeing Cheyennes, he, two officers, and two army surgeons made an inspection of the village. They found an old Sioux man and woman and a young Indian girl. Custer, Hancock, Stanley, and Leavenworth all agreed that when the girl was found she had been raped. Later Indian Agent Wynkoop first implied and then charged that this girl, neither Sioux nor Cheyenne, had been violated by the troops—a charge that was thoroughly discredited by army officers. Wynkoop's accusation was undoubtedly an effort to further discredit the army's relations with the Indians during the spring and summer of 1867.[24]

Wynkoop, immediately after the Indians had fled, judged the Hancock expedition as "disastrous." He maintained in letters to Commissioner N. G. Taylor that the Hancock campaign would end in a general Indian war in which the unprotected settlers and mail station keepers would suffer. The agent also pleaded with Hancock not to destroy the Cheyenne and Sioux village, because such an act would only deepen the antagonism of the Indians. For several days Hancock vacillated whether or not to burn the lodges. The General thought that the raping of the child was sufficient justification in itself. But, as late as April 18, Hancock verbally informed Wynkoop that the village would not be destroyed. Colonel Andrew J. Smith, Seventh Cavalry, supported Wynkoop's position, pointing out that

---

23 George Bent to Hyde, June 5, 1906, Bent Letters, Coe Collection; Elizabeth B. Custer, *Tenting on the Plains*, 560–61.

24 *Reports of Hancock*, 23; Stanley, *Early Travels*, I, 39–40; Custer, *Life on the Plains*, 64; Leavenworth to Commissioner N. G. Taylor, April 15, 1867, Upper Arkansas Agency, Letters Received; *Report, Commissioner of Indian Affairs, 1867*, 312; Wynkoop to Murphy, June 11, 1867, in *Difficulties with Indian Tribes*, 41 Cong., 2 sess., *House Exec. Doc. No. 240*, 31; Colonel Andrew J. Smith to Taylor, October 30, 1867, Department of the Missouri, Letters Sent.

the destruction of the village would only add difficulty in arranging meetings with other Indian groups.[25]

Two reports from Custer, who was trailing the Indians, ended Hancock's doubts. On the morning of April 15, Custer, with eight troops of the Seventh Cavalry, Delaware scouts, Ed Guerrier, Bill Comstock, and "Wild Bill" Hickok, took up the pursuit of the Indians, who were moving in small parties toward Walnut Creek. Taking the advice of the Delawares, Custer left his baggage train behind at Walnut Creek and pressed on ahead rapidly to the Smoky Hill road, reaching there during the night of April 16 and 17. At Downer's station employees of the stage company reported that during the past twenty-four hours small parties of Indians had been crossing the road on their way north. It was assumed that these Indians had committed depredations over a thirty-five mile stretch of the road. Upon Hancock's receipt of the first two messages from Custer on April 18, he issued the order to burn the Cheyenne and Sioux village.[26]

Custer, on April 18, rode the thirty-five miles to Lookout station, where the greatest damage had taken place. There the station house, stables, and forage had been burned and the stock run off. The bodies of the three station attendants "were so horribly burned as scarcely recognizable; the hair was singed from their heads; the skin and flesh burned from the breasts and arms, and their intestines torn out." Custer, in his third message to Hancock, carefully stated that neither he nor the Delaware scouts found "the slightest clue as to what tribe committed the act." But the message came too late, and Hancock informed Sherman on April 19 that, "we utterly destroyed the Sioux and Cheyenne village this morning. What property could not be burned, such as tool, &c., we carried off." The official inventory

[25] Wynkoop to Hancock, April 15, 1867, Office of the Adjutant General, Letters Received; Wynkoop to Taylor, April 15, 18, 1867, Upper Arkansas Agency, Letters Received; Stanley, *Early Travels,* I, 40; Mitchell to Asbury, April 15, 1867, Department of the Missouri, Letters Sent.

[26] W. G. Mitchell to Asbury, April 15, 1867, Department of the Missouri, Letters Sent; Custer to Lieutenant Thomas B. Weir, April 16, 17, 1867, Office of the Adjutant General, Letters Received; Elizabeth B. Custer, *Tenting on the Plains,* 570; Hancock to Sherman, April 19, 1867, Office of the Adjutant General, Letters Received; see also Hancock's journal, in *Difficulties with Indian Tribes,* 65–67, 96, and corrections authorized on the official copy in the Office of the Adjutant General, Letters Received.

listed 140 Sioux and 111 Cheyene lodges destroyed in addition to nearly all of the Indians' camping equipment. The two old Sioux and the girl, who soon died, were sent to Fort Dodge.[27]

Indian Agent Wynkoop reacted bitterly to Hancock's action. Writing to Commissioner Taylor two days after the village had been burned, he claimed "I know of no overt act that the Cheyennes had committed to cause them to be thus punished not even since their flight." He maintained that the Indians of his agency had been forced into war, and he was sustained by Jesse Leavenworth, who offered the opinion that it would have been better if Hancock had never entered the Indian country. After conversing with Leavenworth, Superintendent Murphy informed the commissioner of Indian affairs that the Cheyennes and Sioux, peaceful when Hancock entered their country, were now in full flight, and that no one could anticipate what consequences were in store for the frontier settlements.[28]

Lack of forage and provisions caused Custer to abandon his pursuit of the Indians at Fort Hays. On their way north, the Cheyennes and Sioux ran off stock from a Kansas Pacific Railroad work-party, and Guerrier thought the Indians would regather at Beaver Creek, a tributary of the Republican River. In desperation Custer sent "Wild Bill" Hickok, mounted ingloriously on a mule, to see if forage was available at Fort Harker. Custer, unable to move, sent additional details to Hancock. The attack on Lookout station, according to Custer, occurred on April 15, and was not committed by the occupants of the Pawnee Fork village. "I am confident, however," Custer rationalized, "that the act was committed with their knowledge and approval, which accounts for their hasty flight." Hancock, with Custer's letter in hand, constructed his own timetable and maintained that Cheyenne and Sioux from the Pawnee Fork could have reached the Smoky Hill in time to commit the attacks. Whether or not the Cheyennes and Sioux actually were at fault did not appear to Hancock to be "of much importance, for I am satisfied that the

27 Custer to Weir, April 19, 1867, Hancock to Sherman, April 19, 1867, Office of the Adjutant General, Letters Received; Smith to Taylor, October 30, 1867, Department of the Missouri, Letters Sent; Hancock to Grant, May 23, 1867, Headquarters of the Army, Letters Received; *Difficulties with Indian Tribes,* 71; *Reports of Hancock,* 27.

28 Wynkoop to Taylor, April 21, 1867, Murphy to Taylor, May 13, 1867, Upper Arkansas Agency, Letters Received.

Indian village was a nest of conspirators." In his official report Hancock ignored Custer's information and used the murders on the Smoky Hill as the final reason for the burning of the camp. As Hancock moved toward Fort Dodge, he wrote to Colonel Smith: "It is war against the Cheyennes and Sioux, between the Arkansas and Platte, save for a few small bands on the headwaters of the Republican."[29]

The killing of some Cheyenne warriors west of Fort Dodge gave Wynkoop an additional reason to complain. After the Cheyennes and Sioux had fled, garrisons were alerted by Hancock to watch for Indians moving south. Two companies of the Seventh Cavalry were detached to patrol the Santa Fe Trail west of Fort Dodge toward the Cimarron Crossing with orders which provided that if the Indians did not surrender immediately, they were to be fought "without hesitation." On the morning of April 19, Indians were observed skulking near the cavalry's bivouac at the Cimarron Crossing. Major Wickliffe Cooper, commanding the detachment, sent Lieutenant Berry with twenty troopers to demand the surrender of the Indians, who immediately opened fire. On foot, the Indians "fought until death," wounding one of the detachment. At Fort Dodge, Wynkoop declared that the Indians were guiltless and the cavalry's attack was unprovoked. The reporting officer stated that the troopers killed six Cheyennes, while George Bent, who was in Black Kettle's camp when the survivors arrived, maintained that only two of the four warriors were killed. In any event, these young warriors were something less than guiltless, because Henry Stanley saw the "scalp of a woman with long auburn hair attached to it" taken from the body of one of the dead warriors.[30]

After counciling with Arapahoes and Kiowas at Fort Dodge, Hancock moved his comand back towards Fort Harker. These

[29] Custer to Weir, April 19, 1867, Hancock to Sherman, April 21, 1867, Hancock to Smith, April 21, 1867, Office of the Adjutant General, Letters Received; *Reports of Hancock,* 27.

[30] Lieutenant George H. Wallace to Cooper, April 17, 1867, Cooper to Douglass, Douglass to AAG., April 19, 1867, Fort Dodge, Letters Sent; Wynkoop to Taylor, April 21, 1867, Office of the Adjutant General, Letters Received; Stanley, *Early Travels,* I, 50; George Bent to Hyde, June 5, 1906, Bent Letters, Coe Collection; Grinnell, *Fighting Cheyennes,* 254–58.

Indians, of course, promised not to join the Cheyennes and Sioux in any war against the whites and also promised to inform the army officers of the movements of hostile Indians. En route to Fort Harker in early May, 1867, Hancock received information that six citizens had been killed near Lake Sibley on the Republican River. This confirmed, in Hancock's mind, that a war was impending, and he advocated the removal of all Plains Indians between the Platte and Arkansas rivers through continuous pressure from his forces. Colonel Smith was ordered by Hancock to send a cavalry force against the hostile Cheyennes and Sioux as quickly as possible, taking precaution not to attack the Brulés and Oglalas, who had recently received permission from the peace commission to range as far south as the Smoky Hill River. Many of the officers in the Department of the Missouri, including Custer, considered that the destruction of the village by Hancock would not result in a full-scale Indian war.[31]

Major General Hancock tried to minimize the effect of his actions on Black Kettle's people. A seventy-five-warrior party from Black Kettle's camp made a few passes along the Arkansas River, doing very little damage. Their hostility was lessened when Black Kettle and some of his leading men offered to meet Hancock at Fort Larned. Although Hancock could not come to Fort Larned immediately, the General offered to subsist Black Kettle and his band at some military post until he could be free to explain in person the origins of the renewed skirmishing.[32]

The ineptness with which Hancock handled the Indians in the spring of 1867 is generally conceded as the immediate cause of Indian retaliations along the Kansas frontier. Hancock's burning of the Indian village seems unnecessary, but there are other factors to be considered. In 1867 neither the Dog Soldiers nor their allies, the Sioux, appeared willing to allow either travel or the extension of the

31 "Talk held with Little Raven (head chief of the Arapahoes), Yellow Bear, Beardy, Cut Nose and several warriors present, Fort Dodge, Kansas," April 28, 1867, Office of the Adjutant General, Letters Received; George Bent to Hyde, December 17, 1913, Bent Letters, Coe Collection; *Reports of Hancock*, 33, 35–37, 80; Mitchell to Smith, May 7, 1867, Office of the Adjutant General, Letters Received; Elizabeth B. Custer, *Tenting on the Plains*, 578.

32 George Bent to Hyde, December 17, 1913, Bent Letters, Coe Collection; Mitchell to Wynkoop, Mitchell to Smith, Mitchell to Asbury, May 7, 1867, Department of the Missouri, Letters Sent.

Kansas Pacific Railroad to take place in the Smoky Hill Valley. General Sherman participated in the planning of the expedition, urged its approval, and was fully determined to protect the construction of the railroad at all costs. If Hancock had not moved against the Cheyennes and Sioux, undoubtedly some other campaign would have taken place.

Within a month after Hancock left the Plains, Cheyennes began to take their toll along the Smoky Hill road and upon the railroad crews. Indians attacked a Kansas Pacific engineering party at the track end, and in a four-hour fight tried to seize the camp. Between May 22 and June 24, 1867, Indian raids all but halted the railroad's construction. On June 3, two station keepers west of Fort Wallace tried to round up some stray stock and were ambushed by Cheyennes, who killed the men, scalped them, and hacked off the skull of one of the men at eye level. Reports came into the district and departmental headquarters almost constantly, giving details of new attacks. General Hancock, while inspecting the Smoky Hill route on June 16, stated that every station along the road 170 miles on either side of Fort Wallace had been attacked at least four times. Some of the deaths of station keepers appeared unavoidable, but at least four lives were lost through the individual's own carelessness. Stages were withdrawn from service until the troops could drive the hostiles from the roads. For the greater part of a month, the Cheyennes nearly swept the Smoky Hill road clean. The detachments of soldiers at the stage stations and even at the larger posts at Fort Dodge, Fort Wallace, and Fort Harker could not safely venture from their protecting walls to intercept the big war parties.[33]

For about a week after June 21, 1867, the Cheyennes made Fort Wallace the focal point of their attacks. On that date, when Indians

[33] John D. Perry to Crawford, June 24, 1867, in Samuel J. Crawford, *Kansas in the Sixties*, 255–57; Keough to Lieutenant M. Moylan, May 29, 1867, Keough to Weir, June 4, 7, 1867, Fort Wallace, Letters Sent; Douglas to AAG., Department of the Missouri, June 18, 1867, Fort Dodge, Letters Sent; Captain V. K. Hart to AAAG., District of the Upper Arkansas, June 18, 1867, Fort Harker, Letters Sent, United States Army Command, Records of the War Department, National Archives, Washington, D. C.; Hancock to Sherman, June 16, 1867, Office of the Adjutant General, Letters Received; Marvin H. Garfield, "Defense of the Kansas Frontier, 1866–1867," *KHQ*, Vol. 1, No. 4 (August, 1932), 330–31.

in considerable strength made their appearance at the post, Charles Bent was recognized among the Cheyennes. The warriors tried to overpower a work detail going from the fort to the post's stone quarry. Re-enforced by a detachment from the garrison, the soldiers fought hard with the Cheyennes for two hours, with some hand-to-hand encounters taking place. The garrison's troops lost two men dead, two wounded, and a wagon driver was also mortally wounded.[34]

Not satisfied with their results, the warriors remained in the vicinity, and on June 26 attacked the Pond Creek station just west of Fort Wallace. At the time of the attack, Captain Albert Barnitz, camped near the fort with "G" Company of the Seventh Cavalry, took his troop and fifteen men from the garrison and rode to the relief of the beleaguered station. The Cheyennes lured Captain Barnitz and his men into a trap, and the fighting lasted for three hours. Before the command could extricate itself, the Cheyennes had killed six and wounded eight soldiers. Erroneously, the survivors reported that they had killed fifteen to twenty warriors, one of them being the noted Roman Nose.

Eastern readers of the *Harper's Weekly* were undoubtedly thrilled and horrified by the descriptions provided from these encounters. The correspondent mistook one of the Cheyennes' leaders as Roman Nose. This warrior unhorsed a soldier with his spear and was about to run him through when a corporal barely missed a saber thrust aimed at the Indian. As the supposed Roman Nose turned to meet the new threat, the corporal placed the muzzle of his Spencer rifle on the breast of the savage and fired. "With blood spouting from his wound," the Indian "fell forward on his horse." One powerful warrior was seen to pick up the bugler, Charles Clark, who had been pierced by three arrows, strip off the soldier's clothes as he dashed away, mash the soldier's head to a jelly with his tomahawk, and throw the corpse under his horse's feet. When the body of Sergeant Frederick Wyllyams was recovered, the correspondent regaled his readers with the following bloody description: "His scalp was taken, two balls pierced his brain, and his right brow was cut open with a hatchet. His nose was severed and his throat gashed. The body was

34 Lieutenant James Hale to Weir, June 22, 1867, Fort Wallace, Letters Sent.

opened and the heart laid bare. The legs were cut to the bone, and the arms hacked with knives." Indian encounters, then as today, provided vicarious delights to the American populace.[35]

While the Cheyennes' agent insisted not all of the tribe was hostile, Sherman declared that contrary to treaty rights, the Indians should be removed from the lands between the Platte and Arkansas rivers. While on the scene of the hostilities, Sherman wrote to Secretary of War Stanton: "if fifty (50) Indians are allowed to remain between the Arkansas and Platte we will have to guard every stage station, every train and all Railroad working parties. . . . Rather get them out as soon as possible and it makes little difference whether they be coaxed out by Indian Commissioners or killed." At other times Sherman was more moderate. There was no single cause of the Indian wars, he wrote to his old comrade-in-arms, General Grant, and the conflicts should not be charged solely either to the army or the Bureau of Indian Affairs; the causes arose from the inevitable conflict of races. "The Indians," Sherman knew, "are poor and proud. They are tempted beyond the power of resistance to steal of the herds and flocks they see grazing so peacefully in this valley [South Platte]. To steal they sometimes kill. We in turn cannot discriminate—all look alike and to get the rascals, we are forced to include all." Sherman wanted the secretary of the interior to aid him by defining what war and peace meant and to segregate the hostile from the peaceful. It was impossible to reason with westerners who had lost property or who had seen families killed by marauding Indians; almost universally the frontiersmen clamored for extermination of the Indians. "We, the military," wrote Sherman to Secretary of the Interior Browning, "do not wish this result, because it would be a national disgrace, if we, . . . did not make an effort to prevent it, but if some general plan is not adopted, and that soon, there can be but one result."[36]

[35] Hale to Weir, June 27, 1867, Fort Wallace, Letters Sent; *Report of the Secretary of War for 1867*, 40 Cong., 2 sess., *House Exec. Doc. No. 1*, 46; *Harper's Weekly*, Vol. XI, No. 552 (July 27, 1867), 468.

[36] Morrison to Wynkoop, May 29, 1867, Upper Arkansas, Sherman to Stanton, June 17, 1867 (Copy), Central Superintendency III; Sherman to Grant, June 10, 11, 1867, Office of the Secretary of War, Letters Received, Records of the War Department, National Archives, Washington, D. C.; Sherman to Browning, June 22, 1867, Office of the Adjutant General, Letters Received.

Hoping to quiet the fears of Governor Alexander C. Hunt of Colorado territory, Sherman shifted Lieutenant Colonel Custer and three hundred men of the Seventh Cavalry to the Platte. While Custer awaited at Fort McPherson for Sherman, Pawnee Killer came into Custer's camp and complained that the Cheyennes were "bad Indians," and that he was tired of them. Sherman and Custer were not deceived by Pawnee Killer's visit because they realized that the wily old chief only wanted to learn their plans. On July 17, 1867, Custer moved out of Fort McPherson toward the Republican River, where it was thought most of the Indians harassing the Smoky Hill road were encamped. The detachment set up a bivouac on the Republican River about equidistant between Fort McPherson and Fort Wallace.[37]

Little transpired for several days at Custer's camp. At dawn on June 24, the sharp crack of a carbine from the picket line roused Custer, and he heard his brother Thomas, on duty as officer of the day, dash by shouting, "They are here." The horse-herd guards prevented a party of fifty Indians from stampeding the animals. Retiring as quickly as they struck, the Indians regrouped on a knoll a mile from Custer's camp, there signaling to other parties of warriors who quickly surrounded Custer and the four remaining companies of the Seventh Cavalry, the other portions of Custer's original column being absent on escort duty to Fort Sedgwick and Fort Wallace.

Sending forward an interpreter and guide, Custer tried to council with the Indians. Custer was successful and led six of his officers forward to meet Pawnee Killer and six other Sioux chiefs. Sullenly Pawnee Killer demanded repeatedly to know why Custer had left the Platte, and refused to give any information about his attempt to raid the horse herd. When the parley broke up, Custer sent his troops in a futile pursuit of the Sioux. As soon as the tired and disgusted troopers had returned to camp, a party of warriors appeared on the surrounding bluffs, and Captain Louis McLane Hamilton, a grandson of Alexander Hamilton, rode to attack. After the warriors had lured Hamilton a sufficient distance from the camp, the trap was

---

[37] "Report of Lieutenant General Sherman," October 1, 1867, in *Report of the Secretary of War, 1867*, 35; Custer, *Life on the Plains*, 124–25, 129; Elizabeth B. Custer, *Tenting on the Plains*, 581–83; Davis, "A Summer on the Plains," *loc. cit.*, 298–99, 301.

sprung, and concealed warriors swarmed around Hamilton's men. With courage and cool decision, Captain Hamilton directed his men and beat off three hundred of the Plains' finest warriors. Learning of Hamilton's plight, Custer rode out to his relief, but two miles out the Captain was observed bringing his company in without a casuality.[38]

Pawnee Killer's purpose in harrying Custer became clear a few days later. Soon after establishing his camp on the Republican River, Custer sent his wagons to Fort Wallace for additional supplies and ammunition. On the return trip, five to six hundred Cheyenne and Sioux warriors attacked the train, but the escort, under Lieutenants S. M. Robbins and W. W. Cook, held them off for three hours. These Indians, Custer reported, were led by Roman Nose, whose horse was shot out from under him in one of the attempts to charge the wagon train. The plan seemed to be to put Custer on foot, then intercept the wagon train to gain needed supplies and a few scalps.[39]

The large number of warriors about Fort Wallace led General Sherman to believe that the Dog Soldiers and Sioux were being reenforced by Cheyennes and other Indians living south of the Arkansas River. Sherman, late in June, ordered Custer to shift his force and use Fort Wallace as the base of his operations. Lieutenant Lyman S. Kidder, accompanied by ten troopers and Red Bead, a Sioux scout, was to carry the orders. On June 29, 1867, Lieutenant Kidder and his detachment left Fort Sedgwick for the Republican River.[40]

Lieutenant Kidder never reached Custer. Near Beaver Creek the messengers were observed by some Sioux who told the Dog Soldiers and Pawnee Killer's Brulés that a small party of soldiers was approaching the main encampment of these Indians. Kidder's small detachment was surrounded by the Cheyennes and Sioux in a small ravine. The Cheyennes circled the ravine on horseback to prevent any escape while the main body of Sioux approached the soldiers on

---

[38] Custer to Sherman, July 6, 1867, Office of the Adjutant General, Letters Received; Custer, *Life on the Plains*, 131-33, 135-44; Elizabeth B. Custer, *Tenting on the Plains*, 144-50; Davis, "A Summer on the Plains," *loc. cit.*, 302-303; New York *Tribune*, July 16, 1867.

[39] Custer to Sherman, July 6, 1867, Office of the Adjutant General, Letters Received; Davis, "A Summer on the Plains," *loc. cit.*, 303.

[40] *Report of the Secretary of War, 1867*, 35.

foot through the tall, protective grass. Red Bead, the Sioux guide, called out to the Sioux to let him escape, but he and the others were soon killed. Later, when Custer was moving to Fort Wallace, Bill Comstock and Custer's Delaware scouts discovered the remains of Kidder's detachment near Beaver Creek. Kidder and his men were "brutally hacked and disfigured," while Red Bead lay dead and scalped. But his hair was found near his body indicating that his own people had killed the scout, for the Sioux would not keep another tribesman's scalp as a trophy. Custer reached Fort Wallace on July 15, and with seventy-five picked men, marched to Fort Hays, encountering as he moved eastward more reports of Indian attacks and depredations. The Seventh Cavalry, however, was temporarily withdrawn from the field, and its place was taken by a regiment of Kansas volunteers.[41]

On a personal inspection of the Smoky Hill road and the Kansas Pacific Railroad early in July, 1867, Sherman found that the Kansas press and citizenry had exaggerated the Indian danger. Indians were not responsible either for the termination of the stage service or the slow railroad construction. The stage line, now operated by Wells Fargo and Company, was unprofitable, while the railroad building was hampered more by heavy rains than by Indian raids. Nevertheless, Sherman, under pressure from Governor Samuel J. Crawford of Kansas, allowed the governor to recruit and outfit the Eighteenth Kansas Cavalry to guard the Kansas Pacific's construction crews.[42]

Four companies of volunteers were finally organized as the Eighteenth Kansas Cavalry. After cholera had taken its toll on the recruits at Fort Harker, those fit for duty were sent on to Fort Hays. There Captain George A. Armes of the Tenth Cavalry, a Negro regiment, was convinced by sporadic Indian raids and skirmishes with his troops that a large concentration of Indians was encamped either on the upper Saline or Solomon rivers. Hoping to co-operate with some units of the Seventh Cavalry already in the field, Captain

[41] Grinnell, *Fighting Cheyennes*, 260–61; Custer, *Life on the Plains*, 188–98, 206–11; Davis, "A Summer on the Plains," *loc. cit.,* 306–307.

[42] Sherman to Leet, July 17, 1867, Headquarters of the Army, Letters Received; Correspondence of Kansas Governors, Crawford Copy Book, 47, 48, Kansas State Historical Society, Topeka, Kansas; *Congressional Globe,* 40 Cong., 1 sess., 688; *Report, Secretary of War, 1867,* 36.

Armes took his troop, "F" Company, and two troops of the Eighteenth Kansas and started toward the Solomon and Republican rivers. At Prairie Dog Creek the column made camp, and during the night of August 21 Captain George B. Jenness rode out with about thirty men to investigate what looked to be a campfire some distance away. The Indian camp was deserted, and unable to find their way back in the darkness, the detachment remained for the night. The next morning Jenness' party found the wagon train left behind by Captain Armes, who had moved more rapidly ahead. Then the Indians struck. At the wagon train the volunteers formed a hollow square and prevented hundreds of Indians from overrunning their positon. One of the Indians' leaders, mounted on a magnificent white horse, led the charges. When the other warriors broke under the fire from the troops, the intrepid brave rode over one cavalryman and dashed through the square, emerging without a wound despite the volley of shots fired at him.

Another large group of Indians pinned Captain Armes down while Jenness and the wagon guards were under attack. Intermittent fighting continued until the late afternoon of August 23, when the Indians waved a white flag and asked for a parley. The guides recognized Satanta of the Kiowas, Roman Nose of the Cheyennes, and Charles Bent among the Indians' leaders. Soon after the talk Captain Armes moved his three companies back to Fort Hays, where he reported his losses at three dead, thirty-five wounded, and estimated the Indians' casualties at fifty killed and three times that number wounded.[43]

Even before the last skirmishes took place on the Plains, General Sherman was forced to terminate offensive military operations. Congress established an Indian Peace Commission, and Sherman was unable to do more than patrol the roads and maintain garrisons to check Indian depredations. He was disappointed by the action of Congress because, as he wrote to Grant, he knew that the commissioners could not contact the fighting warriors, "and to talk with the old ones is the same old senseless twaddle."[44]

[43] Armes to Captain H. C. Corbin, August 3, 24, 1867, in George A. Armes, *Ups and Downs of an Army Officer*, 237–40, 244–48; Hancock to Sherman, August 24, 1867, Office of the Adjutant General, Letters Received; George B. Jenness, "The Battle on Beaver Creek," KSHS *Transactions*, 1905–1906, IX, 443–52.

[44] Sherman to Grant, July 19, 1867, Headquarters of the Army, Letters Received.

# 13

## THE TREATY OF MEDICINE LODGE
## ANOTHER PEACE FAILS

THE INDIAN PEACE COMMISSION of 1867 originated from the pressures of various forces on Congress. Reacting to the report of the Joint Special Committee on the Condition of Indian Tribes, to the insistence of Indian sympathizers, and to those who demanded punishment and army control of the Indians, Congress, on July 20, 1867, established the commission to conclude a permanent peace with hostile western tribes. Under the terms of the act, the President was authorized to appoint three general officers to serve as commissioners with Indian Commissioner Nathaniel G. Taylor, Senator John B. Henderson of Missouri, chairman of the Senate Committee on Indian Affairs, Samuel F. Tappan, and John B. Sanborn. The statute appropriated $50,000 for the purposes of the commissioners, who were to separate the hostile from the friendly Indians and, if possible, to place the Indians upon permanent reservations removed from western roads and railroads. When President Johnson appointed Generals Sherman, Harney, and Terry, the commission was complete.[1]

Meeting in St. Louis on August 6, 1867, the commissioners held their preliminary conferences before moving to the Northern Plains. While still in St. Louis, the commissioners sent messages to General Hancock and Superintendent Murphy to arrange for the Indians of the Southern Plains to gather near Fort Larned at an appropriate time. Superintendent Murphy dispatched Isaac L. Butterfield, brother of David A. Butterfield, to those Cheyennes, Arapahoes, and Kiowa-Apaches known to be friendly to the government. The messenger found the tribes and assured their leading chiefs, Black Kettle, Little Raven, and Poor Bear, that the commissioners "will settle

[1] Robert G. Athern, *William Tecumseh Sherman and the Settlement of the West,* 172; 15 U.S. Stat. 17.

with you all your difficulties & mark out a straight road for the future." During this conference Butterfield guaranteed the Indians provisions and safety while at the treaty councils, which would begin after the full moon in October.[2]

When the Cheyennes and Arapahoes arrived at Fort Larned, their attitudes and conditions were in stark contrast. On September 2, 1867, Little Raven and Yellow Bear appeared at Fort Larned with some of their warriors, women, and children—all in an utterly destitute condition—maintaining that they had no peace to make since they had not been at war and blaming the Cheyennes for all of the depredations committed along the Santa Fe route. A day later Black Kettle and seven Cheyennes rode into the post, well dressed and mounted on strong Indian ponies. Where Little Raven was openly friendly to the whites, Black Kettle was "sullen and morose and reluctantly" gave his hand to Major M. W. Kidd, Tenth Cavalry, commanding officer of Fort Larned. While the Indians remained at the post, messengers informed Superintendent Murphy at the mouth of the Little Arkansas that the Indians were ready to discuss the preliminaries of the formal treaty.[3]

Before departing for Fort Larned, Superintendent Murphy gathered information about the Cheyennes and sent additional messengers to round up more of the tribesmen. George Bent, living at that time with Arapahoes on Medicine Lodge Creek, informed Indian Agent Wynkoop that Black Kettle, with little influence outside of his own band, had incurred the ridicule of the Cheyenne soldier societies for his peace overtures. Neither Black Kettle nor the chiefs of the other tribes apparently had much success in deterring the

[2] "Report of the Indian Peace Commissioners," 40 Cong., 2 sess., *House Exec. Doc. No. 97*, 2–3; Sherman to Hancock, Taylor to Murphy, August 7, 1867, Murphy to Little Raven, Black Kettle, and Poor Bear, September 2, 1867, Indian Peace Commission, Separated Correspondence, Records of the Office of the Secretary of the Interior, National Archives, Washington, D. C. (hereafter cited as Indian Peace Commission, Separated Correspondence); Athearn, *Sherman and the Settlement of the West*, 173–83.

[3] Kidd to AAG., Department of the Missouri, September 4, 1867, Murphy to Taylor, September 9, 1867, Indian Peace Commission, Separated Correspondence. Indian Agent Leavenworth was not responsible for the gathering of the Indians as Grinnell asserted in *Fighting Cheyennes*, 270–73, basing his conclusions on George Bent to Hyde, December 17, 1913, Bent Letters, Coe Collection, and Leavenworth to Commissioner of Indian Affairs, September 2, 1867, in *Report, Commissioner of Indian Affairs, 1867*, 314–15.

soldier societies from further raiding, and those chiefs told Bent that "they had talked to the Cheyennes until they are worn out . . . trying to keep them from going to war with the whites." Despite the antagonism between Black Kettle and the soldier societies, he and the other pro-peace chiefs of the Southern Plains Indians were determined to meet the treaty commissioners. To the best of Bent's knowledge, the Cheyennes, other than Black Kettle and his band, knew nothing of the projected peace treaty.[4]

Three emissaries sent by Murphy to the Cheyennes found that tribal discipline had almost completely broken down. Isaac Butterfield, Thomas B. Whitledge, and Ed Guerrier located the camps of the Kiowas, Comanches, Kiowa-Apaches, and Arapahoes and were always told the same story. The chiefs had held many conferences with the Cheyenne warriors, doing all in their power to dissuade them from carrying on the war. One Comanche chief complained that at the end of one council the Cheyennes had become abusive to him and threatened to kill one of his men as an expression of their displeasure. By accident, while traveling between an Arapaho and a Comanche village, Butterfield and his companions were joined by a small party of Cheyennes led by "Grey Head," better known as Grey Beard. The people had secretly left the camps of the soldier societies because Bull Bear, Roman Nose, and other leaders, fearing that their tribesmen would go on the warpath, refused to allow them to leave. Nevertheless, in defiance of their leaders' wishes, a large party of young Cheyennes left their camps in search of plunder and scalps. Ignoring the danger, Guerrier, with a Cheyenne to guide him, set out for the camps of Bull Bear and Roman Nose.

The rumors of Cheyenne hostilities proved to be accurate. While waiting for Guerrier to return, Butterfield and Whitledge rode out a short distance from the Arapaho village with a few young warriors. A short distance from the camp, a party of young Cheyennes appeared, feigned friendship, and then threw off their robes and fired a fusillade at the two men. Only the immediate intervention of the Arapahoes saved their scalps. After waiting for five days for Guerrier's return, Little Raven sent fifty of his best men with Butterfield

4 George Bent to Wynkoop, September [?], 1867, Indian Peace Commission, Separated Correspondence.

and Whitledge for protection on the ride back to Fort Larned. The messengers' report contained little that Superintendent Murphy did not already know. They told the superintendent that the principal chiefs and the old men of the Cheyennes desired peace, but that they had lost all control over the young warriors, who seemed bent on war at any cost. The headstrong youths of the Cheyennes boasted of their easy victories over the whites and claimed that they had lost _ ~e men during the fighting of the preceding summer. Regardless of the actions of the Cheyenne soldier societies, the messengers predicted that the peace faction of the Cheyennes and full delegations from the other four tribes would meet with the treaty commissioners. Even Roman Nose, Superintendent Murphy reported, discountenanced the recent actions of the young warriors and "promised after returning to his village to come in with his people to the place of rendezvous & await" the arrival of the commissioners. Since Roman Nose possessed great influence among the young men of the Cheyennes, Murphy hopefully thought the war leader could recall the Cheyenne war party operating either on or north of the Arkansas River, thereby assuring the treaty councils a better chance of success.[5]

Little Raven, Black Kettle, and Poor Bear were at Fort Larned on September 8, 1867, when Superintendent Murphy arrived at the post. In the talks that followed, Murphy learned that only one Cheyenne war party was raiding for stock along the Smoky Hill River. He also was told that relations between the Cheyenne warriors and the Comanches were strained because the latter had firmly informed the Cheyennes that they as a tribe were determined to sign a peace treaty with the whites. A party of Cheyennes rode into the Comanche camp ready to fight; a group of Kiowa-Apache warriors rode between the warriors of the two tribes, averting bloodshed. The boldness of the Cheyennes, the chiefs thought, resulted from their victories over Major Armes. In these discussions with Superintendent Murphy, the Indians insisted the councils with the Indian Peace Commission could only be held on Medicine Lodge Creek. As their spokesman, Little Raven pointed out that because troops did not always dis-

[5] Isaac L. Butterfield and Thos. B. Whitledge to Murphy [September 15, 1867], Murphy to Taylor, September 15, 1867, Indian Peace Commission, Separated Correspondence.

tinguish between hostile and friendly Indians, they were reluctant to move their people near the army posts on the Arkansas River. Although Superintendent Murphy conceded that the soldier societies had "committed many great outrages, if they will agree to be friendly, I would trust them much more than any of the other tribes."[6]

Superintendent Murphy and Indian Agent Wynkoop departed from Fort Larned on September 17, guided and protected by forty warriors of the Arapahoes, Cheyennes, and Kiowa-Apaches. It took the officials, encumbered with a large train carrying provisions, three days to reach the council grounds sixty miles south of Fort Larned on Medicine Lodge Creek. There fourteen hundred Indians, most of them Arapahoes, awaited Murphy's arrival, and the Arapahoes immediately assumed the responsibility of protecting the whites and the treaty provisions. Some twenty miles away Satanta of the Kiowas and Ten Bears of the Comanches camped with their people. Late in the evening of Murphy's arrival at Medicine Lodge Creek, six young Cheyennes visited the superintendent's camp and agreed to conduct Ed Guerrier to their village with a letter inviting the hostile Cheyennes to the councils. It was determined that the hostile Cheyenne village, under Tall Bull, Bull Bear, Roman Nose, Medicine Arrows, and Big Head, was located three-days' ride to the west on the Cimarron River. "These Cheyennes," Murphy explained to the commissioners, "being fooled by whites so often and many of them but recently from war are very timid, and are determined to understand well who they will be expected to meet before they come." Murphy urged the commisioners to meet the Indians at Medicine Lodge Creek because the council ground, being well supplied with wood, water, and grass, was a favorite resort of the Indians. Admittedly it was expensive to feed the Indians during the councils, but that was the only way the objects of the Indian Peace Commission could be accomplished. Fear of troops and an outbreak of cholera along the Arkansas River also caused the Indians' refusal to venture farther north.[7]

[6] Murphy to Taylor, September 9, 10, 15, 1867, Proceedings of a Council held September 8, 1867, at Fort Larned, with Charles H. Tracy as secretary, Indian Peace Commission, Separated Correspondence.

[7] George Bent to Hyde, July 18, 1905, MSS of the Colorado State Historical Society; Murphy to Taylor, September 21, 1867, to AAG., Department of the Missouri, Indian Peace Commission, Separated Correspondence.

Successful in his quest for the Cheyenne camps, Guerrier returned to Medicine Lodge Creek on September 27 with Roman Nose, Grey Beard, and eight other Cheyenne warriors. The superintendent opened the conversations with a plea for the Cheyennes' attendance at this most important conference, explaining that the commissioner of Indian affairs, hearing of the Cheyennes' problems, was coming to take the tribe "by the hand & make a good road for our peace and happiness." Grey Beard, in particular, remained skeptical. The Cheyenne chief belligerently stated: "A dog will rush to eat provisions. The provisions you bring us make us sick, we can live on buffalo but the main articles that we need we do not see, powder, lead & caps. When you bring us these we will believe you are sincere." Still, Grey Beard was encouraged by the fact that Murphy had come without troops, and advised the superintendent to "keep a strong heart, there are many parties out, but no more shall go out, until we know the result of the treaty with the Commissioners." The sole reason the Cheyennes were still fighting, Grey Beard insisted, was the burning of their village by Hancock: "We are only revenging that one thing." By telling the Cheyennes that the burning of their village was un-authorized by Washington officials, Murphy gained a promise from Grey Beard and Roman Nose to return to their village and take the invitation "to our Chief Medicine Arrow & bring his decision, no matter what it is. Where he goes all of us follow."[8]

Some 2,500 Indians quickly gathered at Medicine Lodge Creek to share in the food and beef brought by Superintendent Murphy. Of this number, however, only 150 Cheyennes, under Black Kettle, remained close at hand; the majority of the tribe stayed on the Cimarron River. While still at the treaty grounds, Murphy began to advise the commissioners. He recommended that not more than two hundred regular troops be used as an escort, and that they should be controlled under the "strictest military discipline" to prevent unfortunate incidents. Murphy also recommended that the Cheyennes be paid for property lost when Hancock burned the Pawnee Fork village; that the five Southern Plains tribes be established on one great reser-

[8] In these conversations Superintendent Murphy called Grey Beard, "White Beard." Proceedings of a Council held at the Arrapahoe Village by Supt. Murphy & Col. D. A. Butterfield with Roman Nose, White Beard & Eight other Cheyenne Warriors, September 27, 1867, Indian Peace Commission, Separated Correspondence.

vation south of the Arkansas River and confederated into one political unit; that the agents be required to live with their charges once they were on the new reservation; and that the Indians be provided with herds of cattle which were not to be killed as long as the Indians could live off the buffalo on the Plains. Through herding and the gradual introduction of agriculture, Murphy hoped that the Indians' nomadic habits might be curtailed. Finally Murphy urged strict control over Indian traders.[9]

Arriving back at Fort Larned on October 8 to escort the commissioners to the treaty ground, Murphy was shocked by the sensational rumors printed in the Kansas press. Contrary to the news stories, Murphy insisted, all was quiet on the Southern Plains, and there was even a good chance that Medicine Arrows, a powerful leader of the Cheyenne soldier societies, would attend the treaty talks. Making little of the rumor that the Cheyennes planned to seize the commissioners, Murphy also stated that "all the other tribes would fight for us." When he learned that the provisions at Medicine Lodge Creek were running low, Murphy urged the commissioners to arrive promptly so that additional supplies could be furnished to the Indians. General Sherman temporarily ordered Major Kidd to stop all wagon trains at Fort Larned, and Murphy complained that "for the sake of a few loads of provisions it would be too bad to spoil our efforts."[10]

The commissioners rested briefly at Fort Larned before making their way to Medicine Lodge Creek. On the afternoon of October 13, 1867, an impressive cavalcade left the post on Pawnee Fork, destined for the council grounds sixty miles to the south. In the party were the seven commissioners; Sherman had been recalled to Washington, and his place was taken by Brigadier General C. C. Augur. In addition to the official party, Governor Crawford, Lieutenant-Governor J. P. Root, and Senator Edward P. Ross of Kansas, eleven newspapermen, and a photographer went along to observe the proceedings. Five hundred cavalrymen from the Seventh Cavalry and a battery of

[9] Murphy to Taylor, October 5, 6, 1867, Indian Peace Commission, Separated Correspondence.

[10] Murphy to Taylor, October 8, 10, 1867, Indian Peace Commission, Separated Correspondence.

Gatling guns were assigned the task of protecting the caravan on its three-day journey. When finally under way, the train consisted of over six hundred officials, camp followers, and soldiers, and sixty-five wagons and ambulances, of which thirty were burdened with food and presents for the Indians.

The Indians were found camping in a natural basin of the Medicine Lodge Valley. At the western extremity of the basin, 250 lodges of Cheyennes stood, representing according to Murphy's figures about fifteen hundred members of the tribe. Others, Murphy explained to the commissioners, were still absent because they had been recently on the war path, "engaged in indiscriminate murder and plunder. They knew that our troops had but recently been hunting them over the plains, killed them whenever they could find them. They could not therefore appreciate this sudden change of policy."[11]

While the commissioners were en route, Roman Nose arrived at the treaty grounds looking for Indian Agent Wynkoop. Revolver in hand, the warrior leader rode at the head of ten of his men directly toward the agent's tent. Knowing that Roman Nose accused him of directing Hancock's troops to the Cheyenne and Sioux villages, Wynkoop fled the camp on a fast horse. George Bent, who was with Murphy and Wynkoop, later claimed that the incident never took place, but it is significant that Roman Nose's presence was never noted at the treaty councils, and it is also doubtful if all of the warrior societies ever came to the treaty grounds.[12]

General Harney took precautions to prevent an unfortunate incident from occurring between the Indians and the escorting troops. He ordered that no enlisted man, teamster, attaché of the commission, or camp follower visit or be in the vicinity of the Indian camps from sundown to sunrise without a written pass from the commanding officer of the military escort. The order was effective in preventing disturbances between the whites and the Indians. However, the Arapahoes and Cheyennes were thoroughly angered when a party of Kaws,

[11] "Report of the Indian Peace Commissioners," 4–5; Stanley, *Early Travels*, I, 216–17, 227; Crawford, *Kansas in the Sixties*, 265; Grinnell, *Fighting Cheyennes*, 273; A. A. Taylor, "Medicine Lodge Peace Council," *Chronicles of Okla.*, Vol. 2, No. 2 (June, 1924), 100–101.

[12] Stanley, *Early Travels*, I, 224, 230; Bent, "Forty Years with the Cheyennes," *The Frontier*, February, 1906, 5.

thought first to be Pawnees, made off with some of their horses. Some of Little Raven's young men ran down the raiders and returned to the villages, and the Arapaho chief warned the assemblage of whites not to be alarmed as his warriors staged a noisy victory celebration.[13]

Cheyenne chiefs played an insignificant role in the councils preceding the Treaty of Medicine Lodge Creek. Black Kettle did little other than accuse other tribes of being the cause of the difficulties between the Cheyennes and the whites. Even Black Kettle did not remain continuously at the council; he was summoned to the soldier societies' camp under the threat of having his horses killed. During the most important talks, on October 19 and 20, only two minor chiefs of the Cheyennes were present, and when called upon, Grey Head, or Grey Beard, simply stated that he could not speak for his people. An appeal by the commissioners brought a small delegation of Cheyenne chiefs headed by Little Robe to Medicine Lodge Creek. Little Robe explained that his people were holding their Medicine Arrow ceremony and that no members of the tribe were allowed to leave the encampment during the four-day ritual. He asked the commissioners to wait and pledged that the whole of the Cheyenne nation would then make a lasting peace. The commissioners, having already completed their treaty with the Kiowas and Comanches, were anxious to depart and after some bickering decided to give the Cheyennes until October 26 to come in. The commissioners knew that the Cheyennes had threatened both the Arapahoes and Comanches for their willingness to sign the treaty and undoubtedly thought that the Cheyennes were unlikely to make their appearance.[14]

Two days after the commissioners' deadline, on October 28, the Cheyennes and Arapahoes signed the Treaty of Medicine Lodge Creek. The tribes acceded to the wishes of the commissioners by agreeing to peace, the right of white travel over emigrant roads

13 Taylor to Kidd, October 18, 1867, General Order No. 3, Headquarters Escort, Indian Peace Commission, October 17, 1867, Indian Peace Commission, Separated Correspondence; Tappan to Anna Tappan, October 23, 1867, Samuel F. Tappan MSS Colorado State Historical Society, Denver, Colorado; Stanley, *Early Travels*, I, 262.

14 Stanley, *Early Travels*, I, 234–35, 236, 245–47, 258–62; Indian Peace Commission to Little Robe, Bull Bear, Tall Bull, Roman Nose and other Chiefs and Headmen of the Cheyenne Nation, October 21, 1867, Taylor to Browning, October 23, 1867, Indian Peace Commission, Separated Correspondence.

through the Southern and Central Plains, the safety of the railroads and their construction, and the cession of all of their lands in Kansas. By signing the treaty, the Cheyennes and Arapahoes accepted, in lieu of their 1865 reservation, lands bounded by the 37th parallel and the Cimarron and Arkansas rivers. The new treaty provided for a resident Indian agent, compulsory schools for their children, a physician, blacksmith, and other permanent agency personnel. Article six provided that any head of a family, either a tribal member or an individual incorporated into the tribe, could select 320 acres of land within the reservation for private use. Legal title to the land remained in the hands of Congress, but protection of the right to the land and its improvements was guaranteed to the agriculturalist. As compensation for previous treaty commitments, the United States government agreed to furnish the Cheyennes and Arapahoes clothing and twenty thousand dollars annually, to be expended for their benefit by the Secretary of the Interior for a period of twenty-five years.

Details of the treaty tried to anticipate and prevent further conflicts between the confederated tribes and the whites. As long as buffalo were in sufficient numbers, the Cheyennes and Arapahoes were given permission to hunt as far north as the Arkansas River. For their part, the tribes pledged themselves not to impede the construction of the railroads in the Platte and Smoky Hill valleys, to abandon all forays against travelers, wagon trains, animal herds, and white settlements, and to "never kill or scalp white men, nor attempt to do them any harm." Since John S. Smith and George and Charles Bent were on hand, we may assume that the provisions of the treaty were fully explained to the Cheyennes. The document was signed by the full Indian Peace Commission and by fourteen Cheyenne chiefs representing the leaders of both the peaceful and hostile factions of the tribe. Among the names of those Cheyennes signing the papers were Black Kettle and Little Robe, acknowledged leaders of the peace faction, and Bull Bear, Tall Bull, White Horse, and Whirlwind, chiefs of the soldier societies.[15]

More than two thousand Cheyennes, including five hundred warriors, accepted presents from the commisoners. The Indians seemed

[15] Stanley, *Early Travels*, I, 227; Taylor, "Medicine Lodge Peace Council," *loc. cit.*, 113; Kappler, *Laws and Treaties*, II, 984–89.

pleased at the generosity of the government, and the Cheyennes loaded their gifts on their ponies and travois. Soon afterwards the Cheyennes departed for their camps on the Cimarron River south of Fort Dodge, where they spent the fall and winter of 1867–68. Much to the consternation of the Kansans and army officers, the presents contained a considerable amount of ammunition intended, of course, for the Indians' use on their winter hunts. Since no agent was as yet able to live among the Cheyennes, the commissioners obtained the services of George Bent and John S. Smith to reside among the tribe and induce them to respect their treaty obligations.

A troublesome problem still remained. Was the entire Cheyenne tribe living on the Southern Plains bound by the provisions of the Treaty of Medicine Lodge? If Commissioner Taylor's estimate of two thousand Cheyennes being present when the gifts were distributed was correct, then the vast majority seemed to be within its provisions. Tall Bull, Bull Bear, Whirlwind, and White Horse signed the document and constituted adequate representation of the warrior element of the tribe. Without an accurate census of the tribe, there is no way of estimating the size of the following of Roman Nose and Medicine Arrows, and we can assume that only a small fraction of the warriors of the Southern Cheyennes abstained from recognizing the treaty by refusing to participate in the division of the presents.[16]

The treaty did not mean that the Cheyennes and Arapahoes intended to abandon their conflicts with other Indian tribes. From their Cimarron River camps the two tribes sent out war parties against the Kaws, who had raided their pony herds on Medicine Lodge Creek. On November 21, 1867, a war party of Cheyenne and Arapaho warriors engaged a well-armed group of Kaws twenty-five miles east of Fort Zarah. In this fight the confederated tribes lost five warriors killed and seven severely wounded; a little later another retaliation was unsuccessful, so the warriors planned to strike the Kaws when spring came. Indian Agent Wynkoop feared "a bloody war" between these tribal foes and realized that large war parties of the Plains Indians would cause alarms along the whole Kansas frontier. The

---

16 Taylor to Browning, November 1, 1867 (Telegram), Indian Peace Commission, Separated Correspondence; Ashton J. H. White to Sherman, November 2, 1867, Office of the Adjutant General, Letters Received; Garfield, "Defense of the Kansas Frontier, 1866–1867," *loc. cit.*, 343–44; Crawford, *Kansas in the Sixties*, 278.

Cheyennes considered their troubles with both the Kaws and Osages so serious that twelve of their chiefs, invited to Washington during the winter of 1867–68, declined the invitation.[17]

The Cheyennes remained in contact with their agent through John S. Smith, who lived in the Cimarron River camps. Generally the Cheyennes caused no difficulties during the winter months, which they passed hunting buffalo and providing themselves with robes for trade and food. By ignoring Smith's information, Wynkoop argued plausibly that the Cheyennes were in need of food and suggested the issuance of flour, sugar, and coffee for the comfort of his charges.[18] Transportation contractors and those interested in supplying provisions undoubtedly had reached the ear of Wynkoop.

Soon old problems arose anew. Since the Cheyennes were successful in their winter hunts, robes were available with which to buy liquor from merchants at Fort Dodge. Quickly the liquor problem got out of hand, and John Smith commented to Superintendent Murphy that it "is certainly a dangerous thing for them to tamper with at this time." The Cheyennes also complained that they had not yet received the large quantities of arms and ammunition promised them at the Treaty of Medicine Lodge, and the presence of a surveying party, which meant roads and railroads to the Indians, also disturbed them.[19]

Isaac L. Butterfield was even more explicit in his warnings than Smith. While trading legally in the Cimarron River villages during January and February, 1868, Butterfield observed that Cheyennes and Arapahoes obtained whisky easily if they possessed sufficient robes. One brave returned from Fort Dodge with five gallons of liquor, and soon the whole camp was drunk. Big Mouth of the Arapahoes, a little later, arrived in his village with eighteen bottles and a keg of "fire water," which caused Butterfield to write that although the

[17] Wynkoop to Murphy, November 30, 1867, January 8, 9, 1868, Upper Arkansas Agency, Letters Received; Wynkoop to Murphy, December 18, 1867, Central Superintendency III; Captain William Thompson to AAAG., District of the Upper Arkansas, November 29, 1867, Fort Dodge, Letters Sent. Grinnell (*Cheyenne Indians,* I, 89), insists that during this period of time the Cheyennes had ten bands.

[18] Smith to Murphy, January 17, 1867, Central Superintendency I; Wynkoop to Murphy, January 21, 1867, Upper Arkansas Agency, Letters Received.

[19] Wynkoop to Murphy, February 1, 1868, Smith to Murphy, February 5, 1868, Upper Arkansas Agency, Letters Received.

Indians did not threaten him or his companions, "it was'nt a very nice situation to be in." Major Douglass, commanding officer at Fort Dodge, admitted that his efforts to check the flow of whisky failed because of the skill and elusiveness of the liquor peddlers.[20]

Indian Agent Wynkoop, despite these problems, remained at Fort Larned and only when food was available for distribution did he make a tour of his agency. Over eighty tons of beef, sixty tons of flour, twenty tons of bacon, five tons of coffee, ten tons of sugar, and four and one-half tons of salt, Wynkoop believed, would go far in keeping the Cheyennes and Arapahoes "content with their lot, and tend toward civilizing them by warning them from their old habits than any plan that could be adopted." The Indian agent conveniently overlooked clear indications that trouble was ahead. Chiefs such as Black Kettle, Little Robe, Medicine Arrows, and Big Jake accepted these provisions either at Fort Dodge or Fort Larned while their young warriors were scouring the Arkansas River Valley looking for their enemies, the Kaws. In their search for foes, the young warriors received the support of their chiefs, who told Wynkoop that since they were the aggrieved parties, "it was necessary for them . . . to strike their enemies once" before they would consider settling the differences.[21]

During April, 1868, it became apparent that the Cheyennes and Arapahoes were dissatisfied with their Medicine Lodge Treaty reservation. Early in that month Lieutenant Frederick H. Beecher, while on patrol with two enlisted men and seven civilians eighty miles northwest of Fort Wallace, found evidences of large Cheyenne and Sioux camps. Although hunting parties of Indians in pursuit of scattered, small herds of buffalo approached within a mile of Beecher's party, no sign of hostility was manifested by the hunters. Knowing that they had been seen, the Cheyennes and Arapahoes informed their agent by April 10 that they intended to move north for the

[20] Butterfield to Murphy, February 5, 1868, Upper Arkansas Agency, Letters Received; Douglass to AAG., Department of the Missouri, March 24, 1868, Fort Dodge, Letters Sent.

[21] Receipt of Subsistence by Wynkoop, Central Superintendency III; Report of Distribution of Subsistence, April 25, 1868, Wynkoop to Murphy, April 10, 1868, Upper Arkansas Agency, Letters Received; Douglass to AAG., Department of the Missouri, March 1, 21, 1868, Fort Dodge, Letters Sent.

spring and summer of 1868 and establish their villages on Pawnee Fork and Walnut Creek.[22]

George Bent's visit to the Moache Utes and Jicarilla Apaches also indicated Cheyenne unwillingness to accept as permanent their new reservation. As an emissary for Black Kettle and Little Raven, Bent initiated efforts to bring peace between his people and the Utes, who had warred with the Cheyennes and Arapahoes for decades. Nothing came of these councils, but they can be explained, perhaps, as an evidence that the two chiefs realized that the Cheyennes and Arapahoes could not be restrained from resuming their wars with the American frontiersmen. The chiefs hoped, it would seem, to move their tribes farther west into the mountains and avoid the troublesome contact with the whites.[23]

Until May, 1868, nothing broke the tranquility of peace. Special Indian Agent Alexander R. Banks traveled without military escort among the Indians of the Upper Arkansas Agency, although he noted the deleterious impact of the encroachment of the railroads and settlements upon the buffalo economy of the Southern Plains Indians. Conditions were developing, however, that would bring unrest to the Kansas frontier once more. Adamantly the leaders of the Cheyennes and Arapahoes refused to settle their disputes with the Kaws until they had struck their enemies once and taken sufficient revenge. The increase in the number of these Indians camping near or north of the Arkansas River quickly brought forth rumors that depredations were soon to follow. General Philip H. Sheridan, who assumed command of the Department of the Missouri in March, 1868, began to note increasing insolence on the part of the Cheyennes, whom he accused of burning down a trader's store at Fort Zarah on May 19 and attacking a citizen wagon train on May 26 near Coyote station on the Smoky Hill road.[24]

---

[22] Captain E. P. Miller to AAAG., District of the Upper Arkansas, April 11, 1868, Fort Wallace, Letters Received; Wynkoop to Murphy, April 10, 1868, Upper Arkansas Agency, Letters Received.

[23] E. B. Dennison to Wynkoop, April 30, 1868, Upper Arkansas Agency, Letters Received.

[24] Banks to Taylor, May 4, 1868, Central Superintendency III; Sheridan to AAG., Military Division of the Missouri, May 27, 1868, Office of the Adjutant General, Letters Received; Sheridan to Sully, May 27, 1868, Department of the Missouri, Letters Sent.

Operating under personal orders from General Sheridan, Lieutenant Beecher kept the Cheyennes under close watch. Uniquely, for a short period of time, army officers and Indian officials agreed that the war scare originated with groups hoping to profit from army contracts. Beecher did not deny that the young warriors were restless and had killed a man four miles from Fort Wallace, but he told General Sheridan that these small, isolated hostilities were undertaken by Indian youths who wanted to count coup to become warriors, and the incidents were not a prelude to general hostilities. William F. ("Buffalo Bill") Cody, however, was not so certain after he was chased back into the forward camp of the Kansas Pacific Railroad by eight Sioux warriors whom the fearless buffalo hunter reported as being determined to lift his scalp.[25]

Late in May, 1868, the Cheyennes organized a large war party of at least three hundred warriors to punish the Kaws. Chiefs of the tribe hid the true purpose of the party by telling Lieutenant Beecher that their young men were going to fight some Pawnees. On June 3 the leaders of the warriors, Tall Bull, Whirlwind, and Little Robe, picked a smaller portion of their warriors to dash through the Kaw camp at Council Grove, Kansas, trying to gain vengeance for the Cheyenne deaths suffered six months before. The surprise attack gained the Cheyennes nothing, and the two tribes refused an attempted mediation by Albert G. Boone. For four hours the Indian foes struggled for an advantage on the surrounding plains, and toward evening the Cheyenne war leader signaled for his braves to withdraw. As the Cheyennes withdrew, they passed through Council Grove, where several buildings belonging to mixed-blood Kaws were burned and the warriors accepted some sugar and coffee from the citizens of the town. In the outlying region the warriors found the farmhouses deserted and appropriated some beeves for food, but the Cheyennes made no effort to molest the settlers. Failing to receive the expected peace overture from the Kaws, the Cheyennes with their three wounded warriors made their way to Fort Larned, where Little Robe visited Indian Agent Wynkoop and reported the events of the raid. Little Robe admitted freely that his young men had

25 Beecher to Sheridan, May 28, June 4, 1868, Philip H. Sheridan Papers, Library of Congress, Washington, D. C. (hereafter cited as Sheridan Papers).

killed some cattle for food. He insisted, however, that while he had seen farmers fleeing with their families to places of safety, the Cheyennes did not disturb any buildings or people other than the Kaws.[26]

General Sheridan quickly learned of the Kaw raid from Lieutenant Beecher. The warriors, Beecher wrote, were adequately armed with rifles, carbines, and revolvers and were well mounted on sturdy Indian ponies of which each warrior seemed to possess at least five. The Cheyennes, the young Lieutenant observed, were not only in possession of ponies but also "enough American horses for a calvy regt. & mules sufficient to stock a good division." Still, Beecher saw no serious trouble arising from the Cheyennes' conflict with the Kaws. Beecher, through John S. Smith and George Bent, further learned that the Cheyennes and Arapahoes expected to be badly cheated by the whites at their annuity payment. When Sheridan's observer asked what they would do when cheated, the Cheyennes' spokesman replied that they would "go home & be poor & cry."[27]

When Superintendent Murphy learned of the Kaw raid, he immediately banned the delivery of the guns and ammunition due the Cheyennes. At the annuity payment attempted by Indian Agent Wynkoop in mid-July at Fort Larned, the Cheyennes refused to take part in the distribution until arms and ammunition were among their goods. The Kansas press interpreted the attitude of the Cheyennes very differently from Wynkoop. The Cheyennes, the newspaper accounts read, threatened General Alfred Sully, who was observing the distribution, and stated that after placing their women and children in safety they would return and seize the arms intended for their use. Sully at the time made no mention of the alleged Cheyenne threat and noted only that the Cheyennes "were cross and sullen." To meet any disturbance, Sully collected as many troops as possible in the vicinity of Fort Larned, and this action seemed to quiet not only the Cheyennes but also the Kiowas and Comanches,

---

[26] Boone to Taylor, June 4, 1868, Wynkoop to Murphy, June 12, 1868, Stover to Murphy, September 10, 1868, in *Report, Commissioner of Indian Affairs, 1868*, 64–66, 261; Asbury to AAAG., District of the Upper Arkansas, Fort Larned, Letters Sent, United States Army Commands, Records of the War Department, National Archives, Washington, D. C.; Garfield, "Defense of the Kansas Frontier, 1868–1869," *KHQ*, Vol. I, No. 5 (November, 1932), 454; Beecher to Sheridan, June 5, 1868, Sheridan Papers.

[27] Beecher to Sheridan, June 13, 1868, Sheridan Papers.

who were "impudent and defiant and refused to remain on their new reservation." After a council with Sully the Cheyennes moved their villages up Pawnee Fork where, George Bent told Beecher, they were well satisfied and planned no outbreak. Commissioner Taylor, when apprised of the Cheyennes' and Arapahoes' irritation, reversed himself and by telegram and letter of July 23, permitted Indian Agent Wynkoop to issue the arms if he thought it "necessary to preserve the peace, and that no evil will result." As the result of their own observations, Murphy and Sully suggested additional Congressional appropriations for food and clothing for the Indians. Unless more supplies were forthcoming, Sully stated, the Indians would soon have to steal rather than starve, "and this will lead to another Indian war, which ... [Sully thought] will take place this fall."[28]

The delay in the delivery of arms and ammunition to the Cheyennes was of short duration. On August 9, 1868, the whole of the Cheyennes appeared at Fort Larned where Wynkoop delivered about 160 revolvers, eight rifles, twelve kegs of powder, one and one-half kegs of lead, and fifteen thousand percussion caps to the Cheyennes. Both Murphy and Wynkoop justified this distribution on the grounds that the Cheyennes were peacefully inclined and that the Indians needed the ammunition for their fall hunt. There is no evidence that General Sully was in any way responsible for the concession to the Cheyennes, as the decision was made and carried out by officials of the Bureau of Indian Affairs.[29]

Within a week after the arms were issued at Fort Larned, a large war party slashed through the Saline and Solomon valleys. Within a few days the warriors, numbering about two hundred Cheyennes,

28 C. E. Mix to Murphy, June 15, 1868, Taylor to Murphy, June 25, 1868, in 40 Cong., 3 sess., *Sen. Exec. Doc. No. 13*, 6; Wynkoop to Murphy, July 20, 1868, Upper Arkansas Agency, Letters Received; Taylor to Murphy, Taylor to Wynkoop, July 23, 1868, in *Report, Commissioner of Indian Affairs, 1868*, 67–68; Murphy to Taylor, July 29, 1868, Central Superintendency III; Beecher to Sheridan, July 22, 1868, Sheridan Papers.

29 Murphy to Taylor, August 1, 1868, Wynkoop to Murphy, August 10, 1868, in *Report, Commissioner of Indian Affairs, 1868*, 68–70; Philip H. Sheridan, *Personal Memoirs of P. H. Sheridan, General, United States Army*, II, 289. The intervention of General Sully in the distribution of arms cannot be sustained but it is generally followed by Garfield, "Defense of the Kansas Frontier, 1868–1869," *loc. cit.*, 455–56, and Carl Coke Rister, *The Southwestern Frontier, 1865–1881*, 106–107.

twenty Sioux who were visiting the Cheyennes at the time, and four Arapahoes, murdered a dozen settlers, outraged, then killed several women, seized several children as prisoners, burned buildings, stole stock, and drove hundreds of settlers from the region. It is impossible to determine exactly why the Cheyennes raided. Lieutenant Beecher furnished General Sheridan with as plausible an explanation as is known. He did not believe that the warriors intended to begin a general war because their families were still vulnerably located on the tributaries of the Republican River. Beecher explained to Sheridan that the warriors had recently suffered a defeat at the hands of the Pawnees. Returning to their camps, the braves found a considerable amount of whisky at the various ranches along the roads, then fell upon the frontier settlements, venting "their rage on the first object they could meet."[30]

The composition of the war party is well established. It consisted of warriors from the camps of Black Kettle, Little Rock, Bull Bear, and Medicine Arrows, and it was led by Red Nose, a Dog Soldier; Man-Who-Breaks-the-Marrow-Bones, a brother of White Antelope, who had been killed at Sand Creek; Tall Wolf, the oldest son of Medicine Arrows; Porcupine Bear, a son of Big Head; and Bear-That-Goes-Alone, a brother of Sand Hill. Indian Agent Wynkoop immediately called for the punishment of those guilty of the outrages, realizing that with such a cross section of the tribe represented it would be difficult to isolate the innocent from the guilty. As the warriors moved south, troops began their pursuit. Some of the men went back to the camps of Black Kettle and crossed the Arkansas River while the greater number of the war party turned north and joined the villages on the Solomon River.[31]

Officials of the Bureau of Indian Affairs reacted in various ways to the news of the raid. Indian Agent Wynkoop stated that while the

[30] "Report of an interview between Colonel E. W. Wynkoop, United States Indian agent, and Little Rock, a Cheyenne chief, held at Fort Larned, Kansas, August 19, 1868, . . . ." in *Report, Commissioner of Indian Affairs, 1868*, 72; "Statement of Edmund Guerriere [*sic*], February 9, 1869, in 41 Cong., 2 sess., *House Exec. Doc. No. 1*, pt. 2, p. 47; Garfield, "Defense of the Kansas Frontier, 1868–1869, *loc. cit.*, 456; Olive A. Clark, "Early Days along the Solomon Valley," KSHS *Collections*, XVII, 723–24; Beecher to Sheridan, August 15, 1868, Sheridan Papers.

[31] *Report, Commissioner of Indian Affairs, 1868*, 72–73.

majority of the Cheyennes and their chiefs regretted the foray, they "were powerless to restrain their young men." Acting Commissioner of Indian Affairs Charles E. Mix conceded that the murders should be punished, but he added, "it would not be right to punish the innocent for acts not committed by them." Superintendent Murphy, thoroughly disillusioned, accused the Cheyennes of plotting the raid at the very time they were making profession of friendship at Fort Larned. "I can," wrote Murphy, "no longer have confidence in what they say or promise. War is surely upon us."[32]

Early in September of 1868, the Cheyennes were credited with more depredations. These forays took place from the Cimarron Crossing westward to the Purgatoire River. After the Cheyennes raided the beef herd on Bogg's Ranch in the Purgatoire Valley on September 8, Captain William H. Penrose took a troop of the Seventh Cavalry and a company of infantry and tried to bring the raiders to bay. Sighting a party of warriors in the distance, Penrose sent forward a lieutenant and ten troopers. After a chase of four miles, the warriors turned on their pursuers, killing two and wounding another in the detachment while suffering the loss of one noted Cheyenne warrior, One Eyed Bull, during the fight. These actions convinced Wynkoop that all of the Indians of his jurisdiction were far south of the Arkansas River and beyond reach of his communications. He therefore asked permission for a leave of absence, which was granted by Superintendent Murphy.[33]

Wynkoop's departure from the Arkansas River was followed by his resignation. On October 7, 1868, after his arrival in Philadelphia, Wynkoop wrote a long letter to Commissioner Mix fully explaining the causes of the outbreak. Shortages of food, arms, and ammunition caused the "wilder elements" among the Cheyennes to become increasingly incensed, and as their anger mounted, they fell upon the frontier settlements in the Saline and Solomon valleys. He recounted the murders at Sand Creek, the wanton destruction of Cheyenne property by Hancock, and the inadequate amount of time given to

---

[32] Wynkoop to Murphy, August 19, 1868, Murphy to Mix, August 22, 1868, in *Report, Commissioner of Indian Affairs, 1868*, 70–71.

[33] Penrose to AAG., Department of the Missouri, September 10, 12, 1868, Fort Lyon, Letters Sent, United States Army Commands, National Archives, Washington, D. C.; Wynkoop to Murphy, September 3, 20, 1868, Upper Arkansas Agency, Letters Received.

the chiefs to surrender the young men guilty of the recent attacks. Congress, by its failure to appropriate a few thousand dollars with which supplies could have been purchased for the Indians, failed to save the lives of the frontiersmen, and had forced the troops into hunting down and destroying innocent Indians "for the faults of the guilty."[34]

Superintendent Murphy condemned the Cheyennes and Arapahoes where Wynkoop had vindicated them. In anger Murphy demanded that the Cheyennes and Arapahoes be held accountable for the recent outrages. The confederated tribes had no reason for the attacks since their annuities had been paid to them and the government had fulfilled every treaty commitment under the peace pact at Medicine Lodge Creek. On their part the tribes had violently broken their treaty pledges by committing gross outrages. He advocated leaving the Cheyennes, especially, in the hands of the military until they sued for peace. Before, Murphy argued, the government had pleaded, coaxed, and bought treaties from the Cheyennes—ineffectively, as experience proved.[35] The clashing ideas of Murphy and Wynkoop undoubtedly precipitated the latter's resignation.

Other debates raged as the army began concentrating troops to fight the Cheyennes. General Sherman entered into a long defense of the use of troops for Samuel F. Tappan, a peace advocate much impressed with Wynkoop's reasoning. Sherman promised Tappan that he would do all that was possible "to segregate the friendly from the hostile, but the latter should now be killed," and to Grant, Sherman maintained that the Cheyennes had broken out without a particle of reason. The issue to Sherman was clear. Either the Indians must give way or the whites must abandon all lands west of the Missouri River—an admission that forty million people were cowed by a few thousand savages. Sherman reminded Tappan that he had approved the generous policy of the Indian Peace Commission and that he had stretched his authority to aid the Indians. But, Sherman continued, "when they laugh at our credulity, rape our women, burn whole trains with their drivers to cinders, and send word that they never

[34] Wynkoop to Mix, October 7, 1868, Murphy to Taylor, December 5, 1868, Upper Arkansas Agency, Letters Received.

[35] Murphy to Mix, September 19, 1868, Central Superintendency III.

intended to keep their treaties, then we must submit or we must fight them. When we come to fighting Indians I will take my code from soldiers and not civilians."[36]

There were also other incidents that supported the military contention of widespread Cheyenne hostility. Shortly after the distribution of annuities at Fort Larned, General Sheridan employed three veteran frontiersmen, William Comstock, Abner S. Grover, and Richard Parr, to work with Lieutenant Beecher in an effort to maintain contact with the Cheyennes and Arapahoes and also to explain governmental policy to the Indians. Comstock and Grover were assigned to the region west of Fort Wallace and Parr to the country of the Saline and Solomon rivers. To gain additional information about the raids on the Saline and Solomon valleys, Lieutenant Beecher sent Comstock and Grover to Turkey Legs, whose camp was known to be on the Solomon River. Their reception cooled when an Indian runner brought news of the fighting in the Saline Valley. At this point Indian and white versions of the events are in conflict. According to the Indians' traditions, Bull Bear, a Dog Soldier chief, personally escorted Comstock and Grover from the camp to safety. A war party returning from the fights to the northeast, however, found the two scouts, killed Comstock, and severely wounded Grover. Grover's account relates that they were ordered from the camp with an escort of seven young braves; as they rode slowly away, the young men dropped behind and suddenly fired upon them from the rear. Several bullets ripped the life from Comstock; Grover, though badly wounded, protected the body of his friend, beat off the Indians until nightfall, and made his way on foot to a place near Monument station on the Kansas Pacific Railroad where a train picked him up. When he could travel Grover was brought to Fort Wallace, where he reported to Captain H. C. Bankhead, commanding the post."[37]

[36] Sherman to Tappan, September 6, 24, 1868, Tappan MSS, Colorado State Historical Society, Denver; Sherman to Grant, September 9, 1868, Headquarters of the Army, Letters Received.

[37] Grinnell, *Fighting Cheyennes,* 263; 40 Cong., 3 sess., *House Exec. Doc. No. 1,* 10–11; Sheridan, *Memoirs,* II, 292–94; *Harper's Weekly,* Vol. XII, No. 612 (September 19, 1868), 606; Captain H. C. Bankhead to AAAG., District of the Upper Arkansas, August 19, 1868, Fort Wallace, Letters Sent; George Bent to Hyde, August 9, 1904, MSS of Colorado State Historical Society, Denver, Colorado.

The raids and continued depredations brought General Sheridan into the field immediately. The governors of Kansas and Colorado insisted upon protection of their frontiers, and the General pledged the former: "It may take until cold weather to catch them, but we will not cease till it is accomplished." The "catching" of the warriors was a difficult task without sufficient troops even for such a competent military officer as Sheridan. In the whole of the Department of the Missouri, Sheridan could muster only 1,200 cavalry, of whom 800 were fit for field duty, and 1,400 infantry for garrison duty at the posts and stations along the roads. To add a mobile striking force to his command, on August 24, 1868, Sheridan ordered his aide, Major George A. Forsyth, to enlist fifty "first class hardy frontiersmen" from Forts Harker and Hays for immediate service against the Indians. When organized, Major Forsyth's command also contained Lieutenant Beecher, Dr. John H. Mooers as surgeon, and Abner S. Grover, recovered from his wounds, as chief scout.[38]

Leaving Fort Hays on August 29, Forsyth's Scouts arrived at Fort Wallace on September 5, remaining there five days. The small force of scouts, well armed with Spencer carbines and revolvers, felt confident as they left Fort Wallace to relieve Sheridan, Kansas, a small settlement thirteen miles east of the post. By the time Forsyth arrived at Sheridan, the Indians had also intercepted a wagon train nearby, killing two Mexican teamsters and then riding away. Trailing the Indians, the command veered north toward the Republican River and its tributaries where Governor Hunt in a previous appeal had claimed the Indians were concentrated. By traveling up the Arikaree fork, Forsyth's scouts picked up the trail of a small Indian war party which they followed for several days. On the evening of September 16, Forsyth selected a camp site on the north bank of the Arikaree. As the campfires were built, the men began to speculate whether the war party, fully aware that Forsyth was trailing them, would return with an overwhelming force of their tribesmen. Lieutenant Beecher said little, but the chief scout, Grover, thought the

[38] Sheridan to Crawford, August 21, 1868, in Crawford, *Kansas in the Sixties,* 292–93; Sheridan to Sherman, October 15, 1868, in 40 Cong., 3 sess., *House Exec. Doc. No. 1,* 17; Sheridan, *Memoirs,* II, 297–98; Garfield, "Defense of the Kansas Frontier, 1868–1869," *loc. cit.,* 457; Forsyth to McKeever, March 31, 1869, Office of the Adjutant General, Letters Received (hereafter cited as Forsyth, *Report*).

Indians were certain to return in strength. Only twelve miles away were three large Indian camps, two of Brulé Sioux under Pawnee Killer and the other composed of Dog Soldiers under Bull Bear, Tall Bull, and White Horse. In the Cheyenne village were also a number of the Sutaio band, led by Black Shin, with whom Roman Nose was living.[39]

The country surrounding Forsyth's camp was ideal for a surprise attack. The Arikaree cuts well below the higher level of the plains at this point, and each side of the stream is lined with broken, low-lying hills. When a small party of Sioux warriors discovered the exact location of Forsyth's camp, six young Sioux and two Cheyenne warriors decided to raid the scouts' horses. Near daybreak, guided by Forsyth's campfires, the raiders managed to stampede only seven animals and also spoiled an opportunity to overwhelm the scouts with one massive charge. As the scouts saddled up their horses to retreat, Indian warriors "seemed to spring from the very earth—out of the tall weeds and bushes along the creek, from the depressions in the ground, and began swarming out over the hills." Major Forsyth ordered his men to occupy a small island in the dry creek bed of the Arikaree where bushes and a stand of cottonwood trees afforded some cover. The sand river bed gave the scouts a clear field of fire around the whole island. With two hundred and fifty rounds of ammunition for each man and trees for protection, the frontiersmen prepared to take a heavy toll of the Indians. A siege, however, would give trouble because their food supply was exhausted.[40]

No massed charge was attempted by the Indians at the outset. The Cheyennes and Sioux circled the island and poured a heavy fire in upon the scouts as they rapidly dug rifle pits with their hands and knives. Most of the Indians broke their charge as they approached

[39] Forsyth, *Report;* Chauncey B. Whitney, "Diary," KSHS *Collections, 1911–12,* XII, 297; George A. Forsyth, "A Frontier Fight," *Harper's New Monthly Magazine,* Vol. XCI, No. 541 (June, 1895), 41–44; George Bent to Hyde, September 3, 1913, Bent Letters, Coe Collection.

[40] The fight took place near the small settlement of Beecher Island, Yuma County, Colorado. John Hurst and Sigmund Shlesinger, "Battle of the Arikaree," KSHS *Collections,* 1919–20, XV, 532; Forsyth, *Report;* Whitney, "Diary," *loc. cit.,* 297; Forsyth, "A Frontier Fight," *loc. cit.,* 42–43, 47; Bankhead to Brevet Colonel J. Schuyler Crosby, September 22, 1868, Fort Wallace, Letters Sent; George Bent to Hyde, June 10, 1904, MSS of Colorado State Historical Society, Denver, Colorado.

the island and only a few warriors rode through the beleaguered scouts. Casualties mounted quickly before the rifle pits were deep enough for adequate protection. Dr. Mooers was struck in the head by a bullet and died three days later, never regaining consciousness; Lieutenant Beecher was shot through the body and lay in agony with a broken back, begging his comrades to shoot him; and Major Forsyth was shot through both legs, one of which was badly shattered between the ankle and knee. Six enlisted scouts were also lost during the early fighting—four of them mortally wounded.

Annihilation seemed inevitable to Forsyth's men; all avenues of escape seemed blocked. About nine-thirty in the morning the warriors massed for their first charge and surged to within a few yards of the island. The scouts poured volley after volley from their seven-shot Spencers into the Indians' ranks, breaking the charge. Twice more that afternoon the warriors returned to destroy the scouts but lost many of their bravest men, including Roman Nose who went down with a bullet through the body. At the end of the day Forsyth's command was in dire peril, twenty-two of fifty-two men either dead or wounded, the animals killed, medical supplies and rations exhausted, and an estimated six hundred Cheyenne and Sioux warriors bent on their extinction. Word to Fort Wallace, eighty-five miles away, was their only hope.

Two scouts, Jack Stilwell and Pierre Trudeau, volunteered to carry the message to Fort Wallace on a mission thought by "Sharp" Grover to be certain death. Using all of their plains' lore to get through the ring of Indians, Stilwell and Trudeau evaded detection. Once, on the morning of September 19, a large war party of Indians appeared directly in their path, and the two scouts took refuge in a buffalo carcass sufficiently intact to afford cover. A rattlesnake, resenting the human intrusion, hissed its warning and coiled to strike, but Stilwell cut short its attack with a well-directed stream of tobacco juice. Reaching the wagon road to Fort Wallace on September 20, they followed it for two more days until they met two Negro troopers of the Tenth Cavalry, a detachment under Brevet Lieutenant Colonel Louis H. Carpenter in the field to co-operate with Forsyth's scouts. The troopers rode on to carry the news to Carpenter's command while the scouts continued on to Fort Wallace.

On the days following Stilwell's and Trudeau's departure, the Indians made no more massed charges. They contented themselves with ringing the island and sniping constantly at the well-entrenched scouts, who suffered no additional casualties. During the siege the men found prickly pears and coyote meat an improvement over putrid horse flesh roasted and boiled. Water, fortunately, was abundant and was obtained by digging in the soft sand of the island. After four days, the men began to despair of their lives; Chauncey Whitney confided to his diary, "My God! Have you deserted us?" Intermittent firing was continued by the Indians until September 22, when they retired to the hills, and two days later the warriors completely abandoned the field of action.

Carpenter's troops were the first to relieve Forsyth's men. On the morning of September 25, 1868, the seventy men of the Tenth Cavalry and the seventeen frontier scouts with Carpenter brought shouts of joy and tears of relief from the scouts on Beecher's Island. On the following day Captain Bankhead arrived from Fort Wallace with one hundred men and two field pieces. No effort was made to follow the departed Indians because Forsyth's command needed immediate medical attention. Two days were spent preparing the badly mauled scouts for travel back to Fort Wallace.[41]

Forsyth's losses are well established, but those of the Indians are disputed. Six members of Forsyth's little command died either on the field of battle or later of wounds, while fifteen others survived their injuries. At the battlefield Forsyth stated that he and his men killed thirty-five warriors, but in his official report he reduced the number to thirty-two. He also claimed that his men wounded at least one hundred warriors during the fighting. Long after the battle Indians minimized their losses and stated that six Cheyennes, one Arapaho, and two Sioux fell before the frontiersmen's carbines. Of these, Roman Nose, the bravest Cheyenne war leader, was the most

---

41 Bankhead to Crosby, September 22, 1868, Lieutenant Hugh Johnson to Carpenter, September 22, 1868; Bankhead to McKeever, October 5, 1868, Fort Wallace, Letters Sent; Forsyth, *Report*; Whitney, "Diary," *loc. cit.*, 298–99; Hurst and Sheslinger, "Battle of the Arikaree," *loc. cit.*, 533–38, 542–45; Forsyth, "A Frontier Right," *loc. cit.*, 47–61; E. A. Brininstool, "The Rescue of Forsyth's Scouts," KSHS *Collections*, XVII, 845–51; George Bent to Hyde, September 25, 1868, MSS of Colorado State Historical Society, Denver, Colorado.

prominent. There is no possibility of reconciling the differences between the contemporary white accounts and those stories told from memory by Cheyennes living during the early twentieth century.[42]

Failing to wipe out Forsyth's scouts, the Indians moved away from the Arikaree Fork. To throw off any pursuit, the large encampments first moved southeast and then reversed their directions to new camps on the Republican River and its tributaries. With additional re-enforcements arriving from the South, Sheridan hoped to concentrate fifteen companies of cavalry to hunt down the Indians on the Central Plains. Sheridan anticipated that his cavalry, including the Fifth Cavalry recently transferred into his department, would intercept the Indians and demand unconditional surrender. At any event, he promised Sherman that the Indians "will not find much quiet for the balance of the season."[43]

Major William B. Royall was temporarily placed in command of units of the Fifth Cavalry to scout in western Kansas. Royall took seven companies of the regiment and headed north from Fort Harker on October 1, 1868, into the Republican Valley. On October 11, Major Royall split his command, sending three companies toward the Republican and a like number toward Beaver Creek. Royall remained in the bivouac with one company. His scouting troops did not find the Indians—rather, the Indians found Royall. Three days after the troops departed, Tall Bull with most of the Dog Soldiers swept through Royall's encampment, killing two troopers and running off twenty-six cavalry mounts. When the full contingent was reunited shortly afterwards, Royall tried to find the elusive Indians and, failing, returned to the Kansas Pacific Railroad.[44]

Not all of the hostiles remained on the Republican River. On October 6 mixed parties of the Cheyennes and Arapahoes appeared near Fort Lyon. Captain Penrose, with only seventy men in his garri-

[42] Forsyth, *Report;* Forsyth to Bankhead, September 19, 1868, in "A Frontier Fight," *loc. cit.,* 59–60; George Bent to Hyde, June 10, 20, 1904, MSS of Colorado State Historical Society, Denver, Colorado; George Bent to Hyde, May 24, 1906, Bent Letters, Coe Collection.

[43] Forsyth, *Report;* Bankhead to Sheridan, September 28, 1868, Sherman to AG., September 28, 1868, Sheridan to Sherman, September 23, 28, 1868, Office of the Adjutant General, Letters Received.

[44] George F. Price, *Across the Continent with the Fifth Cavalry,* 131–32; 40 Cong., 3 sess., *House Exec. Doc. No. 1,* 19.

son fit for field duty, could not attack the Indians who were at least three hundred strong. These warriors, a day after they were first observed near Fort Lyon, intercepted a train of eight wagons ten miles east of Sand Creek, stampeded the oxen, severely wounded one of the eleven men in the train, and seized Mrs. Clara Blinn and her small child. Two hundred Indians kept the wagon train surrounded until October 12, when Captain Penrose, hearing of the attack, sent out a portion of his garrison to save the travelers. Since the wagon master claimed that he recognized Satanta among the Indians, the Cheyennes and Arapahoes might have received some support from the Kiowas.[45]

Major Eugene A. Carr arrived in mid-October, 1868, to assume permanent command of the Fifth Cavalry on the Plains. Intending to join his troops, who were still operating under Royall, Carr left Fort Wallace escorted by two companies of the Tenth Cavalry commanded by Captain Carpenter. When the troops were moving down Beaver Creek on October 17, a party of two hundred Cheyennes opened fire at long range. Retreating to high ground, the cavalry corralled their wagons, dismounted, and repelled a savage charge. The Cheyennes dashed up to the wagons, exhibiting reckless and superb horsemanship, and discharged their guns and bows at point-blank range, losing five warriors. After a six-hour fight the Cheyennes withdrew and disappeared. Major Carr did not continue the search for his command but returned to Fort Wallace on October 21 to await more definite information on the location of his seven companies.[46]

The Cheyennes deny that they ever charged Carpenter's troops. The incident occurred because a young Northern Cheyenne, called Bullet Proof, claimed after the Beecher Island fight the power to protect others from injury or death from white men's guns. Selecting eight other young braves, Bullet Proof dressed them with a sash made of the anterior portions of a four-year-old buffalo hide and

[45] Penrose to AAAG., Department of the Missouri, October 8, 11, 15, 1868, Fort Lyon, Letters Sent.

[46] Report of Brevet Major General E. A. Carr, Commanding Expedition from Fort Lyon, of the Operations of his Command during the Late Campaign against hostile Indians, to General Chauncey McKeever, April 7, 1869, Sheridan Papers (hereafter cited as Carr *Report*).

brought them under the protection of his powerful medicine. Bullet Proof instructed his companions to circle the corralled wagons four times, and if they were unharmed, they could then charge the wagons with impunity. The young men, riding hard, began to circle the wagons, but before the circuit was completed their horses began to drop and Broken Arrow and Bobtail Porcupine were killed. Because Bullet Proof's medicine failed, the young men withdrew and the soldiers were not bothered again. The young medicine man explained the deaths as a result of the failure of the young men to follow his instructions exactly; Bullet Proof incurred no opprobrium from his tribesmen.[47]

Sheridan was determined to keep the Indians on the move. On October 22, 1868, Major Carr joined his troops near Buffalo Tank on the Saline River. The command consisted of seven companies of the Fifth Cavalry, 458 men strong, supplemented by fifty frontier scouts under Lieutenant Silas Pepoon, some of whom had previously served with Forsyth. Major Carr quickly moved his column from the Kansas Pacific Railroad toward the Solomon River, where the Indians were thought to be concentrated. On October 25 the trail of an Indian village was discovered and easily followed until Indians began attacking Carr's advance guard and Pepoon's scouts. Not strong enough to do more than delay the progress of Carr's strong column, the Indians harassed the expedition and lost ten warriors and some ponies. Two hundred warriors, thought to be Cheyennes and Sioux, charged Carr's men, who were pressing forward without wagons or camp equipment. After the Indians fired the dry plain's grasses, the obliterated trail could not be found and Carr was unable to force the Indians to make a stand. Still, Carr made the Indians abandon their winter's supply of new lodge poles, a considerable number of lodges and undressed buffalo robes, and a quantity of their camp equipment. When he returned to Fort Wallace on November 2, Carr estimated that he had captured 130 ponies, killed 20 Indians, and wounded others.[48]

The operations of Forsyth, Royall, and Carr were not total failures

[47] George Bent to Hyde, June 10, 1904, MSS of Colorado State Historical Society; Grinnell, *Fighting Cheyennes*, 293–97.

[48] Carr to Sheridan, October 27, November 1, 1868, Office of the Adjutant General, Letters Received, Carr, *Report*.

in Sheridan's view. By keeping the Indians constantly on the move, they had forced the warriors to join their families in the region of the Antelope Hills in western Indian territory. Sheridan, however, was not content with these small harassing columns and as early as October 9, 1868, he had received approval from the War Department to strike the hostile Cheyennes during the coming winter while the Cheyennes' ponies were weak and thin. When the Indians were immobilized, Sheridan hoped to punish the Indians and bring the wars on the Plains to an end.[49]

[49] 41 Cong., 2 sess., *House Exec. Doc. No. 1*, pt. 2, p. 44.

# 14

## THE END OF FREEDOM

GENERAL SHERIDAN BLAMED THE CHEYENNES for many attacks on the Santa Fe road. Early in September, 1868, small detachments of soldiers moving between posts and civilian wagon trains lost lives and property to Indian warriors. On one occasion a large wagon train with fifty men fought off the Indians for four days while a much smaller train containing only fifteen men met complete destruction. These attacks occurred while Sheridan was at Fort Dodge, where he was visited by Little Raven, Powder Face, and Spotted Wolf of the Arapahoes who told the general that they wanted no part of the war. From his talks with the Arapahoes and army scouts, Sheridan ascertained that the Cheyennes with their families and stock were living on the Cimarron River. He therefore assembled a strong force under the command of Brigadier General Alfred Sully and sent it to attack the Cheyennes.[1]

Nine companies of the Seventh Cavalry and one company of the Third Infantry left Fort Dodge on September 7, 1868. John S. Smith, Ben Clark, and Amos Chapman, intermarried whites among the Cheyennes and Arapahoes who were familiar with the country, were assigned to Sully's command as guides. Several days were spent looking for Indian trails south of the fort. Sully sent ahead Major Joel H. Elliott, senior officer of the Seventh Cavalry troops, with four of his companies to find the Indian villages. Major Elliott saw many old Indian trails but no Indians, and on September 10 the whole com-

[1] Douglas to McKeever, September 3, 1868, Fort Dodge, Letters Sent; General Field Orders No. 1, by command of Brevet Brigadier General Alfred Sully, September 4, 1868, District of the Upper Arkansas, United States Army Commands, Records of the War Department, National Archives, Washington, D. C.; *Record of Engagements with Hostile Indians within the Military Division of the Missouri from 1868 to 1882,* 10; Sheridan to General W. A. Nichols, September 5, 1868, Sheridan Papers.

mand regrouped on the Cimarron River. The first skirmish occurred
when a party of Indians attacked the advance guard of Sully's column
that day. No casualties were suffered by the troops, and units sent
forward to drive off the Indians killed two warriors. After the Indians
disappeared, the troops bivouacked at the confluence of Crooked
Creek and the Cimarron River.

During the night parties of Indians surrounded Sully's camp and
patiently waited for an opportunity to surprise the troops. Breaking
camp on September 11, Sully assigned Captain Louis M. Hamilton
a squadron of the Seventh Cavalry to act as a rear guard. As Hamilton
moved out, two stragglers remaining behind were seized by a strong
party of warriors who dashed out of concealment in a large draw.
The warriors threw the screaming troopers across their ponies and
rode hard for the breaks surrounding the Cimarron River. Captain
Hamilton's determined pursuit of the warriors caused them to drop
the two men, one of whom was killed and the other badly mauled.
Throughout the remainder of the day, as the column marched down
the Cimarron, Sully's men fought the Indians in the hills and breaks,
killing at least eight. Armed with repeating rifles, splendidly mounted,
the Indians were identified by Sully's scouts as Cheyenne Dog Soldiers. Sully marvelled at the discipline with which the Cheyenne
leaders controlled their warriors as they signaled their commands
with a series of bugle calls.

The Indians in their retreat left the Cimarron Valley and took a
stand on Beaver Creek, an upper tributary of the North Canadian
River. Since the Indians occupied high ground in a strong defensive
position, Sully ordered his cavalry to dismount and fight on foot.
After two hours of fighting the Indians slipped away, having suffered
the loss of at least a dozen men. The warriors used many decoys,
made false trails, and harassed the stragglers in an effort to shake
Sully off the trail of their main village. By marching steadily each
day Sully remained close behind the Cheyenne village until the command crossed the South Canadian River. On September 13, in the
sand hills bordering the South Canadian, Sully ran into a well-con-
ceived trap. To protect his men and baggage train, Sully had to dismount his troops and drive the Indians through interminable sand
hills. Unable to fight his way to the Indian village, the general aban-

doned the expedition on the following day and returned to Fort Dodge to wait for additional troops. Cheyenne warriors followed Sully's troops for some distance, thumbing their noses and slapping their buttocks in derision.

Sully's expedition was not a notable success. When he reported that his troops had killed twenty to thirty warriors, Sully probably was optimistic, since the Indians usually enjoyed the better positions and carefully controlled their warriors during all of the engagements. In all the troops suffered only three killed and six wounded. Sully's movements, however, must have demonstrated to Sheridan and Sherman that if the Cheyennes were to be punished, a much stronger force than that commanded by Sully was necessary.[2]

A thoroughly angry Sherman was determined to punish the Cheyennes and their allies. Writing to Secretary of War John M. Schofield, Sherman declared: "All of the Cheyennes and Arapahoes are now at war. Admitting that some of them have not done acts of murder, rape, &c., still they have not restrained those who have, nor have they on demand given up the criminals as they agreed to do." To Schofield, Sherman advocated establishing the Cheyenne and Arapaho Agency at Old Fort Cobb on the Washita River, where the Indian agent could feed the "old, young, and feeble" while the army campaigned against the warriors.[3]

Sherman's wishes were approved after Acting Commissioner of Indian Affairs C. E. Mix received assurances that peaceful Indians gathered at Fort Cobb would be safe from harm. No Indian agents, however, were available for duty at Fort Cobb; Wynkoop was absent on leave and Albert Boone was ill. To care for the Kiowas and Comanches who had promised Sheridan and Brevet Major General

[2] Record for the Month of September, 1868, Fort Dodge, Sully to McKeever, September 16, 1868, Office of the Adjutant General, Letters Received; E. S. Godfrey, "Some Reminiscences, Including an Account of General Sully's Expedition Against the Southern Plains Indians," *Cavalry Journal*, Vol. XXXVI (July, 1927), 421–22, 424–26; E. S. Godfrey, "General Sully's Expedition against the Southern Plains Indians," MSS in Bates Collection, Custer Battlefield National Monument Museum Archives, Crow Agency, Montana; *Record of Engagements*, 11.

[3] Sherman to Schofield, September 17, 1868, in *Report, Commissioner of Indian Affairs, 1868*, 76–77; Sherman to Secretary of War, September 19, 1868 (Copy), Upper Arkansas Agency, Letters Received.

William M. Hazen that they would assemble at Fort Cobb, Captain Henry E. Alvord was ordered to proceed from Fort Arbuckle, Indian territory, to the designated post and assume charge of the Indians. In councils held at Fort Larned on September 20, 1868, Hazen had promised to conduct the Kiowas and Comanches to Fort Cobb himself. When the two tribes failed to appear at Fort Larned on the appointed day, Hazen departed for Fort Cobb, hoping that the Indians were already en route.[4]

Captain Alvord's position at Fort Cobb was fraught with difficulties. He arrived at the Washita River post during mid-October and found several hundred Indians already there and more arriving daily. Soon his slender resources of food were exhausted. In councils with the Kiowas, Comanches, Caddoes, Wichitas, and other affiliated tribes, Alvord soon learned that these Indians did not intend joining the Cheyennes and were ready to promise to act as intermediaries with the Cheyennes under Black Kettle and the whole of the Arapahoes. On October 31, Alvord learned from the assembled chiefs that a large delegation of Cheyennes and Arapahoes had promised to come to Fort Cobb within the week on a mission of friendship. Other information gathered by Alvord was less favorable. Some portions of the Kiowas and Comanches had recently received invitations from both the Cheyennes and Arapahoes to join them in hostilities. The main camp of the Cheyennes, among whom were living a large number of Sioux, was on the South Canadian near the Antelope Hills, and the principal village of the Arapahoes was also near the Cheyennes. These Indians, particularly the Cheyennes and Sioux, were accumulating supplies and ammunition by trading stolen stock to Mexicans.[5]

By the time that Hazen arrived at Fort Cobb on November 7, 1868,

---

[4] Mix to W. T. Otto, September 25, 1868, in *Report, Commissioner of Indian Affairs, 1868*, 77–79; Mix to Otto, September 30, 1868, in 40 Cong., 3 sess., *Sen Exec. Doc. No. 13*, 23–24; Hazen to Sherman, November 10, 1868, Alvord to Roy, October 30, 1868, Sheridan Papers; Hazen to Sherman, June 30, 1869, in *Report of the Commissioner of Indian Affairs, made to the Secretary of the Interior for the Year, 1869*, 388–89; William B. Hazen, "Some Corrections of 'Life on the Plains,' " *Chronicles of Okla.*, Vol. III, No. 3 (September, 1925), 300–301, 303, 304.

[5] Alvord to Roy, October 30, 1868 (Copy), November 5, 1868, Office of the Adjutant General, Letters Received.

about one thousand Caddoes, Wichitas, and members of other small tribes had already assembled for protection. Sherman, in his orders to Hazen, had outlined his duties. Hazen was to provide food and protection for all the Indians assembled at Fort Cobb with the intention of keeping out of the war. Sherman also mentioned the possibility that Sheridan might be forced to pursue the hostiles near Fort Cobb, and in that event Sheridan was already instructed "to do all he can to spare the well-disposed."[6]

Sherman's attitudes were well known to his subordinates. At the Chicago meetings of the Indian Peace Commission, Sherman and other commissioners had voted down the plans of Samuel Tappan and Commissioner Taylor for a soft Indian policy. Subsequently Sherman assured Sheridan that he would be protected from "any efforts that may be attempted in your rear to restrain your purpose or check your troops." Fighting Indians was an "inglorious war" for the regular army to fight and not one "apt to add much to our fame or personal comfort." The Indians, according to Sherman, had a free choice between extermination and survival, and now: "As brave men, and as soldiers of a Government which has exhausted its peace efforts, we, in the performance of a most unpleasant duty, accept the war begun by our enemies and hereby resolve to make its end final." A fine insight into Sherman's Indian views is found in an endorsement made on October 6, 1868, to a communication to the Office of the Adjutant General. Sherman suggested that Fort Cobb was a suitable place "from whence to issue food and clothing to friendly Indians who will be left at the close of the War, a residue which he hopes will be small."[7]

In the course of his duties at Fort Cobb, Hazen learned very little

[6] Sherman to Hazen, October 13, 1868, in Hazen, "Some Corrections of 'Life on the Plains,' " *loc. cit.*, 303; Hazen to Sherman, Office of the Adjutant General, Letters Received.

[7] Athearn, *Sherman and the Settlement of the West*, 227–29; Sherman to Sheridan, October 15, 1868, Office of the Adjutant General, Letters Received. The endorsement was written on a communication registered as M–1316 (1868), however a search for the original document disclosed that it was no longer in the Records of the War Department (see Sherman to AGO., October 6, 1868, Register of Letters Received by the Office of the Adjutant General, Records of the War Department, National Archives, Washington, D. C.).

from the Cheyennes and Arapahoes. Negligence, according to Hazen, had in part caused the most recent outbreak of the two tribes. Neither Wynkoop nor Leavenworth as Indian agents had carried out the terms of the Treaty of Medicine Lodge, and they had failed to establish their charges on reservations. Rather, the Indian agents remained on the Arkansas River, invited the Indians to visit them for their goods and annuities, and provided an opportunity to renew their raids on the Kansas frontier settlements. From some undetermined source, probably John Smith who was at Fort Cobb, Hazen was told that when the Cheyennes and Arapahoes were near Fort Larned, where whisky was abundant, a war party set out after a drinking bout to attack the Pawnees. The warriors were beaten by the Pawnees and, returning south, rode near a homesteader's house on the Saline River. One of the braves went toward the house to ask for something to eat and was warned off by the homesteader. When the Indian continued to ride toward the house, the man fired on the warrior with a shotgun. This fracas opened the war which, Hazen was told, had not been premeditated by the Cheyennes, who at the time were busy trading off the arms issued to them by Indian Agent Wynkoop at Fort Larned. Indecisive policy on the part of the Bureau of Indian Affairs led the Indians to doubt the power of the government. "Old gray headed men," Hazen wrote to Sherman, "laugh when told the Government will punish and say they have been told that since they were children."[8]

On November 20, 1868, Black Kettle and Little Robe, accompanied by Big Mouth and Spotted Wolf of the Arapahoes, appeared voluntarily at Fort Cobb. Black Kettle, speaking only for his camp of 180 lodges, wanted peace. He professed to have no control over any other Cheyenne group. The peace chief maintained that the Cheyennes had not begun the war; the responsibility rested upon the frontiersmen of Kansas who had fired on a Cheyenne war party during the summer of 1868. Black Kettle admitted that after the first hostilities, although he tried to keep his young men at home, they disregarded his wishes. Hazen spoke frankly to the Cheyenne and Arapaho dele-

8 Hazen to Sherman, November 10, 1868, Office of the Adjutant General, Letters Received.

gation. He declined either to offer or make peace and warned the chiefs not to come to Fort Cobb or join the camps of the friendly Kiowas and Comanches.[9]

Hazen did not believe that it was his duty to make peace with Sheridan already in the field. Unless the Cheyennes were punished, Hazen explained to Sherman, any peace would only be temporary and would be broken by the young warriors. The Kiowas and Comanches agreed with Hazen. They told Hazen privately that while the chiefs of the Cheyennes and Arapahoes sincerely desired to end the war, the young men of the tribes rejoiced when no truce was arranged, since it meant that they "would get more mules and that next Spring the Sioux and other northern bands were coming down and would clean out this entire country." On their way back to their camps twenty miles west of the Antelope Hills, the Cheyennes and Arapahoes talked freely of war. Since the Kiowas under Satanta were grumbling about the limited rations provided by Hazen, that officer suggested that two companies of the Tenth Cavalry and two howitzers be transferred from Fort Arbuckle to Fort Cobb for his protection.[10]

Sheridan prepared for his winter campaigns with great care. Supplies were gathered at Forts Dodge, Lyon, and Arbuckle to sustain the troops while they operated in the field against the Cheyennes and Arapahoes. To supplement the strength of his regulars, Sheridan also had the use of the Nineteenth Kansas Volunteers, a regiment of twelve hundred men commanded by Colonel Samuel J. Crawford; a company of scouts under Lieutenant Silas Pepoon; free-lancing frontiersmen such as "California Joe" and his partner, Jack Corbin; and the services of Little Beaver, Hard Rope, and eleven other Osages as trailers for his column.[11]

It was Sheridan's intention to send three columns into the field si-

[9] Records of a conversation held between Colonel and Brevet Major General W. B. Hazen, U. S. A., on special service, and Chiefs of the Cheyenne and Arapahoe tribes of Indians at Ft. Cobb, Indian Territory, November 20, 1868, Office of the Adjutant General, Letters Received.

[10] Hazen to Sherman, November 22, 1868, Hazen to Roy, November 26, 1868, Office of the Adjutant General, Letters Received.

[11] Sheridan to Crawford, October 9, 1868, Office of the Adjutant General, Letters Received; Sheridan, *Memoirs*, II, 311, 318; Custer, *Life on the Plains*, 279–80, 300; *Difficulties with the Indian Tribes*, 169ff.

multaneously. One force under Major Andrew W. Evans was ordered to proceed down the South Canadian from Fort Bascom, New Mexico territory. The combined detachments under Majors E. A. Carr and William H. Penrose were sent from Fort Lyon and were to concentrate their attention on the region of upper Beaver and Wolf creeks. These troops, Sheridan hoped, would drive the Indians toward his command, which would consist of eleven companies of the Seventh Cavalry, twelve companies of the Nineteenth Kansas Volunteers, and four infantry companies. When the preparations were completed, Sheridan left his headquarters at Fort Hays, stopped at Fort Dodge for his escort, and joined the Seventh Cavalry on November 21, 1868, at the site of Camp Supply.[12]

Before Sheridan arrived at Camp Supply, Sully and Custer were bickering over the command of the troops. Custer was spoiling for action and Sully was delaying until the Kansas volunteers arrived. Sheridan broke the stalemate by sending Sully back to Fort Harker where he resumed his duties as the commanding officer of the District of the Upper Arkansas. Obviously Sheridan preferred Custer as the field commander of the Seventh Cavalry.[13]

An early storm struck the Plains while Custer was preparing to take the field. It was foul weather for fighting Indians. Yet the storm served to cover the troop movement, and the Indians were unlikely to move their camps during the severe weather. It was bitterly cold and there was a foot of snow on the ground on November 23, when Custer moved out of Camp Supply with all eleven companies of the Seventh Cavalry, the Osage trailers, and a detachment of frontiersmen. Even the regimental band playing the cheerful marching tune, "The Girl I Left Behind Me," did not console the numbed troopers.

Falling and drifting snow obliterated all Indian trails. As the temperature rose mud and slush slowed Custer's march, so that the

[12] Sheridan to Sherman, November 1, 1869, in 41 Cong., 2 sess., *House Exec. Doc. No. 1*, pt. 2, pp. 44–45; Sheridan to Sherman, November 23, 1868, Office of the Adjutant General, Letters Received; Sheridan, *Memoirs*, II, 308–10; Carl Coke Rister, *Border Command, General Phil Sheridan in the West*, 94ff.

[13] Custer to Lieutenant John F. Westton, November 19, 1868, in *Difficulties with Indian Tribes*, 171; Sheridan to Sherman, November 23, 1868, Office of the Adjutant General, Letters Received; E. S. Godfrey, "Some Reminiscences, Including the Washita Battle, November 27, 1868," *Cavalry Journal*, Vol. XXXVII (October, 1928), 6.

South Canadian River was not reached until the evening of November 25. To speed up the scouting, since no Indians had been seen on the first three days of marching, Custer sent Major Joel H. Elliott with three troops to scout westward along the South Canadian under orders to follow any Indian trail found. Twelve miles up the South Canadian Elliott found a fresh trail leading in a southeasterly direction, and he sent a courier immediately to Custer. Custer ordered Elliott to follow the trail and make camp if the Indians were not overtaken by nightfall. Determined not to allow the Indians to escape, Custer had the remaining troops of the Seventh Cavalry draw one hundred rounds of ammunition for their carbines and revolvers, a little hardtack and coffee, and some forage for their horses; the baggage train was left on the South Canadian with a guard of eighty cavalrymen. Custer drove his men hard, overtook Elliott by nine o'clock in the evening of November 26, and after an hour's rest resumed the march again. Ranging ahead, Osage trailers brought word to Custer at one-thirty on the morning of November 27 that they had discovered an Indian village less than a mile in front of the column. Darkness and the hills bordering the Washita River to the north allowed Custer to withdraw his comand from the immediate vicinity of the village. Custer and his officers reconnoitered and found the Indian village located on the south bank of the Washita River in a strip of heavy timber. After Custer divided the troops of the Seventh Cavalry into four detachments surrounding the village, he ordered his subordinates to begin their attack at the first light of dawn.

Well before dawn on November 27, two companies were stationed above and below the village, and three more waiting south of the camp, while Custer kept four companies with him in the hills north of the Indians' camp. Custer moved his men cautiously to the valley floor and prepared to give the order to charge. Before he could act a single shot rang out from the far side of the village and the Battle of the Washita began. The regimental musicians, on Custer's orders, played "Garry Owen" as the four columns of cavalry swept into the village. The surprise was complete.

Within ten minutes Custer's troops were in possession of the village. Then the real fighting took place. Cheyenne women and children rushed from the village to the river bed seeking concealment while

the warriors remained in the timber or in the ravines bordering the
Washita. The Cheyenne warriors fought desperately to save their
families and were determined to extract a heavy toll before they died.
No quarter was given or asked, warriors and troopers fought hand-to-
hand. While Custer's troops were heavily engaged, some of the
women and children began fleeing toward much larger Indian villages which had not been seen by Custer and his scouts.

Little Rock, a Cheyenne chief, with one Cheyenne man and a
Kiowa, tried to lead some of the women and children down the
Washita toward the other Indian villages. Major Elliott and about
fifteen troopers dashed in pursuit. The men dropped back to fight,
Little Rock was quickly killed, and Elliott apparently overtook the
women and children. By this time the sound of the fighting had
reached the other villages to the east, and large parties of Cheyenne,
Kiowa, and Arapaho warriors were moving up the river to save
Black Kettle's people. A party of Arapahoes, whose camp was nearest
Black Kettle's, surrounded Elliott and his detachment. The Indians
pinned them down, used tall grass and ravines for cover, and easily
overwhelmed Elliott and his men.[14]

Custer's position at Black Kettle's village became untenable as
great numbers of Indian warriors filled the nearby hills. From Black
Kettle's captured sister Custer learned that great numbers of Cheyennes, Arapahoes, Kiowas, Comanches, and Kiowa-Apaches were
in the vicinity. No men could be spared to search for Major Elliott
and his detachment, who had last been seen riding after members of
Black Kettle's village. An ever-increasing number of Indian warriors
pressed attacks upon Custer's seven hundred men until midafternoon,
when Custer feinted a movement of his column toward the lower
Indian villages. At dusk Custer reversed his line of march and did
not halt his movement for six hours or more, granting his men only
an hour's respite. Pressing on rapidly until the afternoon of November 28 and picking up the baggage train en route, Custer made a
camp and dashed off a field note to Sheridan.

Custer grossly exaggerated the magnitude of his victory over the
Cheyennes. He did destroy fifty-one lodges, captured a herd of nearly

[14] George Bent to Hyde, September [?], 1905, MSS of the Colorado State Historical
Society, Denver, Colorado.

nine hundred ponies, and seized stores of Cheyenne lodge skins, arms, food and camping equipment. The elated officer, however, claimed that he and his men counted 103 Indian men dead on the battlefield, including Black Kettle, who with his wife was killed near his tipi during the initial charge. Custer made little mention of the Cheyenne women and children killed during the action and said that he had taken fifty-three women and children prisoners, among whom were the surviving members of Black Kettle's and Little Rock's families. Three reliable sources reduced the number of warriors killed at the Battle of the Washita from Custer's 103 to between 9 and 20 men, and the same sources estimate that the number of women and children killed by Custer's troops ranged between 18 and 40.[15]

Custer's command did not emerge from the fight unscathed. Major Elliott, Lieutenant Hamilton, and nineteen enlisted men were killed; three officers and eleven enlisted men were wounded, and one of these officers, Captain Albert Barnitz, later died of his wounds. The Cheyennes also mutilated Mrs. Clara Blinn and killed her young son by smashing his head against a tree. Another two-year-old white boy was seen being carried off by an Indian woman. When the troops tried to rescue the child, the Cheyenne woman plunged a large knife into his stomach and "ripped out his entrails." Two other white children, however, were rescued by Custer's men.[16]

At Camp Supply, General Sheridan reviewed Custer's men as they entered the post. The Osages led the way, waving the scalps of Black Kettle and other Cheyennes killed in the battle. The general did not wait for Custer's return to issue a general order congratulating the command "for the efficient and gallant services rendered." There was no doubt in Sheridan's mind that Custer had punished the right Indians. He accused members of Black Kettle's band of attacking and pillaging the Smoky Hill and Saline valleys. Sheridan further con-

---

[15] *Report of the Board of Indian Commissioners . . . for 1869*, 43; James S. Morrison to Wynkoop, December 14, 1868, Upper Arkansas Agency, Letters Received; George Bent to Hyde, August 28, 1913, Bent Letters, Coe Collection.

[16] Custer to Sheridan, November 28, 1868, Sheridan Papers; Custer, *Life on the Plains*, 305–52; Godfrey, "The Washita Battle," *loc. cit.*, 11–14; De. B. Randolph Keim, *Sheridan's Troopers on the Border: A Winter Campaign on the Plains*, 110–20; *Record of Engagements*, 15–16; Grinnell, *Fighting Cheyennes*, 300–305.

tended that the trail of the war party followed by Major Elliott led directly to the Washita River camp, and that that camp contained mail, animals, and artifacts seized by the Cheyennes during their widespread raids on the Kansas frontier. "If we can get in one or two more good blows," Sheridan wrote soon after receiving Custer's dispatch, "there will be no more Indian troubles in my department." General Sherman, after learning some of·the news from the Washita, added his congratulations and had no doubt that Sheridan would, by Christmas, "have all these Indians begging for their lives."[17]

The death of Black Kettle did not disturb Sheridan. He characterized Black Kettle's band as the "guiltiest of all," claiming they had "perpetrated cruelties too fiendish for recital." To Sheridan, Black Kettle was nothing but "a worn out and worthless old cypher" who had refused to accept Sheridan's offer of protection and food before any troops were sent into the field. Relying upon a letter written by Ed Guerrier, the scalps and plunder in Black Kettle's village, and a book of Cheyenne pictographs enumerating the recent depredations committed by this band, Sheridan approved of Custer's strike, which "wiped out old Black Kettle and his murderers and rapers of helpless women."[18]

Not content with the Battle of the Washita, Sheridan was fully determined to demonstrate to all of the Southern Plains Indians how helpless they were when the army pursued its objectives. On December 7, Sheridan moved the Seventh Cavalry and the Nineteenth Kansas Volunteers from Camp Supply toward Fort Cobb. En route Sheridan wanted to visit the scene of the Battle of the Washita and, if possible, confirm the fate of Elliott and his detachment. The loss of these men and Custer's retreat from the field of battle without an effort to find them caused Sheridan to question Custer sharply at

---

[17] David L. Spotts, *Campaigning with Custer and the Nineteenth Kansas Volunteer Cavalry on the Washita Campaign, 1868–69, 66*; General Field Orders, No. 6, Headquarters, Department of the Missouri, November 29, 1868, Sheridan to Nichols, November 29, 1868, 40 Cong., 3 sess., *Sen. Exec. Doc. No. 18*, 30, 32; Sheridan to Nichols, December 2, 1868, Office of the Adjutant General, Letters Received; Sherman to Commanding Officer, Fort Hays, Kansas, December 2, 1868, Military Division of the Missouri, Letters Sent.

[18] Sheridan to Sherman, November 1, 1869, 41 Cong., 2 sess., *House Exec. Doc. No. 1*, pt. 2, pp. 47–48.

Camp Supply and led to bitter criticism of Custer among officers of the Seventh Cavalry. At the Washita River Custer and one hundred troopers of his regiment discovered "the stark stiff, naked, and horribly mutilated bodies" of Elliott and his men. In their rage the Indians had mangled the bodies of the soldiers, decapitating some, hacking off arms, feet, and hands, and riddling them with bullets and arrows. Near the scene of the conflict the Indians had abandoned in their flight much property, which was destroyed before the column followed the Indians' trails down the Washita River toward Fort Cobb.[19]

Some of the Indians from the Washita gathered at Fort Cobb and relied on Hazen's guarantee of protection. This promise deterred Sheridan from striking the first village of Indians he encountered, a camp of Kiowas. The Cheyennes and Arapahoes, with some Comanches and about one-half of the Kiowas under Satanta and Satank, fled southward and established themselves on the western slope of the Wichita Mountains. A little later these same Indians moved farther west to the mouth of the Sweetwater River to avoid punishment from Sheridan's powerful force. In the latter village, it was later reported, were 150 Cheyenne and 180 Arapaho lodges. Some of the Kiowas, before Sheridan reached their village in mid-December, began to return to the Washita, ignoring the warnings of George Bent and John Smith that the post was only a trap in which the Indians would be seized as prisoners.[20]

At the Kiowa village messengers from Hazen told Sheridan that the Indians occupying the camps from that point to Fort Cobb could be trusted. Sheridan doubted Hazen, especially when the Kiowas, with the memory of the Battle of the Washita fresh in their minds, bolted. The general then seized Satanta and Lone Wolf, chiefs of

[19] Sheridan to Sherman, December 7, 1868, Office of the Adjutant General, Letters Received; Sheridan, *Memoirs*, II, 317–18; Rister, *Border Command*, 114; Sheridan to Nichols, December 19, 1868, Sheridan Papers; Custer to Crosby, December 22, 1868, 40 Cong., 3 sess., *Sen. Exec. Doc. No. 40*, 3–5.

[20] Custer to Crosby, December 22, 1868, 40 Cong., 3 sess., *Sen. Exec. Doc. No. 40*, 5–6; Sheridan to Sherman, December 19, 1868, Sheridan Papers; Henry E. Alvord, "Summary of information regarding hostile Indians," December 7, 1868, Hazen to Sherman, December 7, 1868, Office of the Adjutant General, Letters Received.

Kiowas, as hostages and threatened to hang the two chiefs unless their bands and families returned to Fort Cobb by December 19. Five days later, after the Kiowas had come in under a flag of truce, Sheridan told them that unless they disassociated themselves from the Cheyennes and Arapahoes, he would "take some of the starch out of them."[21]

Soon after the Battle of the Washita, Indian sympathizers began to criticize Sheridan's and Custer's actions. Barely three months before, Superintendent Murphy had called for an army-dictated peace with the Cheyennes and Arapahoes. At that time the superintendent claimed distrust of all Cheyennes, but now that Black Kettle was dead, Murphy extolled the virtues and services of the chief to the whites. It was Black Kettle, Murphy reminded Commissioner Taylor, who had bought white captives with his own ponies and who had used his influence so vigorously against a general outbreak in the spring of 1867 that he had been forced to flee the Cheyenne camps to safety among the Arapahoes when the warriors threatened his life. Samuel Tappan also sprang to the defense of the Indians, maintaining that the Indian outbreaks were occasioned by nonfulfillment of governmental treaty obligations and outrages perpetrated by the frontiersmen. He demanded the "immediate and unconditional abandonment of the present war policy," the use of the army only as a police force, and the dispensing of justice impartially to both whites and Indians when laws or agreements were broken. The most slashing protest, however, came from former Indian Agent Edward Wynkoop, who represented Black Kettle as the true "noble savage." Reality became soft plastic as Wynkoop molded Black Kettle, fifty-six years old at his death, into "the ruling spirit of his tribe . . . looked upon by all the nomadic tribes of the Plains as a superior—one whose word was law, whose advice was to be heeded. His moral dignity and lofty bearing, combined with his sagacity and intelligence had that moral effect which placed him in the position of a potentate." Twice Black Kettle's love of the white man had been betrayed, once at Sand Creek and now at the Washita,

---

[21] Custer, *Life on the Plains*, 257ff.; Sheridan to Sherman, December 19, 1868; Sheridan Papers; Sheridan to Nichols, December 24, 1868, 40 Cong., 3 sess., *Sen. Exec. Doc. No. 40*, 1–2.

where he met "his death at the hands of white men, in whom he had too often fatally trusted and who triumphantly report the fact of his scalp in their possession."[22]

Sherman took pains to undermine the position of the peace advocates. He forwarded copies of all of Sheridan's reports and noted the differences between the conflict at Sand Creek and that on the Washita. Chivington, Sherman explained, had attacked Cheyennes who were under the protection of the commanding officer at Fort Lyon; Custer's attack was defensible because Hazen had refused to give Black Kettle protection until peace had been made with Sheridan. The information provided from his office, Sherman hoped, would meet "the cry raised by Tappan, Taylor and Co., . . . that Black Kettle's was a friendly camp, and that Custer's battle was a second Sand Creek affair." Sherman assured Sheridan that the latter's conduct met with the hearty approval of General Grant and the secretary of war. Instead of recalling Sheridan from further punishment of the Cheyennes, the divisional commander instructed his field officers to "kill and punish the hostile, rescue the captive white women and children, capture and destroy the ponies, lances, carbines, &c., &c., of the Cheyennes, Arapahoes, and Kiowas," establish them in camps where they could be fed, and start them on the road to self-support.[23]

The columns under Evans and Carr still in the field while Custer and Sheridan were at Fort Cobb did not meet any Cheyennes or Arapahoes during their scouts. Fear of the troops caused the Cheyennes to shift their camps continuously, interfered with their hunting, and led them to make peace overtures to Sheridan. On December 20, 1868, Sheridan sent Mah-wis-sa, Black Kettle's sister, and Iron-Shirt, a Kiowa-Apache chief, to persuade the Cheyennes and Arapahoes to come to Fort Cobb. The messengers found the tribes' camps several

[22] Murphy to Taylor, December 4, 1868, Central Superintendency II; Tappan to Taylor, December 4, 1868, in Report of the Commissioner of Indian Affairs, *Annual Report of the Secretary of the Interior, 1868*, 40 Cong., 3 sess., *House Exec. Doc. No. 1*, 832–36; Wynkoop to Peter Cooper and others, December 23, 1868, Sheridan Papers.

[23] Sherman to Sheridan, Hazen, and Brevet Major General B. H. Grierson, December 23, 1868, Office of the Adjutant General, Letters Received; Sherman to AAG., Washington, D. C., December 12, 1868, Sherman to McKeever, January 16, 1869, Sherman to Sheridan, January 18, 1869, Military Division of the Missouri, Letters Sent.

days' ride west of Fort Cobb and reported to Sheridan that Little
Robe of the Cheyennes and Yellow Bear of the Arapahoes were
anxious for peace; other leaders of the tribes evidently disagreed
with the two peace chiefs and said they would not travel to Fort Cobb
because their ponies were too poor and the distance was too great.[24]

Little Robe, Yellow Bear, and nineteen other leaders of the confederated tribes arrived at Fort Cobb on the night of December 31, 1868.
They came on foot because their ponies were too weak to carry them
and begged for peace on Sheridan's terms, telling him that the "tribes
[were] mourning for their losses, their people starving, their ponies
dying, their dogs all eaten up, and no buffalo." Sheridan accepted
their unconditional surrender and commented, "I can scarcely make
an error in any punishment awarded for they all have blood on
their hands."[25]

Sheridan minced no words with the Cheyenne and Arapaho delegation. Through his interpreter the General told the chiefs that if
their tribes stayed away from Fort Cobb, he would "make war on
them winter and summer as long as I live, or until they are wiped
out." His fiery temper startled the Indians when he told them that
they could not make peace now and commence killing whites again
in the spring. If the chiefs headed by Little Robe and Yellow Bear
were not willing to make a complete peace, Sheridan stated bluntly,
"you can go back and we will fight the thing out." When Sheridan
finished, Little Robe simply said: "It is for you to say what we have
to do."

Repenting his harshness, Sheridan declared, "I am not a bad chief;
I am not a bad man," and promised to treat the Indians justly.
Because Carr's column was believed to be in the region of the Cheyenne and Arapaho villages, Sheridan gave the chiefs a written guarantee to protect their people if they moved immediately in the direction of Fort Cobb. At the conclusion of the council Sheridan was

[24] Evans to AAAG., Headquarters District of New Mexico, January 23, 1869, Carr
to McKeever, April 7, 1869, Sheridan to Nichols, December 24, 1868, Sheridan Papers;
W. S. Nye, *Carbine and Lance: The Story of Old Fort Sill*, 100–107; Custer, *Life on
the Plains*, 414–15, 468, 472–73.

[25] Sheridan to Nichols, January 1, 1869, Sheridan Papers.

still adamant on one point—either total peace or total war; until all of the Cheyennes and Arapahoes surrendered, none of the prisoners taken at the Battle of the Washita would be returned to their people.[26]

Several weeks passed, but the Cheyennes and Arapahoes failed to surrender. While he was waiting for the tribes, Sheridan moved his headquarters from Fort Cobb to Camp Wichita, later to be renamed Fort Sill, on Medicine Bluff Creek just east of the Wichita Mountains. Sheridan decided to wait until mid-January, 1869, before sending out another expedition against the Cheyennes and Arapahoes, whom the General knew to be sharing their camps with the Kiowas under Kicking Bird, Little Heart, and Satank.[27]

Little Robe and Yellow Bear were in the vanguard of the tribes who had surrendered at Fort Sill by January 20, 1869. Sheridan understood that the bulk of their people were on their way in, moving slowly, often leading their ponies, and the General realized that no large campaign was necessary against the Cheyennes and Arapahoes. Sheridan, as the tribes were surrendering, still refused to discuss any peace settlement until all of the bands were at Fort Sill. To hurry the Cheyennes and Arapahoes along, Custer requested Sheridan's permission to take a small, hand-picked detachment to the Indians' camps.[28]

Custer, guided by Little Robe and Yellow Bear, headed southwestward from the Wichita Mountains. The Arapahoes were easily found on Mulberry Creek, a tributary of the Red River. There Little Raven and the Arapahoes, who agreed to start their movement to Fort Sill within three days, did not know the location of the Cheyennes, whom the Arapahoes said were constantly on the move. Little Robe was determined to find his people and left Custer's camp, carefully marking a trail for Custer's scouts to follow. Although Custer's column consisted of only forty sharpshooters under Lieutenant William W. Cooke, the Cheyennes did not desire to talk and fled west-

[26] Interview of General Sheridan with "Little Robe," of the Cheyennes and "Yellow Robe" [Yellow Bear], of the Arapahoes,—representing the warriors of their tribes—January 1, 1869, Sheridan Papers.

[27] Nye, *Carbine and Lance,* 109–13; William Brown Morrison, *Military Posts and Camps in Oklahoma,* 161–62; Sheridan to Sherman, January 8, 1869, Sheridan Papers.

[28] Sheridan to Sherman, Sheridan to McKeever, January 20, 1869, Sheridan to Nichols, January 23, 1869, Sheridan Papers.

ward, causing Custer to return to Fort Sill on February 7, 1869, without completing his mission. Reappraising the situation, Sheridan labeled the actions of the Cheyennes a "breach of faith" and on February 9 contemplated sending the Seventh Cavalry against the Cheyennes. He instructed Majors Carr and Evans to move their troops, if possible, into the region known to be occupied by the tribe.[29]

Sheridan, nevertheless, did not want to act prematurely. In conversations with Sheridan, Lieutenant Colonel Joseph C. Audenreid, Sherman's personal observer at Fort Sill, reported that the Cheyennes' reluctance to surrender could be accounted for partly by John Smith's warning to the tribe that Fort Cobb was a trap—a logical explanation to the tribe because of the great concentration of troops there and at Fort Sill. According to Audenried, Sheridan planned to give Little Robe, in whom the General had confidence, sufficient time to contact his people, then if the chief failed to bring the Cheyennes in, to dismount the Nineteenth Kansas Volunteers, use them as infantry, and personally lead the Seventh Cavalry into the field. As he waited Sheridan learned that Little Raven's Arapahoes had established a camp three miles from Fort Sill on February 11, and he was hopeful that other segments of the tribe would follow their example. Big Mouth with about eighty lodges of Arapahoes declined to surrender and joined the Cheyennes on the Staked Plains.[30]

General Sheridan did not lead the troops against the Cheyennes; the task was assigned to Custer. The election of Ulysses S. Grant to the presidency led to a reshuffling of commands; Sherman assumed Grant's old duties as commanding general of the army; Sheridan became the commanding officer of the Division of the Missouri; and Major General John M. Schofield took charge of the Department of the Missouri. Custer could not march from Fort Sill until March 2, 1869, because of the lack of supplies and the poor condition of the cavalry mounts. His troops consisted of eleven companies of the Seventh Cavalry and ten companies of the Nineteenth Kansas Volunteers. Marching directly to the North Fork of the Red River, Custer

---

[29] Custer, *Life on the Plains,* 478–79, 483–527; Sheridan to McKeever, February 8, 1869, Sheridan to Nichols, February 9, 1869, Sheridan Papers.

[30] Sherman to Audenried, January 11, 1869, Military Division of the Missouri, Letters Sent; Audenried to Sherman, February 8, 12, 1869, Sherman Papers.

divided his command, selected eight hundred of his best mounted men from both regiments, and sent the remainder with the baggage and wagons to the Washita River.[31]

Four days out from Fort Sill smoke was observed ahead which "California Joe" judged could be reached by afternoon. Hard Rope and the Osage scouts were sent ahead to follow the trail of the Indians and reported on the afternoon of February 8 that a small camp of Cheyennes was just a short distance ahead. Deploying his cavalry, Custer charged. His stag hounds, Maida and Blucher, however, outran the cavalry; forewarned, the Indians scattered on foot, leaving behind all of their possessions and ponies. "The battle," a discouraged Kansas volunteer wrote, "resulted in no casualties and no captures except two tents, eleven ponies, some blankets and some buffalo meat they were to have for their evening meal."[32]

Custer maintained the march although his provisions were exhausted and no trails were found for several days. At the mouth of Mulberry Creek the Osages found a single lodge trail which was joined by eleven others. Mo-nah-see-tah, Little Rock's beautiful daughter brought along by Custer to communicate with the Cheyennes, declared the camps and trails at least ten days old. As the troops followed, the trail became larger as more lodges joined it and the remains of the camps seemed fresher. On March 15, Hard Rope, the chief Osage scout, reported back to Custer that a mile or two to the north he had observed a pony herd. The herders also saw the Osages and quickly drove their ponies toward a stand of timber bordering the Sweetwater River. Indians watched Custer, signalling to each other from the sand hills as the officer urged his column to greater speed.

Eight Indians rode toward Custer and sought a parley. From them Custer learned that 260 Cheyenne lodges were stretched out for ten or fifteen miles along the Sweetwater River. Two hundred of these lodges, mostly occupied by Dog Soldiers described by Custer

---

[31] Sheridan, *Memoirs*, II, 345, 347; Athearn, *Sherman and the Settlement of the West*, 240; Custer to Sheridan, March 21, 1869, Sheridan Papers.

[32] Custer, *Life on the Plains*, 536–41; Spotts, *Campaigning with Custer*, 142–43; Custer to Sheridan, March 21, 1869, Sheridan Papers; John McBee, "John McBee's Account of the Expedition of the Nineteenth Kansas," KSHS *Collections*, XVII, 363.

as "the most mischievous, blood thirsty, and barbarous band of Indians that infest the plains," recognized Medicine Arrows' leadership. Farther down the Sweetwater, Little Robe was camped with sixty lodges. Custer claimed that he rode with Medicine Arrows into the larger village to talk while his troops surrounded the Cheyennes. During the course of his conversation with the chief, Custer was informed that the camp contained two women captured earlier on the Kansas frontier, Mrs. Anna Belle Morgan from the Solomon settlements and Miss Sarah C. White from the Republican Valley. Cheyenne tradition varies in some details from Custer's accounts. Custer, Indians related, was taken to Medicine Arrows' lodge by Sand Hill, who had come upon Custer's column while hunting. Inside the lodge Custer was seated beside Medicine Arrows. First Medicine Arrows smoked, then holding the pipe, he asked Custer to smoke and in Cheyenne said: "If you are acting treachery toward us, sometime you and your whole command will be killed." When the ritual was finished, the chief poured the ashes over the toes of Custer's boots to bring the cavalryman bad luck.[33] Once Custer learned that the white women were captives, he ordered his troops not to attack. The Kansas volunteers bitterly resented Custer's order, called him a "coward and traitor," and were with difficulty restrained from plunging into the Cheyenne village by their shouting and cursing officers.

Custer saw that the Cheyennes' ponies were in the village and the Indians were poised for flight. He therefore seized four chiefs as hostages and sent one of them to Little Robe's village, hoping that the peace chief could obtain the release of the white women and a promise from the Cheyennes to surrender. Little Robe's intercession made no impression upon the Cheyennes, and for three days a tense stalemate developed; the Cheyennes demanded a large ransom for their prisoners while Custer demanded unconditional surrender. Finally Custer decided to force the issue. Freeing one of the hostages as a messenger to Little Robe, Custer threatened to hang the three chiefs, Big Head, Dull Knife, also known as Lean Face, and Fat Bear, unless the women were immediately released. A tree was selected and ropes were strung over a limb when a small party of Cheyennes approached with the

[33] George Bent to Hyde, September [?], 1905, MSS of the Colorado State Historical Society, Denver, Colorado.

women wanting to bargain. Custer, however, forced the Cheyennes to deliver the women to the men and officers of the Kansas volunteers. From Mrs. Morgan and Miss White and from his own personal observations, Custer knew that the Cheyennes had been reduced to eating the flesh of dead ponies, mules, and dogs. Before he left the villages, Custer received the assurance of Little Robe and other chiefs that they were tired of war and would make their way to Camp Supply.

With sufficient supplies Custer would have continued to press the Cheyennes. His own men, on their march back to the Washita supply depot, were reduced to eating mules that had died during the day. Custer believed that the seizure of the three hostages would cause the tribe to conform to his demands. After the column's arrival at Camp Supply on March 28, 1869, the three Cheyenne chiefs were sent to Fort Hays, where the Cheyenne women and children seized during the Battle of the Washita were being held. Two of the chiefs, Big Head and Dull Knife, never regained their freedom. The commanding officer at Fort Hays, acting without an interpreter, decided to transfer the chiefs from the prison stockade to a guardhouse for greater security. When the Cheyennes saw the guards entering the stockade with fixed bayonets, they thought they were being led to their execution. Drawing concealed knives, the three Cheyenne chiefs rushed the guards; Big Head was killed by the first volley, Dull Knife received a mortal bayonet wound, and Fat Bear was temporarily stunned when a guard clubbed him with a rifle butt.[34]

Most of the Arapahoes were accounted for at Fort Sill by April 2, 1869, and a few days later three Cheyenne runners appeared before Colonel Benjamin H. Grierson, stating that six hundred of their people would arrive shortly. Little Robe, Minimic, Red Moon, Grey

34 Custer to Sheridan, March 21, 1869, Sheridan Papers; Custer, *Life on the Plains,* 542ff., 600–601; Spotts, *Campaigning with Custer,* 147–48; McBee, "Expedition of the Nineteenth Kansas," *loc. cit.,* 363–64; James A. Hadley, "The Nineteenth Kansas Cavalry and the Conquest of the Plains Indians," KSHS *Collections,* X, 446–56; Horace L. Moore, "The Nineteenth Kansas Cavalry," KSHS *Transactions,* VI, 44–46; George Bent to Hyde, December 11, 1912, Bent Letters, Coe Collection; Colonel Nelson A. Miles to AAG., Department of the Missouri, May 9, 10, 1869, Fort Hays, Letters Sent, United States Army Commands, Records of the War Department, National Archives, Washington, D. C.

Eyes, and several other chiefs, representing sixty-seven lodges, reached Fort Sill on April 7 and claimed that they had been on their way to surrender when Custer's expedition frightened and scattered the tribe. General Hazen, still charged with caring for the Indians at peace, hoped to collect about one thousand Arapahoes and Cheyennes and shift them to Camp Supply, where they could begin reservation life on the lands set aside for them at the Treaty of Medicine Lodge.[35]

On April 19, Red Moon bolted with thirty lodges of Cheyennes. Major Meredith Kidd, sent in immediate pursuit with 150 troopers of the Tenth Cavalry, could not recapture the fleeing Cheyennes, who divested themselves of their lodges and most of the camp equipment. Red Moon's camp apparently intended to join Sand Hill, a Cheyenne chief who up to this time had made no effort to quit fighting. Little Robe and Minimic promised Captain Alvord that the remaining forty-six lodges would make the trip to Camp Supply. However, Alvord feared that even these chiefs would not go to Camp Supply because they had made a strong plea to be allowed to stay with the Comanches. On April 25, the day before the actual movement began, a portion of the remaining Cheyennes mortally wounded a teamster and "left in hot haste for the plains." Other Indians at Fort Sill told the officers that the Cheyennes intended to join their tribe near the Antelope Hills.[36]

Few if any of the Cheyennes proceeded directly to Camp Supply. During the first week in May, 1869, the Cheyennes hunted along the Texas boundary between the Washita and South Canadian rivers. When camped on the Washita, the Cheyennes held a decisive council in which Little Robe, sensing a desire for peace among a majority of the tribe, gave the Dog Soldiers still holding out for war their choice of either agreeing to live on the reservation or leaving the country. Tall Bull and White Horse, the spokesmen of the warrior society, opposed Little Robe and declared that it was their intention to "go north and join the Sioux, that they never would make peace

[35] Grierson to McKeever, April 3, 1869, Grierson to AAG., Department of the Missouri, April 7, 10, 1869, Sheridan Papers.

[36] Alvord to Grierson, April 24, 1869, Sheridan Papers; Lieutenant S. L. Woodward to AAG., Department of the Missouri, April 26, 1869 (Copy), Upper Arkansas Agency, Letters Received.

that compelled them to settle down, they had always been a free nation, and they would remain so or die." John S. Smith's Cheyenne wife, Na-to-mah, said that about 165 lodges of Dog Soldiers left Little Robe's camp, discarded their lodges, and started north.[37]

Defiantly Tall Bull and the Dog Soldiers established themselves on the Republican River and its tributaries. Major E. A. Carr was ordered on May 1, to transfer his troops of the Fifth Cavalry from Fort Lyon to the Platte River and begin a search for the Dog Soldiers. Twelve days later, after finding fresh pony tracks near Beaver Creek, Carr sent Lieutenant E. W. Ward with the troopers and "Buffalo Bill" Cody to make a reconnaissance. Five miles from camp Ward saw the smoke of a large village and retreated toward the main command, but he was quickly surrounded by a large hunting party of Cheyennes and Sioux. Cody dashed through the Indians to appraise Carr of the detachment's desperate plight. As Ward was fighting his way clear, Carr with his whole command assaulted the village and its five hundred warriors. The Indians fought savagely to save their women and children, retreating at dusk and leaving behind twenty-five dead braves. Carr's units, losing four dead and three wounded, pursued the Indians into Nebraska on Spring Creek, where the quarry turned on the column's advanced company. The five hundred warriors broke off their attack and scattered into small parties when Carr's main body of troops appeared, forcing Carr to abandon further pursuit.[38]

In retaliation for Carr's harassment of their village, the Dog Soldiers raided savagely along the Kansas frontier. In the eight days following May 21, Cheyennes and Sioux killed thirteen people and took two prisoners in Republic County, Kansas; tore up two miles of track on the Kansas Pacific near the Fossil Spring station; and killed thirteen settlers, taking two women, Mrs. G. Weichel and Mrs. Suzannah Alderdice, as prisoners. Units of the Seventh Cavalry led by Custer were shifted to the Kansas frontier, but they caught only fleeting glimpses of the Cheyennes and Sioux during their scouts. The major effort to punish the intransigents was entrusted to Major

37 Lieutenant Henry Jackson to McKeever, June 6, 1869, Sheridan Papers.

38 Endorsement by Sheridan, May 18, 1869, on Woodward to AAG., Department of the Missouri, April 26, 1869 (Copy), Upper Arkansas Agency, Letters Received; *Record of Engagements*, 20; Price, *Across the Continent*, 134–35.

Carr, who was given command of eight companies of the Fifth Cavalry and 150 Pawnee scouts under Major Frank J. North. General C. C. Augur's orders were explicit: "Clear the Republican country of Indians." All Indians found in the region were to be considered hostile unless they surrendered willingly and allowed themselves to be disarmed.[39]

Departing from Fort McPherson on June 9, 1869, Carr led his expedition to the Republican Valley. A party of Cheyennes raided the cavalry camp six days later, and thereafter the Dog Soldiers eluded Carr's troops for more than three weeks. The Cheyennes constantly broke and shifted their camps, scattering to higher ground and traveling in small groups until they reached their next predetermined camp. Carr kept his command on the move and used the Pawnees to track down their tribal foes. Early in July, Carr believed that the Cheyennes could not be far away and sent Major William B. Royall with three companies of the Fifth Cavalry and a company of Pawnee scouts to follow a fresh trail. Unobserved by a small party of Cheyennes, Royall's detachment drew near the Indians, and without waiting for orders the Pawnees stripped off their army uniforms, charged the surprised Cheyennes, killed three, and routed the others. The chase brought Royall back to the vicinity of the main body of troops which he joined on July 7.[40]

Tall Bull, the Cheyenne Dog Soldier chief, discouraged by the constant necessity of eluding Carr, hoped to lead his band north of the Platte River. Crossing over to the watershed of the Platte, Tall Bull went into camp at Summit Springs to wait until the high water

[39] Daniel W. Wilder, *Annals of Kansas*, 506–507; Garfield, "Defense of the Kansas Frontier, 1868–69," *loc. cit.*, 469; Clarence Reckmeyer, "The Battle of Summit Springs," *Colo. Magazine,* Vol. VI, No. 6 (November, 1929), 211; Lieutenant Edward Low to Brevet Colonel Lewis Merrill, June 11, 1869, George D. Ruggles, AAG., Department of the Platte to Carr, June 7, 1869, Sheridan Papers; Schofield to AAG., Military Division of the Missouri, October 23, 1869, in 41 Cong., 2 sess., *House Exec. Doc. No. 1,* pt. 2, p. 68; Grinnell, *Two Great Scouts,* 183.

[40] Report of Operations of the Republican River Expedition, Brevet Major General E. A. Carr Commanding, from June 30th to July 20th, 1869, to Brevet Brigadier General George D. Ruggles, Assistant Adjutant General, Department of the Platte, Camp Near Fort Sedgwick, Colorado Territory, July 20, 1869, Sheridan Papers (hereafter cited as *Operations of the Republican River Expedition*); James T. King, "The Republican River Expedition, June–July, 1869," *Nebr. History,* Vol. XLI, No. 3 (September, 1960), 173, 178–79; Grinnell, *Two Great Scouts,* 186–87.

of the Platte subsided.[41] Carr did not think that he could overtake the Cheyennes, but when a small party of Cheyennes tried to stampede his horse herd on July 8, he decided that the main Cheyenne village must be nearby. The trail of Tall Bull's camp led up Frenchman's Fork, then cut through the sand hills marking the divide between the Republican and South Platte rivers. Leaving his baggage train behind, Carr selected his best mounted troops and the Pawnees, then divided his reduced command on July 11 to follow three diverging Cheyenne trails. Carr, a few Pawnees, and one hundred troopers followed the trail leading northwest, and from some low hills southeast of Summit Springs, Carr's Pawnees saw a herd of ponies grazing four miles away. Messengers to Royall's detachment and Frank and Luther North's Pawnees brought the column together, and it moved cautiously from depression to depression in the broken country to within a mile of the Cheyenne village.

The Pawnees stripped for action although no one had yet seen the hostile camp. From the top of the last hill Tall Bull's entire village came into view as the whole column charged. The surprise was complete. Some of the Cheyenne warriors were lounging in their lodges, the ponies were grazing a short distance from the camp, and the women were occupied with the daily routines. The Norths and the Pawnees reached the village first, galloping directly through it while some of the cavalry encircled the camp to cut the Indians off from their ponies.

The Dog Soldiers had two alternatives: flee or die. What few ponies were in the camp were used for women and children; because some families such as Tall Bull's had no horses nearby, they were placed in ravines while the men fought. The Norths were fired upon by an Indian from a ravine, and Frank pulled up abruptly, dismounted, and told his brother to ride away. Frank North reasoned that the Indian would raise his head to see if his shot had struck its target. When the Indian's head appeared above the edge of the ravine, North fired. After the firing ceased North found the body of Tall Bull, the Dog Soldier chief, in the ravine.

[41] Summit Springs is located near the Washington-Logan county line about six miles south of Atwood, Logan County, Colorado, and several miles east of present Colorado State Highway 63.

Some of the Cheyenne warriors scattered to shallow depressions, where they were killed by Carr's troopers or the Pawnee scouts. Luther North remembered especially the bravery of one fifteen-year-old Cheyenne youth. At the outset of the attack the youth was guarding the horse herd and was mounted on a good horse. Instead of fleeing as the troops charged, the boy drove as many horses as he could into the village and joined a small group of warriors trying to keep the Pawnees from the women and children. "There," North related later, "he died like a warrior, no braver man ever lived than that fifteen year old boy." After this action the Norths joined their Pawnees, who had twenty Cheyenne warriors completely surrounded in a draw. Armed only with bows and arrows, the Cheyennes kept their enemies at bay until their arrows were exhausted. One Pawnee, Traveling Bear, killed and scalped four Cheyennes in the draw; Congress later ordered a medal struck honoring the Pawnee's valor.

All afternoon the cavalry and Pawnees chased and killed Cheyennes. Early in the evening the troops began assembling and assessing the magnitude of their victory. They determined that they had killed fifty-two Indians, captured seventeen women and children, and burned eighty-four lodges with all the Cheyennes' food, robes, and camp equipment. Mrs. Weichel, although wounded by Tall Bull, was freed, while Mrs. Alderdice was killed by the chief before he led his wife and child to safety. The plunder taken from the Cheyennes proved conclusively that Tall Bull's band was among the Indians who had raided the Saline and Solomon valleys. The troops found in the Dog Soldiers' lodges a necklace made of human fingers, scalps of white women, clocks, quilts, and wearing apparel. Also recovered were about nine hundred dollars in paper currency and gold coins which the Pawnees and troops gave to Mrs. Weichel.[42]

The surviving Dog Soldiers and their families reassembled on Frenchman's Fork and were harried out of the region. On August 2,

[42] *Operations of the Republican River Expedition*; Proceedings of a Board convened by Special Order No. 17, Headquarters Republican River Expedition, July 11, 1869, Sheridan Papers; Grinnell, *Two Great Scouts*, 191–92, 194–202; Grinnell, *Fighting Cheyennes*, 311–18; Frank J. North, "The Journal of an Indian Fighter: The 1869 Diary of Major Frank J. North," *Nebr. History*, Vol. XXXIX, No. 2 (June, 1958), 138–39; James T. King, "The Republican River Expedition, June–July, 1869, II, The Battle of Summit Springs," *Nebr. History*, Vol. XLI, No. 4 (December, 1960), 281–97.

1869, Major Royall left Fort Sedgwick with a command smaller than that led by Carr, retraced the route to Frenchman's Fork, and tracked the fleeing Dog Soldiers until the Niobrara River was reached. The remnants of Tall Bull's village did not stop their flight until they joined Sioux camps on the White River.[43] The Battle of Summit Springs thus ended Cheyenne occupation and use of the region between the Platte and Arkansas rivers.

Those Cheyennes who had not fled with Tall Bull surrendered at Camp Supply in small groups. Little Robe and Minimic were the first Cheyenne leaders to bring their people to Camp Supply, where Lieutenant Colonel Anderson D. Nelson and a detachment of the Tenth Cavalry were stationed to control the Cheyennes and Arapahoes. About June 20, Medicine Arrows and Buffalo Head arrived at Camp Supply with a few members of their immediate families to observe how the Arapahoes and few Cheyennes were being treated. A few days later Medicine Arrows again left the post, promising to return within a day with the remainder of his band. Colonel Nelson hoped that Medicine Arrows would lead the 165 lodges of Cheyennes camping on the headwaters of the Washita River to the post. To prove to the Cheyennes remaining south of the Arkansas that the government was willing to cease attacking the tribe, the Cheyenne prisoners were delivered to the custody of Little Robe on June 21, 1869. The army, however, could do little more than wait for the Cheyennes to straggle in, because President Grant had already initiated his peace policy and entrusted the care of the Southern Plains Indians to the Society of Friends.[44]

[43] Royall to AAAG., District of the Republican, August 18, 1869, Sheridan Papers; Grinnell, *Fighting Cheyennes,* 316.

[44] Nelson to McKeever, June 22, 1869, Sheridan Papers.

# 15

## RESERVATION LIFE BEGINS

INDIAN POLICY FOR THE SOUTHERN PLAINS underwent sweeping change after Ulysses S. Grant was elected to the presidency. Even before his inauguration, Grant accepted the suggestion that the Society of Friends, or Quakers, furnish a list of their members for service in the Bureau of Indian Affairs. Subsequently, two Quakers, Enoch Hoag as superintendent of the Central Superintendency and Brinton Darlington as agent for the Upper Arkansas Agency, were appointed by President Grant and under their direction the Cheyennes began their reservation life.[1] To further implement the new peace policy, President Grant appointed his former aide-de-camp, Ely S. Parker, commissioner of Indian affairs and in June, 1869, organized a Quaker-dominated Special Indian Commission to inspect Indian reservations and advise the Bureau of Indian affairs.[2]

Agent Brinton Darlington, elderly but alert, arrived on July 6, 1869, at the Upper Arkansas Agency. Immediately serious problems confronted the new agent. Most of the Cheyennes, 240 lodges, were still not at Camp Supply. When faced with a loss of rations, the Cheyennes and Arapahoes still refused to occupy the Medicine Lodge Treaty reservation. They claimed that the boundaries of the reservation had never been fully explained to them and that the waters of the Salt Fork and its tributaries were too brackish for their ponies, rendering the area unfit for their occupation.[3]

[1] Rayner W. Kelsey, *Friends and Indians, 1655–1917*, 167ff.

[2] James D. Richardson (comp.), *A Compilation of the Messages and Papers of the Presidents, 1789–1908*, 7, 23–24.

[3] Darlington to Hoag, October 1, 1869, Central Superintendency I; Seth Bonney to Brevet Brigadier General M. R. Morgan, July 20, 1869, Camp Supply Letter Book, Archives of the University of Oklahoma; Nelson to McKeever, May 28, June 2, 11, 1869, Fort Supply, Letters Sent.

Disregarding the Cheyennes' objections, Darlington built two log cabins and dug a well for his headquarters. The first agency was on Pond Creek, a tributary of the Salt Fork of the Arkansas River, in present Grant County, Oklahoma. No Indians joined Darlington and soon army officers recommended that the agency be shifted to the North Fork of the Canadian River. General Hazen, after visiting Darlington, supported the Cheyenne and Arapaho demands. He claimed that they had never understood the boundaries established at the Medicine Lodge Treaty and they preferred the North Canadian where there was "excellent soil, good water, and a fair amount of timber." Hazen's recommendation was also supported by Lieutenant Pepoon, who, under orders from Colonel Nelson, surveyed the country east of Camp Supply and pointed out a good locale for the agency at the future site of Darlington, Indian territory. Rich bottom land and a gushing spring made Pepoon's selection a feasible location for the Upper Arkansas Agency.[4]

Colonel Nelson was not enthusiastic about removing the Cheyennes and Arapahoes from Camp Supply. He conceded, however, that Pepoon's site was preferable to one that would force the Indians to leave the North Canadian. Captain Seth Bonney, Indian commissary officer at Camp Supply, was more outspoken in his criticism. The Cheyennes and Arapahoes, Bonney believed, were well satisfied at Camp Supply, and if the tribes were shifted very far from Camp Supply, he wrote, "it will require all the Cavalry force in the Department to induce them to 'go in' for rations."[5]

During July and August Little Robe and Minimic were the only Cheyenne chiefs to remain with their people at Camp Supply. Medicine Arrows continued to hold the main villages out on the plains. Darlington at Pond Creek was not in contact with his charges and was helpless since without rations he could not induce the tribes to join him. The impasse was broken when three members of the Special Indian Commission arrived at Camp Supply for a council with the Cheyennes and Arapahoes. The commissioners, Felix A. Brunot, Nathan Bishop, and W. E. Dodge, arriving on August 7,

---

[4] Hazen to Hoag, July 24, 1869, Upper Arkansas Agency, Letters Received; Pepoon to Lieutenant L. K. Orleman, July 22, 1869, Sheridan Papers.

[5] Nelson to Schofield, July 24, 1869, Sheridan Papers; Bonney to Morgan, August 6, 1869, Camp Supply Letter Book.

sent runners immediately to the Cheyenne villages. On August 10, Medicine Arrows arrived at Camp Supply at the head of a Cheyenne delegation.

Little Raven, an Arapaho chief, rather than any of the Cheyennes, assured the success of the talks. Speaking directly to the Cheyennes, Little Raven pleaded for peace. For a long time, Little Raven reminded his friends, the two tribes had lived, made war, and hunted together, and now they must settle down on a reservation and make the best of their opportunities. As the spokesman for the two tribes, Little Raven forcefully set forth certain tribal demands. The two tribes did not want the Medicine Lodge Treaty reservation; they preferred lands along the North Canadian River. They did not desire to live near the thieving Osages or the Kansas frontier. The Arapaho chief wanted traders to be sent among them, but nothing, Little Raven insisted, should be construed as a willingness of the Cheyennes and Arapahoes to abandon their wars against the Pawnees and Utes.

Medicine Arrows accepted Little Raven's proposals and added one of his own. Without specifically mentioning the remnant of Tall Bull's Dog Soldiers, Medicine Arrows obtained the assurance of the commissioners and Colonel Nelson that the band could surrender without fear of reprisals. Before the end of the council Medicine Arrows promised to send five of his principal men out in search of the Dog Soldiers.[6]

President Grant, before receiving the commissioners' report, had by executive order created a new Cheyenne and Arapaho reservation. Utilizing lands already made avaliable by treaties with the Creek, Seminole, Chickasaw, and Choctaw nations, President Grant set aside the region bounded by the Cherokee Outlet on the north, the Cimarron River and ninety-eighth meridian on the east, the Kiowa, Comanche, and Kiowa-Apache reservation on the south, and by the Texas state line on the west. The new reservation contained 4,297,771 acres of land.[7]

Darlington, although not present at the councils, optimistically

[6] Brunot to Parker, August 10, 1869, Central Superintendency III; *Report, Board of Indian Commissioners, 1869*, 11–15.

[7] *Annual Report of the Commissioner of Indian Affairs to the Secretary of the Interior for the Year 1882*, 269–70; Roy Gittinger, *The Formation of the State of Oklahoma, 1803–1906*, 109, 263.

believed that his Indians were prepared to place their children in schools and would labor for the food. However, when the Indian agent approached the Cheyennes at Camp Supply and requested them to place their children in school, the chiefs remained non-committal. Darlington hoped that the example of the "Arapahoe children dressed up neatly and attending school, ... would have an influence on the Cheyennes and induce them to follow." It was evident that the Quakers' school would see few Indian children. Labor by the men of the tribes was emphatically rejected. When Captain Bonney applied to Little Raven for Indian laborers, the Arapaho chief replied: "The Indian dont know how to work. He gets tired too quick."[8] The Cheyennes and Arapahoes were willing to accept rations and live peacefully on the reservation, but Quaker efforts to civilize them by education, Christianity, and agricultural pursuits held no attractions for tribesmen.

In contrast, Colonel Nelson placed little faith in Medicine Arrows' peace statements. The Cheyenne chief planned, Nelson reasoned, to bring in all the warriors of the tribe and utilize their strength to dictate the terms for their life on the reservation. Four days after the conclusion of the council, when Nelson explained that the young men of the tribe by their impertinence and insolence did not manifest much friendship for the whites, the older Cheyennes admitted that they were restrained only with great difficulty. The commanding officer at Camp Supply fully expected "to see their young men set the whole tribe by the ears, and force them on the warpath" before winter. So uneasy were the Cheyennes that Nelson and his troops were constantly on the alert, fearing that "a mere spark may at any time set this whole region in a blaze."[9]

Medicine Arrows did not send the promised messengers to the Dog Soldiers.[10] Some of the Dog Soldiers evidently came to Camp Supply without invitation. Twenty-two lodges from Tall Bull's band arrived from the Republican River in mid-September, including Medi-

[8] Darlington to Parker, August 13, 1869, Upper Arkansas Agency, Letters Received; Elma D. Townsend to Hoag, August 16, 1869, Central Superintendency III; *Report of the Commissioner of Indian Affairs to the Secretary of the Interior, 1869,* 382.

[9] Nelson to AAG., Department of the Missouri, August 14, 1869, Fort Supply, Letters Sent.

[10] Nelson to AAG., Department of the Missouri, August 20, 1869, Sheridan Papers.

cine Arrows' son-in-law, whose wife and four children were among the prisoners taken in the Battle of Summit Springs. When they arrived in Medicine Arrows' camp, Major Milo H. Kidd, temporarily commanding at Camp Supply, believed them to be thoroughly humbled.[11] Others from the Dog Soldier band were chased out of the Republican Valley by continued campaigns led by Lieutenant Colonel Thomas Duncan. Indians tried on September 26, 1869, to cut off Captain Luther North, William Cody, and twenty troopers. The abortive attack led to the discovery and destruction of a large Brulé Sioux village under Pawnee Killer and Whistler, with whom some Dog Soldiers were living. Even after the destruction of the Sioux camps, some of the Dog Soldiers did not choose to go south and, under White Horse, joined the Northern Cheyennes in the Wind River country. General Sheridan, trying to terminate the Cheyenne conflict, ordered his officers in Indian territory to allow the Dog Soldiers to "slip in, family after family," to the new reservation.[12]

Commissioner Parker ordered Darlington to select a new agency site within the territory desired by the Cheyennes and Arapahoes. By August 17 the Indian agent found a location for the new agency which met the commissioner's specifications. The North Canadian Valley at the point where it was crossed by the Fort Harker–Fort Sill military road contained abundant meadows, water, and timber for the agency's use. For once the army and civil officers were in complete agreement, but it would take some time to prepare the Indians for the move from the buffalo range.[13]

Colonel Nelson continued to fret about a Cheyenne outbreak. Buffalo were still plentiful within thirty miles of Camp Supply, and the tribes did not even bother to draw their rations. This independence bothered Nelson. His pessimism was not shared by his superior

11 Kidd to AAG., Department of the Missouri, September 18, 1869, Fort Supply, Letters Sent.

12 Duncan to Forbush, October 7, 1869, Sheridan Papers; *Record of Engagements,* 24–25; Schofield to Hartsuff, August 24, 1869 (Copy); Lieutenant John H. Page to Mitchell, September 11, 1869 (Copy), Upper Arkansas Agency, Letters Received; Endorsement of Philip H. Sheridan, September 7, 1869, to Medicine Arrows' pledge made at Camp Supply, I. T., August 10, 1869, Sheridan Papers.

13 Parker to Hoag, August 13, 1869, Office of Commissioner of Indian Affairs, Letters Sent, Vol. 92, pp. 64–65; Darlington to Hoag, August 17, 1869, Central Superintendency I.

officer, General Schofield, who reasoned that the Indians would not raid while their people were exposed to troops at Camp Supply.[14]

Rations and firearms became troublesome for Darlington. Spokesmen from both tribes complained that the government was trying to drown them with corn. Neither their people nor their ponies would eat the corn, and the chiefs suggested that the grain be exchanged for coffee and sugar. Medicine Arrows was the most outspoken of the chiefs, claiming that General Sheridan had promised them food, peace, and protection if they abandoned the warpath. Now the Cheyennes, finding the rations inedible, were forced to hunt buffalo. Their hunts were not completely satifactory because the officers at Camp Supply refused, in Medicine Arrows' opinion, to allow the Cheyennes to purchase reasonable quantities of guns and ammunition.[15]

Darlington's problems were complicated by constant bickering with Colonel Nelson. The Colonel was reluctant to turn the Cheyennes over completely to the Indian agent's jurisdiction because he believed, as did Captain Bonney, that the "Cheyennes will behave themselves, but if they do it will be from fear of punishment alone." Nelson's attitudes vacillated from day to day. When Darlington first arrived at Camp Supply, the Colonel insisted that the Indian agent was solely responsible for his charges. Within a month he claimed that until the Indians were actually on their reservation, the army exercised complete control over the Indians. On the day following this pronouncement, however, Nelson thought better of his order and acknowledged that the control over the Indians was a proper function of their Indian agent. To add to all these problems, Darlington found it impossible to employ an interpreter when the Department of the Interior refused to adjust its salary scale to meet the army's competition. After three months Darlington managed to hire Ralph Romero as an interpreter, and for the first time the Quaker was able to converse with his Indians.[16]

---

[14] Schofield to Hartsuff, August 24, 1869 (Copy); Darlington to Hoag, August 27, 1869, Upper Arkansas Agency, Letters Received; Bonney to Morgan, August 20, 1869, Camp Supply Letter Book.

[15] Darlington to Hoag, September 2, 4, 1869, Upper Arkansas Agency, Letters Received.

[16] Bonney to Brevet Major W. A. Elderkins, August 21, 1869, Camp Supply Letter Book; Darlington to Hoag, August 27, 1869, Upper Arkansas Agency, Letters Received;

Profit-seekers and hangers-on at the agency were troublesome from the outset. Since the Indians did not use their corn ration, whites suggested that it be accepted and traded to them. Usually the Indians received nothing of value for their corn and became dissatisfied with the swap. By reducing the corn issue by one-half and curtailing trading corn, Darlington remedied one source of dissatisfaction after months of correspondence with his supervisors. When corn was no longer available, the traders placed pressure upon the Cheyennes and Arapahoes for their ponies. This, Darlington claimed, would cause the Indians to raid for more horses or leave them without sufficient stock. Sincere, competent, and honest, Darlington strove constantly to gain the confidence of the chiefs and their people. Nothing he did pleased the army officers because when he did not accede to the Indians' wishes they criticized him, and when he did the officers charged that he was too lenient.[17]

As anticipated, Dog Soldiers under Bull Bear quietly slipped into the Cheyenne villages near Camp Supply. No effort was made to discipline them and Darlington was instructed only to determine their future intentions. Early in November, 1869, Darlington called a general council which was attended by a full delegation of Cheyennes and Arapahoes, including Bull Bear with his young warriors. The warrior chief claimed that he and his braves had abstained from retaliations after Carr's attack. Each day the sun rises, Bull Bear assured Darlington, "makes us have a better feeling towards the white man. If there is any more trouble I trust it will not originate with us. I hope this meeting today will drive away all the clouds." Toward the end of the council Bull Bear asked Darlington to obtain the release of his people seized by Carr.[18]

Parker to Hoag, September 3, 7, 1869, Office of the Commissioner of Indian Affairs, Letters Sent, Vol. 92, pp. 136–37, 155–56; Darlington to Hoag, September 6, October 2, 11, 17, 1869, Central Superintendency I.

17 *Report, Commissioner of Indian Affairs, 1869,* 382–83; Bonney to Morgan, October 1, 1869, Camp Supply Letter Book; Darlington to Hoag, September 24, 1869, Central Superintendency I.

18 Parker to Hoag, October 13, 1869, Office of the Commissioner of Indian Affairs, Letters Sent, Vol. 92, pp. 308–309; Darlington to Hoag, November 6, 11, 1869, Upper Arkansas Agency, Letters Received. Carr's official reports do not mention prisoners, but see Donald F. Danker (ed.), *Man of the Plains: The Recollections of Luther North,* 120.

Darlington saw opportunities to aid the Indians immediately. He hoped that schools and vocational education could begin quickly, recommending his daughter, Mrs. Elma D. Townsend, as teacher and Israel Negus to instruct the Indians in agriculture. Although the Indian agent underestimated the difficulty he would have in establishing these programs, he fully understood the problems with the Indian traders. For generations Indian traders had made exorbitant profits by undervaluing buffalo robes. Somehow the old trading pattern had to be broken and the Indians taught to exchange their robes for wagons, ploughs, harnesses, and agricultural implements of permanent utility. The Indian agent quickly found that his objectives were unobtainable because of the trading monopoly enjoyed by C. F. Tracy and Company.[19]

During the winter of 1869–70, Darlington saw little of the Cheyennes and Arapahoes. Buffalo, still plentiful on the Southern Plains, furnished plenty of meat, lodge skins, and robes for trade. Nothing seemed to seriously disturb the tribes. When Pawnees ran off ninety head of ponies and mules from Little Robe's camp, the Cheyennes merely trailed the thieves to the Arkansas River and then sent messengers to inform Colonel Nelson of their losses. Displaying unusual restraint, Bull Bear's Dog Soldiers rejected a personal invitation from Satanta to join the Kiowas, Comanches, and Kiowa-Apaches for raids into Texas. Colonel Nelson, no longer fearing an outbreak, recommended that the return of Carr's prisoners, some of whom were relatives of Bull Bear, would be beneficial to continued peace.[20]

Darlington maintained constant surveillance over individuals who traded with his charges. Some aspirants for the Indian trade laid their plans carefully and posed grave dangers for the safety of the frontier. Such an individual was W. A. Rankin. Rankin appeared at Camp Supply shortly after Darlington and made his services available to the Indian agent, accompanying the latter in the search for a suitable agency site. Hoping to gain the exclusive right to all Indian

[19] Darlington to Hoag, Isidore Becker to Darlington, Darlington to Becker and J. R. Townsend, November 18, 20, 24, 26, December 25, 1869, Central Superintendency I.

[20] Darlington to Hoag, January 15, 1870, Upper Arkansas Agency, Letters Received; E. Van Horn to Nelson, January 10, 1870, Nelson to AAG., Department of the Missouri, January 15, 23, 1870, Fort Supply, Letters Sent.

trade on the Upper Arkansas Agency, Rankin hinted broadly to Darlington that he "should live like a gentleman and that [Darlington] . . . have some outside support plainly intimating to my understanding that if he was the Licensed Trader for the Agency he would see to that part." Forewarned, J. R. Townsend, Darlington's son-in-law, refused a partnership in the trading venture offered by Rankin. Deterred for the moment, Rankin went to Lawrence, Kansas, where he obtained a trade permit from Superintendent Hoag. Rankin returned to Camp Supply early in January, 1870, with a large supply of gunpowder, lead, and percussion caps, boasting that he was in partnership with Sidney Clarke, a Kansas congressman.

To win friends among the Cheyennes, Rankin visited the camp of Bull Bear. In return for gifts Bull Bear's wife gave Rankin a fine buffalo robe while the chief offered a revolver. Rankin had his eye on a large herd of mules in the possession of the Dog Soldiers and hoped to swap his load of arms and ammunition for a substantial profit. The trader claimed that he had been afraid to refuse the gifts from Bull Bear, who, when Rankin protested, had declared, "me give you, no swap." Before Rankin could arrange for the final trade, Darlington ordered him out of the country. A visiting delegation of Quakers, amazingly enough, believed Rankin's story that Darlington was acting only to protect the previously licensed traders. Even though Darlington was supported in his action by Colonel Nelson, the Indian agent was reprimanded by Superintendent Hoag. Fortunately Commissioner Parker intervened and upheld Darlington's action, preventing a large supply of ammunition from falling into the hands of the Dog Soldiers, who were planning a visit to the Sioux.[21]

Bull Bear and Medicine Arrows held their bands aloof from the agency and the army post at Camp Supply during the early months of 1870. When councils were called to meet touring Quaker committees in the spring of 1870, these chiefs and their people were not represented. Little was accomplished at these councils except exchanges

[21] Nelson to AAG., Department of the Missouri, January 22, 28, April 23, 1870, Fort Supply, Letters Sent; Darlington to Hoag, Rankin to Hoag, January 29, March 12, 1870, Central Superintendency I; Nelson to Darlington, March 28, 1870, Upper Arkansas Agency, Letters Received; Parker to Hoag, March 7, 1870, Office of the Commissioner of Indian Affairs, Letters Sent, Vol. 94, pp. 363–64.

of platitudes between the Indians and the committee members. Benjamin Tatham, of New York, admitted to the assembled Arapahoes and Cheyennes that the transition to civilization would not be easy but urged them to fence and cultivate their land. Let the Indian, Tatham orated, "be industrious and not drink whiskey and he will become rich. . . . Let the Indian appeal to their white brothers for that Justice which they demand for themselves, and their white brothers cannot refuse it without destroying the foundation of their own prosperity." Only one Cheyenne chief attended this council. Ten days later Superintendent Hoag and Thomas Wistar visited Camp Supply and they met a few Cheyennes. The Cheyennes' disdain for councils was fully evident and contrasted clearly to the full delegations from the other nine tribes in western Indian territory.[22]

When the time approached to move the agency down the North Canadian River, Indian opinion was divided. The Arapahoes were willing, but Bull Bear and Medicine Arrows refused to commit themselves to the constraints of reservation life. Darlington used Little Robe as an intermediary and tried to persuade the absent bands to join him at the new agency. Perhaps Medicine Arrows and Bull Bear were only trying to gain the release of Carr's prisoners before joining the others. The basic division among the Cheyennes was revealed by Darington late in April, when he wrote that some of the Cheyennes "look upon our removal as designed to bring them under more rigid control and are fearful it will prove a snare to obtain more complete power and control over them. Others rejoice, trusting and believing they will be benefitted thereby."[23]

Medicine Arrows and Bull Bear never intended to move to the new agency. Messengers from these chiefs indirectly informed Darlington on April 9, 1870, that they intended to move north. Runners failed to find Medicine Arrows' and Bull Bear's camps later in the spring, and Colonel Nelson alerted the troops at Forts Dodge and Lyon for Cheyenne activity. Darlington had never had much confidence in Medicine Arrows' profession of friendship, and therefore

[22] Townsend to Hoag, February 18, 1870, "Speech of Benjamin Tatham, February 24, 1870," Council with Indian Tribes, March 12, 1870, North Fork, Canadian River, Hoag to Parker, April 26, 1870, Central Superintendency II.

[23] Darlington to Hoag, March 26, April 9, 30, 1870, Central Superintendency I.

assumed that the two bands, containing about two hundred people, were among the Sioux in the North Platte country during the summer of 1870.[24]

On May 3, 1870, Darlington shifted his agency to its permanent site near present El Reno, Canadian County, Oklahoma. The Arapahoes quickly followed the Indian agent, but, as had been anticipated, the Cheyennes were slow to move east. Only Stone Calf with thirteen lodges and the families of George Bent and John Smith were with Darlington on May 26. Knowing that most of the Cheyennes were camping near the Antelope Hills with the Kiowas and Comanches, Darlington feared the Cheyennes were raiding travelers and cattle herds. Big Jake, one of Darlington's trusted chiefs, pleaded for peace in the intertribal council held on the South Canadian River. He and other Cheyennes demonstrated their opposition to war by leaving the council early and coming to the agency. Colonel Nelson's information indicated that war was possible. But optimistically Nelson believed that not all of Bull Bear's and Medicine Arrows' bands had followed their chiefs north.[25]

At the new agency Darlington fed the Indians as they came in band by band. With a sawmill completed, buildings were begun and 220 acres of prairie were broken for grain and vegetables. Occasionally a killing, small depredation, or skirmish was reported by the commanding officer at Camp Supply. Only after the buffalo moved to more northerly or higher ranges in the summer heat did the Cheyennes in appreciable numbers begin drawing their rations at the agency.[26]

The Indians stayed with Darlington only briefly. The Cheyennes and Arapahoes complained that the new agency site was too far from the buffalo ranges for their convenience. When supplies ran short

24 Darlington to Hoag, April 9, 1870, Upper Arkansas Agency, Letters Received; Darlington to Hoag, April 30, 1870, Central Superintendency I; Nelson to Commanding Officer, Fort Dodge, April 23, 1870, Fort Supply, Letters Sent; *Report of the Commissioner of Indian Affairs to the Secretary of the Interior, 1870,* 266.

25 Nelson to AAG., Department of the Missouri, Nelson to Pope, May 7, 28, 1870, Fort Supply, Letters Sent; J. A. Covington to Hoag, May 26, 1870, Central Superintendency I; Darlington to Hoag, June 12, 1870, Upper Arkansas Agency, Letters Received.

26 *Report, Commissioner of Indian Affairs, 1870,* 267; Nelson to AAG., Department of the Missouri, June 12, 1870, Fort Supply, Letters Sent.

there was no reason for the Indians to remain. Even the compliant Arapahoes were irked at the equal treatment afforded the Cheyennes. To army officers at Camp Supply, Little Raven and Yellow Bear argued that while they and their people remained at the agency demonstrating their good faith, the Cheyenne chiefs and warriors were permitted to visit the agency for supplies and return immediately to their camps on the South Canadian and Washita rivers.[27]

While Darlington was absent temporarily, the agent's subordinates became worried. Texas militia were out in strength looking for Kiowa and Comanche raiders. Big Jake's large camp was on the Washita River and in danger of being attacked by the Texans, who were not prone to discriminate between hostile and friendly Indians. Young Cheyennes undoubtedly rode with the war parties of the neighboring tribes, and J. R. Townsend, through George Bent, urged Big Jake to move back to the reservation. During the late summer and early fall of 1870, only eight to ten lodges of Indians remained at the agency, while the others would return only when the winter's meat and robes were distributed.[28]

Colonel Nelson, obviously delighted, listened to the Indians' grumblings. The Cheyennes and Arapahoes wanted the traders to purchase their robes at Camp Supply rather than at the agency. George Bent pinpointed the Indians' dissatisfactions. He told Colonel Nelson that the Indians did not want to haul their robes the hundred miles to the agency where the rations were scarce and where some Indians had already died of fever. After their hunts the Indians of both tribes declared that they would not return to the agency. They demanded that the agency be moved back to Camp Supply, that traders come to their western camps, and that annuity goods be issued immediately. Unless these demands were met, the chiefs claimed they would join the neighboring tribes in the spring and resume the war.[29]

[27] *Report, Commissioner of Indian Affairs, 1870,* 266–67; John Murphy, "Reminiscences of the Washita Campaign and the Darlington Indian Agency," *Chronicles of Okla.,* Vol. I, No. 3 (June, 1923), 269; Nelson to Hoag, June 18, 1870, Central Superintendency IV; J. P. Fenlon to Hoag, July 19, 1870, Little Raven and Yellow Bear to Commanding Officer, Camp Supply, I. T., August 23, 1870, Upper Arkansas Agency, Letters Received; Covington to Hoag, August 10, 18, 23, 1870, Central Superintendency I; Nelson to Pope, September 2, 1870, Fort Supply, Letters Sent.

[28] Townsend to Darlington, Townsend to Hoag, September 1, 3, 1870, Central Superintendency I.

Rations drew the Indians back to their agent. Only a week after the chiefs had insisted that they would never return to the agency, a large delegation of Arapahoes talked amicably with Darlington. Some of the chiefs professed interest in houses, wagons, and farming implements. Only one Cheyenne leader expressed a willingness to settle down, and Darlington observed, "there is but little prospect of inducing a large number of either tribe to engage in agricultural pursuits speedily, but . . . with proper encouragement and assistance a few would enter into the work immediately."[30]

During the winter of 1870–71 the army officers predicted war while the Indian agent believed peace would continue. Big Jake, for example, told Colonel Nelson that when spring came and the grass was green, not a white man would be left in the country. "When this war breaks out," Nelson wrote his headquarters, "it will be one the like of which has not been seen on their frontier for some years." Traders returning from the Cheyenne camps in February, 1871, brought much the same information. Kiowa runners were constantly in the Cheyennes' camps, and the Cheyennes were preparing only enough robes to obtain the barest of necessities. Big Jake told A. G. Tracy, a trader, that it was the intention of the Cheyennes to move south and join the Kiowas in war. John S. Smith, acting as interpreter, provided conflicting accounts. First he informed the army officers that he expected trouble in the summer, but to the agency employees Smith stated that "since he was with the Cheyennes, he never found them so friendly or well disposed. . . ."[31]

Brinton Darlington answered the army officers' charges. Visiting

29 Nelson to AAG., Department of the Missouri, September 16, November 2, 1870, Fort Supply, Letters Sent; Darlington to Hoag, October 10, 1870, Central Superintendency I.

30 Darlington to Hoag, November 9, 1870, Upper Arkansas Agency, Letters Received. On November 10, 1870, Darlington listed all Cheyenne chiefs drawing rations. They included Big Jake, Little Robe, Sitting Bear, Heap-of-Birds, Big Horse, Grey Beard, Red Moon, Bears Tongue, Lean Bear, Young Whirlwind, Stone Calf, White Bull, Good Bear, Lone Chief, and Wolf Head (see List of Cheyennes and Arapahoes, Names of Chiefs whose bands have been present & drawing rations . . . Cheyenne and Arapahoe Agency, November 20, 1870, Central Superintendency I).

31 Nelson to AAG., Department of the Missouri, November 18, 1870, Captain W. B. Kennedy to AAAG., Department of the Missouri, March 2, 1871, Captain J. S. Schindel to Lt. Colonel J. W. Davidson, March 22, 1871, Central Superintendency III.

with Red Moon, Little Robe, and Heap of Birds from Grey Beard's village, the Indian agent found no dissatisfaction with either his or the government's policies. Rather Darlington found increased loyalty expressed both to the agency and to the government. To facilitate the Indians' trading, Darlington permitted licensed traders to visit the Indian hunting camps, reducing the Indians' annoyance over the scarcity of trade goods.[32]

Despite the constant war rumors, Darlington found no immediate danger threatening either himself or his employees. Not foolhardy, he still realized that "constant vigilance is our only safety." Toward the end of January, 1871, Big Jake, Red Moon, and three other leading Cheyenne chiefs discussed tribal problems with Darlington. With disarming candor Big Jake told the agent that five of his young men had raided in Texas, where they had killed a man and captured several horses. "They were big fools and had no excuse for the act," Big Jake conceded to Darlington. When the young men returned with their trophies to the camp, the band showed its displeasure by refusing to join the dance held by the young men celebrating their success. Big Jake explained his earlier belligerent talk to the traders and army officers by accusing Colonel Nelson of insulting him and of shooting Cheyenne horses. The principal difficulty, Big Jake asserted, was the inability of the chiefs to keep their young warriors from joining Kiowa and Comanche raids into Texas. Responding to Darlington's inquiry on the possibility of war, Big Jake said: "Why do you ask this? We are at peace. We intend to keep the peace. . . . You need not feel alarmed, . . . your people can come and go in perfect safety." Young Whirlwind, claiming to represent the soldiers within Big Jake's band, pledged himself and his followers to support his chief's peaceful intentions.[33]

No longer seriously worried about an outbreak, Darlington began to outline his plans to aid the Cheyennes and Arapahoes. Education, agricultural instruction, and adequate medical attention were urged by the agent as the means of civilizing his charges. He was

[32] Darlington to Hoag, January 23, 1871, Upper Arkansas Agency, Letters Received.

[33] Darlington to Hoag, January 23, 27, 1871, Covington to Hoag, January 27, 1871, Upper Arkansas Agency, Letters Received.

not deluded that any one of the programs would be immediately popular with the Indians, but ploughed lands and schools should be available if the Indians showed any inclination to use them. Effective medical treatment could possibly attach the Indians more strongly to the agency, especially if doctors could prevent such epidemics as whooping cough, which had caused the death of children during the previous winter.[34]

Darlington's Quaker beliefs created some problems for him when he was confronted with warriors who persisted in depredations and killings. The greater portion of his charges desired peace, Darlington insisted, and if properly assisted would begin to farm at least to a limited extent. Any possible success was slight because some of the young tribesmen refused to abandon raiding and this had a demoralizing effect on others. Some Indians, like some whites, Darlington knew, "cannot be restrained from evil by persuasion." He wanted the hostile activity stopped, but he did not want to call for troops. Therefore he advocated, with some naïveté, the sending of "some discreet and capable person" to live with the Cheyennes and bring the Cheyenne warriors under control.[35]

Tensions lessened when Lieutenant Colonel J. W. Davidson, Tenth Cavalry, replaced Colonel Nelson as commanding officer at Camp Supply. Colonel Davidson reversed his predecessor's policy of allowing no Indian within his post and permitted well-disposed chiefs to visit him at his headquarters. The new commander closely checked the location of the Cheyennes and found them scattered from the Cimarron to the Washita. Only Bull Bear's and Medicine Arrows' camps could not be found, supporting the general belief that those bands were with the Sioux.[36] At the Cheyenne and Arapaho Agency, Captain J. P. Schindel, Sixth Infantry, learned that the five young men reported by Big Jake to be raiding in Texas, were only one of many such groups riding with the Kiowas and Comanches. Further, the officer learned that contraband arms and ammunition were pour-

34 Darlington to Hoag, February 6, 9, 1871, Central Superintendency I.

35 Darlington to Hoag, February 15, 1871, Central Superintendency I.

36 Davidson to AAG., Department of the Missouri, February 11, 1871 (Copy), Upper Arkansas Agency, Letters Received.

ing into the Cheyenne camps through Osages trading without restriction in western Indian territory.[37]

A man with less patience than Brinton Darlington would have given up the struggle, even to maintain peace. Darlington pleaded with the Bureau of Indian Affairs for adequate funds to begin a modest school, break the land, and provide medical assistance. "Shall we endeavor," Darlington asked Hoag, "faithfully to lead these people forward or shall we permit them to sink in discouragement for want of needed assistance?" Grey Beard, leader of eighty-two lodges of Cheyennes and viewed by Darlington as the most volatile chief of the tribe, typified his tribe's attitude when he told the agent that "his men are not prepared yet to commence Farming but they will come into it after awhile."[38]

Mild weather brought renewed assertions that an Indian outbreak was imminent. Dick Curtis, chief interpreter at Camp Supply, wrote a desperate letter to former agent Wynkoop pleading with the latter to come back to the Indian country and: "Talk to them as of old. Make them feel that the Government is doing all that it can for them & satisfy them that they have friends, who are doing all they can for them." From Little Robe, Big Jake, and Minimic, Curtis learned that the outbreak was timed to begin in April. In all probability the rumors that Medicine Arrows and Bull Bear were soon to return added substance to the fears of Curtis and others. Movement of these chiefs with the bulk of the Dog Soldiers to the south was reported from Fort Laramie in March, 1871, and their return would perhaps trigger the outbreak. Lest incidents between the Cheyennes and Kansas frontiersmen occur, Commissioner Parker wanted the Kansas settlers informed that the Cheyennes desired only to pass peacefully to their reservation.[39]

Bull Bear's and Medicine Arrows' Cheyennes moved south in small parties to avoid observation and prevent pursuit. When a party of fifty Indians on March 11, 1871, attacked a wagon on Pawnee River,

[37] Schindel to AAG., Department of the Missouri, February 16, 1871 (Copy), Upper Arkansas Agency, Letters Received.

[38] Darlington to Hoag, March 1, 1871, Upper Arkansas Agency, Letters Received.

[39] Curtis to Wynkoop, March 4, 1871 (Copy), Upper Arkansas Agency, Letters Received; Parker to Hoag, Office of the Commissioner of Indian Affairs, Letters Sent, Vol. 100, pp. 316, 422–23.

officers within the Department of the Missouri immediately assumed that the Cheyennes were guilty. Traveling slowly along routes designated by army officers within the Department of the Platte, the Cheyennes committed no depredations. By March 25 the vanguard of the bands began arriving in the Cheyenne camps near Camp Supply. Taking pity on their utter destitution, Colonel Davidson issued rations to the Dog Soldier band, warning them that if they attempted to leave the reservation again, he would be forced to punish them and return them to their assigned lands.[40]

With spring returning to the Southern Plains, the anticipated war did not begin. Darlington questioned Grey Beard's band closely about an attack upon a railroad surveying party in Kansas, and they absolutely disclaimed any responsibility or intention of disturbing the surveyors. Each succeeding week brought more of the Cheyennes to the agency or its vicinity. Conversations with most of the Cheyenne chiefs two or three times a week led Darlington to assert, "without hesitation, I can say that never since my arrival in this Agency, has the prospect for permanent peace been more flattering." Even those bands who had wintered on the Washita near the Kiowas were at the agency. Grey Beard, Heap of Birds, Big Horse, and Old Whirlwind led their bands in and with the others awaited the arrival of Medicine Arrows so that their religious ceremonies could begin. Unable to raid on the Texas frontier, the young men of the Sutaio band wanted to begin an expedition against the Utes. Heap of Birds, the Sutaio war chief, firmly denied his young men their request.[41]

Darlington delicately maintained the balance necessary to keep the Indians near the agency. Rations were quickly exhausted when the beef contractor as usual was weeks late in delivering cattle. The Cheyennes and Arapahoes, Darlington wrote, "behaved themselves remarkably well for hungry savages, few companies of whites would have conducted themselves as becoming on such short allowance." When Bull Bear, apparently lingering on the Republican River, sent a

[40] D. F. Jones to AAAG., Department of the Missouri, March 11, 1871, and endorsement by General Pope, March 20, 1871, Captain G. S. Carpenter to AAG., Department of the Platte, March 13, 1871, and endorsement by General Augur, March 17, 1871, Davidson to AAG., Department of the Missouri, March 25, 1871 (Copies), Upper Arkansas Agency, Letters Received.

[41] Darlington to Hoag, April 1, 6, 16, 1871, Central Superintendency I.

message to Red Cloud, the Oglala Sioux chief, rumors of war started again.[42] During April, 1871, Bull Bear remained with some Sioux in western Kansas. They caused no trouble, approaching the stations and ranches under a flag of truce to trade robes for blankets and tobacco. Medicine Arrows continued on to the reservation and Darlington received word of his arrival by May 10, but the chief did not visit the agency headquarters. The council of this Cheyenne leader was crucial to peace plans because of his influence among the more restless elements of the tribe. When the Cheyennes scattered for their spring hunt, the inevitable rumors of war again spread.[43]

The agency's routine was not disturbed during the summer of 1871. Kiowas, following the arrest of their chiefs by General Sherman, made every effort to gain the support of the Cheyennes for war, but Darlington, Joseph D. Hoag, and Colonel Davidson, working with Little Robe and Stone Calf, successfully prevented the tribe from responding to the Kiowas' appeals. A few individual warriors undoubtedly rode off to aid the Kiowas, but no significant number of the fighting men became involved in the Texas raids. The fact that Little Robe and Stone Calf were in the East during the summer of 1871 contributed to the Cheyennes' reluctance to disturb peaceful relations with the whites.[44]

Conferring with government and Quaker officials at Philadelphia, Boston, and New York, Little Robe and Stone Calf were objects of much attention. Touring the campus of Harvard College, Little Robe thought the school would be a good place to educate his sons. In Boston, Stone Calf presented some of the Cheyenne complaints. The railroads and the nonfulfillment of treaty promises still rankled the Cheyennes' minds. Stone Calf bluntly stated that the Cheyennes had no use for railroads since the Cheyennes had no goods to trans-

---

[42] Darlington to Hoag, April 25, 29, 1871, Central Superintendency I; Parker to Hoag, April 20, 1871, Commissioner of Indian Affairs, Letters Sent, Vol. 102, p. 3, Office of Indian Affairs, Department of the Interior.

[43] Captain E. Butler to AAG., Department of the Missouri, May 2, 1871 (Copy), Upper Arkansas Agency, Letters Received; Darlington to Hoag, May 10, 22, 1871, Central Superintendency I.

[44] Report of the Commissioner of Indian Affairs to the Secretary of the Interior, 1871, 471.

port. The men who built the railroads and those left behind after the tracks were laid were evil, making almost inevitable clashes with the young Cheyennes. As for the government's promise of agricultural aid, Stone Calf alleged: "We haven't an ax, we haven't an acre of corn growing to-day in our great country that the Government has said they would reserve for us."[45]

Even though the Cheyennes did not raid, Darlington watched his charges constantly through the summer of 1871. George Bent, employed by the agent, remained in the Cheyenne camps on Wolf Creek when the Medicine Arrow ceremonies were conducted. Something would have to be done to stop the flow of whisky into the villages. Without regard for the safety of others, the traders sold liquor indiscriminately to the Indians. Brawls in the Indian camps, drunken boasts requiring fulfillment, or an isolated murder could easily ignite the whole tribe into depredations and war. Only the warning by Darlington that a war party against the Utes would lead to the loss of rations caused the chiefs to keep their young men on the reservation. The younger men of the tribe wanted to use the ammunition promised to Little Robe and Stone Calf in Washington against their enemies rather than on the buffalo hunt as intended by the Indian officials.[46]

Checking Kiowa visitations to the Cheyenne camps was even more difficult. Periodically Kiowa warriors visited the hunting camps to invite the young men of the Cheyennes to join them. The problem was complicated by the fact that the Cheyennes and Kiowas had by this date intermarried, and one of Little Robe's wives was a sister of a Kiowa chief. General Sheridan, dismissing the danger as Indian talk, maintained that the Kiowas were the most cowardly, noisy, and troublesome Indians on the plains and that the other Indians would give them no aid in furtherance of hostilities.[47]

[45] *Third Annual Report of the Board of Indian Commissioners to the President of the United States, 1871,* 25, 28.

[46] Darlington to Hoag, May 27, June 10, 22, July 4, 1871, Central Superintendency I.

[47] *Report, Commissioner of Indian Affairs, 1871,* 472; Darlington to Hoag, July 15, 1871, Central Superintendency I; Davidson to AAG., Department of the Missouri, July 10, 1871, and Sheridan's endorsement, July 24, 1871, Central Superintendency III; Davidson to AAG., Department of the Missouri, July 21, 1871, Fort Supply, Letters Sent.

The Cheyennes knew their agent was pleased with their conduct. To reciprocate, Darlington strove hard to provide sufficient arms and ammunition for hunting. If this could be done, it would emphasize the government's confidence in his wards. At any event, the eight hundred male Indians in both tribes could destroy the agent and his employees with or without the issuance of ammunition and guns. Because Osages, whisky peddlers, and illegal traders provided the Cheyennes and Arapahoes with all of the necessities of war, Darlington saw no reason to continue the prohibition of weapons and ammunition any longer. The Indian agent now began his efforts to have federal marshals placed on the reservation to reduce illegal trade. The Indian fondness for whisky, Darlington insisted, made it impossible to obtain their testimony against the clandestine white traders.[48]

Before leaving for the buffalo ranges, Big Jake, Bull Bear, Grey Beard, Red Moon, and Medicine Arrows paid Darlington a friendly visit at the agency. So amicable were the Cheyennes that a month later when reports drifted back to Darlington that some young Cheyennes had stolen horses in Texas, the agent predicted that the raiders would be condemned by the tribe. The chiefs, with little urging from Darlington, gathered up the stolen stock and turned the animals over to Colonel Davidson. Not even the presence of Pawnees near the Cheyenne and Arapaho reservation caused much of a furor among the tribes. Of course the Cheyenne chiefs objected to the nearness of their hereditary enemies and warned: "Every one that knows anything of the Indians of this Agency are aware that it is unsafe to trifle with them." No tribal conflicts resulted, but some young Cheyennes in October, 1871, killed several Pawnee men who had wandered too far from their main camp.[49]

The Cheyennes made little effort to follow the Arapahoes in either agriculture or education. Big Mouth, a former Arapaho war chief, led some of his people in beginning the cultivation of land. To his own people Big Mouth said: "I have just been gathering my corn and it does me good to look at it and think what we might do. I have

[48] Darlington to Hoag, August 7, 10, 1871, Central Superintendency I.

[49] Darlington to Hoag, August 12, September 21, 1871, Central Superintendency I; Davidson to AAG., Department of the Missouri, September 20, 1871, Fort Supply, Letters Sent.

worked and been tired several times but I am well paid. . . . This is good country and if we go to work now while good white folks are here to help us, we may, like them, have plenty and be happy." Such sentiments buoyed Darlington's hopes that the Cheyennes might follow Big Mouth's example, but no offers came from the Cheyennes controlled by Medicine Arrows, Bull Bear, Red Moon, and Little Robe. Only two Cheyenne families tried agriculture, planting fifteen acres of corn and pumpkins. Eight Cheyenne children found their way into the Quaker school, and these undoubtedly were the offspring of mixed bloods or intermarried whites.[50]

The contrast between the attitudes of army officers and Indian agents became evident when news arrived that the Atlantic and Pacific Railroad intended building its tracks up the North Canadian River. Darlington, realizing that a railroad would bring farmers and pressure for Indian lands, urged the officials in Washington to speed agricultural aid to the Indians. Colonel Davidson, on the other hand, wanted all of the tribes in western Indian territory moved to the area bounded by Indian territory, Kansas, Texas, New Mexico, and Colorado, where they could be more easily controlled. Davidson's suggestion, however, was ignored by the Washington officials.[51]

On Christmas Day, 1871, Medicine Arrows made his appearance at Camp Supply with thirty lodges of his band. Forty more lodges, the chief reported, were en route to the agency from the north, moving slowly because their ponies were in poor condition and because they lacked clothing and robes. Reflecting his desire for freedom and independence, Medicine Arrows could not understand why he was not permitted to roam wherever he chose. These forty lodges of Cheyennes returning to the reservation were evidently the last of those who had moved north when the agency was shifted to its permanent site on the North Canadian River.[52]

With all of their people united, the Cheyennes began hunting

[50] See copy of Big Mouth's speech provided by John F. Williams, dated October 3, 1871, and Hoag to Commissioner H. R. Clum, November 11, 1871, Upper Arkansas Agency, Letters Received; *Report, Commissioner of Indian Affairs, 1871*, 472, 474.

[51] Darlington to Hoag, October 10, 1871, Davidson to Commissioner Francis A. Walker, December 31, 1871, Upper Arkansas Agency, Letters Received.

[52] Lieutenant M. M. Maxon to Darlington, December 25, 1871, Darlington to Hoag, December 29, 1871, Central Superintendency I.

buffalo. John A. Covington, after visiting the hunting camps, reported to Darlington that "all was peace and quietude." Colonel Davidson was less sanguine than Darlington of peace since Medicine Arrows' whole band was back on the reservation. On January 12, 1872, Colonel Davidson seized 1,200 pounds of lead and powder from an authorized trader who was on his way to the Cheyenne hunting camps. The commanding officer at Camp Supply maintained that it would be suicidal to allow unlimited supplies of ammunition to be made available to the Cheyennes, arguing that: "I would as soon think of putting a knife in the hands of a mad man as to sanction unlimited trading of ammunition to these Indians." Through his interpreters and scouts Davidson made an effort to count the population of the Cheyennes. When the enumeration was completed, Davidson stated that the tribe contained 2,300 individuals among whom there were 500 warriors.[53]

Darlington spent the last few months of his life trying to enlarge the area of arable land available for the Cheyennes and Arapahoes. No band of the Cheyennes gave evidence of being troublesome, and even Medicine Arrows assured the agent that when "medicine making" was completed and their ponies got "a little fat," all of the Cheyennes would council with the agent. Darlington therefore devoted most of his time to writing letters to Superintendent Hoag and Commissioner Francis A. Walker which spelled out the necessity for moving the boundary farther to the east. He noted first that the original lands of the proclamation reservation had been diminished when the Wichitas and affiliated tribes were settled on the reservation's southeastern corner. Then, after a careful survey, the eastern boundary of the reservation had been found to be two miles east of the agency buildings. Since much of the western portion of the reservation was unsuited to agriculture, Darlington suggested shifting the eastern boundary twenty miles to the east. After considerable correspondence, the best that Darlington and Hoag could obtain was a concession from Commissioner Walker that those Cheyennes and

[53] Darlington to Hoag, February 3, 1872, Central Superintendency I; Davidson to Darlington, January 22, 1872, Upper Arkansas Agency, Letters Received; Davidson to AAG., Department of the Missouri, January 23, 31, 1872, Fort Supply, Letters Sent.

Arapahoes who could not find suitable lands for farms west of the ninety-eighth meridian could take lands east of that line.[54]

Brinton Darlington became ill in mid-April, 1872, lingering near death until May 1, when he succumbed to "brain fever." Knowing that their agent was seriously ill, the reservation Indians kept the peace so that nothing would disturb his last days. One incident demonstrated the affection of the Cheyennes and Arapahoes for the elderly Quaker. Two wagons bringing goods to the sutler at Camp Supply were surprised by a party of Cheyennes and Arapahoes. Fearing an attack, the whites cut loose a few mules from the wagons and dashed for the post. Captain Orlando H. Moore, Sixth Infantry, temporarily commanding the post, immediately sent two companies of cavalry after the wagons, fully expecting to find that the Indians had stolen what they desired. Instead the troopers found the wagons undisturbed and the remaining mules carefully tied to bushes so they would not wander off. Immediately upon receiving notification of Darlington's death, Superintendent Hoag recommended that John D. Miles, Kickapoo agent in Indian territory, be transferred to the Cheyenne and Arapaho Agency.[55]

Darlington died as he desired, "in the harness," believing that he had brought peace between his Indians and the whites. During his tenure as agent the Cheyennes had hunted buffalo and traded their robes, enjoying considerable prosperity. The winter and spring hunts of 1872 were good and the Cheyennes dressed over ten thousand robes for trade. But shortly after the death of Darlington, the army officers at Camp Supply braced themselves for an Indian war.[56]

An attack upon the mule herd of Captain Moore's transportation train en route from Camp Supply to Fort Hays appeared to herald the outbreak. Since the depredation took place at Bear Creek, thirty-six miles south of Fort Dodge, army officers from post to departmental

54 Covington to Cyrus Beede, March 30, 1872, Darlington to Hoag, March 7, 1872, Central Superintendency I; Walker to Hoag, April 19, May 9, 1872, Office of Indian Affairs, Letters Sent, Vol. 106, pp. 411–12, 514–15, Department of the Interior.

55 Covington to Hoag, May 1, 1872, Central Superintendency I; Hoag to Walker, May [?], 1872, Central Superintendency II; Moore to AAG., Department of the Missouri, April 26, 1872, Fort Supply, Letters Sent.

56 McCusker to Hazen, May 1, 1872, Central Superintendency III.

commanders judged the Cheyennes guilty. Even though the Kiowas rather than the Cheyennes had put the column on foot, the situation was tense: Kiowa warriors insisted on war. In the opinion of Little Raven, the Arapaho chief, cavalry patrols were not safe on the plains, and he sent a detachment back to Camp Supply escorted by a large party of his own warriors.[57]

Colonel Davidson was not put at ease when he talked to Little Robe, Stone Calf, and George Bent. Bent had left the Cheyenne villages in haste, indicating that even the mixed bloods realized an outbreak was near and that no one of white blood was safe among the Indians. The reluctance of Bent and the two chiefs to discuss the temper of the Cheyennes convinced Davidson that a large number of the Cheyenne warriors planned to join the Kiowas. At this date, however, Bent enjoyed no large reputation among the army officers on the frontier. General Pope wrote: "George Bent whose stories Colonel Davidson repeats, is utterly unreliable, and as likely as not came to Camp Supply to obtain rather than give information."[58]

The Cheyennes camped and hunted during the late spring of 1872 from the Antelope Hills to the Cimarron River. Delegations from these villages periodically visited the agency to draw rations, expressing their sorrow at the loss of their beloved agent. Nevertheless, as a tribe, the Cheyennes were unwilling to consider adopting a more settled way of life. Big Jake, Bull Bear, Red Moon, Heap of Birds, and Old Whirlwind expressed the consensus of their people when they told Acting Agent Covington, "we are not yet ready for the corn *road* but will wait a year or two to see how the Arapahoes succeed."[59]

John D. Miles arrived at the agency on May 31, 1872, and found only the Arapahoes near at hand. Some of this tribe were planting corn, pumpkins, and a few other garden vegetables. For the most part the tribes considered the agent's chief function to be the providing of rations and annuity goods. It was obvious to Miles and to Cyrus

[57] Moore to AAG., Department of the Missouri, May 17, 1872 (Copy); Pope to Hoag, May 22, 1872, Central Superintendency III; Davidson to AAG., Department of the Missouri, May 19, 29, June 3, 1872, Fort Supply, Letters Sent.

[58] Davidson to AAG., Department of the Missouri, June 6, 1872, and Pope endorsement, June 19, 1872, Fort Supply, Letters Sent.

[59] Covington to Hoag, June 1, 1872, Central Superintendency I.

*Left,* Stone Calf, Cheyenne chief, and his wife. *Courtesy Bureau of American Ethnology.*

*Below,* Cheyenne Indians at their agency, 1854–55; the man at the extreme right is identified as Friday, a chief. *Courtesy Bureau of American Ethnology.*

Cheyenne and Arapaho chiefs with their interpreters. Seated, left to right: Little Raven (Arapaho), Bird Chief (Arapaho), Little Robe (Cheyenne), Buffalo Good (?) (Wichita); standing: Edmond Guerrier (interpreter), two unidentified men, and McCusker (interpreter). *Courtesy Bureau of American Ethnology.*

Tipis in a Cheyenne camp on the Plains. From a photograph by W. S. Soule. *Courtesy Bureau of American Ethnology.*

Drawings from a Cheyenne notebook captured at the Battle of Summit Springs. *Courtesy State Historical Society of Colorado.*

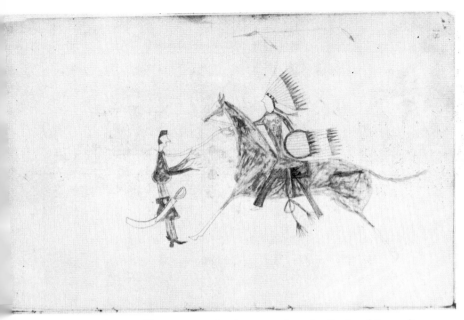

Drawings from a Cheyenne notebook captured at the Battle of Summit
Springs. *Courtesy State Historical Society of Colorado.*

Custer's Washita prisoners, from a photograph made at Fort Dodge. *Courtesy Division of Manuscripts, University of Oklahoma Library.*

Spotted Tail, Roman Nose, and Old Man Afraid of His Horses, Fort Laramie, 1868. *Courtesy Bureau of American Ethnology.*

"Attack at Dawn," the Battle of the Washita. From a painting by Charles Schreyvogel. *Courtesy Library of Congress.*

Beede, chief clerk of the Central Superintendency, that the Kiowas and some of the Cheyennes were wavering on the thin edge of peace and war. If the Kiowa chiefs, Lone Wolf, Kicking Bird, and Stumbling Bear, maintained control of their warriors, no fighting would take place. These chiefs, supported by the Arapahoes and the main body of the Cheyennes, were doing everything they could to restrain the young men. Through Grey Beard the Kiowa chiefs returned some of the mules captured from Captain Moore. The constant goading of Kiowa warriors that the Cheyennes were "squaws" and cowards had some effect. Medicine Arrows' and Old Whirlwind's camps remained with the Kiowas when the main villages moved toward the Cimarron River. As they separated, the Cheyennes complained bitterly that they would be accused of stealing Captain Moore's mules since the attack took place in their country.[60] Colonel Davidson sent runners to the Cheyenne camps, and soon thereafter Stone Calf, Little Robe, and Grey Beard appeared at Camp Supply. At this June 22 talk the chiefs confirmed that the whole of the Kiowa tribe was on the warpath, but they also admitted that two "bad men" from their bands had killed two couriers from Davidson's post.[61]

At both the Cheyenne-Arapaho and the Wichita agencies, Cyrus Beede tried to gain Cheyenne and Arapaho consent to the location of the new agency on the southeastern corner of their reservation. At the Wichita Agency Beede managed to assemble most of the Cheyenne chiefs except Medicine Arrows, Heap of Birds, and Old Whirlwind, who refused to leave the Kiowas. Only twenty lodges of Cheyennes remained with those chiefs, but Beede was not able to obtain any agreement on the reservation problem.[62]

The majority of the Cheyennes clearly favored peace with the whites; that was the only concession the tribe was willing to make. They refused almost unanimously to send their children to the agency school, begin cultivation of crops, or to listen with much tolerance to the Quaker preachment of Christianity's virtues. Jesse R. Town-

60 Miles to Hoag, June 4, 1872, Central Superintendency I; Beede to Hoag, June 16, 1872, Central Superintendency III.

61 Davidson to AAG., Department of the Missouri, June 23, 1872, Fort Supply, Letters Sent.

62 Beede to Hoag, July 22, 24, 1872, Central Superintendency III; *Report of the Commissioner of Indian Affairs to the Secretary of the Interior, 1872*, 250–51.

send, Darlington's son-in-law, summed up the situation accurately when he wrote:

> "The one main obsticle [*sic*] in the way of a more rapid advance, in the moral and religious condition of this people is their deep seated prejudice against their pale faced brothers and their reluctance to in any way, acknowledge the superiority of the whites, their lack of confidence consequent upon being so often and so cruelly deceived by them. And the tenacity with which they cling to their old superstitions, habits and Indian customs, which nothing will eradicate but years of *patient, self-sacrificing, Christian labor.*"[63]

The Cheyennes clung to their pacifistic declarations through the late summer months of 1872. Agent Miles, fearing to disturb the tribe, was reluctant to discuss the final approval of the exchange of the new reservation proclaimed by the President for the Medicine Lodge treaty lands. George Bent and Ed Guerrier refused to broach the subject to the chiefs since it would only cause trouble for themselves and the peace faction. The Cheyennes wanted no more treaties with the white man. Except for the three chiefs with the Kiowas, the Cheyennes moved en masse late in July to the agency, where they again reiterated their determination to reject the Kiowas' war pipes. There was no evidence that Cheyennes in any appreciable strength were raiding with the Kiowas. Still, Miles feared that his tribe would eventually fall under Kiowa influence.[64]

Those Cheyennes who persistently refused to leave the Kiowas were in an ugly mood. When in August, 1872, Richard Jordan and his family were murdered near Ellis, Kansas, Colonel Davidson immediately accused the Kiowas and Cheyennes of the killings. Medicine Arrows vehemently denied that his people were involved in the attack, but the chief seemed, nevertheless, to have considerable knowledge of the incident. A few weeks earlier a party of Northern and a few Southern Cheyennes had left the camps near Camp Supply for a trip to the north. Near Pawnee Fork one of the party's members approached a group of buffalo hunters, laid down his gun, a sign of peace, and was shot down by the whites. When the Indians happened upon the Jordan family, they killed outright all of the family

---

[63] Townsend to Miles, July 31, 1872, Central Superintendency I.

[64] Miles to Hoag, August [1], 12, September 1, 1872, Central Superintendency I.

except Mrs. Jordan. A year later another version of the murders was given in Washington, D. C., by a delegation of Cheyenne chiefs confronted with the incident. They admitted that some Southern Cheyennes had participated in the slaughter and that Mrs. Jordan was repeatedly raped then killed. No motive of revenge was mentioned at Washington and the Southern Cheyennes refused to surrender one of the attackers who was living on the Cheyenne and Arapaho reservation in Indian territory.[65]

During the fall of 1872, Henry E. Alvord arrived on the Washita River to arrange for a delegation to visit the nation's capital and to try to settle down the Kiowas. It was assumed that Alvord's previous relations with the Indians would be useful in the present negotiations. Full delegations from the other tribes in western Indian territory attended the councils; only the Cheyennes remained away. Nevertheless, the Arapahoes sent their representatives to Washington, where they signed an agreement relinquishing title to all lands held under the Treaty of Medicine Lodge. Following the recommendation of Miles and Alvord, Commissioner Walker acknowledged that the Arapahoes were to receive a separate reservation. If they were no longer hampered by the more turbulent Cheyennes, it was thought, the Arapahoes would progress more rapidly towards economic self-sufficiency.[66] But without the concurrence of the Cheyennes, no real settlement of the reservation problem could be achieved. Slowly more of the Cheyennes began to show resentment against the whites. As their grievances mounted, the young men of the tribe became restless and the control of the peace faction slowly disintegrated.

[65] Davidson to AAG., Department of the Missouri, October 20, 1872, Fort Supply, Letters Sent; Lieutenant Colonel Thomas H. Neill to AAG., Department of the Missouri, October 6, 7, 7, 1872, Cheyenne and Arapaho Indian Murders File, Oklahoma State Historical Society; Miles to Commissioner Edward P. Smith, September 29, 1873, Upper Arkansas Agency, Letters Received; Miles to Hoag, November 4, 1873, Central Superintendency I.

[66] Walker to Alvord, July 22, August 10, 1872, Office of Indian Affairs, Letters Sent, Vol. 108, pp. 255–57, 373–74, Department of the Interior; Miles to Hoag, September 16, October 1, 1872, Central Superintendency I.

# 16

## THE LAST WAR

FOR FOUR YEARS the Cheyennes caused comparatively little trouble on the frontier. Resentment began to smolder, however, and Cheyenne raiding parties rode for scalps, plunder, and revenge. Once more the cavalry came to the Southern Plains and broke the Cheyennes' resistance. No one cause explains the last war of the Southern Cheyennes, for grievances accumulated over a period of several years. Some of the irritants could have been prevented; others were inherent in the nature of the frontiersmen and the Cheyennes.

The Cheyennes grumbled about many things during the winter of 1872–73. Agent Miles withheld the Cheyennes' share of the annuities, trying to force them to be more co-operative at the councils. White buffalo hunters, after decimating the herds north of the Arkansas River, were beginning to penetrate the range west of the Cheyenne and Arapaho Reservation. The indiscriminate slaughter of buffalo, the Cheyennes demanded, must be stopped because it constituted "wholesale robbery of what the Indians contended is their own inherited property." There were still enough buffalo for both the Indians and the whites, so the former did nothing more than complain to their agent.[1]

Illegal traders and swarms of whisky peddlers were another matter. Attempting to evade regulations and laws, white traders sent Indians on to the Cheyenne and Arapaho reservation. These Indians, such as John F. Brown, a Seminole, and the old Delaware scout Black Beaver, claimed immunity from regulations because of their Indian blood. If Indians were allowed to trade freely, Miles maintained, he would lose all control over traders, and the reservation

[1] Miles to Hoag, November 5, December 2, 1872, Central Superintendency I.

would soon be flooded with illegal whisky and arms. Since the Indians involved did not own the trade goods, Miles and the Bureau of Indian Affairs terminated this practice quickly.[2]

Stone Calf and Bull Bear complained bitterly when Miles confiscated Black Beaver's three wagonloads of goods. They asserted that the only reason their chiefs went to Washington in the summer of 1872 was to obtain more guns and ammunition. Their demands had been met by the commissioner of Indian affairs, but it now appeared that the agent did not trust his charges enough to let them buy guns and ammunition.[3]

A surveying party appeared in December, 1872, at the eastern boundary of the reservation. The surveyors were intercepted by a party of Cheyenne warriors who wasted few words. If the work party tried to move into the reservation, the whites would lose their scalps. To the Cheyennes surveyors meant railroads, and railroads meant loss of their lands.[4]

The winter of 1872–73 was not a starving time for the Cheyennes, and they remained in good humor. So plentiful were robes that the Cheyennes told Miles to hold their annuity goods and rations until the next summer because they could provide for themselves for the winter. Even an epidemic of disease in their pony herds did not slow down the hunting, for the Cheyennes quickly adopted the white hunters' still-shooting technique. To meet the competition of Kansas traders operating on the reservation's borders, the licensed traders increased their prices for buffalo robes, adding six yards of calico, four cups of sugar, and double the previous amount of beads for each robe. The men of the tribe, however, were disturbed when their women staged a slowdown strike to protest the men's trading the products of their mutual labor for whisky, leaving insufficient robes to barter for cloth, sugar, coffee, and food.

Agent Miles had a personal opportunity to view the effect of whisky upon the Indians. His charges, for their part, were something

[2] Miles to Hoag, December 12, 13, 20, 1872, January 12, 1873, Central Superintendency I.

[3] Miles to Hoag, January 12, 1873, Central Superintendency I.

[4] E. N. Darling to Willis Drummond, commissioner of the General Land Office, December 12, 1872, Upper Arkansas Agency, Letters Received.

less than truthful when questioned on the source of liquor. One day Miles saw twelve hundred Cheyennes "drunk as loons." The Cheyennes told the agent that when they approached a group of white buffalo hunters, the white men ran, leaving behind four ten-gallon kegs of alcohol, so they simply loaded the kegs on their ponies and came back to camp for a drunken orgy that lasted more than a day. Other whisky peddlers operated openly out of Dodge City, Kansas. One man brought a wagonload of bottled whisky to the edge of the reservation and swapped off his entire stock in a matter of a few moments, exchanging one bottle of liquor for one robe.

Miles could not learn from either the chiefs or the warriors where the supplies of whisky were located. Even when a whisky peddler was intercepted by the agency force, the tribesmen refused to give incriminating evidence to the agent or army officers. Finally some women in the Arapaho camps told the agent that most of the liquor came from five ranches located in southern Kansas. Colonel Davidson provided a small detachment of cavalry, and Miles sent J. J. Hoag as his representative to arrest the ranch keepers. The troopers and Hoag took nine men into cusody and returned with a considerable quantity of buffalo robes and ponies. "Will I be backed?" Miles asked Superintendent Hoag, because the agent realized that he was operating without specific authorization from his superiors.[5]

These whisky peddlers, the scum of the frontier, were dangerous to Indians and whites alike. Yet the United States district attorney at Topeka was reluctant to prosecute eight of the men when they arrived for trial. The ninth prisoner, Jack Gallagher (or Gallager) escaped while being escorted to Fort Dodge. Joined by another renegade, Robert Hollis, he returned to Indian territory to recoup his losses. The pair robbed a teamster, then stole a horse and mule from a Caddo chief, and finally murdered a courier of a surveying party for his horse and saddle. Two more gunmen and several deserters from Camp Supply also joined Gallagher and Hollis. Together they held up a stage and ran off the horses. When Amos Chapman and six picked men cornered the desperadoes late in April, 1873, Gallagher

[5] Miles to Hoag, January 16, 1873, Miles to Lee and Reynolds and Wood Brothers, February 1, 1873, Central Superintendency I.

admitted that the country was getting too warm for him and moved on.[6] Without peace officers and courts Miles was powerless to completely stop the flow of whisky into his Indians' camps.

If the Cheyennes had drunk the whisky and remained on the reservation, an incident of greater significance would not have occurred. During a drinking bout some young Cheyennes pledged themselves to join a war party to fight Utes. Led by White Bird, a nephew of Little Robe, seventeen young Cheyenne warriors traveled cautiously into the mountains west of Fort Bascom, New Mexico territory, looking for Utes. Committing no depredations and finding no enemies, the party began its trip back to the reservation. While camped some distance east of Fort Bascom, the young warriors were surprised by troops from the fort who chased them into the hills and severely punished them. Before the Cheyennes could make their escape, one of their number had been killed and four wounded, one of whom they left behind for dead. White Bird was among the three wounded who came back to the camps spoiling for revenge. Little Robe mourned and warned Miles that he did not know if the young men of the tribe could be controlled.[7]

About a month after White Bird's war party returned to the reservation, United States surveyors were working about twenty-five to thirty miles southeast of Camp Supply. Although Indians harassed them occasionally, the men did not believe themselves in immediate danger. On March 18, 1873, Cheyennes wrecked the surveyors' camp and beat the cook with rifle butts and revolvers. A day or two later a large party of Cheyennes appeared and killed E. N. Deming, the chief surveyor, and three of his assistants. Deming, when found, had been scalped and both of his hands were hacked off. At first it appeared that the Cheyennes were not involved, since John Williams, agency blacksmith, who was in the Cimarron camps at the time, heard nothing of the murders. For a month Miles continued at every

[6] Miles to Hoag, April 14, 17, 28, 1873, William M. Lee to [Miles], May 10, 1873, Central Superintendency I.

[7] Miles to Hoag, March 15, 1873, Central Superintendency I; John Williams to Hoag, March 31, Central Superintendency III; Lieutenant Colonel John R. Brooke to AAG., Department of the Missouri, March 15, April 4, 1873, Fort Supply, Letters Sent.

opportunity to question the Cheyennes, and finally Little Robe admitted on April 25 that Foolish Bear, son-in-law of Bull Bear, had committed the attack with forty or fifty other young men. Once revenge upon the whites was taken, the young men joined the bands of Grey Bear, Bull Bear, Old Whirlwind, Medicine Arrows, and White Horse. These bands slipped quietly away from the Cimarron camps and went to the Washita, refusing to come nearer the agency.[8]

The peace chiefs, Little Robe and Big Jake, struggled hard to prevent the young men from making more trouble. Backed by the soldier societies, who whipped young men and killed their horses when they tried to leave the camps, the peace faction slowly gained strength as members of the Washita camps joined Little Robe near the agency. Big Bow, the Kiowa chief, added to the stress when he told the Cheyenne warriors that he would wait a little while more for the release of Satanta and Big Tree. If they were not shortly freed from prison, Big Bow announced, he would ask the Cheyenne men to join him in attacking any white found on the plains.[9]

A Sun Dance was set for early June, 1873, on the Washita. The Cheyennes camping near the agency were required to join the bands on the Washita under pressure from the soldier societies. When Stone Calf refused to leave the agency, soldiers whipped him, slashed his lodge, killed some of his horses, and made him join the rest of the tribe. Young Cheyenne braves, against the wishes of their chiefs, refused to be quiet. Despite the fact that the surveyors were now guarded by a detachment of cavalry from Camp Supply, a small group from the Washita camps rode into the work camp, demanded food, and began shoving some of the surveyors around. When the noncommissioned officer ordered the young braves to leave, they defiantly strung up their bows and left. But before long they fired a volley of arrows and shots into the camp. Amos Chapman encountered these warriors, and they told him that they had approached the camp, asking only for food, and in answer had been fired upon

[8] T. H. Barrett to Miles, April 24, 1873, Cheyenne and Arapaho Depredation Files, Indian Archives, Oklahoma State Historical Society; Williams to Hoag, March 22, 31, 1873, Miles to Hoag, March 29, April 4, 18, 21, 25, 1873, Central Superintendency I.

[9] Miles to Hoag, Miles to Beede, April 28, May 5, 1873, Central Superintendency I; Miles to Hoag, May 19, 1873, Central Superintendency III.

by the troops. Miles did not interpret the affair as anything more than Cheyenne anger at the surveying of the reservation and did not regard it as a war threat.[10]

After the Sun Dance was completed, the Cheyennes dispersed for their summer camps. Little Robe, Stone Calf, White Horse, and Minimic brought their people near Camp Supply, while others hunted on Wolf Creek west of the post. Agent Miles was pleased that the Indians did not renew their contact with the Kansas whisky traders. His pleasure soon changed to sorrow when New Mexicans took over the role of the Kansans. Ben Clark, before leaving the Cheyenne camps near the head of the Washita, promised the tribesmen that he would not reveal their new source of liquor to the agent. The scout also brought back the news that the Cheyennes had displaced Little Robe and Grey Beard as chiefs of the tribe. Evidently the New Mexicans were cleaning out the Cheyennes even more systematically than the Kansans. When the Cheyennes had no more robes, groups of sixty ponies each were swapped for small quantities of whisky. So bad were the conditions in the camps that Ed Guerrier sent his string of ponies to Camp Supply so that they would not be "borrowed" by his relatives and sold for liquor. Miles concluded that it would be safer to bring the Cheyennes to their village sites near the Kansas line, since they might begin raids into Texas to recoup their depleted pony herds. When Miles went out to check the Indians himself, he found that his trusted Little Robe had just returned with a "cargo" of whisky. The chief and his band were "fearfully drunk," and the agent lamented, "we can't move drunken Indians."[11]

Miles sought a delegation of chiefs for a Washington conference. Since the spring of 1873, Miles and Commissioner Smith had planned to bring the Cheyennes and Arapahoes to Washington, where their acceptance of the presidential proclamation would be formalized, and at the same time there would be created two separate reservations— one for the Cheyennes and another for the Arapahoes. Miles quickly

[10] Brooke to AAG., Department of the Missouri, June 3, 1873 (Copy), Central Superintendency III; Miles to Hoag, June 13, 1873, Central Superintendency I.

[11] Miles to Hoag, July 1, 18, 21, 28, August 11, 23, 1873, Clark to Miles, July 22, 1873 (Copy), Central Superintendency I; Brooke to AAG., Department of the Missouri, July 16, 1873, Fort Supply, Letters Sent.

found that it was impossible to find a suitable delegation among the Cheyennes. The warriors of the tribe demanded a voice in the conference and insisted that if their representatives could not accompany the chiefs, no delegation would leave the reservation. But by mid-September, 1873, after a visit from the commissioner of Indian affairs and the secretary of the interior, the Cheyennes acceded to the government's demands and a delegation was organized.[12] Six Cheyenne leaders, Stone Calf, Little Robe, Whirlwind, White Shield, Pawnee, and White Horse, were escorted to Washington for the council.[13]

While these chiefs and warriors were in Washington, a large party of Cheyennes scoured the southeastern portion of Colorado territory looking for Utes. This party, 160 warriors under the soldier chiefs, Spotted Horse, Big Wolf, and One-eyed Bull, alarmed the southeastern Colorado territory, causing hundreds of settlers to flee. Although the secretary of the interior wanted these Cheyennes killed or captured, Generals Pope and Sheridan were surprisingly moderate. General Pope said that since the Cheyennes did not intend to harm the settlers, it would be cheaper to pay for a few depredations than to attack the war party and bring on a war. And Sheridan believed that the Cheyennes killed nothing more than "two chicken cocks in order to get their tail feathers." Two other Cheyenne parties were also absent from the reservation at this time. White Eagle led thirty braves to visit the graves of their comrades near Fort Bascom, and a smaller group under White Wolf and Man-Who-Walks-Under-a-Cloud successfully raided for stock in Texas but lost their loot when hit by a patrol from Camp Supply.[14]

When the six Cheyenne delegates appeared before Commissioner

---

[12] Smith to Hoag, April 14, 1873, Office of Indian Affairs, Letters Sent, Vol. 112, p. 119; Miles to Hoag, August 28, September 22, October 15, 1873, Covington to Hoag, September 15, 1873, Central Superintendency I.

[13] "Cheyenne and Arapahoe Reservation," in 43 Cong., 1 sess., *House Exec. Doc. No. 1*, 3.

[14] Hoag to Pope, October 3, 1873, Upper Arkansas Agency, Letters Received; Covington to Hoag, October 31, 1873, Central Superintendency I; Brooke to AAG., Department of the Missouri, October 27, 1873, Fort Supply, Letters Sent; Pope to Major James Riddle, November 3, 1873, Department of the Missouri, Letters Sent; Sherman to Sheridan, October 8, 1873, Pope to AAG., Division of the Missouri, October 10, 1873, Sheridan to Sherman, October 29, 1873, Office of the Adjutant General, Letters Received.

Edward P. Smith, they were quickly informed of the government's wishes. The commissioner wanted the Cheyennes to accept a permanent reservation and share it with the Northern Cheyennes. Under no circumstances were the Cheyennes to continue their war with the Utes, they were to keep their young men on the reservation and surrender the murderers of the Jordan family. The Southern Cheyenne and Arapaho chiefs accepted the terms of a new treaty outlined by Commissioner Smith and President Grant. Talks hit a snag when the northern divisions of the tribes refused to give up their ranges and move south. From the talks came the agreement that the Cheyennes and Arapahoes were to have separate reservations. That of the Cheyennes would in large part duplicate the lands originally reserved for them by the Treaty of Medicine Lodge. The agreements, however, did not become effective because Congress took no action on the treaty. About the only concession received by the Southern Cheyennes was the reopening of the sale of guns and ammunition under the agent's supervision.[15]

Arriving by railroad at Dodge City, Miles was beset with problems. The horses promised as presents to the chiefs in Washington were not available. Temporarily Miles rented a room for the Cheyenne and Arapaho chiefs in Dodge City to await the horses mistakenly sent to Wichita. During the night some denizens of the barrooms slipped into the room and threw a couple of small packages of red pepper mixed with gunpowder into the stove. The Indians stampeded from the room choking and coughing, and Miles was forced to house the chiefs in an unheated railroad car until the horses arrived from Wichita. Before Miles could get his chiefs safely out of Dodge City, someone succeeded in slipping the chiefs enough whisky to get them "fearfully drunk" and nearly into a brawl.[16]

Conditions during Miles's and the chiefs' absence had not changed. Increased numbers of buffalo hunters were operating south of the Arkansas River, and they were also supplying the Indians with large quantities of liquor. An example of the effects of whisky upon the

[15] Miles to Smith, September 29, 1873, Upper Arkansas Agency, Letters Received; Miles to Hoag, November 4, 14, 23, 1873, Central Superintendency I; 43 Cong., 1 sess., *House Exec. Doc. No. 12,* 1–5.
[16] Miles to Hoag, December 7, 9, 1873, Central Superintendency I.

Cheyennes occurred when the chiefs returned to Camp Supply. In Washington they had promised the commissioner to help the agent check the open use of liquor among the tribes. White Horse found his camp in the midst of a drinking party. The chief tried to destroy the whisky and seize the peddler, but the soldier society members intervened. Angered, White Horse got his gun and shot Bear Shield's horse, collected a few loyal members of his soldier society about him, and escorted the whisky seller from the village.[17]

The licensed reservation traders stayed in close contact with the scattered Cheyenne villages during the winter of 1873–74. Broken into camps varying in size from thirty-five to ninety lodges, the men found plenty of buffalo, and the robe trade was brisk. Confidently the traders predicted that the Cheyennes would not join the Kiowas and Comanches if the latter tribes carried out their threat of war.[18]

Agent Miles tried to concentrate the Cheyennes near the agency to reduce Kiowa and Comanche influence. In late December, 1873, Little Robe admitted to Miles that some young Cheyennes had returned to their villages with thirty-five horses, their share of an intertribal raid into Texas. The agent then banned further sale of guns and ammunition to the Cheyennes. Bull Bear told the agent that it did not matter since the Osages had already sold them all that was necessary for the season. More guns and ammunition were also available between the reservation and the Kansas boundary, where they were openly traded to the Indians by well-supplied outfits from Dodge City and Caldwell.[19]

Early in January, 1874, contrary to their practice in past seasons, Cheyennes began to draw rations at the agency. Apparently the tremendous slaughter of buffalo by the white hunters was beginning to take effect, and the Cheyennes refused to shift their hunting to more westerly ranges. Little Robe, Bull Bear, Big Jake, and Stone Calf claimed all of the Cheyenne camps were quiet, and none of their people talked of war.[20]

After more than a year of requests, the Department of Justice

[17] Miles to Hoag, December 16, 1873, Lee and Reynolds to Miles, December 18, 1873 (Copy), Central Superintendency I.

[18] Lee and Reynolds to Miles, December 18, 1873, Central Superintendency I.

[19] Miles to Hoag, December 26, 1873, Central Superintendency I.

[20] Miles to Hoag, January 13, February 1, 1874, Central Superintendency I.

finally commissioned a deputy United States marshal to co-operate with Miles in stamping out the illegal whisky, gun, and ammunition trade. The new deputy marshal, John H. Talley, and one of Miles's trusted employees, Benjamin Williams, began their first tour early in January, 1874, swinging through the country from Caldwell to Camp Supply. They were to arrest all persons engaged in illicit trade with the Indians or indiscriminately slaughtering the buffalo herds. Two men were powerless to accomplish these purposes and so were supported by a detachment of cavalry from Camp Supply. Williams and the cavalry arrested eleven men and a youth in a hunting camp south of the Kansas line. Carcasses were thickly strewn over the plains. It was easy to identify the buffalo killed by the whites because they did not skin the buffalo hides down the legs as did the Indians. Since the prisoners were charged with no offense other than killing buffalo, Miles was forced to release the hunters—to the intense dissatisfaction of the Indians. The outraged Cheyennes and Arapahoes claimed that the Washington officials had lied to them when they had promised to curtail the slaughter of the buffalo herds.[21]

Eastern tanners paid good prices for buffalo hides after 1871. Millions of the beasts were shot for their hides alone—the best esimate being about 7,500,000 in the years 1872–74. Destruction of the buffalo, for centuries the source of food, shelter, implements, and barter for the Plains Indians, was not to be taken lightly. Officially nothing could be done to check the decimation of the herds in the states of Kansas and Texas or the territories of New Mexico and Colorado. Federal jurisdiction over citizens was limited in this case to the Indian reservations, an area too small to protect adequately the number of buffalo necessary for Indian use. So this constant irritant continued unabated.[22]

If the buffalo slaughter had been the sole grievance of the Indians in 1874, no outbreak would have occurred, but whisky drove the

[21] Miles to Williams, Miles to Hoag, January 2, 10, 1873, Central Superintendency I; Williams to Miles, Miles to Hoag, February 6, 7, March 7, 1874, Central Superintendency III.

[22] Carl Coke Rister, "The Significance of the Destruction of the Buffalo in the Southwest," *Southwestern Historical Quarterly*, Vol. XXXIII, No. 1 (July, 1929), 43, 47–48. The destruction of the buffalo is also well covered in Mari Sandoz, *The Buffalo Hunters* and Wayne Gard, *The Great Buffalo Hunt*.

Indians crazy. What robes they obtained were swapped for liquor instead of food, trade goods, guns, and ammunition. Warriors numbed by the poisonous alcohol hunted little, and their families nearly starved. White men, with the aid of some chiefs, dressed and painted themselves as Cheyennes to avoid detection by federal marshals and employees of the agency. Miles could control his charges, "filled with whiskey, no more than you can control a fire by piling on fuel." A member of a licensed trading firm wrote to Miles from Camp Supply: "The Indians will be hungry and mad very soon and . . . whiskey is more plentiful than good water and all hands in the vicinity are nearly continually drunk."[23]

As band after band of the Cheyennes moved near the agency, rations ran low. On March 21, 1874, Miles warned Hoag, "We will soon be out of rations & thou can then judge our situation." Forced to eat corn and beef instead of buffalo, the Indians grew more and more dissatisfied. No money was available for the purchase of adequate supplies of beef; buffalo were scarce on the reservation; and Miles was concerned that the Cheyennes would join the Kiowas, who were poised for war. Compounding Miles's difficulties were horse thieves who brazenly raided Cheyenne camps within sight of the agency. William Martin, known as "Hurricane Bill" on the Kansas frontier, ran off forty head of ponies from Little Robe's camp. Cheyenne warriors trailed the thieves into Kansas without success. The chiefs were provoked and in blunt terms informed Miles that unless the stock were returned, they would not be able to restrain their young men.[24]

Jack Gallagher, Robert Hollis, and William Martin were the leaders of a cutthroat band infesting the Chisholm Trail from the agency north to the Kansas line. They made their headquarters in the heavy timber on the Cimarron River, from which point they raided for horses and carried on a brisk sale of whisky. Troops managed to chase Gallagher and his bunch out of the country, but this was no sooner accomplished when another nest of thieves moved in.[25]

Finding no buffalo within a hundred miles of the agency and losing

[23] Miles to Hoag, February 21, 1873, A. E. Reynolds to Lee, March 3, 1874 (Copy), Central Superintendency I.

[24] Miles to Hoag, March 2, 21, 28, 31, April 4, 1873, Central Superintendency I.

[25] Miles to Commanding Officer, Camp Supply, April 25, 1874, Miles to Hoag, May 9, 1874, Central Superintendency I.

their ponies to white horse thieves, the Cheyennes decided to move into the Texas Panhandle. About the time the Cheyennes left the agency, a party of young warriors, including Little Robe's son, decided to recover their stolen stock. Failing to find their ponies, the Cheyennes took horses, mules, and cattle near Sun City, Kansas, to replace their losses. Before the young men could leave Kansas, they were overtaken by a company of the Sixth Cavalry, and Little Robe's son and one other young brave were badly wounded. Those few Cheyennes who remained with Miles at the agency continued to suffer losses of their ponies. George Bent had his whole string stolen within sight of the agency, and nothing the United States deputy marshals could do seemed to check the thieves.[26]

Three young boys had better luck than the marshals and agency employees. Just north of the Cimarron River, the youths found a large herd of mules, horses, and ponies hidden in a stand of blackjack. The boys ran off most of the herd and took the animals to their camps. Agent Miles learned that some of the animals belonged to James S. Morrison and the stage line and demanded them from the Cheyennes. Big Horse and White Shield demurred, pointing out to Miles that the Cheyennes still were missing many of their best hunting and war ponies.[27]

Superintendent Hoag fumed futilely in Lawrence. Two deputy marshals were powerless to deal with the bands of ruffians roaming Indian territory. The army officers at Camp Supply were forbidden to intervene when only violations of civil laws were involved. To Hoag the pattern of events and resulting dangers were clear. Citizens in Kansas rob the Indians; the Indians retaliate, trying "to reclaim or retake what is theirs and if they fail they take substitutes if they can. Then our senators ask Congress to furnish the Governor with arms to aid the border settlers and defend themselves against the Indian raiders."[28]

[26] Miles to Hoag, Bent to Miles, May 1, 6, 1874, Central Superintendency I; Major C. E. Compton to AAG., Department of the Missouri, July 16, 1874, Office of the Adjutant General, Letters Received; *Report of the Commissioner of Indian Affairs to the Secretary of the Interior, 1874,* 233.

[27] Miles to Hoag, May 19, 1874 (Copy), Office of the Adjutant General.

[28] Hoag to Smith, April 23, May 18, 1874, Central Superintendency II; Williams to Hoag, May 16, 1874 (Copy), Office of the Adjutant General, Letters Received. After

"I know," Miles wrote Superintendent Hoag, "thou would not advise the restraining of these people here at the Agency in a starving condition and exposed as they were to the frequent raids upon their herds." Miles was not worried that the Cheyennes would agree to war, but events proved the agent wrong. Kiowas sent war pipes to the Cheyennes, whose chiefs still wanted peace. Incidents continued to inflame the minds of the young warriors. In mid-May a small party of Cheyenne hunters approached a camp of railroad surveyors west of the Antelope Hills. The whites did not return the Indians' signs of friendship and opened fire, severely wounding one of the warriors. This brought a threat of retaliation at the first opportunity from the Cheyennes.[29]

Buffalo and whisky were in such abundance west of the reservation that Miles could not attract all of the Cheyennes back to the agency. New Mexican traders were clearing out the Cheyennes' robes and ponies rapidly. "If fifty-two kegs of whiskey in one day will make that article plenty, then whiskey is plenty," Miles told Hoag. After the Sun Dance sponsored by Little Robe's wounded son, the influence of the peace chiefs waned and that of the warriors grew.[30]

By June, 1874, it was apparent that the chiefs could no longer keep their warriors quiet. Even Little Robe and Stone Calf, normally at the head of the peace faction, openly censured Agent Miles for his failure to return the ponies stolen by Kansas horse thieves. Only the Arapahoes remained loyal to the agent, and their chiefs rigidly controlled their young men by firm use of the tribe's warrior societies. The agency force was thoroughly frightened and remained at the reservation only because Powder Face, an Arapaho chief, assured Mrs. Miles that "the white people at the Agency belonged to him, and that he would see that they were protected." One party of Cheyennes ran off stock from the agency, and when Miles requested its return, the Cheyennes told his messenger that he could have the

months of delay, President Grant in June, 1874, permitted the use of troops on the Cheyenne and Arapaho reservation. By then it was too late, because the Cheyennes were already committed to war (see C. Delano to Secretary of War, June 6, 1874, Office of the Adjutant General, Letters Received).

[29] Miles to Hoag, May 12, 16, 1874, Central Superintendency I.

[30] Brooke to AAG., Department of the Missouri, May 18, 1874, Fort Supply, Letters Sent; Miles to Hoag, June 13, 1874, Central Superintendency I.

animals when he sent enough soldiers to take them. Buffalo hunters were attacked near Adobe Walls on June 9, and at least two were killed. A week later Cheyennes in considerable strength rode to the vicinity of Medicine Lodge, Kansas, where they killed and scalped three homesteaders. Frontier settlers in Kansas panicked and fled to larger settlements. On June 21 and 24, Major Charles E. Compton and his escort were attacked by a mixed party of Kiowas and Cheyennes while enroute between Camp Supply and Fort Dodge.[31]

The fight at Adobe Walls was not the beginning of the last Indian war on the Southern Plains—only its best-publicized skirmish. Undoubtedly the strong medicine of the young Comanche, Isatai, added to the young Cheyennes' incentive, for they believed that under Isatai's protection they would not be harmed by the white man's bullets. Many Cheyenne leaders, including Grey Beard and Medicine Water, accepted the Kiowa and Comanche war pipes and were joined by most of the tribe's young men. Little Robe moved back to the agency when he realized that trouble was inevitable. His example would have been followed by others had it not been for the soldier societies.

Warriors from the five tribes of the Southern Plains decided to attack the buffalo hunters and trading settlement at Adobe Walls. Most of the braves were Comanches and Cheyennes, and in all the party consisted of some 250 to 300 men.[32] Isatai directed the movements of the warriors from the Washita River camps to the South Canadian. At dawn on June 27, 1874, the warriors surrounded the hunting post and were ready to attack.

Adobe Walls was usually inhabited by seven or eight men in the stores, blacksmith shop, and saloon. A number of buffalo hunters had been driven to the protection of Adobe Walls by Indian harassment earlier in the month, so that when the war party arrived, twenty-

31 E. C. Lefebvre to Miles, June 14, 1874, Miles to Smith, June 18, 1874, Central Superintendency I; Miles to Smith, June 16, 30, 1874, Upper Arkansas Agency, Letters Received, and Wichita, Kansas, *Beacon*, June 24, 1874.

32 Evidence for accepting a much smaller force of Indians at Adobe Walls than that generally used will be found in Davidson to AAG., Department of the Missouri, July 7, 1874 (Copy), Office of the Adjutant General, Letters Received, and Joseph Kinchen Griffis (Tahan) to Walter S. Campbell, February 28, 1937, Walter S. Campbell Papers, Archives of the University of Oklahoma.

eight men and a woman were either living in the buildings or camping nearby. Many of the men were still not asleep at dawn because
they had spent the night repairing the roof of James Haranahan's
saloon. Among those who had spent the night repairing the damage
caused by the collapse of a cottonwood ridgepole was Bill Dixon, a
buffalo hunter. A few men were walking to their wagons when the
Indians silently drew up in a long line, awaiting Isatai's signal to
charge.

The sun was just rising as Bill Dixon observed a dark mass approaching. At first Dixon thought it was a buffalo herd; then the
speed of the charge and the war whoops of the Indians caused Dixon
to run for his life to the saloon. Three men, caught in the wagons,
were cut down by the Indians in the first charge. Inside the adobe
stores and sod-house saloon, the whites fought desperately, knocking
firing holes in the adobe or using the windows of the saloon to break
the Indians' initial onslaught. The big buffalo guns and Sharps
rifles picked off the circling Indians. Stone Calf's son and Horse
Chief of the Cheyennes fell before the Indians regrouped for another
attempt to destroy the buffalo hunters. During the whole forenoon
the Indians threw themselves against the barricaded whites. The
Indians' bugle calls constantly alerted the besieged men, who would
not be panicked or driven from their cover.

By mid-afternoon the warriors gave up the fight and began to ride
away. Considering the prolonged attack, the Indians' losses were
small; only six Cheyennes and three Comanches were killed, but
many others were seriously wounded. Hippy, a Cheyenne warrior,
seized Isatai to quirt the disgraced medicine man. Other Cheyennes
restrained Hippy because they not only knew the Comanche's medicine had failed, but they also thought Isatai a coward since he had
refused to join them in their charges on Adobe Walls.[33]

At his agency, Miles knew nothing of the fight at Adobe Walls,
but five days later the Indian agent realized that he had an Indian war
on his hands. Peg Leg, a Cheyenne messenger sent to the main camps,

[33] Frederick S. Barde (comp.), *Life and Adventures of "Billy" Dixon of Adobe
Walls, Texas Panhandle*, 218ff.; Rupert N. Richardson, "The Comanche Indians and
the Fight at Adobe Walls," *The Panhandle-Plains Historical Review*, Vol. IV (1931),
24–38; McCusker to Jones, July 20, 1874 (Copy), Office of the Adjutant General,
Letters Received.

returned with the news of Adobe Walls and that five Cheyenne war parties were out looking for scalps. That same night, July 2, Old Whirlwind told Miles that three young Cheyenne braves and a woman had visited his camp and admitted their complicity in killing William Watkins between the Cimarron River and the Kingfisher station. Hastily Miles sent a messenger to Fort Sill for a company of cavalry to guard the agency.[34]

Military action, deprecated by the Quakers, was now necessary. The Cheyennes were beyond control by any other means. Small incidents, individually unimportant, had gradually driven the Cheyennes to abandon the peace. Horse thieves, buffalo hunters, poisonous whisky, lack of rations, restless young men needing trophies and coups for warrior status, and inadequate law enforcement had finally taken their toll.

Miles realized that he needed more than a company of cavalry to subdue the Cheyennes and decided to plead for aid at Lawrence and Fort Leavenworth. The Indian agent gathered a small force of whites from his employees and traders to make the dangerous trip to Caldwell, Kansas. Thirty miles out the body of Watkins was found, scalped and left by the Cheyennes on the road. Re-enforced by a few more men from Kingfisher station, the party found the ranches already deserted. At the site of present Hennessey, Oklahoma, Miles and his escort found a still-smoldering wagon train and the bodies of four men. Patrick Hennessey, the wagon master, recognizable only by his feet and hands, had been tied while still alive to a wagon wheel and burned to death by the Indians. Of his companions George Fand and Thomas Calloway were scalped, but Ed Cook was not mutilated. When Miles arrived at Caldwell, the Indian agent was scared; he wanted protection for his agency and troops immediately to guard the road to Caldwell—otherwise his position was untenable.[35]

At Lawrence, Superintendent Hoag agreed with Agents Miles and Tatum; the warring tribes would have to be chastised by the army. The executive committee of Quakers at Lawrence disagreed. They

34 Miles to Davidson, July 3, 1874, Davidson to AAG., Department of the Missouri, July 5, 1874, Office of the Adjutant General, Letters Received; Miles to Smith, July 10, 1874, Headquarters of the Army, Letters Sent.

35 Miles to Smith, July 7, 1874, Upper Arkansas Agency, Letters Received; Miles to Hoag, July 10, 1874, Central Superintendency I.

found Miles' communications "warlike" in tone and demanded his immediate resignation. Safe at Lawrence, the committee stated that the turmoil caused by the "intrusion of white men, who kill buffalo, trade in whiskey, and steal horses," had brought retaliations from only a few chiefs and young men. An attack on one train, a few ranches, and buffalo hunters did not justify, in the Quakers' opinion, the use of troops upon the Indians. Miles refused to submit his resignation, insisting that "it will not do for us to remain quiet & permit the horrid butchery of innocent persons—this would have been criminal negligence."[36]

General Pope was inclined to do nothing more than protect the agencies, roads, and actual settlers. For the trading firms from Dodge City who opened grog shops or trading posts in the Texas Panhandle, Pope had nothing but contempt. The hunters' camps were inhabited only by ruffians who invaded the Indian country contrary to law, committing "violent and inexcusable outrages upon the Indians." These frontier drifters, Pope wrote to Governor Thomas A. Osborn of Kansas, "have justly earned all that may befall them, and if I were to send troops to the locality of these unlawful establishments, it would be to break them up and not to protect them."[37]

Sheridan disagreed with Pope and wanted troops to take the offensive. A dispatch critical of Pope's stand and intended only for General Sherman and the Secretary of War was published in the Kansas press, arousing Pope's ire. Sheridan, however, maintained his ground and insisted that the buffalo hunters had every legal right to hunt and trade at Adobe Walls, and that Pope could have relieved them without violating the Indians' reservation rights.[38]

Later, as Sheridan prepared expeditions to drive the Indians back to their reservations, he presented his justifications for vigorous action. Unlike Pope, Sheridan blamed the Indians and attributed the trouble to "the immunity with which these tribes have been treated in all their raids into Texas for the past three years." Sheridan conceded that the Indians had cause for complaints against the buffalo hunters, the

[36] Miles to Smith, July 18, 1874, Upper Arkansas Agency, Letters Received, which encloses the report of the Associated Executive Committee of Friends on Indian Affairs.

[37] Pope to Osborn, July 8, 1874, Department of the Missouri, Letters Sent.

[38] Sheridan to Pope, August 21, 1874, Division of the Missouri, Letters Sent.

advance of settlers, whisky peddlers, and surveying parties. Now, however, with the settlers on the plains owning hundreds of thousands of head of stock, it was unreasonable to blame the Indian war upon the frontiersmen, who would suffer in any such conflict. "This outbreak," Sheridan wrote, "does not look to me, as being originated by the actions of bad white men, or the sale of whisky to Indians by traders. It is the result of the restless nature of the Indian who has no profession but arms and naturally seeks for war and plunder when the grazing gets high enough to feed his ponies."[39]

Despite his personal sympathy toward the Indians, General Pope in July, 1874, began his preparations for a campaign. Bickering immediately occurred between the General and the officials of the Bureau of Indian Affairs. Pope wanted to punish those guilty of murders and depredations wherever found, while the Indian officials tried to exclude the troops from the reservations. At best the Department of the Interior was willing to permit the army to punish only those actually engaged in hostilities, to which Pope replied that all Indians in danger pleaded peace and love of white men. By the end of July, Colonel Nelson A. Miles and Lieutenant Colonel Thomas H. Neill were freed from interference of Indian agents and were empowered to "attack all Indians who are, or have been hostile during the present year wherever found" and to seize those who attempted to avoid punishment by surrendering to their agents.[40]

A small peace faction of Cheyennes sought sanctuary at the agency. Perhaps more Cheyennes would have surrendered if the agent could have assured them of protection from the troops. Six young Cheyennes appeared at Old Whirlwind's camp near the agency on August 7, 1874, and they stated that nearly the whole Cheyenne tribe was moving towards their reservation. A severe drought was sapping their ponies' strength, and it was the decision of the tribal council to "call the trouble square." All of the war parties were back in camp, and the soldier societies were in control of their people. The warriors, however, would not allow the peace chiefs to leave the villages and

[39] Sheridan to AAG., United States Army, October 1, 1874, Division of the Missouri, Letters Sent.

[40] Pope to Hoag, Pope to Neill, July 27, 29, August 1, 22, 1874, Department of the Missouri, Letters Sent.

undoubtedly preferred to dictate the terms of the tribe's surrender to the agent. Little Robe was punished by the soldiers, and his horses were shot when he tried to leave the main camps. Still, Little Robe, White Shield, and Pawnee joined Old Whirlwind at the agency and from them Miles learned more of Cheyenne raids.[41]

The hostiles gave no evidence of abandoning the war. Medicine Water, leading a large Cheyenne war party, overwhelmed a surveying party about forty-five miles southwest of Fort Dodge on August 26, 1874. After the attack Medicine Water's warriors retreated to the main Cheyenne village located on a tributary of Beaver Creek one hundred miles west of Camp Supply. Except for the 280 Cheyennes, including 80 warriors, at the agency, the tribe was willing to take its chances and try to evade the column concentrating under Colonel Miles at Camp Supply.[42]

"I propose now," General Sheridan declared, "if let alone to settle the Indian matter in the Southwest forever." The Cheyennes, Sheridan believed, were the most formidable of the Southern Plains tribes, and if they were punished and subdued the backbone of Indian resistance would be cracked. By this time, however, it was impossible to isolate the Cheyennes because their camps were thoroughly mixed with those of the Kiowas and Comanches. Therefore Sheridan planned to send five separate columns into the field: Miles was assigned to move south and west from Camp Supply; Major William R. Price was to move east from Fort Union, New Mexico territory; Colonel Ranald S. Mackenzie was to march north from Fort Concho, Texas; Colonel Davidson was to push west from Fort Sill; and, Lieutenant Colonel George P. Buell's command was to operate between those of Davidson and Mackenzie.[43]

[41]McCusker to Smith, Miles to Smith, July 28, August 8, 19, 1874, Upper Arkansas Agency, Letters Received.

[42] S. A. Gillette to Commanding Officer, Fort Dodge, August 31, 1874, Office of the Adjutant General, Letters Received; Miles to Smith, October 24, 1874 (Copy), Upper Arkansas Agency, Letters Received; *Report, Commissioner of Indian Affairs, 1874*, 234.

[43] Sheridan to Sherman, Sheridan to Pope, August 13, 18, September 15, 1874, Division of the Missouri, Letters Sent; Pope to Price, August 12, 1874, Department of the Missouri, Letters Sent; Nye, *Carbine and Lance*, 282,

Elements of Miles's command were the first to come into contact with the hostiles. Organized at Fort Dodge, the column consisted of eight companies of the Sixth Cavalry, four companies of the Fifth Infantry, and thirty-nine scouts and guides. On August 14, 1874, Major Compton preceded the main body of troops to Camp Supply, while a scouting party of guides and cavalry under Lieutenant F. D. Baldwin rode west to Palo Duro Creek, then south to Adobe Walls. Baldwin's detachment arrived at the hunting outpost in time to repulse another Indian attack on the buffalo hunters. About 150 warriors lurked about Baldwin's troops and were able to cut off one unwary hunter and lance him within sight of the soldiers. From Adobe Walls Baldwin proceeded down the South Canadian and surprised a small party of Indians, killing one and wounding another. The Cheyennes, Kiowas, and Comanches, unaware of other columns soon to take to the field, withdrew to the southwest, gradually consolidating into one large village as they moved.[44]

Talking to scouts and guides, Miles thought the hostiles' strength was seriously underestimated. On the Sweetwater the guides picked up the broad trail of an Indian village, which the command followed for four days. Before dawn on August 30, Miles ordered Lieutenant Baldwin and the scouts forward, and as they entered a narrow defile, they were attacked by a large body of Cheyennes. Fighting dismounted, the scouts held their ground while Miles deployed the large command, using the cavalry on the flanks and the infantry and artillery in the center. As the command advanced, the Indians fought hard in a rearguard action through the rough country for five hours until they were driven across the Red River. Although the Indians escaped, Miles's command destroyed one large village in a canyon of the Tule River and several other small camps nearby. Delayed by six hundred warriors, which meant that some Comanches and Kiowas must have been in the fight, Miles took no prisoners and was unable to capture the Indians' pony herds. Miles was temporarily forced to abandon further pursuit of the Indians because his provisions and forage were exhausted, and he returned to his supply depot on the

[44] 44 Cong., 1 sess., *House Exec. Doc. No. 1*, Part 2, p. 78; Barde (comp.), *Adventures of "Billy" Dixon*, 246–51.

Washita River. Sheridan viewed Miles's activities as successful beyond his expectations. Henceforth, Sheridan wrote: "All captured Indians must be treated as prisoners of war, and all captured stock as government property. All surrenders must be total and absolute, and arms of every description delivered up."[45]

Some Cheyenne war parties eluded the cavalry net in the Texas Panhandle and raided the road north of the agency and into Kansas. Medicine Water again was the leader of these parties. On September 11 near the Kansas-Colorado boundary, the family of John German, making their way from Georgia to Colorado territory, were intercepted by Medicine Water. The father, mother, and an older sister were killed, and four young girls were seized as captives. A few weeks later another party of Cheyennes, twenty-five strong, headed for the Chisholm Trail while Miles's wife and children were being escorted to Caldwell by ten soldiers. Terrified at the thought of his family being captured by the Cheyennes, he sent for an additional company of cavalry to re-enforce the escort. "The Cheyennes," the frightened agent wrote, "exasperated by their losses & encouraged by their successes, will fight like demons and will scour the whole country."[46]

General Pope's strategy was simple and effective. He hoped to keep the Indians moving and under pressure "until the cold weather and starvation force them in when they will be at your [Miles's] mercy." The only real problem was to supply the five columns with sufficient supplies to maintain an effective force in the field.[47]

After the fight with Miles, the combined Indian village moved to the rim of the Staked Plains, seeking refuge in the Palo Duro Canyon. Operating out of Fort Concho, Colonel Mackenzie, with eight com-

[45] Miles to AAG., Department of the Missouri, September 1, 1874, Office of the Adjutant General, Letters Received; Sheridan to AAG., Department of the Missouri, October 6, 1874, Division of the Missouri, Letters Sent; 44 Cong., 1 sess., *House Exec. Doc. No. 1*, Part 2, pp. 78–79; Nelson A. Miles, *Personal Recollections and Observations* . . . , 167–68.

[46] Pope to Miles, September 18, 1874, Department of the Missouri, Letters Sent; Miles to Smith, September 26, 1874, Upper Arkansas Agency, Letters Received; Grace E. Meredith (ed.), *Girl Captives of the Cheyennes: A True Story of the Capture and Rescue of Four Pioneer Girls*, 17ff.

[47] Pope to Miles, Pope to Sheridan, September 13, 18, 1874, Department of the Missouri, Letters Sent.

panies of the Fourth Cavalry and five companies of the Tenth Infantry, penetrated into the Texas Panhandle and began tracking down the Indian village. Diversions failed to deceive Mackenzie's Seminole and Tonkawa scouts, and they found hundreds of tipis on the floor of the deep canyon. At daybreak on September 27, Mackenzie's cavalry led their horses down the face of the canyon walls. The attack was a complete surprise and successful, although few casualties were suffered by the Indians. When Mackenzie was finished in the Palo Duro Canyon, he had destroyed perhaps as many as four hundred lodges, captured fourteen hundred ponies, and burned the Indians' supply of pemmican. On the next morning, September 28, Mackenzie mopped up five small camps at the mouth of Cañon Blanco on the Red River.[48]

After Mackenzie's punishing attack the Indians had no rest. Lieutenant Colonel Buell, moving to the east of Mackenzie's line of march, intercepted a small Indian camp on October 9, 1874. The Indians' flight led Buell to still larger camps, containing nearly five hundred lodges in all, which Buell destroyed, capturing large numbers of Indian ponies.[49]

The vigor of the campaigns had an immediate effect upon the Cheyennes. Small groups began to split off from the main Cheyenne camps. White Horse, for example, a Dog Soldier chief who had been in the Mackenzie fight, surrendered on October 20, 1874, to Lieutenant Colonel Neill at the agency. Eleven warriors, one old man, thirteen women, and White Horse escaped from the control of the soldier societies in the confusion of the attack. They had lost most of their horses to Mackenzie, but they still had 134 ponies with which to make the ride to the agency. From White Horse and his people Neill and Agent Miles learned that Grey Beard was assuming control of the Cheyennes. Smaller groups of completely irreconcilable elements of the tribe were beginning to consider a move to the Powder River country. Medicine Water reportedly was the leader of the latter faction, and he was revealed by the prisoners as head of the war

[48] William H. Leckie, "The Military Conquest of the Southern Plains Indians" (Ph.D. dissertation, University of Oklahoma, 1954), 347–52; Nye, *Carbine and Lance,* 284–90.

[49] Buell to Miles, October 18, 1874, Office of the Adjutant General; Drum to AAG., United States Army, October 24, 1874, Division of the Missouri, Letters Sent.

parties guilty of killing Short's surveying party, the Hennessey wagon train, and the capturing of the German family.[50]

Grey Beard knew that the only hope to avoid the troops was to stay in the rough country bordering the rivers of the Texas Panhandle. Although there was talk of moving north en masse, this idea was discarded, and the main camps hoped to winter on the Staked Plains. Staying clear of the troops was difficult because the Cheyenne ponies were used up and they had lost many to Mackenzie and Buell. One small party of Cheyenne warriors tried to raid the Caddo horse herds near the Wichita Agency only to be discovered and repulsed by the Caddoes. Three of the young Cheyenne men were killed, six decided to take their chances by surrendering to the "soldier chief" at the agency, and the rest fled back to Grey Beard's camps.[51]

Late in October, 1874, General Sheridan visited the agencies in western Indian territory. While Sheridan was at the Cheyenne and Arapaho agency, he witnessed at firsthand the audacity of the Kansas horse thieves. On the night of October 27, some renegades ran off seventy-five head of ponies from the friendly Cheyennes and Arapahoes. This was more than the fiery little cavalryman could stand, and he immediately ordered a detachment of cavalry to "pursue and punish at all hazards" the thieves. Guided by James S. Morrison, who had lost some of the stock, troops from Fort Dodge overtook the raiders on the North Fork of the Pawnee. Most of the Indians' animals were recovered, two whites were killed, and two others made their escape. Friend Miles approved the summary punishment meted out by the troops, since criminals tried at Fort Smith, Arkansas, were liberated too quickly in the Indian agent's judgment.[52]

Portions of Davidson's, Buell's, Mackenzie's, and Miles's columns continued to pursue the Cheyennes during November. Only on one occasion did the Cheyennes mete out any punishment to the troops. On November 6, 1874, Lieutenant H. J. Farnsworth and twenty-

[50] Neill to AAG., Department of the Missouri, October 20, 1874, Office of the Adjutant General; Miles to Smith, October 20, 24, 26, 1874, Upper Arkansas Agency, Letters Received.

[51] Miles to Smith, October 23, 26, 1874, George Washington (Caddo chief) to Miles, October 24, 1874, Upper Arkansas Agency, Letters Received.

[52] Miles to Smith, October 28, 1874, Upper Arkansas Agency, Letters Received; Lefebvre and Talley to Tough, December 31, 1874 (Copy), Central Superintendency I.

eight men of the Eighth Cavalry were patrolling McClellan's Creek.
Scouts from a Cheyenne war party of about one hundred men observed the troopers and waited in ambush. Despite the advantage of
surprise and superiority in numbers of almost four to one, the Cheyennes could not pin down the cavalrymen, who fought their way
free and returned to Miles's supply depot on the Washita. The Cheyennes killed one of the men, wounding one slightly and three seriously. How many Cheyennes died in the skirmish is not known;
Farnsworth reported that personally he saw four Cheyennes killed.[53]

Simultaneously, on November 8, small columns from Miles's and
Davidson's commands struck separate Cheyenne camps. Lieutenant
Baldwin with an infantry and a cavalry company supported by a
field howitzer drove Grey Beard's village out of the breaks north of
McClellan's Creek. The infantry stormed through the Indian camp,
riding in wagons, and firing over the backs of the mules. Once the
camp was taken, the cavalry continued in pursuit of the Cheyennes
for twelve miles. Again the Cheyennes eluded capture, but they
lost much of the camp equipment and two of the younger German
sisters, Adelaide, aged five, and Julia, aged seven.[54]

Farther to the west Davidson's command destroyed fifty Cheyenne
lodges in the Red River hills on November 8. Picking 160 of his best
mounted men, Davidson sent them in hot pursuit. For two or three
days the Cheyennes fought off the cavalry, enabling their people to
scatter into rough country. This band abandoned its pack animals,
carrying camping utensils, to the troops so that they could flee
unimpeded. A week later the Texas Plains were covered by frozen
sleet, and Davidson's suffering command was forced to return to its
supply base. Operating independently out of Davidson's column,
Major Compton and a battalion of cavalry chased a small band of
Cheyennes over 370 miles through the sand hills of the South Canadian without ever contacting the Indians.[55]

53 Farnsworth to Field Adjutant, Wingate Battalion, November 7, 1874 (Copy),
Central Superintendency III.

54 Sheridan to AAG., Department of the Missouri, November 17, 1874, Division of
the Missouri, Letters Sent.

55 Buell to AAG., Department of Texas, November 8, 1874, Augur to Whipple, November 17, 1874 (Copies), Central Superintendency III; Davidson to Augur, November
23, 1874, Davidson to Captain C. H. Carleton, November 17, 1874, Office of the Adjutant
General, Letters Received.

After remounting his command, Miles returned to the field. One battalion under Captain C. A. Hartwell followed some trails leading away from McClellan's Creek. On November 29, 1874, near the head of Muster Creek, Hartwell drove a large number of Cheyennes from their villages. Less than a week later, a detachment of the Sixth Cavalry struck a Cheyenne camp forty miles north of the Sweetwater River, capturing some ponies and destroying a quantity of ammunition and food.[56]

Suffering from lack of shelter and food, virtually without sound ponies, the Cheyennes under Grey Beard, Stone Calf, Medicine Arrows, Medicine Water, Red Moon, Big Jake, Young Whirlwind, and Minimic still made little effort to surrender. The total count of Cheyennes at the agency late in November, 1874, did not exceed four hundred. Among this number were 128 warriors who had either been captured in small groups by troops or who, facing starvation, had voluntarily surrendered to Lieutenant Colonel Neill. Stone Calf, with thirty-five more braves, supposedly was in favor of giving up the fight; neither he nor his men appeared as expected at the agency. Medicine Arrows also seemed to be weakening, for the old medicine arrow priest sent one of his young men to Colonel W. H. Lewis, commanding at Camp Supply. At first the young warrior agreed to lead a detachment of cavalry to Medicine Arrows' camp so that it could be escorted to the agency. Because something aroused the brave's suspicion, he slipped away, and Medicine Arrows' camp fled back to Grey Beard's village on the South Canadian River, where the bulk of the hostiles were gathered.[57]

Eagle and Hawk Leader were typical of those Cheyennes who no longer accepted the discipline of the soldier societies. Members of Medicine Water's camp, they and nine other warriors broke away. En route to the agency they were jumped by troops and lost their ponies, lodges, food, and camping equipment. They had no alternative other than surrender. On December 14, 1874, Little Shield and a larger number surrendered and informed Agent Miles that the

[56] 44 Cong., 1 sess., *House Exec. Doc. No. 1*, Part 2, p. 81.

[57] Covington to Smith, November 28, 1874, W. D. Whipple, AAG., Department of the Missouri to AG., United States Army, November 11, 1874 (Copy), Upper Arkansas Agency, Letters Received; Lewis to Neill, November 15, 1874, Fort Supply, Letters Sent.

two older German sisters were being held in the camps of Medicine
Water and Sand Hill. From Little Shield's people, Miles learned that
the German sisters had been frequently traded for ponies and other
property among the hostiles. The Cheyennes believed that when peace
was restored they could exact a large ransom for the two teen-aged
prisoners.[58]

As winter weather came, portions of Medicine Water's and Grey
Beard's bands began making the ride back to the agency to surrender.
Medicine Water talked again of escaping north with his brother
Man-on-the-Clouds, Antelope, and their families. One German sister
was taken by Long Back from Medicine Water's village to Stone
Calf's camp; the other remained with Wolf Robe in Grey Beard's
camp. One party of about fifty Cheyennes from the Texas Panhandle
was trailed across the reservation and captured by Lieutenant Maxon
near Kingfisher station. During the last part of December, 1874,
troops began encountering parties from these two bands of hostiles
within fifteen miles of the agency attempting to slip into the camps
of Little Robe unnoticed. Others feared punishment; Medicine
Arrows thought that the agent or officers would seize possession of the
sacred medicine arrows. Fox Tail, Medicine Arrows' son who, in the
winter of 1866–67, murdered William Bent's Mexican employee, reported that his father and White Antelope with about thirteen lodges
had been chased by troops several times and so finally had decided
to join the Northern Cheyennes. In particular Agent Miles wanted
Medicine Arrows taken because of his influence among the Cheyennes
of his reservation. If Medicine Arrows made good his escape, Miles
feared that the medicine arrows' priest would be joined by Grey
Beard's 120-lodge village.[59]

By the end of 1874 the army's expeditions had killed few Cheyennes in combat. Agent Miles informed Commissioner Smith that

58 Miles to Smith, December 15, 1874, Central Superintendency I.

59 Miles to Smith, December 15, 22, 1874, Upper Arkansas Agency, Letters Received; Miles to Jonathan Richards, December 29, 1874, Central Superintendency III;
Neill to Captain A. S. P. Keyes, December 21, 1874, Major G. W. Schofield to Post
Adjutant, Fort Sill, December 31, 1874, Office of the Adjutant General; Miles to Smith,
December 29, 1874, Records of the Cheyenne and Arapahoe Agency, Records of the Office
of Indian Affairs, National Archives. (At this point the Records of the Upper Arkansas Agency become the Records of the Cheyenne and Arapahoe Agency and hereafter will be cited as Cheyenne and Arapahoe Agency.)

troops had killed only seventeen Cheyenne warriors. Ninety-seven Cheyenne warriors known to have been actively hostile were under guard at the agency, and about thirty or forty more were confined to the prisoner camp under mere suspicion. According to Miles' calculations, between 1,550 to 1,650 Cheyennes were still in the hostile camps.[60]

The expedition led by Colonel Miles from Camp Supply on January 2, 1875, led to the surrender of a majority of the hostile Cheyennes. The column remained in the field for a month and, on its march, noted that the Cheyennes were making their way back to the reservation. Thereafter Miles kept only enough cavalry patrols operating in the Texas Panhandle to push the Indians toward the agency.[61]

After surrendering, Cheyenne warriors began identifying members of the raiding parties. Big Moccasin pointed out that Bear's Heart and Limpy were among the men who had attacked Short's surveyors and had also aided in the butchering of the German family. Chief Killer, already confined at Fort Sill, was declared to be a participant in both attacks. This information, it had been decided in December, 1874, would be used in trying the Indians before a military commission. Knowing full well that Cheyenne warriors bitterly opposed imprisonment and leg irons, Miles feared a mass attempt by the prisoners to break for freedom. Still, the agent thought that to allow those guilty to go "unpunished, increases their impudence and audacity, and renders an agent powerless to control them or do them good."[62]

Lieutenant Colonel Neill early in January, 1875, offered Stone Calf's band the privilege of surrendering without reprisals if the German sisters were immediately freed. The message probably divided the Cheyennes, because Grey Beard stayed on the plains while Stone Calf's people separated from the former group and began moving to the reservation. Grey Beard, the Sutaio chief, merely told Neill's messenger he would let the whites send a few more messengers and then he would make his own terms. The Cheyennes who

[60] Miles to Smith, December 31, 1874, Miles to Hoag, January 14, 1874, Central Superintendency I.

[61] R. Williams to Major James Riddle, January 16, 1875, Department of the Missouri, Letters Sent; 44 Cong., 1 sess., *House Exec. Doc. No. 1*, Part 2, pp. 81–82.

[62] Miles to Smith, January 3, 1875, Cheyenne and Arapahoe Agency, Letters Received.

were not yet willing to surrender raided for horses and provisions and enjoyed partial success. Howling Wolf, Minimic's son, led a large party of warriors into Mexico, toward the head of Red River, and to the Wichita Agency, acquiring some food and fresh horses.[63]

Medicine Arrows, Medicine Water, and White Antelope decided to abandon the Southern Plains and started across Kansas. On January 8, 1875, Lieutenant F. S. Hinkle, operating out of Fort Wallace, intercepted a camp of about twenty people and captured four warriors, including a lesser chief, Long-haired Bear. Ten days after Hinkle encountered the camp, Man-on-the-Clouds, and Yellow Hair, Medicine Water's brother and mother, came to the agency. When Cheyenne women told Yellow Hair that the army intended to hang her son, the two fled in terror back to the plains. Medicine Arrows and White Antelope were trailed to Northern Cheyenne villages near Camp Robinson, Nebraska. Captain W. H. Jordan refused to arrest Medicine Arrows, since the chief had committed "no overt act" in the Department of the Platte and the 250 Cheyenne warriors would come to Medicine Arrows' aid. After resting either among the Sioux or their northern kinsmen, Medicine Arrows and White Antelope moved on to the Powder River.[64]

The refusal of Grey Beard, Medicine Arrows, Medicine Water, and White Antelope to surrender convinced Agent Miles that the Cheyennes were not yet whipped. Many of the tribe, Miles informed Commissioner Smith, were willing to accept blankets and food and cause no more trouble, but, "The majority of the fighting element," Miles insisted, "would prefer to die rather than submit to prison life. And not until they are completely overpowered will they think or feel differently." Even after five young warriors, part of Howling Wolf's raiders, surrendered and informed the Indian agent that Stone Calf was willing to surrender both of the German sisters, Miles urged a

[63] Miles to Smith, January 20, 1875, Cheyenne and Arapahoe Agency, Letters Received.

[64] Miles to Smith, January 20, 1875, Jordan to AAG., Department of the Platte, February 5, 1875 (Copy), Cheyenne and Arapahoe Agency, Letters Received; Neill to AAG., Department of the Missouri, January 18, 1875, Captain W. Hawley to Commanding Officer, District of the Black Hills, February 5, 1875, Hawley to AAG., Department of the Platte, February 6, 1875, Hambright to AAG., Department of the Missouri, January 29, 1875, Office of the Adjutant General, Letters Received.

vigorous campaign against the Cheyennes. The Cheyennes, wrote the agent, "are now powerless to resist a force and would readily yield to any reasonable demand backed up by a manifest force. Comparative rest, a recruit of stock, and prospective grass will very likely . . . change their minds."[65]

A vanguard of Stone Calf's village, consisting of forty-nine Cheyennes, arrived at the agency on February 9, 1875, and announced that it was the decision of the tribal council to free the German girls. Foolish Bear, Bull Bear's son, who was guilty of killing the surveyor E. N. Deming in the spring of 1873, was among those who came in from Stone Calf's camp, and he stated that the Cheyennes intended to trade the girls for a favorable surrender. On the same day the four warriors taken by Lieutenant Hinkle arrived at the agency as prisoners and confirmed the agent's suspicions that Medicine Arrows and White Antelope had arrived among the Northern Cheyennes.[66]

Benjamin Williams and James S. Morrison, agency employees hunting with some Arapahoes near the site of Black Kettle's death on the Washita River, were visited on February 14, 1875, by Stone Calf and other Cheyenne chiefs who wanted to use the German sisters to free their warriors held by Lieutenant Colonel Neill. Medicine Water and some young men talked bravely of not being tired of fighting. Since they had some fresh ponies, they maintained that they were not going to surrender to the army. Nine days later Stone Calf arrived at the agency with fifteen of his soldiers and tried to negotiate with Neill. Dejected when he could gain nothing by the surrender of his captives, Stone Calf agreed to accompany an ambulance back to his camp for the German girls. Catherine Elizabeth and Sophia Louisa German arrived at Darlington on March 1, 1875, and began immediately to point out Cheyenne men who had murdered their relatives and who had forced sexual relations upon them.[67]

By Lieutenant Colonel Neill's count, 821 Cheyennes surrendered

[65] Miles to Smith, January 20, February 6, 1875, Cheyenne and Arapahoe Agency, Letters Received.

[66] Miles to Smith, February 10, 1875, Cheyenne and Arapahoe Agency, Letters Received.

[67] Miles to Smith, February 18, 24, March 2, 1875, Cheyenne and Arapahoe Agency, Letters Received.

at the agency on March 6, 1875. Stone Calf, Grey Beard, Heap-of-Birds, Red Moon, Bull Bear, Minimic and even Medicine Water and Wolf Robe, leaders of the younger warrior element, were in custody. Two hundred and forty of these people were warriors, and they surrendered to Neill their worn-out ponies and useless guns. A considerable number of warriors with the tribe's best horses and arms hung back, determined to join Medicine Arrows and White Antelope in the north if the army's treatment of those who surrendered "looked too rough." George Bent, aided by Sand Hill, interviewed each family in the hostile camp and found that eighty-three men and a few women were still missing. When the German sisters could identify only four warriors as among those who attacked their family, Miles was certain that many of the most dangerous and intransigent were going to flee to the north. Sophia German also pointed out a Cheyenne woman who "chopped my mother's head open with an ax."[68]

By mid-March, 1875, conditions were quiet at the agency. Trusted Cheyennes and Arapahoes were permitted to hunt buffalo in the western reaches of the reservation escorted only by two agency employees. The officers at the agency as quietly as possible rounded up those Cheyenne warriors and chiefs most guilty of bringing on the war and placed them in leg irons and close confinement. Agent Miles took a temporary leave of absence from his post to rest from the strain of his duties.[69]

On April 6, 1875, the Cheyennes broke loose again. Black Horse, a young warrior judged to be dangerous and guilty of crimes, was being placed in leg irons by the army blacksmith. Taunted by Chey-

[68] Miles to Smith, March 9, 12, 15, 1875, Cheyenne and Arapahoe Agency, Letters Received; *Report of the Commissioner of Indian Affairs to the Secretary of the Interior, 1875,* 268–69. Catherine German related most of her experiences to Mrs. Miles. The younger sister, Sophia, was spared indignities for the most part, but Catherine was traded three times, finally coming into the possession of Long Back. Although Long Back did not mistreat Catherine, he permitted young Cheyenne men upon payment of horses or other property to visit his lodge and have sexual intercourse with the young woman. Sometimes Long Back's wife forced Catherine from the lodge to get wood and water. Unprotected, she would be raped by as many as six young Cheyennes before she could regain the lodge's safety (see Miles to Smith, March 19, 1875, Cheyenne and Arapahoe Agency, Letters Received).

[69] Covington to Smith, March 19, 1875, Cheyenne and Arapahoe Agency, Letters Received.

enne women, Black Horse knocked the blacksmith down, ran from the enclosure, and was shot down by the guard. Some of the shots strayed into the camp of the hostiles, arousing them into a state of frenzy. The Cheyenne warriors sent a volley of bullets and arrows into the soldiers' camp and dashed across the North Canadian to a sand hill, where they immediately dug rifle pits and opened caches of arms and ammunition secreted there for just such an emergency. Three companies of cavalry and some infantry, supported by a Gatling gun, surrounded the sand hill and tried until darkness to dislodge the Cheyennes. The troops dug in for the night, set up a ring of sentries, and waited for dawn to renew their assault. Despite all precautions the Cheyennes, having lost six dead warriors, fled during the night, leaving the troops to guard empty rifle pits. During the sand hill fight, the Cheyennes wounded three soldiers severely and sixteen others less dangerously.[70]

All but sixty-six Cheyenne men had to be rounded up again. Acting Agent Covington thought that since the families of the men were still in the camps of Little Robe and Old Whirlwind, there would be less difficulty in bringing the men back. From Lawrence, Kansas, Miles ordered that no Cheyennes be received back at the agency without enrollment of all males over ten years of age, an exact count of women and children, and the stripping from the Cheyennes of all weapons and emblems of war. The fight convinced Miles that the Cheyennes were well armed and able to resist the seizure of their leaders or to move their reservation from western Indian territory.[71]

The Cheyenne men stampeded from their camps near the agency more from fear and panic than for any other reason. They thought that the volley fired at Black Horse signaled an attack on their camp by the troops. Two-thirds of the absent Cheyenne warriors communicated with their families, remained about ninety miles northwest of Darlington on the Cimarron, east of the Salt Plains, and made no threat or effort to flee north. A small camp of warriors, about eighty

---

[70] Covington to Smith, April 7, 1875, Cheyenne and Arapahoe Agency, Letters Received; Neill to AAG., United States Army, April 7, 1875, in 44 Cong., 1 sess., *House Exec. Doc. No. 1*, Part 2, pp. 86–88; *Report, Commissioner of Indian Affairs, 1875*, 269.

[71] Covington to Smith, April 10, 1875, Cheyenne and Arapahoe Agency, Letters Received; Miles to Covington, April 10, 1875, Miles to Hoag, April 15, 1875, Central Superintendency I.

in number, fled immediately to the Antelope Hills, and they, it was believed, would be more difficult to reconcile.[72]

Three companies of cavalry under Captain William A. Rafferty, Sixth Cavalry, were sent up the Cimarron River after the main group of absentees. When the troops approached the camp, the younger men and women rode rapidly up the Cimarron to join the camp near the Antelope Hills and make a break for the Northern Cheyennes. The Antelope Hill group was comprised largely of those warriors who had never surrendered at the agency. Returning to the agency, Miles counted 1,336 Cheyennes at Darlington with 389 of their number from Little Robe's and Old Whirlwind's peace faction.[73]

Red Moon, three weeks after the sand hill fight, was the first to bring his band back to the agency. Smaller camps of others followed, especially after General Pope authorized an invitation for the remaining absentees to return, guaranteeing no more arrests.[74]

Agent Miles and the army officers believed they had under control the worst of the ringleaders of the 1874 uprising. They selected thirty-one men and one woman for eventual imprisonment at Fort Marion, Florida. Among the prisoners were the chiefs, Grey Beard, Heap-of-Birds, Bear Shield, and Minimic, and the warrior leaders, Medicine Water, Long Back, Big Moccasin, and Howling Wolf. Two of the prisoners, Grey Beard and Lean Bear, never reached Fort Marion. Grey Beard was shot while attempting to escape from the railroad car carrying them to Florida, and Lean Bear went berserk. The other prisoners, exhibiting something less than loyalty to their absent comrades, accused Grey Beard and Lean Bear of bringing all the troubles on the Cheyennes, hoping to absolve themselves from further punishment.[75]

A month after the revolt of April 6, 1875, Miles estimated there were 678 Cheyennes absent from the agency. This is far too large a number, but Miles arrived at the figure by overestimating the popu-

72 Covington to Smith, April 18, 1875, Central Superintendency I.

73 Miles to Smith, April 22, 24, 1875, Cheyenne and Arapahoe Agency, Letters Received.

74 Miles to Smith, April 29, 1875, Central Superintendency I.

75 Miles to Smith, April 29, 1875, Lieutenant R. H. Pratt to Post Adjutant, Fort Marion, Pratt to AG., United States Army, June 30, November 5, 1875, Cheyenne and Arapahoe Agency, Letters Received.

lation of the Cheyennes.[76] How many Cheyennes decided to make a dash for the Northern Cheyenne country cannot be accurately determined. Sand Hill and his son, Yellow Horse, with less than twenty people crossed the Arkansas. But the greatest number trying to escape were led by Bull Elk. As far as Miles could tell, Bull Elk's group contained about two hundred men, women, and children.[77]

General Pope wired Major H. A. Hambright, Nineteenth Infantry, commanding at Fort Wallace, to intercept and return those Cheyennes in flight to the country north of the Platte River. Immediately Lieutenant Austin Henely, with forty men of the Sixth Cavalry, started to search for the Cheyennes on the Smoky Hill. Finding no Cheyennes, Henely decided to scout along Sappa Creek and its tributaries, and on the North Fork of that stream on April 22, he encountered three buffalo hunters who claimed that they had been robbed by a large Indian party. During the following day Henely's command found the Cheyenne camp, captured all but a few of the ponies, and forced the warriors to dig rifle pits in the low creek bed. Fighting on foot, the troopers kept the Cheyennes pinned down from higher ground. As warrior after warrior rose from cover, each was picked off by the troopers. When the firing ceased, Henely inspected the rifle pits and found nineteen men and eight women and children lying dead. The Lieutenant judged one of the Cheyennes from his dress to have been a chief of considerable rank, and another was an important medicine man. Henely took no prisoners and killed more Cheyennes than the combined columns had during the winter campaign of 1874-75. No one expressed much sympathy for the Cheyennes because the troops had found a memorandum book which contained Indian sketches of the Battle of Adobe Walls, the attack on Major Lyman's supply train, and perhaps another on the slaughter of the German family.[78]

Some Cheyennes, nevertheless, by mid-May had found their way to

[76] In August, 1875, Miles stated that 2,055 Cheyennes were charged to his agency of whom 1,611 were present, 411 absent, and 33 held prisoners in Florida (see, *Report, Commissioner of Indian Affairs, 1875,* 268). Two months earlier Miles stated that if all of the Cheyennes were present, they would number 2,200 people.

[77] Miles to Smith, May 8, 1875, Cheyenne and Arapahoe Agency, Letters Received.

[78] Henely to Post Adjutant, Fort Wallace, April 26, 1875, in 44 Cong., 1 sess., *House Exec. Doc. No. 1,* Part 2, pp. 89-92.

the Red Cloud Agency. Troops from Fort Robinson followed the trail of about two hundred Southern Cheyennes and failed to overtake them. Northern Arapahoes reported to Agent Martin Gibbons that fifty Southern Cheyenne men with their families passed through their camps en route to the Powder River country.[79]

In August, 1875, the "stampeders" began drifting back from the north. From them it was learned that Little Bull and Turkey Wailing, both noted warriors among the Cheyennes, had been killed by Lieutenant Henely. Practically all of the Southern Cheyennes were waiting anxiously at the Red Cloud Agency for permission to make the trip to Indian territory. Sand Hill, suffering from a bad wound acquired during the fight on Sappa Creek, wanted to rejoin his band in the south. Failing to acquire the necessary passes, small camps of Cheyennes made their way over the Central Plains, leaving behind a few irreconcilables who later would exact some revenge at the Battle of the Little Big Horn.[80]

The days of freedom were ended. The warpath, the buffalo hunt, the thrill of horse raids were all in the past. Rations, schools, Christianity, and the cultivation of land were unsatisfactory substitutes, but the Southern Cheyennes were powerless to contest the superior force of the white man. Stripped of their reservation several decades later by land hungry American farmers and speculators, the Cheyennes declined as disease, despair, and lethargy took their toll. The Southern Cheyennes clung stubbornly to their institutions until finally, in the 1930's, some recognition of their culture was granted by the United States government.

[79] Gibbons to Smith, May 19, 1875, Red Cloud Agency, Letters Received, Records of the Office of Indian Affairs, National Archives.

[80] Covington to Smith, August 9, 25, 1875, Miles to Smith, December 8, 1875, Cheyenne and Arapahoe Agency, Letters Received; Stanley Vestal, *Sitting Bull: Champion of the Sioux,* 143ff.

# BIBLIOGRAPHY

I. ARCHIVAL MATERIALS

1. *Denver, Colorado*

a. Colorado Division of State Archives and Public Records
   John Evans Collection, Indian Affairs.
b. Colorado State Historical Society
   Diary of Samuel F. Tappan.
   Edward W. Wynkoop Manuscript Colorado History.
   George Bent Letters.
   Samuel F. Tappan Manuscripts.
   Scott J. Anthony Letters.
c. Denver Public Library, Western History Department
   George Bent Letters.

2. *Norman, Oklahoma*

The Archives of the University of Oklahoma
   Camp Supply Letter Book.
   Walter S. Campbell Papers.

3. *Oklahoma City, Oklahoma*

Oklahoma State Historical Society
   Cheyenne and Arapaho Indian Depredation File.
   Cheyenne and Arapaho Indian Murder File.

4. *St. Louis, Missouri*

Missouri Historical Society
   Chouteau Collections.
   Chouteau-Papin Collection.
   Manuscript Journal of S. W. Kearny.
   William Clark Papers.

*Bibliography*

5. *Topeka, Kansas*

Kansas State Historical Society
  Correspondence of Kansas Governors.
  Manuscript Autobiography of Samuel F. Tappan.
  William Clark Papers.

6. *Washington, D. C.*

a. Bureau of American Ethnology
  Benjamin Clark. "Extracts from manuscript on ethnology and philology of the Cheyennes." MS No. 3449.
b. Library of Congress
  Philip H. Sheridan Papers.
  William T. Sherman Papers.
c. National Archives
  Records of the Department of the Interior.
    Office of Indian Affairs, Letters Sent.
    Office of the Secretary of the Interior, Separated Correspondence, Indian Peace Commission.
  Records of the Office of Indian Affairs.
    Central Superintendency, Field Office Files, Letters Received.
    Central Superintendency, Field Office Files, Letters Sent.
    Central Superintendency, Letters Received.
    Cheyenne and Arapahoe Agency, Letters Received.
    Cheyenne and Arapahoe Agency, Heirship Files.
    Colorado Superintendency, Letters Received.
    Office of the Commissioner of Indian Affairs, Letters Sent.
    Office of Indian Affairs, Letters Sent.
    Red Cloud Agency, Letters Received.
    St. Louis Superintendency, Letters Received.
    Upper Arkansas Agency, Letters Received.
    Upper Platte Agency, Letters Received.
  Records of the War Department.
    Headquarters of the Army, Letters Received.
    Office of the Adjutant General, Letters Received.
    Office of the Adjutant General, Register of Letters Received.
    Office of the Secretary of War, Letters Received.
    United States Army Commands.
      Department of the Missouri.
        District of Colorado, Letters Sent.

Headquarters in the Field, Letters Sent.
Letters Sent.
Fort Dodge, Letters Sent.
Fort Harker, Letters Sent.
Fort Hays, Letters Sent.
Fort Laramie, Letters Sent.
Fort Larned, Letters Sent.
Fort Leavenworth, Letters Sent.
Fort Lyon, Letters Sent.
Fort Supply, Letters Sent.
Fort Wallace, Letters Sent.
Military Division of the Missouri, Letters Sent.

## 7. *Other Depositories*

Bates Collection. Custer Battlefield National Monument Museum Archives, Crow Agency, Montana.
George Bent Letters. William Robertson Coe Collection, Yale University Library, New Haven, Connecticut.

## II. GOVERNMENT DOCUMENTS

### 1. *Congressional*

Abert, J. W. *Report of Lieut. J. W. Abert of His Examination of New Mexico in the Years 1846–'47.* 30 Cong., 1 sess., *Sen. Exec. Doc. No. 23,* 1847.
*Annual Report of the Secretary of War.* 1865–75.
*Cheyenne and Arapahoe Reservation.* 43 Cong., 1 sess., *House Exec. Doc. No. 12,* 1873.
*Condition of the Indian Tribes.* Report of the Joint Special Committee, appointed under Joint Resolution of March 3, 1865, with Appendix. 39 Cong., 2 sess., *Sen. Report No. 156,* 1867.
*Council with the Sioux Indians at Fort Pierre.* 34 Cong., 1 sess., *House Exec. Doc. No. 130,* 1856.
*Difficulties with Indian Tribes.* 41 Cong., 2 sess., *House Exec. Doc. No. 240,* 1870.
Emory, W. H. *Notes of a Military Reconnaissance, from Fort Leavenworth, in Missouri, to San Diego, in California, including Part of the Arkansas, Del Norte, and Gila Rivers.* 30 Cong., 1 sess., *House Exec. Doc. No. 41,* 1848.

*Engagement between United States Troops and Sioux Indians.* 33 Cong., 2 sess., *House Exec. Doc. No. 63,* 1854.

Kearny, S. W. *Report of a summer campaign to the Rocky mountains, &c., in 1845.* 29 Cong., 1 sess., *House Exec. Doc. No. 2,* 1846.

*Letter of the Secretary of the Interior communicating in compliance with a resolution of the Senate of the 8th instant, information touching the origin and progress of Indian hostilities on the frontier.* 40 Cong., 1 sess., *Sen. Exec. Doc. No. 13,* 1868.

*Massacre of Cheyenne Indians.* Report of the Joint Committee on the Conduct of the War. 38 Cong., 2 sess., *Sen. Report No. 142,* 1865.

*Protection Across the Continent.* 39 Cong. 2 sess., *House Exec. Doc. No. 23,* 1867.

*Report of General Harney, Commander of the Sioux Expedition.* 34 Cong., 1 sess., *Sen. Exec. Doc. No. 1,* 1855.

*Report of the Board of Indian Commissioners.* 1869, 1871.

*Report of the Commissioner of Indian Affairs.* 1824–75, 1882.

*Report of the Indian Peace Commissioners.* 40 Cong., 2 sess., *House Exec. Doc. No. 97,* 1868.

*Report of the Secretary of War.* Communicating, In compliance with a resolution of the Senate of February 4, 1867, a copy of the evidence taken at Denver and Fort Lyon, Colorado Territory, by a military commission, ordered to inquire into the Sand Creek massacre, November, 1864. 39 Cong., 2 sess., *Sen. Exec. Doc. No. 26,* 1867.

*Reports of Explorations and Surveys to Ascertain the Most Practicable and Economical Route to the Pacific Ocean.* 12 vols. 33 Cong., 2 sess., *Sen. Exec. Doc. No. 78,* 1855–60.

Sawyer[s], James A. "Wagon Road From Niobrara to Virginia City," 39 Cong., 1 sess., *House Exec. Doc. No. 58,* 1866.

*House Executive Documents*: 15 Cong., 1 sess., *No. 197;* 19 Cong., 1 sess., *No. 117;* 24 Cong., 1 sess., *No. 181;* 30 Cong., 2 sess., *No. 1;* 32 Cong., 1 sess., *No. 2;* 33 Cong., 2 sess., *No. 36;* 34 Cong., 3 sess., *No. 1,* Vol. II; 35 Cong., 1 sess., *No. 1,* Vol. II; 40 Cong., 3 sess., *No. 1;* 41 Cong., 2 sess., *No. 1,* Pt. 2; 44 Cong., 1 sess., *No. 1,* Pt. 2.

*Senate Executive Documents*: 18 Cong., 2 sess., *No. 7;* 22 Cong., 1 sess., *No. 90;* 24 Cong., 1 sess., *No. 209;* 29 Cong., 1 sess., *No. 438;* 30 Cong., 1 sess., *No. 1;* 30 Cong., 1 sess., *No. 23;* 34 Cong., 2 sess., *No. 58;* 34 Cong., 1 and 2 sess., *No. 91;* 39 Cong., 2 sess., *No. 15;* 39 Cong., 2 sess., *No. 16;* 40 Cong., 1 sess., *No. 7;* 40 Cong., 3 sess., *No. 13;* 40 Cong., 3 sess., *No. 18,* Pt. 2; 40 Cong., 3 sess., *No. 40.*

*Senate Miscellaneous Document No. 7,* 31 Cong., 1 sess.

2. *General Government Documents*

*American State Papers,* Military Affairs. Vol. V. Washington, 1860.

*Congressional Globe.* 39 Cong., 2 sess., Pt. 2.

"Journal of a march of a detachment of dragoons, under the command of Colonel Dodge, during the summer of 1835," *American State Papers,* Military Affairs, Vol. VI. Washington, 1861.

Kappler, Charles J., comp. and ed. *Indian Affairs: Laws and Treaties.* 4 vols. Washington, 1904, 1913, 1927.

*Record of Engagements with Hostile Indians within the Military Division of the Missouri from 1868 to 1882.* Washington, 1882.

Richardson, James D., comp. *A Compilation of the Messages and Papers of the Presidents, 1789–1908.* Vol. 7. Washington, 1909.

*United States Statutes at Large.* Vols. 7, 10, 12.

United States War Department. *The War of Rebellion. A Compilation of the Official Records of the Union and Confederate Armies.* Four series, 128 vols. Washington, 1880–1901.

III. NEWSPAPERS

Denver, Colorado, *Republican.*

Denver, Colorado, *Rocky Mountain News.*

Kansas City, Missouri, *Journal of Commerce.*

Lawrence, Kansas, *Daily Tribune.*

New York *Tribune.*

Omaha, Nebraska, *Advertizer.*

Omaha, Nebraska, *Nebraskian.*

St. Louis, Missouri, *Missouri Republican.*

Wichita, Kansas, *Beacon.*

IV. PRIMARY SOURCES

Abel, Annie Heloise, ed. *The Official Correspondence of James S. Calhoun.* Washington, 1915.

Armes, George A. *Ups and Downs of an Army Officer.* Washington, 1900.

Bandel, Eugene. *Frontier Life in the Army, 1854–1861.* Ed. by Ralph P. Bieber. Glendale, 1932.

Barde, Frederick S., comp. *Life and Adventures of "Billy" Dixon of Adobe Walls, Texas Panhandle.* Guthrie, Oklahoma, c.1914.

Beckwourth, James P. *The Life and Adventures of James P. Beckwourth.* Ed. by T. D. Bonner. New York, 1931.

Bell, Captain John R. *The Journal of Captain John R. Bell.* Ed. by Harlin M. Fuller and LeRoy R. Hafen. Glendale, 1957.

Bieber, Ralph P., ed. *Southern Trails to California in 1849.* Glendale, 1937.

Bruff, J. Goldsborough. *Gold Rush: The Journals, Drawings, and Other Papers of J. Goldsborough Bruff.* Ed. by Georgia Willis Read and Ruth Gaines. New York, 1949.

Carter, Clarence E., ed. *The Territorial Papers of the United States.* Vols. 2–25. Washington, 1934–.

Carvalho, S. N. *Incidents of Travel and Adventure in the Far West; with Colonel Frémont's Last Expedition.* New York, 1857.

Carver, Jonathan. *Three Years' Travel throughout the Interior Part of North America . . .* Walpole, New Hampshire, 1813.

Chittenden, Hiram Martin, and Alfred Talbot Richardson. *Life, Letters and Travels of Father Pierre-Jean De Smet, S.J., 1801–1873.* 4 vols. New York, 1905.

Cooke, Philip St. George. *Scenes and Adventures in the Army: Or, Romance of Military Life.* Philadelphia, 1857.

Crawford, Samuel J. *Kansas in the Sixties.* Chicago, 1911.

Culbertson, Thaddeus A. *Journal of an Expedition to the Mauvaises Terres and the Upper Missouri in 1850.* Bureau of American Ethnology Bulletin No. 147. Ed. by John Francis McDermott. Washington, 1952.

Custer, Elizabeth B. *Tenting on the Plains.* London, 1888.

Custer, George A. *My Life on the Plains.* Ed. by Milo Milton Quaife. Chicago, 1952.

Danker, Donald F., ed. *Man of the Plains: The Recollections of Luther North.* Lincoln, Nebraska, 1961.

Dawson, Nicholas. *Narrative of Nicholas "Cheyenne" Dawson to California in '41 & '49, and Texas in '51.* Ed by Charles L. Camp. San Francisco, 1933.

Fowler, Jacob. *The Journal of Jacob Fowler.* Ed. by Elliott Coues. New York, 1898.

Frémont, John Charles. *Memoirs of My Life.* 2 vols. Chicago and New York, 1887.

———. *Report of the Exploring Expedition to the Rocky Mountains in the Year 1842, and to Oregon and North Carolina in the Years 1843–'44.* Washington, 1845.

Garrard, Lewis H. *Wah-to-yah and the Taos Trail.* Ed. by Ralph P. Bieber. Glendale, 1938.

Gibson, George Rutledge. *Journal of a Soldier under Kearny and Doniphan, 1846–1847.* Ed. by Ralph P. Bieber. Glendale, 1935.

Gregg, Josiah. *Commerce of the Prairies.* Ed. by Max L. Moorhead. Norman, 1954.

Grinnell, George Bird. *The Cheyenne Indians: Their History and Ways of Life.* 2 vols. New Haven, 1923.

———. *The Fighting Cheyennes.* Norman, c. 1956.

Hafen, LeRoy R., ed. *Colorado Gold Rush.* Glendale, 1941.

———, ed. *Overland Routes to the Gold Fields, 1859.* Glendale, 1942.

———, ed. *Pike's Peak Gold Rush Guidebook of 1859.* Glendale, 1941.

———, and Ann W. Hafen, eds. *Central Route to the Pacific.* Glendale, 1957.

———, and ———, eds. *Relations with the Indians of the Plains, 1857–1861.* Glendale, 1959.

———, and ———, eds. *To the Rockies and Oregon, 1839–1842.* Glendale, 1955.

Hancock, Winfield Scott. *Reports of Major General Hancock upon Indian Affairs with Accompanying Exhibits.* Washington, [1867].

Henry, Alexander, and David Thompson. *New Light on the Early History of the Greater Northwest: The Manuscript Journals of Alexander Henry and David Thompson, 1799–1814.* Ed. by Elliott Coues. 3 vols. New York, 1897.

Holman, Albert M. *Pioneering in the Northwest.* Sioux City, Iowa, 1924.

Hughes, John Taylor. *Doniphan's Expedition and the Conquest of New Mexico and California.* Ed. by William E. Connelley. Topeka, 1907.

Hyde, George E. "Life of George Bent." Typescript. Western History Department, Denver Public Library, Denver, Colorado.

James, Edwin. *Account of an Expedition from Pittsburgh to Rocky Mountains, Performed in the Years 1819 and '20.* 2 vols. Philadelphia, 1823.

Johnston, Abraham Robinson. *Marching with the Army of the West, 1846–1848.* Ed. by Ralph P. Bieber. Glendale, 1936.

Keim, De. B. Randolph. *Sheridan's Troopers on the Border: A Winter Campaign on the Plains.* Philadelphia, 1870.

La Vérendrye, Pierre Gaultier de Varrenes de. *Journals and Letters of Pierre Gaultier de Varrenes de la Vérendrye and His Sons.* Ed. by Lawrence J. Burpee. Toronto, 1927.

Lewis, Meriwether, and William Clark. *Original Journals of the Lewis and Clarke Expedition, 1804–1806.* Ed. by Reuben Gold Thwaites. 8 vols. New York, 1904.

Lowe, Percival G. *Five Years a Dragoon, '49 to '54, and Other Adventures on the Great Plains.* Kansas City, 1906.

Luttig, John C. *Journal of a Fur-Trading Expedition on the Upper Missouri, 1812–1813*. Ed. by Stella M. Drumm. St. Louis, 1920.

Magoffin, Susan Shelby. *Down the Santa Fé Trail into Mexico: The Diary of Susan Shelby Magoffin, 1846–1847*. Ed. by Stella M. Drumm. New Haven, 1926.

Margry, Pierre. *Découvertes et établissements des français dans l'ouest et dans sud de l'Amérique Septentrionale, 1614–1754. Memoires et documents originaux decueillis et pub. par P. Margry*. 6 vols. Paris, 1879–88.

Meredith, Grace E., ed. *Girl Captives of the Cheyennes: A True Story of the Capture and Rescue of Four Pioneer Girls*. Los Angeles, 1927.

Miles, Nelson A. *Personal Recollections and Observations* . . . . Chicago, 1897.

Mooney, James. *Calendar History of the Kiowa Indians. Seventeenth Annual Report* of the Bureau of American Ethnology. Washington, 1898.

Morgan, Lewis Henry. *The Indian Journals, 1859–1862*. Ann Arbor, c.1959.

Morse, Jedidiah. *A Report to the Secretary of War*. New Haven, 1822.

Parkman, Francis. *The Journals of Francis Parkman*. Ed. by Mason Wade. 2 vols. New York, 1947.

Perrin du Lac, M. *Travels through the Two Louisianas, and among the Savage Nations of the Missouri . . . in 1801, 1802, & 1803*. London, 1807.

Preuss, Charles. *Exploring with Frémont: The Private Diaries of Charles Preuss. Trans. and ed. by Erwin G. and Elizabeth K. Gudde*. Norman, c.1958.

Price, George F. *Across the Continent with the Fifth Cavalry*. New York, 1833.

Robinson, Jacob S. *A Journal of the Santa Fe Expedition under Colonel Doniphan*. Ed. by Carl L. Cannon. Princeton, 1932.

Royce, Charles C., comp. *Indian Land Cessions in the United States. Eighteenth Annual Report* of the Bureau of American Ethnology. Washington, 1899.

Ruxton, George Frederick. Ruxton of the Rockies. Collected by Clyde and Mae Reed Porter; ed. by LeRoy R. Hafen. Norman, c.1950.

Sage, Rufus B. *His Letters and Papers, 1836–1847, with an annotated reprint of his "Scenes" in the Rocky Mountains and in Oregon, California, New Mexico, Texas, and the Grand Prairies*. Ed. by LeRoy R. and Ann W. Hafen. 2 vols. Glendale, 1956.

Sheridan, Philip H. *Personal Memoirs of P. H. Sheridan, General, United States Army*. 2 vols. New York, 1888.

Spotts, David L. *Campaigning with Custer and the Nineteenth Kansas Volunteer Cavalry on the Washita Campaign, 1868–'69.* Los Angeles, 1928.

Stanley, Henry M. *My Early Travels and Adventures in America and Asia.* 2 vols. New York, 1905.

Stansbury, Howard. *Exploration and Survey of the Valley of the Great Salt Lake of Utah.* Philadelphia, 1852.

Stuart, Robert. *On the Oregon Trail: Robert Stuart's Journal of Discovery.* Ed. by Kenneth A. Spaulding. Norman, c.1953.

Talbot, Theodore. *The Journals of Theodore Talbot, 1843 and 1849–52.* Ed. by Charles H. Carey. Portland, Oregon, 1931.

Thompson, David. *David Thompson's Narratives of his Explorations in Western America, 1784–1812.* Ed. by J. B. Tyrrell. Toronto, 1916.

Thwaites, Reuben Gold, ed. *Early Western Travels, 1748–1846.* 32 vols. Cleveland, 1904–1907.

Twitchell, Ralph Emerson. *The Spanish Archives of New Mexico.* 2 vols. Cedar Rapids, 1914.

Ware, Eugene F. *The Indian War of 1864.* Topeka, 1911.

Williams, Joseph. *Narrative of a Tour from the State of Indiana to the Oregon Territory in the Years 1841–2.* In *To the Rockies and Oregon, 1839–1842.* Ed. by LeRoy R. and Ann W. Hafen. Glendale, 1955.

Wislizenus, A. *Memoir of a Tour to Northern Mexico, Connected with Col. Doniphan's Expedition, in 1846 and 1847.* Washington, 1848.

Wright, Robert M. "Reminiscences of Robert M. Wright." Typescript. Kansas State Historical Society, Topeka.

## V. SECONDARY WORKS

Albright, George Leslie. *Official Explorations for Pacific Railroads, 1853–1855.* University of California *Publications in History,* XI. Berkeley, 1921.

Athearn, Robert G. *William Tecumseh Sherman and the Settlement of the West.* Norman, c.1956.

Bancroft, Hubert Howe. *History of Nevada, Colorado, and Wyoming.* 2 vols. San Francisco, 1890.

Billington, Ray Allen. *Westward Expansion, A History of the American Frontier.* New York, 1949.

Brower, J. V. *The Mississippi River and Its Sources.* Minnesota Historical Society *Collections,* IX. Minneapolis, 1893.

Bushnell, David I., Jr. *Villages of the Algonquian, Siouan, and Caddoan*

*Tribes West of the Mississippi.* Bureau of American Ethnology *Bulletin No. 77.* Washington, 1922.

Campbell, Walter S. See Stanley Vestal.

Castel, Albert. *A Frontier State at War: Kansas, 1861–1865.* Ithaca, c.1958.

Chambers, William Nisbet. *Old Bullion Benton: Senator from the New West.* Boston, c.1956.

Clark, William P. *The Indian Sign Language.* Philadelphia, 1885.

Cleland, Robert Glass. *From Wilderness to Empire, A History of California.* Ed. by Glenn S. Dumke. New York, 1959.

Colton, Ray C. *The Civil War in the Western Territories: Arizona, Colorado, New Mexico, and Utah.* Norman, c.1959.

Curtis, Edward S. *The North American Indian.* 20 vols. Norwood, Massachusetts, c. 1907–1930.

Davidson, Gordon Charles. *The North West Company.* Berkeley, 1918.

De Voto, Bernard. *Across the Wide Missouri.* Boston, c.1947.

Dodge, Richard I. *Our Wild Indians.* Hartford, Connecticut, 1882.

———. *The Plains of the Great West.* New York, 1877.

Dorsey, George A. *The Arapaho Sun Dance: The Ceremony of the Offerings Lodge.* Field Columbian Museum *Publication No. 75, Anthropological Series,* IV. Chicago, 1903.

———. *The Cheyenne: Ceremonial Organization.* Field Columbian Museum *Publication No. 99, Anthropological Series,* Vol. IX, No. 1. Chicago, March, 1905.

———. *The Cheyenne: The Sun Dance.* Field Columbian Museum *Publication No. 103, Anthropological Series,* Vol. IX, No. 2. Chicago, May, 1905.

———, and Alfred L. Kroeber. *Traditions of the Arapaho.* Field Columbian Museum *Anthropological Series,* V. Chicago, 1903.

Dunn, J. P. *Massacres of the Mountains, A History of the Indian Wars of the Far West.* New York. 1886.

Ewers, John C. *The Blackfeet: Raiders on the Northwestern Plains.* Norman, c. 1958.

———. *Teton Dakota: History and Ethnology.* Berkeley, 1937.

Fritz, Percy Stanley. *Colorado, the Centennial State.* New York, 1941.

Gard, Wayne. *The Great Buffalo Hunt.* New York, 1959.

Gittinger, Roy. *The Formation of the State of Oklahoma, 1803–1906.* Norman, 1939.

Grinnell, George Bird. *When Buffalo Ran.* New Haven, c.1920.

———. *Two Great Scouts.* Cleveland, 1928.

Hafen, LeRoy R. *The Overland Mail, 1849–1862.* Cleveland, 1926.

———. *The Southwest Historical Series,* IX, Introduction. Glendale, 1941.

———, and Carl Coke Rister. *Western America.* 2d ed. New York, 1950.

———, and Francis Marion Young. *Fort Laramie and the Pageant of the West, 1834–1890.* Glendale, 1938.

Haney, Lewis Henry. *A Congressional History of Railways in the United States, 1850–1887.* University of Wisconsin *Economics and Political Science Series,* Vol. 6, No. 1. Madison, 1910.

Hayden, F. V. *Contributions to the Ethnography and Philology of the Indian Tribes of the Missouri Valley.* Philadelphia, 1862.

Hilger, Sister M. Inez. *Arapaho Child Life and Its Cultural Background.* Bureau of American Ethnology *Bulletin No. 148.* Washington, 1952.

Hodge, Frederick W. *Handbook of American Indians North of Mexico.* Bureau of American Ethnology *Bulletin No. 30.* 2 vols. Washington, 1910.

Hoopes, Alban W. *Indian Affairs and Their Administration with Special Reference to the Far West, 1849–1860.* Philadelphia, 1932.

Hyde, George E. *Indians of the High Plains.* Norman, c.1959.

———. *The Pawnee Indians.* [Denver], c.1951.

———. *Red Cloud's Folk: A History of the Oglala Sioux Indians.* Norman, 1937.

Jablow, Joseph. *The Cheyenne in Plains Indian Trade Relations, 1795–1840.* New York, 1950.

Jackson, W. Turrentine. *Wagon Roads West.* Berkeley, 1952.

Johnson, Harrison. *Johnson's History of Nebraska.* Omaha, 1880.

Kelsey, Rayner W. *Friends and Indians, 1655–1917.* Philadelphia, 1917.

Laubin, Reginald, and Gladys Laubin. *The Indian Tipi: Its History, Construction, and Use.* Norman, c. 1957.

Lavender, David. *Bent's Fort.* Garden City, New York, 1954.

Leckie, William H. "The Military Conquest of the Southern Plains Indians." Unpublished Ph.D. dissertation, University of Oklahoma, 1954.

Lesley, Lewis Burt. *Uncle Sam's Camels.* Cambridge, 1929.

Llewellyn, Karl N., and E. Adamson Hoebel. *The Cheyenne Way: Conflict and Case Law in Primitive Jurisprudence.* Norman, 1941.

Lowie, Robert H. *The Assiniboine.* American Museum of Natural History *Anthropological Papers,* Vol. IV, Pt. 1. New York, 1907.

———. *The Crow Indians.* New York, 1935.

———. *Indians of the Plains.* New York, 1954.

———. *Primitive Society.* New York, c.1920.

McReynolds, Edwin C. *Oklahoma: A History of the Sooner State.* Norman, c.1954.

Malin, James C. *Indian Policy and Westward Expansion.* University of Kansas *Humanistic Studies,* Vol. II, No. 3. Lawrence, November, 1921.

Mishkin, Bernard. *Rank and Warfare among the Plains Indians. Monographs of the American Ethnological Society,* III. New York, 1940.

Monaghan, Jay [James]. *The Overland Trail.* Indianapolis, c.1947.

Mooney, James. *The Cheyenne Indians. Memoirs of the American Anthropological Association,* I. Lancaster, Pennsylvania, 1905–1907.

———. *The Ghost-Dance Religion and the Sioux Outbreak of 1890. Fourteenth Annual Report* of the Bureau of American Ethnology. Washington, 1896.

Moorhead, Max L. *New Mexico's Royal Road: Trade and Travel on the Chihuahua Trail.* Norman, c.1958.

Morrison, William Brown. *Military Posts and Camps in Oklahoma.* Oklahoma City, 1936.

Morton, Arthur S. *A History of the Canadian West to 1870–71.* London, n.d.

Nevins, Allan. *Frémont, the West's Greatest Adventurer.* 2 vols. New York, 1928.

Nute, Grace Lee. *Rainy River Country.* St. Paul, 1950.

Nye, W. S. *Carbine and Lance: The Story of Old Fort Sill.* Norman, 1938.

Parkman, Francis. *A Half-Century of Conflict.* 2 vols. Boston, 1897.

———. *La Salle and the Discovery of the Great West.* 2 vols. Boston, 1897.

———. *The Oregon Trail, Sketches of Prairie and Rocky Mountain Life.* Boston, 1904.

Pelzer, Louis. *Marches of the Dragoons in the Mississippi Valley.* Iowa City, 1917.

Riggs, Stephen Return. *Dakota Grammar, Texts, and Ethnography. Contributions to North American Ethnology,* IX. Washington, 1893.

Rister, Carl Coke. *Border Command: General Phil Sheridan in the West.* Norman, 1944.

———. *The Southwestern Frontier, 1865–1881.* Cleveland, 1928.

Roe, Frank Gilbert. *The Indian and the Horse.* Norman, c.1955.

———. *The North American Buffalo: A Critical Study of the Species in Its Wild State.* Toronto, 1951.

Root, Frank A., and William Elsey Connelley. *The Overland Stage to California.* Topeka, 1901.

Russel, Robert R. *Improvement of Communication with the Pacific Coast as an Issue in American Politics, 1783–1864.* Cedar Rapids, 1948.

Sabin, Edwin L. *Kit Carson Days.* 2 vols. New York, 1935.

Sandoz, Mari. *The Buffalo Hunters.* New York, c.1954.

———. *Cheyenne Autumn.* New York, c.1953.

Service, Elman R. *A Profile of Primitive Culture.* New York, c.1958.

Smiley, Jerome C. *Semi-Centennial History of the State of Colorado.* 2 Vols. Chicago, 1913.

Smith, Elbert B. *Magnificent Missourian: The Life of Thomas Hart Benton.* Philadelphia, 1958.

Smith, Maurice Greer. *Political Organization of the Plains Indians, with Special Reference to the Council. University Studies* of the University of Nebraska, Vol. XXIV, Nos. 1 and 2. Lincoln, 1925.

Spring, Agnes Wright. *Caspar Collins: The Life and Exploits of an Indian Fighter of the Sixties.* New York, 1927.

Strong, William Duncan. *An Introduction to Nebraska Archaeology.* Smithsonian *Miscellaneous Collections,* Vol. XCIII, No. 10. Washington, 1935.

Vestal, Stanley [Walter S. Campbell]. *Jim Bridger, Mountain Man.* New York, 1946.

———. *Sitting Bull: Champion of the Sioux.* Norman, c.1957.

Wagner, Henry R. *The Plains and the Rockies.* Revised by Charles L. Camp. 3 ed. Columbus, Ohio, 1953.

Wallace, Ernest, and E. Adamson Hoebel. *The Comanches: Lords of the South Plains.* Norman, c.1952.

Warren, Sidney. *Fartherest Frontier, the Pacific Northwest.* New York, 1949.

Watkins, Albert, ed. *Notes of the Early History of the Nebraska Country. Publications* of the Nebraska State Historical Society, XX. Lincoln, 1922.

Wedel, Waldo Rudolph. *An Introduction to Pawnee Archaeology.* Bureau of American Ethnology *Bulletin No. 112.* Washington, 1936.

Wilder, Daniel W. *Annals of Kansas.* Topeka, 1875.

Willison, George F. *Here They Dug the Gold.* New York, c.1946.

Wissler, Clark. *North American Indians of the Plains.* American Museum of Natural History *Handbook Series No. 1.* New York, 1927.

———. *The Relations of Nature to Man in Aboriginal America.* New York, 1926.

———, ed. *Societies of the Plains Indians.* American Museum of Natural History *Anthropological Papers,* XI. New York, 1916.

Young, Otis E. *The First Military Escort on the Santa Fe Trail, 1829.* Glendale, 1952.

———. *The West of Philip St. George Cooke, 1809–1895.* Glendale, 1955.

Zornow, William Frank. *Kansas: A History of the Jayhawk State.* Norman, 1957.


VI. Articles and Essays

Anderson, Robert. "The Buffalo Men, A Cheyenne Ceremony of Petition Deriving from the Sutaio," *Southwestern Journal of Anthropology*, Vol. XII, No. 1 (Spring, 1956).

Ashley, Susan R. "Reminiscences of Early Colorado," *Colorado Magazine*, Vol. XIV, No. 2 (March, 1937).

Benedict, Ruth Fulton. "The Concept of the Guardian Spirit in North America," *Memoirs* of the American Anthropological Association, No. 29. Menasha, Wisconsin, 1923.

———. "The Vision in Plains Culture," *American Anthropologist*, N.S., Vol. XXIV, No. 1 (January–March, 1922).

Bent, Charles. "The Charles Bent Papers," *New Mexico Historical Review*, Vol. XXX, No. 2 (April, 1955).

Bent, George. "Forty Years with the Cheyennes," ed. by George E. Hyde, *The Frontier*, October, 1905–February, 1906.

Bidwell, John. "The First Emigrant Train to California," *Century Magazine*, Vol. XLI, No. 1, (November, 1890).

Block, Augusta Hauck. "Lower Boulder and St. Vrain Valley Home Guards and Fort Junction," *Colorado Magazine*, Vol. XVI, No. 5 (September, 1939).

Brininstool, E. A. "The Rescue of Forsyth's Scouts," *Collections* of the Kansas State Historical Society. XVII. Topeka, 1928.

Burkey, Elmer R. "The Site of the Murder of the Hungate Family by Indians in 1864," *Colorado Magazine*, Vol. XII, No. 4 (July, 1935).

Clark, Olive A. "Early Days along the Solomon Valley," *Collections* of the Kansas State Historical Society, XVII, Topeka, 1928.

Comfort, A. J. "Indian Mounds near Fort Wadsworth, Dakota Territory," *Report of the Smithsonian Institution . . . for the Year 1871.* Washington, 1873.

Connelley, William E. "A Journal on the Santa Fe Trail," *Mississippi Valley Historical Review*, Vol. XII, Nos. 1 and 2 (June, September, 1925).

Davis, Theodore. "A Summer on the Plains," *Harper's New Monthly Magazine*, Vol. XXXVI, No. 213 (February, 1868).

DeLand, Charles Edmund. "Basil Clement (Claymore)," *South Dakota Historical Collections*, XI. Pierre, n.d.

Dixon, James W. "Across the Plains with General Hancock," *Journal of the Military Service Institution of the United States*, Vol. VII, No. 26 (June, 1886).

Dorsey, George A. "How the Pawnees Captured the Cheyenne Medicine Arrows," *American Anthropologist*, N.S., Vol. V, No. 4 (October–December, 1903).

Eggan, Fred. "The Cheyenne and Arapaho Kinship System," *Social Anthropology of North American Tribes*. Ed. by Fred Eggan. Chicago, c.1955.

Ellis, Elmer. "Colorado's First Fight for Statehood," 1865–1868," *Colorado Magazine*, Vol. VIII, No. 1 (January, 1931).

Fairfield, S. H. "The Eleventh Kansas Regiment at Platte Bridge," *Kansas Historical Collections*, VIII. Topeka, 1904.

Ford, Lemuel. "Captain Ford's Journal of an Expedition to the Rocky Mountains," ed. by Louis Pelzer, *Mississippi Valley Historical Review*, Vol. XII, No. 4 (March, 1926).

Forsyth, George A. "A Frontier Fight," *Harper's New Monthly Magazine*, Vol. XCI, No. 541 (June, 1895).

Fynn, Arthur J. "Fur and Forts of the Rocky Mountain West," *Colorado Magazine*, Vol. IX, No. 2 (March, 1932).

Garfield, Marvin H. "The Military Post as a Factor in the Frontier Defense of Kansas, 1865–1869," *Kansas Historical Quarterly*, Vol. I, No. 1 (November, 1931).

———. "Defense of the Kansas Frontier, 1866–1869," *Kansas Historical Quarterly*, Vol I, Nos. 4 and 5 (August, November, 1932).

"General Sully's Expedition against the Southern Plains Indians," MS in Bates Collection, Custer Battlefield National Monument Museum Archives, Crow Agency, Montana.

Godfrey, E. S. "Some Reminiscences, Including an Account of General Sully's Expedition Against the Southern Plains Indians," *Cavalry Journal*, Vol. XXXVI (July, 1927).

———. "Some Reminiscences, Including the Washita Battle, November 27, 1868," *Cavalry Journal*, Vol. XXXVII (October, 1928).

Green, James. "Incidents of the Indian Outbreak of 1864," *Publications* of the Nebraska State Historical Society, XIX. Lincoln, 1919.

Grinnell, George Bird. "Bent's Old Fort and Its Builders," *Collections of* the Kansas State Historical Society, 1919–22, XV. Topeka, 1923.

————. "The Cheyenne Medicine Lodge," *American Anthropologist*, N.S., Vol. XVI, No. 2 (April–June, 1914).

————. "Coup and Scalp among the Plains Indians," *American Anthropologist*, N.S., Vol. XII, No. 2 (April–June, 1910).

————. "Early Cheyenne Villages," *American Anthropologist*, N.S., Vol. XX, No. 4 (October–December, 1918).

————. "Great Mysteries of the Cheyenne," *American Anthropologist*, N.S., Vol. XII, No. 4 (October–December, 1910).

————. "Social Organization of the Cheyennes," *International Congress of Americanists, Thirteenth Session, Held in New York in 1902*. Easton, Pennsylvania, 1905.

————. "Some Early Cheyenne Tales," *Journal of American Folk-Lore*, N.S., Vol. XX–XXI, Nos. 78 and 82 (July–September, 1907, October–December, 1908).

Hadley, James Albert. "The Nineteenth Kansas Cavalry and the Conquest of the Plains Indians," *Collections* of the Kansas State Historical Society, X. Topeka, 1908.

Hafen, LeRoy R. "Fraeb's Last Fight and How Battle Creek Got Its Name," *Colorado Magazine*, Vol. VII, No. 3 (May, 1930).

————. "Old Fort Lupton and Its Founder," *Colorado Magazine*, Vol. VI, No. 6 (November, 1929).

————, ed. "A Report from the First Indian Agent of the Upper Platte and Arkansas," *New Spain and the Anglo-American West. Historical Contributions presented to Herbert Eugene Bolton*. 2 vols. Lancaster, Pennsylvania, c.1932.

————. "When Was Bent's Fort Built," *Colorado Magazine*, Vol. XXXI, No. 2 (April, 1954).

Hagerty, Leroy W. "Indian Raids Along the Platte and Little Blue Rivers, 1864–1865," *Nebraska History*, Vol. XXVIII, No. 4 (October–December, 1947).

Haines, Francis. "The Northward Spread of Horses among the Plains Indians," *American Anthropologist*, N.S., Vol. XL, No. 3 (July–September, 1938).

Hazen, William B. "Some Corrections of 'Life on the Plains,' " *Chronicles of Oklahoma*, Vol. III, No. 3 (September, 1925).

Hilger, Sister M. Inez. "Notes on Cheyenne Child Life," *American Anthropologist*, N.S., Vol. XLVIII, No. 1 (January–March, 1946).

Hoopes, Alban W. "Thomas S. Twiss, Indian Agent on the Upper Platte,

1855–1861," *Mississippi Valley Historical Review*, Vol. XX, No. 3 (December, 1933).

Hornaday, William T. "The Extermination of the American Bison, with a Sketch of Its Discovery and Life History," Smithsonian Institution *Annual Report, 1887.* 2 pts. Washington, 1889.

Hurst, John, and Sigmund Shlesinger. "Battle of the Arikaree," *Collections* of the Kansas State Historical Society, 1919–22. Topeka, 1923.

"The Indian War," *Harper's Weekly*, Vol. XII, No. 612 (September 19, 1868).

Jackson, W. Turrentine. "The Army Engineers as Road Surveyors and Builders in Kansas and Nebraska, 1854–1858," *Kansas Historical Quarterly*, Vol. XVII, No. 1 (February, 1949).

Jenness, George B. "The Battle on Beaver Creek," *Transcriptions* of the Kansas State Historical Society, 1905–1906, IX. Topeka, 1906.

Kennerly, James. "Diary of James Kennerly," ed. by Edgar B. Wesley, Missouri Historical Society *Collections*, VI. St. Louis, n.d.

King, James T. "The Republican River Expedition, June–July, 1869," *Nebraska History*, Vol. XLI, Nos. 3 and 4 (September, December, 1960).

Kingman, Samuel A. "Diary of Samuel A. Kingman at Indian Treaty of 1865," *Kansas Historical Quarterly*, Vol. I, No. 5 (November, 1932).

Kroeber, A. L. "Cheyenne Tales," *Journal of American Folk-Lore*, N.S., Vol. XIII, No. 50 (July–September, 1900).

"Late Indian Outrages," *Harper's Weekly*, Vol. XI, No. 552 (July 27, 1867).

LeRaye, Charles. "The Journal of Charles LeRaye," South Dakota *Historical Collections*, IV. Sioux Falls, South Dakota, 1908.

Lowie, Robert H. "Ceremonialism in North America," *American Anthropologist*, N.S., Vol. XVI, No. 4 (October–December, 1914).

———. "Plains Indians Age-Societies: Historical and Comparative Summary," American Museum of Natural History *Anthropological Papers*, XI. New York, 1916.

Lubers, H. L. "William Bent's Family and the Indians of the Plains," *Colorado Magazine*, Vol. XIII, No. 1 (January, 1936).

McBee, John. "John McBee's Account of the Expedition of the Nineteenth Kansas," ed. by William E. Connelley, *Collections* of the Kansas State Historical Society, XVII. Topeka, Kansas, 1928.

Mallery, Garrick. "Pictographs of the North American Indians. A Preliminary Paper," *Fourth Annual Report* of the Bureau of American Ethnology. Washington, 1886.

Merrill, Rev. Moses. "Extracts from the Diary of Rev. Moses Merrill, a Missionary to the Otoe Indians from 1832 to 1840," *Transactions and Reports* of the Nebraska State Historical Society, IV. Lincoln, 1892.

Michelson, Truman. "The Narrative of a Southern Cheyenne Woman," Smithsonian *Miscellaneous Collections,* Vol. XXCVII, No. 5. Washington, 1932.

Moore, Horace L. "The Nineteenth Kansas Cavalry," *Transactions* of the Kansas State Historical Society, VI. Topeka, 1900.

Mulloy, William. "The Northern Plains," *Archeology of Eastern United States.* Ed. by James B. Griffin. Chicago, c.1952.

Murphy, John. "Reminiscences of the Washita Campaign and of the Darlington Indian Agency," *Chronicles of Oklahoma,* Vol. I, No. 3 (June, 1923).

*Niles' Register,* January 15, 1825; October 25, 1845.

North, Frank J. "The Journal of an Indian Fighter: The 1869 Diary of Major Frank J. North," ed. by Donald F. Danker, *Nebraska History,* Vol. XXXIX, No. 2 (June, 1958).

Nute, Grace Lee. "Hudson's Bay Company Posts in Minnesota Country," *Minnesota History,* Vol. XXII, No. 3 (September, 1941).

Palmer, H. E. "History of the Powder River Indian Expedition of 1865," *Transactions and Reports* of the Nebraska State Historical Society, II. Lincoln, 1887.

Peck, Robert Morris. "Recollections of Early Times in Kansas Territory," Kansas *Historical Collections,* VIII. Topeka, 1904.

Perrine, Fred S. "Military Escorts on the Santa Fe Trail," *New Mexico Historical Review,* Vol. III, No. 3 (July, 1928).

Pond, Peter. "Journal of Peter Pond," *Collections* of the State Historical Society of Wisconsin, XVIII. Madison, 1908.

Provinse, John H. "The Underlying Sanctions of Plains Indian Culture," *Social Anthropology of North American Tribes.* Ed. by Fred Eggan. Chicago, c.1955.

Reckmeyer, Clarence. "The Battle of Summit Springs," *Colorado Magazine,* Vol. VI, No. 6 (November, 1929).

Richardson, Rupert N. "The Comanche Indians and the Fight at Adobe Walls," *The Panhandle-Plains Historical Review,* Vol. IV (1931).

Riggs, S. R. "Mounds of Minnesota Valley," Minnesota Historical Society *Collections,* I. St. Paul, 1902.

Rister, Carl Coke. "The Significance of the Destruction of the Buffalo in the Southwest," *Southwestern Historical Quarterly,* Vol. XXXIII, No. 1 (July, 1929).

Robinson, De Lorme W. "Editorial Notes on Historical Sketch of North and South Dakota," South Dakota *Historical Collections,* I. Aberdeen, South Dakota, 1902.

Sayr, Major Hal. "Major Hal Sayr's Diary of the Sand Creek Campaign," ed. by Lynn I. Perrigo, *Colorado Magazine,* Vol. XV, No. 2 (March, 1938).

*Science Magazine,* November 4, 1887.

Seger, John H. "Cheyenne Marriage Customs," *Journal of American Folk-Lore,* N.S., Vol. XI, No. 43 (October–December, 1898).

Spier, Leslie. "The Sun Dance of the Plains Indians: Its Development and Diffusion," American Museum of Natural History, *Anthropological Papers,* Vol. XVI, Pt. 7. New York, 1921.

Stoner, W. H. Letter to J. B. Weston, *Publications* of the Nebraska State Historical Society, XIX. Lincoln, 1919.

Strong, William Duncan. "From History to Prehistory in the Northern Great Plains," Smithsonian *Miscellaneous Collections,* C. Washington, 1940.

Swanton, John R. "Some Neglected Data Bearing on Cheyenne, Chippewa, and Dakota History," *American Anthropologist,* N.S., Vol. XXXII, No. 1 (January–March, 1930).

Taylor, A. A. "Medicine Lodge Peace Council," *Chronicles of Oklahoma,* Vol. II, No. 2 (June, 1924).

Taylor, Jackson, Jr. "Early Days at Wetmore and on the Hardscrabble," *Colorado Magazine,* Vol. VIII, No. 3 (May, 1931).

Trudeau, Jean Baptiste. "Trudeau's Journal," South Dakota *Historical Collections,* VII. Pierre, 1914.

Wedel, Waldo R. "Culture Sequence in the Central Great Plains," Smithsonian *Miscellaneous Collections,* C. Washington, 1940.

Wetmore, Major Alphonso. "Diary of a Journey to Santa Fe, 1828," *Missouri Historical Review,* Vol. VIII, No. 4 (July, 1914).

Whitney, Chauncey B. "Diary of Chauncey B. Whitney," *Collections* of of the Kansas State Historical Society, 1911–12. XII. Topeka, 1912.

Will, George F. "Archaeology of the Missouri Valley," American Museum of Nautral History *Anthropological Papers,* XXII. New York, 1924.

———. "The Cheyenne Indians in North Dakota," *Proceedings* of the Mississippi Valley Historical Association for the year 1913–14, VII. Cedar Rapids, 1914.

Williamson, T. S. "Who Were the First Men," Minnesota Historical Society *Collections,* I. St. Paul, 1902.

Wissler, Clark. "Diffusion of Culture in the Plains of North America,"

*Congrès International des Américanistes, XVᵉ Session.* 2 vols. Quebec, 1907.

———. "Societies and Ceremonial Associations in the Oglala Division of the Teton-Dakota," American Museum of Natural History, *Anthropological Papers,* XI. New York, 1916.

Wolf, Captain Lambert Brown. "Extracts from Diary of Captain Lambert Brown Wolf," ed. by George A. Root, *Kansas Historical Quarterly,* Vol. I, No. 3 (May, 1932).

# LIST OF ABBREVIATIONS
## USED IN FOOTNOTES

| | |
|---|---|
| *Amer. Anthr.* | *American Anthropologist* |
| AMNH *Anthropological Papers* | American Museum of Natural History *Anthropological Papers* |
| BAE *Annual Report* | Bureau of American Ethnology *Annual Report* |
| BAE *Bulletin* | Bureau of American Ethnology *Bulletin* |
| *Chronicles of Okla.* | *Chronicles of Oklahoma* |
| *Colo. Magazine* | *Colorado Magazine* |
| Field Mus. *Anthropological Series* | Field Columbian Museum *Anthropological Series* |
| *Jour. Amer. Folk-Lore* | *Journal of American Folk-Lore* |
| Kansas *HC* | Kansas *Historical Collections* |
| *KHQ* | *Kansas Historical Quarterly* |
| KSHS *Collections* | *Collections* of the Kansas State Historical Society |
| KSHS *Transactions* | Kansas State Historical Society *Transactions* |
| *MHR* | *Missouri Historical Review* |
| *Minn. History* | *Minnesota History* |
| MinnHS *Collections* | Minnesota Historical Society *Collections* |
| MoHS *Collections* | Missouri Historical Society *Collections* |
| *MVHR* | *Mississippi Valley Historical Review* |
| *Nebr. History* | *Nebraska History* |

| | |
|---|---|
| *NMHR* | *New Mexico Historical Review* |
| NSHS *Publications* | *Publications* of the Nebraska State Historical Society |
| NSHS *Transactions and Reports* | *Transactions and Reports* of the Nebraska State Historical Society |
| *Proceedings*, MVHA | *Proceedings* of the Mississippi Valley Historical Association |
| SD *Historical Collections* | South Dakota *Historical Collections* |
| SHSWis *Collections* | *Collections* of the State Historical Society of Wisconsin |
| Smithsonian *AR* | Smithsonian Institution *Annual Report* |
| Smithsonian *MC* | Smithsonian *Miscellaneous Collections* |
| Smithsonian *Report* | *Report* of the Smithsonian Institution for the year ——— |

# INDEX

Abert, Lieutenant James W.: 98ff., 107
Alights-on-the-Cloud: 94
Alvord, Captain Henry E.: 321, 339, 371
Anthony, Major Scott J.: 170, 209–10, 214–16, 219; criticizes Chivington, 222–23
Arapaho Indians: 143–47, 163, 200–201; influence on Cheyenne migrations, 17–19; on Arkansas River, 19; relations with neighboring tribes, 19; range of, 24; alliance with Cheyennes, 77–78; contact Frémont, 86; on South Platte, 93; impressed by Army guns, 98; hostility of, 104–105; description of, 105–106; population of, 107; conflict with Cheyennes, 109–10
Arikaras: relations with Cheyennes, 10, 14, 80
Arkansas River Cheyennes: *see* Southern Cheyennes
Arkansas River Valley: 156
Armes, Captain George A.: 287–88
Arrow Renewal ceremony: 57–58
Ashcraft, Granville: 195
Atchison, David R.: 116
Atkinson, General Henry: makes

treaty with Cheyennes: 22–23
Audenreid, Lieutenant Colonel Joseph C.: 335
Augur, Brigadier General C. C.: 295

Babbitt, Almon W.: 135
Bankhead, Captain H. C.: 309, 313
Banks, Alexander R.: 302
Barnitz, Captain Albert: 283, 328
Bates, Lieutenant A. E.: 262
Battle of Adobe Walls: 384–86
Battle of Arikaree: 310–13
Battle of Summit Springs: 342–43
Battle of the Washita: 325–28
Beale, Lieutenant Edward F.: 125
Beall, Major Benjamin L.: 113
Bear (Brulé Sioux chief): 129–30
Bear's Heart: 398
Bear-That-Goes-Alone: 306
Bear Tooth (Arapaho chief): 20–21
Beaver: 177
Beckwourth, James P.: 87, 90–91, 216–17, 224–25, 227
Beecher, Lieutenant Frederick H.: 301, 303–306, 309–12
Beede, Cyrus: 368–69
Bent, Charles (brother of William): 78–79, 83–84; contacts Cheyennes, 24–25; asks for protection

428

from illegal traders, 91–92; murder of, 104–105

Bent, Charles (son of William): 185, 253, 256, 260, 263, 269, 283, 288, 298

Bent, George: 177, 185, 196, 203, 207, 220, 225, 227–28, 230–31, 253, 260, 269, 276, 280, 290–91, 296, 298–99, 302, 304–305, 355–56, 363, 367, 370, 383, 401

Bent, Robert (son of William): 146, 150, 217

Bent, William: 92, 102–103n., 104, 114, 123–24, 132, 138, 141, 143–44, 146–49, 155, 179, 186, 196, 199, 207, 236–37, 240–41, 243, 256–57, 260–63

Bent, St. Vrain and Company: 24ff., 77, 87, 90–92, 109, 114

Benton, Thomas Hart: 106, 124

Bent's Fort: 25–26, 79, 82, 94, 98, 105, 107, 109, 111–15, 236

Big Bow (Kiowa chief): 376

Big Crow: 226

Big Head: 258, 293, 337–38

Big Horse: 383

Big Jake: 301, 356–58, 376

Big Left Hand: 101

Big Moccasin: 398

Big Mouth (Arapaho chief): 153, 198, 240, 323, 335, 364–65

Big Timbers, on Arkansas River: 98, 111

Big Tree (Kiowa chief): 376

Big Wolf: killed by Captain Nichols, 213

Bird, Asbury: 186

Bissonnette, Joseph: 169

Black Bear (Northern Arapaho chief): 253–54

Black Beaver: 372–73

Black Horse (Kiowa chief): 128

Black Horse: 401–402

Black Kettle: 149, 156, 206–10, 213–15, 218–19, 224–25, 228, 234, 240, 242, 258, 261, 263, 281, 289–92, 294, 297, 301, 321, 323, 327, 329, 331–32

Black Shin: 311

Blackwell, Jefferson: 90

Blinn, Mrs. Clara: 315, 328

Blunt, Major General James G.: 198, 209–10

Bobtail Porcupine: 316

Bogy, Charles: 263–64

Bogy, Lewis V.: 270

Bonney, Captain Seth: 346, 348, 350

Boone, Albert G.: 149, 152–54, 156, 160, 181, 303

Booth, Captain Henry: 199

Bowstring society: 82

Bradbury, John: 18

Bridger, James: 88, 118–19, 250, 252

Broken Arrow: 316

Broken Hand: *see* Thomas Fitzpatrick

Brown, B. Gratz: 118ff.

Brown, J. S.: 190

Brown, John F.: 372–73

Brown, Orlando: 115

Browning, Orville H.: 270

Brulé Sioux: 157, 270, 281, 285–87, 311

Bryan, Lieutenant Francis T.: 132–33, 135–36

Buell, Lieutenant Colonel George P.: 393

Buffalo: 30–31, 98, 100–101, 372, 381–82

Buffalo (Long Chief): 162

Buffalo Head: 344
Bull Bear: 168, 209–11, 225, 264, 273, 276, 291, 293, 309, 311, 351, 353–55, 361, 373, 380
Bull Elk: 404
Bullet Proof (Northern Cheyenne): 315–16
Bull Hump (Comanche chief): 81, 83
Burton, Lieutenant Augustus W.: 185
Butterfield, David A.: 241, 264, 269
Butterfield, Isaac L.: 289–92, 300–301
Butterfield's Overland Despatch route: 196

Caddoes: 239, 321–22
"California Joe" (Moses E. Milner): 324, 336
Camp Supply: 328, 344, 346–47
Camp Weld: 176–77, 185, 210–12
Carleton, Major General James H.: 215
Carpenter, Brevet Lieutenant Colonel Louis H.: 311–12, 315–16
Carr, Major Eugene A.: 315–16, 332, 340–43
Carson, Kit: 86, 88, 106, 117–18, 177, 237–38, 240
Carvalho, S. N.: 125–26
Chambers, A. B.: 118ff.
Chapman, Amos: 318, 374–76
Charbonneau, Baptiste: 87
Chase, Lieutenant George H.: 195
Cherry Creek, Colorado territory: 143–45, 148
Cheyenne Indians: 200–201; myths of, 3–4; food of, 4, 28, 84–85, 103; lodges of, 4, 6, 14, 29; clothing of, 4, 34–35; original habitat of, 4, 27; French contact with, 4–5; in New Mexico, 5, 16; occupy Minnesota River Valley, 5–6; conflicts with Crees, 6; conflict with Assiniboins, 6, 15; village sites of, 6; arms of, 6; trade goods of, 6; occupy Sheyenne River Valley, 6–7; move from Sheyenne River, 7–9; acquire horses, 6, 8–9; trade with Chippewas, 7–8; agriculture of, 9–10, 28; Missouri River sites of, 9–10; population increase of, 10; act as intermediaries in fur trade, 10ff.; trade furs, 10ff., 12–13, 16–17; White Man myth of, 10–11, 14; economy of, 11; conflict with Sioux, 12, 14–15, 84; on Cheyenne River, 12–13; act as intermediaries for Arapahoes, 13, 18–19; observations of Lewis and Clark concerning, 13–17; trade with Arikaras, 13–14; trade at Arikara villages, 18; range of, 13–14, 24, 92; population of, 14–15, 21–22, 92, 107, 132; near Black Hills, 15; near beaver streams, 15; request traders, 15; conflict with Teton Sioux, 15–16, 19; on sources of Platte River, 16; near Arapahoes, 16; conflict with Crows, 17; conflict with Kiowas, 18, 23; on Arkansas River, 19ff., 107; claim Arkansas River Valley, 108; trade on Missouri River, 20; Hairy Rope band of, 21; hunt horses in Cimarron Valley, 21; horse herds of, 21; dispersal of tribe, 21–22, 89, 113; range in Republican and Smoky Hill val-

leys, 22, 101; sign treaty of 1825,
22–23; range west of Black Hills,
22–23; trade at Cherry River, 23;
precede Bent to Arkansas River,
24; shift to Arkansas River, 26;
migrations of, 26; joined by Sutaios, 27; historic tales of, 27–28;
search for better range, 27–28;
culture-heroes of, 28; sacred
Medicine Hat of, 28; acquire corn,
28; cultural influences upon, 28–
29; cultural change of, 29; adapt
to Great Plains environment, 29–
30; transportation of, 29–30, 35–
36; Plains Indians traits of, 30;
dependence upon buffalo of, 30–
31; animal meat used by, 31;
hunting techniques of, 31–32;
labor of women, 32–33, 36–37,
103; uses of buffalo by, 32–33;
utensils of, 33–34; pottery of, 34;
use of hides by, 34–35; ornaments of, 35, 126; sexual behavior of, 35, 37–38, 48; influence of women, 36–37; courtship
of, 37–38; marriage customs
among, 38–39, 45; role of widows
among, 39; death customs of, 39;
love of children, 40; childlife,
40–41; names of, 40–41; boys'
training, 41–42; practice of counting coup, 42–43; consider horses
as wealth, 43; visions of, 43–45;
self-torture among, 43–45;
family unit of, 45–46; kinship system of, 46–49; religion of,
50ff., 102; gods of, 50–51; attrib-
ute powers to animals and birds,
51–53; celebrate Ceremony of the
Buffalo, 52–53; shamans, 53–55;

medicine of, 54; prayers of, 55;
priests of, 55, 59–60; taboos of,
55–56; medicine arrows of, 56–
57; loss of medicine arrows, 58–
59; buffalo hat, 59–60; power of
fetishes among, 60–61; military
societies of, 67–69; Contraries,
69–70; government among, 70–
73; origin of chiefs' council, 70–
71; selection of chiefs' council,
71–72; power of chiefs, 72–73;
division of bands, 73–75, 142–
43, 153; migration from Missouri
River, 77; description of, 77–78,
84, 89–90, 96–97, 108; alliance
with Arapahoes, 77–78; population on Arkansas River, 78; conflict with Comanches, 78; conflict with Pawness, 78–81, 102,
110, 113, 125; peace with Pawnees, 79–80; described by Captain Ford, 79; conflict with Arikaras, 80; conflict with Potawatomis, 80–81; conflict with Kiowas
and Comanches, 81–83; peace
with Kiowas and Comanches,
82–83; create disturbance on
Overland route, 85; occupy South
Platte River, 86–87; contact Frémont, 86–87; in Fraeb fight, 87–
88; hostile to whites in 1842,
88–89; on North Platte River,
89; murders among, 89–90;
liquor among, 90–92; on South
Platte River, 91; raid Shoshonis,
93; use Republican River buffalo
range, 93; conflict with Delawares, 94; trade with Comanches,
97; impact of routes upon, 100;
decline of, 100–101; diseases

among, 101, 113–14; offer to revenge Charles Bent, 104; foes of in 1847, 108; alliances of,108–109; conflict with Arapahoes, 109–10; struggle for buffalo range, 110; attend councils at Bent's Fort, 112–13; contact forty-niners, 113; cholera among, 113–14; with Sumner's command, 117; peace with Shoshonis, 119, 121; horsemanship of, 120; baptism of, 120–21; adopt Shoshoni children, 121; lands defined by Treaty of Fort Laramie, 121; condition of 1853, 123; accused of raids, 124; raid Frémont's horses, 125; with allies attack Pawnees, 127–28; celebrate Pawnee victory, 127; defeated by Eastern Indians, 128; power of charms, 128; unity until 1850's, 128–29, 133; accede to Harney's demands, 130–31; raid on Platte route, 131; threaten William Bent, 131; proceeds of hunting, 132; fight at Upper Platte Bridge, 133; attack on Little Blue River, 133–34; threaten Pawnees, 134; raid near Fort Kearny, 134–35; deliver prisoners, 136; seek peace, 136; Sumner's campaign against, 137–40; meet Sumner on Solomon River, 138–39; village destroyed by Sumner, 140; flee from Sumner, 140; explain raids before Sumner campaign, 142; seek treaty, 143–44; relations with Colorado settlers, 145; visit William Bent, 147; divisions of emerge, 147; on South Platte,

159; discontent among, 162–63; refuse to negotiate treaty, 165; raid Irwin-Jackman herd, 176–77; attacked by Dunn, 179–80; raid South Platte, 182–83; attacked at Cedar Bluffs, 183–84; grievances of in 1864, 187

Chief Killer: 398

Chisholm, Jesse: 237, 239

Chivington, John M.: 162–63, 170–71, 176, 180–81, 183–84, 187, 189, 191, 197–98, 203, 207–209, 210–16ff., 217n., 218, 220–21

Chouteau, Auguste Pierre: trades on Arkansas River, 19–20

Chouteau, Pierre, Jr., and Company: 109

Clark, Ben: 318, 377

Clark, Charles: 283

Clark, William: 23; issues license to Charles Bent at Bent's Fort, 26

Clarke, Sidney: 353

Cody, William F. ("Buffalo Bill"): 303, 340, 349

Cole, Colonel Nelson: 249–50, 254–55

Colley, S. G.: 156–59, 161–62, 164–66, 172, 175, 197, 199–200, 207, 212

Collins, Lieutenant Caspar: 248–49

Collins, Lieutenant Colonel William O.: 176, 180, 229–30

Colorado territory: seeks Cheyenne lands, 144–45; organic statute of, 160–61n.; statehood movement in, 197–98

Comanche Indians: 78, 146, 158, 189, 193, 198, 228, 239, 291–92, 304–305, 320–21, 324, 327, 385–86

Compton, Major Charles E.: 385, 391, 395
Comstock, William: 262, 278, 287, 309
Connor, Brigadier General P. Edward: 245, 249ff.
Contraries: 69–70
Cook, Lieutenant W. W.: 286
Cooke, Captain Philip St. George: 92; describes Cheyennes, 96
Cooke, Lieutenant William W.: 334
Cooley, D. N.: 261
Cooper, Colonel Samuel: 118
Cooper, Major Wickliffe: 280
Corbin, Jack: 324
Covington, John A.: 366, 402
Crawford, Samuel J.: 287, 324
Crazy Dog society (Northern Cheyennes): 247
Crooked Lance society: 226, 253
Crow Chief: 177
Crows: conflict with Cheyennes, 17
Culbertson, Alex: 120
Curtis, Dick: predicts outbreak in 1871, 360
Curtis, Major General Samuel R.: 144, 175–76, 189, 193–99, 202, 206–207, 211–12, 215–16, 221–22
Custard, Sergeant Amos J.: 248
Custer, Lieutenant Colonel George A.: 275–79, 285–87, 325–28, 334–38
Custer, Captain Thomas: 285

Dark: 137, 139
Darlington, Brinton: 345–48, 350–53, 355, 357–60, 364, 366–67
Darrah, Thomas J.: 190
Davidson, Captain Joseph C.: 191

Davidson, Lieutenant Colonel J. W.: 359, 365–67, 395
Davis, Theodore: 272
Dawson, Nicholas: 85
Delawares: 94
Deming, E. N.: 375–76, 400
DeMun, Jules: trades on Arkansas River, 19–20
Denver, Colorado territory: 145, 191–92, 204
Denver, James W.: 144–45
De Smet, Pierre Jean: 84–85, 120–21
Dixon, Bill: 386
Dodge City: 380
Dodge, Major General Grenville M.: 231–33, 235–40, 257
Dodge, Colonel Henry: 76–80
Dog Soldiers: 68, 73, 75, 152, 168, 178, 180, 185, 224–25, 242, 245, 253, 256–57, 259–60, 262, 270, 275, 281, 286–87, 311, 314, 319, 336–37, 339–43, 347–49, 352, 361
Dohasan (Kiowa chief): 239
Dole, William P.: 153, 192, 212
Doolittle, James R.: 233–34ff.
Dougherty, John: 76–77
Douglass, Major Henry: 301
Downing, Major Jacob: 178, 182–84
Dryer, Major Hiram: 257, 259
Dull Knife (Northern Cheyenne): 133, 253
Duncan, Lieutenant Colonel Thomas: 349
Dunn, Lieutenant Clark: 178, 180–81, 191, 221

Eayre, Lieutenant George S.: 176–77, 185–88
Elliott, Major Joel H.: 318, 326–27, 329–30

Ellsworth, Lieutenant William: 229
Evans, Major Andrew W.: 332
Evans, John: 158–63, 165–66, 168–69ff., 171, 173, 188–89, 191–95. 197–98, 201–204, 210–12

Fall Leaf (Delaware chief): 138–39, 209, 272
Farnsworth, Lieutenant H. J.: 393–94
Fat Bear: 337
Fetterman, Brevet Lieutenant Colonel William J.: 268
Fitzpatrick, Thomas (Broken Hand): 24, 85, 88–89, 94, 106ff., 108–109, 111–12, 115–16, 118f., 122–23, 125
Fleming, Lieutenant Hugh B.: 129
Fletcher, Mary: 258
Flying Arrow: 79
Ford, Colonel James H.: 232–34
Ford, Captain Lemuel: 77, 79
Forsyth, Major George A.: 55, 310–13
Forsyth, Thomas: 98
Fort Atkinson: 116–17, 124–25, 140–41
Fort Bridger: 93
Fort Cobb: 234, 320–22, 329–30
Fort Collins: 163
Fort Cottonwood: 202, 206
Fort Dodge: 269, 300–301
Fort Harker: 197n., 269, 281, 287, 314
Fort Hays: 279, 387–88, 310
Fort Kearny: 134, 201–203, 231
Fort Laramie: 250, 266
Fort Larned: 153, 156, 158, 164, 174, 196, 198, 209, 236, 257, 273, 275, 281, 290, 304–305, 321

Fort Leavenworth: 97
Fort Lupton: 90, 114
Fort Lyon: 163, 166, 182, 199, 209, 214–15, 216, 235, 267, 314–15
Fort McPherson: 266, 285, 341
Fort Mann: 110–12
Fort Rankin: 226–29
Fort Riley: 196, 206, 272
Fort St. Vrain: 87, 89, 105, 114
Fort Sedgwick: 286
Fort Sill: 334–35
Fort Wallace: 262–63, 282–83, 286–87, 310, 313, 316
Fort Zarah: 197n., 236, 261, 264, 302
Fowler, Jacob: trades with Plains Indians, 21
Fox Tail: 264, 272
Fraeb, Henry: fights with Indians, 87–88
Frémont, Lieutenant John Charles: 86ff., 92–94, 125–27
Friday (Arapaho chief): 165
Fur trade on Arkansas River: 114

Gallagher, Jack: 374, 382
Gantt, Captain John: 76, 90
Garrard, Lewis H.: describes Cheyennes, 102–105
German, Adelaide and Julia: 395
German, Catherine Elizabeth and Sophia Louisa: 400–401n.
German, John: 392
Gerry, Elbridge: 166–67, 180, 204–205
Gilpin, William: 110–12, 153
Goodale, Tim: 137–38
Grant, Ulysses S.: 267, 347
Grattan, Lieutenant John L.: 129–30

Grattan Massacre: 129–30
Gray Thunder: 81–82
Greeley, Horace: 145–46
Greenwood, A. B.: 148–49
Grey Beard: 276, 291, 294, 297, 360, 377, 385, 393–94, 398, 403
Grinnell, George Bird: ix, 25, 63, 166, 171
Grover, Abner S.: 309–12
Guerrier, Edmond G.: 218–20, 225, 258–60, 273–74, 276–79, 291, 293–94, 370, 377
Guerrier, William: 133
Gunnison, Captain John: 124–25

Hairy Rope band: chiefs of, 21
Hall, Benjamin F.: 161–62
Halleck, Major General Henry W.: 222, 233
Hamilton, Captain Louis McLane: 285–86, 319, 328
Hancock, Major General Winfield Scott: 265–66, 268ff., 277–82
Hard Rope (Osage): 324, 336
Hardscrabble: 109
Hardy, Captain David L.: 181–82
Harlan, James: 236, 238
Harney, Major General William S.: 130–31, 296
Hartwell, Captain C. A.: 396
Harvey, Thomas A.: 106
Hawkins, Lieutenant George W.: 162
Hayden, Captain J.: 153
Hazen, Brevet Major General William M.: 320–24, 330, 339, 346
Heap of Birds: 358
Heap of Whips: 145
Hedges, Nathaniel D.: 253

Henely, Lieutenant Austin: strikes Southern Cheyennes: 404
Hennessey, Patrick: killed by Southern Cheyennes, 387
Henning, Major B. C.: 214–16
Henry, Alexander: 7–9
Heth, Lieutenant Henry: 124
Hickok, James Butler ("Wild Bill"): 272, 278
High-Back-Wolf: 142
High-Backed-Wolf: 78
Hinkle, Lieutenant F. S.: attacks fleeing Southern Cheyennes, 399
Hippy: 386
Hoag, Enoch: 345, 353–54, 366, 383, 387
Hoffman, Major William: 131, 136
Holladay: Ben: 207, 228
Hollis, Robert: 374, 382
Horse Chief: 386
Horse thieves: 382–83
Howling Wolf: 398–99
Hungate, Nathan Ward: murder of, 190–91
Hunt, Alexander C.: 285

Indian Peace Commission of 1867: 288; members of, 289, 295
Indians: tribes near Black Hills, 15
Indian traders: 352
Intermarried whites: 122–23, 154, 157
Iron Shirt (Kiowa-Apache chief): 332
Irwin, W. R.: 263–64
Isatai (Comanche): 385–86

James, Edwin: describes Arkansas River trade, 20
Janisse, Antoine: 166–67

Janisse, Nicholas: 250–51
Jenness, Captain George B.: 288
Johnson, Andrew: 234
Jones, F. F.: 273
Jones, H. L.: 188
Jordan, Richard: murder of, 370–71
Jordan, Captain W. H.: 399

Kansas: Indian raids, 1864, 196–98
Kansas Pacific Railroad: 281–82, 287
Kaws: 296–97; raided by Southern Cheyennes, 303–304
Kearny, Colonel Stephen Watts: 94–97
Ketcham, H. T.: 174–75
Kicking Bird (Kiowa chief): 334
Kidd, Colonel James H.: 252
Kidd, Major Meredith W.: 290, 295, 339
Kidd, Major Milo H.: 349
Kidder, Lieutenant Lyman S.: 286–87
Kingman, Samuel: 244
Kingsbury, Lieutenant Gaines P.: 76–80
Kiowa-Apaches: 189, 239, 264, 291–92, 327
Kiowas: 23, 146, 148, 158, 176, 189, 193, 198, 228, 238–39, 270, 280–81, 291, 304–305, 320–21, 324, 327, 331, 357, 363, 369

Laidlaw, William: notes Cheyenne migration, 25–26
La Salle, Sieur de: contacts Cheyennes, 4–5
La Vérendryes: alleges Cheyenne contact, 7

Lea, Luke: 116
Lean Bear: 155; killed by Eayre, 186–87
Lean Chief: 103
Lean Face: 337
Leavenworth, Jesse H.: 158, 163–64, 232–34, 237, 239–40, 260, 277, 279
Left Hand (Arapaho chief): 155, 170, 214
Leg-in-the-Water: 224
LeRaye, Charles: trades with Cheyennes, 13
Limpy: 398
Liquor trade: 89–92, 109, 154, 163–64, 174, 300, 363, 372–75, 377, 380–82, 384
Little Beaver (Osage): 324
Little Bull: 405
Little Chief: 148, 179n.
Little Grey Head: 135
Little Heart (Kiowa chief): 164, 166, 334
Little Moon: 78–79
Little Mountain (Kiowa chief): 83, 199
Little Raven (Arapaho chief): 83, 145, 170, 172, 214, 225, 228, 240, 242, 289–93, 318, 347–48, 356
Little Robe: 168, 224, 240, 258–59, 263, 273, 297, 301, 303–304, 323, 333–34, 339, 346, 354, 358, 362–63, 375–77, 384, 390
Little Rock: 327
Little Spotted Crow: 135
Little Thunder (Brulé Sioux (chief): 130, 245
Little Wolf: 81–82, 155
Lone Wolf (Kiowa chief): 330–31

Long, Stephen: encounters Plains Indian encampment: 20–21
Long Chin (Brulé Sioux chief): 137
Long Chin (Cheyenne chief): 167, 204
Loree, John: 165, 175–76
Lupton, Lancaster P.: 90
Luttig, John: description of Cheyennes, 16–17

McCook, Major General Alexander McD.: 235
McFerran, Colonel J. C.: 205
McGaa, William: 191–92
McKenny, Major T. I.: 193
Mackenzie, Colonel Ranald S.: 392–93
Mah-wis-sa: 332
Mandans: contact Cheyennes, 10; fear Cheyennes, 14
Man-Shot-by-a-Ree: 204
Man-Who-Breaks-the Marrow-Bones: 306
Many Whips (Arapaho chief): 165
Martin, William: 382
Massaum ceremony: 61–62
Maxwell, Lucien: 86
Medicine Arrow ceremonies: 363
Medicine Arrows (Southern Cheyenne chief): 82, 258, 293, 295, 299–301, 337, 344, 347–48, 350, 353–55, 362, 365, 396–97, 399–400
Medicine Lodge: *see* Sun Dance
Medicine Water: 94, 385, 392–93
Medicine Wolf: 276
Miles, John D.: 367–70, 372–75, 379–80, 382, 384, 387, 397, 402

Miles, Colonel Nelson A.: 389–91, 397
Military societies: 67–69, 72–73
Miller, Robert C.: 141ff., 143–44
Minimic: 207–208, 339, 346
Mitchell, Brigadier General Robert B.: 176, 189, 195, 202, 206, 227, 232
Mitchell, D. D.: 115–16, 181ff., 119–20
Mix, Charles E.: 154, 192, 307, 320
Mooers, Dr. John H.: 310, 312
Mo-nah-see-tah: 336
Moonlight, Colonel Thomas: 227, 246
Moore, Captain Orlando H.: 367–68
Morrison, James S.: 393, 400
Murie, Lieutenant James: 252
Murphy, Captain Edward B.: 203
Murphy, Thomas: 256, 260–61, 263, 279, 289–90, 292–96, 300, 304–305, 307–308, 331

Na-to-mah: 340
Nebraska territory: Indian raids in 1864, 201
Negus, Israel: 352
Neill, Lieutenant Colonel Thomas H.: 389
Nelson, Lieutenant Colonel Anderson D.: 344, 346, 348, 350, 355–56
Neva (Arapaho chief): 170, 191, 214
New Bent's Fort: 124–25, 127, 131–32
Nichols, Captain David H.: 213
North, Major Frank J.: 250–52, 254–55, 341–42

North, Captain Luther: 342–43, 349

North, Robert: 172, 191–92

Northern Arapahoes: 171, 193, 231, 248, 252–54

Northern Cheyennes: x, 157, 168–69, 193, 270

Notee, John (Arapaho): 191

O'Brien, Captain Nicholas J.: 226–27

Oglala Sioux: 17, 120, 153, 253, 281

Old Bark (Ugly Face): 91, 94, 100, 104, 127

Old Whirlwind: 127–28

One Eye: 207–208

One Eyed Bull: 307

Osages: 360, 380

Osborn, Thomas A.: 388

Overland road: Indian raids in 1864, 203

Overland route: 200–201, 206, 213–14

Owl Woman: 147, 217

Parker, Colonel Ely S.: 271, 345, 353, 360

Parkman, Francis: describes Cheyennes, 105–106

Parr, Richard: 309

Pattie, James Ohio: notes Cheyenne range, 22

Pawnee Killer (Sioux chief): 224, 231, 275, 285–86, 349

Pawnees: 58–59, 78–81, 102, 110, 206, 269, 352, 364, 390

Pawnee Scouts: 250–52, 254, 341–43

Peg Leg: 386

Penrose, Captain William H.: 307, 314–15

Pepoon, Lieutenant Silas: 316, 324, 346

Perrin du Lac, François Marie: description of Cheyenne Indians, 12

Philibert, Joseph: contacts Cheyennes on Arkansas, 19

Pierce, John: 161

Pike, Albert: 152, 155

Pike's Peak gold rush: 143

Plains Indians: Confederate agents among, 152, 154–55

Platte Bridge: 247–48

Plumb, Lieutenant Colonel Preston B.: 247

Poisal, John: 122

Poor Bear (Kiowa-Apache chief): 239, 289, 292

Pope, Major General John: 231, 235, 239–40, 245–46, 378, 388–89, 392

Porcupine Bear: 82, 306

Potawatomis: conflict with Cheyennes, 81

Powder Face (Arapaho chief): 318; protects agency, 384

Preuss, Charles: 86, 89

Price, Confederate Major General Sterling: 105, 198

Prowers, John: 181

Pueblo: 105, 109; establishment of, 90

Rafferty, Captain William A.: 403

Railroad surveys: through Cheyenne range: 124–26

Rankin, W. A.: 352–53

Ransom, George: 234

Red Bead (Sioux): 286–87
Red Bull: 251–52
Red Moon: 339, 358, 403
Red Nose: 306
Red Shield society: 82
Republican River: buffalo range, 93
Reynal, Antoine (also Raynal): 205
Ribble, Captain Henry H.: 213
Richardson, Albert D.: 145–46
Riley, Major Bennet: protects Santa Fe trade, 23
Ripley, W. D.: 178
Road surveys: through Cheyenne range, 124–26, 132–33
Robbins, Lieutenant S. M.: 286
Robinson, A. M.: 146, 148, 152
Roman Nose: 55–56, 255, 262, 275–76, 288, 291–94, 296, 299, 311; killed at Battle of Arikaree, 312
Roman Nose (Northern Arapaho): 191
Romero, Ralph: 350
Ross, Edward P.: 295
Rowland, Captain E. S.: 254
Royall, Major William B.: 314–15, 341, 344
Ruchare, John: 109

Sage, Rufus: 89–90, 93
St. Vrain, Céran: 102, 114
St. Vrain, Marcellus: 87
Sanborn, Captain George L.: 178, 183, 195
Sanborn, Major General John B.: 237–40, 242
Sand Creek Massacre: 195ff.
Sand Hill: 397, 401, 404
Sand Hill fight: 401–403

Santa Fe trade: need for protection, 23–24
Satank (Kiowa chief): 82–83, 330, 334
Satanta (Kiowa chief): 199, 288, 293, 330–31, 324, 352, 376
Sawyers, James A.: 253
Schofield, General John M.: 163, 320, 335, 350
Sedgwick, Major John: 138, 148, 152
Shamans: 53–55, 101
Shavehead (Comanche chief): 83
Sheridan, General Philip H.: 302, 309–10, 314, 316–18, 322, 324–25, 328–30, 333–35, 349, 363, 378, 388–93
Sherman, General William Tecumseh: 266–72, 281, 284–85, 287–88, 295, 308–309, 320, 322–23, 332
Shoshonis: 93, scouts killed by Cheyennes, 118
Shoup, Colonel George L.: 210, 216
Sioux Indians: 13, 84, 119, 163, 165, 185, 192–93, 200–201, 228, 231, 234, 248, 252, 255, 259, 273, 276, 279, 316, 321, 324
Slim Face (Mi-ah-tose): 101–102
Smith, Colonel Andrew J.: 277–78, 281
Smith, Edward P.: 378–79
Smith, Jack: 150
Smith, John S.: 102n., 102–104, 122, 145, 166–67, 170, 172, 187, 210, 218, 260, 298–300, 304, 318, 323, 335, 357
Smith, General Persifer F.: 137
Southern Arapahoes: 148–59, 174–76, 200, 208, 214–15, 225, 240,

263, 280–81, 290–91, 296–97, 321, 323, 327, 330, 345, 347; surrender at Fort Sill, 328; initiate agriculture, 364–65; separate reservation recommended for, 371

Southern Cheyennes: 152–53, 181–82, 193, 228, 245, 252, 270, 286, 290, 305; offer to punish Kiowas, 148; sign Treaty of Fort Wise, 148–51; lands of, 149–50; agree to amendments to Treaty of Fort Wise, 154–55; population of, 155, 299, 366; description of, 155–56; discontent among, 156; agriculture recommended for, 157; peaceful in 1862, 157–58; cattle and sheep raising recommended for, 158–59; commit depredations on Santa Fe route, 160; attend council with Evans, 167–68; peaceful during winter 1863–64, 174; raid Utes, 175–76, 378; peaceful during spring, 1864, 181–82, 184; reports of hostility, 187–88; successful raids, 1864, 189; raids in 1864, 194; fight Captain Murphy, 203; raid Santa Fe route, 205; surrender prisoners, 208; move near Fort Lyon, 1864, 214–15; numbers at Sand Creek, 218; numbers killed at Sand Creek, 219–20; chiefs killed at Sand Creek, 222; take vengeance after Sand Creek, 224ff.; attack Julesburg, 225–29; move north, 229ff.; fight at Mud Spring, 229–30; pursued by Collins, 230–31; raid Santa Fe road, 234–35; sign truce, 240; north of

Platte River, 245ff.; attack Platte route, 1865, 245–48; attack Smoky Hill road, 256; move south, 256; oppose Smoky Hill road, 258, 263–64; sign amendments to Treaty of Little Arkansas, 264; Hancock's campaign against, 271ff.; raids in 1867, 271; raid Kansas Pacific Railroad, 279; attend Treaty of Medicine Lodge, 293ff.; sign Treaty of Medicine Lodge, 298; raid Kaws, 299, 303–304; seek peace with Utes, 302; raid Kansas frontier, 305–306; at Battle of Arikaree, 311–12; losses at Battle of Arikaree, 313–14; raid near Fort Lyon, 315; evade Sully, 318–20; at Battle of the Washita, 326–29; losses at Battle of the Washita, 327; surrender at Fort Sill, 328; prisoners at Fort Hays, 328, 334; flee from Sheridan's troops, 330; surrender at Fort Cobb, 333; take white captives, 337; flee Fort Sill, 339; surrender at Camp Supply, 344; refuse lands of Treaty of Medicine Lodge, 345, 347; proclamation reservation of, 347; raid with Kiowas and Comanches, 359–60, 362; refuse to farm, 365; respect Darlington, 367; council with Davidson, 369; attitudes toward reservation policy, 369–70; murder Jordan family, 370–71; causes of outbreak, 1874, 372–73; war against Utes, 1873, 375; visit Washington, 378, 379; harassed in Dodge City, 379–80; raid for horses, 383;

at Adobe Walls, 385–86; campaign against, 390ff.; return to reservation, 393ff., 405; hostiles weaken, 396–97; surrender in 1875, 401; Fort Marion prisoners, 403; flee north in 1875, 404–405
South Platte Valley: settlement of, 161
Special Indian Commission: 345–47
Speyer, Albert: 97
Spotted Horse (Northern Cheyenne): 169, 262–63
Spotted Tail (Brulé Sioux chief): 224, 231
Spotted Wolf (Arapaho chief): 318, 323
Standing-in-Water: 209
Stanley, Henry M.: 272–74, 277, 280
Stanton, Edwin M.: 202, 232, 235
Starved Bear: 142
Stewart, Captain George H.: 134–36, 142
Stilwell, Lieutenant George H.: 180
Stilwell, Jack: 312–13
Stone Calf: 355, 373, 384, 399–400; visits East, 362–63
Storm (Arapaho chief): 240
Stuart, Lieutenant Jeb: 140
Sturgis, Captain S. D.: 148
Sugar (or "Sheshepaskut," Chippewa chief): in Cheyenne–Chippewa conflict, 7–9
Sully, Brigadier General Alfred: 245, 304, 318–20, 325
Sumner, Colonel Edwin Vos: 117, 137–42, 144

Sun Dance (Medicine Lodge): 62–66, 167, 376, 384
Sutaios: 361; join Cheyennes, 9–10

Tabeau, Pierre-Antoine: establishes Cheyenne–trader contact, 12
Tall Bear: 142, 155, 168
Tall Bull: 55, 225, 273–74, 276, 293, 303, 311, 314, 340–42
Talley, John H.: 381
Tall Wolf: 306
Tappan, Samuel F.: 220, 308, 322, 331
Tatham, Benjamin: 354
Taylor, I. C.: 257–58, 261–62
Taylor, Nathaniel G.: 277, 279, 305, 322
Teller, Henry M.: 197–98
Ten Bears (Comanche chief): 293
Teton Sioux: conflict with Cheyennes, 19
Thompson, David: on Cheyenne–Chippewa conflict, 7–9
Tobacco (Cheyenne chief): 104; death, 107–108
Townsend, Mrs. Elma D.: 352
Townsend, J. R.: 353, 356, 369–70
Tracy, C. F. and Company: 352
Treaty of Fort Laramie: 116ff., 118–19, 121–23
Treaty of Fort Wise: 148–51
Treaty of Little Arkansas: 241ff.
Treaty of Medicine Lodge: 289ff.
Trudeau, Pierre: 312–13
Turkey Wailing: 405
Twiss, Thomas S.: 130, 136–37
Two Wolves: 168

Usher, Jacob P.: 231–32, 234

Utes: 161, 175–76, 203, 267, 375, 378

Van Wormer, Isaac P.: 190
Vargas, Don Diego de: reports contact with Cheyennes, 5

Walker, Francis A.: 366–67; recommends separate reservation for Southern Arapahoes, 371
Walker, Lieutenant Colonel Samuel: 250, 254–55
Walking Whirlwind: 79
Wallen, Major Henry D.: 193
Ward, Lieutenant E. W.: 340
Ware, Captain Eugene F.: 179, 228–29
Watkins, William: 387
Wells Fargo and Company: 287
Wetmore, Alphonso: notes Cheyenne horse raids, 23
Wharton, Captain H. W.: 134
Whirlwind: 303, 387, 389–90
Whistler (Sioux chief): 349
White Antelope: 142, 148–49, 155, 168, 209–11, 213–14, 219, 397, 400
White Bird: 375
White Bull: 137, 139
White Crow: 79
White Horse: 225, 273, 275–76, 311, 349, 380, 393
Whitely, Simeon: 210
White Shield: 383, 390
Whitfield, John W.: 127–32
Whitledge, Thomas B.: 291–92

Whitney, Chauncey: 313
Who-Walks-with-His-Toes-Turned-Out (Wan-ne-sah-ta): 119–20
Wichitas: 239, 320–21
Williams, Benjamin: 381, 400
Williams, John: 375
Wilson, Captain Luther: 218
Wislizenus, Adolphus: 97
Wistar, Thomas: 354
Wolf Chief: 186–87
Wyllyams, Sergeant Frederick: 283–84
Wynkoop, Edward W.: 184–87, 189, 199–200, 207–208, 210–11, 214, 257–61, 264–65, 270, 272–75, 277, 279, 290, 293, 296, 299–301, 304–307; councils with Southern Cheyennes, 208, 261–62; resigns as Indian agent, 307–308; eulogizes Black Kettle, 331–32

Yamparika Comanches: 155
Yellow Bear (Arapaho chief): 333, 356
Yellow Buffalo (Kiowa chief): 170
Yellow Horse: 404
Yellow Wolf (Cheyenne chief): 25, 81, 94, 100, 107–108; notes decline of Cheyennes, 100–101; asks for agricultural aid, 107–108; signs Treaty of Fort Laramie, 122–23; killed at Sand Creek, 222
Yellow Woman: 147, 199
Young Whirlwind: 358